Excel® 2019
Power Programming
with VBA

Excel® 2019 Power Programming with VBA

Michael Alexander

Dick Kusleika

Previously by John Walkenbach

WILEY

Excel® 2019 Power Programming with VBA

Published by
John Wiley & Sons, Inc.
10475 Crosspoint Boulevard
Indianapolis, IN 46256
www.wiley.com

Copyright © 2019 by John Wiley & Sons, Inc., Indianapolis, Indiana

Published simultaneously in Canada

ISBN: 978-1-119-51492-3
ISBN: 978-1-119-51494-7 (ebk)
ISBN: 978-1-119-51491-6 (ebk)

Manufactured in the United States of America

C10009406_041219

For general information on our other products and services please contact our Customer Care Department within the United States at (877) 762-2974, outside the United States at (317) 572-3993 or fax (317) 572-4002.

Wiley publishes in a variety of print and electronic formats and by print-on-demand. Some material included with standard print versions of this book may not be included in e-books or in print-on-demand. If this book refers to media such as a CD or DVD that is not included in the version you purchased, you may download this material at http://booksupport.wiley.com. For more information about Wiley products, visit www.wiley.com.

Library of Congress Control Number: 2019936928

About the Authors

Michael Alexander is a Microsoft Certified Application Developer (MCAD) and author of several books on advanced business analysis with Microsoft Access and Microsoft Excel. He has more than 20 years of experience consulting and developing Microsoft Office solutions. Mike has been named a Microsoft MVP for his ongoing contributions to the Excel community. You can find Mike at www.datapigtechnologies.com.

Dick Kusleika is a 12-time Microsoft Excel MVP and has been working with Microsoft Office for more than 20 years. Dick develops Access- and Excel-based solutions for his clients and has conducted training seminars on Office products in the United States and Australia. Dick also writes a popular Excel-related blog at www.dailydoseofexcel.com.

About the Technical Editors

Doug Holland is an Architect Evangelist at Microsoft Corporation, working with partners to drive digital transformation through technologies such as the Microsoft Cloud, Office 365, and HoloLens. He holds a master's degree in software engineering from Oxford University and lives in Northern California with his wife and five children.

Guy Hart-Davis is the author of an improbable number of computer books on a bizarre range of topics. If you had been wondering who was responsible for the *Word 2000 Developer's Handbook*, *AppleScript: A Beginner's Guide*, *iMac Portable Genius*, or *Samsung Galaxy S8 Maniac's Guide*, you need wonder no more.

Credits

Associate Publisher
Jim Minatel

Senior Editorial Assistant
Devon Lewis

Editorial Manager
Pete Gaughan

Production Manager
Katie Wisor

Project Editor
Gary Schwartz

Production Editor
Barath Kumar Rajasekaran

Technical Editors
Doug Holland
Guy Hart-Davis

Copy Editor
Kim Wimpsett

Proofreader
Nancy Bell

Indexer
Johnna VanHoose Dinse

Cover Designer
Wiley

Cover Image
© Rost-9D/Getty Images

Acknowledgments

Our deepest thanks to the professionals at John Wiley & Sons for all the hours of work put into bringing this book to life. Thanks also to Doug Holland and Guy Hart-Davis for suggesting numerous improvements to the examples and text in this book. A special thank-you goes out to our families for putting up with all the time spent locked away on this project. Finally, we'd like to thank John Walkenbach for his many years of work on the previous editions of this book. His efforts in curating Excel knowledge have been instrumental, not only in helping millions of Excel users to achieve their learning goals but also in inspiring countless Excel MVPs to share their expertise with the Excel community.

Contents at a Glance

Contents

Contents

Contents

Contents

Contents

Contents

Contents

Contents

Introduction

For most of us, the path to Excel VBA programming starts with the need to perform some task that can't be done with the standard tools in Excel. That task is different for each of us. Maybe that task is to create separate workbooks automatically for all the rows in a data set. Maybe that task is to automate the emailing of dozens of reports. Whatever that task is for you, you can bet that someone has started their own journey into Excel VBA with the same need.

The beautiful thing about Excel VBA is that you don't have to be an expert to start solving problems with it. You can learn just enough to solve a particular problem, or you can go further and discover ways to handle all kinds of automation scenarios.

Whatever your goals may be, *Excel 2019 Power Programming with VBA* will help you harness the power of the VBA language to automate tasks, work smarter, and be more productive.

Topics Covered

This book focuses on Visual Basic for Applications (VBA), the programming language built into Excel (and other applications that make up Microsoft Office). More specifically, it shows you how to write programs that automate various tasks in Excel. This book covers everything from recording simple macros through creating sophisticated user-oriented applications and utilities.

You can approach this book in any way you please. You can read it from cover to cover, or you can skip around, picking up useful tidbits here and there. VBA programming is often a task-oriented endeavor. So, if you're faced with a challenging task, you might try the index first to see where the book might specifically address your problem.

This book does *not* cover Microsoft Visual Studio Tools for Office (VSTO), a technology that uses Visual Basic .NET and Microsoft Visual C#. VSTO can also be used to control Excel and other Microsoft Office applications.

As you may know, Excel 2019 is available for other platforms. For example, you can use Microsoft's Excel Web App in your browser and even iPads and tablets. These versions do not support VBA. In other words, this book is for the desktop version of Excel 2019 for Windows.

What You Need to Know

This is not a book for beginning Excel users. If you have no experience with Excel, a better choice might be the *Excel 2019 Bible* (Wiley, 2018), which provides comprehensive coverage of all the features of Excel and is meant for users of all levels.

To get the most out of this book, you should be a relatively experienced Excel user who knows how to do the following:

- Create workbooks, insert sheets, save files, and so on
- Navigate through a workbook
- Use the Excel Ribbon user interface
- Enter formulas
- Use Excel's worksheet functions
- Name cells and ranges
- Use basic Windows features, such as file management techniques and the Clipboard

What You Need to Have

Excel is available in several versions, including a web version and a version for tablets and phones. This book was written exclusively for the desktop version of Microsoft Excel 2019 for Windows. If you plan to develop applications that will be used in earlier versions of Excel, we strongly suggest you use the earliest version of Excel that your target audience will be using. Over the last few years, Microsoft has adopted an agile release cycle for the web version of Excel with Office 365, generating release updates practically on a monthly basis.

It is important to have a full installation of Excel, and if you want to try the more advanced chapters involving communication between Excel and other Office applications, you will need a full installation of Office.

The version of Windows you use is not important. Any computer system that can run Windows will suffice, but you'll be much better off with a fast machine with plenty of memory. Excel is a large program, and using it on a slower system or a system with minimal memory can be extremely frustrating.

Please note that this book is not applicable to Microsoft Excel for Mac.

Conventions Used in This Book

Take a minute to skim this section and learn about some of the typographic conventions used throughout this book.

Excel commands

Excel uses a context-sensitive Ribbon menu system. The words along the top (such as Insert and View) are known as *tabs*. Click a tab, and the Ribbon of icons displays the commands that are most suited to the task at hand. Each icon has a name that is (usually) displayed next to or below the icon. The icons are arranged in groups, and the group name appears below the icons.

The convention used in this book is to indicate the tab name, followed by the group name, followed by the icon name. So, for example, the command used to toggle word wrap in a cell is indicated as follows:

> Home ⇨ Alignment ⇨ Wrap Text

Clicking the first tab, labeled File, takes you to the Backstage window. The Backstage window has commands along the left side of the window. To indicate Backstage commands, we use the word *File*, followed by the command. For example, the following command displays the Excel Options dialog box:

> File ⇨ Options

Visual Basic Editor commands

Visual Basic Editor is the window in which you will work with your VBA code. VB Editor uses the traditional menu-and-toolbar interface. A command like the following means to click the Tools menu and select the References menu item:

> Tools ⇨ References

Keyboard conventions

You need to use the keyboard to enter data. In addition, you can work with menus and dialog boxes directly from the keyboard—a method that you might find easier if your hands are already positioned over the keys.

Input

Inputs that you are supposed to type from the keyboard will appear in boldface—for example, enter **=SUM(B2: B50)** in cell B51.

Lengthier inputs will appear on a separate line in a monospace font. For example, we might instruct you to enter the following formula:

```
=VLOOKUP(StockNumber,PriceList,2)
```

VBA code

This book contains many snippets of VBA code, as well as complete procedure listings. Each listing appears in a monospace font, and each line of code occupies a separate line.

(We copied these listings directly from the VBA module and pasted them into our word processors.) To make the code easier to read, we often use one or more tabs to create indentations. Indentation is optional, but it does help to delineate statements that go together.

If a line of code doesn't fit on a single line in this book, we use the standard VBA line continuation sequence: at the end of a line, a space followed by an underscore character indicates that the line of code extends to the next line. For example, the following two lines are a single code statement:

```
columnCount = Application.WorksheetFunction. _
CountA(Range("A:A")) + 1
```

You can enter this code either on two lines, exactly as shown, or on a single line without the space and underscore character.

Functions, filenames, and named ranges

Excel's worksheet functions appear in uppercase font, like so: "Enter a SUM formula in cell C20." For VBA procedure names, properties, methods, and objects, we often use mixed uppercase and lowercase letters to make these names easier to read.

Typographical conventions

Anything that you're supposed to type using the keyboard appears in **bold**. Lengthy input usually appears on a separate line. Here's an example:

```
="Part Name: " &VLOOKUP(PartNumber,PartList,2)
```

Names of the keys on your keyboard appear in normal type. When two keys should be pressed simultaneously, they're connected with a plus sign, like this: "Press Ctrl+C to copy the selected cells."

The four "arrow" keys are collectively known as the *navigation keys*.

Excel built-in worksheet functions appear in monofont in uppercase like this: "Note the SUMPRODUCT function used in cell C20."

Mouse conventions

You'll come across some of the following mouse-related terms, which are all standard fare.

Mouse pointer   This is the small graphic figure that moves on-screen when you move your mouse. The mouse pointer is usually an arrow, but it changes shape when you move to certain areas of the screen or when you're performing certain actions.

Point   Move the mouse so that the mouse pointer is on a specific item; for example, "Point to the Save button on the toolbar."

Click   Press the left mouse button once and release it immediately.

Right-click Press the right mouse button once and release it immediately. The right mouse button is used in Excel to open shortcut menus that are appropriate for whatever is currently selected.

Double-click Press the left mouse button twice in rapid succession.

Drag Press the left mouse button and keep it pressed while you move the mouse. Dragging is often used to select a range of cells or to change the size of an object.

What the Icons Mean

Throughout the book, we use icons to call your attention to points that are particularly important.

NOTE
We use Note icons to tell you that something is important—perhaps a concept that could help you master the task at hand or something fundamental for understanding subsequent material.

TIP
Tip icons indicate a more efficient way of doing something or a technique that might not be obvious.

 These icons are used to refer to other section or chapters that have more to say on a subject.

CAUTION
We use caution icons when the operation that we're describing can cause problems if you're not careful.

ON THE WEB
These icons indicate that an example file is available on the book's website. See the section "What's on the Website" later in this introduction.

How This Book Is Organized

The chapters of this book are grouped into five main parts.

Part I: Introduction to Excel VBA

In Part I, we introduce you to VBA, providing the programming fundamentals that you will need to create and manage Excel subroutines and functions. Chapter 1 sets the stage with a conceptual overview of Excel application development. Chapters 2 through 6 cover everything you need to know to start coding in VBA. Chapter 7 rounds out your introduction to VBA with many useful examples.

Part II: Advanced VBA Techniques

Part II covers additional techniques that are often considered advanced. Chapters 8 and 9 discuss how to use VBA to work with pivot tables and charts (including Sparkline graphics). Chapter 10 discusses various techniques that you can use to interact with other applications (such as Word and Outlook). Chapter 11 concludes Part II with a discussion on how to work with files and external data sources, including how to control Power Query from VBA.

Part III: Working with UserForms

The four chapters in Part III cover custom dialog boxes (*UserForms*). Chapter 12 presents some built-in alternatives to creating custom UserForms. Chapter 13 provides an introduction to UserForms and the various controls that you can use. Chapters 14 and 15 present many examples of custom dialog boxes, ranging from basic to advanced.

Part IV: Developing Excel Applications

The chapters in Part IV deal with important elements of creating user-oriented applications. Chapter 16 offers a hands-on discussion of creating add-ins. Chapters 17 and 18 discuss how to modify Excel's Ribbon and shortcut menus. Chapter 19 demonstrates several ways to provide online help for your applications. In Chapter 20, we present a primer on developing user-oriented applications. Chapter 21 rounds out your exploration of Excel VBA programming with some information regarding compatibility.

Part V: Appendix

Part V includes an appendix that offers a reference guide to all the statements and functions exposed to VBA as keywords.

How to Use This Book

The topics in this book get more advanced as you progress through it, so you can work through the material from front to back and build your skills as you go. You can also use this book as a reference that you can consult when you need help with the following situations:

- You're stuck while trying to do something
- You need to do something that you've never done before
- You have some time on your hands, and you're interested in learning something new about VBA

The index is comprehensive, and each chapter typically focuses on a single broad topic. Don't be discouraged if some of the material is over your head. Most VBA programmers get by just fine by using only a subset of the language.

What's on the Website

Nearly everything discussed in this book has examples with it. You can (and should) download the many useful examples included with this book.

The files are located at www.wiley.com/go/excel2019powerprogramming.

Part I

Introduction to Excel VBA

IN THIS PART

Essentials of Spreadsheet Application Development

IN THIS CHAPTER

Discovering the basic steps involved in spreadsheet application development

Determining end users' needs

Planning applications to meet users' needs

Developing and testing your applications

Documenting your development efforts and writing user documentation

What Is a Spreadsheet Application?

For the purposes of this book, a *spreadsheet application* is a spreadsheet file (or group of related files) that is designed so that someone other than the developer can perform specific tasks without extensive training. According to this definition, most of the spreadsheet files that you've developed probably don't qualify as spreadsheet applications. You may have dozens or hundreds of spreadsheet files on your hard drive, but it's a safe bet that most of them aren't designed for others to use.

A good spreadsheet application does the following:

- Enables the end user to perform a task that he or she probably would not be able to do otherwise.
- Provides the appropriate solution to the problem. (A spreadsheet environment isn't always the optimal approach.)
- Accomplishes what it is supposed to do. This prerequisite may be obvious, but it's not at all uncommon for applications to fail this test.
- Produces accurate results and is free of bugs.
- Uses appropriate and efficient methods and algorithms to accomplish its job.
- Traps errors before the user is forced to deal with them.
- Does not allow the user to delete or modify important components accidentally (or intentionally).

- Has a clear and consistent user interface so that the user always knows how to proceed.
- Has well-documented formulas, macros, and user interface elements that allow for subsequent changes, if necessary.
- Is designed so that it can be modified in simple ways without making major changes. A basic fact is that a user's needs change over time.
- Has an easily accessible help system that provides useful information on at least the major procedures.
- Is designed to be portable and to run on any system that has the proper software (in this case, a copy of a supported version of Excel).

It should come as no surprise that it is possible to create spreadsheet applications for many different usage levels, ranging from a simple fill-in-the-blank template to an extremely complex application that uses a custom interface and may not even look like a spreadsheet.

Steps for Application Development

There is no simple, surefire recipe for developing an effective spreadsheet application. Everyone has his or her own style for creating such applications. In addition, every project is different and therefore requires its own approach. Finally, the demands and technical expertise of the people with whom (or for whom) you work also play a role in how the development process proceeds.

Spreadsheet developers typically perform the following activities:

- Determine the needs of the user(s)
- Plan an application that meets these needs
- Determine the most appropriate user interface
- Create the spreadsheet, formulas, macros, and user interface
- Test and debug the application
- Attempt to make the application bulletproof
- Make the application aesthetically appealing and intuitive
- Document the development effort
- Develop user documentation and Help systems
- Distribute the application to the user
- Update the application when necessary

Not all of these steps are required for each application, and the order in which these activities are performed varies from project to project. We describe each of these activities in the pages that follow. For most of these items, we cover the technical details in subsequent chapters.

Determining User Needs

When you undertake a new Excel project, one of your first steps is to identify exactly what the end users require. Failure to assess the end users' needs thoroughly early on often results in additional work later when you have to adjust the application so that it does what it was supposed to do in the first place.

In some cases, you'll be intimately familiar with the end users—you may even be an end user yourself. In other cases (for example, if you're a consultant developing a project for a new client), you may know little or nothing about the users or their situations.

How do you determine the needs of the user? If you've been asked to develop a spreadsheet application, it's a good idea to meet with the end users and ask specific questions. Better yet, get everything in writing, create flow diagrams, pay attention to minor details, and do anything else to ensure that the product you deliver is the product that is needed.

Here are some guidelines that may help make this phase easier:

- Don't assume that you know what the user needs. Second-guessing at this stage almost always causes problems later.
- If possible, talk directly to the end users of the application, not just their supervisor or manager.
- Learn what, if anything, is currently being done to meet the users' needs. You might be able to save some work by simply adapting an existing application. At the very least, looking at current solutions will familiarize you with the operation.
- Identify the resources available at the users' site. For example, try to determine whether you must work around any hardware or software limitations.
- If possible, determine the specific hardware systems that will be used. If your application will be used on slow systems, you need to take that into account.
- Identify which versions of Excel are in use. Keep in mind that users can have versions of Excel running on macOS, mobile platforms, and Windows. These have to be taken into account when planning an automated Excel solution. Although Microsoft does everything in its power to urge users to upgrade to the latest version of the software, the majority of Excel users don't.
- Understand the skill levels of the end users. This information will help you design the application appropriately.
- Determine how long the application will be used and whether any changes are anticipated during the lifetime of the project. Knowing this information may influence the amount of effort that you put into the project and help you plan for changes.

Finally, don't be surprised if the project specifications change before you complete the application. This occurrence is common, and you're in a better position if you expect changes rather than being surprised by them. Just make sure that your contract (if you have one) addresses the issue of changing specifications.

Planning an Application That Meets User Needs

After you determine the end users' needs, it's tempting to jump right in and start fiddling around in Excel. Take it from those who suffer from this problem: try to restrain yourself. Builders don't construct a house without a set of blueprints, and you shouldn't build a spreadsheet application without some type of plan. The formality of your plan depends on the scope of the project and your general style of working, but you should spend at least *some* time thinking about what you're going to do and coming up with a plan of action.

Before rolling up your sleeves and settling down at your keyboard, you'll benefit by taking some time to consider the various ways that you can approach the problem. This planning period is where a thorough knowledge of Excel pays off. Avoiding blind alleys rather than stumbling into them is always a good idea.

If you ask a dozen Excel experts to design an application based on precise specifications, chances are that you'll get a dozen different implementations of the project that meet those specifications. Of those solutions, some will be better than the others because Excel often provides several options to accomplish a task. If you know Excel inside and out, you'll have a good idea of the potential methods at your disposal, and you can choose the one most appropriate for the project at hand. Often, a bit of creative thinking yields an unusual approach that's vastly superior to other methods.

Consider some general options at the beginning stage of this planning period, such as the following:

File structure Think about whether you want to use one workbook with multiple sheets, several single-sheet workbooks, or a template file.

Data structure You should always consider how your data will be structured and also determine whether you will be using external database files, data sources stored on the cloud, or storing everything in worksheets.

Add-in or workbook file In some cases, an add-in may be the best choice for your final product, or perhaps you might use an add-in with a standard workbook.

Version of Excel Will your Excel application be used with Excel 2019 only, or will your application also need to run on earlier versions of Excel? What about versions of Excel running on other platforms, such as macOS or mobile devices? These considerations are important because each new version of Excel adds features that aren't available in previous versions.

Error handling Error handling is a major issue with applications. You need to determine how your application will detect and deal with errors. For example, if your application performs pivot table operations on the active sheet, you need to be able to handle a case in which a pivot table does not exist on the sheet that is active.

Use of special features   If your application needs to summarize a lot of data, you may want to consider using Excel's pivot table feature, or you may want to use Excel's data validation feature as a check for valid data entry.

Performance issues   The time to start thinking about increasing the speed and efficiency of your application is in the development stage, not when the application is complete and users are complaining.

Level of security   As you may know, Excel provides several protection options to restrict access to particular elements of a workbook. For example, you can lock cells so that formulas cannot be changed, and you can assign a password to prevent unauthorized users from viewing or accessing specific files. Determining up front exactly what you need to protect—and what level of protection is necessary—will make your job easier.

> **NOTE**
>
> Be aware that Excel's protection features aren't 100 percent effective—far from it. If you desire complete and absolute security for your application, Excel probably isn't the best platform.

You'll probably have to deal with many other project-specific considerations in this phase. Consider all options, and don't settle on the first solution that comes to mind.

Another design consideration is remembering to plan for change. You'll do yourself a favor if you make your application as generic as possible. For example, don't write a procedure that works with only a specific range of cells. Rather, write a procedure that accepts any range as an argument. When the inevitable changes are requested, such a design makes it easier for you to carry out the revisions. Also, you may find that the work that you do for one project is similar to the work that you do for another. Keep reusability in mind when you are planning a project.

Avoid letting the end user completely guide your approach to a problem. For example, suppose that you meet with a manager who tells you that the department needs an application to write text files that will be imported into another application. Don't confuse the user's need with the solution. The user's real need is to share data. Using an intermediate text file to do it is just one possible solution; better ways to approach the problem may exist. In other words, don't let the users define their problem by stating it in terms of a solution approach. Determining the best approach is *your* job.

Determining the Most Appropriate User Interface

When you develop spreadsheets that others will use, you need to pay special attention to the user interface. By *user interface*, we mean the method by which the user interacts with the application and executes your VBA macros.

Since the introduction of Excel 2007, some of these user interface decisions are irrelevant. Custom menus and toolbars are, for all intents and purposes, obsolete. Consequently, developers must learn how to work with the Ribbon.

Excel provides several features that are relevant to user interface design:

- Ribbon customization
- Shortcut menu customization
- Shortcut keys
- Custom dialog boxes (UserForms)
- Message boxes and input boxes
- Controls (such as a ListBox or a CommandButton) placed directly on a worksheet

We discuss these features briefly in the following sections and cover them more thoroughly in later chapters.

Customizing the Ribbon

As a developer, you have a fair amount of control over the Ribbon including which tabs and commands are available when your Excel application opens. Although Excel allows end users to modify the Ribbon, making UI changes via code isn't a simple task.

 See Chapter 17, "Working with the Ribbon," for information about working with the Ribbon.

Customizing shortcut menus

Excel allows the VBA developer to customize the right-click shortcut menus. Right-click menus can offer users a way to trigger an action easily without having to move too far from the range in which they are working. Figure 1.1 illustrates a customized shortcut menu that appears when a cell is right-clicked.

FIGURE 1.1

A customized shortcut menu

 Chapter 18, "Working with Shortcut Menus," describes how to work with shortcut menus using VBA, including some limitations due to the single document interface introduced in Excel 2013.

Creating shortcut keys

Another user interface option at your disposal is a custom shortcut key. Excel lets you assign a Ctrl key (or Shift+Ctrl key) combination to a macro. When the user presses the key combination, the macro executes.

There are two caveats, however. First, make it clear to the user which keys are active and what they do. Second, do not assign a key combination that's already used for something else. A key combination that you assign to a macro takes precedence over the built-in shortcut keys. For example, Ctrl+S is a built-in Excel shortcut key used to save the current file. If you assign this key combination to a macro, you lose the capability to save the file with Ctrl+S. Remember that shortcut keys are case sensitive, so you can use a combination such as Ctrl+Shift+S.

Creating custom dialog boxes

Anyone who has used a personal computer for any length of time is undoubtedly familiar with dialog boxes. Consequently, custom Excel dialog boxes can play a major role in the user interfaces that you design for your applications. Figure 1.2 shows an example of a custom dialog box.

FIGURE 1.2

A dialog box created with Excel's UserForm feature

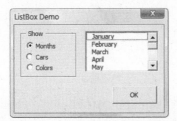

A custom dialog box is known as a *UserForm*. A UserForm can solicit user input, get a user's options or preferences, and direct the flow of your entire application. The elements that make up a UserForm (buttons, drop-down lists, check boxes, and so on) are called *controls*—more specifically, *ActiveX controls*. Excel provides a standard assortment of ActiveX controls, and you can also incorporate third-party controls.

After adding a control to a dialog box, you can link it to a worksheet cell so that it doesn't require any macros (except a simple macro to display the dialog box). Linking a control to a cell is easy, but it's not always the best way to get user input from a dialog box. Most of the time, you want to develop VBA macros that work with your custom dialog boxes.

 We cover UserForms in detail in Part III.

Using ActiveX controls on a worksheet

Excel also lets you add UserForm ActiveX controls to a worksheet's *drawing layer* (an invisible layer on top of a sheet that holds pictures, charts, and other objects). Figure 1.3 shows a simple worksheet model with several UserForm controls inserted directly in the worksheet. This sheet contains the following ActiveX controls: a CheckBox, a ScrollBar, and two sets of OptionButtons. This workbook uses no macros. Rather, the controls are linked to worksheet cells.

FIGURE 1.3

You can add UserForm controls to worksheets and link them to cells.

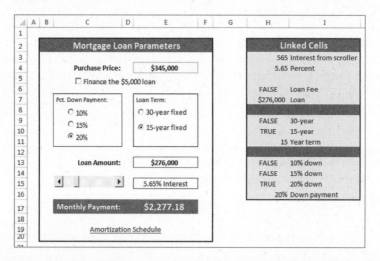

ON THE WEB

This workbook is available on this book's website. The file is named worksheet controls.xlsx.

Perhaps the most common control is a CommandButton. By itself, a CommandButton doesn't do anything, so you need to attach a macro to each CommandButton.

Using dialog box controls directly in a worksheet often eliminates the need for custom dialog boxes. You can often greatly simplify the operation of a spreadsheet by adding a few ActiveX controls (or form controls) to a worksheet. These ActiveX controls let the user make choices by operating familiar controls rather than making entries in cells.

Access these controls by using the Developer ⇨ Controls ⇨ Insert command (see Figure 1.4). If the Developer tab isn't on the Ribbon, add it by using the Customize Ribbon tab of the Excel Options dialog box.

FIGURE 1.4

Using the Ribbon to add controls to a worksheet

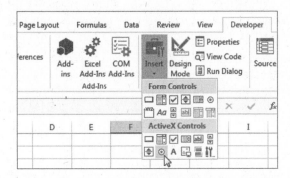

The controls come in two types: form controls and ActiveX controls. Both sets of controls have their advantages and disadvantages. Generally, form controls are easier to use, but ActiveX controls are a bit more flexible. Table 1.1 summarizes these two classes of controls.

TABLE 1.1   ActiveX Controls versus Form Controls

	ActiveX Controls	Form Controls
Excel versions	97, 2000, 2002, 2003, 2007, 2010, 2013, 2016, 2019	5, 95, 97, 2000, 2002, 2003, 2007, 2010, 2013, 2016, 2019
Controls available	CheckBox, TextBox, Command Button, OptionButton, ListBox, ComboBox, ToggleButton, Spin Button, ScrollBar, Label, Image (and others can be added)	GroupBox, Button, Check Box, OptionButton, List-Box, DropDown (ComboBox), ScrollBar, Spinner
Macro code storage	In the code module for the sheet	In any standard VBA module
Macro name	Corresponds to the control name (for example, CommandButton1_ Click)	Any name you specify
Correspond to	UserForm controls	Pre–Excel 97 dialog sheet controls
Customization	Extensive, using the Properties box	Minimal
Respond to events	Yes	Click or Change events only

Executing the development effort

After you identify user needs, determine the approach you'll take to meet those needs, and decide on the components that you'll use for the user interface. Next, it's time to get down to the nitty-gritty and start creating the application. This step, of course, constitutes a great deal of the total time you spend on a particular project.

How you go about developing the application depends on your personal style and the nature of the application. Except for simple fill-in-the-blanks template workbooks, your application will probably use macros. Creating macros in Excel is easy, but creating *good* macros is difficult.

Concerning Yourself with the End User

In this section, we discuss the important development issues that surface as your application becomes more and more workable and as the time to package and distribute your work grows nearer.

Testing the application

How many times have you used a commercial software application, only to have it bomb out on you at a crucial moment? Most likely, the problem was caused by insufficient testing that didn't catch all of the bugs. All nontrivial software has bugs, but in the best software, the bugs are simply more obscure. As you'll see, you sometimes must work around the bugs in Excel to get your application to perform properly.

After you create your application, you need to test it. Testing is one of the most crucial steps; it's not uncommon to spend as much time testing and debugging an application as you did creating it. Actually, you should be doing a great deal of testing during the development phase. After all, whether you're writing a VBA routine or creating formulas in a worksheet, you want to make sure that the application is working the way it's supposed to work.

Like standard compiled applications, spreadsheet applications that you develop are prone to bugs. A *bug* can be defined as (1) something that does happen but shouldn't happen while a program (or application) is running, or (2) something that doesn't happen when it should happen. Both species of bugs are equally nasty, and you should plan on devoting a good portion of your development time to testing the application under all reasonable conditions and fixing any problems that you find.

It's important to test thoroughly any spreadsheet application that you develop for others. And depending on its eventual audience, you may want to make your application bullet-proof. In other words, try to anticipate all the errors and screw-ups that could possibly occur and make concerted efforts to avoid them—or, at least, to handle them gracefully. This foresight not only helps the end user but also makes it easier on you and protects your reputation. Also, consider using beta testing—your end users are likely candidates because they're the ones who will be using your product. (See the upcoming sidebar "What about beta testing?")

Although you can't conceivably test for all possibilities, your macros should be able to handle common types of errors. For example, what if the user enters a text string instead of a numeric value? What if the user tries to run your macro when a workbook isn't open? What if the user cancels a dialog box without making any selections? What happens if the user presses Ctrl+F6 and jumps to the next window? When you gain experience, these types of issues become very familiar, and you account for them without even thinking.

What about beta testing?

Software manufacturers typically have a rigorous testing cycle for new products. After extensive internal testing, the pre-release product is usually sent to a group of interested users for *beta testing*. This phase often uncovers additional problems that are usually corrected before the product's final release.

If you're developing an Excel application that more than a few people will use, you may want to consider a beta test. This test enables your intended users to use your application in its proposed setting on different hardware (usually).

The beta period should begin after you've completed all of your own testing and you feel that the application is ready to distribute. You'll need to identify a group of users to help you. The process works best if you distribute everything that will ultimately be included in your application: user documentation, the installation program, help, and so on. You can evaluate the beta test in a number of ways, including face-to-face discussions, email, questionnaires, and phone calls.

You almost always become aware of problems that you need to correct or improvements that you need to make before you undertake a widespread distribution of the application. Of course, a beta-testing phase takes additional time, and not all projects can afford that luxury.

Making the application bulletproof

If you think about it, destroying a spreadsheet is fairly easy. Erasing one critical formula or value can cause errors throughout the entire worksheet—and perhaps even other dependent worksheets. Even worse, if the damaged workbook is saved, it replaces the good copy on disk. Unless a backup procedure is in place, the user of your application may be in trouble, and *you* will probably be blamed for it.

Obviously, you can easily see why you need to add some protection when users—especially novices—will be using your worksheets. Excel provides several techniques for protecting worksheets and parts of worksheets.

Lock specific cells   You can lock specific cells (by using the Protection tab in the Format Cells dialog box) so that users can't change them. Locking takes effect only when the document is protected with the Review ➪ Changes ➪ Protect Sheet command. The Protect Sheet dialog box has options that allow you to specify which actions users can perform on a protected sheet (see Figure 1.5).

FIGURE 1.5

Using the Protect Sheet dialog box to specify what users can and can't do

Hide the formulas in specific cells   You can hide the formulas in specific cells (by using the Protection tab in the Format Cells dialog box) so that others can't see them. Again, hiding takes effect only when the document is protected by choosing the Review ➪ Changes ➪ Protect Sheet command.

Protect an entire workbook   You can protect an entire workbook—the structure of the workbook, the window position and size, or both. Use the Review ➪ Protect ➪ Protect Workbook command for this purpose.

Lock objects on the worksheet   Use the Properties section in the task pane to lock objects (such as shapes) and prevent them from being moved or changed. To access this section of the task pane, right-click the object and choose Size and Properties. Locking objects takes effect only when the document is protected using the Review ➪ Protect ➪ Protect Sheet command. By default, all objects are locked.

Hide rows, columns, sheets, and documents   You can hide rows, columns, sheets, and entire workbooks. Doing so helps prevent the worksheet from looking cluttered, and it also provides some modest protection against prying eyes.

Designate an Excel workbook as read-only recommended   You can designate an Excel workbook as read-only recommended (and use a password) to ensure that the file can't be overwritten with any changes. You make this designation in the General Options dialog box. Display this dialog box by choosing File ➪ Save As, choosing a directory, and then clicking the Tools button found on the Save As dialog box. Choose General Options to specify the appropriate password.

Assign a password   You can assign a password to prevent unauthorized users from opening your file. Choose File ➪ Info ➪ Protect Workbook ➪ Encrypt with Password.

Use a password-protected add-in   You can use a password-protected add-in, which doesn't allow the user to change anything on their worksheets.

Excel passwords are not foolproof

Be aware that Excel passwords can often be easily circumvented using commercially available password-breaking programs. Don't think of password protection as foolproof. Sure, it will be effective for the casual user. But if someone *really* wants to break your password, he or she probably can.

1

Making the application aesthetically appealing and intuitive

If you've used many different software packages, you've undoubtedly seen examples of poorly designed user interfaces, difficult-to-use programs, and just plain ugly screens. If you're developing spreadsheets for other people, you should pay particular attention to how the application looks.

How a computer program looks can make all the difference in the world to users, and the same is true of the applications that you develop with Excel. Beauty, however, is in the eye of the beholder. If your skills lean more in the analytical direction, consider enlisting the assistance of someone with a more aesthetic sensibility to provide help with design.

End users appreciate a good-looking user interface, and your applications will have a much more polished and professional look if you devote additional time to design and aesthetic considerations. An application that looks good demonstrates that its developer cared enough about the product to invest extra time and effort. Take the following suggestions into account:

Strive for consistency When designing dialog boxes, for example, try to emulate the look and feel of Excel's dialog boxes whenever possible. Be consistent with formatting, fonts, text size, and colors.

Keep it simple A common mistake that developers make is trying to cram too much information into a single screen or dialog box. A good rule is to present only one or two chunks of information at a time.

Break down input screens If you use an input screen to solicit information from the user, consider breaking it up into several, less-crowded screens. If you use a complex dialog box, you may want to break it up by using a `MultiPage` control, which lets you create a familiar tabbed dialog box.

Don't overdo color Use color sparingly. It's easy to overdo color and make the screen look gaudy.

Monitor typography and graphics Pay attention to numeric formats and use consistent typefaces, font sizes, and borders.

Evaluating aesthetic qualities is subjective. When in doubt, strive for simplicity and clarity.

Creating a user Help system

With regard to user documentation, it's a best practice to provide users with paper-based documentation or electronic documentation (or both). Providing electronic help is standard fare in Windows applications. Fortunately, your Excel applications can also provide help—even context-sensitive help. Developing help text takes quite a bit of additional effort, but for a large project it may be worth it.

Another point to consider is support for your application. In other words, who gets the phone call if the user encounters a problem? If you aren't prepared to handle routine questions, you need to identify someone who is. In some cases, you want to arrange it so that only highly technical or bug-related issues escalate to the developer.

 In Chapter 19, "Providing Help for Your Applications," we discuss several alternatives for providing help for your applications.

Documenting the development effort

Putting a spreadsheet application together is one thing. Making it understandable for other people is another. As with traditional programming, it's important that you thoroughly document your work. Such documentation helps if you need to go back to it (and you will), and it helps anyone else whom you might pass it onto.

How do you document a workbook application? You can either store the information in a worksheet or use another file. You can even use a paper document if you prefer. Perhaps the easiest way is to use a separate worksheet to store your comments and key information for the project. For VBA code, use comments liberally. (VBA text preceded with an apostrophe is ignored because that text is designated as a comment.) Although an elegant piece of VBA code can seem perfectly obvious to you today, when you come back to it in a few months, your reasoning may be completely obscured unless you use the VBA comment feature.

Distributing the application to the user

You've completed your project, and you're ready to release it to the end users. How do you go about distributing it? You can choose from many ways to distribute your application, and the method that you choose depends on many factors.

You could just hand over a download link or thumb drive, scribble a few instructions, and be on your way. Or, you may want to install the application yourself—but this approach isn't always feasible. Another option is to develop an official setup program that performs the task automatically. You can write such a program in a traditional programming language, purchase a generic setup program, or write your own in VBA.

Excel incorporates technology to enable developers to sign their applications digitally. This process is designed to help end users identify the author of an application, to ensure that the project has not been altered, and to help prevent the spread of macro viruses or other potentially destructive code. To sign a project digitally, you first apply for a digital certificate from a formal certificate authority (or you can self-sign your project by creating your own digital certificate). Refer to the Help system or the Microsoft website for additional information.

Updating the application when necessary

After you distribute your application, you're finished with it, right? You can sit back, enjoy yourself, and try to forget about the problems that you encountered (and solved) during development. In rare cases, yes, you may be finished. More often, however, the users of your application won't be completely satisfied. Sure, your application adheres to all of the *original* specifications, but things change. Seeing an application working often causes the user to think of other things that the application could be doing.

When you need to update or revise your application, you'll appreciate that you designed it well in the first place and that you fully documented your efforts.

Other Development Issues

You need to keep several other issues in mind when developing an application—especially if you don't know exactly who will be using the application. If you're developing an application that will have widespread use (a shareware application, for example), you have no way of knowing how the application will be used, what type of system it will run on, or what other software will be running concurrently.

The user's installed version of Excel

Although Excel 2019 is available, many large corporations are still using earlier versions of Excel. Unfortunately, there is no guarantee that an application developed for, say, Excel 2010 will work perfectly with later versions of Excel. If you need your application to work with a variety of Excel versions, the best approach is to work with the lowest version—and then test it thoroughly with all other versions.

Also, be aware of any security updates or new changes to Excel released with service packs (for stand-alone versions of Excel). If some of your users are on Office 365, be aware that Microsoft has adopted an agile release cycle, allowing it to release updates to Office 365 practically on a monthly basis. This is great news for those who love seeing new features added to Excel. It's not so great if you're trying to manage compatibility with your application. Although rare, some changes introduced in these releases can cause certain components of your application no longer to work as designed.

 Compatibility issues are discussed in Chapter 21, "Understanding Compatibility Issues."

Language issues

Consider yourself fortunate if all of your end users have the English language version of Excel. Non-English versions of Excel aren't always 100 percent compatible, so that means additional testing on your part. In addition, keep in mind that two users can both be using the English language version of Excel yet use different Windows regional settings. In some cases, you may need to be aware of potential problems.

 We briefly discuss language issues in Chapter 21.

System speed

Although system speed and processing power has become less of an issue on modern PCs and devices, testing your application for performance and speed is still a recommended best practice. A procedure that executes almost instantaneously on your system may take several seconds to execute on another system. In the world of computers, several seconds may be unacceptable.

> **TIP**
>
> When you gain more experience with VBA, you'll discover that there are ways to get the job done and there are ways to get the job done *fast*. It's a good idea to get into the habit of coding for speed. Other chapters in this book can certainly help you out in this area.

Video modes

As you probably know, users' video displays vary widely. Higher-resolution displays and even dual displays are becoming increasingly common. Just because you have a super-high-resolution monitor, you can't assume that everyone else does.

Video resolution can be a problem if your application relies on specific information being displayed on a single screen. For example, if you develop an input screen that fills the screen in 1280 × 1024 mode, users with a 1024 × 768 display won't be able to see the whole input screen without scrolling or zooming.

Also, it's important to realize that a *restored* (that is, not maximized or minimized) workbook is displayed at its previous window size and position. In the extreme case, it's possible that a window saved by using a high-resolution display may be completely off the screen when opened on a system running in a lower resolution.

Unfortunately, you can't automatically scale things so that they look the same regardless of the display resolution. In some cases, you can zoom the worksheet (using the Zoom control in the status bar), but doing so reliably may be difficult. Unless you're certain about the video resolution that the users of your application will use, you should probably design your application so that it works with the lowest common denominator—800 × 600 or 1024 × 768 mode.

As you will discover later in the book, you can determine the user's video resolution by using Windows API calls from VBA. In some cases, you may want to adjust things programmatically, depending on the user's video resolution.

Introducing Visual Basic for Applications

IN THIS CHAPTER

Using Excel's macro recorder

Working with the Visual Basic Editor

Understanding the Excel Object Model

Diving into the Range object

Knowing where to turn for help

Getting a Head Start with the Macro Recorder

A *macro* is essentially Visual Basic for Applications (VBA) code that you can call to execute any number of actions. In Excel, macros can be written or recorded.

Excel programming terminology can be a bit confusing. A recorded macro is technically no different from a VBA procedure that you create manually. The terms *macro* and *VBA procedure* are often used interchangeably. Many Excel users call any VBA procedure a macro. However, when most people think of macros, they think of recorded macros.

Recording a macro is like programming a phone number into your smartphone. First you manually enter and save a number. Then when you want, you can redial the number with the touch of a button. Just like on a smartphone, you can record your actions in Excel while you perform them. While you record, Excel gets busy in the background, translating and storing your keystrokes and mouse clicks to VBA code. After a macro is recorded, you can play back those actions any time you want.

The absolute best way to become familiar with VBA, without question, is simply to turn on the macro recorder and record some of the actions that you perform in Excel. This approach is a quick way to learn the relevant VBA syntax for a task.

In this section, you'll explore macros and learn how you can use the macro recorder to start familiarizing yourself with VBA.

Creating your first macro

To start recording your first macro, you first need to find the macro recorder, which is on the Developer tab. Unfortunately, Excel comes out of the box with the Developer tab hidden—you may not see it on your version of Excel at first. To display this tab, follow these steps:

1. Choose File ⇨ Excel Options.
2. In the Excel Options dialog box, select Customize Ribbon.
3. In the list box on the right, place a check mark next to Developer.
4. Click OK to return to Excel.

Now that you have the Developer tab showing in the Excel Ribbon, you can start up the macro recorder by selecting the Record Macro command found in the Code group on the Developer tab. This activates the Record Macro dialog box, as shown in Figure 2.1.

FIGURE 2.1

The Record Macro dialog box

> **NOTE**
>
> Note that you can also get to the Macro Recorder by selecting View ⇨ Macros ⇨ Macros ⇨ Record Macros. However, if you plan to work with VBA macros, you'll want to make sure that the Developer tab is visible in order to gain access to the full gamut of developer features.

Here are the four parts of the Record Macro dialog box:

Macro Name This should be self-explanatory. Excel gives a default name to your macro, such as Macro1, but you should give your macro a name more descriptive of what it actually does. For example, you might name a macro that formats a generic table as FormatTable.

Shortcut Key Every macro needs an event, or something to happen, for it to run. This event can be a button press, a workbook opening, or, in this case, a keystroke combination. When you assign a shortcut key to your macro, entering that combination of keys triggers your macro to run. This is an optional field.

Store Macro In This Workbook is the default option. Storing your macro in This Workbook simply means that the macro is stored along with the active Excel file. The next time you open that particular workbook, the macro is available to run. Similarly, if you send the workbook to another user, that user can run the macro as well (provided the macro security is properly set by your user—more on that later in this chapter).

Description This is an optional field, but it can come in handy if you have numerous macros in a workbook or if you need to give a user a more detailed description about what the macro does. The description is also useful for distinguishing one macro from another when you have multiple workbooks open or you have macros stored in the Personal Macro Workbook.

With the Record Macro dialog box open, follow these steps to create a simple macro that enters your name into a worksheet cell:

1. Enter a new single-word name for the macro to replace the default Macro1 name. A good name for this example is MyName.

2. Assign the shortcut key Ctrl+Shift+N to this macro by entering uppercase **N** in the edit box labeled Shortcut Key.

3. Click OK to close the Record Macro dialog box and begin recording your actions.

4. Type your name into the active cell and press Enter.

5. Choose Developer ⇨ Code ⇨ Stop Recording. Alternatively, you can click the Stop Recording icon in the status bar (the square icon on left side of the status bar).

Examining your macro

Excel stored your newly recorded macro in a new module that it created automatically and named Module1. To view the code in this module, you must activate the Visual Basic Editor. You can activate the VB Editor in either of two ways:

- Press Alt+F11.
- Choose Developer ⇨ Code ⇨ Visual Basic.

In the VB Editor, the Project window displays a list of all open workbooks and add-ins. This list is displayed as a tree diagram on the left of the screen, which you can expand or collapse. The code that you recorded previously is stored in Module1 in the current workbook. When you double-click Module1, the code in the module appears in the Code window.

NOTE

If you don't see a Project window in the VB Editor, you can activate it by going up to the menu and selecting View ⇨ Project Explorer. Alternatively, you can use the keyboard shortcut Ctrl+R.

The macro should look something like this:

```
Sub MyName()
'' MyName Macro
'' Keyboard Shortcut: Ctrl+Shift+N
ActiveCell.FormulaR1C1 = "Michael Alexander"
End Sub
```

The macro recorded is a `Sub` procedure that is named `MyName`. The statements tell Excel what to do when the macro is executed.

Notice that Excel inserted some comments at the top of the procedure. These comments are some of the information that appeared in the Record Macro dialog box. These comment lines (which begin with an apostrophe) aren't really necessary, and deleting them has no effect on how the macro runs. If you ignore the comments, you'll see that this procedure has only one VBA statement.

```
ActiveCell.FormulaR1C1 = "Michael Alexander"
```

This single statement causes the name you typed while recording to be inserted into the active cell.

Testing your macro

Before you recorded this macro, you set an option that assigned the macro to the Ctrl+Shift+N shortcut key combination. To test the macro, return to Excel by using either of the following methods:

- Press Alt+F11.
- Click the View Microsoft Excel button on the standard toolbar in the VB Editor window.

When Excel is active, activate a worksheet. (It can be in the workbook that contains the VBA module or in any other workbook.) Select a cell and press Ctrl+Shift+N. The macro immediately enters your name into the cell.

> **NOTE**
>
> In the preceding example, notice that you selected your target cell before you started recording your macro. This step is important. If you select a cell while the macro recorder is turned on, the actual cell that you selected will be recorded into the macro. In such a case, the macro would always format that particular cell, and it would not be a general-purpose macro.

Editing your macro

After you record a macro, you can make changes to it. For example, assume that you want your name to be bold. You could re-record the macro, but this modification is simple, so editing the code is more efficient. Press Alt+F11 to activate the VB Editor window. Then activate `Module1` and insert `ActiveCell.Font.Bold = True`, as demonstrated in the following sample code:

```
ActiveCell.Font.Bold = True
```

The edited macro appears as follows:

```
Sub MyName()
''  MyName Macro
''  Keyboard Shortcut: Ctrl+Shift+N
    ActiveCell.Font.Bold = True
    ActiveCell.FormulaR1C1 = "Michael Alexander"
End Sub
```

Test this new macro, and you'll see that it performs as it should.

Comparing absolute and relative macro recording

Now that you've read about the basics of the macro recorder interface, it's time to go deeper and begin recording a more complex macro. The first thing you need to understand before you begin is that Excel has two modes for recording: absolute reference and relative reference.

Recording macros with absolute references

Excel's default recording mode is in absolute reference. As you may know, the term *absolute reference* is often used in the context of cell references found in formulas. When a cell reference in a formula is an absolute reference, it does not automatically adjust when the formula is pasted to a new location.

The best way to understand how this concept applies to macros is to try it. Open the Chapter 2 Sample.xlsm file and record a macro that counts the rows in the Branchlist worksheet. (See Figure 2.2.)

FIGURE 2.2

Your pretotaled worksheet containing two tables

	A	B	C	D	E	F	G	H	I
1		Region	Market	Branch			Region	Market	Branch
2		NORTH	BUFFALO	601419			SOUTH	CHARLOTTE	173901
3		NORTH	BUFFALO	701407			SOUTH	CHARLOTTE	301301
4		NORTH	BUFFALO	802202			SOUTH	CHARLOTTE	302301
5		NORTH	CANADA	910181			SOUTH	CHARLOTTE	601306
6		NORTH	CANADA	920681			SOUTH	DALLAS	202600
7		NORTH	MICHIGAN	101419			SOUTH	DALLAS	490260
8		NORTH	MICHIGAN	501405			SOUTH	DALLAS	490360
9		NORTH	MICHIGAN	503405			SOUTH	DALLAS	490460
10		NORTH	MICHIGAN	590140			SOUTH	FLORIDA	301316
11		NORTH	NEWYORK	801211			SOUTH	FLORIDA	701309
12		NORTH	NEWYORK	802211			SOUTH	FLORIDA	702309
13		NORTH	NEWYORK	804211			SOUTH	NEWORLEANS	601310
14		NORTH	NEWYORK	805211			SOUTH	NEWORLEANS	602310
15		NORTH	NEWYORK	806211			SOUTH	NEWORLEANS	801607

NOTE

The sample dataset used in this chapter can be found on this book's companion website. See this book's introduction for more on the companion website.

Follow these steps to record the macro:

1. Before recording, make sure that cell A1 is selected.

2. Select Record Macro from the Developer tab.

3. Name the macro AddTotal.

4. Choose This Workbook in the Store Macro In drop-down.

5. Click OK to start recording.

   At this point, Excel is recording your actions. While Excel is recording, perform the following steps:

6. Select cell A16, and type **Total** in the cell.

7. Select the first empty cell in Column D (D16), type = COUNTA(D2:D15), and then press Enter. This gives a count of branch numbers at the bottom of column D. The COUNTA function is used to catch any branch numbers stored as text.

8. Click Stop Recording on the Developer tab to stop recording the macro.

The formatted worksheet should look like something like the one in Figure 2.3.

FIGURE 2.3

Your post-totaled worksheet

	A	B	C	D	E	F	G	H	I
1		Region	Market	Branch			Region	Market	Branch
2		NORTH	BUFFALO	601419			SOUTH	CHARLOTTE	173901
3		NORTH	BUFFALO	701407			SOUTH	CHARLOTTE	301301
4		NORTH	BUFFALO	802202			SOUTH	CHARLOTTE	302301
5		NORTH	CANADA	910181			SOUTH	CHARLOTTE	601306
6		NORTH	CANADA	920681			SOUTH	DALLAS	202600
7		NORTH	MICHIGAN	101419			SOUTH	DALLAS	490260
8		NORTH	MICHIGAN	501405			SOUTH	DALLAS	490360
9		NORTH	MICHIGAN	503405			SOUTH	DALLAS	490460
10		NORTH	MICHIGAN	590140			SOUTH	FLORIDA	301316
11		NORTH	NEWYORK	801211			SOUTH	FLORIDA	701309
12		NORTH	NEWYORK	802211			SOUTH	FLORIDA	702309
13		NORTH	NEWYORK	804211			SOUTH	NEWORLEANS	601310
14		NORTH	NEWYORK	805211			SOUTH	NEWORLEANS	602310
15		NORTH	NEWYORK	806211			SOUTH	NEWORLEANS	801607
16	Total			14					

To see your macro in action, delete the total row that you just added and play back your macro by following these steps:

1. Select Macros from the Developer tab.

2. Find and select the AddTotal macro that you just recorded.

3. Click the Run button.

If all goes well, the macro plays back your actions perfectly and gives your table a total. Here's the thing: no matter how hard you try, you can't make the AddTotal macro work on the second table. Why? Because you recorded it as an absolute macro.

To understand what this means, examine the underlying code. To examine the code, select Macros from the Developer tab to get the Macro dialog box illustrated in Figure 2.4. The Macro dialog box will, by default, list the macros available in all open Excel workbooks (including any Add-ins that you may have installed). You can limit the list to only those macros contained in the active workbook by changing the Macros In setting to This Workbook.

FIGURE 2.4

The Excel Macro dialog box

Select the AddTotal macro and click the Edit button. This opens the Visual Basic Editor to show you the code that was written when you recorded your macro.

```
Sub AddTotal()
    Range("A16").Select
    ActiveCell.FormulaR1C1 = "Total"
    Range("D16").Select
    ActiveCell.FormulaR1C1 = "=COUNTA(R[-14]C:R[-1]C)"
End Sub
```

Pay particular attention to line 2 and line 4 of the macro. When you asked Excel to select cell range A16 and then D16, those cells are exactly what it selected. Because the macro was recorded in absolute reference mode, Excel interpreted your range selection as absolute. In other words, if you select cell A16, that cell is what Excel gives you. In the next section, you will examine what the same macro looks like when recorded in relative reference mode.

Recording macros with relative references

In the context of Excel macros, relative means *relative to the currently active cell*. Thus, you should use caution with your active cell choice—both when you record the relative reference macro and when you run it.

First, make sure that the Chapter 2 Sample.xlsm file is open. (This file is available on this book's companion website.) Then use the following steps to record a relative-reference macro:

1. Select the Use Relative References toggle button from the Developer tab, as shown in Figure 2.5.

FIGURE 2.5

Recording a macro with relative references

2. Before recording, make sure that cell A1 is selected.
3. Select Record Macro from the Developer tab.
4. Name the macro AddTotalRelative.
5. Choose This Workbook in the Store Macro In drop-down.
6. Click OK to start recording.
7. Select cell A16 and type **Total** in the cell.
8. Select the first empty cell in Column D (D16), type = **COUNTA(D2:D15)**, and then press Enter.
9. Click Stop Recording on the Developer tab to stop recording the macro.

At this point, you have recorded two macros. Take a moment to examine the code for your newly created macro.

Select Macros from the Developer tab to open the Macro dialog box. Here, choose the AddTotalRelative macro and click Edit.

Again, this opens the Visual Basic Editor to show you the code that was written when you recorded your macro. This time, your code looks something like the following:

```
Sub AddTotalRelative()
    ActiveCell.Offset(15, 0).Range("A1").Select
    ActiveCell.FormulaR1C1 = "Total"
    ActiveCell.Offset(0, 3).Range("A1").Select
    ActiveCell.FormulaR1C1 = "=COUNTA(R[-14]C:R[-1]C)"
End Sub
```

Notice that there are no references to any specific cell ranges at all (other than the starting point "A1"). Let's take a moment to look at what the relevant parts of this VBA code really mean.

Notice that in line 2, Excel uses the Offset property of the active cell. This property tells the cursor to move a certain number of cells up or down and a certain number of cells left or right.

The Offset property code tells Excel to move 15 rows down and 0 columns across from the active cell (in this case, A1). There's no need for Excel to select a cell explicitly, as it did when recording an absolute reference macro.

To see this macro in action, delete the total row and do the following:

1. Select cell A1.
2. Select Macros from the Developer tab.
3. Find and select the AddTotalRelative macro.
4. Click the Run button.
5. Now select cell F1.
6. Select Macros from the Developer tab.
7. Find and select the AddTotalRelative macro.
8. Click the Run button.

Notice that this macro, unlike your previous macro, works on both sets of data. Because the macro applies the totals relative to the currently active cell, the totals are applied correctly.

For this macro to work, you simply need to ensure that

- You've selected the correct starting cell before running the macro.
- The block of data has the same number of rows and columns as the data on which you recorded the macro.

Ideally, this simple example has given you a firm grasp of macro recording of both absolute and relative references.

Other macro recording concepts

At this point, you should feel comfortable recording your own Excel macros. Next are some of the other important concepts you'll need to keep in mind when writing or recording macros.

By default, Excel workbooks are given the standard file extension .xlsx. Be aware that files with the .xlsx extension cannot contain macros. If your workbook contains macros and then you save that workbook as an .xlsx file, all VBA code is removed automatically. Luckily, Excel will warn you that your macro content will be removed when saving a workbook with macros as an .xlsx file.

If you want to retain the macros, you must save your file as an Excel Macro-Enabled Workbook. This gives your file an .xlsm extension. The idea is that all workbooks with an .xlsx file extension are automatically known to be safe, whereas you can recognize .xlsm files as a potential threat.

Alternatively, you can save your workbook as an Excel 97-2003 Workbook (with the .xls extension). The .xls file type can contain macros, but it doesn't support some of the modern features of Excel such as conditional formatting icons and pivot table slicers. You would typically use this file type only if there is a specific reason, such as that you need to have your workbook interact with an add-in that works only with .xls files.

Macro security in Excel

With the release of Office 2010, Microsoft introduced significant changes to its Office security model. One of the most significant changes is the concept of trusted documents. Without getting into the technical minutiae, a *trusted document* is essentially a workbook that you have deemed safe by enabling macros.

If you open a workbook that contains macros, you will see a yellow bar message under the Ribbon stating that macros (active content) have, in effect, been disabled.

If you click Enable, it automatically becomes a trusted document. This means that you no longer are prompted to enable the content as long as you open that file on your computer. The basic idea is that if you told Excel that you "trust" a particular workbook by enabling macros, it is highly likely that you will enable macros each time you open it. Thus, Excel remembers that you've enabled macros before and inhibits any further messages about macros for that workbook.

This is great news for you and your clients. After enabling your macros just one time, they won't be annoyed by the constant messages about macros, and you won't have to worry that your macro-enabled dashboard will fall flat because macros have been disabled.

Trusted locations

If the thought of any macro message coming up (even one time) unnerves you, you can set up a trusted location for your files. A *trusted location* is a directory that is deemed a safe zone where only trusted workbooks are placed. A trusted location allows you and your clients to run a macro-enabled workbook with no security restrictions as long as the workbook is in that location.

To set up a trusted location, follow these steps:

1. Select the Macro Security button on the Developer tab. This activates the Trust Center dialog box.

2. Click the Trusted Locations button. This opens the Trusted Locations menu (see Figure 2.6), which shows you all the directories that are considered trusted.

3. Click the Add New Location button.

4. Click Browse to find and specify the directory that will be considered a trusted location.

FIGURE 2.6

The Trusted Locations tab allows you to add directories that are considered trusted.

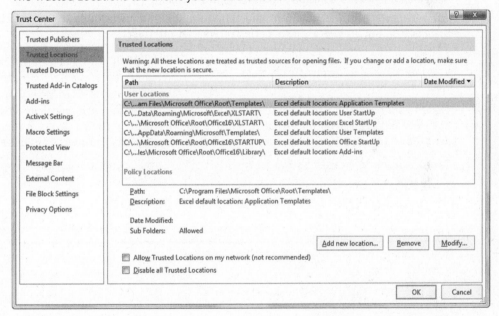

After you specify a trusted location, any Excel file that is opened from this location will have macros automatically enabled.

Storing macros in your Personal Macro Workbook

Most user-created macros are designed for use in a specific workbook, but you may want to use some macros in all of your work. You can store these general-purpose macros in the Personal Macro Workbook so that they're always available to you. The Personal Macro Workbook is loaded whenever you start Excel. This file, named `Personal.xlsb`, doesn't exist until you record a macro using Personal Macro Workbook as the destination.

To record the macro in your Personal Macro Workbook, select the Personal Macro Workbook option in the Record Macro dialog box before you start recording. This option is in the Store Macro In drop-down list (refer to Figure 2.1 in the section "Creating Your First Macro").

If you store macros in the Personal Macro Workbook, you don't have to remember to open the Personal Macro Workbook when you load a workbook that uses macros. When you want to exit, Excel asks whether you want to save changes to the Personal Macro Workbook.

> **NOTE**
>
> The Personal Macro Workbook normally is in a hidden window to keep it out of the way.

Assigning a macro to a button and other form controls

When you create macros, you may want to have a clear and easy way to run each macro. A basic button can provide a simple but effective user interface.

As luck would have it, Excel offers a set of form controls designed specifically for creating user interfaces directly on spreadsheets. There are several different types of form controls, from buttons (the most commonly used control) to scrollbars.

The idea behind using a form control is simple. You place a form control on a spreadsheet and then assign a macro to it—that is, a macro you've already recorded. When a macro is assigned to the control, that macro is executed, or played, when the control is clicked.

Take a moment to create a button for the AddTotalRelative macro you created earlier. Here's how:

1. Click the Insert button on the Developer tab (see Figure 2.7).

FIGURE 2.7

You can find the form controls on the Developer tab.

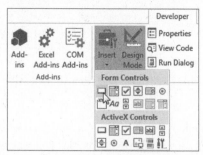

2. Select the Button control from the drop-down list that appears.
3. Click the location where you want to place your button.

   When you drop the button control onto your spreadsheet, the Assign Macro dialog box, as shown in Figure 2.8, activates and asks you to assign a macro to this button.

FIGURE 2.8

Assign a macro to the newly added button.

4. Select the macro that you want to assign to the button and then click OK.

At this point, you have a button that runs your macro when you click it. Keep in mind that all the controls in the Form Controls group (shown in Figure 2.7) work in the same way as the command button in that you right-click and choose Assign Macro to specify a macro to trigger with the control.

> **NOTE**
>
> Notice the form controls and ActiveX controls in Figure 2.7. Although they look similar, they're quite different. Form controls are designed specifically for use on a spreadsheet, and ActiveX controls are typically used on Excel user forms. As a general rule, you should always use form controls when working on a spreadsheet. Why? Form controls need less overhead, so they perform better, and configuring form controls is far easier than configuring their ActiveX counterparts.

Placing a macro on the Quick Access toolbar

You can also assign a macro to a button in Excel's Quick Access toolbar. The Quick Access toolbar sits either above or below the Ribbon. You can add a custom button that will run your macro by following these steps:

1. Right-click your Quick Access toolbar and select Customize Quick Access Toolbar. This will open the dialog box illustrated in Figure 2.9.

2. Select Macros from the Choose Commands From drop-down list on the left.

3. Select the macro that you want to add and click the Add button.

4. Click the Modify button to choose an icon for your macro and provide a friendly display name.

5. Click the OK button.

FIGURE 2.9

Adding a macro to the Quick Access toolbar

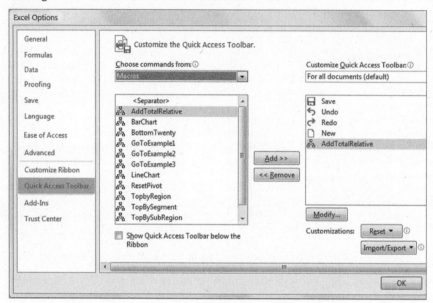

Working with the Visual Basic Editor

The Visual Basic Editor is a separate application that runs when you open Excel. To see this hidden VBE environment, you'll need to activate it. The quickest way to activate the VBE is to press Alt+F11 when Excel is active. To return to Excel, press Alt+F11 again.

You can also activate the VBE by using the Visual Basic command on Excel's Developer tab.

Understanding VBE components

Figure 2.10 shows the VBE program with some of the key parts identified. Chances are that your VBE program window won't look exactly like what you see in Figure 2.10. The VBE contains several windows and is highly customizable. You can hide windows, rearrange windows, dock windows, and so on.

Menu bar

The VBE menu bar works just like every other menu bar you've encountered. It contains commands that you use to do things with the various components in the VBE. You will also find that many of the menu commands have shortcut keys associated with them.

The VBE also features shortcut menus. You can right-click virtually anything in the VBE and get a shortcut menu of common commands.

FIGURE 2.10

The VBE with significant elements identified

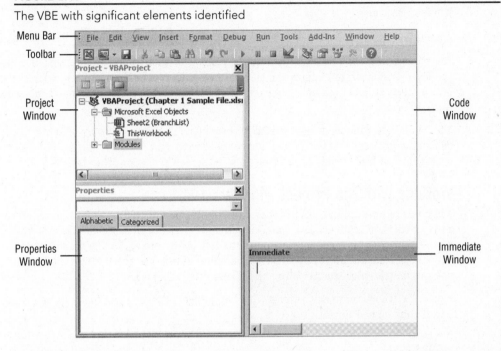

Toolbar

The Standard toolbar, which is directly under the menu bar by default, is one of four VBE toolbars available. You can customize the toolbars, move them around, display other toolbars, and so on. If you're so inclined, use the View ➪ Toolbars command to work with VBE toolbars. Most people just leave them as they are.

Project window

The Project window displays a tree diagram that shows every workbook currently open in Excel (including add-ins and hidden workbooks). Double-click items to expand or contract them. You'll explore this window in more detail in the "Working with the Project Window" section later in this chapter.

If the Project window is not visible, press Ctrl+R or use the View ➪ Project Explorer command. To hide the Project window, click the Close button in its title bar. Alternatively, right-click anywhere in the Project window and select Hide from the shortcut menu.

Code window

A Code window contains VBA code. Every object in a project has an associated Code window. To view an object's Code window, double-click the object in the Project window. For example, to view the Code window for the Sheet1 object, double-click Sheet1 in the Project window. Unless you've added some VBA code, the Code window will be empty.

You find out more about Code windows later in this chapter's "Working with a Code Window" section.

Immediate window

The Immediate window may or may not be visible. If it isn't visible, press Ctrl+G or use the View ⇨ Immediate Window command. To close the Immediate window, click the Close button in its title bar (or right-click anywhere in the Immediate window and select Hide from the shortcut menu).

The Immediate window is most useful for executing individual VBA statements and for debugging your code. If you're just starting out with VBA, this window won't be all that useful, so feel free to hide it and free up some screen space for other things.

Working with the Project window

When you're working in the VBE, each Excel workbook and add-in that's open is a project. You can think of a project as a collection of objects arranged as an outline. You can expand a project by clicking the plus sign (+) at the left of the project's name in the Project window. Contract a project by clicking the minus sign (-) to the left of a project's name. Or, you can double-click the items to expand and contract them.

Figure 2.11 shows a Project window with two projects listed: a workbook named Book1 and a workbook named Book2.

FIGURE 2.11

This Project window lists two projects. They are expanded to show their objects.

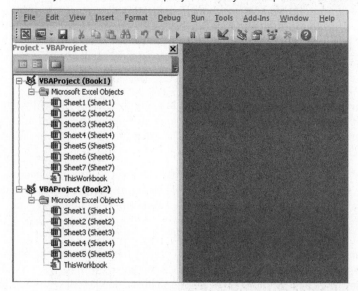

Every project expands to show at least one node called Microsoft Excel Objects. This node expands to show an item for each sheet in the workbook (each sheet is considered an object), and another object called ThisWorkbook (which represents the Workbook object). If the project has any VBA modules, the project listing also shows a Modules node.

Adding a new VBA module

When you record a macro, Excel automatically inserts a VBA module to hold the recorded code. The workbook that holds the module for the recorded macro depends on where you chose to store the recorded macro, just before you started recording.

In general, a VBA module can hold three types of code.

Declarations   One or more information statements that you provide to VBA. For example, you can declare the data type for variables you plan to use or set some other module-wide options.

Sub procedures   A set of programming instructions that performs some action. All recorded macros will be Sub procedures.

Function procedures   A set of programming instructions that returns a single value (similar in concept to a worksheet function, such as Sum).

A single VBA module can store any number of Sub procedures, Function procedures, and declarations. How you organize a VBA module is completely up to you. Some people prefer to keep all of their VBA code for an application in a single VBA module; others like to split up the code into several different modules. It's a personal choice, just like arranging furniture.

Follow these steps to add a new VBA module manually to a project:

1. Select the project's name in the Project window.
2. Choose Insert ⇨ Module.

Or you can do the following:

1. Right-click the project's name.
2. Choose Insert ⇨ Module from the shortcut menu.

The new module is added to a Modules folder in the Project window (see Figure 2.12). Any module that you create in a given workbook is placed in this Modules folder.

Removing a VBA module

You may want to remove a code module that is no longer needed. To do so, follow these steps:

1. Select the module's name in the Project window.
2. Choose File ⇨ Remove xxx, where xxx is the module name. Note that Excel will ask if you want to export the module before removing it. You can click Yes if you want to save the module for backup purposes or for importing into another workbook.

FIGURE 2.12

Code modules are visible in the Project window in a folder called Modules.

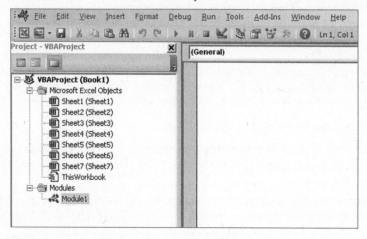

Or you can do the following:

1. Right-click the module's name in the Project window.
2. Choose Remove *xxx* from the shortcut menu.

> **NOTE**
>
> You can remove VBA modules, but there is no way to remove the other code modules such as those for the Sheet objects or for This Workbook.

Working with a Code window

As you become proficient with VBA, you spend lots of time working in Code windows. Macros that you record are stored in a module, and you can type VBA code directly into a VBA module.

Minimizing and maximizing windows

Code windows are much like workbook windows in Excel. You can minimize them, maximize them, resize them, hide them, rearrange them, and so on. Most people find it much easier to maximize the Code window on which they're working. Doing so lets you see more code and keeps you from getting distracted.

To maximize a Code window, click the maximize button in its title bar (right next to the X). Or, just double-click its title bar to maximize it. To restore a Code window to its original size, click the Restore button. When a window is maximized, its title bar isn't really visible, so you'll find the Restore button to the right of the Type a Question for Help box.

Sometimes, you may want to have two or more Code windows visible. For example, you may want to compare the code in two modules or copy code from one module to another. You can arrange the windows manually or use the Window ⇨ Tile Horizontally or Window ⇨ Tile Vertically command to arrange them automatically.

You can quickly switch among Code windows by pressing Ctrl+Tab. If you repeat that key combination, you keep cycling through all the open Code windows. Pressing Ctrl+Shift+Tab cycles through the windows in reverse order.

Minimizing a Code window gets it out of the way. You can also click the window's Close button in a Code window's title bar to close the window completely. (Closing a window just hides it; you won't lose anything.) To open it again, just double-click the appropriate object in the Project window. Working with these Code windows sounds more difficult than it really is.

Getting VBA code into a module

Before you can do anything meaningful, you must have some VBA code in the VBA module. You can get VBA code into a VBA module in three ways.

- Use the Excel macro recorder to record your actions and convert them to VBA code.
- Enter the code directly.
- Copy the code from one module and paste it into another.

You have discovered the excellent method for creating code by using the Excel Macro recorder. However, not all tasks can be translated to VBA by recording a macro. You often have to enter your code directly into the module. Entering code directly basically means either typing the code yourself or copying and pasting code you have found from somewhere else.

Entering and editing text in a VBA module works as you might expect. You can select, copy, cut, paste, and do other things to the text.

A single line of VBA code can be as long as you like. However, you may want to use the line-continuation character to break up lengthy lines of code. To continue a single line of code (also known as a *statement*) from one line to the next, end the first line with a space followed by an underscore (_). Then continue the statement on the next line. Here's an example of a single statement split into three lines:

```
Selection.Sort Key1:=Range("A1"), _
    Order1:=xlAscending, Header:=xlGuess, _
    Orientation:=xlTopToBottom
```

This statement would perform exactly the same way if it were entered in a single line (with no line-continuation characters). Notice that the second and third lines of this statement are indented. Indenting is optional, but it helps clarify the fact that these lines are not separate statements.

The VBE has multiple levels of undo and redo. If you deleted a statement that you shouldn't have, use the Undo button on the toolbar (or press Ctrl+Z) until the statement appears again. After undoing, you can use the Redo button to perform the changes you've undone.

Are you ready to enter some real, live code? Try the following steps:

1. Create a new workbook in Excel.

2. Press Alt+F11 to activate the VBE.

3. Click the new workbook's name in the Project window.

4. Choose Insert ⇨ Module to insert a VBA module into the project.

5. Type the following code into the module:

```
Sub GuessName()
    Dim Msg as String
    Dim Ans As Long
    Msg = "Is your name " & Application.UserName & "?"
    Ans = MsgBox(Msg, vbYesNo)
    If Ans = vbNo Then MsgBox "Oh, never mind."
    If Ans = vbYes Then MsgBox "I must be clairvoyant!"
End Sub
```

6. Make sure that the cursor is located anywhere within the text you typed, and press F5 to execute the procedure.

> **TIP**
>
> F5 is a shortcut for the Run ⇨ Run Sub/UserForm command.

When you enter the code listed in step 5, you might notice that the VBE makes some adjustments to the text you enter. For example, after you type the Sub statement and press Enter, the VBE automatically inserts the End Sub statement. And if you omit the space before or after an equal sign, the VBE inserts the space for you. Also, the VBE changes the color and capitalization of some text. This is all perfectly normal. It's just the VBE's way of keeping things neat and readable.

If you followed the previous steps, you just created a VBA Sub procedure, also known as a *macro*. When you press F5, Excel executes the code and follows the instructions. In other words, Excel evaluates each statement and does what you told it to do. You can execute this macro any number of times—although it tends to lose its appeal after a few dozen executions.

This simple macro uses the following concepts:

- Defining a Sub procedure (the first line)
- Declaring variables (the Dim statements)
- Assigning values to variables (Msg and Ans)

- Concatenating (joining) strings of text (using the & operator)
- Using a built-in VBA function (MsgBox)
- Using built-in VBA constants (vbYesNo, vbNo, and vbYes)
- Using an If-Then construct (twice)
- Ending a Sub procedure (the last line)

As mentioned previously, you can copy and paste code into a VBA module. For example, a Sub or Function procedure that you write for one project might also be useful in another project. Instead of wasting time reentering the code, you can activate the module and use the normal copy and paste procedures (Ctrl+C to copy and Ctrl+V to paste). After pasting it into a VBA module, you can modify the code as necessary.

Alternatively, you can right-click your module and select the Export File option. This allows you to save your module as a .bas file. Once you have your .bas file, you can open another workbook, open the VBE, and then choose File ⇨ Import File to import the saved .bas file.

Customizing the VBA environment

If you're serious about becoming an Excel programmer, you'll spend a lot of time with VBA modules on your screen. To help make things as comfortable as possible, the VBE provides quite a few customization options.

When the VBE is active, choose Tools ⇨ Options. You'll see a dialog box with four tabs: Editor, Editor Format, General, and Docking. Take a moment to explore some of the options found on each tab.

The Editor tab

Figure 2.13 shows the options accessed by clicking the Editor tab of the Options dialog box. Use the options in the Editor tab to control how certain things work in the VBE.

The Auto Syntax Check option   The Auto Syntax Check setting determines whether the VBE pops up a dialog box if it discovers a syntax error while you're entering your VBA code. The dialog box tells roughly what the problem is. If you don't choose this setting, the VBE flags syntax errors by displaying them in a different color from the rest of the code, and you don't have to deal with any dialog boxes popping up on your screen.

The Require Variable Declaration option   If the Require Variable Declaration option is set, the VBE inserts the following statement at the beginning of each new VBA module you insert: Option Explicit. Changing this setting affects only new modules, not existing modules. If this statement appears in your module, you must explicitly define each variable you use. Using a Dim statement is one way to declare variables.

The Auto List Members option   If the Auto List Members option is set, the VBE provides some help when you're entering your VBA code. It displays a list that would logically complete the statement you're typing. This is one of the best features of the VBE.

The Auto Quick Info option   If the Auto Quick Info option is selected, the VBE displays information about functions and their arguments as you type. This is similar to the way Excel lists the arguments for a function as you start typing a new formula.

The Auto Data Tips option   If the Auto Data Tips option is set, VBE displays the value of the variable over which your cursor is placed when you're debugging code. This is turned on by default and often quite useful. There is no reason to turn this option off.

The Auto Indent setting   The Auto Indent setting determines whether the VBE automatically indents each new line of code the same as the previous line. Most Excel developers are keen on using indentations in their code, so this option is typically kept on.

The Tab Width setting   The Tab Width setting is used to increase or decrease the number of spaces used when indenting code or pressing the Tab key on the keyboard.

The Drag-and-Drop Text Editing option   The Drag-and-Drop Text Editing option, when enabled, lets you copy and move text by dragging and dropping with your mouse.

The Default to Full Module View option   The Default to Full Module View option sets the default state for new modules. (It doesn't affect existing modules.) If set, procedures in the Code window appear as a single scrollable list. If this option is turned off, you can see only one procedure at a time.

The Procedure Separator option   When the Procedure Separator option is turned on, separator bars appear at the end of each procedure in a Code window. Separator bars provide a nice visual line between procedures, making it easy to see where one piece of code ends and where another starts.

FIGURE 2.13

The Editor tab in the Options dialog box

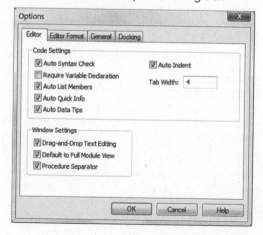

The Editor Format tab

Figure 2.14 shows the Editor Format tab of the Options dialog box. With this tab, you can customize the way the VBE looks.

The Code Colors option   The Code Colors option lets you set the text color and background color displayed for various elements of VBA code. This is largely a matter of personal preference. Most Excel developers stick with the default colors, but if you like to change things up, you can play around with these settings.

The Font option   The Font option lets you select the font that's used in your VBA modules. For best results, stick with a fixed-width font such as Courier New. In a fixed-width font, all characters are the same width. This makes your code more readable because the characters are nicely aligned vertically, and you can easily distinguish multiple spaces (which is sometimes useful).

The Size setting   The Size setting specifies the point size of the font in the VBA modules. This setting is a matter of personal preference determined by your video display resolution and how good your eyesight is.

The Margin Indicator Bar option   This option controls the display of the vertical margin indicator bar in your modules. You should keep this turned on; otherwise, you won't be able to see the helpful graphical indicators when you're debugging your code.

FIGURE 2.14

Change the VBE's looks with the Editor Format tab.

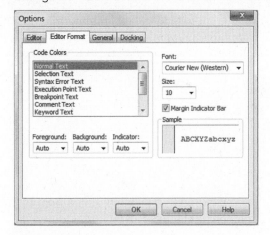

The General tab

Figure 2.15 shows the options available on the General tab in the Options dialog box. In almost every case, the default settings are just fine. The most important setting on the General tab is Error Trapping. If you are just starting your Excel macro writing career, it's best to leave the Error Trapping set to Break on Unhandled Errors. This ensures that Excel warns you of errors as you type your code—as opposed to waiting until you try to run your macro.

FIGURE 2.15

The General tab of the Options dialog box

The Docking tab

Figure 2.16 shows the Docking tab. These options determine how the various windows in the VBE behave. When a window is docked, it is fixed in place along one of the edges of the VBE program window. This makes it much easier to identify and locate a particular window. If you turn off all docking, you have a big, confusing mess of windows. Generally, the default settings work fine.

FIGURE 2.16

The Docking tab of the Options dialog box

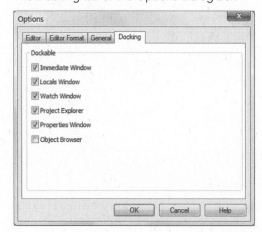

VBA Fundamentals

VBA is an object-oriented programming language. The basic concept of *object-oriented programming* is that a software application (Excel in this case) consists of various individual objects. An Excel application contains workbooks, worksheets, cells, charts, pivot tables, shapes, and the list goes on. Each object has its own set of attributes, which are called *properties*, and its own set of actions, called *methods*.

You can think of this concept just as you would of the objects you encounter every day, such as your computer or your car. Each of those objects has attributes, such as height, weight, and color. They also have their own distinct actions. For instance, your computer boots up, and your program starts.

VBA objects also have their identifiable attributes and actions. A workbook, for example, is an object with attributes (properties), such as its name, the number of worksheets it contains, and the date it was created. A workbook object also has actions (methods) such as Open, Close, and Save.

In Excel, you deal with objects such as workbooks, worksheets, and ranges on a daily basis. You likely think of each of these "objects" as all part of Excel, not really separating them in your mind. However, Excel thinks about these internally as all part of a hierarchical model called the Excel Object Model. The *Excel Object Model* is a clearly defined set of objects that are structured according to the relationships among them.

Understanding objects

In the real world, you can describe everything you see as an object. When you look at your house, it is an object. Your house has rooms; those rooms are also separate objects. Those rooms may have closets. Those closets are likewise objects. As you think about your house, the rooms, and the closets, you may see a hierarchical relationship among them. Excel works in the same way.

In Excel, the *Application object* is the all-encompassing object—similar to your house. Inside the Application object, Excel has a workbook. Inside a workbook is a worksheet. Inside that is a range. These are all objects that live in a hierarchical structure.

To point to a specific object in VBA, you can traverse the object model. For example, to get to cell A1 on Sheet 1, you can enter this code:

```
Application.ThisWorkbook.Sheets("Sheet1").Range("A1").Select
```

In most cases, the object model hierarchy is understood, so you don't have to type every level. Entering this code also gets you to cell A1 because Excel infers that you mean the active workbook and the active sheet:

```
Range("A1").Select
```

Indeed, if you have your cursor already in cell A1, you can simply use the `ActiveCell` object, negating the need to spell out the range.

```
Activecell.Select
```

Understanding collections

Many of Excel's objects belong to collections. Your house sits within a neighborhood, for example, which is a collection of houses called a neighborhood. Each neighborhood sits in a collection of neighborhoods called a city. Excel considers collections to be objects themselves.

In each Workbook object, you have a collection of Worksheets. The Worksheets collection is an object that you can call upon through VBA. Each worksheet in your workbook lives in the Worksheets collection.

If you want to refer to a worksheet in the Worksheets collection, you can refer to it by its position in the collection as an index number starting with 1 or by its name as quoted text. If you run these two lines of code in a workbook that has only one worksheet and that worksheet is called MySheet, they both do the same thing:

```
Worksheets(1).Select
Worksheets("MySheet").Select
```

If you have two worksheets in the active workbook that have the names MySheet and YourSheet, in that order, you can refer to the second worksheet by typing either of these statements:

```
Worksheets(2).Select
Worksheets("YourSheet").Select
```

If you want to refer to a worksheet in a workbook called MySheet in a particular workbook that is not active, you must qualify the worksheet reference and the workbook reference. Here's an example:

```
Workbooks("MyData.xlsx").Worksheets("MySheet").Select
```

Understanding properties

Properties are essentially the characteristics of an object. Your house has a color, a square footage, an age, and so on. Some properties can be changed, like the color of your house. Other properties can't be changed, like the year your house was constructed.

Likewise, an object in Excel, like the Worksheet object, has a sheet name property that can be changed, and a Rows.Count row property that cannot.

You refer to the property of an object by referring to the object and then the property. For instance, you can change the name of your worksheet by changing its Name property.

In this example, you are renaming Sheet1 to MySheet:

```
Sheets("Sheet1").Name = "MySheet"
```

Some properties are read-only, which means you can't assign a value to them directly—for instance, the Text property of a cell. The Text property gives you the formatted appearance of value in a cell, but you cannot overwrite or change it.

Some properties have arguments that further specify the property value. For instance, this line of code uses the RowAbsolute and ColumnAbsolute arguments to return the address of cell A1 as an absolute reference (A 1).

```
MsgBox Range("A1").Address(RowAbsolute:=True, ColumnAbsolute:=True)
```

Specifying properties for the active object

When you're working with Excel, only one workbook at a time can be active. In that workbook, only one sheet can be active. And if the sheet is a worksheet, one cell is the active cell (even if a multicell range is selected). VBA knows about active workbooks, worksheets, and cells, and it lets you refer to these active objects in a simplified manner.

This method of referring to objects is often useful because you won't always know the exact workbook, worksheet, or range on which you want to operate. VBA makes object referencing easy by providing properties of the Application object. For example, the Application object has an ActiveCell property that returns a reference to the active cell. The following instruction assigns the value 1 to the active cell:

```
ActiveCell.Value = 1
```

In the preceding example, we omitted the reference to the Application object and to the active worksheet because both are assumed. This instruction will fail if the active sheet isn't a worksheet. For example, if VBA executes this statement when a chart sheet is active, the procedure halts and you get an error message.

If a range is selected in a worksheet, the active cell is a cell within the selected range. In other words, the active cell is always a single cell (never a multicell range).

The Application object also has a Selection property that returns a reference to whatever is selected, which may be a single cell (the active cell), a range of cells, or an object such as ChartObject, TextBox, or Shape.

Table 2.1 lists the other Application properties that are useful when working with cells and ranges.

TABLE 2.1 Some Useful Properties of the Application Object

Property	Object Returned
ActiveCell	The active cell.
ActiveChart	The active chart sheet or chart contained in a ChartObject on a worksheet. This property is Nothing if a chart isn't active.
ActiveSheet	The active sheet (worksheet or chart sheet).
ActiveWindow	The active window.
ActiveWorkbook	The active workbook.
Selection	The object selected. It could be a Range object, Shape, ChartObject, and so on.
ThisWorkbook	The workbook that contains the VBA procedure being executed. This object may or may not be the same as the ActiveWorkbook object.

The advantage of using these properties to return an object is that you don't need to know which cell, worksheet, or workbook is active, and you don't need to provide a specific reference to it. This allows you to write VBA code that isn't specific to a particular workbook, sheet, or range. For example, the following instruction clears the contents of the active cell, even though the address of the active cell isn't known:

```
ActiveCell.ClearContents
```

The example that follows displays a message that tells you the name of the active sheet:

```
MsgBox ActiveSheet.Name
```

If you want to know the name and directory path of the active workbook, use a statement like this:

```
MsgBox ActiveWorkbook.FullName
```

If a range on a worksheet is selected, you can fill the entire range with a value by executing a single statement. In the following example, the `Selection` property of the `Application` object returns a `Range` object that corresponds to the selected cells. The instruction simply modifies the `Value` property of this `Range` object, and the result is a range filled with a single value.

```
Selection.Value = 12
```

If something other than a range is selected (such as a `ChartObject` or a `Shape`), the preceding statement generates an error because `ChartObject` and `Shape` objects don't have a `Value` property.

The following statement, however, enters a value of 12 into the `Range` object that was selected before a non-`Range` object was selected. If you look up the `RangeSelection` property in the Help system, you find that this property applies only to a `Window` object.

```
ActiveWindow.RangeSelection.Value = 12
```

To find out how many cells are selected in the active window, access the `Count` property. Here's an example:

```
MsgBox ActiveWindow.RangeSelection.Count
```

Understanding methods

Methods are the actions that can be performed with an object. It helps to think of methods as verbs. You can paint your house, so in VBA, that translates to something like `house.paint`.

A simple example of an Excel method is the `Select` method of the `Range` object.

```
Range("A1").Select
```

Another is the `Copy` method of the `Range` object.

```
Range("A1").Copy
```

Some methods have arguments that can dictate how they are applied. For instance, the `Paste` method can be used more effectively by explicitly defining the `Destination` argument.

```
ActiveSheet.Paste Destination:=Range("B1")
```

More about arguments

An issue that often leads to confusion among new VBA programmers concerns arguments. Some methods use arguments to clarify further the action to be taken, and some properties use arguments to specify additionally the property value. In some cases, one or more of the arguments are optional.

Consider the `Protect` method for a workbook object. Check the Help system, and you'll find that the `Protect` method takes three arguments: `Password`, `Structure`, and `Windows`. These arguments correspond to the options in the Protect Structure and Windows dialog box.

If you want to protect a workbook named `MyBook.xlsx`, for example, you might use a statement like this:

```
Workbooks("MyBook.xlsx").Protect "xyzzy", True, False
```

In this case, the workbook is protected with a password (argument 1). Its structure is protected (argument 2) but not its windows (argument 3).

If you don't want to assign a password, you can use a statement like this:

```
Workbooks("MyBook.xlsx").Protect , True, False
```

The first argument is omitted, and we specified the placeholder by using a comma.

You can make your code more readable by using named arguments. Here's an example of how you use named arguments for the preceding example:

```
Workbooks("MyBook.xlsx").Protect Structure:=True, Windows:=False
```

Using named arguments is a good idea, especially for methods that have many optional arguments and also when you need to use only a few of them. When you use named arguments, you don't need to use a placeholder for missing arguments.

For properties (and methods) that return a value, you must use parentheses around the arguments. For example, the `Address` property of a Range object takes five optional arguments. Because the `Address` property returns a value, the following statement isn't valid because the parentheses are omitted:

```
MsgBox Range("A1").Address False ' invalid
```

The proper syntax for such a statement requires parentheses as follows:

```
MsgBox Range("A1").Address(False)
```

You can also write the statement using a named argument:

```
MsgBox Range("A1").Address(RowAbsolute:=False)
```

These nuances will become clearer as you gain more experience with VBA.

Deep Dive: Working with Range Objects

Much of the work that you will do in VBA involves cells and ranges in worksheets. That being the case, let's take some time to use the Range object as a case study on how to explore and get familiar with a specific object.

Finding the properties of the Range object

Open the Visual Basic Editor and then go up to the menu and click Help ➪ Microsoft Visual Basic for Applications Help. You'll be taken to the Microsoft Developer Network (MSDN) website. While on MSDN, search for the word *Range* to see the page for the Range object. There you will discover that the Range object exposes three properties that can be used to manipulate your worksheets via VBA.

- The Range property of a Worksheet or Range class object
- The Cells property of a Worksheet object
- The Offset property of a Range object

The Range property

The Range property returns a Range object. If you consult the Help system for the Range property, you learn that this property has two syntaxes.

```
object.Range(cell1)
object.Range(cell1, cell2)
```

The Range property applies to two types of objects: a Worksheet object or a Range object. Here, cell1 and cell2 refer to placeholders for terms that Excel recognizes as identifying the range (in the first instance) and delineating the range (in the second instance). The following are a few examples of using the Range property.

You've already seen examples like the following one earlier in the chapter. The instruction that follows simply enters a value into the specified cell. In this case, it puts the value 12.3 into cell A1 on Sheet1 of the active workbook.

```
Worksheets("Sheet1").Range("A1").Value = 12.3
```

The Range property also recognizes defined names in workbooks. Therefore, if a cell is named Input, you can use the following statement to enter a value into that named cell:

```
Worksheets("Sheet1").Range("Input").Value = 100
```

The example that follows enters the same value in a range of 20 cells on the active sheet. If the active sheet isn't a worksheet, the statement causes an error message.

```
ActiveSheet.Range("A1:B10").Value = 2
```

The next example produces the same result as the preceding example:

```
Range("A1", "B10") = 2
```

The sheet reference is omitted, however, so the active sheet is assumed. Also, the `Value` property is omitted, so the default property (which is `Value` for a `Range` object) is assumed. This example also uses the second syntax of the `Range` property. With this syntax, the first argument is the cell at the top left of the range, and the second argument is the cell at the lower right of the range.

The following example uses the Excel range intersection operator (a space) to return the intersection of two ranges. In this case, the intersection is a single cell, C6. Therefore, this statement enters 3 in cell C6:

```
Range("C1:C10 A6:E6") = 3
```

Finally, if the range you're referencing is a noncontiguous range (a range where not all the cells are adjacent to each other), you can use commas to serve as a union operator. For example, the following statement enters the value 4 in five cells that make up a noncontiguous range. Note that the commas are within the quote marks.

```
Range("A1,A3,A5,A7,A9") = 4
```

So far, all the examples have used the `Range` property on a `Worksheet` object. As mentioned, you can also use the `Range` property on a `Range` object. For example, the following line of code treats the `Range` object as if it were the upper-left cell in the worksheet, and then it enters a value of 5 in the cell that *would be* B2. In other words, the reference returned is relative to the upper-left corner of the `Range` object. Therefore, the statement that follows enters a value of 5 into the cell directly to the right and one row below the active cell:

```
ActiveCell.Range("B2") = 5
```

Fortunately, you can access a cell relative to a range in a much clearer way—the `Offset` property. We discuss this property after the next section.

The Cells property

Another way to reference a range is to use the `Cells` property. You can use the `Cells` property, like the `Range` property, on `Worksheet` objects and `Range` objects. Check the Help system, and you see that the `Cells` property has three syntaxes.

```
object.Cells(rowIndex, columnIndex)
object.Cells(rowIndex)
object.Cells
```

Some examples demonstrate how to use the `Cells` property. The first example enters the value 9 in cell A1 on `Sheet1`. In this case, we're using the first syntax, which accepts the index number of the row (from 1 to 1048576) and the index number of the column (from 1 to 16384):

```
Worksheets("Sheet1").Cells(1, 1) = 9
```

Here's an example that enters the value 7 in cell D3 (that is, row 3, column 4) in the active worksheet:

```
ActiveSheet.Cells(3, 4) = 7
```

You can also use the `Cells` property on a `Range` object. When you do so, the `Range` object returned by the `Cells` property is relative to the upper-left cell of the referenced `Range`. Confusing? Probably. An example may help clear up any confusion. The following instruction enters the value 5 in the active cell. Remember, in this case, the active cell is treated as if it were cell A1 in the worksheet.

```
ActiveCell.Cells(1, 1) = 5
```

> **NOTE**
>
> The real advantage of this type of cell referencing will be apparent when you explore variables and looping (in Chapter 3, "VBA Programming Fundamentals"). In most cases, you don't use actual values for the arguments; rather, you use variables.

To enter a value of 5 in the cell directly below the active cell, you can use the following instruction:

```
ActiveCell.Cells(2, 1) = 5
```

Think of the preceding example as though it said this: "Start with the active cell and consider this cell as cell A1. Place 5 in the cell in the second row and the first column."

The second syntax of the `Cells` property uses a single argument that can range from 1 to 17,179,869,184. This number is equal to the number of cells in an Excel worksheet. The cells are numbered starting from A1 and continuing right and then down to the next row. The 16,384th cell is XFD1; the 16,385th cell is A2.

The next example enters the value 2 into cell SZ1 (which is the 520th cell in the worksheet) of the active worksheet:

```
ActiveSheet.Cells(520) = 2
```

To display the value in the last cell in a worksheet (XFD1048576), use this statement:

```
MsgBox ActiveSheet.Cells(17179869184)
```

You can also use this syntax with a `Range` object. In this case, the cell returned is relative to the `Range` object referenced. For example, if the `Range` object is A1:D10 (40 cells), the `Cells` property can have an argument from 1 to 40 and can return one of the cells in the `Range` object. In the following example, a value of 2000 is entered in cell A2 because A2 is the 5th cell (counting from the top, to the right, and then down) in the referenced range:

```
Range("A1:D10").Cells(5) = 2000
```

> **NOTE**
>
> In the preceding example, the argument for the `Cells` property isn't limited to values between 1 and 40. If the argument exceeds the number of cells in the range, the counting continues as if the range were taller than it actually is. Therefore, a statement like the preceding one could change the value in a cell that's outside the range A1:D10. The statement that follows, for example, changes the value in cell A11:
>
> ```
> Range("A1:D10").Cells(41) = 2000
> ```

The third syntax for the `Cells` property simply returns all cells on the referenced worksheet. Unlike the other two syntaxes, in this one, the return data isn't a single cell. This example uses the `ClearContents` method on the range returned by using the `Cells` property on the active worksheet. The result is that the content of every cell on the worksheet is cleared.

```
ActiveSheet.Cells.ClearContents
```

Getting information from a cell

If you need to get the contents of a cell, VBA provides several properties. The following are the most commonly used properties:

- The `Formula` property returns the formula in a single cell, if the cell has one. If the cell doesn't contain a formula, it returns the value in the cell. The `Formula` property is a read/write property. Variations on this property include `FormulaR1C1`, `FormulaLocal`, and `FormulaArray`. (Consult the Help system for details.)

- The `Value` property returns the raw, unformatted value in the cell. This property is a read/write property.

- The `Text` property returns the text that is displayed in the cell. If the cell contains a numeric value, this property includes all the formatting, such as commas and currency symbols. The `Text` property is a read-only property.

- The `Value2` property is just like the `Value` property, except that it doesn't use the `Date` and `Currency` data types. Rather, this property converts `Date` and `Currency` data types to `Variants` containing `Doubles`. If a cell contains the date 5/1/2019, the `Value` property returns it as a `Date`, while the `Value2` property returns it as a double (for example, 43586).

The Offset property

The `Offset` property, like the `Range` and `Cells` properties, also returns a `Range` object. But unlike the other two methods discussed, the `Offset` property applies only to a `Range` object and no other class. Its syntax is as follows:

```
object.Offset(rowOffset, columnOffset)
```

The `Offset` property takes two arguments that correspond to the relative position from the upper-left cell of the specified `Range` object. The arguments can be positive (down or to the right), negative (up or to the left), or 0. The example that follows enters a value of 12 into the cell directly below the active cell:

```
ActiveCell.Offset(1,0).Value = 12
```

The next example enters a value of 15 in the cell directly above the active cell:

```
ActiveCell.Offset(-1,0).Value = 15
```

If the active cell is in row 1, the `Offset` property in the preceding example generates an error because it can't return a `Range` object that doesn't exist.

The `Offset` property is useful, especially when you use variables in looping procedures. We discuss these topics in the next chapter.

When you record a macro using the relative reference mode, Excel uses the `Offset` property to reference cells relative to the starting position (that is, the active cell when macro recording begins). For example, we used the macro recorder to generate the following code. We started with the cell pointer in cell B1, entered values into B1:B3, and then returned to B1.

```
Sub Macro1()
    ActiveCell.FormulaR1C1 = "1"
    ActiveCell.Offset(1, 0).Range("A1").Select
    ActiveCell.FormulaR1C1 = "2"
    ActiveCell.Offset(1, 0).Range("A1").Select
    ActiveCell.FormulaR1C1 = "3"
    ActiveCell.Offset(-2, 0).Range("A1").Select
End Sub
```

The macro recorder uses the `FormulaR1C1` property. Normally, you want to use the `Value` property to enter a value in a cell. However, using `FormulaR1C1` or even `Formula` produces the same result. Also, the generated code references cell A1—a cell that wasn't even involved in the macro. This notation is a quirk in the macro recording procedure that makes the code more complex than necessary. You can delete all references to Range ("A1"), and the macro still works perfectly.

```
Sub Modified_Macro1()
    ActiveCell.FormulaR1C1 = "1"
    ActiveCell.Offset(1, 0).Select
    ActiveCell.FormulaR1C1 = "2"
    ActiveCell.Offset(1, 0).Select
    ActiveCell.FormulaR1C1 = "3"
    ActiveCell.Offset(-2, 0).Select
End Sub
```

In fact, you can enter this much more efficient version of the macro. In this version, you don't do any selecting.

```
Sub Macro1()
    ActiveCell = 1
    ActiveCell.Offset(1, 0) = 2
    ActiveCell.Offset(2, 0) = 3
End Sub
```

Essential Concepts to Remember

In this section, we cover some additional essential concepts for would-be VBA gurus. These concepts will become clearer when you work with VBA and read subsequent chapters:

Objects have unique properties and methods. Each object has its own set of properties and methods. Some properties and methods are common to various objects. For example, many objects in Excel have a `Name` property and a `Delete` method.

You can manipulate objects without selecting them. This idea may be contrary to how you normally think about manipulating objects in Excel. After all, to work with an object in Excel, you have to select that object manually first, right?

Well, this is not so when using VBA. It's usually more efficient to perform actions on objects without selecting them first.

However, when you record a macro, Excel records every step you take, *including* selecting objects before you work with them. These are unnecessary steps that may make your macro run more slowly. You can generally remove the lines of code in your recorded macro that selects objects.

It's important that you understand the concept of collections. Most of the time, you refer to an object indirectly by referring to the collection in which it's located. For example, to access a `Workbook` object named `Myfile`, reference the `Workbooks` collection as follows:

```
Workbooks("Myfile.xlsx")
```

This reference returns an object, which is the workbook with which you're concerned.

Properties can return a reference to another object. For example, in the following statement, the `Font` property returns a `Font` object contained in a `Range` object. Bold is a property of the `Font` object, not the `Range` object.

```
Range("A1").Font.Bold = True
```

You can refer to the same object in many ways. Assume that you have a workbook named `Sales`, and it's the only workbook open. Then assume that this workbook has one worksheet, named `Summary`. You can refer to the sheet in any of the following ways:

```
Workbooks("Sales.xlsx").Worksheets("Summary")
Workbooks(1).Worksheets(1)
Workbooks(1).Sheets(1)
Application.ActiveWorkbook.ActiveSheet
ActiveWorkbook.ActiveSheet
ActiveSheet
```

The method that you use is usually determined by how much you know about the workspace. For example, if more than one workbook is open, the second and third methods aren't reliable. If you want to work with the active sheet (whatever it may be), any of the last three methods would work. To be absolutely sure that you're referring to a specific sheet on a specific workbook, the first method is your best choice.

About the code examples

Throughout this book, we present many small snippets of VBA code to make a point or to provide an example. In some cases, this code consists of a single statement, or only an *expression*, which isn't a valid instruction by itself.

For example, the following is an expression:

```
Range("A1").Value
```

To test an expression, you must evaluate it. The MsgBox function is a handy tool for this:

```
MsgBox Range("A1").Value
```

To try these examples, put the statement in a procedure in a VBA module, like this:

```
Sub Test()
    ' statement goes here
End Sub
```

Then put the cursor anywhere in the procedure and press F5 to execute it. Also, make sure that the code is being executed in the proper context. For example, if a statement refers to Sheet1, make sure that the active workbook has a sheet named Sheet1.

If the code is just a single statement, you can use the VBE Immediate window. The Immediate window is useful for executing a statement immediately, without having to create a procedure. If the Immediate window isn't displayed, press Ctrl+G in the VBE.

Just type the VBA statement in the Immediate window and press Enter. To evaluate an expression in the Immediate window, precede the expression with a question mark (?), which is a shortcut for Print. For example, you can type the following in the Immediate window:

```
? Range("A1").Value
```

The result of this expression is displayed in the next line of the Immediate window.

Don't Panic—You Are Not Alone

If this is your first exposure to VBA, you're probably a bit overwhelmed by objects, properties, and methods. That's normal. No one is going to be a VBA expert in one day. VBA is a journey of time and practice. The good news is that you won't be alone on this journey. There are plenty of resources out there that can help you on your path. This section highlights a few resources you can leverage when you need a push in the right direction.

Read the rest of the book

Don't forget, the name of this chapter is "Introducing Visual Basic for Applications." The remainder of this book covers many additional details and provides many useful and informative examples.

Let Excel help write your macro

One of the best places to get macro help is the macro recorder in Excel. When you record a macro with the macro recorder, Excel writes the underlying VBA for you. After recording, you can review the code, see what the recorder is doing, and then try to turn the code it creates into something more suited to your needs. For example, let's say you need a macro that refreshes all the pivot tables in your workbook and clears all of the filters in each pivot table.

Writing this macro from a blank canvas would be a daunting task. Instead, you can start the macro recorder and record yourself refreshing all the pivot tables and clearing all the filters. Once you've stopped recording, you can review the macro and make any changes that you deem necessary.

Use the Help system

To a new Excel user, the Help system may seem like a clunky mechanism that returns a perplexing list of topics that has nothing to do with the topic you're searching. The truth is, however, once you learn how to use the Excel Help system effectively, it's often the fastest and easiest way to get extra help on a topic.

You just need to remember two basic tenets of the Excel Help system: location matters when asking for help, and you need to be connected to the Internet to use Excel's Help system.

Location matters when asking for help

In Excel, there are actually two Help systems: one providing help on Excel features and another providing help on VBA programming topics. Instead of doing a global search with your criteria, Excel throws your search criteria only against the Help system that is relevant to your current location. This essentially means that the help you get is determined by the area of Excel in which you're working. So, if you need help on a topic that involves macros and VBA programming, you'll need to be in the Visual Basic Editor while performing your search. This will ensure that your keyword search is performed on the correct Help system.

You need to be connected to the Internet

When you search for help on a topic, Excel checks to see if you're connected to the Internet. If you are, Excel takes you to the MSDN website where you can search for the topic on which you need help. If you aren't connected to the Internet, Excel gives you a message telling you that you need to be online to use Help.

Use the Object Browser

The *Object Browser* is a handy tool that lists every property and method available for every object. When you are in the VBE, you can bring up Object Browser in any of the following three ways:

- Press F2.
- Choose View ➪ Object Browser.
- Click the Object Browser button on the Standard toolbar.

The Object Browser is shown in Figure 2.17.

The drop-down list in the upper-left corner of Object Browser includes a list of all object libraries to which you have access:

- Excel itself
- MSForms (if user forms are utilized in your workbook)

FIGURE 2.17

The Object Browser is a great reference source.

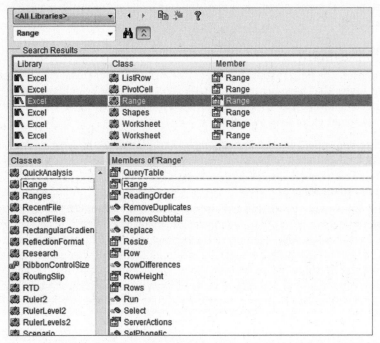

- Office (objects common to all Microsoft Office applications)
- Stdole (OLE automation objects)
- VBA
- The current project (the project that's selected in Project Explorer) and any workbooks referenced by that project

Your selection in this upper-left drop-down list determines what is displayed in the Classes window, and your selection in the Classes window determines what is visible in the Members Of panel.

After you select a library, you can search for a particular text string to get a list of properties and methods that contain the text. You do so by entering the text in the second drop-down list and then clicking the binoculars (Search) icon.

1. Select the library of interest.

   If you're not sure which object library is appropriate, you can select <All Libraries>.

2. Enter the object you're seeking in the drop-down list below the library list.

3. Click the binoculars icon to begin the text search.

The Search Results window displays the matching text. Select an object to display its classes in the Classes window. Select a class to display its members (properties, methods, and constants). Pay attention to the bottom pane, which shows more information about the object. You can press F1 to go directly to the appropriate help topic.

Object Browser may seem complex at first, but its usefulness to you will increase over time.

Pilfer code from the Internet

All the macro syntax you will ever need has likely been documented somewhere on the Internet. In many ways, programming has become less about the code one creates from scratch and more about how to take existing code and apply it creatively to a particular scenario.

If you are stuck trying to create a macro for a particular task, fire up your favorite online search engine and simply describe the task you are trying to accomplish. For the best results, enter **Excel VBA** before your description.

For example, if you are trying to write a macro that deletes all the blank rows in a worksheet, search for *Excel VBA delete blank rows in a worksheet*. You can bet two months' salary that someone out there on the Internet has tackled the same problem. Nine times out of 10, you will find some example code that will give you the nugget of information you need to jump-start some ideas for building your own macro.

Leverage user forums

If you find yourself in a bind, you can post your question in a forum to get customized guidance based on your scenario.

User forums are online communities that revolve around a particular topic. In these forums, you can post questions and have experts offer advice on how to solve particular problems. The folks answering the questions are typically volunteers who have a passion for helping the community solve real-world challenges.

There are many forums dedicated to all things Excel. To find an Excel Forum, enter the words **Excel Forum** in your favorite online search engine.

Here are a few tips for getting the most out of user forums:

- Always read and follow the forum rules before you get started. These rules often include advice on posting questions and community etiquette guidelines.
- Use concise and accurate subject titles for your questions. Don't create forum questions with abstract titles like "Need Advice" or "Please Help."
- Keep the scope of your questions as narrow as possible. Don't ask questions like "How do I build an invoicing macro in Excel?"
- Be patient. Remember that the folks answering your questions are volunteers who typically have day jobs. Give the community some time to answer your question.

- Check back often. After posting your question, you may receive requests for more details about your scenario. Do everyone a favor and return to your posting either to review the answers or respond to follow-up questions.
- Thank the expert who answered your question. If you receive an answer that helps you, take a moment to post a thank you to the expert who helped you out.

Visit expert blogs

There are a few dedicated Excel gurus who share their knowledge through blogs. These blogs are often treasure troves of tips and tricks, offering nuggets that can help build up your skills. Best of all, they are free!

Although these blogs will not necessarily speak to your particular needs, they offer articles that advance your knowledge of Excel and can even provide general guidance on how to apply Excel in practical business situations.

Here is a starter list of a few of the best Excel blogs on the Internet today:

```
http://chandoo.org
http://www.contextures.com
http://www.datapigtechnologies.com/blog
http://www.dailydoseofexcel.com
http://www.excelguru.ca/blog
http://www.mrexcel.com
```

Mine YouTube for video training

Some of us learn better if we watch a task being done. If you find that you absorb video training better than online articles, consider mining YouTube. There are dozens of channels run by amazing folks who have a passion for sharing knowledge. You'll be surprised at how many free high-quality video tutorials you'll find.

Go to www.youtube.com and search for the words *Excel VBA*.

Learn from the Microsoft Office Dev Center

The Microsoft Office Dev Center is a site dedicated to helping new developers get a quick start in programming Office products. You can get to the Excel portion of this site by going to

https://msdn.microsoft.com/en-us/library/office/fp179694.aspx

Although the site can be a bit difficult to navigate, it's worth a visit to see all of the free resources, including sample code, tools, step-by-step instructions, and much more.

Dissect the other Excel files in your organization

Like finding gold in your backyard, the existing files in your organization are often a treasure trove for learning. Consider cracking open those Excel files that contain macros and take a look under the covers. See how others in your organization use macros. Try to go through the macros line by line and see if you can spot new techniques. You may even stumble upon entire chunks of useful code that you can copy and implement in your own workbooks.

Ask your local Excel genius

Do you have an Excel genius in your company, department, organization, or community? Make friends with that person today. Most Excel experts love sharing their knowledge. Don't be afraid to approach your local Excel guru to ask questions or seek out advice on how to tackle macro problems.

2

VBA Programming Fundamentals

IN THIS CHAPTER

Understanding VBA language elements, including variables, data types, constants, and arrays

Using VBA built-in functions

Manipulating objects and collections

Controlling the execution of your procedures

VBA Language Elements: An Overview

If you've used other programming languages, much of the information in this chapter may sound familiar. However, VBA has a few unique wrinkles, so even experienced programmers may find some new information.

This chapter explores the VBA *language elements*, which are the keywords and control structures that you use to write VBA routines.

To get the ball rolling, take a look at the following VBA Sub procedure. This simple procedure, which is stored in a VBA module, calculates the sum of the first 100 positive integers. When the code finishes executing, the procedure displays a message with the result.

```
Sub VBA_Demo()
    ' This is a simple VBA Example
    Dim Total As Long, i As Long
    Total = 0
    For i = 1 To 100
        Total = Total + i
    Next i
    MsgBox Total
End Sub
```

This procedure uses some common VBA language elements, including the following:

- A comment (the line that begins with an apostrophe)
- A variable declaration statement (the line that begins with Dim)

- Two variables (`Total` and `i`)
- Two assignment statements (`Total = 0` and `Total = Total + i`)
- A looping structure (`For - Next`)
- A VBA function (`MsgBox`)

You will explore all of these language elements in subsequent sections of this chapter.

> **NOTE**
>
> VBA procedures need not manipulate any objects. The preceding procedure, for example, doesn't do anything with objects. It simply works with numbers.

Entering VBA code

VBA code, which resides in a VBA module, consists of instructions. The accepted practice is to use one instruction per line. This standard isn't a requirement, however; you can use a colon to separate multiple instructions on a single line. The following example combines four instructions on one line:

```
Sub OneLine()
    x= 1: y= 2: z= 3: MsgBox x + y + z
End Sub
```

Most programmers agree that code is easier to read if you use one instruction per line.

```
Sub MultipleLines()
  x = 1
  y = 2
  z = 3
  MsgBox x + y + z
End Sub
```

Each line can be as long as you like; the VBA module window scrolls to the left when you reach the right side. However, reading very long lines of code while having to scroll is not a particularly pleasant. For lengthy lines, it's considered a best practice to use VBA's line continuation sequence: a space followed by an underscore (_). Here's an example:

```
Sub LongLine()
  SummedValue = _
    Worksheets("Sheet1").Range("A1").Value + _
    Worksheets("Sheet2").Range("A1").Value
End Sub
```

When you record macros, Excel often uses the line continuation sequence to break a long statement into multiple lines.

After you enter an instruction, VBA performs the following actions to improve readability:

- **It inserts spaces between operators.** If you enter `Ans=1+2` (without spaces), for example, VBA converts it to the following:

```
Ans = 1 + 2
```

- **It adjusts the case of the letters for keywords, properties, and methods.** If you enter the following text:

```
Result=activesheet.range("a1").value=12
```

VBA converts it to the following:

```
Result = ActiveSheet.Range("a1").Value = 12
```

Notice that text within quotation marks (in this case, "a1") isn't changed.

- **Because VBA variable names aren't case-sensitive, the VBE, by default, adjusts the names of all variables with the same letters so that their case matches the case of letters that you most recently typed.** For example, if you first specify a variable as `myvalue` (all lowercase) and then enter the variable as `MyValue` (mixed case), the VBA changes all other occurrences of the variable to `MyValue`. An exception occurs if you declare the variable with `Dim` or a similar statement; in this case, the variable name always appears as it was declared.

- **VBA scans the instruction for syntax errors.** If VBA finds an error, it changes the color of the line and might display a message describing the problem. In the Visual Basic Editor, choose the Tools ⇨ Options command to display the Options dialog box, where you control the error color (use the Editor Format tab) and whether the error message is displayed (use the Auto Syntax Check option in the Editor tab).

Comments

A *comment* is descriptive text embedded in your code and ignored by VBA. It's a good idea to use comments liberally to describe what you're doing because an instruction's purpose isn't always obvious.

You can use a complete line for your comment, or you can insert a comment *after* an instruction on the same line. A comment is indicated by an apostrophe. VBA ignores any text that follows an apostrophe—except when the apostrophe is contained within quotation marks—up until the end of the line. For example, the following statement doesn't contain a comment, even though it has an apostrophe:

```
Msg = "Can't continue"
```

The following example shows a VBA procedure with three comments:

```
Sub CommentDemo()
'       This procedure does nothing of value
        x = 0 'x represents nothingness
'       Display the result
        MsgBox x
End Sub
```

Although the apostrophe is the preferred comment indicator, you can also use the Rem keyword to mark a line as a comment. Here's an example:

```
Rem -- The next statement prompts the user for a filename
```

The Rem keyword (short for *Remark*) is essentially a holdover from older versions of BASIC, and it is included in VBA for the sake of compatibility. Unlike the apostrophe, Rem can be written only at the beginning of a line, not on the same line as another instruction.

The following are a few general tips on making the best use of comments:

- Use comments to describe briefly the purpose of each procedure that you write.
- Use comments to describe changes you make to a procedure.
- Use comments to indicate you're using functions or constructs in an unusual or a nonstandard manner.
- Use comments to describe the purpose of variables so that you and other people can decipher otherwise cryptic names.
- Use comments to describe workarounds that you develop to overcome Excel bugs or limitations.
- Write comments *while* you code rather than afterward.
- When you've completed all coding, take some time to go back and tidy up your comments, removing any comments that are no longer needed and expanding on comments that may be incomplete or a bit too cryptic.

TIP

In some cases, you may want to test a procedure without including a particular instruction or group of instructions. Instead of deleting the instruction, convert it to a comment by inserting an apostrophe at the beginning. VBA then ignores the instruction when the routine is executed. To convert the comment back to an instruction, just delete the apostrophe.

The Visual Basic Editor offers an Edit toolbar containing tools to assist you in editing your code. In particular, there are two handy buttons that enable you to comment and uncomment entire blocks of code at once.

Note that the Edit toolbar isn't displayed by default. To display this toolbar, choose View ⇨ Toolbars ⇨ Edit.

You can select several lines of code at once and then click the Comment Block button on the Edit toolbar to convert the selected lines to comments. The Uncomment Block button converts a group of comments back into uncommented code.

Variables, Data Types, and Constants

VBA's main purpose is to manipulate data. Some data resides in objects, such as worksheet ranges. Other data is stored in variables that you create.

You can think of a *variable* as a named storage location in your computer's memory. Variables can accommodate a wide variety of *data types*—from simple Boolean values (True or False) to large, double-precision values (see the following section). You assign a value to a variable by using the equal sign operator (more about this process in the upcoming section "Assignment Statements").

You make your life easier if you get into the habit of making your variable names as descriptive as possible. VBA does, however, have a few rules regarding variable names.

- You can use alphabetic characters, numbers, and some punctuation characters, but the first character must be alphabetic.
- VBA doesn't distinguish between case. To make variable names more readable, programmers often use mixed case (for example, InterestRate rather than interestrate).
- You can't use spaces or periods. To make variable names more readable, programmers often use the underscore character (Interest _ Rate).
- You can't embed special type declaration characters (#, $, %, &, or !) in a variable name.
- Variable names can be as long as 254 characters—but using such long variable names isn't recommended.

The following list contains some examples of assignment expressions that use various types of variables. The variable names are to the left of the equal sign. Each statement assigns the value to the right of the equal sign to the variable on the left.

```
x = 1
InterestRate = 0.075
LoanPayoffAmount = 243089.87
DataEntered = False
x = x + 1
MyNum = YourNum * 1.25
UserName = "Bob Johnson"
DateStarted = #12/14/2012#
```

VBA has many *reserved words*, which are words that you can't use for variable or procedure names. If you attempt to use one of these words, you get an error message. For example, although the reserved word Next might make a very descriptive variable name, the following instruction generates a syntax error:

```
Next = 132
```

Unfortunately, syntax error messages aren't always descriptive. If the Auto Syntax Check option is turned on, you get the error `Compile error: Expected: variable`. If Auto Syntax Check is turned off, attempting to execute this statement results in `Compile error: Syntax error`. It would be more helpful if the error message were something like `Reserved word used as a variable`. So, if an instruction produces a strange error message, check the VBA Help system to ensure that your variable name doesn't have a special use in VBA.

Defining data types

VBA makes life easy for programmers because it can automatically handle all the details involved in dealing with data. Some programming languages, however, are *strictly typed*, which means that the programmer must explicitly define the data type for every variable used.

Data type refers to how data is stored in memory—as integers, real numbers, strings, and so on. Although VBA can take care of data typing automatically, it does so at a cost: slower execution and less efficient use of memory. As a result, letting VBA handle data typing may present problems when you're running large or complex applications. Another advantage of explicitly declaring your variables as a particular data type is that VBA can perform some additional error checking at the compile stage. These errors might otherwise be difficult to locate.

Table 3.1 lists VBA's assortment of built-in data types. (Note that you can also define custom data types, which are covered later in this chapter in the section "User-Defined Data Types.")

> **NOTE**
>
> The `Decimal` data type is unusual because you can't declare it. In fact, it is a subtype of a variant. You need to use the VBA `CDec` function to convert a variant to the `Decimal` data type.

Generally, it's best to use the data type that uses the smallest number of bytes yet still can handle all the data that will be assigned to it. When VBA works with data, execution speed is partially a function of the number of bytes that VBA has at its disposal. In other words, the fewer the bytes used by the data, the faster that VBA can access and manipulate the data.

For worksheet calculation, Excel uses the `Double` data type, so that's a good choice for processing numbers in VBA when you don't want to lose any precision. For integer calculations, you can use the `Integer` type (which is limited to values less than or equal to 32,767). Otherwise, use the `Long` data type. In fact, using the `Long` data type even for values less than 32,767 is recommended because this data type may be a bit faster than using the `Integer` type. When dealing with Excel worksheet row numbers, you want to

TABLE 3.1 VBA Built-in Data Types

Data Type	Bytes Used	Range of Values
Byte	1 byte	0 to 255.
Boolean	2 bytes	True or False.
Integer	2 bytes	–32,768 to 32,767.
Long	4 bytes	–2,147,483,648 to 2,147,483,647.
Single	4 bytes	–3.402823E38 to –1.401298E-45 (for negative values); 1.401298E-45 to 3.402823E38 (for positive values).
Double	8 bytes	–1.79769313486232E308 to –4.94065645841247E-324 (negative values); 4.94065645841247E-324 to 1.79769313486232E308 (for positive values).
Currency	8 bytes	–922,337,203,685,477.5808 to 922,337,203,685,477.5807.
Decimal	12 bytes	+/–79,228,162,514,264,337,593,543, 950,335 with no decimal point; +/–7.9228162514264337593543950335 with 28 places to the right of the decimal.
Date	8 bytes	January 1, 0100 to December 31, 9999.
Object	4 bytes	Any object reference.
String (variable length)	10 bytes + string length	0 to approximately 2 billion characters.
String (fixed length)	Length of string	1 to approximately 65,400 characters.
Variant (with numbers)	16 bytes	Any numeric value up to the range of a double data type. It can also hold special values, such as Empty, Error, Nothing, and Null.
Variant (with characters)	22 bytes + string length	0 to approximately 2 billion.
User-defined	Varies	Varies by element.

use the Long data type because the number of rows in a worksheet exceeds the maximum value for the Integer data type.

Declaring variables

If you don't declare the data type for a variable that you use in a VBA routine, VBA uses the default data type, Variant. Data stored as a Variant acts like a chameleon: it changes type, depending on what you do with it.

The following procedure demonstrates how a variable can assume different data types:

```
Sub VariantDemo()
    MyVar = True
    MyVar = MyVar * 100
    MyVar = MyVar / 4
    MyVar = "Answer: " & MyVar
    MsgBox MyVar
End Sub
```

In the VariantDemo procedure, MyVar starts as a Boolean. The multiplication operation converts it to an Integer. The division operation converts it to a Double. Finally, it's concatenated with text to make it a String. The MsgBox statement displays the final string: Answer: -25.

To demonstrate further the potential problems in dealing with Variant data types, try executing this procedure:

```
Sub VariantDemo2()
    MyVar = "123"
    MyVar = MyVar + MyVar
    MyVar = "Answer: " & MyVar
    MsgBox MyVar
End Sub
```

The message box displays Answer: 123123. This is probably *not* what you wanted. When dealing with variants that contain text strings, the + operator will join (concatenate) the strings together rather than perform addition.

Determining a data type

You can use the VBA TypeName function to determine the data type of a variable. Here's a modified version of the VariantDemo procedure. This version displays the data type of MyVar at each step.

```
Sub VariantDemo3()
    MyVar = True
    MsgBox TypeName(MyVar)
    MyVar = MyVar * 100
    MsgBox TypeName(MyVar)
    MyVar = MyVar / 4
    MsgBox TypeName(MyVar)
    MyVar = "Answer: " & MyVar
    MsgBox TypeName(MyVar)
    MsgBox MyVar
End Sub
```

Thanks to VBA, the data type conversion of undeclared variables is automatic. This process may seem like an easy way out, but remember that you sacrifice speed and memory—and you run the risk of errors that you may not even know about.

Declaring each variable in a procedure before you use it is an excellent habit. Declaring a variable tells VBA its name and data type. Declaring variables provides two main benefits.

- **Your programs run faster and use memory more efficiently.** The default data type, `Variant`, causes VBA to perform time-consuming checks repeatedly and reserve more memory than necessary. If VBA knows the data type, it doesn't have to investigate, and it can reserve just enough memory to store the data.

- **You avoid problems involving misspelled variable names.** This benefit assumes that you use `Option Explicit` to force yourself to declare all variables (see the next section). Say that you use an undeclared variable named `CurrentRate`. At some point in your routine, however, you insert the statement `CurentRate = .075`. This misspelled variable name, which is difficult to spot, will likely cause your routine to give incorrect results.

Forcing yourself to declare all variables

To force yourself to declare all the variables that you use, include the following as the first instruction in your VBA module:

```
Option Explicit
```

When this statement is present, VBA won't even execute a procedure if it contains an undeclared variable name. VBA issues the error message shown in Figure 3.1, and you must declare the variable before you can proceed.

FIGURE 3.1

VBA's way of telling you that your procedure contains an undeclared variable

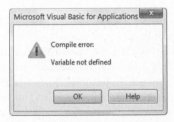

Scoping variables

A variable's *scope* determines in which modules and procedures you can use the variable. Table 3.2 lists the three ways in which a variable can be scoped.

TABLE 3.2   Variable Scope

Scope	To Declare a Variable with This Scope
Single procedure	Include a `Dim` or `Static` statement within the procedure.
Single module	Include a `Dim` or `Private` statement before the first procedure in a module.
All modules	Include a `Public` statement before the first procedure in a module.

We discuss each scope further in the following sections.

A note about the examples in this chapter

This chapter contains many examples of VBA code, usually presented in the form of simple procedures. These examples demonstrate various concepts as simply as possible. Most of these examples don't perform any particularly useful task; in fact, the task can often be performed in a different (perhaps more efficient) way. In other words, don't use these examples in your own work. Subsequent chapters provide many more code examples that *are* useful.

Local variables

A *local variable* is one declared within a procedure. You can use local variables only in the procedure in which they're declared. When the procedure ends, the variable no longer exists, and Excel frees up the memory that the variable used. If you need the variable to retain its value when the procedure ends, declare it as a `Static` variable. (See the section "Static variables" later in this chapter.)

The most common way to declare a local variable is to place a `Dim` statement between a `Sub` statement and an `End Sub` statement. `Dim` statements usually are placed right after the `Sub` statement, before the procedure's code.

> **NOTE**
>
> `Dim` is a shortened form of *Dimension*. In old versions of BASIC, this statement was used exclusively to declare the dimensions for an array. In VBA, the `Dim` keyword is used to declare any variable, not just arrays.

The following procedure uses six local variables declared by using `Dim` statements:

```
Sub MySub()
    Dim x As Integer
    Dim First As Long
    Dim InterestRate As Single
    Dim TodaysDate As Date
    Dim UserName As String
    Dim MyValue
'          - [The procedure's code goes here] -
End Sub
```

Notice that the last `Dim` statement in the preceding example doesn't declare a data type; it simply names the variable. As a result, that variable becomes a variant.

You also can declare several variables with a single `Dim` statement. Here's an example:

```
Dim x As Integer, y As Integer, z As Integer
Dim First As Long, Last As Double
```

CAUTION

Unlike some languages, VBA doesn't let you declare a group of variables to be a particular data type by separating the variables with commas. For example, the following statement, although valid, does *not* declare all the variables as integers:

```
Dim i, j, k As Integer
```

In VBA, only `k` is declared to be an integer; the other variables are declared variants. To declare `i`, `j`, and `k` as integers, use this statement:

```
Dim i As Integer, j As Integer, k As Integer
```

If a variable is declared with a local scope, other procedures in the same module can use the same variable name, but each instance of the variable is unique to its own procedure.

In general, local variables are the most efficient because VBA frees up the memory that they use when the procedure ends.

Module-wide variables

Sometimes, you want a variable to be available to all procedures in a module. If so, just declare the variable *before* the module's first procedure (outside of any procedures or functions).

In the following example, the `Dim` statement is the first instruction in the module. Both `Procedure1` and `Procedure2` have access to the `CurrentValue` variable.

```
Dim CurrentValue as Long
Sub Procedure1()
' - [Code goes here] -
End Sub
```

```
Sub Procedure2()
' - [Code goes here] -
End Sub
```

The value of a module-wide variable retains its value when a procedure ends normally (that is, when it reaches the `End Sub` or `End Function` statement). An exception is if the procedure is halted with an `End` statement. When VBA encounters an `End` statement, all variables in all modules lose their values.

Public variables

To make a variable available to all the procedures in all the VBA modules in a project, declare the variable at the module level (before the first procedure declaration) by using the `Public` keyword rather than `Dim`. Here's an example:

```
Public CurrentRate as Long
```

The `Public` keyword makes the `CurrentRate` variable available to any procedure in the VBA project, even those in other modules in the project. You must insert this statement before the first procedure in a module (any module). This type of declaration must appear in a standard VBA module, not in a code module for a sheet or a UserForm.

Static variables

Static variables are a special case. They're declared at the procedure level, and they retain their value when the procedure ends normally. However, if the procedure is halted by an `End` statement, static variables *do* lose their values. Note that an `End` statement is not the same as an `End Sub` statement.

You declare static variables by using the `Static` keyword.

```
Sub MySub()
    Static Counter as Long
    '- [Code goes here] -
End Sub
```

Working with constants

A variable's value may change while a procedure is executing (that's why it's called a *variable*). Sometimes, you need to refer to a named value or string that never changes: a *constant*.

Using constants throughout your code in place of hard-coded values or strings is an excellent programming practice. For example, if your procedure needs to refer to a specific value (such as an interest rate) several times, it's better to declare the value as a constant and use the constant's name rather than its value in your expressions. Not only does this technique make your code more readable, it also makes it easier to change should the need arise—you have to change only one instruction rather than several.

Declaring constants

You declare constants with the `Const` statement. Here are some examples:

```
Const NumQuarters as Integer = 4
Const Rate = .0725, Period = 12
Const ModName as String = "Budget Macros"
Public Const AppName as String = "Budget Application"
```

The second example doesn't declare a data type. Consequently, VBA determines the data type from the value. The `Rate` variable is a `Double`, and the `Period` variable is an `Integer`. Because a constant never changes its value, you normally want to declare your constants as a specific data type.

Like variables, constants have a scope. If you want a constant to be available within a single procedure only, declare it after the `Sub` or `Function` statement to make it a local constant. To make a constant available to all procedures in a module, declare it before the first procedure in the module. To make a constant available to all modules in the workbook, use the `Public` keyword and declare the constant before the first procedure in a module. Here's an example:

```
Public Const InterestRate As Double = 0.0725
```

> **NOTE**
>
> If your VBA code attempts to change the value of a constant, you get an error (`Assignment to constant not permitted`). This message is what you would expect. A constant is a constant, not a variable.

Using predefined constants

Excel and VBA make available many predefined constants, which you can use without declaring. In fact, you don't even need to know the value of these constants to use them. The macro recorder generally uses constants rather than actual values. The following procedure uses a built-in constant (`xlLandscape`) to set the page orientation to landscape for the active sheet:

```
Sub SetToLandscape()
    ActiveSheet.PageSetup.Orientation = xlLandscape
End Sub
```

It's often useful to record a macro just to discover the various constants that can be used. And, if you have the `AutoList Members` option turned on, you can often get some assistance while you enter your code (see Figure 3.2). In many cases, VBA lists all the constants that you can assign to a property.

The actual value for `xlLandscape` is 2 (which you can discover by using the Immediate window). The other built-in constant for changing paper orientation is `xlPortrait`, which

FIGURE 3.2

VBA displays a list of constants that you can assign to a property.

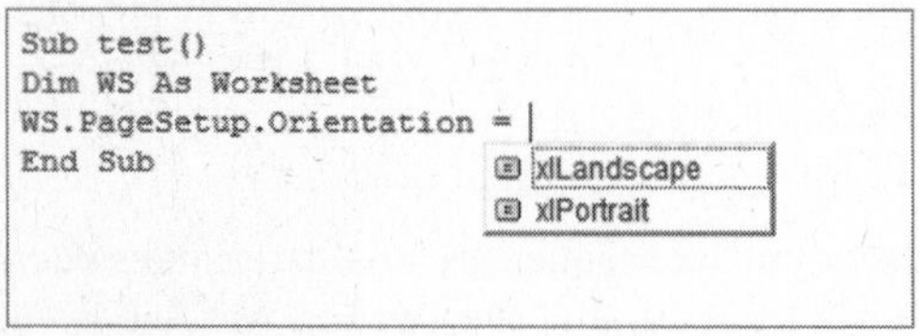

```
Sub test()
Dim WS As Worksheet
WS.PageSetup.Orientation = |
End Sub                    ⊠ xlLandscape
                           ⊠ xlPortrait
```

has a value of 1. Obviously, if you use the built-in constants, you don't really need to know their values.

> **NOTE**
>
> The Object Browser can display a list of all Excel and VBA constants. In the VBE, press F2 to bring up the Object Browser.

Working with strings

Like Excel, VBA can manipulate both numbers and text (strings). There are two types of strings in VBA.

- *Fixed-length strings* are declared with a specified number of characters. The maximum length is 65,535 characters.
- *Variable-length strings* theoretically can hold up to 2 billion characters.

Each character in a string requires 1 byte of storage, plus a small amount of storage for the header of each string. When you declare a variable with a `Dim` statement as data type `String`, you can specify the length if you know it (that is, a fixed-length string), or you can let VBA handle it dynamically (a variable-length string).

In the following example, the `MyString` variable is declared to be a string with a maximum length of 50 characters. `YourString` is also declared as a string; but it's a variable-length string, so its length is not fixed.

```
Dim MyString As String * 50
Dim YourString As String
```

Working with dates

You can use a string variable to store a date, but if you do, it's not a real date (meaning that you can't perform date calculations with it). Using the `Date` data type is a better way to work with dates.

A variable defined as a date uses 8 bytes of storage and can hold dates ranging from January 1, 0100, to December 31, 9999. That's a span of nearly 10,000 years—more than enough for even the most aggressive financial forecast! The `Date` data type is also useful for storing time-related data. In VBA, you specify dates and times by enclosing them between two hash marks (#).

 In Chapter 5, "Creating Function Procedures," we describe some relatively simple VBA functions that enable you to create formulas that work with pre-1900 dates in a worksheet.

About Excel's date bug

It is commonly known that Excel has a date bug: it incorrectly assumes that the year 1900 is a leap year. Even though there was no February 29, 1900, Excel accepts the following formula and displays the result as the 29th day of February 1900:

```
=Date(1900,2,29)
```

VBA doesn't have this date bug. The VBA equivalent of Excel's DATE function is DateSerial. The following expression (correctly) returns March 1, 1900:

```
DateSerial(1900,2,29)
```

Therefore, Excel's date serial number system doesn't correspond exactly to the VBA date serial number system. These two systems return different values for dates between January 1, 1900, and February 28, 1900.

Here are some examples of declaring variables and constants as Date data types:

```
Dim Today As Date
Dim StartTime As Date
Const FirstDay As Date = #1/1/2019#
Const Noon = #12:00:00#
```

If you use a message box to display a date, it's displayed according to your system's short date format. Similarly, a time is displayed according to your system's time format (either 12- or 24-hour). You can modify these system settings by using the Regional Settings option in the Windows Control Panel.

Assignment Statements

An *assignment statement* is a VBA instruction that evaluates an expression and assigns the result to a variable or an object. Excel's Help system defines *expression* as "a combination of keywords, operators, variables, and constants that yields a string, number, or object. An expression can perform a calculation, manipulate characters, or test data."

Much of the work done in VBA involves developing (and debugging) expressions. If you know how to create formulas in Excel, you'll have no trouble creating expressions in VBA. With a worksheet formula, Excel displays the result in a cell. The result of a VBA expression, on the other hand, can be assigned to a variable or used as a property value.

VBA uses the equal sign (=) as its assignment operator. The following are examples of assignment statements (the expressions are to the right of the equal sign):

```
x = 1
x = x + 1
x = (y * 2) / (z * 2)
FileOpen = True
FileOpen = Not FileOpen
Range("TheYear").Value = 2010
```

Often, expressions use functions. These functions can be built-in VBA functions, Excel's worksheet functions, or custom functions that you develop in VBA. We discuss built-in VBA functions later in this chapter (see the upcoming section "Built-in Functions").

> **TIP**
> Expressions can be complex. You may want to use the line continuation sequence (space followed by an underscore) to make lengthy expressions easier to read.

Operators play a major role in VBA. Familiar operators describe mathematical operations, including addition (+), multiplication (*), division (/), subtraction (–), exponentiation (^), and string concatenation (&). Less familiar operators are the backslash (\) operator (used in integer division) and the Mod operator (used in modulo arithmetic). The Mod operator returns the remainder of one number divided by another. For example, the following expression returns 2:

```
17 Mod 3
```

VBA also supports the same comparison operators used in Excel formulas: equal to (=), greater than (>), less than (<), greater than or equal to (>=), less than or equal to (<=), and not equal to (<>).

With one exception, the order of precedence for operators in VBA is exactly the same as in Excel (see Table 3.3). And, of course, you can use parentheses to change the default order of precedence.

TABLE 3.3   Operator Precedence

Operator	Operation	Order of Precedence
^	Exponentiation	1
* and /	Multiplication and division	2
+ and -	Addition and subtraction	3
&	Concatenation	4
=, <, >, <=, >=, <>	Comparison	5

> **CAUTION**
>
> The negation operator (a minus sign) is handled differently in VBA. In Excel, the following formula returns 25:
>
> ```
> =-5^2
> ```
>
> In VBA, x equals –25 after this statement is executed.
>
> ```
> x = -5 ^ 2
> ```
>
> VBA performs the exponentiation operation first and then applies the negation operator. The following statement returns 25:
>
> ```
> x = (-5) ^ 2
> ```

In the statement that follows, x is assigned the value 10 because the multiplication operator has a higher precedence than the addition operator:

```
x = 4 + 3 * 2
```

To avoid ambiguity, you may prefer to write the statement as follows:

```
x = 4 + (3 * 2)
```

In addition, VBA provides a full set of logical operators, shown in Table 3.4. For complete details on these operators (including examples), use the VBA Help system.

TABLE 3.4   VBA Logical Operators

Operator	What It Does
Not	Performs a logical negation on an expression
And	Performs a logical conjunction on two expressions
Or	Performs a logical disjunction on two expressions
Xor	Performs a logical exclusion on two expressions
Eqv	Performs a logical equivalence on two expressions
Imp	Performs a logical implication on two expressions

The following instruction uses the Not operator to toggle the gridline display in the active window. The DisplayGridlines property takes a value of either True or False. Therefore, using the Not operator changes False to True and True to False.

```
ActiveWindow.DisplayGridlines = Not ActiveWindow.DisplayGridlines
```

The following expression performs a logical And operation. The MsgBox statement displays True only when Sheet1 is the active sheet *and* the active cell is in Row 1. If either or both of these conditions aren't true, the MsgBox statement displays False.

```
MsgBox ActiveSheet.Name = "Sheet1" And ActiveCell.Row = 1
```

The following expression performs a logical Or operation. The MsgBox statement displays True when either Sheet1 *or* Sheet2 is the active sheet.

```
MsgBox ActiveSheet.Name = "Sheet1" Or ActiveSheet.Name = "Sheet2"
```

Arrays

An *array* is a group of elements of the same type that have a common name. You refer to a specific element in the array by using the array name and an index number. For example, you can define an array of 12 string variables so that each variable corresponds to the name of a month. If you name the array MonthNames, you can refer to the first element of the array as MonthNames(0), the second element as MonthNames(1), and so on, up to MonthNames(11).

Declaring arrays

You declare an array with a Dim or Public statement, just as you declare a regular variable. You can also specify the number of elements in the array. You do so by specifying the first index number, the keyword To, and the last index number—all inside parentheses. For example, here's how to declare an array comprising exactly 100 integers:

```
Dim MyArray(1 To 100) As Integer
```

> **TIP**
>
> When you declare an array, you need to specify only the upper index, in which case VBA assumes that 0 is the lower index. Therefore, the two statements that follow have the same effect:
>
> ```
> Dim MyArray(0 To 100) As Integer
> Dim MyArray(100) As Integer
> ```
>
> In both cases, the array consists of 101 elements.

By default, VBA assumes zero-based arrays. If you would like VBA to assume that 1 is the lower index for all arrays that declare only the upper index, include the following statement before any procedures in your module:

```
Option Base 1
```

Declaring multidimensional arrays

The array examples in the preceding section are one-dimensional arrays. VBA arrays can have up to 60 dimensions, although you'll rarely need more than three dimensions (a 3D array). The following statement declares a 100-integer array with two dimensions (2D):

```
Dim MyArray(1 To 10, 1 To 10) As Integer
```

You can think of the preceding array as occupying a 10 × 10 matrix. To refer to a specific element in a 2D array, you need to specify two index numbers. For example, here's how you can assign a value to an element in the preceding array:

```
MyArray(3, 4) = 125
```

The following is a declaration for a 3D array that contains 1,000 elements (visualize this array as a cube):

```
Dim MyArray(1 To 10, 1 To 10, 1 To 10) As Integer
```

Reference an item in the array by supplying three index numbers.

```
MyArray(4, 8, 2) = 0
```

Declaring dynamic arrays

A *dynamic array* doesn't have a preset number of elements. You declare a dynamic array with a blank set of parentheses.

```
Dim MyArray() As Integer
```

Before you can use a dynamic array in your code, however, you must use the ReDim statement to tell VBA how many elements are in the array. You can use a variable to assign the number of elements in an array. Often the value of the variable isn't known until the procedure is executing. For example, if the variable x contains a number, you can define the array's size by using this statement:

```
ReDim MyArray (1 To x)
```

You can use the ReDim statement any number of times, changing the array's size as often as you need. When you change an array's dimensions, the existing values are destroyed. If you want to preserve the existing values, use ReDim Preserve. Here's an example:

```
ReDim Preserve MyArray (1 To y)
```

Arrays crop up later in this chapter when we discuss looping (see the section "Looping blocks of instructions").

3

Object Variables

An *object variable* is one that represents an entire object, such as a range or a worksheet. Object variables are important for two reasons.

- They can simplify your code significantly.
- They can make your code execute more quickly.

Object variables, like normal variables, are declared with the Dim or Private or Public statement. For example, the following statement declares InputArea as a Range object variable:

```
Dim InputArea As Range
```

Use the Set keyword to assign an object to the variable. Here's an example:

```
Set InputArea = Range("C16:E16")
```

To see how object variables simplify your code, examine the following procedure, which doesn't use an object variable:

```
Sub NoObjVar()
    Worksheets("Sheet1").Range("A1").Value = 124
    Worksheets("Sheet1").Range("A1").Font.Bold = True
    Worksheets("Sheet1").Range("A1").Font.Italic = True
    Worksheets("Sheet1").Range("A1").Font.Size = 14
    Worksheets("Sheet1").Range("A1").Font.Name = "Cambria"
End Sub
```

This routine enters a value into cell A1 of Sheet1 on the active workbook, applies some formatting, and changes the fonts and size. That's a lot of typing. To reduce wear and tear on your fingers (and make your code more efficient), you can condense the routine with an object variable.

```
Sub ObjVar()
    Dim MyCell As Range
    Set MyCell = Worksheets("Sheet1").Range("A1")
    MyCell.Value = 124
    MyCell.Font.Bold = True
    MyCell.Font.Italic = True
    MyCell.Font.Size = 14
    MyCell.Font.Name = "Cambria"
End Sub
```

After the variable MyCell is declared as a Range object, the Set statement assigns an object to it. Subsequent statements can then use the simpler MyCell reference in place of the lengthy Worksheets("Sheet1").Range("A1") reference.

The true value of object variables will become apparent when we discuss looping later in this chapter.

User-Defined Data Types

VBA lets you create custom, or *user-defined*, data types. A *user-defined data type* can ease your work with some types of data. For example, if your application deals with customer information, you may want to create a user-defined data type named `CustomerInfo`.

```
Type CustomerInfo
    Company As String
    Contact As String
    RegionCode As Long
    Sales As Double
End Type
```

After you create a user-defined data type, you use a `Dim` statement to declare a variable as that type. Usually, you define an array. Here's an example:

```
Dim Customers(1 To 100) As CustomerInfo
```

Each of the 100 elements in this array consists of four components (as specified by the user-defined data type, `CustomerInfo`). You can refer to a particular component of the record as follows:

```
Customers(1).Company = "Acme Tools"
Customers(1).Contact = "Tim Robertson"
Customers(1).RegionCode = 3
Customers(1).Sales = 150674.98
```

3

You can also work with an element in the array as a whole. For example, to copy the information from `Customers(1)` to `Customers(2)`, use this instruction:

```
Customers(2) = Customers(1)
```

The preceding example is equivalent to the following instruction block:

```
Customers(2).Company = Customers(1).Company
Customers(2).Contact = Customers(1).Contact
Customers(2).RegionCode = Customers(1).RegionCode
Customers(2).Sales = Customers(1).Sales
```

Built-in Functions

Like most programming languages, VBA has a variety of *built-in functions* that simplify calculations and operations. Many VBA functions are similar (or identical) to Excel worksheet functions. For example, the VBA function `UCase`, which converts a string argument to uppercase, is equivalent to the Excel worksheet function `UPPER`.

 Appendix A contains a complete list of VBA functions, with a brief description of each. All are thoroughly described in the VBA Help system.

TIP

To get a list of VBA functions while you're writing your code, type **VBA** followed by a period (.).V BE displays a list of all its members, including functions (see Figure 3.3). The functions are preceded by a green icon. If this technique doesn't work for you, make sure that the Auto List Members option is selected. Choose Tools ⇨ Options and then click the Editor tab.

FIGURE 3.3

Displaying a list of VBA functions in VBE

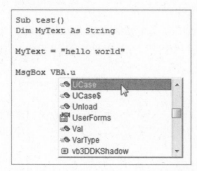

You use functions in VBA expressions in much the same way that you use functions in worksheet formulas. Here's a simple procedure that calculates the square root of a variable (using the VBA Sqr function), stores the result in another variable, and then displays the result:

```
Sub ShowRoot()
    Dim MyValue As Double
    Dim SquareRoot As Double
    MyValue = 25
    SquareRoot = Sqr(MyValue)
    MsgBox SquareRoot
End Sub
```

The VBA Sqr function is equivalent to the Excel SQRT worksheet function.

You can use many (but not all) of Excel's worksheet functions in your VBA code. The WorksheetFunction object, which is contained in the Application object, holds all the worksheet functions that you can call from your VBA procedures.

To use a worksheet function in a VBA statement, just precede the function name with this:

```
Application.WorksheetFunction
```

The following example demonstrates how to use an Excel worksheet function in a VBA procedure. Excel's infrequently used ROMAN function converts a decimal number into a Roman numeral.

```
Sub ShowRoman()
    Dim DecValue As Long
    Dim RomanValue As String
    DecValue = 1939
    RomanValue = Application.WorksheetFunction.Roman(DecValue)
    MsgBox RomanValue
End Sub
```

When you execute this procedure, the MsgBox function displays the string MCMXXXIX.

Keep in mind that you can't use worksheet functions that have an equivalent VBA function. For example, VBA can't access the Excel SQRT worksheet function because VBA has its own version of that function, Sqr. Therefore, the following statement generates an error:

```
MsgBox Application.WorksheetFunction.Sqrt(123) 'error
```

 In Chapter 5, you will discover that you can use VBA to create custom worksheet functions that work just like Excel's built-in worksheet functions.

The MsgBox function

The MsgBox function is one of the most useful VBA functions. Many of the examples in this chapter use this function to display the value of a variable.

This function often is a good substitute for a simple custom dialog box. It's also a useful debugging tool because you can insert MsgBox functions at any time to pause your code and display the result of a calculation or an assignment.

Most functions return a single value, which you assign to a variable. The MsgBox function not only returns a value but also displays a dialog box to which the user can respond. The value returned by the MsgBox function represents the user's response to the dialog box. You can use the MsgBox function even when you have no interest in the user's response but want to take advantage of the message display.

The official syntax of the MsgBox function has five arguments (those in square brackets are optional).

```
MsgBox(prompt[, buttons][, title][, helpfile, context])
```

> prompt: Required. The message displayed in the pop-up display.
>
> buttons: Optional. A value that specifies which buttons and which icons, if any, appear in the message box. Use built-in constants—for example, vbYesNo.
>
> title: Optional. The text that appears in the message box's title bar. The default is Microsoft Excel.
>
> helpfile: Optional. The name of the Help file associated with the message box.
>
> context: Optional. The context ID of the Help topic, which represents a specific Help topic to display. If you use the context argument, you must also use the helpfile argument.

You can assign the value returned to a variable, or you can use the function by itself without an assignment statement. This example assigns the result to the variable Ans:

```
Dim Ans As Long
Ans = MsgBox("Continue?", vbYesNo + vbQuestion, "Tell me")
If Ans = vbNo Then Exit Sub
```

Note that we used the sum of two built-in constants (vbYesNo + vbQuestion) for the buttons argument. Using vbYesNo displays two buttons in the message box: one labeled Yes and one labeled No. Adding vbQuestion to the argument also displays a question mark icon. When the first statement is executed, Ans contains one of two values, represented by the constant vbYes or vbNo. In this example, if the user clicks the No button, the procedure ends.

See Chapter 12, "Leveraging Custom Dialog Boxes," for more information about the MsgBox function.

Manipulating Objects and Collections

As an Excel programmer, you'll spend a lot of time working with objects and collections. Therefore, you want to know the most efficient ways to write your code to manipulate these objects and collections. VBA offers two important constructs that can simplify working with objects and collections.

- With-End With constructs
- For Each-Next constructs

With-End With constructs

The With-End With construct enables you to perform multiple operations on a single object. To start understanding how the With-End With construct works, examine the following procedure, which modifies six properties of a selection's formatting. (The selection is assumed to be a Range object.)

```
Sub ChangeFont1()
    Selection.Font.Name = "Cambria"
    Selection.Font.Bold = True
    Selection.Font.Italic = True
    Selection.Font.Size = 12
    Selection.Font.Underline = xlUnderlineStyleSingle
    Selection.Font.ThemeColor = xlThemeColorAccent1
End Sub
```

You can rewrite this procedure using the With-End With construct. The following procedure performs exactly like the preceding one:

```
Sub ChangeFont2()
    With Selection.Font
        .Name = "Cambria"
        .Bold = True
        .Italic = True
        .Size = 12
        .Underline = xlUnderlineStyleSingle
        .ThemeColor = xlThemeColorAccent1
    End With
End Sub
```

Some people think that the second incarnation of the procedure is more difficult to read. Remember, though, that the objective is increased speed. Although the first version may be more straightforward and easier to understand, a procedure that uses the With-End With construct to change several properties of an object can be faster than the equivalent procedure that explicitly references the object in each statement.

3

For Each-Next constructs

Recall from the preceding chapter that a *collection* is a group of related objects. For example, the `Workbooks` collection is a collection of all open `Workbook` objects. You can also work with many other collections.

Suppose you want to perform some action on all objects in a collection. Or suppose you want to evaluate all objects in a collection and take action under certain conditions. These occasions are perfect for the `For Each-Next` construct because you don't have to know how many elements are in a collection to use the `For Each-Next` construct.

The syntax of the `For Each-Next` construct is as follows:

```
For Each element In collection
    [instructions]
    [Exit For]
    [instructions]
Next [element]
```

The following procedure uses the `For Each-Next` construct with the Worksheets collection in the active workbook. When you execute the procedure, the `MsgBox` function displays each worksheet's `Name` property. (If five worksheets are in the active workbook, the `MsgBox` function is called five times.)

```
Sub CountSheets()
    Dim Item as Worksheet
    For Each Item In ActiveWorkbook.Worksheets
        MsgBox Item.Name
    Next Item
End Sub
```

The next example uses `For Each-Next` to cycle through all objects in the Windows collection and count the number of windows that are hidden:

```
Sub HiddenWindows()
    Dim iCount As Integer
    Dim Win As Window
```

```
        iCount = 0
    For Each Win In Windows
        If Not Win.Visible Then iCount = iCount + 1
    Next Win
    MsgBox iCount & " hidden windows."
End Sub
```

For each window, if the window is hidden, the iCount variable is incremented. When the loop ends, the message box displays the value of iCount.

Here's an example that closes all workbooks except the active workbook. This procedure uses the If-Then construct to evaluate each workbook in the Workbooks collection:

```
Sub CloseInactive()
    Dim Book as Workbook
    For Each Book In Workbooks
    If Book.Name <> ActiveWorkbook.Name Then Book.Close
    Next Book
End Sub
```

A common use for the For Each-Next construct is to loop through all of the cells in a range. The next example of For Each-Next is designed to be executed after the user selects a range of cells. Here, the Selection object acts as a collection that consists of Range objects because each cell in the selection is a Range object. The procedure evaluates each cell and uses the VBA UCase function to convert its contents to uppercase. (Numeric cells are not affected.)

```
Sub MakeUpperCase()
    Dim Cell as Range
    For Each Cell In Selection
    Cell.Value = UCase(Cell.Value)
    Next Cell
End Sub
```

VBA provides a way to exit a For-Next loop before all the elements in the collection are evaluated. Do this with an Exit For statement. The example that follows selects the first negative value in Row 1 of the active sheet:

```
Sub SelectNegative()
    Dim Cell As Range
    For Each Cell In Range("1:1")
        If Cell.Value < 0 Then
            Cell.Select
            Exit For
        End If
    Next Cell
End Sub
```

This example uses an If-Then construct to check the value of each cell. If a cell is negative, it's selected, and then the loop ends when the Exit For statement is executed.

Controlling Code Execution

Some VBA procedures start at the top and progress line by line to the bottom. Macros that you record, for example, always work in this fashion. Often, however, you need to control the flow of your routines by skipping over some statements, executing some statements multiple times, and testing conditions to determine what the routine does next.

The preceding section describes the `For Each-Next` construct, which is a type of loop. This section discusses the additional ways of controlling the execution of your VBA procedures.

- `GoTo` statements
- `If-Then` constructs
- `Select Case` constructs
- `For-Next` loops
- `Do While` loops
- `Do Until` loops

GoTo statements

The most straightforward way to change the flow of a program is to use a `GoTo` statement. This statement simply transfers program execution to a new instruction, which must be preceded by a label (a text string followed by a colon, or a number with no colon). VBA procedures can contain any number of labels, but a `GoTo` statement can't branch outside a procedure.

The following procedure uses the VBA `InputBox` function to get the user's name. If the name is not *Howard*, the procedure branches to the `WrongName` label and ends. Otherwise, the procedure executes some additional code. The `Exit Sub` statement causes the procedure to end.

```
Sub GoToDemo()
    UserName = InputBox("Enter Your Name:")
    If UserName <> "Howard" Then GoTo WrongName
    MsgBox ("Welcome Howard...")
'       -[More code here] -
    Exit Sub
WrongName:
    MsgBox "Sorry. Only Howard can run this macro."
End Sub
```

This simple procedure works, but it's not an example of good programming. In general, you should use the `GoTo` statement only when you have no other way to perform an action. In fact, the only time you *really* need to use a `GoTo` statement in VBA is for error handling (refer to Chapter 4, "Working with VBA Sub Procedures").

Finally, it goes without saying that the preceding example is *not* intended to demonstrate an effective security technique!

If-Then constructs

Perhaps the most commonly used instruction grouping in VBA is the If-Then construct. This common instruction is one way to endow your applications with decision-making capability. Good decision-making is the key to writing successful programs.

The basic syntax of the If-Then construct is as follows:

```
If condition Then true_instructions [Else false_instructions]
```

The If-Then construct is used to execute one or more statements conditionally. The Else clause is optional. If included, the Else clause lets you execute one or more instructions when the condition that you're testing isn't True.

The following procedure demonstrates an If-Then structure without an Else clause. The example deals with time, and VBA uses a date-and-time serial number system similar to Excel's. The time of day is expressed as a fractional value—for example, noon is represented as .5. The VBA Time function returns a value that represents the time of day, as reported by the system clock.

In the following example, a message is displayed if the time is before noon. If the current system time is greater than or equal to .5, the procedure ends, and nothing happens.

```
Sub GreetMe1()
    If Time < 0.5 Then MsgBox "Good Morning"
End Sub
```

Another way to code this routine is to use multiple statements, as follows:

```
Sub GreetMe1a()
    If Time < 0.5 Then
        MsgBox "Good Morning"
    End If
End Sub
```

Note that the If statement has a corresponding End If statement. In this example, only one statement is executed if the condition is True. You can, however, place any number of statements between the If and End If statements.

If you want to display a different greeting when the time of day is after noon, add another If-Then statement, as follows:

```
Sub GreetMe2()
    If Time < 0.5 Then MsgBox "Good Morning"
    If Time >= 0.5 Then MsgBox "Good Afternoon"
End Sub
```

Notice that we used >= (greater than or equal to) for the second If-Then statement. This covers the remote chance that the time is precisely 12 p.m.

3

Another approach is to use the `Else` clause of the `If-Then` construct. Here's an example:

```
Sub GreetMe3()
    If Time < 0.5 Then MsgBox "Good Morning" Else _
        MsgBox "Good Afternoon"
End Sub
```

Notice that we used the line continuation sequence; `If-Then-Else` is actually a single statement.

If you need to execute multiple statements based on the condition, use this form:

```
Sub GreetMe3a()
    If Time < 0.5 Then
        MsgBox "Good Morning"
        ' Other statements go here
    Else
        MsgBox "Good Afternoon"
        ' Other statements go here
    End If
End Sub
```

If you need to expand a routine to handle three conditions (for example, morning, afternoon, and evening), you can use either three `If-Then` statements or a form that uses `ElseIf`. The first approach is simpler.

```
Sub GreetMe4()
    If Time < 0.5 Then MsgBox "Good Morning"
    If Time >= 0.5 And Time < 0.75 Then MsgBox "Good Afternoon"
    If Time >= 0.75 Then MsgBox "Good Evening"
End Sub
```

The value 0.75 represents 6 p.m.—three-quarters of the way through the day and a good point at which to call it an evening.

In the preceding examples, every instruction in the procedure gets executed, even if the first condition is satisfied (that is, it's morning). A more efficient procedure would include a structure that ends the routine when a condition is found to be `True`. For example, it might display the "Good Morning" message in the morning and then exit without evaluating the other, superfluous conditions. True, the difference in speed is inconsequential when you design a procedure as small as this routine. For more complex applications, however, you need another syntax.

```
If condition Then
    [true_instructions]
[ElseIf condition-n Then
    [alternate_instructions]]
[Else
    [default_instructions]]
End If
```

Here's how you can use this syntax to rewrite the `GreetMe` procedure:

```
Sub GreetMe5()
    If Time < 0.5 Then
        MsgBox "Good Morning"
    ElseIf Time >= 0.5 And Time < 0.75 Then
        MsgBox "Good Afternoon"
    Else
        MsgBox "Good Evening"
    End If
End Sub
```

With this syntax, when a condition is `True`, the conditional statements are executed, and the `If-Then` construct ends. In other words, the extraneous conditions aren't evaluated. Although this syntax makes for greater efficiency, some find the code to be more difficult to understand.

The following procedure demonstrates yet another way to code this example. It uses nested `If-Then-Else` constructs (without using `ElseIf`). This procedure is efficient and also easy to understand. Note that each `If` statement has a corresponding `End If` statement.

```
Sub GreetMe6()
    If Time < 0.5 Then
        MsgBox "Good Morning"
    Else
        If Time >= 0.5 And Time < 0.75 Then
            MsgBox "Good Afternoon"
        Else
            If Time >= 0.75 Then
                MsgBox "Good Evening"
            End If
        End If
    End If
End Sub
```

The following is another example that uses the simple form of the `If-Then` construct. This procedure prompts the user for a value for `Quantity` and then displays the appropriate discount based on that value. Note that `Quantity` is declared as a `Variant` data type. This is because `Quantity` contains an empty string (not a numeric value) if `InputBox` is cancelled. To keep the procedure simple, it doesn't perform any other error checking. For example, it doesn't ensure that the quantity entered is a non-negative numeric value.

```
Sub Discount1()
    Dim Quantity As Variant
    Dim Discount As Double
    Quantity = InputBox("Enter Quantity: ")
    If Quantity = "" Then Exit Sub
    If Quantity >= 0 Then Discount = 0.1
    If Quantity >= 25 Then Discount = 0.15
```

```
            If Quantity >= 50 Then Discount = 0.2
            If Quantity >= 75 Then Discount = 0.25
            MsgBox "Discount: " & Discount
        End Sub
```

Notice that every `If-Then` statement in this procedure is always executed, and the value for `Discount` can change. The final value, however, is the desired value.

The following procedure is the previous one rewritten to use the alternate syntax. In this alternate version, only the `If-Then` statement that evaluates to `True` is actually executed.

```
        Sub Discount2()
            Dim Quantity As Variant
            Dim Discount As Double
            Quantity = InputBox("Enter Quantity: ")
            If Quantity = "" Then Exit Sub
            If Quantity >= 0 And Quantity < 25 Then
                Discount = 0.1
            ElseIf Quantity < 50 Then
                Discount = 0.15
            ElseIf Quantity < 75 Then
                Discount = 0.2
            Else
                Discount = 0.25
            End If
            MsgBox "Discount: " & Discount
        End Sub
```

VBA's IIf function

VBA offers an alternative to the `If-Then` construct: the `IIf` function. This function takes three arguments and works much like Excel's `IF` worksheet function. The syntax is as follows:

```
    IIf(expr, truepart, falsepart)
```

`expr`: (Required) Expression you want to evaluate

`truepart`: (Required) Value or expression returned if `expr` is `True`

`falsepart`: (Required) Value or expression returned if `expr` is `False`

The following instruction demonstrates the use of the `IIf` function. The message box displays `Zero` if cell A1 contains a 0 or is empty and displays `Nonzero` if cell A1 contains anything else.

```
    MsgBox IIf(Range("A1") = 0, "Zero", "Nonzero")
```

It's important to understand that the third argument (`falsepart`) is always evaluated, even if the first argument (`expr`) is `True`. Therefore, the following statement generates a division-by-zero error if the value of n is 0 (zero):

```
    MsgBox IIf(n = 0, 0, 1 / n)
```

Select Case constructs

The Select Case construct is useful for choosing among three or more options. This construct also works with two options, and it is a good alternative to If-Then-Else. The syntax for Select Case is as follows:

```
Select Case testexpression
    [Case expressionlist-n
        [instructions-n]]
    [Case Else
        [default_instructions]]
End Select
```

The following example of a Select Case construct shows another way to code the GreetMe examples presented in the preceding section:

```
Sub GreetMe()
    Dim Msg As String
    Select Case Time
        Case Is < 0.5
            Msg = "Good Morning"
        Case 0.5 To 0.75
            Msg = "Good Afternoon"
        Case Else
            Msg = "Good Evening"
    End Select
    MsgBox Msg
End Sub
```

And here's a rewritten version of the Discount example using a Select Case construct. This procedure assumes that Quantity is always an integer value. For simplicity, the procedure performs no error checking.

```
Sub Discount3()
    Dim Quantity As Variant
    Dim Discount As Double
    Quantity = InputBox("Enter Quantity: ")
    Select Case Quantity
    Case ""
        Exit Sub
    Case 0 To 24
        Discount = 0.1
    Case 25 To 49
        Discount = 0.15
    Case 50 To 74
        Discount = 0.2
    Case Is >= 75
        Discount = 0.25
    End Select
    MsgBox "Discount: " & Discount
End Sub
```

3

The Case statement also can use a comma to separate multiple values for a single case. The following procedure uses the VBA Weekday function to determine whether the current day is a weekend (that is, the Weekday function returns 1 or 7). The procedure then displays an appropriate message.

```
Sub GreetUser1()
    Select Case Weekday(Now)
        Case 1, 7
            MsgBox "This is the weekend"
        Case Else
            MsgBox "This is not the weekend"
    End Select
End Sub
```

The following example shows another way to code the previous procedure:

```
Sub GreetUser2()
    Select Case Weekday(Now)
        Case 2, 3, 4, 5, 6
            MsgBox "This is not the weekend"
        Case Else
            MsgBox "This is the weekend"
    End Select
End Sub
```

Here's another way to code the procedure, using the To keyword to specify a range of values:

```
Sub GreetUser3()
    Select Case Weekday(Now)
        Case 2 To 6
            MsgBox "This is not the weekend"
        Case Else
            MsgBox "This is the weekend"
    End Select
End Sub
```

To demonstrate the flexibility of VBA, here is a final example in which each case is evaluated until one of the expressions evaluates to True:

```
Sub GreetUser4()
    Select Case True
        Case Weekday(Now) = 1
            MsgBox "This is the weekend"
        Case Weekday(Now) = 7
            MsgBox "This is the weekend"
        Case Else
            MsgBox "This is not the weekend"
    End Select
End Sub
```

Any number of instructions can be written after each Case statement, and they're all executed if that case evaluates to True. If you use only one instruction per case, as in the preceding example, you might want to put the instruction on the same line as the Case keyword (but don't forget the VBA statement-separator character, the colon). This technique makes the code more compact. Here's an example:

```
Sub Discount3()
    Dim Quantity As Variant
    Dim Discount As Double
    Quantity = InputBox("Enter Quantity: ")
    Select Case Quantity
        Case "": Exit Sub
        Case 0 To 24: Discount = 0.1
        Case 25 To 49: Discount = 0.15
        Case 50 To 74: Discount = 0.2
        Case Is >= 75: Discount = 0.25
    End Select
    MsgBox "Discount: " & Discount
End Sub
```

> **TIP**
>
> VBA exits a Select Case construct as soon as a True case is found. Therefore, for maximum efficiency, you should check the most likely case first.

Select Case structures can also be nested. The following procedure, for example, uses the VBA TypeName function to determine what is selected (a range, nothing, or anything else). If a range is selected, the procedure executes a nested Select Case and tests for the number of cells in the range. If one cell is selected, it displays One cell is selected. Otherwise, it displays a message with the number of selected rows.

```
Sub SelectionType()
    Select Case TypeName(Selection)
        Case "Range"
            Select Case Selection.Count
Case 1
MsgBox "One cell is selected"
Case Else
MsgBox Selection.Rows.Count & " rows"
            End Select
        Case "Nothing"
            MsgBox "Nothing is selected"
        Case Else
            MsgBox "Something other than a range"
    End Select
End Sub
```

This procedure also demonstrates the use of `Case Else`, a catchall case. You can nest `Select Case` constructs as deeply as you need, but make sure that each `Select Case` statement has a corresponding `End Select` statement.

This procedure demonstrates the value of using indentation in your code to clarify the structure. For example, take a look at the same procedure without the indentations:

```
Sub SelectionType()
Select Case TypeName(Selection)
Case "Range"
Select Case Selection.Count
Case 1
MsgBox "One cell is selected"
Case Else
MsgBox Selection.Rows.Count & " rows"Case "Nothing"
MsgBox "Nothing is selected"
Case Else
MsgBox "Something other than a range"
End Select
End Sub
```

Fairly incomprehensible, eh?

Looping blocks of instructions

Looping is the process of repeating a block of instructions. You might know the number of times to loop, or the number may be determined by the values of variables in your program.

The following code, which enters consecutive numbers into a range, demonstrates what is considered to be a *bad loop*. The procedure uses two variables to store a starting value (`StartVal`) and the total number of cells to fill (`NumToFill`). This loop uses the `GoTo` statement to control the flow. If the `iCount` variable, which keeps track of how many cells are filled, is less than the value of `NumToFill`, the program control loops back to `DoAnother`.

```
Sub BadLoop()
    Dim StartVal As Integer
    Dim NumToFill As Integer
    Dim iCount As Integer
    StartVal = 1
    NumToFill = 100
    ActiveCell.Value = StartVal
    iCount = 1
DoAnother:
    ActiveCell.Offset(iCount, 0).Value = StartVal + iCount
    iCount = iCount + 1
    If iCount < NumToFill Then GoTo DoAnother Else Exit Sub
End Sub
```

This procedure works as intended, so why is it an example of bad looping? Programmers generally frown on using a GoTo statement when not absolutely necessary. Using GoTo statements to loop is contrary to the concept of structured coding. (See the "What is structured programming?" sidebar.) A GoTo statement makes the code much more difficult to read because representing a loop using line indentations is almost impossible. In addition, this type of unstructured loop makes the procedure more susceptible to error. Furthermore, using lots of labels results in *spaghetti code*—code that appears to have little or no structure and has a tangled flow.

Because VBA has several structured looping commands, you almost never have to rely on GoTo statements for your decision-making.

For-Next loops

The simplest type of a good loop is a For-Next loop. Its syntax is as follows:

```
For counter = start To end [Step stepval]
    [instructions]
    [Exit For]
    [instructions]
Next [counter]
```

What is structured programming?

Hang around with programmers, and sooner or later you'll hear the term *structured programming*. You'll also discover that structured programs are considered superior to unstructured programs.

So, what is structured programming, and can you do it with VBA?

The basic premise of structured programming is that a routine or code segment should have only one entry point and one exit point. In other words, a body of code should be a stand-alone unit, and program control should not jump into or exit from the middle of this unit. As a result, structured programming rules out the GoTo statement. When you write structured code, your program progresses in an orderly manner and is easy to follow—as opposed to spaghetti code, in which a program jumps around.

A structured program is easier to read and understand than an unstructured one. More important, it's also easier to modify.

VBA is a structured language. It offers standard structured constructs, such as If-Then-Else and Select Case and the For-Next, Do Until, and Do While loops. Furthermore, VBA fully supports modular code construction.

If you're new to programming, form good structured programming habits early.

The following is an example of a For-Next loop that doesn't use the optional Step value or the optional Exit For statement. This routine executes the Sum = Sum + Sqr(Count) statement 100 times and displays the result, that is, the sum of the square roots of the first 100 integers.

```
Sub SumSquareRoots()
    Dim Sum As Double
    Dim Count As Integer
    Sum = 0
    For Count = 1 To 100
        Sum = Sum + Sqr(Count)
    Next Count
    MsgBox Sum
End Sub
```

In this example, Count (the loop counter variable) starts out as 1 and increases by 1 each time the loop repeats. The Sum variable simply accumulates the square roots of each value of Count.

> **CAUTION**
>
> When you use For-Next loops, it's important to understand that the loop counter is a normal variable—nothing special. As a result, it's possible to change the value of the loop counter in the block of code executed between the For and Next statements. Changing the loop counter inside a loop, however, is a bad practice and can cause unpredictable results. You should take precautions to ensure that your code doesn't change the loop counter.

You can also use a Step value to skip some values in the loop. Here's the same procedure rewritten to sum the square roots of the odd numbers between 1 and 100:

```
Sub SumOddSquareRoots()
    Dim Sum As Double
    Dim Count As Integer
    Sum = 0
    For Count = 1 To 100 Step 2
        Sum = Sum + Sqr(Count)
    Next Count
    MsgBox Sum
End Sub
```

In this procedure, Count starts out as 1 and then takes on values of 3, 5, 7, and so on. The final value of Count used in the loop is 99. When the loop ends, the value of Count is 101.

A Step value in a For-Next loop can also be negative. The procedure that follows deletes rows 2, 4, 6, 8, and 10 of the active worksheet:

```
Sub DeleteRows()
    Dim RowNum As Long
    For RowNum = 10 To 2 Step -2
        Rows(RowNum).Delete
    Next RowNum
End Sub
```

You may wonder why we used a negative Step value in the DeleteRows procedure. If you use a positive Step value, as shown in the following procedure, incorrect rows are deleted.

That's because the rows below a deleted row get a new row number. For example, when row 2 is deleted, row 3 becomes the new row 2. Using a negative `Step` value ensures that the correct rows are deleted.

```vba
Sub DeleteRows2()
    Dim RowNum As Long
    For RowNum = 2 To 10 Step 2
        Rows(RowNum).Delete
    Next RowNum
End Sub
```

The following procedure performs the same task as the `BadLoop` example at the beginning of the "Looping blocks of instructions" section. We eliminate the `GoTo` statement, however, converting a bad loop into a good loop that uses the `For-Next` structure.

```vba
Sub GoodLoop()
    Dim StartVal As Integer
    Dim NumToFill As Integer
    Dim iCount As Integer
    StartVal = 1
    NumToFill = 100
    For iCount = 0 To NumToFill - 1
        ActiveCell.Offset(iCount, 0).Value = StartVal + iCount
    Next iCount
End Sub
```

`For-Next` loops can also include one or more `Exit For` statements in the loop. When this statement is encountered, the loop terminates immediately, and control passes to the statement following the `Next` statement of the current `For-Next` loop. The following example demonstrates the use of the `Exit For` statement. This procedure determines which cell has the largest value in Column A of the active worksheet:

```vba
Sub ExitForDemo()
    Dim MaxVal As Double
    Dim Row As Long
    MaxVal = Application.WorksheetFunction.Max(Range("A:A"))
    For Row = 1 To 1048576
        If Cells(Row, 1).Value = MaxVal Then
            Exit For
        End If
    Next Row
    MsgBox "Max value is in Row " & Row
    Cells(Row, 1).Activate
End Sub
```

The maximum value in the column is calculated by using the Excel MAX function, and the value is assigned to the `MaxVal` variable. The `For-Next` loop checks each cell in the column. If the cell being checked is equal to `MaxVal`, the `Exit For` statement terminates the loop, and the statements following the `Next` statement are executed. These statements display the row of the maximum value and activate the cell.

> **NOTE**
>
> The `ExitForDemo` procedure is presented to demonstrate how to exit from a `For-Next` loop. However, it's not the most efficient way to activate the largest value in a range. In fact, a single statement does the job.
>
> ```
> Range("A:A").Find(Application.WorksheetFunction.Max _
> (Range("A:A"))).Activate
> ```

The previous examples use relatively simple loops. But you can have any number of statements in the loop, and you can even nest `For-Next` loops inside other `For-Next` loops. Here's an example that uses nested `For-Next` loops to initialize a 10 × 10 × 10 array with the value –1. When the procedure is finished, each of the 1,000 elements in `MyArray` contains –1.

```
Sub NestedLoops()
    Dim MyArray(1 to 10, 1 to 10, 1 to 10)
    Dim i As Integer, j As Integer, k As Integer
    For i = 1 To 10
        For j = 1 To 10
            For k = 1 To 10
                MyArray(i, j, k) = -1
            Next k
        Next j
    Next i
'        [More code goes here]
End Sub
```

Do While loops

This section describes another type of looping structure available in VBA. Unlike a For-Next loop, a Do While loop executes as long as a specified condition is met.

A Do While loop can have either of two syntaxes. Here's the first:

```
Do [While condition]
    [instructions]
    [Exit Do]
    [instructions]
Loop
```

Here's the second:

```
Do
    [instructions]
    [Exit Do]
    [instructions]
Loop [While condition]
```

As you can see, VBA lets you put the While condition at the beginning or the end of the loop. The difference between these two syntaxes involves the point at which the condition is evaluated. In the first syntax, the contents of the loop may never be executed. In the second syntax, the statements inside the loop are always executed at least one time.

The following examples insert a series of dates into the active worksheet. The dates correspond to the days in the current month, and the dates are entered in a column beginning at the active cell.

The first example demonstrates a Do While loop that tests the condition at the beginning of the loop: The EnterDates1 procedure writes the dates of the current month to a worksheet column, beginning with the active cell.

```
Sub EnterDates1()
'       Do While, with test at the beginning
    Dim TheDate As Date
    TheDate = DateSerial(Year(Date), Month(Date), 1)
    Do While Month(TheDate) = Month(Date)
        ActiveCell = TheDate
        TheDate = TheDate + 1
        ActiveCell.Offset(1, 0).Activate
    Loop
End Sub
```

This procedure uses a variable, TheDate, which contains the dates that are written to the worksheet. This variable is initialized with the first day of the current month. Inside the loop, the value of TheDate is entered into the active cell, TheDate is incremented, and the next cell is activated. The loop continues while the month of TheDate is the same as the month of the current date.

The following procedure has the same result as the EnterDates1 procedure, but it uses the second Do While loop syntax, which checks the condition at the end of the loop.

```
Sub EnterDates2()
'       Do While, with test at the end
    Dim TheDate As Date
    TheDate = DateSerial(Year(Date), Month(Date), 1)
    Do
        ActiveCell = TheDate
        TheDate = TheDate + 1
        ActiveCell.Offset(1, 0).Activate
    Loop While Month(TheDate) = Month(Date)
End Sub
```

Do While loops can also contain one or more Exit Do statements. When an Exit Do statement is encountered, the loop ends immediately, and control passes to the statement following the Loop statement.

Do Until loops

The Do Until loop structure is similar to the Do While structure. The difference is evident only when the condition is tested. In a Do While loop, the loop executes *while* the condition is True; in a Do Until loop, the loop executes *until* the condition is True.

Do Until also has two syntaxes. Here's the first way:

```
Do [Until condition]
    [instructions]
    [Exit Do]
    [instructions]
Loop
```

Here's the second way:

```
Do
    [instructions]
    [Exit Do]
    [instructions]
Loop [Until condition]
```

The two examples that follow perform the same action as the Do While date entry examples in the previous section. The difference in these two procedures is where the condition is evaluated (at the beginning or the end of the loop). Here is the first example:

```
Sub EnterDates3()
'       Do Until, with test at beginning
    Dim TheDate As Date
    TheDate = DateSerial(Year(Date), Month(Date), 1)
    Do Until Month(TheDate) <> Month(Date)
        ActiveCell = TheDate
        TheDate = TheDate + 1
        ActiveCell.Offset(1, 0).Activate
    Loop
End Sub
```

Here is the second example:

```
Sub EnterDates4()
'       Do Until, with test at end
    Dim TheDate As Date
    TheDate = DateSerial(Year(Date), Month(Date), 1)
    Do
        ActiveCell = TheDate
        TheDate = TheDate + 1s
        ActiveCell.Offset(1, 0).Activate
    Loop Until Month(TheDate) <> Month(Date)
End Sub
```

The following example was originally presented for the `Do While` loop but has been rewritten to use a `Do Until` loop. The only difference is the line with the `Do` statement. This example makes the code a bit clearer because it avoids the negative required in the `Do While` example.

```
Sub DoUntilDemo1()
    Dim LineCt As Long
    Dim LineOfText As String
    Open "c:\data\textfile.txt" For Input As #1
    LineCt = 0
    Do Until EOF(1)
        Line Input #1, LineOfText
        Range("A1").Offset(LineCt, 0) = UCase(LineOfText)
        LineCt = LineCt + 1
    Loop
    Close #1
End Sub
```

> **NOTE**
>
> VBA supports yet another type of loop, `While Wend`. This looping structure is included primarily for compatibility purposes. Here's how the date entry procedure looks when it's coded to use a `While Wend` loop:
>
> ```
> Sub EnterDates5()
>     Dim TheDate As Date
>     TheDate = DateSerial(Year(Date), Month(Date), 1)
>     While Month(TheDate) = Month(Date)
>         ActiveCell = TheDate
>         TheDate = TheDate + 1
>         ActiveCell.Offset(1, 0).Activate
>     Wend
> End Sub
> ```

3

Working with VBA Sub Procedures

IN THIS CHAPTER

Declaring and creating VBA Sub procedures

Executing procedures

Passing arguments to a procedure

Using error-handling techniques

An example of developing a useful procedure

About Procedures

A *procedure* is a series of VBA statements that resides in a VBA module, which you access in the Visual Basic Editor (VBE). A module can hold any number of procedures. A procedure holds a group of VBA statements that accomplishes a desired task. Most VBA code is contained in procedures.

You have a number of ways to *call*, or execute, procedures. A procedure is executed from beginning to end, but it can also be ended prematurely.

> **TIP**
>
> A procedure can be any length, but many people prefer to avoid creating extremely long procedures that perform many different operations. You may find it easier to write several smaller procedures, each with a single purpose, and then design a main procedure that calls those other procedures. This approach can make your code easier to maintain.

Some procedures are written to receive arguments. An *argument* is information that is used by the procedure and that is passed to the procedure when it is executed. Procedure arguments work much like the arguments that you use in Excel worksheet functions. Instructions within the procedure perform operations using these arguments, and the results of the procedure are usually based on those arguments.

Although this chapter focuses on Sub procedures, VBA also supports Function procedures, which we discuss in Chapter 5, "Creating Function Procedures." Chapter 7, "VBA Programming Examples and Techniques," has many additional examples of procedures, both Sub and Function, that you can incorporate into your work.

Declaring a Sub procedure

A procedure declared with the Sub keyword must adhere to the following syntax:

```
[Private | Public][Static] Sub name ([arglist])
    [instructions]
    [Exit Sub]
    [instructions]
End Sub
```

Here's a description of the elements that make up a Sub procedure:

Private: Optional. Indicates that the procedure is accessible only to other procedures in the same module.

Public: Optional. Indicates that the procedure is accessible to all other procedures in all other modules in the workbook. If used in a module that contains an Option Private Module statement, the procedure is not available outside the project (other workbooks or Microsoft Office applications that may attempt to call the procedures in the module).

Static: Optional. Indicates that the procedure's variables are preserved when the procedure ends.

Sub: Required. The keyword that indicates the beginning of a procedure.

name: Required. Any valid procedure name.

arglist: Optional. Represents a list of variables, enclosed in parentheses, that receive arguments passed to the procedure. Use a comma to separate arguments. If the procedure uses no arguments, a set of empty parentheses is required.

instructions: Optional. Represents valid VBA instructions.

Exit Sub: Optional. Forces an immediate exit from the procedure prior to its formal completion.

End Sub: Required. Indicates the end of the procedure.

> **NOTE**
> With a few exceptions, all VBA instructions in a module must be contained in procedures. Exceptions include module-level variable declarations, user-defined data type definitions, and a few other instructions that specify module-level options (for example, Option Explicit).

Naming procedures

Every procedure must have a name. The rules governing procedure names are generally the same as those for variable names. Ideally, a procedure's name should describe what its contained processes do. A good rule is to use a name that includes a verb and a noun (for example, `ProcessDate`, `Print Report`, `Sort_Array`, or `CheckFilename`). Unless you're writing a quick and dirty procedure that you'll use once and delete, avoid meaningless names such as `DoIt`, `Update`, and `Fix`.

Some programmers use sentence-like names that describe the procedure (for example, `WriteReportToTextFile` and `Get_Print_Options_` and `_Print_Report`).

Note that the first letter of each word in the example procedure names are uppercase. This technique is called *Pascal casing*, and it is generally considered a best practice.

Scoping a procedure

In the preceding chapter, we noted that a variable's *scope* determines the modules and procedures in which you can use the variable. Similarly, a procedure's scope determines which other procedures can call it.

Public procedures

By default, procedures are *public procedures*; that is, they can be called by other procedures in any module in the workbook. It's not necessary to use the `Public` keyword, but programmers often include it for clarity. The following two procedures are both public:

```
Sub First()
' ... [code goes here] ...
End Sub
Public Sub Second()
' ... [code goes here] ...
End Sub
```

Private procedures

Private procedures can be called by other procedures in the same module but not by procedures in other modules.

> **NOTE**
>
> When a user displays the Macro dialog box (by pressing Alt+F8), Excel shows only public procedures. Therefore, if you have procedures that are designed to be called only by other procedures in the same module, you should make sure that those procedures are declared as `Private`. Doing so prevents the user from viewing and selecting these procedures from the Macro dialog box.

4

The following example declares a private procedure named `MySub`:

```
Private Sub MySub()
' ... [code goes here] ...
End Sub
```

Excel's macro recorder creates new `Sub` procedures called `Macro1`, `Macro2`, and so on. Unless you modify the recorded code, these procedures are all public procedures, and they will never use any arguments.

Executing Sub Procedures

In this section, we describe the various ways to *execute*, or call, a VBA `Sub` procedure:

- You can call `Sub` procedure with the Run ⇨ Run Sub/UserForm command (in the VBE menu). You can also call a `Sub` procedure by pressing the F5 shortcut key, or you can click the Run Sub/UserForm button on the Standard toolbar. These methods all assume that the cursor is within a procedure.
- You can call a `Sub` procedure from Excel's Macro dialog box.
- You can call a `Sub` procedure by using the Ctrl key shortcut assigned to the procedure (assuming that you assigned one).
- You can call a `Sub` procedure by clicking, on a worksheet, a button or shape assigned to the procedure.
- You can call a `Sub` procedure from another procedure that you write. `Sub` and `Function` procedures can execute other procedures.
- You can call a `Sub` procedure from an icon added to the Quick Access toolbar.
- You can call a `Sub` procedure from a button added to the Ribbon.
- You can call a `Sub` procedure from a customized shortcut menu.
- You can specify that a `Sub` procedure be run when an event occurs, such as opening the workbook, saving the workbook, closing the workbook, changing a cell's value, or activating a sheet.
- Finally, you can run a `Sub` procedure from the Immediate window in VBE. Just type the name of the procedure, including any arguments that may apply, and press Enter.

We discuss these methods of executing procedures in the following sections.

> **NOTE**
>
> In many cases, a procedure won't work properly unless it's executed in the appropriate context. For example, if a procedure is designed to work with the active worksheet, it will fail if a chart sheet is active. A good procedure incorporates code that checks for the appropriate context and exits gracefully if it can't proceed.

Executing a procedure with the Run Sub/UserForm command

The VBE Run ⇨ Run Sub/UserForm menu command is used primarily to test a procedure while you're developing it. You would never require a user to activate VBE to execute a procedure. Choose Run ⇨ Run Sub/UserForm in VBE to execute the current procedure (in other words, the procedure that contains the cursor). Or, press F5 or use the Run Sub/UserForm button on the Standard toolbar.

If the cursor isn't located within a procedure, VBE displays its Macro dialog box so that you can select a procedure to execute.

Executing a procedure from the Macro dialog box

Choose Excel's View ⇨ Macros ⇨ Macros command to display the Macro dialog box, as shown in Figure 4.1. You can also press Alt+F8 or choose Developer ⇨ Code ⇨ Macros to access this dialog box. Use the Macros In drop-down box to limit the scope of the macros displayed (for example, show only the macros in the active workbook).

FIGURE 4.1

The Macro dialog box

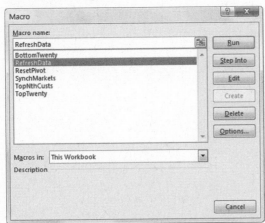

The Macro dialog box does *not* display the following:

- `Function` procedures
- `Sub` procedures declared with the `Private` keyword
- `Sub` procedures that require one or more arguments
- `Sub` procedures contained in add-ins
- Event procedures stored in code modules for objects such as `ThisWorkbook`, `Sheet1`, or `UserForm1`

> **TIP**
>
> Even though procedures stored in an add-in are not listed in the Macro dialog box, you still can execute such a procedure if you know the name. Simply type the procedure name in the Macro Name field in the Macro dialog box and then click Run.

Executing a procedure with a Ctrl+shortcut key combination

You can assign a Ctrl+shortcut key combination to any `Sub` procedure that doesn't use any arguments. If you assign the Ctrl+U key combo to a procedure named `UpdateCustomer List`, for example, pressing Ctrl+U executes that procedure.

When you begin recording a macro, the Record Macro dialog box gives you the opportunity to assign a shortcut key. However, you can assign a shortcut key at any time. To assign a Ctrl shortcut key to a procedure (or to change a procedure's shortcut key), follow these steps:

1. Activate Excel and display the Macro dialog box (Alt+F8 is one way to do that).

2. Select the appropriate procedure from the list box in the Macro dialog box.

3. Click the Options button to display the Macro Options dialog box (see Figure 4.2).

FIGURE 4.2

The Macro Options dialog box lets you assign a Ctrl key shortcut and an optional description to a procedure.

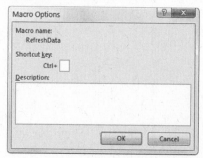

4. Enter a character into the Ctrl+ text box.

   Note: The character that you enter into the Ctrl+ text box is case-sensitive. If you enter a lowercase *s*, the shortcut key combo is Ctrl+S. If you enter an uppercase *S*, the shortcut key combo is Ctrl+Shift+S.

5. Enter a description (optional). If you enter a description for a macro, it's displayed at the bottom of the Macro dialog box when the procedure is selected in the list box.

6. Click OK to close the Macro Options dialog box and then click Cancel to close the Macro dialog box.

CAUTION

If you assign one of Excel's predefined shortcut key combinations to a procedure, your key assignment takes precedence over the predefined key assignment. For example, Ctrl+S is the Excel predefined shortcut key for saving the active workbook. But if you assign Ctrl+S to a procedure, pressing Ctrl+S no longer saves the active workbook when that macro is available.

TIP

The following keyboard keys are *not* used by Excel 2019 for Ctrl+key combinations: J, M, and Q. Excel doesn't use too many Ctrl+Shift+key combinations, and they are used for obscure commands.

Executing a procedure from the Ribbon

Excel's Ribbon user interface was introduced in Excel 2007. In that version, customizing the Ribbon required writing XML code to add a new button (or other control) to the Ribbon. Note that you modify the Ribbon in this way outside of Excel, and you can't do it using VBA.

Beginning with Excel 2010, users can modify the Ribbon directly from Excel. Just right-click any part of the Ribbon and choose Customize the Ribbon from the shortcut menu. It's a simple matter to add a new control to the Ribbon and assign a VBA macro to the control. However, this must be done manually. In other words, it's not possible to use VBA to add a control to the Ribbon.

 Refer to Chapter 17, "Working with the Ribbon," for more information about customizing the Ribbon.

Executing a procedure from a customized shortcut menu

You can also execute a macro by clicking a menu item in a customized shortcut menu. A shortcut menu appears when you right-click an object or range in Excel. It's fairly easy to write VBA code that adds a new item to any of Excel's shortcut menus.

 Refer to Chapter 18, "Working with Shortcut Menus," for more information about customizing shortcut menus.

Executing a procedure from another procedure

One of the most common ways to execute a procedure is to call it from another VBA procedure. You have three ways to do this.

- Enter the procedure's name, followed by its arguments (if any) separated by commas. Do not enclose the argument list in parentheses.
- Use the `Call` keyword followed by the procedure's name and then its arguments (if any) enclosed in parentheses and separated by commas. The `Call` keyword is technically optional, as you don't need it to run the specified procedure. However, many Excel developers still use it as a clear indicator that another procedure is being called.
- Use the `Run` method of the `Application` object. The `Run` method is useful when you need to run a procedure whose name is assigned to a variable. You can then pass the variable as an argument to the `Run` method.

Here's a simple `Sub` procedure that takes two arguments. The procedure displays the product of the two arguments.

```
Sub AddTwo (arg1, arg2)
    MsgBox arg1 + arg2
End Sub
```

The following three statements demonstrate three different ways to execute the AddTwo procedure and pass two arguments. All three have the same result.

```
AddTwo 12, 6
Call AddTwo (12, 6)
Run "AddTwo", 12, 6
```

> **TIP**
>
> Even though it's optional, consider always using the `Call` keyword. It not only makes it perfectly clear that another procedure is being called, but the `Call` keyword also comes in handy when you want to search for all of the instances in your code where you're explicitly calling other procedures.

Perhaps the best reason to use the Run method is when the procedure name is assigned to a variable. In fact, it's the only way to execute a procedure in such a way. The following over-simplified example demonstrates this. The Main procedure uses the VBA WeekDay function to determine the day of the week (an integer between 1 and 7, beginning with Sunday). The SubToCall variable is assigned a string that represents a procedure name. The Run method then calls the appropriate procedure (either WeekEnd or Daily).

```
Sub Main()
    Dim SubToCall As String
    Select Case WeekDay(Now)
            Case 1, 7: SubToCall = "WeekEnd"
            Case Else: SubToCall = "Daily"
    End Select
    Application.Run SubToCall
End Sub

Sub WeekEnd()
    MsgBox "Today is a weekend"
    ' Code to execute on the weekend
    ' goes here
End Sub

Sub Daily()
    MsgBox "Today is not a weekend"
    ' Code to execute on the weekdays
    ' goes here
End Sub
```

> **NOTE**
>
> Note that the last example is included to illustrate the concept of the Run keyword. However, it's generally considered a bad practice to call a procedure through a variable or string because the VBA compiler will not be able to confirm that the specified procedure actually exists. In other words, the name of the procedure to be run isn't supplied to the code until run-time. This introduces the chance for error, as supplying an invalid or even misspelled procedure name during run-time will cause the code to fail.

Calling a procedure in a different module

If VBA can't locate a called procedure in the current module, it looks for public procedures in other modules in the same workbook.

If you need to call a private procedure from another procedure, both procedures must reside in the same module.

You can't have two procedures with the same name in the same module, but you can have identically named procedures in different modules within the project. You can force VBA to execute an *ambiguously named procedure,* that is, another procedure in a different module that has the same name. To do so, precede the procedure name with the module name and a dot.

For example, assume that you define procedures named MySub in Module1 and Module2. If you want a procedure in Module2 to call the MySub in Module1, you can use either of the following statements:

```
Module1.MySub
Call Module1.MySub
```

If you do not differentiate between procedures that have the same name, you get the aptly named Ambiguous name detected error message.

Calling a procedure in a different workbook

In some cases, you may need your procedure to execute another procedure defined in a different workbook. To do so, you have two options: either establish a reference to the other workbook or use the Run method and specify the workbook name explicitly.

To add a reference to another workbook, choose VBE's Tools ⇨ References command. Excel displays the References dialog box (see Figure 4.3), which lists all available references, including all open workbooks. Select the box that corresponds to the workbook that you want to add as a reference and then click OK. After you establish a reference, you can call procedures in the workbook as if they were in the same workbook as the calling procedure.

FIGURE 4.3

The References dialog box lets you establish a reference to another workbook.

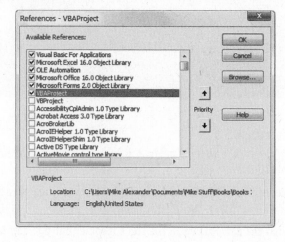

A referenced workbook doesn't have to be open when you create the reference; the referenced workbook is treated like a separate object library. Use the Browse button in the References dialog box to establish a reference to a workbook that isn't open.

When you open a workbook that contains a reference to another workbook, the referenced workbook is opened automatically.

> **NOTE**
>
> The workbook names that appear in the list of references are listed by their VBE project names. By default, every project is initially named *VBAProject*. Therefore, the list may contain several identically named items (but the full path of the selected item appears at the bottom of the dialog box). To distinguish a project, change its name in the Project Properties dialog box. Click the project name in the Project window and then choose Tools ⇨ *xxxx* Properties (where *xxxx* is the current project name). In the Project Properties dialog box, click the General tab and change the name displayed in the Project Name field.

The list of references displayed in the References dialog box also includes object libraries and ActiveX controls that are registered on your system. Excel 2019 workbooks always include references to the following object libraries:

- Visual Basic for Applications
- Microsoft Excel 17.0 Object Library
- OLE Automation
- Microsoft Office 17.0 Object Library
- Microsoft Forms 2.0 Object Library (this reference is included only if your project includes a UserForm)

> **NOTE**
>
> Any additional references to other workbooks that you add are also listed in your project outline in the Project Explorer window in VBE. These references are listed under a node called *References*.

If you've established a reference to a workbook that contains the YourSub procedure, for example, you can use either of the following statements to call YourSub:

```
YourSub
Call YourSub
```

To identify precisely a procedure in a different workbook, specify the project name, module name, and procedure name by using the following syntax:

```
YourProject.YourModule.YourSub
```

Alternatively, you can use the `Call` keyword.

```
Call YourProject.YourModule.YourSub
```

Another way to call a procedure in a different workbook is to use the `Run` method of the `Application` object. This technique doesn't require that you establish a reference, but the workbook that contains the procedure must be open. The following statement executes the `Consolidate` procedure located in a workbook named `budget macros.xlsm`:

```
Application.Run "'budget macros.xlsm'!Consolidate"
```

Note that the workbook name is enclosed in single quotes. That syntax is necessary only if the filename includes one or more space characters. Here's an example of calling a procedure in a workbook that doesn't have any spaces:

```
Application.Run "budgetmacros.xlsm!Consolidate"
```

Why call other procedures?

If you're new to programming, you may wonder why anyone would ever want to call a procedure from another procedure. You may ask, "Why not just put the code from the called procedure into the calling procedure and keep things simple?"

One reason is to clarify your code. The simpler your code, the easier it is to read, maintain, and modify. Smaller routines are easier to decipher and then debug. Examine the accompanying procedure, which does nothing but call other procedures. This procedure is easy to follow.

```
Sub Main()
    Call GetUserOptions
    Call ProcessData
    Call CleanUp
    Call CloseAllFiles
End Sub
```

Calling other procedures also eliminates redundancy. Suppose that you need to perform an operation at 10 different places in your routine. Rather than enter the code 10 times, you can write a procedure to perform the operation and then simply call the procedure 10 times. Also, if you need to make a change, you make it only 1 time rather than 10 times.

Also, you may have a series of general-purpose procedures that you use frequently. If you store these in a separate module, you can import the module to your current project and then call these procedures as needed—which is much easier than copying and pasting the code into your new procedures.

Creating several small procedures rather than a single large one is often considered good programming practice. A modular approach not only makes your job easier, but it also makes life easier for the people who wind up working with your code.

Executing a procedure by clicking an object

Excel provides a variety of objects that you can place on a worksheet or chart sheet; you can attach a macro to any of these objects. These objects fall into several classes.

- ActiveX controls
- Forms controls
- Inserted objects (Shapes, SmartArt, WordArt, charts, and pictures)

> **NOTE**
>
> The Developer ➪ Controls ➪ Insert drop-down list contains two types of controls that you can insert on a worksheet: form controls and ActiveX controls. Form controls are designed specifically for use on a spreadsheet, and ActiveX controls are typically used on Excel UserForms. As a general rule, you should always use form controls when working on a spreadsheet. Form controls perform better on spreadsheets, and they are easier to configure.
>
> Unlike form controls, you can't use ActiveX controls to execute just any macro. An ActiveX control executes a specially named macro. For example, if you insert an ActiveX button control named `CommandButton1`, clicking the button executes a macro named `CommandButton1 _ Click`, which must be located in the code module for the sheet on which the control was inserted.
>
> Refer to Chapter 13, "Introducing UserForms," for information about using controls on worksheets.

To assign a procedure to a Button object from the form controls, follow these steps:

1. Choose Developer ➪ Controls ➪ Insert and click the Button icon in the Form Controls group.

2. Click the worksheet to create a button with the default height and width, or you can drag your mouse on the worksheet to create your button using your own preferred height and width.

   Excel jumps right in and displays the Assign Macro dialog box (see Figure 4.4).

3. Select the macro that you want to assign to the button and then click OK.

You can always change the macro assignment by right-clicking the button and choosing Assign Macro.

To assign a macro to a Shape, SmartArt, WordArt, or picture, right-click the object and choose Assign Macro from the shortcut menu.

To assign a macro to an embedded chart, press Ctrl and click the chart (to select the chart as an object). Then right-click and choose Assign Macro from the shortcut menu.

4

FIGURE 4.4

Assigning a macro to a button

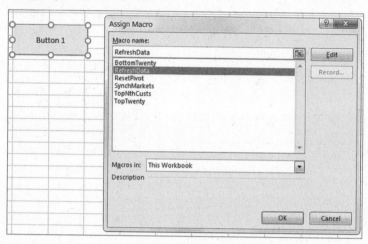

Executing a procedure when an event occurs

You might want a procedure to execute when a particular event occurs, such as opening a workbook, entering data into a worksheet, saving a workbook, or clicking a Command Button ActiveX control. A procedure that is executed when an event occurs is an *event-handler procedure*. Event-handler procedures are characterized by the following:

- They have special names that are made up of an object, an underscore, and the event name. For example, the procedure that is executed when a workbook is opened is `Workbook_Open`.
- They're stored in the Code module for the particular object (for example, ThisWorkbook or Sheet1).

 Chapter 6, "Understanding Excel's Events," is devoted to event-handler procedures.

Executing a procedure from the Immediate window

You also can execute a procedure by entering its name in the Immediate window of VBE. (If the Immediate window isn't visible, press Ctrl+G.) The Immediate window executes VBA statements while you enter them. To execute a procedure, simply enter the name of the procedure in the Immediate window and press Enter.

This method can be useful when you're developing a procedure because you can insert commands to display results in the Immediate window. The following procedure demonstrates this technique:

```
Sub ChangeCase()
    Dim MyString As String
    MyString = "This is a test"
    MyString = UCase(MyString)
    Debug.Print MyString
End Sub
```

Figure 4.5 shows what happens when you enter **ChangeCase** in the Immediate window: the Debug.Print statement displays the result immediately.

FIGURE 4.5

Executing a procedure by entering its name in the Immediate window

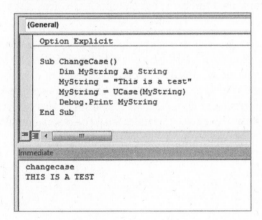

Passing Arguments to Procedures

A procedure's *arguments* provide it with data that it uses in its instructions. The data that's passed by an argument can be any of the following:

- A variable
- A constant
- An expression
- An array
- An object

You are probably familiar with many of Excel's worksheet functions. Arguments for procedures are similar.

- A procedure may not require any arguments.
- A procedure may require a fixed number of arguments.
- A procedure may accept an indefinite number of arguments.
- A procedure may require some arguments, leaving others optional.
- A procedure may have all optional arguments.

For example, a few of Excel's worksheet functions, such as RAND and NOW, use no arguments. Others, such as COUNTIF, require two arguments. Others still, such as SUM, can use up to 255 arguments. Still other worksheet functions have optional arguments. The PMT function, for example, can have five arguments (three are required; two are optional).

Most of the procedures that you've seen so far in this book have been declared without arguments. They were declared with just the Sub keyword, the procedure's name, and a set of empty parentheses. Empty parentheses indicate that the procedure does not accept arguments.

The following example shows two procedures. The Main procedure calls the ProcessFile procedure three times (the Call statement is in a For-Next loop). Before calling Process-File, however, a three-element array is created. Inside the loop, each element of the array becomes the argument for the procedure call. The ProcessFile procedure takes one argument (named TheFile). Note that the argument goes inside parentheses in the Sub statement. When ProcessFile finishes, program control continues with the statement after the Call statement.

```
Sub Main()
    Dim File(1 To 3) As String
    Dim i as Integer
    File(1) = "dept1.xlsx"
    File(2) = "dept2.xlsx"
    File(3) = "dept3.xlsx"
    For i = 1 To 3
        Call ProcessFile(File(i))
    Next i
End Sub

    Sub ProcessFile(TheFile)
    Workbooks.Open FileName:=TheFile
'        ...[more code here]...
    End Sub
```

You can also pass *literals* (that is, not variables) to a procedure. Here's an example:

```
Sub Main()
    Call ProcessFile("budget.xlsx")
End Sub
```

You can pass an argument to a procedure in two ways.

By reference   Passing an argument by reference passes the memory address of the variable. Changes to the argument within the procedure are made to the original variable. This is the default method of passing an argument.

By value   Passing an argument by value passes a *copy* of the original variable. Consequently, changes to the argument within the procedure are not reflected in the original variable.

The following example demonstrates this concept. The argument for the Process procedure is passed by reference (the default method). After the Main procedure assigns a value of 12 to MyValue, it calls the Process procedure and passes MyValue as the argument. The Process procedure multiplies the value of its argument (named YourValue) by 10. When Process ends and program control passes back to Main, the MsgBox function displays 120.

```
Sub Main()
    Dim MyValue As Integer
    MyValue = 12
    Call Process(MyValue)
    MsgBox MyValue
End Sub
Sub Process(YourValue)
    YourValue = YourValue * 10
End Sub
```

If you don't want the called procedure to modify any variables passed as arguments, you can modify the called procedure's argument list so that arguments are passed to it by *value* rather than by *reference*. To do so, precede the argument with the ByVal keyword. This technique causes the called routine to work with a copy of the passed variable's data—not the data itself. In the following procedure, for example, the changes made to YourValue in the Process procedure do not affect the MyValue variable in Main. As a result, the MsgBox function displays 12 and not 120.

```
Sub Process(ByVal YourValue)
    YourValue = YourValue * 10
End Sub
```

In most cases, you'll be content to use the default reference method of passing arguments. However, if your procedure needs to use data passed to it in an argument—and you must keep the original data intact—you'll want to pass the data by value.

A procedure's arguments can mix and match by value and by reference. Arguments preceded with ByVal are passed by value; all others are passed by reference.

NOTE

If you pass a variable defined as a user-defined data type to a procedure, it must be passed by reference. Attempting to pass it by value generates an error.

4

Because we didn't declare a data type for any of the arguments in the preceding examples, all of the arguments have been of the `Variant` data type. But a procedure that uses arguments can define the data types directly in the argument list. The following is a `Sub` statement for a procedure with two arguments of different data types. The first is declared as an integer, and the second is declared as a string.

```
Sub Process(Iterations As Integer, TheFile As String)
```

When you pass arguments to a procedure, the data that is passed as the argument must match the argument's data type. For example, if you call `Process` in the preceding example and pass a string variable for the first argument, you get an error: `ByRef argument type mismatch`.

> **NOTE**
>
> Arguments are relevant to both `Sub` procedures and `Function` procedures. In fact, arguments are more often used in `Function` procedures. In Chapter 5, where we focus on `Function` procedures, we provide additional examples of using arguments with your routines, including how to handle optional arguments.

Using public variables vs. passing arguments to a procedure

In Chapter 3, "VBA Programming Fundamentals," we point out how a variable declared as `Public` (at the top of the module) is available to all procedures in the module. In some cases, you may want to access a `Public` variable rather than pass the variable as an argument when calling another procedure.

For example, the procedure that follows passes the value of `MonthVal` to the `ProcessMonth` procedure:

```
Sub MySub()
    Dim MonthVal as Integer
    ' ... [code goes here]
    MonthVal = 4
    Call ProcessMonth(MonthVal)
    ' ... [code goes here]
End Sub
```

An alternative approach, which doesn't use an argument, is as follows:

```
Public MonthVal as Integer
Sub MySub()
'... [code goes here]
    MonthVal = 4
    Call ProcessMonth2
'... [code goes here]
End Sub
```

In the revised code, because `MonthVal` is a public variable, the `ProcessMonth2` procedure can access it, thus eliminating the need for an argument for the `ProcessMonth2` procedure.

Error-Handling Techniques

When a VBA procedure is running, errors can (and probably will) occur. These include either *syntax errors* (which you must correct before you can execute a procedure) or *run-time errors* (which occur while the procedure is running). This section deals with run-time errors.

> **CAUTION**
>
> For error-handling procedures to work, the Break on All Errors setting *must* be turned off. In VBE, choose Tools ⇨ Options and click the General tab in the Options dialog box. If Break on All Errors is selected, VBA ignores your error-handling code. You'll usually want to use the Break on Unhandled Errors option.

Normally, a run-time error causes VBA to stop, and the user sees a dialog box that displays the error number and a description of the error. A good application doesn't make the user deal with these messages. Rather, it incorporates error-handling code to trap errors and take appropriate actions. At the very least, your error-handling code can display a more meaningful error message than the one VBA pops up.

Trapping errors

You can use the On Error statement to specify what happens when an error occurs. Basically, you have two choices.

- **Ignore the error and let VBA continue.** Your code can later examine the Err object to determine what the error was and then take action, if necessary.
- **Jump to a special error-handling section of your code to take action.** This section is placed at the end of the procedure and is also marked by a label.

To cause your VBA code to continue when an error occurs, insert the following statement in your code:

```
On Error Resume Next
```

Some errors are inconsequential, and you can ignore them without causing a problem. However, you might want to determine what the error was. When an error occurs, you can use the Err object to determine the error number. You can use the VBA Error function to display the text that corresponds to the Err.Number value. For example, the following statement displays the same information as the normal Visual Basic error dialog box (the error number and the error description):

```
MsgBox "Oops! Can't find the object being referenced. " & _
    "Error " & Err & ": " & Error(Err.Number)
```

Figure 4.6 shows a VBA error message, and Figure 4.7 shows the same error displayed in a message box. You can, of course, make the error message a bit more meaningful to your end users by using more descriptive text.

4

FIGURE 4.6

VBA error messages aren't always user friendly.

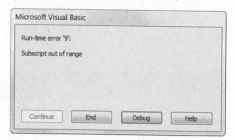

FIGURE 4.7

You can create a message box to display the error code and description.

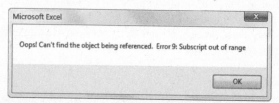

> **NOTE**
>
> Referencing `Err` is equivalent to accessing the `Number` property of the `Err` object. Therefore, the following two statements have the same effect:
>
> ```
> MsgBox Err
> MsgBox Err.Number
> ```

You also use the `On Error` statement to specify a location in your procedure to jump to when an error occurs. You use a label to mark the location. Here's an example:

```
On Error GoTo ErrorHandler
```

Error-handling examples

The first example demonstrates an error that you can safely ignore. The `SpecialCells` method selects cells that meet a certain criterion.

> **NOTE**
>
> The `SpecialCells` method is equivalent to choosing the Home ⇨ Editing ⇨ Find & Select ⇨ Go To Special command. The Go To Special dialog box provides you with a number of choices. For example, you can select cells that contain a numeric constant (nonformula).

In the example that follows, which doesn't use any error handling, the `SpecialCells` method selects all the cells in the current range selection that contain a formula. If no cells in the selection qualify, VBA displays the error message shown in Figure 4.8.

```
Sub SelectFormulas()
    Selection.SpecialCells(xlFormulas).Select
' ...[more code goes here]
End Sub
```

FIGURE 4.8

The SpecialCells method generates this error if no cells are found.

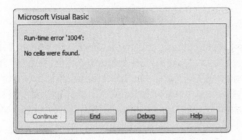

```
Microsoft Visual Basic

Run-time error '1004':

No cells were found.

   Continue        End        Debug        Help
```

The following is a variation that uses the `On Error Resume Next` statement to prevent the error message from appearing:

```
Sub SelectFormulas2()
    On Error Resume Next
    Selection.SpecialCells(xlFormulas).Select
    On Error GoTo 0
'         ...[more code goes here]
End Sub
```

The `On Error GoTo 0` statement restores normal error handling for the remaining statements in the procedure.

The following procedure uses an additional statement to determine whether a specific error did occur. If so, the user is informed by a message.

```
Sub SelectFormulas3()
    On Error Resume Next
    Selection.SpecialCells(xlFormulas).Select
    If Err.Number = 1004 Then MsgBox "No formula cells were found."
    On Error GoTo 0
'         ...[more code goes here]
End Sub
```

4

If the `Number` property of `Err` is equal to anything other than 0, an error occurred. The `If` statement checks to see whether `Err.Number` is equal to 1004 and displays a message box if it is. In this example, the code is checking for a specific error number. To check for any error, use a statement like this:

```
If Err.Number <> 0 Then MsgBox "An error occurred."
```

The next example demonstrates error handling by jumping to a label:

```
Sub ErrorDemo()
    On Error GoTo Handler
    Selection.Value = 123
    Exit Sub
Handler:
    MsgBox "Cannot assign a value to the selection."
End Sub
```

The procedure attempts to assign a value to the current selection. If an error occurs (for example, a range isn't selected or the sheet is protected), the assignment statement results in an error. The `On Error` statement specifies a jump to the handler label if an error occurs. Note the use of the `Exit Sub` statement before the label. This statement prevents the error-handling code from being executed if no error occurs. If this statement is omitted, the error message is displayed even if an error does not occur.

Sometimes, you can take advantage of an error to get information. The example that follows simply checks whether a particular workbook is open. It doesn't use any error handling.

```
Sub CheckForFile1()
    Dim FileName As String
    Dim FileExists As Boolean
    Dim book As Workbook
    FileName = "BUDGET.XLSX"
    FileExists = False
'       Cycle through all open workbooks
    For Each book In Workbooks
        If UCase(book.Name) = FileName Then FileExists = True
    Next book
'       Display appropriate message
    If FileExists Then
        MsgBox FileName & " is open."
    Else
        MsgBox FileName & " is not open."
    End If
End Sub
```

Here, a `For Each-Next` loop cycles through all objects in the `Workbooks` collection. If the workbook is open, the `FileExists` variable is set to `True`. Finally, a message is displayed that tells the user whether the workbook is open.

You can rewrite the preceding routine to use error handling to determine whether the file is open. In the example that follows, the On Error Resume Next statement causes VBA to ignore any errors. The next instruction attempts to reference the workbook by assigning the workbook to an object variable (by using the Set keyword). If the workbook isn't open, an error occurs. The If-Then-Else structure checks the value property of Err and displays the appropriate message. This procedure uses no looping, so it's slightly more efficient.

```
Sub CheckForFile()
    Dim FileName As String
    Dim x As Workbook
    FileName = "BUDGET.XLSX"
    On Error Resume Next
    Set x = Workbooks(FileName)
    If Err = 0 Then
        MsgBox FileName & " is open."
    Else
        MsgBox FileName & " is not open."
    End If
    On Error GoTo 0
End Sub
```

 Chapter 7 includes several additional examples that use error handling.

A Realistic Example That Uses Sub Procedures

Up to this point, the code examples covered in this chapter have been presented for demonstration purposes and not very useful on their own. The remainder of this chapter will walk you through a real-life exercise that demonstrates many of the concepts covered in this and the preceding two chapters.

This section describes the development of a useful utility. More important, you will explore the *process* of analyzing a problem and then solving it with VBA.

ON THE WEB

You can find the completed application, named sheet sorter.xlsm, on this book's website.

The goal

The goal of this exercise is to develop a utility that rearranges a workbook by alphabetizing its sheets (something that Excel can't do on its own). If you tend to create workbooks that consist of many sheets, you know that locating a particular sheet can be difficult. If the sheets are ordered alphabetically, however, it's easier to find a desired sheet.

Project requirements

Where to begin? One way to get started is to list the requirements for your application. When you develop your application, you can check your list to ensure that you're covering all of the bases.

Here's the list of requirements for this example application:

- It should sort the sheets (that is, worksheets and chart sheets) in the active workbook in ascending order of their names.
- It should be easy to execute.
- It should always be available. In other words, the user shouldn't have to open a workbook to use this utility.
- It should work properly for any workbook that's open.
- It should trap errors gracefully and not display any cryptic VBA error messages.

What you know

Often, the most difficult part of a project is figuring out where to start. It's often helpful to start by listing things that you know about Excel that may be relevant to the project requirements. For this scenario, you know the following:

- Excel doesn't have a command that sorts sheets, so you're not reinventing the wheel.
- The macro recorder can't be used to record the sorting of worksheets, as new worksheets (that didn't exist at the time of recording) will likely be added by the user sometime in the future. That being said, a recorded macro might provide some helpful guidance on the correct syntax to use.
- Sorting the sheets will require moving some or all of them. You can manually move a sheet easily by dragging its sheet tab.
- *Mental note*: Turn on the macro recorder and drag a sheet to a new location to find out what kind of code this action generates.
- Excel also has a Move or Copy dialog box, which is displayed when you right-click a sheet tab and choose Move or Copy. Would recording a macro of this command generate different code than moving a sheet manually?
- You'll need to know how many sheets are in the active workbook. You can get this information with VBA.
- You'll need to know the names of all of the sheets. Again, you can get this information with VBA.
- Excel has a command that sorts data in worksheet cells.
- *Mental note*: Maybe you can transfer the sheet names to a range and use this feature. Or maybe VBA has a sorting method of which you can take advantage.
- You will need a way to test the code on workbooks other than the one in which you're working. This means that you will need to store the macro in the Personal Macro workbook so that you can use it with other workbooks.
- *Mental note*: Create a dummy workbook for testing.

The approach

After detailing what you know, you can start listing the series of steps needed to accomplish the actual task. In this case, you will need VBA to do the following:

1. Identify the active workbook.

2. Get a list of all of the sheet names in the workbook.

3. Count the sheets.

4. Sort the sheet names (somehow).

5. Rearrange the sheets so that they correspond to the sorted sheet names.

> **TIP**
>
> It's likely that you will not know exactly how to code the steps needed to accomplish the task you have in mind. Don't let this discourage you. The truth is that many developers rarely know the exact syntax needed off the top of their heads. Rest assured that you will eventually be able to find the correct syntax by using a combination of the macro recorder, the VBA Help system, and examples found on the Internet.

Some preliminary recording

The best place to start any VBA procedure is the macro recorder; it's a developer's best friend. Let's start by figuring out the VBA syntax for moving sheets around.

You can turn on the macro recorder and specify that the macro should be placed in the Personal Macro Workbook (because you want to test the code on workbooks other than the one in which you're working). Once the macro starts recording, you can drag Sheet3 before Sheet1 and then stop recording. A review of the recorded macro code shows that Excel used the Move method.

```
Sub Macro1()
    Sheets("Sheet3").Select
    Sheets("Sheet3").Move Before:=Sheets(1)
End Sub
```

A quick search in the VBA Help system tells us that the Move method moves a sheet to a new location in the workbook. It also takes an argument that specifies the location for the sheet. This must be why the recorded macro included Before:=Sheets(1).

So far, so good. Now you need to find out how many sheets are in the active workbook. Searching VBA Help for the word Count tells us that it's a property of a collection. This means that all collections such as Sheets, Rows, Cells, and Shapes have a Count property. Good to know.

To test out this newly acquired piece of information, you can fire up the Visual Basic Editor, activate the Immediate window, and then type the following:

```
? ActiveWorkbook.Sheets.Count
```

4

Figure 4.9 shows the result. Success!

FIGURE 4.9

Using the VBE Immediate window to test a statement

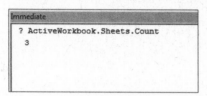

Okay. What about the sheet names? Time for another test. You can enter the following statement in the Immediate window:

```
? ActiveWorkbook.Sheets(1).Name
```

This returns the name of the first sheet (Sheet3), which is correct because you moved it while recording the macro. More good information to keep in mind.

You can now take this information to construct a simple For Each-Next construct (covered in Chapter 3 of this book).

```
Sub Test()
    For Each Sheet In ActiveWorkbook.Sheets
        MsgBox Sheet.Name
    Next Sheet
End Sub
```

Running this procedure displays three message boxes, each showing a different sheet name. Great. Now you know how to get a list of sheet names.

So, what about sorting? A quick search of the VBA Help system tells you that the Sort method applies to a Range object. Thus, one option is to transfer the sheet names to a range and then sort the range, but that seems like overkill for this application. A better option would be to dump the sheet names into an array of strings and then sort the array by using VBA code.

 Check out Chapter 3 for a refresher on arrays.

Initial setup

At this point, you know enough to start writing the procedure. Before doing so, however, you need to set up a test workbook. This test workbook will allow you to re-create the steps we determined at the start of this endeavor.

1. Create an empty workbook with five worksheets, named Sheet1, Sheet2, Sheet3, Sheet4, and Sheet5.

2. Move the sheets around randomly so that they aren't in any particular order. Just click and drag the sheet tabs.

3. Save the workbook as `Test.xlsx`.

4. Activate VBE and select the `Personal.xlsb` project in the Project window.

   If `Personal.xlsb` doesn't appear in the Project window in VBE, it means that you've never used the Personal Macro Workbook. To have Excel create this workbook for you, simply record a macro (any macro) and specify the Personal Macro Workbook as the destination for the macro.

5. Insert a new VBA module in `Personal.xlsb` (choose Insert ⇨ Module).

6. Create an empty `Sub` procedure called `SortSheets` (see Figure 4.10).

FIGURE 4.10

An empty procedure in a module located in the Personal Macro Workbook

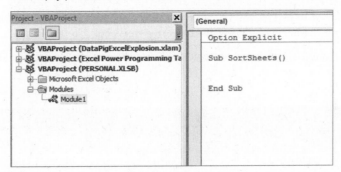

You can store this macro in any module in the Personal Macro Workbook. However, keeping each group of related macros in a separate module is a good idea. That way, you can easily export the module and import it into a different project later.

7. Activate Excel and choose Developer ⇨ Code ⇨ Macros to display the Macro dialog box.

8. In the Macro dialog box, select the `SortSheets` procedure and click the Options button to assign a shortcut key to this macro.

   The Ctrl+Shift+S key combination is a good choice.

Code writing

Now it's time to write some code. You know that you need to put the sheet names into an array consisting of text (so the array needs to have the data type `String`), but because you don't know yet how many sheets there will be in any given workbook, you use a `Dim` statement with empty parentheses to declare the array. You can use `ReDim` once you know the actual number of sheets.

4

As you can see in the following code, you loop through all of the sheets in the active workbook and insert each sheet's name into the `SheetNames` array. You also add a `MsgBox` function within the loop just to give ourselves a visual indicator that the sheets' names are indeed being entered into the array.

```
Sub SortSheets()
'        Sorts the sheets of the active workbook
    Dim SheetNames() as String
    Dim i as Long
    Dim SheetCount as Long
    SheetCount = ActiveWorkbook.Sheets.Count
    ReDim SheetNames(1 To SheetCount)
    For i = 1 To SheetCount
        SheetNames(i) = ActiveWorkbook.Sheets(i).Name
        MsgBox SheetNames(i)
    Next i
End Sub
```

It's a best practice to test as you go. So, test the code to see five message boxes appear, each displaying the name of a sheet in the active workbook. So far, so good.

You can now remove the `MsgBox` statement. (These message boxes become annoying after a while.)

TIP

Rather than use the `MsgBox` function to test your work, you can use the `Print` method of the `Debug` object to display information in the Immediate window. For this example, use the following statement in place of the `MsgBox` statement:

```
Debug.Print SheetNames(i)
```

This technique is much less intrusive than using `MsgBox` statements. Just make sure you remember to remove the statement when you're finished.

At this point, the `SortSheets` procedure simply creates an array of sheet names corresponding to the sheets in the active workbook. Two steps remain: sort the elements in the `SheetNames` array and then rearrange the sheets to correspond to the sorted array.

Writing the Sort procedure

Now that you have the sheet names in the `SheetNames` array, you can start thinking about sorting. One option is to insert the sorting code in the `SortSheets` procedure, but a better approach is to write a general-purpose sorting procedure that you can reuse with other projects. (Sorting arrays is a common operation.)

The thought of writing a sorting procedure seems daunting, but you can search the Internet to find commonly used routines that you can use or adapt. A quick search of VBA sorting procedures leads us to the bubble sort method. Although it's not a fast technique, it's easy to code. Blazing speed isn't a requirement in this application.

The bubble sort method uses a nested For-Next loop to evaluate each array element. If the array element is greater than the next element, the two elements swap positions. The code includes a nested loop, so this evaluation is repeated for every pair of items (that is, $n - 1$ times).

 In Chapter 7, you will explore some other sorting routines and compare them in terms of speed.

Here is the sorting procedure pulled together with the help of a few examples found on the Internet:

```
Sub BubbleSort(List() As String)
'       Sorts the List array in ascending order
    Dim First As Long, Last As Long
    Dim i As Long, j As Long
    Dim Temp As String
    First = LBound(List)
    Last = UBound(List)
    For i = First To Last - 1
        For j = i + 1 To Last
            If List(i) > List(j) Then
                Temp = List(j)
                List(j) = List(i)
                List(i) = Temp
            End If
        Next j
    Next i
End Sub
```

This procedure accepts one argument: a one-dimensional array named List. An array passed to a procedure can be of any length. It uses the LBound function to assign the lower bound of the array and the UBound function to assign the upper bound of the array to the variables First and Last, respectively.

Here's a little temporary procedure that you can use to test the BubbleSort procedure:

```
Sub SortTester()
    Dim x(1 To 5) As String
    Dim i As Long
    x(1) = "dog"
    x(2) = "cat"
    x(3) = "elephant"
    x(4) = "aardvark"
    x(5) = "bird"
    Call BubbleSort(x)
```

4

```
      For i = 1 To 5
          Debug.Print i, x(i)
      Next i
  End Sub
```

The `SortTester` routine creates an array of five strings, passes the array to `BubbleSort`, and then displays the sorted array in the Immediate window (see Figure 4.11). By the way, it's often helpful to create temporary procedures for testing. Once you're done with testing, you can simply delete them.

FIGURE 4.11

Using a temporary procedure to test the BubbleSort code

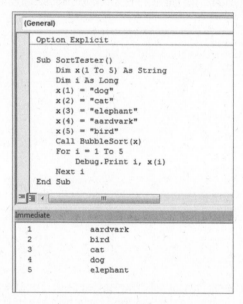

Now that you're satisfied that the `BubbleSort` procedure works reliably, you can modify `SortSheets` by adding a call to the `BubbleSort` procedure, passing the `SheetNames` array as an argument. At this point, the code looks like the following:

```
Sub SortSheets()
    Dim SheetNames() As String
    Dim SheetCount as Long
    Dim i as Long
    SheetCount = ActiveWorkbook.Sheets.Count
    ReDim SheetNames(1 To SheetCount)
    For i = 1 To SheetCount
```

```
        SheetNames(i) = ActiveWorkbook.Sheets(i).Name
    Next i
    Call BubbleSort(SheetNames)
End Sub

Sub BubbleSort(List() As String)
'       Sorts the List array in ascending order
    Dim First As Long, Last As Long
    Dim i As Long, j As Long
    Dim Temp As String
    First = LBound(List)
    Last = UBound(List)
    For i = First To Last - 1
        For j = i + 1 To Last
            If List(i) > List(j) Then
                Temp = List(j)
                List(j) = List(i)
                List(i) = Temp
            End If
        Next j
    Next i
End Sub
```

When the `SheetSort` procedure ends, it contains an array that consists of the sorted sheet names in the active workbook. To verify this, you can display the array contents in the VBE Immediate window by adding the following code at the end of the `SortSheets` procedure (if the Immediate window is not visible, press Ctrl+G):

```
For i = 1 To SheetCount
    Debug.Print SheetNames(i)
Next i
```

So far, so good. The next step is to write some code to rearrange the sheets to correspond to the sorted items in the `SheetNames` array.

The code that you recorded earlier proved useful. Remember the instruction that was recorded when you moved a sheet to the first position in the workbook?

```
Sheets("Sheet3").Move Before:=Sheets(1)
```

You can write a `For-Next` loop that will go through each sheet and move it to its corresponding sheet location, specified in the `SheetNames` array.

```
For i = 1 To SheetCount
    Sheets(SheetNames(i)).Move Before:=Sheets(i)
Next i
```

For example, the first time through the loop, the loop counter `i` is 1. The first element in the sorted `SheetNames` array is (in this example) `Sheet1`. Therefore, the expression for the `Move` method in the loop evaluates to the following:

```
Sheets("Sheet1").Move Before:= Sheets(1)
```

4

The second time through the loop, the expression evaluates to the following:

```
Sheets("Sheet2").Move Before:= Sheets(2)
```

This is what the `SortSheets` procedure looks like with the added code:

```
Sub SortSheets()
    Dim SheetNames() As String
    Dim SheetCount as Long
    Dim i as Long
    SheetCount = ActiveWorkbook.Sheets.Count
    ReDim SheetNames(1 To SheetCount)
    For i = 1 To SheetCount
        SheetNames(i) = ActiveWorkbook.Sheets(i).Name
    Next i
    Call BubbleSort(SheetNames)
    For i = 1 To SheetCount
        ActiveWorkbook.Sheets(SheetNames(i)).Move _
            Before:=ActiveWorkbook.Sheets(i)
    Next i
End Sub
```

It's time to clean things up. Let's make sure that all the variables used in the procedures are declared. Let's also add some comments and blank lines to make the code easier to read.

```
Sub SortSheets()
'          This routine sorts the sheets of the
'          active workbook in ascending order.
'          Use Ctrl+Shift+S to execute
    Dim SheetNames() As String
    Dim SheetCount As Long
    Dim i As Long
'          Determine the number of sheets & ReDim array
    SheetCount = ActiveWorkbook.Sheets.Count
    ReDim SheetNames(1 To SheetCount)
'        Fill array with sheet names
    For i = 1 To SheetCount
        SheetNames(i) = ActiveWorkbook.Sheets(i).Name
    Next i
'        Sort the array in ascending order
    Call BubbleSort(SheetNames)
'              Move the sheets
    For i = 1 To SheetCount
        ActiveWorkbook.Sheets(SheetNames(i)).Move _
            Before:= ActiveWorkbook.Sheets(i)
    Next i
End Sub
```

You can test the code by adding a few more sheets to `Test.xlsx` and changing some of the sheet names.

More testing

Just because the procedure works with the Test.xlsx workbook doesn't mean that it will work with all workbooks. To test it further, you can open a few other workbooks and try running the sort procedure on each workbook.

It soon becomes apparent that there are few issues with the code.

- Workbooks with many sheets take a long time to sort because the screen continually updates during the move operations.
- The sorting procedure you chose seems to be case-sensitive. For example, a sheet named SUMMARY (all uppercase) appears before a sheet named Sheet1. According to the BubbleSort procedure, an uppercase U is "greater than" a lowercase h.
- If there are no workbooks open, the code fails.
- If the workbook's structure is protected, the Move method fails.
- After sorting, the last sheet in the workbook becomes the active sheet. Changing the user's active sheet isn't a good practice; it's better to keep the user's original sheet active.
- If the code is interrupted by pressing Ctrl+Break, VBA displays an error message.
- The macro can't be reversed (that is, the Undo command is disabled when a macro is executed). If the user accidentally triggers the sorting procedure, the only way to get back to the original sheet order is by doing it manually.

Fixing the problems

Fixing the screen-updating problem is a breeze. You can insert the following instruction to turn off screen updating while the sheets are being moved.

```
Application.ScreenUpdating = False
```

This statement causes Excel's windows to freeze while the macro is running. A beneficial side effect is that it also speeds up the macro considerably. After the macro completes its operation, screen updating is turned back on automatically.

It is also easy to fix the problem with the BubbleSort procedure. You can use VBA's UCase function to convert the sheet names to uppercase for the comparison. This causes all of the comparisons to be made by using uppercase versions of the sheet names. The corrected line reads as follows:

```
If UCase(List(i)) > UCase(List(j)) Then
```

> **TIP**
>
> Another way to solve the "case" problem is to add the following statement to the top of your module:
>
> ```
> Option Compare Text
> ```
>
> This statement causes VBA to perform string comparisons based on a case-insensitive text sort order. In other words, *A* is considered the same as *a*.

4

To prevent the error message that appears when no workbooks are visible, you can add a simple check to see whether an active workbook is available. If no active workbook is available, you simply exit the procedure. This statement can go at the top of the SortSheets procedure:

```
If ActiveWorkbook Is Nothing Then Exit Sub
```

There's usually a good reason that a workbook's structure is protected. The best approach is to not attempt to unprotect the workbook. Rather, the code should display a message box warning and let the user unprotect the workbook and re-execute the macro. Testing for a protected workbook structure is easy—the ProtectStructure property of a Workbook object returns True if a workbook is protected.

```
'          Check for protected workbook structure
If ActiveWorkbook.ProtectStructure Then
    MsgBox ActiveWorkbook.Name & " is protected.", _
        vbCritical, "Cannot Sort Sheets."
    Exit Sub
End If
```

If the workbook's structure is protected, the user sees a message box like the one shown in Figure 4.12.

FIGURE 4.12

This message box tells the user that the sheets cannot be sorted.

To reactivate the original active sheet after the sorting is performed, you can add some code to assign the original sheet to an object variable (OldActive) and then activate that sheet when the routine is finished. Here's the statement that assigns the variable:

```
Set OldActive = ActiveSheet
```

This statement activates the original active worksheet.

```
OldActive.Activate
```

Pressing Ctrl+Break normally halts a macro, and VBA usually displays an error message. However, because you want to avoid VBA error messages, you can insert a command to prevent this situation. From the VBA Help system, you discover that the Application object has an `EnableCancelKey` property that can disable Ctrl+Break. So, you can add the following statement at the top of the routine:

```
Application.EnableCancelKey = xlDisabled
```

> **CAUTION**
>
> Be careful when you disable the Cancel key. If your code gets caught in an infinite loop, you can't break out of it. For best results, insert this statement *only after you're sure* that everything is working properly.

To prevent the problem of inadvertently starting the sort procedure, you can add a simple message box asking the user to confirm the action. The following statement is placed before the Ctrl+Break key is disabled:

```
If MsgBox("Sort the sheets in the active workbook?", _
    vbQuestion + vbYesNo) <> vbYes Then Exit Sub
```

When users execute the `SortSheets` procedure, they see the message box in Figure 4.13.

FIGURE 4.13

This message box appears before the sheets are sorted.

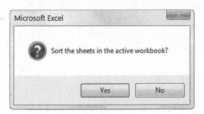

After all these adjustments are implemented, the `SortSheets` procedure looks like this:

```
Option Explicit
Sub SortSheets()
    ' This routine sorts the sheets of the
    ' active workbook in ascending order.
    ' Use Ctrl+Shift+S to execute
    Dim SheetNames() As String
    Dim i As Long
    Dim SheetCount As Long
    Dim OldActiveSheet As Object
    If ActiveWorkbook Is Nothing Then Exit Sub ' No active workbook
    SheetCount = ActiveWorkbook.Sheets.Count
    ' Check for protected workbook structure
    If ActiveWorkbook.ProtectStructure Then
```

```
        MsgBox ActiveWorkbook.Name & " is protected.", _
            vbCritical, "Cannot Sort Sheets."
        Exit Sub
    End If

    ' Make user verify
    If MsgBox("Sort the sheets in the active workbook?", _
        vbQuestion + vbYesNo) <> vbYes Then Exit Sub
    ' Disable Ctrl+Break
    Application.EnableCancelKey = xlDisabled
    ' Get the number of sheets
    SheetCount = ActiveWorkbook.Sheets.Count
    ' Redimension the array
    ReDim SheetNames(1 To SheetCount)
    ' Store a reference to the active sheet
    Set OldActiveSheet = ActiveSheet
    ' Fill array with sheet names
    For i = 1 To SheetCount
        SheetNames(i) = ActiveWorkbook.Sheets(i).Name
    Next i
    ' Sort the array in ascending order
    Call BubbleSort(SheetNames)
    ' Turn off screen updating
    Application.ScreenUpdating = False
    ' Move the sheets
    For i = 1 To SheetCount
        ActiveWorkbook.Sheets(SheetNames(i)).Move _
            Before:=ActiveWorkbook.Sheets(i)
    Next i
    ' Reactivate the original active sheet
    OldActiveSheet.Activate
End Sub
```

Utility availability

Because the SortSheets macro is stored in the Personal Macro Workbook, it's available whenever Excel is running. At this point, you can execute the macro by selecting the macro's name from the Macro dialog box (Alt+F8 displays this dialog box) or by pressing Ctrl+Shift+S. Another option is to add a command to the Ribbon.

To add a command, follow these steps:

1. Right-click any area of the Ribbon and choose Customize the Ribbon.

2. Use the controls in the box on the right to specify a Ribbon tab and then click the New Group button to create a group on the specified tab. You can right-click your new group to rename it.

Figure 4.14 illustrates a new group named Sort Sheets in the View tab. Note that you can't add a command to any of Excel's pre-existing groups.

3. In the Customize Ribbon tab of the Excel Options dialog box, choose Macros from the Choose Commands From drop-down list and find the macro that you want to add.

4. Add the macro to your newly created group.

FIGURE 4.14

Adding a new command to the Ribbon

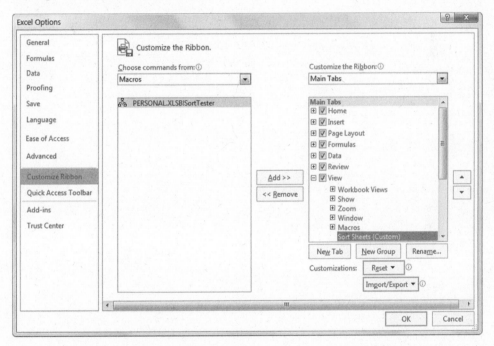

Evaluating the project

There you have it. The utility meets all the original project requirements: it sorts all of the sheets in the active workbook, it can be executed easily, and it's always available for use with any workbook.

> **NOTE**
>
> The procedure still has one slight problem: the sorting is strict and may not always be "logical." For example, after sorting, Sheet10 is placed before Sheet2. Most would want Sheet2 to be listed before Sheet10. Solving that problem is possible, but it is beyond the scope of this introductory exercise.

Creating Function Procedures

IN THIS CHAPTER

- Understanding the difference between `Sub` procedures and `Function` procedures
- Creating custom functions
- Looking at `Function` procedures and `Function` arguments
- Creating a function that emulates Excel's `SUM` function
- Using functions that enable you to work with pre-1900 dates in your worksheets
- Debugging functions, dealing with the Insert Function dialog box, and using add-ins to store custom functions
- Calling the Windows application programming interface (API) to perform otherwise impossible feats

Sub Procedures vs. Function Procedures

A VBA `Function` is a procedure that performs calculations and returns a value. You can use these functions in your Visual Basic for Applications (VBA) code or in worksheet formulas.

VBA enables you to create `Sub` procedures and `Function` procedures. You can think of a `Sub` procedure as a command that either the user or another procedure can execute. `Function` procedures, on the other hand, usually return a single value (or an array), just like Excel worksheet functions and VBA built-in functions. As with built-in functions, your `Function` procedures can use arguments.

`Function` procedures are versatile, and you can use them in two situations.

- As part of an expression in a VBA procedure
- In formulas that you create in a worksheet

In fact, you can use a `Function` procedure anywhere you can use an Excel worksheet function or a VBA built-in function. The only exception is that you can't use a VBA function in a data validation formula. You can, however, use a custom VBA function in a conditional formatting formula.

We cover `Sub` procedures in the preceding chapter and `Function` procedures in this chapter.

Chapter 7, "VBA Programming Examples and Techniques," has many useful and practical examples of Function procedures. You can incorporate many of these techniques into your work.

Why Create Custom Functions?

You're undoubtedly familiar with Excel worksheet functions; even novices know how to use the most common worksheet functions, such as SUM, AVERAGE, and IF. Excel includes more than 450 predefined worksheet functions that you can use in formulas. In addition, you can create custom functions by using VBA.

With all the functions available in Excel and VBA, you might wonder why you'd ever need to create new functions. The answer is to simplify your work. With a bit of planning, custom functions are useful in worksheet formulas and VBA procedures.

Often, for example, you can create a custom function that can significantly shorten your formulas. And shorter formulas are more readable and easier to work with. The trade-off, however, is that custom functions are usually much slower than built-in functions. And, of course, the user must enable macros to use these functions.

When you create applications, you may notice that some procedures repeat certain calculations. In such cases, consider creating a custom function that performs the calculation. Then you can call the function from your procedure. A custom function can eliminate the need for duplicated code, thus reducing errors.

An Introductory Function Example

Without further ado, this section presents an example of a VBA Function procedure.

The following is a custom function defined in a VBA module. This function, named REMOVEVOWELS, uses a single argument. The function returns the argument, but with all the vowels removed.

```
Function REMOVEVOWELS(Txt) As String
' Removes all vowels from the Txt argument
    Dim i As Long
    RemoveVowels = ""
    For i = 1 To Len(Txt)
        If Not UCase(Mid(Txt, i, 1)) Like "[AEIOU]" Then
    REMOVEVOWELS = REMOVEVOWELS & Mid(Txt, i, 1)
        End If
    Next i
End Function
```

This function certainly isn't the most useful function, but it demonstrates some key concepts related to functions. We explain how this function works later in the "Analyzing the custom function" section.

> **CAUTION**
>
> When you create custom functions that will be used in a worksheet formula, make sure that the code resides in a normal VBA module (use Insert ⇨ Module to create a normal VBA module). If you place your custom functions in a code module for a UserForm, a sheet, or ThisWorkbook, they won't work in your formulas. Your formulas will return a #NAME? error.

Using the function in a worksheet

When you enter a formula that uses the REMOVEVOWELS function, Excel executes the code to get the result that's returned by the function. Here's an example of how you'd use the function in a formula:

```
=REMOVEVOWELS(A1)
```

See Figure 5.1 for examples of this function in action. The formulas are in column B, and they use the text in column A as their arguments. As you can see, the function returns the single argument, but with the vowels removed.

FIGURE 5.1

Using a custom function in a worksheet formula

	A	B
1	Every good boy does fine.	vry gd by ds fn.
2	antidisestablishmentarianism	ntdsstblshmntrnsm
3	Microsoft Excel	Mcrsft xcl
4	abcdefghijklmnopqrstuvwxyz	bcdfghjklmnpqrstvwxyz
5	A failure to communicate.	flr t cmmnct.
6	This sentence has no vowels.	Ths sntnc hs n vwls.
7	Vowels: AEIOU	Vwls:
8	Humuhumunukunukuapua'a is a fish	Hmhmnknkp's fsh
9	Honorificabilitudinitatibus	Hnrfcbltdnttbs
10	Do you like custom worksheet functions?	D y lk cstm wrksht fnctns?

Actually, the function works like any built-in worksheet function. You can insert it in a formula by choosing Formulas ⇨ Function Library ⇨ Insert Function or by clicking the Insert Function icon to the left of the formula bar. Either of these actions displays the Insert Function dialog box. In the Insert Function dialog box, your custom functions are located, by default, in the User Defined category.

You can also nest custom functions and combine them with other elements in your formulas. For example, the following formula nests the REMOVEVOWELS function inside Excel's UPPER function. The result is the original string (minus vowels), converted to uppercase.

```
=UPPER(REMOVEVOWELS(A1))
```

5

Using the function in a VBA procedure

In addition to using custom functions in worksheet formulas, you can use them in other VBA procedures. The following VBA procedure, which is defined in the same module as the custom REMOVEVOWELS function, first displays an input box to solicit text from the user. Then the procedure uses the VBA built-in MsgBox function to display the user input after the REMOVEVOWELS function processes it (see Figure 5.2). The original input appears as the caption in the message box.

```
Sub ZapTheVowels()
    Dim UserInput as String
    UserInput = InputBox("Enter some text:")
    MsgBox REMOVEVOWELS(UserInput), vbInformation, UserInput
End Sub
```

Figure 5.2 shows text entered into an input box and the result displayed in a message box.

FIGURE 5.2

Using a custom function in a VBA procedure

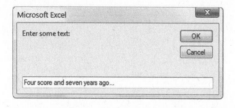

Analyzing the custom function

Function procedures can be as complex as you need them to be. Most of the time, they're more complex and much more useful than this sample procedure. Nonetheless, an analysis of this example may help you understand what is happening.

Here's the code, again:

```
Function REMOVEVOWELS(Txt) As String
' Removes all vowels from the Txt argument
    Dim i As Long
    REMOVEVOWELS = ""
```

```
        For i = 1 To Len(Txt)
            If Not UCase(Mid(Txt, i, 1)) Like "[AEIOU]" Then
                REMOVEVOWELS = REMOVEVOWELS & Mid(Txt, i, 1)
            End If
        Next i
    End Function
```

Note that the procedure starts with the keyword `Function`, rather than `Sub`, followed by the name of the function (REMOVEVOWELS). This custom function uses only one argument (Txt), enclosed in parentheses. `As String` defines the data type of the function's return value. Excel uses the `Variant` data type if no data type is specified.

The second line is an optional comment that describes what the function does. This line is followed by a `Dim` statement, which declares the variable (i) used in the procedure as type `Long`.

The next five instructions make up a `For-Next` loop. The procedure loops through each character in the input and builds the string. The first instruction in the loop uses VBA's `Mid` function to return a single character from the input string and converts this character to uppercase. That character is then compared to a list of characters by using Excel's `Like` operator. In other words, the `If` clause is true if the character isn't A, E, I, O, or U. In such a case, the character is appended to the REMOVEVOWELS variable.

When the loop is finished, REMOVEVOWELS consists of the input string with all the vowels removed. This string is the value that the function returns.

The procedure ends with an `End Function` statement.

Keep in mind that you can do the coding for this function in a number of ways. Here's a function that accomplishes the same result, but it is coded differently:

```
    Function REMOVEVOWELS(txt) As String
    ' Removes all vowels from the Txt argument
        Dim i As Long
        Dim TempString As String
        TempString = ""
        For i = 1 To Len(txt)
            Select Case ucase(Mid(txt, i, 1))
                Case "A", "E", "I", "O", "U"
                    'Do nothing
                Case Else
                    TempString = TempString & Mid(txt, i, 1)
            End Select
        Next i
        REMOVEVOWELS = TempString
    End Function
```

In this version, we used a string variable (TempString) to store the vowels string as it's being constructed. Then, before the procedure ends, we assigned the contents of

5

`TempString` to the function's name. This version also uses a `Select Case` construct rather than an `If-Then` construct.

ON THE WEB

Both versions of this function are available at this book's website. The file is named `remove vowels.xlsm`.

What custom worksheet functions can't do

When you develop custom functions, it's important to understand a key distinction between functions that you call from other VBA procedures and functions that you use in worksheet formulas. `Function` procedures used in worksheet formulas must be passive. For example, code in a `Function` procedure can't manipulate ranges or change things on the worksheet. An example can help make this limitation clear.

You may be tempted to write a custom worksheet function that changes a cell's formatting. For example, it may be useful to have a formula that uses a custom function to change the color of text in a cell based on the cell's value. Try as you might, however, such a function is impossible to write. No matter what you do, the function won't change the worksheet. Remember, a function simply returns a value. It can't perform actions with objects.

That said, we should point out one notable exception. You can change the text in a cell comment by using a custom VBA function. Here's an example function that does just that:

```
Function MODIFYCOMMENT(Cell As Range, Cmt As String)
    Cell.Comment.Text Cmt
End Function
```

Here's an example of using this function in a formula. The formula replaces the comment in cell A1 with new text. The function won't work if cell A1 doesn't have a comment.

```
=MODIFYCOMMENT(A1,"Hey, I changed your comment")
```

Function Procedures

A `Function` procedure has much in common with a `Sub` procedure. (For more information on `Sub` procedures, see Chapter 4, "Working with VBA Sub Procedures.")

The syntax for declaring a function is as follows:

```
[Public | Private][Static] Function name ([arglist])[As type]
    [instructions]
    [name = expression]
    [Exit Function]
    [instructions]
    [name = expression]
End Function
```

The `Function` procedure contains the following elements:

`Public`: Optional. Indicates that the `Function` procedure is accessible to all other procedures in all other modules in all active Excel VBA projects.

`Private`: Optional. Indicates that the `Function` procedure is accessible only to other procedures in the same module.

`Static`: Optional. Indicates that the values of variables declared in the `Function` procedure are preserved between calls.

`Function`: Required. Indicates the beginning of a procedure that returns a value or other data.

`name`: Required. Any valid `Function` procedure name, which must follow the same rules as a variable name.

`arglist`: Optional. A list of one or more variables that represent arguments passed to the `Function` procedure. The arguments are enclosed in parentheses. Use a comma to separate pairs of arguments.

`type`: Optional. The data type returned by the `Function` procedure.

`instructions`: Optional. Any number of valid VBA instructions.

`Exit Function`: Optional. A statement that forces an immediate exit from the `Function` procedure before its completion.

`End Function`: Required. A keyword that indicates the end of the `Function` procedure.

A key point to remember about a custom function written in VBA is that a value is always assigned to the function's name a minimum of one time, generally when it has completed execution.

To create a custom function, start by inserting a VBA module. You can use an existing module, as long as it's a normal VBA module. Enter the keyword `Function` followed by the function name and a list of its arguments (if any) in parentheses and then press Enter on your keyboard. Note that the VBE will automatically insert the `End Function` statement.

Insert the VBA code that performs the work, making sure that the appropriate value is assigned to the term corresponding to the function name at least once in the body of the `Function` procedure.

Function names must adhere to the same rules as variable names. If you plan to use your custom function in a worksheet formula, be careful if the function name is also a cell address. For example, if you use something like ABC123 as a function name, you can't use the function in a worksheet formula, because ABC123 is a cell address. If you do so, Excel displays a #REF! error.

The best advice is to avoid using function names that are also cell references, including named ranges. And avoid using function names that correspond to Excel's built-in function names. In the case of a function name conflict, Excel always uses its built-in function.

5

A function's scope

In Chapter 4, we discuss the concept of a procedure's scope (public or private). The same discussion applies to functions: a *function's scope* determines whether it can be called by procedures in other modules or in worksheets.

Here are a few things to keep in mind about a function's scope:

- If you don't declare a function's scope, its default scope is Public.
- Functions declared As Private don't appear in Excel's Insert Function dialog box. Therefore, when you create a function that should be used only in a VBA procedure, you should declare it Private so that users don't try to use it in a formula.
- If your VBA code needs to call a function that's defined in another workbook, set up a reference to the other workbook by choosing the Visual Basic Editor (VBE) Tools ⇨ References command.
- You do not have to establish a reference if the function is defined in an add-in. Such a function is available for use in all workbooks.

Executing function procedures

Although you can execute a Sub procedure in many ways, you can execute a Function procedure in only four ways.

- Call it from another procedure
- Use it in a worksheet formula
- Use it in a formula that's used to specify conditional formatting
- Call it from the VBE Immediate window

From a procedure

You can call custom functions from a VBA procedure the same way that you call built-in functions. For example, after you define a function called SUMARRAY, you can enter a statement like the following:

```
Total = SUMARRAY(MyArray)
```

This statement executes the SUMARRAY function with MyArray as its argument, returns the function's result, and assigns it to the Total variable.

You also can use the Run method of the Application object. Here's an example:

```
Total = Application.Run ("SUMARRAY", "MyArray")
```

The first argument for the Run method is the function name. Subsequent arguments represent the arguments for the function. The arguments for the Run method can be literal strings (as shown in the preceding example), numbers, expressions, or variables.

In a worksheet formula

Using custom functions in a worksheet formula is like using built-in functions except that you must ensure that Excel can locate the Function procedure. If the Function procedure is in the same workbook, you don't have to do anything special. If it's in a different workbook, you may have to tell Excel where to find it.

You can do so in three ways.

Precede the function name with a file reference: For example, if you want to use a function called COUNTNAMES that's defined in an open workbook named Myfuncs. xlsm, you can use the following reference:

```
=Myfuncs.xlsm!COUNTNAMES(A1:A1000)
```

If you insert the function with the Insert Function dialog box, the workbook reference is inserted automatically.

Set up a reference to the workbook: You do so by choosing the VBE Tools ⇨ References command. If the function is defined in a referenced workbook, you don't need to use the worksheet name. Even when the dependent workbook is assigned as a reference, the Paste Function dialog box continues to insert the workbook reference (although it's not necessary).

Create an add-in: When you create an add-in from a workbook that has Function procedures, you don't need to use the file reference when you use one of the functions in a formula. The add-in must be installed, however. We discuss add-ins in Chapter 16, "Creating and Using Add-Ins."

You'll notice that, unlike Sub procedures, your Function procedures don't appear in the Macro dialog box when you issue the Developer ⇨ Code ⇨ Macros command. In addition, you can't choose a function when you issue the VBE Run ⇨ Sub/UserForm command (or press F5) if the cursor is located in a Function procedure. (You get the Macro dialog box that lets you choose a macro to run.) Therefore, you need to do a bit of extra up-front work to test your functions while you're developing them. One approach is to set up a simple procedure that calls the function. If the function is designed to be used in worksheet formulas, you'll want to enter a simple formula to test it.

In a conditional formatting formula

When you specify conditional formatting, one of the options is to create a formula. The formula must be a logical formula (that is, it must return either TRUE or FALSE). If the formula returns TRUE, the condition is met, and formatting is applied to the cell.

You can use custom VBA functions in your conditional formatting formulas. For example, here's a simple VBA function that returns TRUE if its argument is a cell that contains a formula:

```
Function CELLHASFORMULA(cell) As Boolean
    CELLHASFORMULA = cell.HasFormula
End Function
```

After defining this function in a VBA module, you can set up a conditional formatting rule so that cells that contain a formula contain different formatting.

5

1. Select the range that will contain the conditional formatting. For example, select A1:G20.

2. Choose Home ➪ Styles ➪ Conditional Formatting ➪ New Rule.

3. In the New Formatting Rule dialog box, select the option labeled Use a Formula to Determine Which Cells to Format.

4. Enter this formula in the formula box, but make sure that the cell reference argument corresponds to the upper-left cell in the range that you selected in step 1:

   `=CELLHASFORMULA(A1)`

5. Click the Format button to specify the formatting for cells that meet this condition.

6. Click OK to apply the conditional formatting rule to the selected range.

Cells in the range that contain a formula will display the formatting you specified. In the New Formatting Rule dialog box shown in Figure 5.3, we specify a custom function in a formula.

FIGURE 5.3

Using a custom VBA function for conditional formatting

> **NOTE**
>
> The `ISFORMULA` worksheet function (introduced in Excel 2013) works exactly like the custom `CELLHAS FORMULA` function. But the `CELLHASFORMULA` function is still useful if you plan to share your workbook with others who are still using Excel 2010 or earlier versions.

From the VBE Immediate Window

The final way to call a `Function` procedure is from the VBE Immediate window. This method is generally used only for testing. Figure 5.4 shows an example. The `?` character is a shortcut for the `Debug.Print` command (used to print results to the Immediate window).

FIGURE 5.4

Calling a Function procedure from the Immediate window

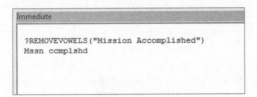

```
Immediate

?REMOVEVOWELS("Mission Accomplished")
Mssn ccmplshd
```

Function Arguments

Keep in mind the following points about `Function` procedure arguments:

- Arguments can be variables (including arrays), constants, literals, or expressions.
- Some functions don't have arguments.
- Some functions have a fixed number of required arguments (from 1 to 60).
- Some functions have a combination of required and optional arguments.

> **NOTE**
>
> If your formula uses a custom worksheet function and it returns `#VALUE!`, your function has an error. The error may be caused by logical errors in your code or by passing incorrect arguments to the function. See the "Debugging Functions" section later in this chapter.

Function Examples

In this section, we present a series of examples that demonstrate how to use arguments effectively with functions. By the way, this discussion applies also to `Sub` procedures.

Functions with no argument

Like `Sub` procedures, `Function` procedures need not have arguments. Excel, for example, has a few built-in functions that don't use arguments, including RAND, TODAY, and NOW. You can create similar functions.

This section contains examples of functions that don't use an argument.

Here's a simple example of a function that doesn't use an argument. The following function returns the `UserName` property of the `Application` object. This is the name that appears in the Excel Options dialog box (General tab) and is stored in the Windows Registry.

```
Function USER()
    ' Returns the name of the current user
    USER = Application.UserName
End Function
```

When you enter the following formula, the cell returns the name of the current user:

```
=USER()
```

NOTE

When you use a function with no arguments in a worksheet formula, you must include a set of empty parentheses. This requirement isn't necessary if you call the function in a VBA procedure, although including the empty parentheses does make it clear that you're calling a function.

There is no need to use this function in another procedure because you can simply access the `UserName` property directly in your code.

The `USER` function demonstrates how you can create a *wrapper* function that returns a property or the result of a VBA function. The following are three additional wrapper functions that take no argument:

```
Function EXCELDIR() As String
    ' Returns the directory in which Excel is installed
    EXCELDIR = Application.Path
End Function

Function SHEETCOUNT()
    ' Returns the number of sheets in the workbook
    SHEETCOUNT = Application.Caller.Parent.Parent.Sheets.Count
End Function

Function SHEETNAME()
    ' Returns the name of the worksheet
    SHEETNAME = Application.Caller.Parent.Name
End Function
```

You can probably think of other potentially useful wrapper functions. For example, you can write a function to display the template's location (`Application.TemplatesPath`), the default file location (`Application.DefaultFilePath`), and the version of Excel

(Application.Version). Also, note that Excel 2013 introduced a worksheet function, SHEETS, that makes the SHEETCOUNT function obsolete.

Here's another example of a function that doesn't take an argument. Most people use Excel's RAND function to fill a range of cells quickly with values. But the RAND function forces random values to be changed whenever the worksheet was recalculated. So, after using the RAND function, most people will convert the formulas to values.

As an alternative, you could use VBA to create a custom function that returns static random numbers that do not change. The custom function follows:

```
Function STATICRAND()
    ' Returns a random number that doesn't
    ' change when recalculated
    STATICRAND = Rnd()
End Function
```

If you want to generate a series of random integers between 0 and 1,000, you can use a formula such as the following:

```
=INT(STATICRAND()*1000)
```

The values produced by this formula never change when the worksheet is calculated normally. However, you can force the formula to recalculate by pressing Ctrl+Alt+F9.

Controlling function recalculation

When you use a custom function in a worksheet formula, when is it recalculated?

Custom functions behave like Excel's built-in worksheet functions. Normally, a custom function is recalculated only when any of the function's arguments are modified. You can, however, force functions to recalculate more frequently. Adding the following statement to a Function procedure makes the function recalculate whenever the sheet is recalculated. If you're using automatic calculation mode, a calculation occurs whenever any cell is changed.

```
Application.Volatile True
```

The Volatile method of the Application object has one argument (either True or False). Marking a Function procedure as volatile forces the function to be calculated whenever recalculation occurs for any cell in the worksheet.

For example, the custom STATICRAND function can be changed to emulate Excel's RAND function using the Volatile method.

```
Function NONSTATICRAND()
    ' Returns a random number that changes with each calculation
    Application.Volatile True
    NONSTATICRAND = Rnd()
End Function
```

5

Using the `False` argument of the `Volatile` method causes the function to be recalculated only when one or more of its arguments change as a result of a recalculation.

To force an entire recalculation, including nonvolatile custom functions, press Ctrl+Alt+F9. This key combination will, for example, generate new random numbers for the `STATICRAND` function presented in this chapter.

A function with one argument

This section describes a function for sales managers who need to calculate the commissions earned by their sales forces. The calculations in this example are based on the following table:

Monthly Sales	Commission Rate
0–$9,999	8.0%
$10,000–$19,999	10.5%
$20,000–$39,999	12.0%
$40,000+	14.0%

Note that the commission rate is nonlinear and also depends on the month's total sales. Employees who sell more earn a higher commission rate.

You can calculate commissions for various sales amounts entered in a worksheet in several ways. If you're not thinking too clearly, you can waste lots of time and come up with a lengthy formula such as this one:

```
=IF(AND(A1>=0,A1<=9999.99),A1*0.08,
IF(AND(A1>=10000,A1<=19999.99),A1*0.105,
IF(AND(A1>=20000,A1<=39999.99),A1*0.12,
IF(A1>=40000,A1*0.14,0))))
```

This approach is bad for a couple of reasons. First, the formula is overly complex, making it difficult to understand. Second, the values are hard-coded into the formula, making the formula difficult to modify.

A better (non-VBA) approach is to use a lookup table function to compute the commissions. For example, the following formula uses VLOOKUP to retrieve the commission value from a range named `Table` and multiplies that value by the value in cell A1:

```
=VLOOKUP(A1,Table,2)*A1
```

Yet another approach (that eliminates the need to use a lookup table) is to create a custom function such as the following:

```
Function COMMISSION(Sales)
    Const Tier1 = 0.08
    Const Tier2 = 0.105
```

```
        Const Tier3 = 0.12
        Const Tier4 = 0.14
        ' Calculates sales commissions
        Select Case Sales
            Case 0 To 9999.99: COMMISSION = Sales * Tier1
            Case 10000 To 19999.99: COMMISSION = Sales * Tier2
            Case 20000 To 39999.99: COMMISSION = Sales * Tier3
            Case Is >= 40000: COMMISSION = Sales * Tier4
        End Select
    End Function
```

After you enter this function in a VBA module, you can use it in a worksheet formula or call the function from other VBA procedures.

Entering the following formula into a cell produces a result of 3,000; the amount (25,000) qualifies for a commission rate of 12 percent:

```
=COMMISSION(25000)
```

Even if you don't need custom functions in a worksheet, creating Function procedures can make your VBA coding much simpler. For example, if your VBA procedure calculates sales commissions, you can use the same function and call it from a VBA procedure. Here's a tiny procedure that asks the user for a sales amount and then uses the COMMISSION function to calculate the commission due:

```
Sub CalcComm()
    Dim Sales as Long
    Sales = InputBox("Enter Sales:")
    MsgBox "The commission is " & COMMISSION(Sales)
End Sub
```

The CalcComm procedure starts by displaying an input box that asks for the sales amount. Then it displays a message box with the calculated sales commission for that amount.

This Sub procedure works, but it's crude. The following is an enhanced version with a bit of error handling. It also displays formatted values and keeps looping until the user clicks No (see Figure 5.5).

```
Sub CalcComm()
    Dim Sales As Long
    Dim Msg As String, Ans As String
    ' Prompt for sales amount
    Sales = Val(InputBox("Enter Sales:", _
    "Sales Commission Calculator"))
    ' Exit if canceled
    If Sales = 0 Then Exit Sub
    ' Build the Message
    Msg = "Sales Amount:" & vbTab & Format(Sales, "$#,##0.00")
    Msg = Msg & vbCrLf & "Commission:" & vbTab
    Msg = Msg & Format(COMMISSION(Sales), "$#,##0.00")
    Msg = Msg & vbCrLf & vbCrLf & "Another?"
```

5

```
        ' Display the result and prompt for another
        Ans = MsgBox(Msg, vbYesNo, "Sales Commission Calculator")
        If Ans = vbYes Then CalcComm
    End Sub
```

FIGURE 5.5

Using a function to display the result of a calculation

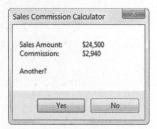

This function uses two VBA built-in constants: `vbTab` represents a tab (to space the output), and `vbCrLf` specifies a carriage return and line feed (to skip to the next line). VBA's `Format` function displays a value in a specified format (in this case, with a dollar sign, a comma, and two decimal places).

In both examples, the `Commission` function must be available in the active workbook; otherwise, Excel displays an error message saying that the function isn't defined.

Use arguments, not cell references

All ranges that are used in a custom function should be passed as arguments. Consider the following function, which returns the value in A1, multiplied by 2:

```
Function DOUBLECELL()
    DOUBLECELL = Range("A1") * 2
End Function
```

Although this function works, at times it may return an incorrect result. Excel's calculation engine can't account for ranges in your code that aren't passed as arguments. Therefore, in some cases, all precedents may not be calculated before the function's value is returned. The DOUBLECELL function should be written as follows, with A1 passed as the argument:

```
Function DOUBLECELL(cell)
    DOUBLECELL = cell * 2
End Function
```

A function with two arguments

Imagine that the aforementioned hypothetical sales managers implement a new policy to help reduce turnover: The total commission paid is increased by 1 percent for every year that the salesperson has been with the company.

We modified the custom COMMISSION function (defined in the preceding section) so that it takes two arguments. The new argument represents the number of years. Call this new function COMMISSION2.

```
Function COMMISSION2(Sales, Years)
    ' Calculates sales commissions based on
    ' years in service
    Const Tier1 = 0.08
    Const Tier2 = 0.105
    Const Tier3 = 0.12
    Const Tier4 = 0.14
    Select Case Sales
        Case 0 To 9999.99: COMMISSION2 = Sales * Tier1
        Case 10000 To 19999.99: COMMISSION2 = Sales * Tier2
        Case 20000 To 39999.99: COMMISSION2 = Sales * Tier3
        Case Is >= 40000: COMMISSION2 = Sales * Tier4
    End Select
    COMMISSION2 = COMMISSION2 + (COMMISSION2 * Years / 100)
End Function
```

Pretty simple, right? We just added the second argument (Years) to the Function statement and included an additional computation that adjusts the commission.

Here's an example of how you can write a formula using this function (it assumes that the sales amount is in cell A1 and the number of years the salesperson has worked is in cell B1):

```
=COMMISSION2(A1,B1)
```

ON THE WEB

All commission-related examples are available on this book's website, in a file named commission functions.xlsm.

A function with an array argument

A Function procedure also can accept one or more arrays as arguments, process the array(s), and return a single value. The array can also consist of a range of cells.

The following function accepts an array as its argument and returns the sum of its elements:

```
Function SUMARRAY(List) As Double
    Dim Item As Variant
    SumArray = 0
```

```
        For Each Item In List
            If WorksheetFunction.IsNumber(Item) Then _
                SUMARRAY = SUMARRAY + Item
        Next Item
    End Function
```

Excel's ISNUMBER function checks to see whether each element is a number before adding it to the total. Adding this simple error-checking statement eliminates the type-mismatch error that occurs when you try to perform arithmetic with something other than a number.

The following procedure demonstrates how to call this function from a Sub procedure. The MakeList procedure creates a 100-element array and assigns a random number to each element. Then the MsgBox function displays the sum of the values in the array by calling the SUMARRAY function.

```
    Sub MakeList()
        Dim Nums(1 To 100) As Double
        Dim i As Integer
        For i = 1 To 100
            Nums(i) = Rnd * 1000
        Next i
        MsgBox SUMARRAY(Nums)
    End Sub
```

Note that the SUMARRAY function doesn't declare the data type of its argument (it's a Variant type). Because it's not declared as a specific numeric type, the function also works in your worksheet formulas in which the argument is a Range object. For example, the following formula returns the sum of the values in A1:C10:

```
    =SUMARRAY(A1:C10)
```

You might notice that, when used in a worksheet formula, the SUMARRAY function works very much like Excel's SUM function. One difference, however, is that SUMARRAY doesn't accept multiple arguments. Understand that this example is for educational purposes only. Using the SUMARRAY function in a formula offers no advantages over the Excel SUM function.

ON THE WEB

This example, named `array argument.xlsm`, is available on this book's website.

A function with optional arguments

Many of Excel's built-in worksheet functions use optional arguments. An example is the LEFT function, which returns characters from the left side of a string. Its syntax is as follows:

```
    LEFT(text,num_chars)
```

The first argument is required, but the second is optional. If the optional argument is omitted for the LEFT function, Excel assumes a value of 1. Therefore, the following two formulas return the same result:

```
=LEFT(A1,1)
=LEFT(A1)
```

The custom functions that you develop in VBA also can have optional arguments. You specify an optional argument by preceding the argument's name with the keyword Optional. In the argument list, optional arguments must appear after any required arguments.

The following is a simple function example that returns the user's name. The function's argument is optional.

```
Function USER(Optional UpperCase As Variant)
    If IsMissing(UpperCase) Then UpperCase = False
    USER = Application.UserName
    If UpperCase Then USER = UCase(USER)
End Function
```

If the argument is False or omitted, the user's name is returned without any changes. If the argument is True, the user's name is converted to uppercase (using the VBA UCase function) before it's returned. Note that the first statement in the procedure uses the VBA IsMissing function to determine whether the argument was supplied. If the argument is missing, the statement sets the UpperCase variable to False (the default value).

All of the following formulas are valid, and the first two produce the same result:

```
=USER()
=USER(False)
=USER(True)
```

> **NOTE**
> If you need to determine whether an optional argument was passed to a function, you must declare the optional argument as a Variant data type. Then you can use the IsMissing function in the procedure, as demonstrated in this example. In other words, the argument for the IsMissing function must always be a Variant data type.

The following is another example of a custom function that uses an optional argument. This function randomly chooses one cell from an input range and returns that cell's contents. If the second argument is True, the selected value changes whenever the worksheet is recalculated (that is, the function is made volatile). If the second argument is False (or omitted), the function isn't recalculated unless one of the cells in the input range is modified.

```
Function DRAWONE(Rng As Variant, Optional Recalc As Variant = False)
'                Chooses one cell at random from a range

'                Make function volatile if Recalc is True
Application.Volatile Recalc
```

5

```
'                           Determine a random cell
    DRAWONE = Rng(Int((Rng.Count) * Rnd + 1))
End Function
```

Note that the second argument for DRAWONE includes the Optional keyword, along with a default value.

All the following formulas are valid, and the first two have the same effect:

```
=DRAWONE(A1:A100)
=DRAWONE(A1:A100,False)
=DRAWONE(A1:A100,True)
```

This function might be useful for choosing lottery numbers, picking a winner from a list of names, and so on.

ON THE WEB

This function is available on this book's website. The filename is `draw.xlsm`.

A function that returns a VBA array

VBA includes a useful function called Array. The Array function returns a variant that contains an array (that is, multiple values). If you're familiar with array formulas in Excel, you have a head start on understanding VBA's Array function. You enter an array formula into a cell by pressing Ctrl+Shift+Enter. Excel inserts curly braces around the formula to indicate that it's an array formula.

NOTE

It's important to understand that the array returned by the Array function isn't the same as a normal array made up of elements of the Variant data type. In other words, a variant array isn't the same as an array of variants.

The MONTHNAMES function, which follows, is a simple example that uses VBA's Array function in a custom function:

```
Function MONTHNAMES ()
    MONTHNAMES = Array("Jan", "Feb", "Mar", "Apr","May", "Jun", _
    "Jul", "Aug", "Sep", "Oct", "Nov", "Dec")
End Function
```

The MONTHNAMES function returns a horizontal array of month names. You can create a multicell array formula that uses the MONTHNAMES function. Here's how to use it:

1. Make sure that the function code is present in a VBA module.

2. In a worksheet, select multiple cells in a row (start by selecting 12 cells).

3. Enter the formula that follows (without the braces) and press Ctrl+Shift+Enter.

   `{=MONTHNAMES()}`

What if you'd like to generate a vertical list of month names? No problem; just select a vertical range, enter the following formula (without the braces), and then press Ctrl+Shift+Enter:

```
{=TRANSPOSE(MONTHNAMES())}
```

This formula uses the Excel TRANSPOSE function to convert the horizontal array to a vertical array.

The following example is a variation on the MONTHNAMES function:

```
Function MonthNames(Optional MIndex)
    Dim AllNames As Variant
    Dim MonthVal As Long
    AllNames = Array("Jan", "Feb", "Mar", "Apr", "May", "Jun", _
    "Jul", "Aug", "Sep", "Oct", "Nov", "Dec")
    If IsMissing(MIndex) Then
        MONTHNAMES = AllNames
    Else
        Select Case MIndex
            Case Is >= 1
'               Determine month value (for example, 13=1)
                MonthVal = ((MIndex - 1) Mod 12)
                MONTHNAMES = AllNames(MonthVal)
            Case Is <= 0 ' Vertical array
                MONTHNAMES = Application.Transpose(AllNames)
        End Select
    End If
End Function
```

Note that we use the VBA IsMissing function to test for a missing argument. In this situation, it isn't possible to specify the default value for the missing argument in the argument list of the function because the default value is defined in the function. You can use the IsMissing function only if the optional argument is a variant.

This enhanced function uses an optional argument that works as follows:

- If the argument is missing, the function returns a horizontal array of month names.
- If the argument is less than or equal to 0, the function returns a vertical array of month names. It uses Excel's TRANSPOSE function to convert the array.
- If the argument is greater than or equal to 1, the function returns the month name that corresponds to the argument value.

NOTE

This procedure uses the Mod operator to determine the month value. The Mod operator returns the remainder after dividing the first operand by the second. Keep in mind that the AllNames array is zero-based and that indices range from 0 to 11. In the statement that uses the Mod operator, 1 is subtracted from the function's argument. Therefore, an argument of 13 returns 0 (corresponding to Jan), and an argument of 24 returns 11 (corresponding to Dec).

5

You can use this function in a number of ways, as illustrated in Figure 5.6.

FIGURE 5.6

Different ways of passing an array or a single value to a worksheet

	A	B	C	D	E	F	G	H	I	J	K	
1	Jan	Feb	Mar	Apr	May	Jun	Jul	Aug	Sep	Oct	Nov	Dec
2												
3		1	Jan		Jan		Mar					
4		2	Feb		Feb							
5		3	Mar		Mar							
6		4	Apr		Apr							
7		5	May		May							
8		6	Jun		Jun							
9		7	Jul		Jul							
10		8	Aug		Aug							
11		9	Sep		Sep							
12		10	Oct		Oct							
13		11	Nov		Nov							
14		12	Dec		Dec							
15												

Range A1:L1 contains the following formula entered as an array. Start by selecting A1:L1, enter the formula (without the braces), and then press Ctrl+Shift+Enter.

```
{=MONTHNAMES()}
```

Range A3:A14 contains integers from 1 to 12. Cell B3 contains the following (nonarray) formula, which was copied to the 11 cells below it:

```
=MONTHNAMES(A3)
```

Range D3:D14 contains the following formula entered as an array:

```
{=MONTHNAMES(-1)}
```

Cell F3 contains this (nonarray) formula:

```
=MONTHNAMES(3)
```

> **NOTE**
> To enter an array formula, you must press Ctrl+Shift+Enter (and don't enter the curly braces).

> **NOTE**
> The lower bound of an array, created using the `Array` function, is determined by the lower bound specified with the `Option Base` statement at the top of the module. If there is no `Option Base` statement, the default lower bound is 0.

A function that returns an error value

In some cases, you might want your custom function to return a particular error value. Consider the following REMOVEVOWELS function, which we presented earlier in this chapter:

```
Function REMOVEVOWELS(Txt) As String
'               Removes all vowels from the Txt argument
    Dim i As Long
    RemoveVowels = ""
    For i = 1 To Len(Txt)
        If Not UCase(Mid(Txt, i, 1)) Like "[AEIOU]" Then
            REMOVEVOWELS = REMOVEVOWELS & Mid(Txt, i, 1)
        End If
    Next i
End Function
```

When used in a worksheet formula, this function removes the vowels from its single-cell argument. If the argument is a numeric value, this function returns the value as a string. You may prefer that the function returns an error value (#N/A), rather than the numeric value converted to a string.

You may be tempted simply to assign a string that looks like an Excel formula error value. Here's an example:

```
REMOVEVOWELS = "#N/A"
```

Although the string *looks* like an error value, other formulas that may reference it don't treat it as such. To return a *real* error value from a function, use the VBA CVErr function, which converts an error number to a real error.

Fortunately, VBA has built-in constants for the errors that you want to return from a custom function. These errors are Excel formula error values and not VBA run-time error values. These constants are as follows:

- xlErrDiv0 (for #DIV/0!)
- xlErrNA (for #N/A)
- xlErrName (for #NAME?)
- xlErrNull (for #NULL!)
- xlErrNum (for #NUM!)
- xlErrRef (for #REF!)
- xlErrValue (for #VALUE!)

5

To return a #N/A error from a custom function, you can use a statement like this:

```
REMOVEVOWELS = CVErr(xlErrNA)
```

The revised REMOVEVOWELS function follows. This function uses an If-Then construct to take a different action if the argument isn't text. It uses Excel's ISTEXT function to determine whether the argument is text. If the argument is text, the function proceeds normally. If the cell doesn't contain text (or is empty), the function returns the #N/A error.

```
Function REMOVEVOWELS (Txt) As Variant
' Removes all vowels from the Txt argument
' Returns #VALUE if Txt is not a string
    Dim i As Long
    RemoveVowels = ""
    If Application.WorksheetFunction.IsText(Txt) Then
        For i = 1 To Len(Txt)
            If Not UCase(Mid(Txt, i, 1)) Like "[AEIOU]" Then
                REMOVEVOWELS = REMOVEVOWELS & Mid(Txt, i, 1)
            End If
        Next i
    Else
        REMOVEVOWELS = CVErr(xlErrNA)
    End If
End Function
```

> **NOTE**
>
> Note that we also changed the data type for the function's return value. Because the function can now return something other than a string, we changed the data type to Variant.

A function with an indefinite number of arguments

Some Excel worksheet functions take an indefinite number of arguments. A familiar example is the SUM function, which has the following syntax:

```
SUM(number1,number2,...)
```

The first argument is required, but you can specify as many as 254 additional arguments. Here's an example of a SUM function with four range arguments:

```
=SUM(A1:A5,C1:C5,E1:E5,G1:G5)
```

You can even mix and match the argument types. For example, the following example uses three arguments: The first is a range, the second is a value, and the third is an expression.

```
=SUM(A1:A5,12,24*3)
```

You can create Function procedures that have an indefinite number of arguments. The trick is to use an array as the last (or only) argument, preceded by the keyword ParamArray.

NOTE

ParamArray can apply only to the last argument in the procedure's argument list. It's always a Variant data type and always an optional argument (although you don't use the Optional keyword).

The following is a function that can have any number of single-value arguments. (It doesn't work with multicell range arguments.) It simply returns the sum of the arguments.

```
Function SIMPLESUM(ParamArray arglist() As Variant) As Double
    For Each arg In arglist
        SIMPLESUM = SIMPLESUM + arg
    Next arg
End Function
```

To modify this function so that it works with multicell range arguments, you need to add another loop, which processes each cell in each of the arguments.

```
Function SIMPLESUM (ParamArray arglist() As Variant) As Double
    Dim cell As Range
    For Each arg In arglist
        For Each cell In arg
            SIMPLESUM = SIMPLESUM + cell
        Next cell
    Next arg
End Function
```

The SIMPLESUM function is similar to Excel's SUM function, but it's not nearly as flexible. Try it by using various types of arguments, and you'll see that it fails if any of the cells contain a nonvalue, or even if you use a literal value for an argument.

Emulating Excel's SUM Function

In this section, we present a custom function called MYSUM. Unlike the SIMPLE-SUM function listed in the preceding section, the MYSUM function emulates Excel's SUM function (almost) perfectly.

Before you look at the code for MYSUM, take a minute to think about the Excel SUM function. It is versatile: it can have as many as 255 arguments (even "missing" arguments), and the arguments can be numerical values, cells, ranges, text representations of numbers, logical values, and even embedded functions. For example, consider the following formula:

```
=SUM(B1,5,"6",,TRUE,SQRT(4),A1:A5,D:D,C2*C3)
```

This perfectly valid formula contains all the following types of arguments, listed here in the order of their presentation:

- A single-cell reference
- A literal value
- A string that looks like a value

5

- A missing argument
- A logical TRUE value
- An expression that uses another function
- A simple range reference
- A range reference that includes an entire column
- An expression that calculates the product of two cells

The MYSUM function (see Listing 5.1) handles all of these argument types.

ON THE WEB

A workbook containing the MYSUM function is available on this book's website. The file is named mysum function.xlsm.

LISTING 5.1   MYSUM Function

```
Function MYSUM(ParamArray args() As Variant) As Variant
  ' Emulates Excel's SUM function
  ' Variable declarations
    Dim i As Variant
    Dim TempRange As Range, cell As Range
    Dim ECode As String
    Dim m, n
    MYSUM = 0
  ' Process each argument
    For i = 0 To UBound(args)
     ' Skip missing arguments
       If Not IsMissing(args(i)) Then
        ' What type of argument is it?
          Select Case TypeName(args(i))
             Case "Range"
               ' Create temp range to handle full row or column ranges
               Set TempRange = Intersect(args(i).Parent.
UsedRange, args(i))
               For Each cell In TempRange
                 If IsError(cell) Then
                   MYSUM = cell ' return the error
                   Exit Function
                 End If
                 If cell = True Or cell = False Then
                   MYSUM = MYSUM + 0
                 Else
                   If IsNumeric(cell) Or IsDate(cell) Then _
                     MYSUM = MYSUM + cell
                   End If
               Next cell
             Case "Variant()"
               n = args(i)
```

```
            For m = LBound(n) To UBound(n)
                MYSUM = MYSUM(MYSUM, n(m)) 'recursive call
            Next m
        Case "Null" 'ignore it
        Case "Error" 'return the error
            MYSUM = args(i)
            Exit Function
        Case "Boolean"
         ' Check for literal TRUE and compensate
            If args(i) = "True" Then MYSUM = MYSUM + 1
        Case "Date"
            MYSUM = MYSUM + args(i)
        Case Else
            MYSUM = MYSUM + args(i)
        End Select
    End If
    Next i
End Function
```

Figure 5.7 shows a workbook with various formulas that use SUM (column E) and MYSUM (column G). As you can see, the functions return identical results.

FIGURE 5.7

Comparing SUM with MYSUM

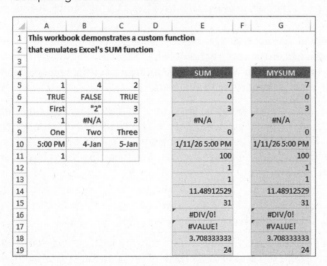

MYSUM is a close emulation of the SUM function, but it's not perfect. It cannot handle operations on arrays. For example, this array formula returns the sum of the squared values in range A1:A4:

```
{=SUM(A:A4^2)}
```

169

This formula returns a #VALUE! error:

```
{=MYSUM(A1:A4^2)}
```

If you're interested in learning how the MYSUM function works, create a formula that uses the function. Then set a breakpoint in the code and step through the statements line by line. (See the section "Debugging Functions" later in this chapter.) Try this for several different argument types, and you'll soon have a good feel for how the MYSUM function works.

As you study the code for MYSUM, keep the following points in mind:

- Missing arguments (determined by the IsMissing function) are simply ignored.
- The procedure uses the VBA TypeName function to determine the type of argument (Range, Error, and so on). Each argument type is handled differently.
- For a range argument, the function loops through each cell in the range, determines the type of data in the cell, and (if appropriate) adds its value to a running total.
- The data type for the function is Variant because the function needs to return an error if any of its arguments contain an error value.
- If an argument contains an error (for example, #DIV/0!), the MYSUM function simply returns the error—just as Excel's SUM function does.
- Excel's SUM function considers a text string to have a value of 0 unless it appears as a literal argument (that is, as an actual value, not a variable). Therefore, MYSUM adds the cell's value only if it can be evaluated as a number. (The MYSUM function uses the IsNumeric function to determine whether a string can be evaluated as a number.)
- For range arguments, the function uses the Intersect method to create a temporary range that consists of the intersection of the range and the sheet's used range. This technique handles cases in which a range argument consists of a complete row or column, which would take forever to evaluate.

You may be curious about the relative speeds of SUM and MYSUM. The MYSUM function, of course, is much slower, but just how much slower depends on the speed of your system and the formulas themselves. However, the point of this example is *not* to create a new SUM function. Rather, it demonstrates how to create custom worksheet functions that look and work like those built into Excel.

Extended Date Functions

A common complaint among Excel users is the inability to work with dates prior to 1900. For example, genealogists often use Excel to keep track of birth and death dates. If either of those dates occurs in a year prior to 1900, calculating the number of years the person lived isn't possible.

We created a series of functions that take advantage of the fact that VBA can work with a much larger range of dates. The earliest date recognized by VBA is January 1, 0100.

> **CAUTION**
>
> Beware of calendar changes if you use dates prior to 1752. Differences between the historical American, British, Gregorian, and Julian calendars can result in inaccurate computations.

The functions are as follows:

- XDATE(y,m,d,fmt): Returns a date for a given year, month, and day. As an option, you can provide a date-formatting string.
- XDATEADD(xdate1,days,fmt): Adds a specified number of days to a date. As an option, you can provide a date-formatting string.
- XDATEDIF(xdate1,xdate2): Returns the number of days between two dates.
- XDATEYEARDIF(xdate1,xdate2): Returns the number of full years between two dates (useful for calculating ages).
- XDATEYEAR(xdate1): Returns the year of a date.
- XDATEMONTH(xdate1): Returns the month of a date.
- XDATEDAY(xdate1): Returns the day of a date.
- XDATEDOW(xdate1): Returns the day of the week of a date (as an integer between 1 and 7).

Figure 5.8 shows a workbook that uses some of these functions.

FIGURE 5.8

The Extended Date functions used in formulas

	A	B	C	D	E	F	G	H
5								
6	**President**	**Year**	**Month**	**Day**	**XDATE**	**XDATEDIF**	**XDATEYEARDIF**	**XDATEDOW**
7	George Washington	1732	2	22	February 22, 1732	102,475	280	Friday
8	John Adams	1735	10	30	October 30, 1735	101,129	276	Sunday
9	Thomas Jefferson	1743	4	13	April 13, 1743	98,407	269	Saturday
10	James Madison	1751	3	16	March 16, 1751	95,513	261	Tuesday
11	James Monroe	1758	4	28	April 28, 1758	92,913	254	Friday
12	John Quincy Adams	1767	7	11	July 11, 1767	89,552	245	Saturday
13	Andrew Jackson	1767	3	15	March 15, 1767	89,670	245	Sunday
14	Martin Van Buren	1782	12	5	December 5, 1782	83,926	229	Thursday
15	William Henry Harrison	1773	2	9	February 9, 1773	87,512	239	Tuesday
16	John Tyler	1790	3	29	March 29, 1790	81,255	222	Monday
17	James K. Polk	1795	11	2	November 2, 1795	79,211	216	Monday
18	Zachary Taylor	1784	11	24	November 24, 1784	83,206	227	Wednesday
19	Millard Fillmore	1800	1	7	January 7, 1800	77,684	212	Tuesday
20	Franklin Pierce	1804	11	23	November 23, 1804	75,903	207	Friday
21	James Buchanan	1791	4	23	April 23, 1791	80,865	221	Saturday
22	Abraham Lincoln	1809	2	12	February 12, 1809	74,361	203	Sunday
23	Andrew Johnson	1808	12	29	December 29, 1808	74,406	203	Thursday

5

Keep in mind that the date returned by these functions is a *string*, not a real date. Therefore, you can't perform mathematical operations on the returned value using Excel's standard operators. You can, however, use the return value as an argument for other Extended Date functions.

The functions are surprisingly simple. For example, here's the listing for the XDATE function:

```
Function XDATE(y, m, d, Optional fmt As String) As String
    If IsMissing(fmt) Then fmt = "Short Date"
    XDATE = Format(DateSerial(y, m, d), fmt)
End Function
```

The arguments for XDATE are as follows:

- y: Required. A four-digit year (0100–9999).
- m: Required. A month number (1–12).
- d: Required. A day number (1–31).
- fmt: Optional. A date format string.

If the fmt argument is omitted, the date is displayed using the system's *short date* setting (as specified in the Windows Control Panel).

If the m or d argument exceeds a valid number, the date rolls over into the next year or month. For example, a month of 13 is interpreted as January of the next year.

ON THE WEB

The VBA code for the Extended Data functions is available on this book's website. The filename is extended date function.xlsm. You can also download documentation for these functions in the extended date functions help.pdf document.

Debugging Functions

When you're using a formula in a worksheet to test a Function procedure, VBA run-time errors don't appear in the all-too-familiar, pop-up error box. If an error occurs, the formula simply returns an error value (#VALUE!). The lack of a pop-up error message doesn't present a problem for debugging functions because you have several possible workarounds.

- Place MsgBox functions at strategic locations to monitor the value of specific variables. Message boxes in Function procedures do pop up when the procedure is executed. But make sure that you have only one formula in the worksheet that uses your function; otherwise, message boxes will appear for each formula that is evaluated, which will quickly become annoying.

- Test the procedure by calling it from a Sub procedure, not from a worksheet formula. Run-time errors are displayed in the usual manner, and you can either fix the problem (if you know it) or jump right into using Debugger.

- Set a breakpoint in the function and then step through the function. You then can access all standard VBA debugging tools. To set a breakpoint, move the cursor to the statement at which you want to pause execution and then choose Debug ⇨ Toggle Breakpoint (or press F9). When the function is executing, press F8 to step through the procedure line by line.

■ Use one or more temporary `Debug.Print` statements in your code to write values to the VBE Immediate window. For example, if you want to monitor a value inside a loop, use something like the following routine:

```
Function VOWELCOUNT(r) As Long
    Dim Count As Long
    Dim i As Long
    Dim Ch As String * 1
    Count = 0
    For i = 1 To Len(r)
        Ch = UCase(Mid(r, i, 1))
        If Ch Like "[AEIOU]" Then
            Count = Count + 1
            Debug.Print Ch, i
        End If
    Next i
    VOWELCOUNT = Count
End Function
```

In this case, the values of two variables, `Ch` and `i`, are printed to the Immediate window whenever the `Debug.Print` statement is encountered. Figure 5.9 shows the result when the function has an argument of `Tucson, Arizona`.

FIGURE 5.9

Use the Immediate window to display results while a function is running.

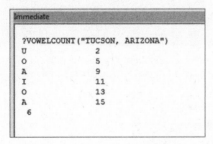

Dealing with the Insert Function Dialog Box

Excel's Insert Function dialog box is a handy tool. When you're creating a worksheet formula, this tool lets you select a particular worksheet function from a list of functions. These functions are grouped into various categories to make locating a particular function easier. When you select a function and click OK, the Function Arguments dialog box activates to help insert the function's arguments.

The Insert Function dialog box also displays your custom worksheet functions. By default, custom functions are listed under the User Defined category. The Function Arguments dialog box prompts you for a custom function's arguments.

The Insert Function dialog box enables you to search for a function by keyword. Unfortunately, you can't use this search feature to locate custom functions created in VBA.

> **NOTE**
>
> Custom `Function` procedures defined with the `Private` keyword don't appear in the Insert Function dialog box. If you develop a function that's intended to be used only in your other VBA procedures, you should declare it by using the `Private` keyword. However, declaring the function as `Private` doesn't prevent it from being used in a worksheet formula. It just prevents the display of the function in the Insert Function dialog box.

Using the MacroOptions method

You can use the `MacroOptions` method of the `Application` object to make your functions appear just like built-in functions. Specifically, this method enables you to do the following:

- Provide a description of the function.
- Specify a function category.
- Provide descriptions for the function arguments.

> **TIP**
>
> Another useful advantage of using the `MacroOptions` method is that it allows Excel to autocorrect the capitalization of your functions. For instance, if you create a function called `MyFunction` and you enter the formula `=myfunction(a)`, Excel will automatically change the formula to `=MyFunction(a)`. This behavior provides a quick and easy way to tell whether you've misspelled the function name. (If the lowercase letters do not autoadjust, the function name is misspelled.)

The following is an example of a procedure that uses the `MacroOptions` method to provide information about a function:

```
Sub DescribeFunction()
Dim FuncName As String
    Dim FuncDesc As String
    Dim FuncCat As Long
    Dim Arg1Desc As String, Arg2Desc As String

    FuncName = "DRAWONE"
    FuncDesc = "Displays the contents of a random cell from a range"
    FuncCat = 5
    Arg1Desc = "The range that contains the values"
    Arg2Desc = "(Optional) If False or missing, a new cell is
selected when "
```

```
        Arg2Desc = Arg2Desc & "recalculated. If True, a new cell is
    selected "
        Arg2Desc = Arg2Desc & "when recalculated."

        Application.MacroOptions _
            Macro:=FuncName, _
            Description:=FuncDesc, _
            Category:=FuncCat, _
            ArgumentDescriptions:=Array(Arg1Desc, Arg2Desc)
    End Sub
```

This procedure uses variables to store the information, and the variables are used as arguments for the `MacroOptions` method. The function is assigned to function category 5 (Lookup & Reference). Note that descriptions for the two arguments are indicated by using an array as the last argument for the `MacroOptions` method.

> **NOTE**
>
> The capability to provide argument descriptions was introduced in Excel 2010. If the workbook that contains the function is opened in a version prior to Excel 2010, the arguments won't display the descriptions.

Figure 5.10 shows the Insert Function and Function Arguments dialog boxes after executing this procedure.

FIGURE 5.10

The Insert Function and Function Arguments dialog boxes for a custom function

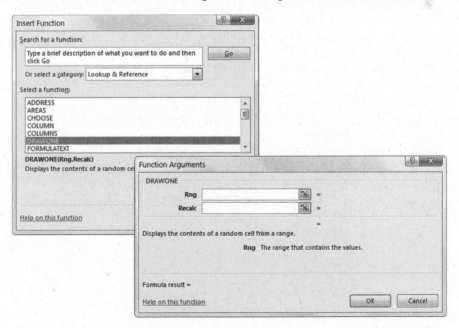

You need to execute the DescribeFunction procedure only one time. After doing so, the information assigned to the function is stored in the workbook. You can also omit arguments for the MacroOptions method. For example, if you don't need the arguments to have descriptions, just omit the ArgumentDescriptions argument in the code.

 For information on creating a custom help topic accessible from the Insert Function dialog box, refer to Chapter 19, "Providing Help for Your Applications."

Specifying a function category

If you don't use the MacroOptions method to specify a different category, your custom worksheet functions appear in the User Defined category in the Insert Function dialog box. You may prefer to assign your function to a different category. Assigning a function to a category also causes it to appear in the drop-down controls in the Formulas ⇨ Function Library group on the Ribbon.

Table 5.1 lists the category numbers that you can use for the Category argument for the MacroOptions method. A few of these categories (10–13) aren't normally displayed in the Insert Function dialog box. If you assign your function to one of these categories, the category will appear in the dialog box.

TABLE 5.1 Function Categories

Category Number	Category Name
0	All (no specific category)
1	Financial
2	Date & Time
3	Math & Trig
4	Statistical
5	Lookup & Reference
6	Database
7	Text
8	Logical
9	Information
10	Commands
11	Customizing
12	Macro Control
13	DDE/External
14	User Defined

Category Number	Category Name
15	Engineering
16	Cube
17	Compatibility*
18	Web**

* The Compatibility category was introduced in Excel 2010.

** The Web category was introduced in Excel 2013.

TIP

You can also create custom function categories. Instead of using a number for the `Category` argument for `MacroOptions`, use a text string. The statement that follows creates a new function category named `VBA Functions` and assigns the `COMMISSION` function to this category:

```
Application.MacroOptions Macro:="COMMISSION",_
Category:="VBA Functions"
```

Adding a function description manually

As an alternative to using the `MacroOptions` method to provide a function description, you can use the Macro dialog box.

NOTE

If you don't provide a description for your custom function, the Insert Function dialog box displays `No help available`.

Follow these steps to provide a description for a custom function:

1. Create your function in VBE.

2. Activate Excel, making sure that the workbook that contains the function is the active workbook.

3. Choose Developer ⇨ Code ⇨ Macros (or press Alt+F8). The Macro dialog box lists available procedures, but your function won't be in the list.

4. In the Macro Name box, type the name of your function.

5. Click the Options button to display the Macro Options dialog box.

6. In the Description box, enter the function description. The Shortcut Key field is irrelevant for functions.

7. Click OK and then click Cancel.

5

After you perform the preceding steps, the Insert Function dialog box displays the description that you entered in step 6 when the function is selected.

Using Add-Ins to Store Custom Functions

You may prefer to store frequently used custom functions in an add-in file. A primary advantage is that you can use those functions in any workbook when the add-in is installed.

In addition, you can use the functions in formulas without a filename qualifier. Assume that you have a custom function named ZAPSPACES that is stored in Myfuncs.xlsm. To use this function in a formula in a workbook other than Myfuncs.xlsm, you need to enter the following formula:

```
=Myfuncs.xlsm!ZAPSPACES(A1)
```

If you create an add-in from Myfuncs.xlsm and the add-in is loaded, you can omit the file reference and enter a formula such as the following:

```
=ZAPSPACES(A1)
```

 We discuss add-ins in Chapter 16.

> **CAUTION**
>
> A potential problem with using add-ins to store custom functions is that your workbook is dependent on the add-in file. If you need to share your workbook with a colleague, you also need to share a copy of the add-in that contains the functions.

Using the Windows API

VBA can borrow methods from other files that have nothing to do with Excel or VBA—for example, the *Dynamic Link Library* (DLL) files that Windows and other software uses. As a result, you can do things with VBA that would otherwise be outside the language's scope.

The *Windows API* is a set of functions available to Windows programmers. When you call a Windows function from VBA, you're accessing the Windows API. Many of the Windows resources used by Windows programmers are available in DLLs, which store programs and functions and are linked at run-time rather than at compile time.

64-bit Excel and API functions

Using Windows API functions in your code became a bit more challenging when Excel became available in both 32-bit and 64-bit versions. If you want your code to be compatible with the 32-bit and the 64-bit versions of Excel, you need to declare your API functions twice, using compiler directives to ensure that the correct declaration is used.

For example, the following declaration works with 32-bit Excel versions, but it causes a compile error with 64-bit Excel:

```
Declare Function GetWindowsDirectoryA Lib "kernel32" _
(ByVal lpBuffer As String, ByVal nSize As Long) As Long
```

In many cases, making the declaration compatible with 64-bit Excel is as simple as adding `PtrSafe` after the `Declare` keyword. The following declaration is compatible with both the 32-bit and 64-bit versions of Excel:

```
Declare PtrSafe Function GetWindowsDirectoryA Lib "kernel32" _
(ByVal lpBuffer As String, ByVal nSize As Long) As Long
```

However, the code will fail in Excel 2007 and earlier versions because the `PtrSafe` keyword is not recognized by those versions.

In Chapter 21, "Understanding Compatibility Issues," we describe how to make API function declarations compatible with all versions of 32-bit Excel and 64-bit Excel.

Windows API examples

Before you can use a Windows API function, you must declare the function at the top of your code module. If the code module is for UserForm, sheet, or ThisWorkbook, you must declare the API function as `Private`.

An API function must be declared precisely. The declaration statement tells VBA the following:

- Which API function you're using
- In which library the API function is located
- The API function's arguments

After you declare an API function, you can use it in your VBA code.

Determining the Windows directory

This section contains an example of an API function that displays the name of the Windows directory—something that's not possible using standard VBA statements. This code works with Excel 2010 and later.

5

Here's the API function declaration:

```
Declare PtrSafe Function GetWindowsDirectoryA Lib "kernel32" _
(ByVal lpBuffer As String, ByVal nSize As Long) As Long
```

This function, which has two arguments, returns the name of the directory in which Windows is installed. After calling the function, the Windows directory is contained in `lpBuffer`, and the length of the directory string is contained in `nSize`.

After inserting the `Declare` statement at the top of your module, you can access the function by calling the `GetWindowsDirectoryA` function. The following is an example of calling the function and displaying the result in a message box:

```
Sub ShowWindowsDir()
    Dim WinPath As String * 255
    Dim WinDir As String
    WinPath = Space(255)
    WinDir = Left(WinPath, GetWindowsDirectoryA (WinPath, Len(WinPath)))
    MsgBox WinDir, vbInformation, "Windows Directory"
End Sub
```

Executing the `ShowWindowsDir` procedure displays a message box with the Windows directory.

Often, you'll want to create a *wrapper* for API functions. In other words, you create your own function that uses the API function. This greatly simplifies using the API function. Here's an example of a wrapper VBA function:

```
Function WINDOWSDIR() As String
    ' Returns the Windows directory
    Dim WinPath As String * 255
    WinPath = Space(255)
    WINDOWSDIR=Left(WinPath,GetWindowsDirectoryA
(WinPath,Len(WinPath)))
End Function
```

After declaring this function, you can call it from another procedure.

```
MsgBox WINDOWSDIR()
```

You can even use the function in a worksheet formula.

```
=WINDOWSDIR()
```

ON THE WEB

This example is available on this book's website. The filename is `windows directory.xlsm`.

The reason for using API calls is to perform actions that would otherwise be impossible (or at least very difficult). If your application needs to find the path of the Windows directory, you could search all day and not find a function in Excel or VBA to do the trick. But knowing how to access the Windows API may solve your problem.

Detecting the Shift key

Here's another example of using an API function. Suppose that you've written a VBA macro that will be executed by clicking a button on a worksheet. Furthermore, suppose that you want the macro to perform differently if the user presses the Shift key when the button is clicked. VBA doesn't provide a way to detect whether the Shift key is pressed. But you can use the GetKeyState API function to find out. The GetKeyState function tells you whether a particular key is pressed. It takes a single argument, nVirtKey, which represents the code for the key in which you're interested.

The following code demonstrates how to detect whether the Shift key is pressed when the Button_Click event-handler procedure is executed. Note that we define a constant for the Shift key (using a hexadecimal value) and then use this constant as the argument for GetKeyState. If GetKeyState returns a value less than zero, it means that the Shift key was pressed; otherwise, the Shift key wasn't pressed. This code isn't compatible with Excel 2007 and earlier versions.

```
Declare PtrSafe Function GetKeyState Lib "user32" _
  (ByVal nVirtKey As Long) As Integer
Sub Button_Click()
    Const VK_SHIFT As Integer = &H10
    If GetKeyState(VK_SHIFT) < 0 Then
        MsgBox "Shift is pressed"
    Else
        MsgBox "Shift is not pressed"
    End If
End Sub
```

Learning more about API functions

Working with the Windows API functions can be tricky. Many programming reference books list the declarations for common API calls and often provide examples. Usually, you can simply copy the declarations and use the functions without understanding the details. Many Excel programmers take a cookbook approach to API functions. The Internet has dozens of reliable examples that you can copy and paste. Or search the Web for a file named Win32API_PtrSafe.txt. This file, from Microsoft, contains many examples of declaration statements.

5

FIGURE 5.11

Using Windows API functions to determine which keys were pressed

 Chapter 7 has several additional examples of using Windows API functions.

Understanding Excel's Events

IN THIS CHAPTER

Recognizing the types of events that Excel can monitor

Figuring out what you need to know to work with events

Exploring examples of `Workbook` events and `Worksheet` events

Using `Application` events to monitor all open workbooks

Seeing examples of processing time-based events and keystroke events

What You Should Know About Events

In many of the example macros in this book, there will be code implemented as event procedures, which are procedures that automatically trigger upon the occurrence of an event. An *event* is nothing more than an action that takes place during a session in Excel.

Everything that happens in Excel happens to an object through an event. A few examples of events are opening a workbook, adding a worksheet, changing a value in a cell, saving a workbook, double-clicking a cell, and the list goes on. The nifty thing is that you can tell Excel to run a certain macro or piece of code when a particular event occurs.

Excel is programmed to monitor many different events. These events can be classified as follows:

Workbook events Events that occur for a particular workbook. Examples of such events include `Open` (the workbook is opened or created), `BeforeSave` (the workbook is about to be saved), and `NewSheet` (a new sheet is added).

Worksheet events Events that occur for a particular worksheet. Examples include `Change` (a cell on the sheet is changed), `SelectionChange` (the user moves the cell indicator), and `Calculate` (the worksheet is recalculated).

Chart events Events that occur for a particular chart. These events include `Select` (an object in the chart is selected) and `SeriesChange` (a value of a data point in a series is changed).

Application events   Events that occur for the application (Excel). Examples include `NewWorkbook` (a new workbook is created), `WorkbookBeforeClose` (any workbook is about to be closed), and `SheetChange` (a cell in any open workbook is altered). To monitor `Application`-level events, you need to use a class module.

UserForm events   Events that occur for a particular UserForm or an object contained on the UserForm. For example, a UserForm has an `Initialize` event (occurs before the UserForm is displayed), and a `CommandButton` on a UserForm has a `Click` event (occurs when the button is clicked).

Events not associated with objects   The final category consists of two useful `Application`-level events that we call `On` events: `OnTime` and `OnKey`. These work in a different manner than other events.

In the following sections, you'll explore a few examples that demonstrate some of these events.

Understanding event sequences

Some actions trigger multiple events. For example, when you insert a new worksheet into a workbook, three `Application`-level events are triggered:

`WorkbookNewSheet`: Occurs when a new worksheet is added

`SheetDeactivate`: Occurs when the active worksheet is deactivated

`SheetActivate`: Occurs when the newly-added worksheet is activated

> **NOTE**
>
> Event sequencing is a bit more complicated than you might think. The preceding events are `Application`-level events. When adding a new worksheet, additional events occur at the workbook level and at the worksheet level.

At this point, just keep in mind that events fire in a particular sequence, and knowing that sequence may be critical when writing event-handler procedures. Later in this chapter, we describe how to determine the order of the events that occur for a particular action (see "Monitoring Application-level events").

Where to put event-handler procedures

VBA newcomers often wonder why their event-handler procedures aren't being executed when the corresponding event occurs. The answer is almost always because these procedures are located in the wrong place.

In the Visual Basic Editor (VBE) window, each project (one project per workbook) is listed in the Project window. The project components are arranged in a collapsible list, as shown in Figure 6.1.

FIGURE 6.1

The components for each VBA project are listed in the Project window.

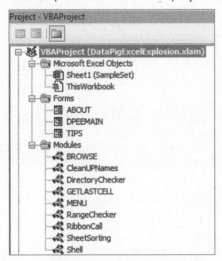

Each of the following components has its own code module:

Sheet objects   For example, Sheet1, Sheet2, and so on. Use this module for event-handler code related to the particular worksheet.

Chart objects   Namely, chart sheets. Use this module for event-handler code related to the chart.

ThisWorkbook object   Use this module for event-handler code related to the workbook.

General VBA modules   You never put event-handler procedures in a general (that is, nonobject) module.

UserForm objects   Use this module for event-handler code related to the UserForm or controls on the UserForm.

Class modules   Use class modules for special-purpose event handlers, including application-level events and events for embedded charts.

Even though the event-handler procedure must be located in the correct module, the procedure can call other standard procedures stored in other modules. For example, the following event-handler procedure, located in the module for the ThisWorkbook object, calls a procedure named WorkbookSetup, which you can store in a regular VBA module:

```
Private Sub Workbook_Open()
    Call WorkbookSetup
End Sub
```

Disabling events

By default, all events are enabled. To disable all events, execute the following VBA instruction:

```
Application.EnableEvents = False
```

To enable events, use this instruction:

```
Application.EnableEvents = True
```

> **NOTE**
>
> Disabling events does *not* apply to events triggered by UserForm controls, for example, the `Click` event generated by clicking a `CommandButton` control on a UserForm.

Why would you need to disable events? One common reason is to prevent an infinite loop of cascading events.

For example, suppose that cell A1 of your worksheet must always contain a value of less than or equal to 12. You can write some code that is executed whenever data is entered in a cell to validate the cell's contents. In this case, you're monitoring the `Change` event for a Worksheet with a procedure named `Worksheet_Change`. Your procedure checks the user's entry, and if the entry isn't less than or equal to 12, it displays a message and then clears that entry. The problem is that clearing the entry with your VBA code generates a new `Change` event, so your event-handler procedure is executed again. This is not what you want to happen, so you need to disable events before you clear the cell and then enable events again so that you can monitor the user's next entry.

Another way to prevent an infinite loop of cascading events is to declare a `Static` Boolean variable at the beginning of your event-handler procedure, such as the following:

```
Static AbortProc As Boolean
```

Whenever the procedure needs to make its own changes, set the `AbortProc` variable to `True` (otherwise, make sure that it's set to `False`). Insert the following code at the top of the procedure:

```
If AbortProc Then
    AbortProc = False
    Exit Sub
End if
```

The event procedure is reentered, but the `True` state of `AbortProc` causes the procedure to end. In addition, `AbortProc` is reset to `False`.

 For a practical example of validating data, see "Monitoring a range to validate data entry," later in this chapter.

> **CAUTION**
>
> Disabling events in Excel applies to all workbooks. For example, if you disable events in your procedure and then open another workbook that has, say, a `Workbook_Open` procedure, that procedure will not execute.

Entering event-handler code

Every event-handler procedure has a predetermined name, and you can't change those names. The following are some examples of event-handler procedure names:

- `Worksheet_SelectionChange`
- `Workbook_Open`
- `Chart_Activate`
- `Class_Initialize`

You can declare the procedure by typing it manually, but a much better approach is to let VBE declare it for you.

Figure 6.2 shows the code module for the `ThisWorkbook` object. To insert a procedure declaration, select Workbook from the Object drop-down list on the left. Then select the event from the Procedure drop-down list on the right. When you do so, you get a procedure shell that contains the procedure declaration line and an `End Sub` statement.

FIGURE 6.2

The best way to create an event procedure is to let the VBE do it for you.

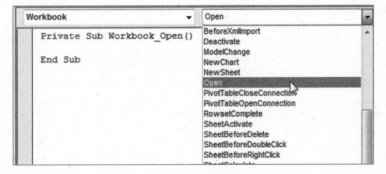

For example, if you select Workbook from the objects list and Open from the procedures list, VBE inserts the following (empty) procedure:

```
Private Sub Workbook_Open()

End Sub
```

Your VBA code, of course, goes between these two statements.

NOTE

Note that as soon as you select an item from the Object drop-down (for example, Workbook or Worksheet), VBE inserts a procedure declaration automatically. Usually, the procedure definition is not the one you want. Simply choose the event you want from the Procedure drop-down list on the right and then delete the one that was generated automatically.

Event-handler procedures that use arguments

Some event-handler procedures use an argument list. For example, you may need to create an event-handler procedure to monitor the `SheetActivate` event for a workbook. If you use the technique described in the preceding section, VBE creates the following procedure in the code module for the `ThisWorkbook` object:

```
Private Sub Workbook_SheetActivate(ByVal Sh As Object)

End Sub
```

This procedure uses one argument (`Sh`), which represents the sheet that was activated. In this case, `Sh` is declared as an Object data type rather than a `Worksheet` data type because the activated sheet can also be a chart sheet.

Your code can use the data passed as an argument. The following procedure is executed whenever a sheet is activated. It displays the type and name of the activated sheet by using VBA's `TypeName` function and accessing the `Name` property of the object passed in the argument.

```
Private Sub Workbook_SheetActivate(ByVal Sh As Object)
    MsgBox TypeName(Sh) & vbCrLf & Sh.Name
End Sub
```

Figure 6.3 shows the message that appears when `Sheet3` is activated.

FIGURE 6.3

This message box was triggered by a SheetActivate event.

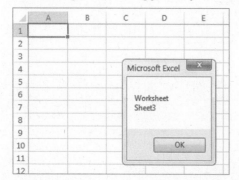

Several event-handler procedures use a `Boolean` argument named `Cancel`. For example, the declaration for a workbook's `BeforePrint` event is as follows:

```
Private Sub Workbook_BeforePrint(Cancel As Boolean)
```

The value of `Cancel` passed to the procedure is `False`. However, your code can set `Cancel` to `True`, which will cancel the printing. The following example demonstrates this:

```
Private Sub Workbook_BeforePrint(Cancel As Boolean)
    Dim Msg As String, Ans As Integer
    Msg = "Have you loaded the 5164 label stock?"
    Ans = MsgBox(Msg, vbYesNo, "About to print...")
    If Ans = vbNo Then Cancel = True
End Sub
```

The `Workbook_BeforePrint` procedure is executed before the workbook is printed. This routine displays the message box shown in Figure 6.4. If the user clicks the No button, `Cancel` is set to `True`, and nothing is printed.

FIGURE 6.4

Clicking No cancels the print operation by changing the Cancel argument in the event-handler procedure.

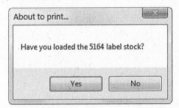

TIP

The `BeforePrint` event also occurs when the user previews a worksheet.

Unfortunately, Excel doesn't provide a sheet-level `BeforePrint` event. Therefore, your code can't determine which sheet is about to be printed. Often, you can assume that the `ActiveSheet` is the sheet that will be printed. However, there is no way to detect whether the user requests that the entire workbook be printed.

Getting Acquainted with Workbook-Level Events

Workbook-level events occur in a particular workbook. Table 6.1 lists the commonly used workbook events, along with a brief description of each. Consult the Help system for a complete list of `Workbook`-level events. Workbook event-handler procedures are stored in the code module for the `ThisWorkbook` object.

TABLE 6.1 **Commonly Used Workbook Events**

Event	Action That Triggers the Event
`Activate`	The workbook is activated.
`AddinInstall`	The workbook is installed as an add-in.
`AddinUninstall`	The workbook is uninstalled as an add-in.
`AfterSave`	The workbook has been saved.
`BeforeClose`	The workbook is about to be closed.
`BeforePrint`	The workbook (or anything in it) is about to be printed or previewed.
`BeforeSave`	The workbook is about to be saved.
`Deactivate`	The workbook is deactivated.
`NewSheet`	The new sheet is created in a workbook.
`Open`	The workbook is opened.
`SheetActivate`	Any sheet is activated within the workbook.
`SheetBeforeDoubleClick`	Any worksheet in the workbook is double-clicked. This event occurs before the default double-click action.
`SheetBeforeRightClick`	Any worksheet in the workbook is right-clicked. This event occurs before the default right-click action.
`SheetCalculate`	Any worksheet in the workbook is calculated (or recalculated).
`SheetChange`	Any worksheet in the workbook is changed by the user or by an external link.
`SheetDeactivate`	Any sheet in the workbook is deactivated.
`SheetFollowHyperlink`	A hyperlink on a sheet in the workbook is clicked.
`SheetPivotTableUpdate`	A pivot table in the workbook is changed or refreshed.
`SheetSelectionChange`	The selection on any worksheet in the workbook is changed.
`WindowActivate`	Any workbook window is activated.
`WindowDeactivate`	Any workbook window is deactivated.
`WindowResize`	Any workbook window is resized.

If you need to monitor events for any workbook, you need to work with `Application`-level events (see "Monitoring with Application Events," later in this chapter). The remainder of this section presents examples of using `Workbook`-level events. All the example procedures that follow must be located in the code module for the `ThisWorkbook` object. If you put them into any other type of code module, they won't work.

The Open event

One of the most common monitored events is the `Open` event for a workbook. This event is triggered when the workbook (or add-in) is opened and executes the procedure named `Workbook_Open`. A `Workbook_Open` procedure is often used for tasks such as these:

- Displaying welcome messages.
- Opening other workbooks.
- Setting up shortcut menus.
- Activating a particular sheet or cell.
- Ensuring that certain conditions are met. For example, a workbook may require that a particular add-in be installed.
- Setting up certain automatic features. For example, you can define key combinations (see the section "The OnKey event" later in this chapter).
- Setting a worksheet's `ScrollArea` property (which isn't stored with the workbook).
- Setting `UserInterfaceOnly` protection for worksheets so that your code can operate on protected sheets. This setting is an argument for the `Protect` method and isn't stored with the workbook.

> **NOTE**
>
> Creating event-handler procedures doesn't guarantee that they will be executed. If the user holds down the Shift key when opening a workbook, the workbook's `Workbook_Open` procedure won't execute. And, of course, the procedure won't execute if the workbook is opened with macros disabled.

The following is an example of a `Workbook_Open` procedure. It uses the VBA Weekday function to determine the day of the week. If it's Friday, a message box appears, reminding the user to submit a weekly report. If it's not Friday, nothing happens.

```
Private Sub Workbook_Open()
If Weekday(Now) = vbFriday Then
    Msg = "Today is Friday. Make sure that you "
    Msg = Msg & "submit the TPS Report."
    MsgBox Msg, vbInformation
End If
End Sub
```

The Activate event

The following procedure is executed whenever the workbook is activated. This procedure simply maximizes the active window. If the workbook window is already maximized, the procedure has no effect.

```
Private Sub Workbook_Activate()
    ActiveWindow.WindowState = xlMaximized
End Sub
```

The SheetActivate event

The following procedure is executed whenever the user activates any sheet in the workbook. If the sheet is a worksheet, the code selects cell A1. If the sheet isn't a worksheet, nothing happens. This procedure uses the VBA function to ensure that the activated sheet is a worksheet (as opposed to a chart sheet).

```
Private Sub Workbook_SheetActivate(ByVal Sh As Object)
    If TypeName(Sh) = "Worksheet" Then Range("A1").Select
End Sub
```

The following procedure demonstrates an alternative method that doesn't require checking the sheet type. In this procedure, the error is just ignored.

```
Private Sub Workbook_SheetActivate(ByVal Sh As Object)
    On Error Resume Next
    Range("A1").Select
End Sub
```

The NewSheet event

The following procedure is executed whenever a new sheet is added to the workbook. The sheet is passed to the procedure as an argument. Because a new sheet can be a worksheet or a chart sheet, this procedure determines the sheet type. If it's a worksheet, the code adjusts the width of all columns and inserts a date and time stamp in cell A1 on the new sheet.

```
Private Sub Workbook_NewSheet(ByVal Sh As Object)
    If TypeName(Sh) = "Worksheet" Then
        Sh.Cells.ColumnWidth = 35
        Sh.Range("A1") = "Sheet added " & Now()
    End If
End Sub
```

The BeforeSave event

The BeforeSave event occurs after the Save command is given but before the workbook is saved.

As you know, choosing the File ⇨ Save command sometimes brings up the Save As dialog box. This dialog box appears if the workbook has never been saved or if it was opened in read-only mode.

When the Workbook_BeforeSave procedure is executed, it receives the argument (SaveAsUI) that indicates whether the Save As dialog box will be displayed. The following example demonstrates how to use the SaveAsUI argument:

```
Private Sub Workbook_BeforeSave _
(ByVal SaveAsUI As Boolean, Cancel As Boolean)
    If SaveAsUI Then
        MsgBox "Make sure you save this file on drive J."
    End If
End Sub
```

When the user attempts to save the workbook, the `Workbook_BeforeSave` procedure is executed. If the save operation will display Excel's Save As dialog box, the `SaveAsUI` variable is `True`. The `Workbook_BeforeSave` procedure checks this variable and displays a message only if the Save As dialog box will be displayed. If the procedure sets the `Cancel` argument to `True`, the file won't be saved (or the Save As dialog box won't be shown).

The Deactivate event

The following example demonstrates the Deactivate event. This procedure is executed whenever the workbook is deactivated and essentially never lets the user deactivate the workbook. One way to trigger the `Deactivate` event is to activate a different workbook window. When the `Deactivate` event occurs, the code reactivates the workbook and displays a message.

```
Private Sub Workbook_Deactivate()
    Me.Activate
    MsgBox "Sorry, you may not leave this workbook"
End Sub
```

This example also illustrates the importance of understanding event sequences. If you try this procedure, you'll see that it works well if the user attempts to activate another workbook. However, it's important to understand that the workbook `Deactivate` event is also triggered by the following actions:

- Closing the workbook
- Opening a new workbook
- Minimizing the workbook

In other words, this procedure may not perform as it was originally intended. When programming event procedures, you need to make sure that you understand all of the actions that can trigger the events.

The BeforePrint event

The `BeforePrint` event occurs when the user requests a print or a print preview but before the printing or previewing occurs. The event uses a `Cancel` argument, so your code can cancel the printing or previewing by setting the `Cancel` variable to `True`. Unfortunately, you can't determine whether the `BeforePrint` event was triggered by a print request or by a preview request.

Updating a header or footer

Excel's page header and footer options are flexible, but these options don't include a common request: the capability to print the contents of a specific cell in the header or footer. The `Workbook_BeforePrint` event provides a way to display the current contents of a cell in the header or footer when the workbook is printed. The following code updates each sheet's left footer whenever the workbook is printed or previewed. Specifically, it inserts the contents of cell A1 on `Sheet1`.

```
Private Sub Workbook_BeforePrint(Cancel As Boolean)
    Dim sht As Object
    For Each sht In ThisWorkbook.Sheets
        sht.PageSetup.LeftFooter = Worksheets("Sheet1").Range("A1")
    Next sht
End Sub
```

This procedure loops through each sheet in the workbook and sets the LeftFooter property of the PageSetup object to the value in cell **A1** on Sheet1.

Hiding columns before printing

The example that follows uses a Workbook_BeforePrint procedure to hide columns B:D in Sheet1 before printing or previewing:

```
Private Sub Workbook_BeforePrint(Cancel As Boolean)
    'Hide columns B:D on Sheet1 before printing
    Worksheets("Sheet1").Range("B:D").EntireColumn.Hidden = True
End Sub
```

Ideally, you would want to unhide the columns after printing has occurred. It would be nice if Excel provided an AfterPrint event, but that event doesn't exist. However, there is a way to unhide the columns automatically. The modified procedure that follows schedules an OnTime event, which calls a procedure named UnhideColumns five seconds after printing or previewing:

```
Private Sub Workbook_BeforePrint(Cancel As Boolean)
    'Hide columns B:D on Sheet1 before printing
    Worksheets("Sheet1").Range("B:D").EntireColumn.Hidden = True
    Application.OnTime Now()+ TimeValue("0:00:05"), "UnhideColumns"
End Sub
```

The UnhideColumns procedure goes in a standard VBA module.

```
Sub UnhideColumns()
    Worksheets("Sheet1").Range("B:D").EntireColumn.Hidden = False
End Sub
```

ON THE WEB

This example, named `hide columns before printing.xlsm`, is available on the book's website.

 For more information about OnTime events, see the section "The OnTime event" later in this chapter.

The BeforeClose event

The `BeforeClose` event occurs after the Close command is given but before a workbook is closed. This event is often used with a `Workbook_Open` event handler. For example, you might use the `Workbook_Open` procedure to add shortcut menu items for your workbook and then use the `Workbook_BeforeClose` procedure to delete the shortcut menu items when the workbook is closed. That way, the custom menu is available only when the workbook is open.

Unfortunately, the `Workbook_BeforeClose` event isn't implemented very well. For example, if you attempt to close a workbook that hasn't been saved, Excel displays a prompt asking whether you want to save the workbook before closing, as shown in Figure 6.5. The problem is that the `Workbook_BeforeClose` event has already occurred by the time the user sees this message. If the user cancels, your event-handler procedure has already executed.

FIGURE 6.5

When this message appears, Workbook_BeforeClose has already done its thing.

Consider this scenario: you need to display custom shortcut menus when a particular workbook is open. Therefore, your workbook uses a `Workbook_Open` procedure to create the menu items when the workbook is opened and a `Workbook_BeforeClose` procedure to remove the menu items when the workbook is closed. These two event-handler procedures follow. Both of these call other procedures, which aren't shown here.

```
Private Sub Workbook_Open()
    Call CreateShortcutMenuItems
End Sub
Private Sub Workbook_BeforeClose(Cancel As Boolean)
    Call DeleteShortcutMenuItems
End Sub
```

As we noted earlier, the Excel "Do you want to save . . ." prompt is displayed *after* the `Workbook_BeforeClose` event handler runs. So, if the user clicks Cancel, the workbook remains open, but the custom menu items have already been deleted.

One solution to this problem is to bypass Excel's prompt and write your own code in the Workbook_BeforeClose procedure to ask the user to save the workbook. The following code demonstrates this solution:

```
Private Sub Workbook_BeforeClose(Cancel As Boolean)
    Dim Msg As String
    If Me.Saved = False Then
        Msg = "Do you want to save the changes you made to "
        Msg = Msg & Me.Name & "?"
        Ans = MsgBox(Msg, vbQuestion + vbYesNoCancel)
        Select Case Ans
            Case vbYes
                Me.Save
            Case vbCancel
                Cancel = True
                Exit Sub
        End Select
    End If
    Call DeleteShortcutMenuItems
    Me.Saved = True
End Sub
```

This procedure checks the `Saved` property of the `Workbook` object to determine whether the workbook has been saved. If so, no problem—the `DeleteShortcutMenuItems` procedure is executed, and the workbook is closed. But if the workbook hasn't been saved, the procedure displays a message box similar to the one that Excel would normally show (see Figure 6.6). The following lists details the effect of clicking each of the three buttons:

Yes: The workbook is saved, the shortcut menu items are deleted, and the workbook is closed.

No: The code sets the `Saved` property of the `Workbook` object to `True` (but doesn't actually save the file), deletes the menu items, and closes the file.

Cancel: The `BeforeClose` event is canceled, and the procedure ends without deleting the shortcut menu items.

FIGURE 6.6

A message displayed by the Workbook_BeforeClose event procedure

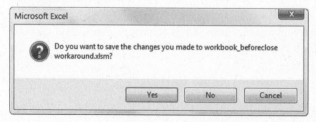

ON THE WEB

A workbook with this example is available on the book's website in the `workbook_beforeclose` work-around.xlsm file.

Examining Worksheet Events

The events for a `Worksheet` object are some of the most useful, because most of what happens in Excel occurs on a worksheet. Monitoring these events can make your applications perform feats that would otherwise be impossible.

Table 6.2 lists the available worksheet events, with a brief description of each.

TABLE 6.2 Worksheet Events

Event	Action That Triggers the Event
Activate	The worksheet is activated.
BeforeDelete	The worksheet is about to be deleted.
BeforeDoubleClick	The worksheet is double-clicked.
BeforeRightClick	The worksheet is right-clicked.
Calculate	The worksheet is calculated (or recalculated).
Change	Cells on the worksheet are changed by the user or by an external link.
Deactivate	The worksheet is deactivated.
FollowHyperlink	A hyperlink on the sheet is clicked.
LensGalleryRender	A callout gallery has been activated and has finished rendering all icons.
PivotTableAfter-ValueChange	A calculated field in a pivot table on the sheet has recalculated.
PivotTableBefore-AllocateChanges	The user has chosen to apply changes to an OLAP pivot table's data source.
PivotTableBefore-CommitChanges	The user has chosen to apply changes to an OLAP pivot table's data source.
PivotTableBefore-DiscardChanges	The user has chosen to roll back the changes made to an OLAP pivot table's data source.
PivotTableChangeSync	A pivot table on the sheet has changed or has been refreshed.
PivotTableUpdate	A pivot table on the sheet is updated or refreshed.
SelectionChange	The selection on the worksheet is changed or refreshed.
TableUpdate	A query table on the sheet has completed updating data from the internal data model.

> **TIP**
>
> Remember that the code for a worksheet event must be stored in the code module for the specific worksheet.

> **TIP**
>
> To activate the module for a worksheet and display its code sheet, right-click the sheet tab and then choose View Code.

The Change event

The Change event occurs when any cell in a worksheet is changed by the user or by a VBA procedure. The Change event does not occur when a calculation generates a different value for a formula or when an object is added to the sheet.

When the Worksheet_Change procedure is executed, it receives a Range object as its Target argument. This Range object represents the changed cell or range that triggered the event. The following procedure is executed whenever the worksheet is changed. It displays a message box that shows the address of the Target range.

```
Private Sub Worksheet_Change(ByVal Target As Range)
    MsgBox "Range " & Target.Address & " was changed."
End Sub
```

To get a better feel for the types of actions that generate a Change event for a worksheet, enter the preceding procedure in the code module for a Worksheet object. After entering this procedure, activate Excel and make some changes to the worksheet using various techniques. Every time the Change event occurs, you'll see a message box that displays the address of the range that was changed.

When you run this procedure, you'll discover some interesting quirks. Some actions that should trigger the event don't, and other actions that shouldn't trigger the event do!

- Changing the formatting of a cell doesn't trigger the Change event (as expected). But copying and pasting formatting *does* trigger the Change event. Choosing the Home ⇨ Editing ⇨ Clear ⇨ Clear Formats command also triggers the event.
- Merging cells doesn't trigger the Change event, even if the contents of some of the merged cells are deleted in the process.
- Adding, editing, or deleting a cell comment doesn't trigger the Change event.
- Pressing Delete generates an event, even if the cell is empty to start with.
- Cells that are changed by using Excel commands may or may not trigger the Change event. For example, sorting a range or using Goal Seek to change a cell does not trigger the event. But using the spellchecker does.
- If your VBA procedure changes the contents of a cell, it *does* trigger the Change event.

As you can see from the preceding list, it's not a good idea to rely on the Change event to detect cell changes for critical applications.

Monitoring a specific range for changes

The Change event occurs when any cell on the worksheet is changed. But, in most cases, all you care about are changes made to a specific cell or range. When the Worksheet_ Change event handler procedure is called, it receives a Range object as its argument. This Range object represents the cell or cells that were changed.

Assume that your worksheet has a range named InputRange and you'd like to monitor changes made only within this range. There is no Change event for a Range object, but you can perform a quick check in the Worksheet_Change procedure.

```
Private Sub Worksheet_Change(ByVal Target As Range)
    Dim MRange As Range
    Set MRange = Range("InputRange")
    If Not Intersect(Target, MRange) Is Nothing Then _
        MsgBox "A cell in the input range has been changed."
End Sub
```

This example uses a Range object variable named MRange, which represents the worksheet range that you want to monitor for changes. The procedure uses the VBA Intersect function to determine whether the Target range (passed to the procedure in its argument) intersects with MRange. The Intersect function returns an object that consists of all cells contained in both of its arguments. If the Intersect function returns Nothing, the ranges have no cells in common. The Not operator is used so that the expression returns True if the ranges *do* have at least one cell in common. Therefore, if the changed range has any cells in common with the range named InputRange, a message box is displayed. Otherwise, the procedure ends and nothing happens.

Monitoring a range to make formulas bold

The following example monitors a worksheet, and it also makes formula entries bold and nonformula entries not bold:

```
Private Sub Worksheet_Change(ByVal Target As Range)
    Dim cell As Range
    For Each cell In Target
        If cell.HasFormula Then cell.Font.Bold = True
    Next cell
End Sub
```

Because the object passed to the Worksheet_Change procedure can consist of a multicell range, the procedure loops through each cell in the Target range. If the cell has a formula, the cell is made bold. Otherwise, the Bold property is set to False.

The procedure works, but it has a problem. What if the user deletes a row or column? In that case, the Target range consists of a huge number of cells. The For-Each loop would take a long time to examine them all—and it wouldn't find any formulas.

The modified procedure listed next solves this problem by changing the `Target` range to the intersection of the `Target` range and the worksheet's used range. The check to ensure that `Target Is Not Nothing` handles the case in which an empty row or column outside the used range is deleted.

```vba
Private Sub Worksheet_Change(ByVal Target As Range)
    Dim cell As Range
    Set Target = Intersect(Target, Target.Parent.UsedRange)
    If Not Target Is Nothing Then
        For Each cell In Target
            cell.Font.Bold = cell.HasFormula
        Next cell
    End If
End Sub
```

ON THE WEB

This example, named `make formulas bold.xlsm`, is available on the book's website.

CAUTION

A `Worksheet_Change` procedure may affect Excel's Undo feature, a potentially serious side effect. Excel's Undo stack is destroyed whenever an event procedure makes a change to the worksheet. In the preceding example, making a cell entry triggers a formatting change, which destroys the Undo stack.

Monitoring a range to validate data entry

Excel's data validation feature is a useful tool, but it suffers from a potentially serious problem. When you paste data into a cell that uses data validation, the pasted value not only fails to get validated but also deletes the validation rules associated with the cell! This fact makes the data validation feature practically worthless for critical applications. In this section, we demonstrate how you can use the `Change` event for a worksheet to create your own data validation procedure.

ON THE WEB

The book's website contains two versions of this example. One (named `validate entry1.xlsm`) uses the `EnableEvents` property to prevent cascading `Change` events; the other (named `validate entry2.xlsm`) uses a `Static` variable. See "Disabling events" earlier in this chapter.

The `Worksheet_Change` procedure that follows is executed when a user changes a cell. The validation is restricted to the range named `InputRange`. Values entered into this range must be integers between 1 and 12.

```vba
Private Sub Worksheet_Change(ByVal Target As Range)
    Dim VRange As Range, cell As Range
    Dim Msg As String
```

```
        Dim ValidateCode As Variant
        Set VRange = Range("InputRange")

        If Intersect(VRange, Target) Is Nothing Then Exit Sub

        For Each cell In Intersect(VRange, Target)
            ValidateCode = EntryIsValid(cell)
            If TypeName(ValidateCode) = "String" Then
                Msg = "Cell " & cell.Address(False, False) & ":"
                Msg = Msg & vbCrLf & vbCrLf & ValidateCode
                MsgBox Msg, vbCritical, "Invalid Entry"
                Application.EnableEvents = False
                cell.ClearContents
                cell.Activate
                Application.EnableEvents = True
            End If
        Next cell
    End Sub
```

The Worksheet_Change procedure creates a Range object (named VRange) that represents the worksheet range that is validated. Then it loops through each cell in the Target argument, which represents the cell or cells that were changed. The code determines whether each cell is contained in the range to be validated. If so, it passes the cell as an argument to a custom function (EntryIsValid), which returns True if the cell is a valid entry.

If the entry isn't valid, the EntryIsValid function returns a string that describes the problem, and the user is informed by a message box (see Figure 6.7). When the message box is dismissed, the invalid entry is cleared from the cell, and the cell is activated. Note that events are disabled before the cell is cleared. If events weren't disabled, clearing the cell would produce a Change event that causes an endless loop.

Also, note that entering an invalid value clears Excel's Undo stack.

FIGURE 6.7

This message box describes the problem when the user makes an invalid entry.

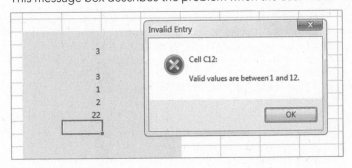

The `EntryIsValid` function procedure is shown here:

```
Private Function EntryIsValid(cell) As Variant
' Returns True if cell is an integer between 1 and 12
' Otherwise it returns a string that describes the problem

    ' Numeric?
    If Not WorksheetFunction.IsNumber (cell) Then
        EntryIsValid = "Non-numeric entry."
        Exit Function
    End If

    ' Integer?
    If CInt(cell) <> cell Then
        EntryIsValid = "Integer required."
        Exit Function
    End If

    ' Between 1 and 12?
    If cell < 1 Or cell > 12 Then
        EntryIsValid = "Valid values are between 1 and 12."
        Exit Function
    End If

    ' It passed all the tests
    EntryIsValid = True
End Function
```

The preceding technique works, but setting it up is tedious. Wouldn't it be nice if you could take advantage of Excel's data validation feature yet ensure that the data validation rules aren't deleted if the user pastes data into the validation range? The next example does the trick:

```
Private Sub Worksheet_Change(ByVal Target As Range)
    Dim VT As Long
    'Do all cells in the validation range
    'still have validation?

    On Error Resume Next
    VT = Range("InputRange").Validation.Type

    If Err.Number <> 0 Then
        Application.Undo
        MsgBox "Your last operation was canceled." & _
            "It would have deleted data validation rules.", _
vbCritical
    End If
End Sub
```

This event procedure checks the validation type of `InputRange`, the range that is *supposed* to contain the data validation rules. If the `VT` variable contains an error, one or more cells in the `InputRange` no longer contain data validation. In other words, the worksheet changes probably resulted from data being copied into the range that contains data validation. If that's the case, the code executes the `Undo` method of the `Application` object and reverses the user's action. Then it displays the message box shown in Figure 6.8.

FIGURE 6.8

The Worksheet_Change procedure ensures that data validation isn't deleted.

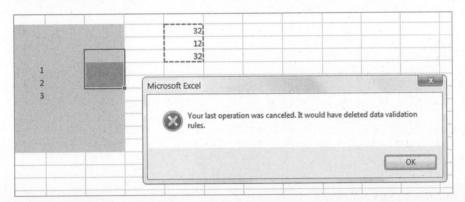

NOTE

This procedure works correctly only if all cells in the validation range contain the same type of data validation.

NOTE

A nice side benefit to using this procedure is that the Undo stack isn't destroyed.

ON THE WEB

This example, named `validate entry3.xlsm`, is available on the book's website.

The SelectionChange event

The following procedure demonstrates the `SelectionChange` event. It's executed whenever the user makes a new selection in the worksheet.

```
Private Sub Worksheet_SelectionChange(ByVal Target As Range)
    Cells.Interior.ColorIndex = xlNone
    With ActiveCell
        .EntireRow.Interior.Color = RGB(219, 229, 241)
```

```
            .EntireColumn.Interior.Color = RGB(219, 229, 241)
        End With
    End Sub
```

This procedure shades the row and column of the active cell, which makes identifying the active cell easy. The first statement removes the background color for all cells in the worksheet. Next, the entire row and column of the active cell is shaded. Figure 6.9 shows the shading in effect.

FIGURE 6.9

Moving the cell cursor shades the active cell's row and column.

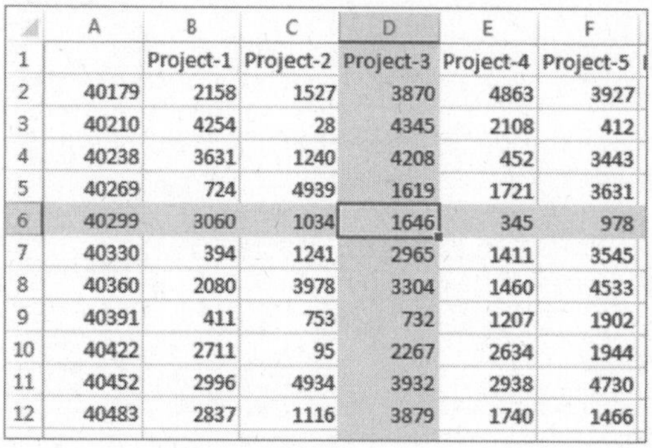

◢	A	B	C	D	E	F
1		Project-1	Project-2	Project-3	Project-4	Project-5
2	40179	2158	1527	3870	4863	3927
3	40210	4254	28	4345	2108	412
4	40238	3631	1240	4208	452	3443
5	40269	724	4939	1619	1721	3631
6	40299	3060	1034	1646	345	978
7	40330	394	1241	2965	1411	3545
8	40360	2080	3978	3304	1460	4533
9	40391	411	753	732	1207	1902
10	40422	2711	95	2267	2634	1944
11	40452	2996	4934	3932	2938	4730
12	40483	2837	1116	3879	1740	1466

You won't want to use the procedure if your worksheet contains any background shading because the shading will be wiped out. The exceptions are tables with a style applied and background colors resulting from conditional formatting. In both of these instances, the background color *is* maintained. Keep in mind, however, that executing the Worksheet_SelectionChange macro destroys the Undo stack, so using this technique essentially disables Excel's Undo feature.

ON THE WEB

This example, named `shade active row and column.xlsm`, is available on the book's website.

The BeforeDoubleClick event

You can set up a VBA procedure to be executed when the user double-clicks a cell. In the following example (which is stored in the code window for a Sheet object), double-clicking a cell toggles the cell's style. If the cell style is "Normal", it applies the "Good" style. If the style is "Good", it applies the "Normal" style.

```
    Private Sub Worksheet_BeforeDoubleClick _
        (ByVal Target As Range, Cancel As Boolean)
        If Target.Style = "Good" Then
            Target.Style = "Normal"
```

```
      Else
          Target.Style = "Good"
      End If
      Cancel = True
  End Sub
```

If `Cancel` is set to True, the default double-click action doesn't occur. In other words, double-clicking the cell won't put Excel into cell edit mode. Keep in mind that every-double click also destroys the Undo stack.

The BeforeRightClick event

When the user right-clicks in a worksheet, Excel displays a shortcut menu. If, for some reason, you'd like to prevent the shortcut menu from appearing in a particular sheet, you can trap the `RightClick` event. The following procedure sets the `Cancel` argument to `True`, which cancels the `RightClick` event and thereby cancels the shortcut menu and then displays a message box:

```
Private Sub Worksheet_BeforeRightClick _
    (ByVal Target As Range, Cancel As Boolean)
    Cancel = True
    MsgBox "The shortcut menu is not available."
End Sub
```

Keep in mind that the user can still access the shortcut menu by using Shift+F10. However, only a tiny percentage of Excel users are aware of that keystroke combination.

 To find out how to intercept the Shift+F10 key combination, see "The OnKey event" later in this chapter. Chapter 18, "Working with Shortcut Menus," describes other methods for disabling shortcut menus.

The following is another example that uses the `BeforeRightClick` event. This procedure checks to see whether the cell that was right-clicked contains a numeric value. If so, the code displays the Number tab of the Format Cells dialog box and sets the `Cancel` argument to `True` (avoiding the normal shortcut menu display). If the cell doesn't contain a numeric value, nothing special happens—the shortcut menu is displayed as usual.

```
Private Sub Worksheet_BeforeRightClick _
    (ByVal Target As Range, Cancel As Boolean)
    If IsNumeric(Target) And Not IsEmpty(Target) Then
        Application.CommandBars.ExecuteMso ("NumberFormatsDialog")
        Cancel = True
    End If
End Sub
```

Note that the code makes an additional check to determine whether the cell is not empty. This check is added because VBA considers empty cells to be numeric.

Using the Object Browser to locate events

The Object Browser is a useful tool that can help you learn about objects and their properties and methods. It can also help you find out which objects support a particular event. For example, say you'd like to find out which objects support the MouseMove event. Activate VBE and press F2 to display the Object Browser window. Make sure that <All Libraries> is selected; then type **MouseMove** and click the binoculars icon.

The Object Browser displays a list of matching items. Events are indicated with a small yellow lightning bolt icon next to the event name. Click the event you are looking for and check the status bar at the bottom of the list for the appropriate usage syntax.

Monitoring with Application Events

In earlier sections, we discussed Workbook events and Worksheet events. Those events are monitored for a particular workbook. If you want to monitor events for all open workbooks or all worksheets, you use Application-level events.

> **NOTE**
> Creating event-handler procedures to handle Application events always requires a class module and some setup work.

Table 6.3 lists commonly used Application events with a brief description of each. Consult the Help system for details.

Enabling Application-level events

To use Application-level events, you need to do the following:

1. Insert a new class module.

2. Set a name for this class module in the Properties window under *Name*. By default, VBA gives each new class module a default name like Class1, Class2, and so on. You may want to give your class module a more meaningful name, such as clsApp.

3. In the class module, declare a public Application object by using the With-Events keyword. Here's an example:

```
Public WithEvents XL As Application
```

4. Create a variable that you'll use to refer to the declared Application object in the class module. It should be a module-level object variable declared in a regular VBA module (not in the class module). Here's an example:

```
Dim X As New
```

TABLE 6.3 Commonly Used Events Recognized by the Application Object

Event	Action That Triggers the Event
AfterCalculate	A calculation has been completed, and no outstanding queries exist.
NewWorkbook	A new workbook is created.
SheetActivate	Any sheet is activated.
SheetBeforeDoubleClick	Any worksheet is double-clicked. This event occurs before the default double-click action.
SheetBeforeRightClick	Any worksheet is right-clicked. This event occurs before the default right-click action.
SheetCalculate	Any worksheet is calculated (or recalculated).
SheetChange	Cells in any worksheet are changed by the user or by an external link.
SheetDeactivate	Any sheet is deactivated.
SheetFollowHyperlink	A hyperlink is clicked.
SheetPivotTableUpdate	Any pivot table is updated.
SheetSelectionChange	The selection changes on any worksheet except a chart sheet.
WindowActivate	Any workbook window is activated.
WindowDeactivate	Any workbook window is deactivated.
WindowResize	Any workbook window is resized.
WorkbookActivate	Any workbook is activated.
WorkbookAddinInstall	A workbook is installed as an add-in.
WorkbookAddinUninstall	Any add-in workbook is uninstalled.
WorkbookBeforeClose	Any open workbook is closed.
WorkbookBeforePrint	Any open workbook is printed.
WorkbookBeforeSave	Any open workbook is saved.
WorkbookDeactivate	Any open workbook is deactivated.
WorkbookNewSheet	A new sheet is created in any open workbook.
WorkbookOpen	A workbook is opened.

5. Connect the declared object with the `Application` object. This step is often done in a `Workbook_Open` procedure. Here's an example:

```
Set X.XL = Application
```

6. Write event-handler procedures for the `XL` object in the class module.

Determining when a workbook is opened

The example in this section keeps track of every workbook that is opened by storing information in a comma-separated variable (CSV) text file. You can import this file into Excel.

We start by inserting a new class module and naming it `clsApp`. The code in the class module is as follows:

```
Public WithEvents AppEvents As Application
Private Sub AppEvents_WorkbookOpen (ByVal Wb As Excel.Workbook)
    Call UpdateLogFile(Wb)
End Sub
```

This code declares `AppEvents` as an `Application` object with events. The `AppEvents_WorkbookOpen` procedure will be called whenever a workbook is opened. This event-handler procedure calls `UpdateLogFile` and passes the `Wb` variable, which represents the workbook that was opened. We then added a VBA module and inserted the following code:

```
Dim AppObject As New clsApp
Sub Init()
' Called by Workbook_Open
    Set AppObject.AppEvents = Application
End Sub
Sub UpdateLogFile(Wb)
    Dim txt As String
    Dim Fname As String
    txt = Wb.FullName
    txt = txt & "," & Date & "," & Time
    txt = txt & "," & Application.UserName
    Fname = Application.DefaultFilePath & "\logfile.csv"
    Open Fname For Append As #1
    Print #1, txt
    Close #1
    MsgBox txt
End Sub
```

Note at the top that the `AppObject` variable is declared as type `clsApp` (the name of the class module). The call to `Init` is in the `Workbook_Open` procedure, which is in the code module for `ThisWorkbook`. This procedure is as follows:

```
Private Sub Workbook_Open()
    Call Init
End Sub
```

The `UpdateLogFile` procedure opens a text file, or it creates the text file if it doesn't exist. The procedure then writes key information about the workbook that was opened: the filename and full path, the date, the time, and the username.

The `Workbook_Open` procedure calls the `Init` procedure. Therefore, when the workbook opens, the `Init` procedure creates the object variable. The final statement uses a message box to display the information that was written to the CSV file. You can delete this statement if you prefer not to see that message.

ON THE WEB

This example, named `log workbook open.xlsm`, is available on the book's website.

Monitoring Application-Level events

To get a feel for the event-generation process, you may find it helpful to see a list of events that get generated as you go about your work.

Figure 6.10 illustrates a workbook (`ApplicationEventTracker.xlsm`) found with the sample files for this chapter. This workbook displays descriptions for various `Application`-level events as they occur. You might find this workbook helpful when learning about the types and sequence of events that occur.

FIGURE 6.10

This workbook uses a class module to monitor all Application-level events.

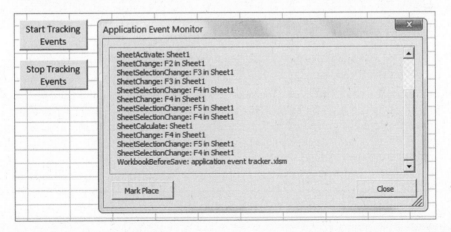

ON THE WEB

This example is available on the book's website in the `ApplicationEventTracker.xlsm` file.

The workbook contains a class module with 21 procedures defined—one for each of the commonly used Application-level events.

Accessing events not associated with an object

The events that we discussed earlier in this chapter are all associated with an object (Application, Workbook, Sheet, and so on). In this section, we discuss two additional rogue events: OnTime and OnKey. Instead of being associated with an object, these events are accessed by using methods of the Application object.

The OnTime event

The OnTime event occurs at a specified time of day. The following example demonstrates how to program Excel so that it beeps and displays a message at 3 p.m.:

```
Sub SetAlarm()
    Application.OnTime TimeValue("15:00:00"), "DisplayAlarm"
End Sub

Sub DisplayAlarm()
    Beep
    MsgBox "Wake up. It's time for your afternoon break!"
End Sub
```

In this example, the SetAlarm procedure uses the OnTime method of the Application object to set up the OnTime event. This method takes two arguments: the time (3 p.m., in the example) and the procedure to execute when the time occurs (DisplayAlarm in the example). After SetAlarm is executed, the DisplayAlarm procedure will be called at 3 p.m., displaying the message shown in Figure 6.11.

FIGURE 6.11

This message box was programmed to display at a particular time of day.

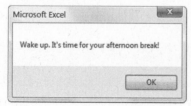

If you want to schedule an event relative to the current time—for example, 20 minutes from now—you can write an instruction like this:

```
Application.OnTime Now + TimeValue("00:20:00"), "DisplayAlarm"
```

You can also use the `OnTime` method to schedule a procedure on a particular day. The following statement runs the `DisplayAlarm` procedure at 12:01 a.m. on April 1, 2020:

```
Application.OnTime DateSerial(2020, 4, 1) + _
    TimeValue("00:00:01"), "DisplayAlarm"
```

> **NOTE**
>
> The `OnTime` method has two additional arguments. If you plan to use this method, you should refer to the online help for complete details.

The two procedures that follow demonstrate how to program a repeated event. In this case, cell A1 is updated with the current time every five seconds. Executing the `UpdateClock` procedure writes the time to cell A1 and also programs another event five seconds later. This event reruns the `UpdateClock` procedure. To stop the events, execute the `Stop-Clock` procedure (which cancels the event). Note that `NextTick` is a module-level variable that stores the time for the next event.

> **ON THE WEB**
>
> This example, named `ontime event demo.xlsm`, is available on the book's website.

```
Dim NextTick As Date
Sub UpdateClock()
' Updates cell A1 with the current time
    ThisWorkbook.Sheets(1).Range("A1") = Time
' Set up the next event five seconds from now
    NextTick = Now + TimeValue("00:00:05")
    Application.OnTime NextTick, "UpdateClock"
End Sub

Sub StopClock()
' Cancels the OnTime event (stops the clock)
    On Error Resume Next
    Application.OnTime NextTick, "UpdateClock", , False
End Sub
```

> **CAUTION**
>
> The `OnTime` event persists even after the workbook is closed. In other words, if you close the workbook without running the `StopClock` procedure, the workbook will reopen itself in five seconds (assuming that Excel is still running). To prevent this, use a `Workbook_BeforeClose` event procedure that contains the following statement:

```
Call StopClock
```

The OnKey event

While you're working, Excel constantly monitors what you type. Because of this monitoring, you can set up a keystroke or a key combination that, when pressed, executes a particular procedure. The only time that these keystrokes won't be recognized is when you're entering a formula or working with a dialog box.

> **CAUTION**
>
> It's important to understand that creating a procedure to respond to an OnKey event isn't limited to a single workbook. The re-mapped keystroke is valid in all open workbooks, not just the one in which you created the event procedure.
>
> Also, if you set up an OnKey event, make sure that you provide a way to cancel the event. A common way to do this is to use the Workbook_BeforeClose event procedure.

An OnKey event example

The following example uses the OnKey method to set up an OnKey event. This event reassigns the PgDn and PgUp keys. After the Setup_OnKey procedure is executed, pressing PgDn executes the PgDn_Sub procedure, and pressing PgUp executes the PgUp_Sub procedure. The net effect is that pressing PgDn moves the cursor down one row and pressing PgUp moves the cursor up one row. Key combinations that use PgUp and PgDn aren't affected. So, for example, Ctrl+PgDn will continue to activate the next worksheet in a workbook.

```
Sub Setup_OnKey()
    Application.OnKey "{PgDn}", "PgDn_Sub"
    Application.OnKey "{PgUp}", "PgUp_Sub"
End Sub
Sub PgDn_Sub()
    On Error Resume Next
    ActiveCell.Offset(1, 0).Activate
End Sub
Sub PgUp_Sub()
    On Error Resume Next
    ActiveCell.Offset(-1, 0).Activate
End Sub
```

> **ON THE WEB**
>
> This example, named onkey event demo.xlsm, is available on the book's website.

In the previous examples, we use On Error Resume Next to ignore any errors that are generated. For example, if the active cell is in the first row, trying to move up one row causes an error. Also, if the active sheet is a chart sheet, an error will occur because there is no such thing as an active cell in a chart sheet.

By executing the following procedure, you cancel the OnKey events and return these keys to their normal functionality:

```
Sub Cancel_OnKey()
    Application.OnKey "{PgDn}"
    Application.OnKey "{PgUp}"
End Sub
```

Contrary to what you might expect, using an empty string as the second argument for the OnKey method does *not* cancel the OnKey event. Rather, it causes Excel to simply ignore the keystroke and do nothing. For example, the following instruction tells Excel to ignore Alt+F4 (the percent sign represents the Alt key):

```
Application.OnKey "%{F4}", ""
```

 Although you can use the OnKey method to assign a shortcut key for executing a macro, it's better to use the Macro Options dialog box for this task. For more details, see Chapter 4, "Working with VBA Sub Procedures."

Key Codes

In the previous section, note that the PgDn keystroke appears in braces. Table 6.4 shows the key codes that you can use in your OnKey procedures.

TABLE 6.4 Key Codes for the OnKey Event

Key	Code
Backspace	{BACKSPACE} or {BS}
Break	{BREAK}
Caps Lock	{CAPSLOCK}
Delete or Del	{DELETE} or {DEL}
Down Arrow	{DOWN}
End	{END}
Enter	~ (tilde)
Enter (on the numeric keypad)	{ENTER}
Escape	{ESCAPE} or {ESC}
Home	{HOME}
Ins	{INSERT}
Left Arrow	{LEFT}
NumLock	{NUMLOCK}
PgDn	{PGDN}

Continues

TABLE 6.4 *(continued)*

Key	Code
PgUp	{PGUP}
Right Arrow	{RIGHT}
Scroll Lock	{SCROLLLOCK}
Tab	{TAB}
Up Arrow	{UP}
F1 through F15	{F1} through {F15}

You can also specify keys combined with Shift, Ctrl, and Alt. To specify a key combined with another key or keys, use the following symbols:

Shift: Plus sign (+)

Ctrl: Caret (^)

Alt: Percent sign (%)

For example, to assign a procedure to the Ctrl+Shift+A key, use this code:

```
Application.OnKey "^+A", "SubName"
```

To assign a procedure to Alt+F11 (which is normally used to switch to the VB Editor window), use this code:

```
Application.OnKey "%{F11}", "SubName"
```

Disabling shortcut menus

Earlier in this chapter, we discussed a `Worksheet_BeforeRightClick` procedure that disabled the right-click shortcut menu. The following procedure is placed in the `This-Workbook` code module:

```
Private Sub Worksheet_BeforeRightClick _
(ByVal Target As Range, Cancel As Boolean)Cancel = True
    MsgBox "The shortcut menu is not available."
End Sub
```

The user could still display the shortcut menu by pressing Shift+F10. To intercept the Shift+F10 key combination, add these procedures to a standard VBA module:

```
Sub SetupNoShiftF10()
    Application.OnKey "+{F10}", "NoShiftF10"
End Sub
Sub TurnOffNoShiftF10()
    Application.OnKey "+{F10}"
End Sub
Sub NoShiftF10()
    MsgBox "Nice try, but that doesn't work either."
End Sub
```

After the `SetupNoShiftF10` procedure is executed, pressing Shift+F10 displays the message box shown in Figure 6.12. Remember that the `Worksheet_BeforeRightClick` procedure is valid only in its own workbook. The Shift+F10 key event, on the other hand, applies to all open workbooks.

FIGURE 6.12

Pressing Shift+F10 displays this message.

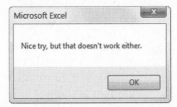

ON THE WEB

The book's website contains a workbook that includes all the `OnKey` procedures. The file, named `no shortcut menus.xlsm`, includes workbook event-handler procedures: `Workbook_Open` executes the `SetupNoShiftF10` procedure, and `Workbook_BeforeClose` calls the `TurnOffNoShiftF10` procedure.

VBA Programming Examples and Techniques

Learning by Example

Most beginning VBA programmers benefit from hands-on examples. A well-thought-out example usually communicates a concept much better than a description of the underlying theory. Therefore, instead of taking you through a painful review of every nuance of VBA, this chapter guides you through demonstrations of useful Excel programming techniques.

Here, you will walk through examples that solve practical problems while furthering your knowledge of VBA. This includes the following:

- Working with ranges
- Working with workbooks and sheets
- VBA techniques
- Functions that are useful in your VBA procedures
- Functions that you can use in worksheet formulas
- Windows API calls

 Subsequent chapters in this book present additional feature-specific examples: charts, pivot tables, events, UserForms, and so on.

Working with Ranges

The examples in this section demonstrate how to manipulate worksheet ranges with VBA.

Specifically, we provide examples of copying a range, moving a range, selecting a range, identifying types of information in a range, prompting for a cell value, determining the first empty cell in a column, pausing a macro to allow the user to select a range, counting cells in a range, looping through the cells in a range, and several other commonly used range-related operations.

Copying a range

Excel's macro recorder is useful not so much for generating usable code but for discovering the names of relevant objects, methods, and properties. The code that's generated by the macro recorder isn't always the most efficient, but it can usually provide you with several clues.

For example, recording a simple copy-and-paste operation generates five lines of VBA code.

```
Sub Macro1()
    Range("A1").Select
    Selection.Copy
    Range("B1").Select
    ActiveSheet.Paste
    Application.CutCopyMode = False
End Sub
```

Note that the generated code selects cell A1, copies it, and then selects cell B1 and performs the paste operation. But in VBA, you don't need to select an object to work with it. You would never learn this important point by mimicking the preceding recorded macro code, where two statements incorporate the Select method. You can replace this procedure with the following much simpler routine, which doesn't select any cells. It also takes advantage of the fact that the Copy method can use an argument that represents the destination for the copied range.

```
Sub CopyRange()
    Range("A1").Copy Range("B1")
End Sub
```

Both macros assume that a worksheet is active and that the operation takes place on the active worksheet. To copy a range to a different worksheet or workbook, simply qualify the range reference for the destination. The following example copies a range from Sheet1 in File1.xlsx to Sheet2 in File2.xlsx. Because the references are fully qualified, this example works regardless of which workbook is active.

```
Sub CopyRange2()
    Workbooks("File1.xlsx").Sheets("Sheet1").Range("A1").Copy _
        Workbooks("File2.xlsx").Sheets("Sheet2").Range("A1")
End Sub
```

Another way to approach this task is to use object variables to represent the ranges, as shown in the code that follows. Using object variables is especially useful when your code will use the ranges at some other point.

```
Sub CopyRange3()
    Dim Rng1 As Range, Rng2 As Range
    Set Rng1 = Workbooks("File1.xlsx").Sheets("Sheet1").Range("A1")
    Set Rng2 = Workbooks("File2.xlsx").Sheets("Sheet2").Range("A1")
    Rng1.Copy Rng2
End Sub
```

As you might expect, copying isn't limited to one single cell at a time. The following procedure, for example, copies a large range. Note that the destination consists of only a single cell (which represents the upper-left cell of the destination range). Using a single cell for the destination works just like it does when you copy and paste a range manually in Excel.

```
Sub CopyRange4()
    Range("A1:C800").Copy Range("D1")
End Sub
```

Moving a range

The VBA instructions for moving a range are similar to those for copying a range, as the following example demonstrates. The difference is that you use the Cut method instead of the Copy method. Note that you need to specify only the upper-left cell for the destination range.

The following example moves 18 cells (in A1:C6) to a new location, beginning at cell H1:

```
Sub MoveRange1()
    Range("A1:C6").Cut Range("H1")
End Sub
```

Copying a variably sized range

In many cases, you need to copy a range of cells, but you don't know the exact row and column dimensions of the range. For example, you might have a workbook that tracks weekly sales, and the number of rows changes weekly when you add new data.

Figure 7.1 shows a common type of worksheet. This range consists of several rows, and the number of rows changes each week. Because you don't know the exact range address at any given time, writing a macro to copy the range requires additional coding.

The following macro demonstrates how to copy this range from Sheet1 to Sheet2 (beginning at cell A1). It uses the CurrentRegion property, which returns a Range object that corresponds to the block of cells around a particular cell (in this case, A1).

```
Sub CopyCurrentRegion2()
    Range("A1").CurrentRegion.Copy Sheets("Sheet2").Range("A1")
End Sub
```

FIGURE 7.1

The number of rows in the data range changes every week.

◢	A	B	C	
1	Week	Total Sales	New Customers	
2	1	71,831	92	
3	2	51,428	13	
4	3	86,302	93	
5	4	76,278	89	
6	5	68,053	11	
7	6	75,636	80	
8	7	47,464	22	
9				

> **NOTE**
>
> Using the `CurrentRegion` property is equivalent to choosing the Home ⇨ Editing ⇨ Find & Select ⇨ Go To Special command and selecting the Current Region option (or by using the Ctrl+Shift+* shortcut to select the current region). To see how the `CurrentRegion` selection works, record your actions while you issue that command. Generally, the `CurrentRegion` property setting consists of a rectangular block of cells surrounded by one or more blank rows or columns.

If the range to be copied is a table (specified by choosing Insert ⇨ Tables ⇨ Table), you can use code like this (assuming the table is named `Table1`):

```
Sub CopyTable()
    Range("Table1[#All]").Copy Sheets("Sheet2").Range("A1")
End Sub
```

Tips for working with ranges

When you work with ranges, keep the following points in mind:

- Your code doesn't need to select a range to work with it.

- You can't select a range that's not on the active worksheet. So, if your code *does* select a range, its worksheet must be active. You can use the `Activate` method of the `Worksheets` collection to activate a particular sheet.

- Remember that the macro recorder doesn't always generate the most efficient code. Often, you can create your macro by using the recorder and then edit the code to make it more efficient.

- Using named ranges in your VBA code is a good idea. For example, refer to `Range("Total")` rather than `Range("D45")`. In the latter case, if you add a row above row 45, the cell address will change. You would then need to modify the macro so that it uses the correct range address (D46).

- If you rely on the macro recorder when selecting ranges, make sure that you record the macro using relative references. Choose Developer ⇨ Code ⇨ Use Relative References to toggle this setting.

- When running a macro that works on each cell in the current range selection, the user might select entire columns or rows. In most cases, you don't want to loop through every cell in the selection. Your macro should create a subset of the selection consisting of only the nonblank cells. See the section "Looping through a selected range efficiently" later in this chapter.

- Excel allows multiple selections. For example, you can select a range, press Ctrl, and select another range. You can test for multiple selections in your macro and take appropriate action. See the section "Determining the type of selected range" later in this chapter.

Selecting or otherwise identifying various types of ranges

Much of the work that you'll do in VBA will involve working with ranges—either selecting a range or identifying a range so that you can do something with the cells.

In addition to the CurrentRegion property (which we discussed earlier), you should also be aware of the End method of the Range object. The End method takes one argument, which determines the direction in which the selection is extended. The following statement selects a range from the active cell to the last nonempty cell in that column:

```
Range(ActiveCell, ActiveCell.End(xlDown)).Select
```

Here's a similar example that uses a specific cell as the starting point:

```
Range(Range("A2"), Range("A2").End(xlDown)).Select
```

As you might expect, three other constants, xlUp, xlToLeft, and xlToRight, can be used as an argument to the End method to extend a range in the three other directions.

> **CAUTION**
>
> Be careful when using the End method with the ActiveCell property. If the active cell is at the perimeter of a range or if the range contains one or more empty cells, the End method may not produce the desired results.

> **ON THE WEB**
>
> This book's website includes a workbook that demonstrates several common types of range selections. When you open this workbook, named range selections.xlsm, the code adds a new menu item to the shortcut menu that appears when you right-click a cell: Selection Demo. This menu contains commands that enable the user to make various types of selections, as shown in Figure 7.2.

The following macro is in the example workbook. The SelectCurrentRegion macro simulates pressing Ctrl+Shift+*.

```
Sub SelectCurrentRegion()
    ActiveCell.CurrentRegion.Select
End Sub
```

FIGURE 7.2

This workbook uses a custom shortcut menu to demonstrate how to select variably sized ranges by using VBA.

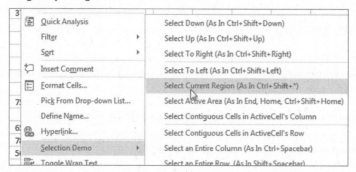

Often, you won't want to select the cells. Rather, you'll want to work with them in some way (for example, format them). You can easily adapt the cell-selecting procedures. The following procedure was adapted from SelectCurrentRegion. This procedure doesn't select cells; it applies formatting to the range defined as the current region around the active cell. You can adapt the other procedures in the example workbook in this manner.

```
Sub FormatCurrentRegion()
    ActiveCell.CurrentRegion.Font.Bold = True
End Sub
```

Another way to refer to a range

If you look at VBA code written by others, you may notice a different way to reference a range. For example, the following statement selects a range:

`[C2:D8].Select`

The range address is surrounded by square brackets, and the range address is not enclosed in quote marks. The preceding statement is equivalent to

`Range("C2:D8").Select`

Using square brackets is a shortcut for the Evaluate method of the Application object. In this example, it's a shortcut for the following:

`Application.Evaluate("C2:D8").Select`

This may save a few keystrokes when entering the code, but it ends up being a bit slower than the normal type of referencing because it takes time to evaluate a text string and determine that it's a range reference.

Resizing a range

The Resize property of a Range object makes it easy to change the size of a range. The Resize property takes two arguments, RowSize and ColumnSize, that represent the total number of rows and the total number of columns in the resized range.

For example, after executing the following statement, the MyRange object variable is 20 rows by 5 columns (range A1:E20):

```
Set MyRange = Range("A1")
Set MyRange = MyRange.Resize(20, 5)
```

After the following statement is executed, the size of MyRange is increased by one row. Note that the second argument is omitted, so the number of columns does not change.

```
Set MyRange = MyRange.Resize(MyRange.Rows.Count + 1)
```

A more practical example involves changing the definition of a range name. Assume a workbook has a range named Data. Your code needs to extend the named range by adding an additional row. This code snippet will do the job:

```
With Range("Data")
    .Resize(.Rows.Count + 1).Name = "Data"
End With
```

Prompting for a cell value

The following procedure demonstrates how to ask the user for a value and then insert it into cell A1 of the active worksheet:

```
Sub GetValue1()
    Range("A1").Value = InputBox("Enter the value")
End Sub
```

Figure 7.3 shows how the input box looks.

FIGURE 7.3

The InputBox function gets a value from the user to be inserted into a cell.

This procedure has a problem, however. If the user clicks the Cancel button in the input box, the procedure deletes any data already in the cell. The following modification takes no action if the Cancel button is clicked (which results in an empty string for the UserEntry variable):

```
Sub GetValue2()
    Dim UserEntry As Variant
    UserEntry = InputBox("Enter the value")
    If UserEntry <> "" Then Range("A1").Value = UserEntry
End Sub
```

In many cases, you'll need to validate the user's entry in the input box. For example, you may require a number between 1 and 12. The following example demonstrates one way to validate the user's entry. In this example, an invalid entry is ignored, and the input box is displayed again. This cycle keeps repeating until the user enters a valid number or clicks Cancel.

```
Sub GetValue3()
    Dim UserEntry As Variant
    Dim Msg As String
    Const MinVal As Integer = 1
    Const MaxVal As Integer = 12
    Msg = "Enter a value between " & MinVal & " and " & MaxVal
    Do
        UserEntry = InputBox(Msg)
        If UserEntry = "" Then Exit Sub
        If IsNumeric(UserEntry) Then
            If UserEntry >= MinVal And UserEntry <= MaxVal Then Exit Do
        End If
        Msg = "Your previous entry was INVALID."
        Msg = Msg & vbNewLine
        Msg = Msg & "Enter a value between " & MinVal & " and " & MaxVal
    Loop
    ActiveSheet.Range("A1").Value = UserEntry
End Sub
```

As you can see in Figure 7.4, the code also changes the message displayed if the user makes an invalid entry.

FIGURE 7.4

Validate a user's entry with the VBA InputBox function.

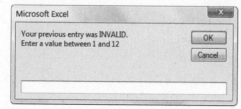

Entering a value in the next empty cell

A common requirement is to enter a value into the next empty cell in a column or row. The following example prompts the user for a name and a value and then enters the data into the next empty row (see Figure 7.5).

```vba
Sub GetData()
    Dim NextRow As Long
    Dim Entry1 As String, Entry2 As String
    Do
'       Determine next empty row
        NextRow = Cells(Rows.Count, 1).End(xlUp).Row + 1

'       Prompt for the data
        Entry1 = InputBox("Enter the name")
        If Entry1 = "" Then Exit Sub
        Entry2 = InputBox("Enter the amount")
        If Entry2 = "" Then Exit Sub

'       Write the data
        Cells(NextRow, 1) = Entry1
        Cells(NextRow, 2) = Entry2
    Loop
End Sub
```

FIGURE 7.5

A macro for inserting data into the next empty row in a worksheet

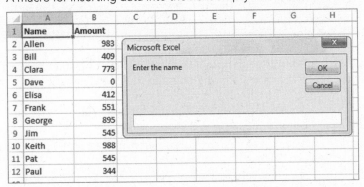

225

To keep things simple, this procedure doesn't perform any validation. The loop continues indefinitely. We use Exit Sub statements to get out of the loop when the user clicks Cancel in the input box.

ON THE WEB

The GetData procedure is available on the book's website in the next empty cell.xlsm file.

Note the statement that determines the value of the NextRow variable. If you don't understand how this statement works, try the manual equivalent: activate the last cell in column A (cell A1048576), press End, and then press the up-arrow key. At this point, the last non-blank cell in column A will be selected. The Row property returns this row number, which is incremented by 1 to get the row of the cell below it (the next empty row). Rather than hard-code the last cell in column A, we used Rows.Count so that this procedure will be compatible with all versions of Excel (including versions before Excel 2007 where the rows on a worksheet were capped at 65,536).

This technique of selecting the next empty cell has a slight glitch. If the column is empty, it will calculate row 2 as the next empty row. Writing additional code to account for this possibility would be fairly easy.

Pausing a macro to get a user-selected range

In some situations, you may need an interactive macro. For example, you can create a macro that pauses while the user specifies a range of cells. The procedure in this section describes how to do this with Excel's InputBox method.

NOTE

Don't confuse Excel's InputBox method with VBA's InputBox function. Although these two items have the same name, they're not the same. For example, the InputBox method includes a Type argument that allows you to limit what sort of data can be input. See Chapter 12, "Leveraging Custom Dialog Boxes," for a complete discussion of both the method and the function.

The Sub procedure that follows demonstrates how to pause a macro and let the user select a range. The code then inserts a formula into each cell of the specified range.

```
Sub GetUserRange()
    Dim UserRange As Range

    Prompt = "Select a range for the random numbers."
    Title = "Select a range"

'   Display the Input Box
    On Error Resume Next
    Set UserRange = Application.InputBox( _
```

```
        Prompt:=Prompt, _
        Title:=Title, _
        Default:=ActiveCell.Address, _
        Type:=8) 'Range selection
    On Error GoTo 0

'   Was the Input Box canceled?
    If UserRange Is Nothing Then
        MsgBox "Canceled."
    Else
        UserRange.Formula = "=RAND()"
    End If
End Sub
```

Figure 7.6 shows the input box.

FIGURE 7.6

Use an input box to pause a macro.

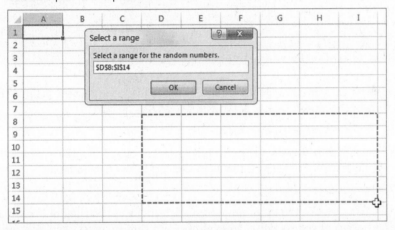

Specifying a `Type` argument of 8 for the `InputBox` method is the key to this procedure. `Type` argument 8 tells Excel that the input box should accept only a valid range.

Also note the use of `On Error Resume Next`. This statement ignores the error that occurs if the user clicks the Cancel button. If the user clicks Cancel, the `UserRange` object variable isn't defined. This example displays a message box with the text `Canceled`. If the user clicks OK, the macro continues. Using `On Error GoTo 0` resumes normal error handling.

By the way, you don't need to check for a valid range selection. Excel takes care of this task for you. If the user types an invalid range address, Excel displays a message box with instructions on how to select a range.

Counting selected cells

You can create a macro that works with the range of cells selected by the user. Use the Count property of the Range object to determine how many cells are contained in a range selection (or any range, for that matter). For example, the following statement displays a message box that contains the number of cells in the current selection:

```
MsgBox Selection.Count
```

> **CAUTION**
>
> With the larger worksheet size introduced in Excel 2007, the Count property can generate an error. The Count property uses the Long data type, so the largest value that it can store is 2,147,483,647. For example, if the user selects 2,048 complete columns (2,147,483,648 cells), the Count property generates an error. Fortunately, Microsoft added a new property beginning with Excel 2007: CountLarge. CountLarge uses the Double data type, which can handle values up to 1.79+E^308.
>
> The bottom line? In the vast majority of situations, the Count property will work fine. If there's a chance that you may need to count more cells (such as all cells in a worksheet), use CountLarge instead of Count.

If the active sheet contains a range named Data, the following statement assigns the number of cells in the Data range to a variable named CellCount:

```
CellCount = Range("Data").Count
```

You can also determine how many rows or columns are contained in a range. The following expression calculates the number of columns in the currently selected range:

```
Selection.Columns.Count
```

And, of course, you can use the Rows property to determine the number of rows in a range. The following statement counts the number of rows in a range named Data and assigns the number to a variable named RowCount:

```
RowCount = Range("Data").Rows.Count
```

Determining the type of selected range

Excel supports several types of range selections.

- A single cell
- A contiguous range of cells
- One or more entire columns
- One or more entire rows
- An entire worksheet
- Any combination of the preceding (that is, a multiple selection)

As a result, when your VBA procedure processes a user-selected range, you can't make any presumptions about what that range might be. For example, the range selection might consist of two areas, say A1:A10 and C1:C10. (To make a multiple selection, press Ctrl while you select the ranges with your mouse.)

In the case of a multiple range selection, the Range object comprises separate areas. To determine whether a selection is a multiple selection, use the Areas method, which returns an Areas collection. This collection represents all of the ranges in a multiple range selection.

You can use an expression such as the following to determine whether a selected range has multiple areas:

```
NumAreas = Selection.Areas.Count
```

If the NumAreas variable contains a value greater than 1, the selection is a multiple selection.

The following is a function named AreaType, which returns a text string that describes the type of range selection:

```
Function AreaType(RangeArea As Range) As String
'    Returns the type of a range in an area
    Select Case True
        Case RangeArea.Cells.CountLarge = 1
            AreaType = "Cell"
        Case RangeArea.CountLarge = Cells.CountLarge
            AreaType = "Worksheet"
        Case RangeArea.Rows.Count = Cells.Rows.Count
            AreaType = "Column"
        Case RangeArea.Columns.Count = Cells.Columns.Count
            AreaType = "Row"
        Case Else
            AreaType = "Block"
    End Select
End Function
```

This function accepts a Range object as its argument and returns one of five strings that describe the area: Cell, Worksheet, Column, Row, or Block. The function uses a Select Case construct to determine which of five comparison expressions is True. For example, if the range consists of a single cell, the function returns Cell. If the number of cells in the range is equal to the number of cells in the worksheet, it returns Worksheet. If the number of rows in the range equals the number of rows in the worksheet, it returns Column. If the number of columns in the range equals the number of columns in the worksheet, the function returns Row. If none of the Case expressions is True, the function returns Block.

Note that we used the CountLarge property when counting cells. As we noted previously in this chapter, the number of selected cells could potentially exceed the limit of the Count property.

FIGURE 7.7

A VBA procedure analyzes the currently selected range.

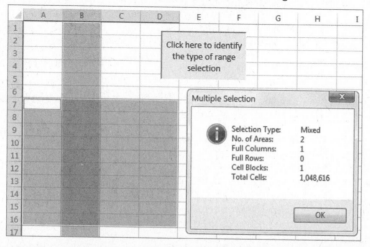

NOTE

You might be surprised to discover that Excel allows multiple selections to be identical. For example, if you hold down Ctrl and click five times in cell A1, the selection will have five identical areas. The `RangeDescription` procedure takes this possibility into account and doesn't count the same cell multiple times. Also note that Excel displays progressively darker shading for overlapping range selections.

Looping through a selected range efficiently

A common task is to create a macro that evaluates each cell in a range and performs an operation if the cell meets a certain criterion. The procedure that follows is an example of such a macro. The `ColorNegative` procedure sets the cell's background color to red for cells that contain a negative value. For non-negative value cells, it sets the background color to none.

NOTE

This example is for educational purposes only. Using Excel's conditional formatting feature is a much better approach.

```
Sub ColorNegative()
'   Makes negative cells red
    Dim cell As Range
    If TypeName(Selection) <> "Range" Then Exit Sub
    Application.ScreenUpdating = False
    For Each cell In Selection
        If cell.Value < 0 Then
            cell.Interior.Color = RGB(255, 0, 0)
        Else
            cell.Interior.Color = xlNone
        End If
    Next cell
End Sub
```

The ColorNegative procedure certainly works, but it has a serious flaw. For example, what if the used area on the worksheet were small, but the user selects an entire column? Or ten columns? Or the entire worksheet? You don't need to process all of those empty cells, and the user would probably give up long before your code churns through all those cells.

A better solution (ColorNegative2) follows. In this revised procedure, we create a Range object variable, WorkRange, which consists of the intersection of the user's selected range and the worksheet's used range.

```
Sub ColorNegative2()
'   Makes negative cells red
    Dim WorkRange As Range
    Dim cell As Range
    If TypeName(Selection) <> "Range" Then Exit Sub
    Application.ScreenUpdating = False
    Set WorkRange = Application.Intersect(Selection, ActiveSheet
.UsedRange)
    For Each cell In WorkRange
        If cell.Value < 0 Then
            cell.Interior.Color = RGB(255, 0, 0)
        Else
            cell.Interior.Color = xlNone
        End If
    Next cell
End Sub
```

Figure 7.8 shows an example; the entire column D is selected (1,048,576 cells). The range used by the worksheet, however, is B2:I16. Therefore, the intersection of these ranges is D2:D16, which is a much smaller range than the original selection. Needless to say, the time difference between processing 15 cells versus processing 1,048,576 cells is significant.

The ColorNegative2 procedure is an improvement, but it's still not as efficient as it could be because it processes empty cells. A third revision, ColorNegative3, is quite a bit longer but much more efficient. We use the SpecialCells method to generate two sub-sets of the selection: one subset (ConstantCells) includes only the cells with numeric

FIGURE 7.8

Using the intersection of the used range and the selected ranged results in fewer cells to process.

	A	B	C	D	E	F	G	H	I
1									
2		-5	0	-7	3	-3	7	-6	-9
3		-5	-6	-6	-10	-1	10	9	-10
4		-2	5	1	4	-3	3	-8	-3
5		1	8	-3	-8	1	8	8	6
6		0	-4	-3	3	-1	7	5	2
7		-10	4	1	8	1	-8	7	9
8		5	-4	-1	7	10	-1	8	-3
9		1	4	1	-8	-2	-1	-6	8
10		-8	-3	10	-1	7	6	7	9
11		0	-2	-2	-1	9	7	7	7
12		10	4	7	6	10	-10	10	4
13		-5	-1	9	7	0	8	6	9
14		3	-4	10	-10	9	-9	2	-4
15		4	9	0	8	4	7	-1	-4
16		0	1	9	-9	2	7	-7	0
17									

constants, and the other subset (FormulaCells) includes only the cells with numeric formulas. The code processes the cells in these subsets by using two For Each-Next constructs. The net effect is that only nonblank, nontext cells are evaluated, thus speeding up the macro considerably.

```
Sub ColorNegative3()
'    Makes negative cells red
    Dim FormulaCells As Range, ConstantCells As Range
    Dim cell As Range
    If TypeName(Selection) <> "Range" Then Exit Sub
    Application.ScreenUpdating = False

'    Create subsets of original selection
    On Error Resume Next
    Set FormulaCells = Selection.SpecialCells(xlFormulas, xlNumbers)
    Set ConstantCells = Selection.SpecialCells(xlConstants, xlNumbers)
    On Error GoTo 0

'    Process the formula cells
    If Not FormulaCells Is Nothing Then
        For Each cell In FormulaCells
            If cell.Value < 0 Then
                cell.Interior.Color = RGB(255, 0, 0)
            Else
                cell.Interior.Color = xlNone
            End If
```

```
                Next cell
        End If

'       Process the constant cells
        If Not ConstantCells Is Nothing Then
            For Each cell In ConstantCells
                If cell.Value < 0 Then
                    cell.Interior.Color = RGB(255, 0, 0)
                Else
                    cell.Interior.Color = xlNone
                End If
            Next cell
        End If
    End Sub
```

> **NOTE**
>
> The `On Error` statement is necessary because the `SpecialCells` method generates an error if no cells qualify.

> **ON THE WEB**
>
> A workbook that contains the three `ColorNegative` procedures is available on this book's website in the `efficient looping.xlsm` file.

Deleting all empty rows

The following procedure deletes all empty rows in the active worksheet. This routine is fast and efficient because it doesn't check all rows. It checks only the rows in the used range, which is determined by using the `UsedRange` property of the `Worksheet` object.

```
    Sub DeleteEmptyRows()
        Dim LastRow As Long
        Dim r As Long
        Dim Counter As Long
        Application.ScreenUpdating = False
        LastRow = ActiveSheet.UsedRange.Rows.Count+ActiveSheet.UsedRange
    .Rows(1).Row-1
        For r = LastRow To 1 Step -1
            If Application.WorksheetFunction.CountA(Rows(r)) = 0 Then
                Rows(r).Delete
                Counter = Counter + 1
            End If
        Next r
        Application.ScreenUpdating = True
        MsgBox Counter & " empty rows were deleted."
    End Sub
```

The first step is to determine the last used row and then assign this row number to the LastRow variable. This calculation isn't as simple as you might think because the used range may or may not begin in row 1. Therefore, LastRow is calculated by determining the number of rows in the used range, adding the first row number in the used range, and subtracting 1.

The procedure uses Excel's COUNTA worksheet function to determine whether a row is empty. If this function returns 0 for a particular row, the row is empty. Note that the procedure works on the rows from bottom to top and also uses a negative step value in the For-Next loop. This negative step value is necessary because deleting rows causes all subsequent rows to move up in the worksheet. If the looping occurred from top to bottom, the counter in the loop wouldn't be accurate after a row is deleted.

The macro uses another variable, Counter, to keep track of how many rows were deleted. This number is displayed in a message box when the procedure ends.

ON THE WEB

A workbook that contains this example is available on this book's website in a file named delete empty rows.xlsm.

Duplicating rows a variable number of times

The example in this section demonstrates how to use VBA to create duplicates of a row. Figure 7.9 shows a worksheet for an office raffle. Column A contains the name, and column B contains the number of tickets purchased by each person. Column C contains a random number (generated by the RAND function). The winner will be determined by sorting the data based on column C (the highest random number wins).

FIGURE 7.9

The goal is to duplicate rows based on the value in column B.

	A	B	C
1	Name	Number of Tickets	Random
2	Alan	1	0.385122758
3	Barbara	2	0.737801364
4	Charlie	1	0.72032982
5	Dave	5	0.823130612
6	Frank	3	0.974566594
7	Gilda	1	0.831766496
8	Huber	1	0.581869402
9	Inz	2	0.697289004
10	Mark	1	0.338082585
11	Norah	10	0.99269247
12	Penelope	2	0.678444158
13	Rance	1	0.257724913
14	Wendy	2	0.929109316

The macro duplicates the rows so that each person will have a row for each ticket purchased. For example, Barbara purchased two tickets, so she should have two rows (and two chances to win).

The procedure to insert the new rows is shown here:

```
Sub DupeRows()
    Dim cell As Range
'   First cell with number of tickets
    Set cell = Range("B2")
    Do While Not IsEmpty(cell)
        If cell > 1 Then
            Range(cell.Offset(1, 0), cell.Offset(cell.Value - 1, _
                0)).EntireRow.Insert
            Range(cell, cell.Offset(cell.Value - 1, 1)).EntireRow.FillDown
        End If
        Set cell = cell.Offset(cell.Value, 0)
    Loop
End Sub
```

The cell object variable is initialized to cell B2, the first cell that has a number. The loop inserts new rows and then copies the row using the FillDown method. The cell variable is incremented to the next person, and the loop continues until an empty cell is encountered. Figure 7.10 shows a portion of the worksheet after running this procedure.

FIGURE 7.10

New rows were added, according to the value in column B.

	A	B	C
1	Name	Number of Tickets	Random
2	Alan	1	0.363036928
3	Barbara	2	0.033243987
4	Barbara	2	0.476445932
5	Charlie	1	0.676207587
6	Dave	5	0.053251416
7	Dave	5	0.701853459
8	Dave	5	0.621100984
9	Dave	5	0.01907403
10	Dave	5	0.54046886
11	Frank	3	0.98366256
12	Frank	3	0.012200271
13	Frank	3	0.674546551
14	Gilda	1	0.115380601
15	Huber	1	0.466506991
16	Inz	2	0.189600728
17	Inz	2	0.848909178
18	Mark	1	0.300738796

Determining whether a range is contained in another range

The following `InRange` function accepts two arguments, both `Range` objects. The function returns `True` if the first range is contained in the second range. This function can be used in a worksheet formula, but it's more useful when called by another procedure.

```
Function InRange(rng1, rng2) As Boolean
'    Returns True if rng1 is a subset of rng2
    On Error GoTo ErrHandler
    If Union(rng1, rng2).Address = rng2.Address Then
        InRange = True
        Exit Function
    End If
ErrHandler:
    InRange = False
End Function
```

The `Union` method of the `Application` object returns a `Range` object that represents the union of two `Range` objects. The union consists of all the cells from both ranges. If the address of the union of the two ranges is the same as the address of the second range, the first range is contained in the second range.

If the two ranges are in different worksheets, the `Union` method generates an error. The `On Error` statement handles this situation by directing execution to the error handler where the function is set to `False`.

Determining a cell's data type

Excel provides a number of built-in functions that can help determine the type of data contained in a cell. Examples of these functions are `ISTEXT`, `ISLOGICAL`, and `ISERROR`. In addition, VBA includes functions such as `IsEmpty`, `IsDate`, and `IsNumeric`.

The following function, named `CellType`, accepts a range argument and returns a string (Blank, Text, Logical, Error, Date, Time, or Number) that describes the data type of the upper-left cell in the range.

```
Function CellType(Rng) As String
'    Returns the cell type of the upper-left cell in a range
    Dim TheCell As Range
    Set TheCell = Rng.Range("A1")
```

```
    Select Case True
        Case IsEmpty(TheCell)
            CELLTYPE = "Blank"
        Case TheCell.NumberFormat = "@"
            CELLTYPE = "Text"
        Case Application.IsText(TheCell)
            CELLTYPE = "Text"
        Case Application.IsLogical(TheCell)
            CELLTYPE = "Logical"
        Case Application.IsErr(TheCell)
            CELLTYPE = "Error"
        Case IsDate(TheCell)
            CELLTYPE = "Date"
        Case InStr(1, TheCell.Text, ":") <> 0
            CELLTYPE = "Time"
        Case IsNumeric(TheCell)
            CELLTYPE = "Number"
    End Select
End Function
```

You can use this function in a worksheet formula or from another VBA procedure. In Figure 7.11, the function is used in formulas in column B. These formulas use data in column A as the argument. Column C is just a description of the data.

FIGURE 7.11

Using a function to determine the type of data in a cell

⟋	A	B	C
1	145.4	Number	A simple value
2	8.6	Number	Formula that returns a value
3	Budget Sheet	Text	Simple text
4	FALSE	Logical	Logical formula
5	TRUE	Logical	Logical value
6	#DIV/0!	Error	Formula error
7	9/17/2012	Date	Formula that returns a date
8	4:00 PM	Time	A time
9	1/13/10 5:25 AM	Date	A date and a time
10	143	Text	Value preceded by apostrophe
11	434	Text	Cell formatted as Text
12	A1:C4	Text	Text with a colon
13		Blank	Empty cell
14		Text	Cell with a single space
15		Text	Cell with an empty string (single apostrophe)

Note the use of the Set TheCell statement. The CellType function accepts a range argument of any size, but this statement causes it to operate on only the upper-left cell in the range (which is represented by the TheCell variable).

ON THE WEB

A workbook that contains this function is available on this book's website in the `celltype function.xlsm` file.

Reading and writing ranges

Many VBA tasks involve transferring values either from an array to a range or from a range to an array. Excel reads from ranges much faster than it writes to ranges because (presumably) the latter operation involves the calculation engine. The WriteReadRange procedure that follows demonstrates the relative speeds of writing and reading a range.

This procedure creates an array and then uses For-Next loops to write the array to a range and then read the range back into the array. It calculates the time required for each operation by using the VBA Timer function.

```
Sub WriteReadRange()
    Dim MyArray()
    Dim Time1 As Double
    Dim NumElements As Long, i As Long
    Dim WriteTime As String, ReadTime As String
    Dim Msg As String

    NumElements = 250000
    ReDim MyArray(1 To NumElements)

'   Fill the array
    For i = 1 To NumElements
        MyArray(i) = i
    Next i

'   Write the array to a range
    Time1 = Timer
    For i = 1 To NumElements
        Cells(i, 1) = MyArray(i)
    Next i
    WriteTime = Format(Timer - Time1, "00:00")

'   Read the range into the array
    Time1 = Timer
    For i = 1 To NumElements
        MyArray(i) = Cells(i, 1)
    Next i
    ReadTime = Format(Timer - Time1, "00:00")
```

```
'   Show results
    Msg = "Write: " & WriteTime
    Msg = Msg & vbCrLf
    Msg = Msg & "Read: " & ReadTime
    MsgBox Msg, vbOKOnly, NumElements & " Elements"
End Sub
```

The results of the timed test will be presented in the form of a message box telling you how long it took to write and read 250,000 elements to and from an array (see Figure 7.12).

FIGURE 7.12

Displaying the time to write to a range and read from a range, using a loop

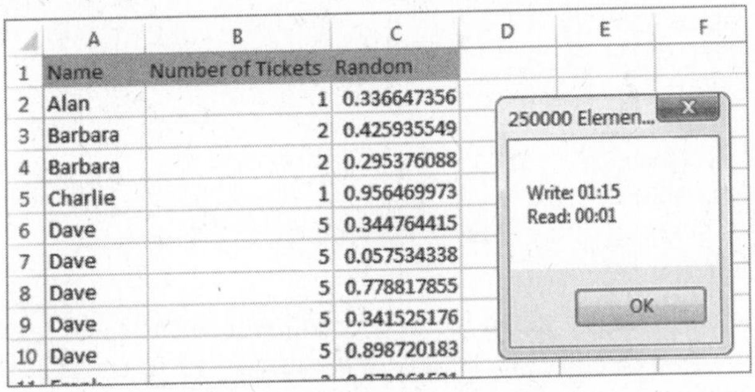

A better way to write to a range

The example in the preceding section uses a For-Next loop to transfer the contents of an array to a worksheet range. In this section, we demonstrate a more efficient way to accomplish this task.

Start with the example that follows, which illustrates the most obvious (but not the most efficient) way to fill a range. This example uses a For-Next loop to insert its values in a range.

```
Sub LoopFillRange()
'   Fill a range by looping through cells

    Dim CellsDown As Long, CellsAcross As Integer
    Dim CurrRow As Long, CurrCol As Integer
    Dim StartTime As Double
    Dim CurrVal As Long

'   Get the dimensions
    CellsDown = InputBox("How many cells down?")
    If CellsDown = 0 Then Exit Sub
```

239

```
        CellsAcross = InputBox("How many cells across?")
        If CellsAcross = 0 Then Exit Sub

    '   Record starting time
        StartTime = Timer

    '   Loop through cells and insert values
        CurrVal = 1
        Application.ScreenUpdating = False
        For CurrRow = 1 To CellsDown
            For CurrCol = 1 To CellsAcross
                ActiveCell.Offset(CurrRow - 1, _
                  CurrCol - 1).Value = CurrVal
                CurrVal = CurrVal + 1
            Next CurrCol
        Next CurrRow

    '   Display elapsed time
        Application.ScreenUpdating = True
        MsgBox Format(Timer - StartTime, "00.00") & " seconds"
    End Sub
```

The example that follows demonstrates a much faster way to produce the same result. This code inserts the values into an array and then uses a single statement to transfer the contents of an array to the range.

```
Sub ArrayFillRange()
'   Fill a range by transferring an array

    Dim CellsDown As Long, CellsAcross As Integer
    Dim i As Long, j As Integer
    Dim StartTime As Double
    Dim TempArray() As Long
    Dim TheRange As Range
    Dim CurrVal As Long

'   Get the dimensions
    CellsDown = InputBox("How many cells down?")
    If CellsDown = 0 Then Exit Sub
    CellsAcross = InputBox("How many cells across?")
    If CellsAcross = 0 Then Exit Sub

    '   Record starting time
    StartTime = Timer

    '   Redimension temporary array
    ReDim TempArray(1 To CellsDown, 1 To CellsAcross)
```

```
'   Set worksheet range
    Set TheRange = ActiveCell.Range(Cells(1, 1), _
      Cells(CellsDown, CellsAcross))

'   Fill the temporary array
    CurrVal = 0
    Application.ScreenUpdating = False
    For i = 1 To CellsDown
        For j = 1 To CellsAcross
            TempArray(i, j) = CurrVal + 1
            CurrVal = CurrVal + 1
        Next j
    Next i

'   Transfer temporary array to worksheet
    TheRange.Value = TempArray

'   Display elapsed time
    Application.ScreenUpdating = True
    MsgBox Format(Timer - StartTime, "00.00") & " seconds"
End Sub
```

On the author's system, using the loop method to fill a 1000 × 250-cell range (250,000 cells) took 15.80 seconds. The array transfer method took only 0.15 seconds to generate the same results—more than 100 times faster! The moral of this story? If you need to transfer large amounts of data to a worksheet, avoid looping whenever possible.

NOTE

The timing results are highly dependent on the presence of formulas. Generally, you'll get faster transfer times if no workbooks are open that contain formulas or if you set the calculation mode to Manual.

ON THE WEB

A workbook that contains the `WriteReadRange`, `LoopFillRange`, and `ArrayFillRange` procedures is available on this book's website. The file is named `loop vs array fill range.xlsm`.

Transferring one-dimensional arrays

The example in the preceding section involves a two-dimensional array, which works out nicely for row-and-column-based worksheets.

When transferring a one-dimensional array to a range, the range must be horizontal—that is, one row with multiple *columns*. If you need the data in a vertical range instead, you must first transpose the array to make it vertical. You can use Excel's TRANSPOSE function to do this. The following example transfers a 100-element array to a vertical worksheet range (A1:A100):

```
Range("A1:A100").Value = Application.WorksheetFunction.
Transpose(MyArray)
```

Transferring a range to a variant array

This section discusses yet another way to work with worksheet data in VBA. The following example transfers a range of cells to a two-dimensional variant array. Then message boxes display the upper bounds for each dimension of the variant array.

```
Sub RangeToVariant()
    Dim x As Variant
    x = Range("A1:L600").Value
    MsgBox UBound(x, 1)
    MsgBox UBound(x, 2)
End Sub
```

In this example, the first message box displays 600 (the number of rows in the original range), and the second message box displays 12 (the number of columns). You'll find that transferring the range data to a variant array is virtually instantaneous.

The following example reads a range (named data) into a variant array, performs a simple multiplication operation on each element in the array, and then transfers the variant array back to the range:

```
Sub RangeToVariant2()
    Dim x As Variant
    Dim r As Long, c As Integer

'    Read the data into the variant
    x = Range("data").Value

'    Loop through the variant array
    For r = 1 To UBound(x, 1)
        For c = 1 To UBound(x, 2)
'            Multiply by 2
            x(r, c) = x(r, c) * 2
        Next c
    Next r

'    Transfer the variant back to the sheet
    Range("data") = x
End Sub
```

You'll find that this procedure runs amazingly fast. Working with 30,000 cells took less than 1 second on this author's computer.

Selecting cells by value

The example in this section demonstrates how to select cells based on their value. Oddly, Excel doesn't provide a direct way to perform this operation. The SelectByValue procedure follows. In this example, the code selects cells that contain a negative value, but you can easily change the code to select cells based on other criteria.

```vba
Sub SelectByValue()
    Dim Cell As Object
    Dim FoundCells As Range
    Dim WorkRange As Range

    If TypeName(Selection) <> "Range" Then Exit Sub

'   Check all or selection?
    If Selection.CountLarge = 1 Then
        Set WorkRange = ActiveSheet.UsedRange
    Else
        Set WorkRange = Application.Intersect(Selection, ActiveSheet _
.UsedRange)
    End If

'   Reduce the search to numeric cells only
    On Error Resume Next
    Set WorkRange = WorkRange.SpecialCells(xlConstants, xlNumbers)
    If WorkRange Is Nothing Then Exit Sub
    On Error GoTo 0

'   Loop through each cell, add to the FoundCells range if it qualifies
    For Each Cell In WorkRange
        If Cell.Value < 0 Then
            If FoundCells Is Nothing Then
                Set FoundCells = Cell
            Else
                Set FoundCells = Union(FoundCells, Cell)
            End If
        End If
    Next Cell

'   Show message, or select the cells
    If FoundCells Is Nothing Then
```

```
                MsgBox "No cells qualify."
        Else
                FoundCells.Select
                MsgBox "Selected " & FoundCells.Count & " cells."
        End If
    End Sub
```

The procedure starts by checking the selection. If it's a single cell, the used range of the worksheet is searched. If the selection is at least two cells, only the selected range is searched. The range to be searched is further refined by using the SpecialCells method to create a Range object that consists only of the numeric constants.

The code in the For-Next loop examines the cell's value. If it meets the criterion (less than 0), the cell is added to the FoundCells Range object by using the Union method. Note that you can't use the Union method for the first cell. If the FoundCells range contains no cells, attempting to use the Union method will generate an error. Therefore, the code checks whether FoundCells is Nothing.

When the loop ends, the FoundCells object will consist of the cells that meet the criterion (or will be Nothing if no cells were found). If no cells are found, a message box appears saying so. Otherwise, the cells are selected, and a message box displays the number of cells selected.

ON THE WEB

This example is available on this book's website in the select by value.xlsm file.

Copying a noncontiguous range

If you've ever attempted to copy a noncontiguous range selection, you discovered that Excel doesn't support such an operation. Attempting to do so displays the following error message:

```
    That command cannot be used on multiple selections.
```

An exception is when you attempt to copy a multiple selection that consists of entire rows or columns or when the multiple selections are in the same row(s) or same column(s). Excel *does* allow those operations. But when you paste the copied cells, all blanks are removed.

When you encounter a limitation in Excel, you can often circumvent it by creating a macro. The example in this section is a VBA procedure that allows you to copy a multiple selection to another location.

```
    Sub CopyMultipleSelection()
        Dim SelAreas() As Range
        Dim PasteRange As Range
        Dim UpperLeft As Range
        Dim NumAreas As Long, i As Long
        Dim TopRow As Long, LeftCol As Long
```

```
        Dim RowOffset As Long, ColOffset As Long

        If TypeName(Selection) <> "Range" Then Exit Sub

'       Store the areas as separate Range objects
        NumAreas = Selection.Areas.Count
        ReDim SelAreas(1 To NumAreas)
        For i = 1 To NumAreas
            Set SelAreas(i) = Selection.Areas(i)
        Next

'       Determine the upper-left cell in the multiple selection
        TopRow = ActiveSheet.Rows.Count
        LeftCol = ActiveSheet.Columns.Count
        For i = 1 To NumAreas
            If SelAreas(i).Row < TopRow Then TopRow = SelAreas(i).Row
            If SelAreas(i).Column < LeftCol Then LeftCol = SelAreas(i)
.Column
        Next
        Set UpperLeft = Cells(TopRow, LeftCol)

'       Get the paste address
        On Error Resume Next
        Set PasteRange = Application.InputBox _
          (Prompt:="Specify the upper-left cell for the paste range:", _
          Title:="Copy Multiple Selection", _
          Type:=8)
        On Error GoTo 0
'       Exit if canceled
        If TypeName(PasteRange) <> "Range" Then Exit Sub

'       Make sure only the upper-left cell is used
        Set PasteRange = PasteRange.Range("A1")

'       Copy and paste each area
        For i = 1 To NumAreas
            RowOffset = SelAreas(i).Row - TopRow
            ColOffset = SelAreas(i).Column - LeftCol
            SelAreas(i).Copy PasteRange.Offset(RowOffset, ColOffset)
        Next i
    End Sub
```

Figure 7.13 shows the prompt to select the destination location.

ON THE WEB

This book's website contains a workbook with this example, plus another version that warns the user if data will be overwritten. The file is named copy multiple selection.xlsm.

FIGURE 7.13

Using Excel's InputBox method to prompt for a cell location

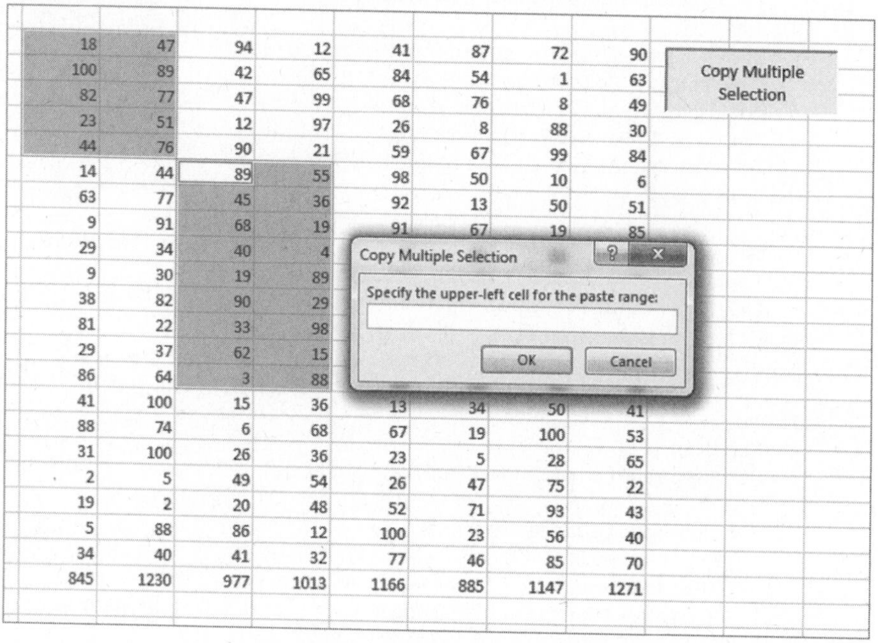

Working with Workbooks and Sheets

The examples in this section demonstrate various ways to use VBA to work with workbooks and worksheets.

Saving all workbooks

The following procedure loops through all of the workbooks in the Workbooks collection and saves each file that has been saved previously:

```
Public Sub SaveAllWorkbooks()
    Dim Book As Workbook
    For Each Book In Workbooks
        If Book.Path <> "" Then Book.Save
    Next Book
End Sub
```

Note the use of the Path property. If a workbook's Path property is empty, the file has never been saved (it's a newly created workbook). This procedure ignores such workbooks and saves only the workbooks that have a nonempty Path property.

A more efficient approach also checks the Saved property. This property is True if the workbook has not been changed since it was last saved. The SaveAllWorkbooks2 procedure doesn't save files that don't need to be saved.

```
Public Sub SaveAllWorkbooks2()
    Dim Book As Workbook
    For Each Book In Workbooks
        If Book.Path <> "" Then
            If Book.Saved <> True Then
                Book.Save
            End If
        End If
    Next Book
End Sub
```

Saving and closing all workbooks

The following procedure loops through the Workbooks collection. The code saves and closes all workbooks.

```
Sub CloseAllWorkbooks()
    Dim Book As Workbook
    For Each Book In Workbooks
        If Book.Name <> ThisWorkbook.Name Then
            Book.Close savechanges:=True
        End If
    Next Book
    ThisWorkbook.Close savechanges:=True
End Sub
```

The procedure uses an If statement in the For-Next loop to determine whether the workbook is the one that contains the code. This statement is necessary because closing the workbook that contains the procedure would end the code, and subsequent workbooks wouldn't be affected. After all the other workbooks are closed, the workbook that contains the code closes itself.

Hiding all but the selection

The example in this section hides all rows and columns in a worksheet except those in the current range selection:

```
Sub HideRowsAndColumns()
    Dim row1 As Long, row2 As Long
    Dim col1 As Long, col2 As Long

    If TypeName(Selection) <> "Range" Then Exit Sub

'   If last row or last column is hidden, unhide all and quit
    If Rows(Rows.Count).EntireRow.Hidden Or _
      Columns(Columns.Count).EntireColumn.Hidden Then
```

```
        Cells.EntireColumn.Hidden = False
        Cells.EntireRow.Hidden = False
        Exit Sub
    End If

    row1 = Selection.Rows(1).Row
    row2 = row1 + Selection.Rows.Count - 1
    col1 = Selection.Columns(1).Column
    col2 = col1 + Selection.Columns.Count - 1

    Application.ScreenUpdating = False
    On Error Resume Next
'   Hide rows
    Range(Cells(1, 1), Cells(row1 - 1, 1)).EntireRow.Hidden = True
    Range(Cells(row2 + 1, 1), Cells(Rows.Count, 1)).EntireRow _
.Hidden = True
'   Hide columns
    Range(Cells(1, 1), Cells(1, col1 - 1)).EntireColumn.Hidden = True
    Range(Cells(1, col2 + 1), Cells(1, Columns.Count)).EntireColumn _
.Hidden = True
End Sub
```

Figure 7.14 shows an example. If the range selection consists of a noncontiguous range, the first area is used as the basis for hiding rows and columns. Note that it's a toggle. Executing the procedures when the last row or last column is hidden unhides all rows and columns.

FIGURE 7.14

All rows and columns are hidden, except for a range (G7:L19).

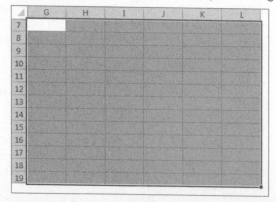

ON THE WEB

A workbook with this example is available on this book's website in the `hide rows and columns.xlsm` file.

Creating a hyperlink table of contents

The CreateTOC procedure inserts a new worksheet at the beginning of the active workbook. It then creates a table of contents, in the form of a list of hyperlinks to each worksheet.

```
Sub CreateTOC()
    Dim i As Integer
    Sheets.Add Before:=Sheets(1)
    For i = 2 To Worksheets.Count
      ActiveSheet.Hyperlinks.Add _
        Anchor:=Cells(i, 1), _
        Address:="", _
        SubAddress:="'" & Worksheets(i).Name & "'!A1", _
        TextToDisplay:=Worksheets(i).Name
    Next i
End Sub
```

It's not possible to create a hyperlink to a chart sheet, so the code uses the Worksheet collection rather than the Sheets collection.

Figure 7.15 shows an example of a hyperlink table of contents that contains worksheets composed of month names.

FIGURE 7.15

Hyperlinks to each worksheet, created by a macro

ON THE WEB

A workbook with this example is available on this book's website in the create hyperlinks.xlsm file.

Synchronizing worksheets

If you use multisheet workbooks, you probably know that Excel can't synchronize the sheets in a workbook. In other words, there is no automatic way to force all sheets to have the same selected range and upper-left cell. The VBA macro that follows uses the active worksheet as a base and then performs the following on all other worksheets in the workbook:

- Selects the same range as the active sheet
- Makes the upper-left cell the same as the active sheet

The following is the listing for the procedure:

```vba
Sub SynchSheets()
'   Duplicates the active sheet's active cell and upper-left cell
'   Across all worksheets
    If TypeName(ActiveSheet) <> "Worksheet" Then Exit Sub
    Dim UserSheet As Worksheet, sht As Worksheet
    Dim TopRow As Long, LeftCol As Integer
    Dim UserSel As String

    Application.ScreenUpdating = False

'   Remember the current sheet
    Set UserSheet = ActiveSheet

'   Store info from the active sheet
    TopRow = ActiveWindow.ScrollRow
    LeftCol = ActiveWindow.ScrollColumn
    UserSel = ActiveWindow.RangeSelection.Address

'   Loop through the worksheets
    For Each sht In ActiveWorkbook.Worksheets
        If sht.Visible Then 'skip hidden sheets
            sht.Activate
            Range(UserSel).Select
            ActiveWindow.ScrollRow = TopRow
            ActiveWindow.ScrollColumn = LeftCol
        End If
    Next sht

'   Restore the original position
    UserSheet.Activate
    Application.ScreenUpdating = True
End Sub
```

ON THE WEB

A workbook with this example is available on this book's website in the synchronize sheets.xlsm file.

VBA Techniques

The examples in this section illustrate common VBA techniques that you might be able to adapt for your own projects.

Toggling a Boolean property

A *Boolean property* is one that is either `True` or `False`. The easiest way to toggle a Boolean property is to use the `Not` operator, as shown in the following example, which toggles the `WrapText` property of a selection:

```
Sub ToggleWrapText()
'   Toggles text wrap alignment for selected cells
    If TypeName(Selection) = "Range" Then
        Selection.WrapText = Not ActiveCell.WrapText
    End If
End Sub
```

You can modify this procedure to toggle other Boolean properties.

Note that the active cell is used as the basis for toggling. When a range is selected and the property values in the cells are inconsistent (for example, some cells are bold and others are not), Excel uses the active cell to determine how to toggle. If the active cell is bold, for example, all cells in the selection are made not bold when you click the Bold button. This simple procedure mimics the way Excel works, which is usually the best practice.

Note also that this procedure uses the `TypeName` function to check whether the selection is a range. If the selection isn't a range, nothing happens.

You can use the `Not` operator to toggle many other properties. For example, to toggle the display of row and column borders in a worksheet, use the following code:

```
ActiveWindow.DisplayHeadings = Not ActiveWindow.DisplayHeadings
```

To toggle the display of gridlines in the active worksheet, use the following code:

```
ActiveWindow.DisplayGridlines = Not ActiveWindow.DisplayGridlines
```

Displaying the date and time

If you understand the serial number system that Excel uses to store dates and times, you won't have any problems using dates and times in your VBA procedures.

The `DateAndTime` procedure displays a message box with the current date and time, as depicted in Figure 7.16. This example also displays a personalized message in the message box's title bar.

The procedure uses the `Date` function as an argument for the `Format` function. The result is a string with a nicely formatted date. We used the same technique to get a nicely formatted time.

FIGURE 7.16

A message box displaying the date and time

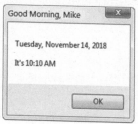

```
Sub DateAndTime()
'    Displays the current date and time
    Dim TheDate As String, TheTime As String
    Dim Greeting As String
    Dim FullName As String, FirstName As String
    Dim SpaceInName As Long

    TheDate = Format(Date, "Long Date")
    TheTime = Format(Time, "Medium Time")

'   Determine greeting based on time
    Select Case Time
        Case Is < TimeSerial(12, 0, 0): Greeting = "Good Morning, "
        Case Is >= TimeSerial(17, 0, 0): Greeting = "Good Evening, "
        Case Else: Greeting = "Good Afternoon, "
    End Select

'   Last saved
    LastSaved = "Document Last Saved: " & _
      ActiveWorkbook.BuiltinDocumentProperties(12)

'   Append user's first name to greeting
    FullName = Application.UserName
    SpaceInName = InStr(1, FullName, " ", 1)

'   Handle situation when name has no space
    If SpaceInName = 0 Then SpaceInName = Len(FullName)
    FirstName = Left(FullName, SpaceInName)
    Greeting = Greeting & FirstName

'   Show the message
    MsgBox TheDate & vbCrLf & vbCrLf & "It's " & TheTime, vbOKOnly, _
Greeting
End Sub
```

In the preceding example, we used named formats (Long Date and Medium Time) to ensure that the macro will work properly regardless of the user's international settings. You can, however, use other formats. For example, to display the date in mm/dd/yy format, you can use a statement like the following:

```
TheDate = Format(Date, "mm/dd/yy")
```

We used a Select Case construct to base the greeting displayed in the message box's title bar on the time of day. VBA time values work just as they do in Excel. If the time is less than .5 (noon), it's morning. If it's greater than .7083 (5 p.m.), it's evening. Otherwise, it's afternoon. We took the easy way out and used VBA's TimeValue function, which returns a time value from a string.

The next series of statements determines the user's first name, as recorded in the General tab in Excel's Options dialog box. We used the VBA InStr function to locate the first space in the user's name. The MsgBox function concatenates the date and time but uses the built-in vbCrLf constant to insert a line break between them. vbOKOnly is a predefined constant that returns 0, causing the message box to appear with only an OK button. The final argument is the Greeting, constructed earlier in the procedure.

> **NOTE**
>
> The DateAndTime procedure is available on this book's website, in a file named date and time.xlsm.

Displaying friendly time

If you're not a stickler for 100 percent accuracy, you might like the FT function, listed here. FT, which stands for *friendly time,* displays a time difference in words.

```
Function FT(t1, t2)
    Dim SDif As Double, DDif As Double

    If Not (IsDate(t1) And IsDate(t2)) Then
        FT = CVErr(xlErrValue)
        Exit Function
    End If

    DDif = Abs(t2 - t1)
    SDif = DDif * 24 * 60 * 60

    If DDif < 1 Then
        If SDif < 10 Then FT = "Just now": Exit Function
        If SDif < 60 Then FT = SDif & " seconds ago": Exit Function
        If SDif < 120 Then FT = "a minute ago": Exit Function
        If SDif < 3600 Then FT = Round(SDif / 60, 0) & _
          "minutes ago": Exit Function
        If SDif < 7200 Then FT = "An hour ago": Exit Function
        If SDif < 86400 Then FT = Round(SDif / 3600, 0) & _
          " hours ago": Exit Function
```

```
        End If
        If DDif = 1 Then FT = "Yesterday": Exit Function
        If DDif < 7 Then FT = Round(DDif, 0) & " days ago": Exit Function
        If DDif < 31 Then FT = Round(DDif / 7, 0) & " weeks ago": Exit
    Function
        If DDif < 365 Then FT = Round(DDif / 30, 0) & " months ago": Exit
    Function
        FT = Round(DDif / 365, 0) & " years ago"
    End Function
```

Figure 7.17 shows examples of this function used in formulas. If you actually have a need for such a way to display time differences, this procedure leaves lots of room for improvement. For example, you can write code to prevent displays such as *1 months ago* and *1 years ago*.

FIGURE 7.17

Using a function to display time differences in a friendly manner

	A	B	C
1	**Time1**	**Time 2**	**Time Difference**
2	3/30/2018 8:45 AM	3/30/2018 8:46 AM	a minute ago
3	3/30/2018 8:45 AM	4/1/2018 1:33 AM	2 days ago
4	3/30/2018 8:45 AM	4/13/2018 1:47 AM	2 weeks ago
5	3/30/2018 8:45 AM	5/1/2018 2:20 PM	1 months ago
6	3/30/2018 8:45 AM	6/28/2018 2:04 PM	3 months ago
7	3/30/2018 8:45 AM	1/24/2019 11:37 AM	10 months ago
8	3/30/2018 8:45 AM	4/21/2019 11:09 PM	1 years ago
9	3/30/2018 8:45 AM	6/16/2026 4:25 PM	8 years ago
10			

> **NOTE**
>
> This example is available on this book's website. The file is named `friendly time.xlsm`.

Getting a list of fonts

If you need to get a list of all installed fonts, you'll find that Excel doesn't provide a direct way to retrieve that information. The technique described here takes advantage of the fact that Excel still supports the old CommandBar properties and methods for compatibility with pre–Excel 2007 versions. These properties and methods were used to work with tool-bars and menus.

The ShowInstalledFonts macro displays a list of the installed fonts in column A of the active worksheet. It creates a temporary toolbar (a CommandBar object), adds the Font control, and reads the font names from that control. The temporary toolbar is then deleted.

```
    Sub ShowInstalledFonts()
        Dim FontList As CommandBarControl
        Dim TempBar As CommandBar
        Dim i As Long
```

```
'   Create temporary CommandBar
    Set TempBar = Application.CommandBars.Add
    Set FontList = TempBar.Controls.Add(ID:=1728)

'   Put the fonts into column A
    Range("A:A").ClearContents
    For i = 0 To FontList.ListCount - 1
        Cells(i + 1, 1) = FontList.List(i + 1)
    Next i

'   Delete temporary CommandBar
    TempBar.Delete
End Sub
```

TIP

As an option, you can display each font name in the actual font (as shown in Figure 7.18). To do so, add this statement inside the For-Next loop:

```
Cells(i + 1, 1).Font.Name = FontList.List(i + 1)
```

Be aware, however, that using many fonts in a workbook can eat up lots of system resources and could even crash

ON THE WEB

This procedure is available on the book's website in the list fonts.xlsm file.

FIGURE 7.18

Listing font names in the actual fonts

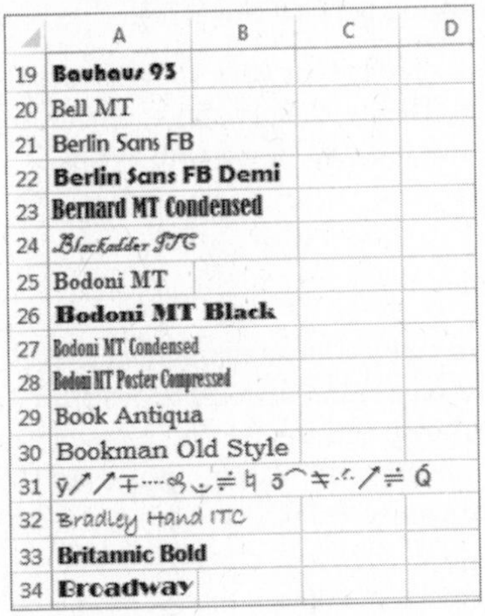

Sorting an array

Although Excel has a built-in command to sort worksheet ranges, VBA doesn't offer a method to sort arrays. One viable (but cumbersome) work-around is to transfer your array to a worksheet range, sort it by using Excel's commands, and then return the result to your array. This method is surprisingly fast, but if you need something faster, use a sorting routine written in VBA.

In this section, we cover four different sorting techniques.

Worksheet sort A *worksheet sort* transfers an array to a worksheet range, sorts it, and transfers it back to the array. This procedure accepts an array as its only argument.

Bubble sort A *bubble sort* is a simple sorting technique (also used in the Chapter 4 sheet-sorting example). Although easy to program, the bubble-sorting algorithm tends to be slow, especially with many elements.

Quick sort A *quick sort* is a much faster sorting routine than bubble sort, but it is also more difficult to understand. This technique works only with `Integer` and `Long` data types.

Counting sort A *counting sort* is lightning fast but difficult to understand. Like the quick sort, this technique works only with `Integer` and `Long` data types.

> **ON THE WEB**
>
> The book's website includes a workbook application that demonstrates these sorting methods. This workbook, named `sorting demo.xlsm`, is useful for comparing these techniques with arrays of varying sizes. However, you can also copy the procedures and use them in your code.

The worksheet sort algorithm is amazingly fast, especially when you consider that the array is transferred to the sheet, sorted, and then transferred back to the array.

The bubble sort algorithm is the simplest and is reasonably fast with small arrays, but for larger arrays (more than 10,000 elements), forget it. The quick sort and counting sort algorithms are blazingly fast, but they're limited to `Integer` and `Long` data types.

Figure 7.19 shows the dialog box for this project.

Processing a series of files

One common use for macros is to perform repetitive tasks. The example in this section demonstrates how to execute a macro that operates on several different files stored on disk. This example, which may help you set up your own routine for this type of task, prompts the user for a file specification and then processes all matching files. In this case, processing consists of importing the file and entering a series of summary formulas that describe the data in the file.

FIGURE 7.19

Comparing the time required to perform sorts of various array sizes

```vba
Sub BatchProcess()
    Dim FileSpec As String
    Dim i As Integer
    Dim FileName As String
    Dim FileList() As String
    Dim FoundFiles As Integer

'   Specify path and file spec
    FileSpec = ThisWorkbook.Path & "\" & "text??.txt"
    FileName = Dir(FileSpec)

'   Was a file found?
    If FileName <> "" Then
        FoundFiles = 1
        ReDim Preserve FileList(1 To FoundFiles)
        FileList(FoundFiles) = FileName
    Else
        MsgBox "No files were found that match " & FileSpec
        Exit Sub
    End If

'   Get other filenames
    Do
        FileName = Dir
        If FileName = "" Then Exit Do
        FoundFiles = FoundFiles + 1
        ReDim Preserve FileList(1 To FoundFiles)
        FileList(FoundFiles) = FileName & "*"
    Loop
```

```
'    Loop through the files and process them
    For i = 1 To FoundFiles
        Call ProcessFiles(FileList(i))
    Next i
End Sub
```

The matching filenames are stored in an array named FoundFiles, and the procedure uses a For-Next loop to process the files. Within the loop, the processing is done by calling the ProcessFiles procedure, which follows. This simple procedure uses the OpenText method to import the file and then inserts five formulas. You may, of course, substitute your own routine in place of this one.

```
Sub ProcessFiles(FileName As String)
'    Import the file
    Workbooks.OpenText FileName:=FileName, _
      Origin:=xlWindows, _
      StartRow:=1, _
      DataType:=xlFixedWidth, _
      FieldInfo:= _
      Array(Array(0, 1), Array(3, 1), Array(12, 1))
'    Enter summary formulas
    Range("D1").Value = "A"
    Range("D2").Value = "B"
    Range("D3").Value = "C"
    Range("E1:E3").Formula = "=COUNTIF(B:B,D1)"
    Range("F1:F3").Formula = "=SUMIF(B:B,D1,C:C)"
End Sub
```

 For more information about working with files using VBA, refer to Chapter 11, "Working with External Data and Files."

Some Useful Functions for Use in Your Code

In this section, we present some custom utility functions that you may find useful in your own applications and that may provide inspiration for creating similar functions. These functions are most useful when called from another VBA procedure. Therefore, they're declared by using the Private keyword so that they won't appear in Excel's Insert Function dialog box.

ON THE WEB
The examples in this section are available on the book's website in the `vba utility functions.xlsm` file.

The FileExists function

The `FileExists` function takes one argument (a path with a filename) and returns `True` if the file exists.

```
Private Function FileExists(fname) As Boolean
'    Returns TRUE if the file exists
     FileExists = (Dir(fname) <> "")
End Function
```

The FileNameOnly function

The `FileNameOnly` function accepts one argument (a path with a filename) and returns only the filename. In other words, it strips out the path.

```
Private Function FileNameOnly(pname) As String
'    Returns the filename from a path/filename string
     Dim temp As Variant
     length = Len(pname)
     temp = Split(pname, Application.PathSeparator)
     FileNameOnly = temp(UBound(temp))
End Function
```

The function uses the VBA `Split` function, which accepts a string (that includes delimiter characters) and returns a variant array that contains the elements between the delimiter characters. In this case, the `temp` variable contains an array that consists of each text string between the `Application.PathSeparator` (usually a backslash character). For another example of the `Split` function, see the section "Extracting the nth element from a string" later in this chapter.

If the argument is `c:\excel files\backup\budget.xlsx`, the function returns the string `budget.xlsx`.

The `FileNameOnly` function works with any path and filename (even if the file *does not* exist). If the file exists, the following function is a simpler way to strip the path and return only the filename:

```
Private Function FileNameOnly2(pname) As String
     FileNameOnly2 = Dir(pname)
End Function
```

The PathExists function

The `PathExists` function accepts one argument (a path) and returns `True` if the path exists.

```
Private Function PathExists(pname) As Boolean
'   Returns TRUE if the path exists
    If Dir(pname, vbDirectory) = "" Then
      PathExists = False
    Else
      PathExists = (GetAttr(pname) And vbDirectory) = vbDirectory
    End If
End Function
```

The RangeNameExists function

The RangeNameExists function accepts a single argument (a range name) and returns True if the range name exists in the active workbook.

```
Private Function RangeNameExists(nname) As Boolean
'   Returns TRUE if the range name exists
    Dim n As Name
    RangeNameExists = False
    For Each n In ActiveWorkbook.Names
        If UCase(n.Name) = UCase(nname) Then
            RangeNameExists = True
            Exit Function
        End If
    Next n
End Function
```

Another way to write this function follows. This version attempts to create an object variable using the name. If doing so generates an error, the name doesn't exist.

```
Private Function RangeNameExists2(nname) As Boolean
'   Returns TRUE if the range name exists
    Dim n As Range
    On Error Resume Next
    Set n = Range(nname)
    If Err.Number = 0 Then RangeNameExists2 = True _
      Else RangeNameExists2 = False
End Function
```

The SheetExists function

The SheetExists function accepts one argument (a worksheet name) and returns True if the worksheet exists in the active workbook.

```
Private Function SheetExists(sname) As Boolean
'   Returns TRUE if sheet exists in the active workbook
    Dim x As Object
    On Error Resume Next
    Set x = ActiveWorkbook.Sheets(sname)
```

```
     If Err.Number = 0 Then SheetExists = True Else SheetExists = False
End Function
```

The WorkbookIsOpen function

The WorkbookIsOpen function accepts one argument (a workbook name) and returns True if the workbook is open.

```
Private Function WorkbookIsOpen(wbname) As Boolean
'    Returns TRUE if the workbook is open
    Dim x As Workbook
    On Error Resume Next
    Set x = Workbooks(wbname)
    If Err.Number = 0 Then WorkbookIsOpen = True _
        Else WorkbookIsOpen = False
End Function
```

Testing for membership in a collection

The following function procedure is a generic function that you can use to determine whether an object is a member of a collection:

```
Private Function IsInCollection_
  (Coln As Object, Item As String) As Boolean
    Dim Obj As Object
    On Error Resume Next
    Set Obj = Coln(Item)
    IsInCollection = Not Obj Is Nothing
End Function
```

This function accepts two arguments: the collection (an object) and the item (a string) that might or might not be a member of the collection. The function attempts to create an object variable that represents the item in the collection. If the attempt is successful, the function returns True; otherwise, it returns False.

You can use the IsInCollection function in place of three other functions listed in this chapter: RangeNameExists, SheetExists, and WorkbookIsOpen. To determine whether a range named Data exists in the active workbook, call the IsInCollection function with this statement:

```
MsgBox IsInCollection(ActiveWorkbook.Names, "Data")
```

To determine whether a workbook named Budget is open, use this statement:

```
MsgBox IsInCollection(Workbooks, "budget.xlsx")
```

To determine whether the active workbook contains a sheet named Sheet1, use this statement:

```
MsgBox IsInCollection(ActiveWorkbook.Worksheets, "Sheet1")
```

Retrieving a value from a closed workbook

VBA doesn't include a method to retrieve a value from a closed workbook file. You can, however, take advantage of Excel's capability to work with linked files. This section contains a custom VBA function (GetValue, which follows) that retrieves a value from a closed workbook. It does so by calling an *XLM macro*, which is an old-style macro used in versions before Excel 5. Fortunately, Excel still supports this old macro system.

```
Private Function GetValue(path, file, sheet, ref)
'    Retrieves a value from a closed workbook
    Dim arg As String

'    Make sure the file exists
    If Right(path, 1) <> "\" Then path = path & "\"
    If Dir(path & file) = "" Then
        GetValue = "File Not Found"
        Exit Function
    End If

'    Create the argument
    arg = "'" & path & "[" & file & "]" & sheet & "'!" & _
        Range(ref).Range("A1").Address(, , xlR1C1)

'    Execute an XLM macro
    GetValue = ExecuteExcel4Macro(arg)
End Function
```

The GetValue function takes four arguments.

   path: The drive and path to the closed file (for example, "d:\files")

   file: The workbook name (for example, "budget.xlsx")

   sheet: The worksheet name (for example, "Sheet1")

   ref: The cell reference (for example, "C4")

The following Sub procedure demonstrates how to use the GetValue function. It displays the value in cell A1 in Sheet1 of a file named 2019budget.xlsx, located in the XLFiles\Budget directory on drive C.

```
Sub TestGetValue()
    Dim p As String, f As String
    Dim s As String, a As String

    p = "c:\XLFiles\Budget"
    f = "2019budget.xlsx"
    s = "Sheet1"
    a = "A1"
    MsgBox GetValue(p, f, s, a)
End Sub
```

Another example follows. This procedure reads 1,200 values (100 rows and 12 columns) from a closed file and then places the values into the active worksheet.

```
Sub TestGetValue2()
    Dim p As String, f As String
    Dim s As String, a As String
    Dim r As Long, c As Long

    p = "c:\XLFiles\Budget"
    f = "2019Budget.xlsx"
    s = "Sheet1"
    Application.ScreenUpdating = False
    For r = 1 To 100
        For c = 1 To 12
            a = Cells(r, c).Address
            Cells(r, c) = GetValue(p, f, s, a)
        Next c
    Next r
End Sub
```

An alternative is to write code that turns off screen updating, opens the file, gets the value, and then closes the file. Unless the file is very large, the user won't even notice that a file is being opened.

> **NOTE**
>
> The GetValue function doesn't work in a worksheet formula. However, there is no need to use this function in a formula. You can simply create a link formula to retrieve a value from a closed file.

> **ON THE WEB**
>
> This example is available on this book's website in the value from a closed workbook.xlsm file. The example uses a file named myworkbook.xlsx for the closed file.

Some Useful Worksheet Functions

The examples in this section are custom functions that you can use in worksheet formulas. Remember, you must define these Function procedures in a VBA module (not a code module associated with ThisWorkbook, a Sheet, or a UserForm).

> **ON THE WEB**
>
> The examples in this section are available on the book's website in the worksheet functions.xlsm file.

Returning cell formatting information

This section contains a number of custom functions that return information about a cell's formatting. These functions are useful if you need to sort data based on formatting (for example, sort in such a way that all bold cells are together).

> **CAUTION**
>
> You'll find that these functions aren't always updated automatically because changing formatting doesn't trigger Excel's recalculation engine. To force a global recalculation (and update all custom functions), press Ctrl+Alt+F9.
>
> Alternatively, you can add the following statement to your function:
>
> ```
> Application.Volatile
> ```
>
> When this statement is present, pressing F9 will recalculate the function.

The following function returns TRUE if its single-cell argument has bold formatting. If a range is passed as the argument, the function uses the upper-left cell of the range.

```
Function ISBOLD(cell) As Boolean
'   Returns TRUE if cell is bold
    ISBOLD = cell.Range("A1").Font.Bold
End Function
```

Note that this function works only with explicitly applied formatting. It doesn't work for formatting applied using conditional formatting. Excel 2010 introduced DisplayFormat, a new object that takes conditional formatting into account. Here's the ISBOLD function rewritten so that it works also with bold formatting applied as a result of conditional formatting:

```
Function ISBOLD(cell) As Boolean
'   Returns TRUE if cell is bold, even if from conditional formatting
    ISBOLD = cell.Range("A1").DisplayFormat.Font.Bold
End Function
```

The following function returns TRUE if its single-cell argument has italic formatting:

```
Function ISITALIC(cell) As Boolean
'   Returns TRUE if cell is italic
    ISITALIC = cell.Range("A1").Font.Italic
End Function
```

Both functions will return an error if the cell has mixed formatting—for example, if only *some* characters are bold. The following function returns TRUE only if all characters in the cell are bold:

```
Function ALLBOLD(cell) As Boolean
'   Returns TRUE if all characters in cell are bold
    If IsNull(cell.Font.Bold) Then
        ALLBOLD = False
    Else
        ALLBOLD = cell.Font.Bold
```

```
        End If
    End Function
```

You can simplify the ALLBOLD function as follows:

```
Function ALLBOLD (cell) As Boolean
'    Returns TRUE if all characters in cell are bold
    ALLBOLD = Not IsNull(cell.Font.Bold)
End Function
```

The FILLCOLOR function returns an integer that corresponds to the color index of the cell's interior. The actual color depends on the applied workbook theme. If the cell's interior isn't filled, the function returns −4142. This function doesn't work with fill colors applied in tables (created with Insert ⇨ Tables ⇨ Table) or pivot tables. You need to use the DisplayFormat object to detect that type of fill color, as we described previously.

```
Function FILLCOLOR(cell) As Integer
'    Returns an integer corresponding to
'    cell's interior color
    FILLCOLOR = cell.Range("A1").Interior.ColorIndex
End Function
```

A talking worksheet

The SAYIT function uses Excel's text-to-speech generator to "speak" its argument (which can be literal text or a cell reference):

```
Function SAYIT(txt)
    Application.Speech.Speak (txt)
    SAYIT = txt
End Function
```

This function has some amusing possibilities, but it can also be useful. For example, use the function in a formula like this:

```
=IF(SUM(A:A)>25000,SAYIT("Goal Reached"))
```

If the sum of the values in column A exceeds 25,000, you'll hear the synthesized voice tell you that the goal has been reached. You can use the Speak method also at the end of a lengthy procedure. That way, you can do something else and get an audible notice when the procedure ends.

Displaying the date when a file was saved or printed

An Excel workbook contains several built-in document properties, accessible from the BuiltinDocumentProperties property of the Workbook object. The following function returns the date and time that the workbook was last saved:

```
Function LASTSAVED()
    Application.Volatile
    LASTSAVED = ThisWorkbook. _
        BuiltinDocumentProperties("Last Save Time")
End Function
```

The date and time returned by this function are the same date and time that appear in the Related Dates section of Backstage view when you choose File ⇨ Info. Note that the Auto-Save feature also affects this value. In other words, the "Last Save Time" value is not necessarily the last time the file was saved by the *user*.

The following function is similar to LASTSAVED, but it returns the date and time when the workbook was last printed or previewed. If the workbook has never been printed or pre-viewed, the function returns a #VALUE error.

```
Function LASTPRINTED()
    Application.Volatile
    LASTPRINTED = ThisWorkbook. _
      BuiltinDocumentProperties("Last Print Date")
End Function
```

If you use these functions in a formula, you might need to force a recalculation (by pressing F9) to get the current values of these properties.

> **NOTE**
>
> Quite a few additional built-in properties are available, but Excel doesn't use all of them. For example, attempting to access the `Number of Bytes` property will generate an error. For a list of all built-in properties, consult the Help system.

The preceding LASTSAVED and LASTPRINTED functions are designed to be stored in the workbook in which they're used. In some cases, you may want to store the function in a different workbook (for example, personal.xlsb) or in an add-in. Because these functions reference ThisWorkbook, they won't work correctly. The following are more general-purpose versions of these functions. These functions use Application.Caller, which returns a Range object that represents the cell that calls the function. The use of Parent.Parent returns the workbook (that is, the parent of the parent of the Range object—a Workbook object). This topic is explained further in the next section.

```
Function LASTSAVED2()
    Application.Volatile
    LASTSAVED2 = Application.Caller.Parent.Parent. _
      BuiltinDocumentProperties("Last Save Time")
End Function
```

Understanding object parents

As you know, Excel's object model is a hierarchy: objects are contained in other objects. At the top of the hierarchy is the Application object. Excel contains other objects, and these objects contain other objects, and so on. The following hierarchy depicts how a Range object fits into this scheme:

Application object

Workbook object

Worksheet object

Range object

In the lingo of object-oriented programming, a Range object's parent is the Worksheet object that contains it. A Worksheet object's parent is the Workbook object that contains the worksheet, and a Workbook object's parent is the Application object.

How can you put this information to use? Examine the SheetName VBA function that follows. This function accepts a single argument (a range) and returns the name of the worksheet that contains the range. It uses the Parent property of the Range object. The Parent property returns an object: the object that contains the Range object.

```
Function SHEETNAME(ref) As String
    SHEETNAME = ref.Parent.Name
End Function
```

The next function, WORKBOOKNAME, returns the name of the workbook for a particular cell. Note that it uses the Parent property twice. The first Parent property returns a Worksheet object, and the second Parent property returns a Workbook object.

```
Function WORKBOOKNAME(ref) As String
    WORKBOOKNAME = ref.Parent.Parent.Name
End Function
```

The APPNAME function that follows carries this exercise to the next logical level, accessing the Parent property three times (the parent of the parent of the parent). This function returns the name of the Application object for a particular cell. It will, of course, always return Microsoft Excel.

```
Function APPNAME(ref) As String
    APPNAME = ref.Parent.Parent.Parent.Name
End Function
```

Counting cells between two values

The following function, named COUNTBETWEEN, returns the number of values in a range (first argument) that fall between the values represented by the second and third arguments:

```
Function COUNTBETWEEN(InRange, num1, num2) As Long
'   Counts number of values between num1 and num2
    With Application.WorksheetFunction
        If num1 <= num2 Then
            COUNTBETWEEN = .CountIfs(InRange, ">=" & num1, _
                InRange, "<=" & num2)
        Else
            COUNTBETWEEN = .CountIfs(InRange, ">=" & num2, _
                InRange, "<=" & num1)
        End If
    End With
End Function
```

Note that this function uses Excel's COUNTIFS function. The CountBetween function is essentially a wrapper that can simplify your formulas.

> **NOTE**
>
> COUNTIFS was introduced in Excel 2007, so this function won't work with previous versions of Excel.

The following is an example formula that uses the COUNTBETWEEN function. The formula returns the number of cells in A1:A100 that are greater than or equal to 10 and less than or equal to 20.

```
=COUNTBETWEEN(A1:A100,10,20)
```

The function accepts the two numeric arguments in either order. The following formula is equivalent to the preceding one:

```
=COUNTBETWEEN(A1:A100,20,10)
```

Using this VBA function is simpler than entering the following (somewhat confusing) formula:

```
=COUNTIFS(A1:A100,">=10",A1:A100,"<=20")
```

The formula approach is faster, however.

Determining the last nonempty cell in a column or row

In this section, we present two useful functions: LASTINCOLUMN returns the contents of the last nonempty cell in a column, and LASTINROW returns the contents of the last nonempty cell in a row. Each function accepts a range as its single argument. The range argument can be a complete column (for LASTINCOLUMN) or a complete row (for LASTINROW). If the supplied argument isn't a complete column or row, the function uses the column or row of the upper-left cell in the range. For example, the following formula returns the last value in column B:

```
=LASTINCOLUMN(B5)
```

The following formula returns the last value in row 7:

```
=LASTINROW(C7:D9)
```

The LASTINCOLUMN function follows:

```
Function LASTINCOLUMN(rng As Range)
'   Returns the contents of the last non-empty cell in a column
    Dim LastCell As Range
    Application.Volatile
    With rng.Parent
        With .Cells(.Rows.Count, rng.Column)
            If Not IsEmpty(.Value) Then
                LASTINCOLUMN = .Value
```

```
            ElseIf IsEmpty(.End(xlUp)) Then
                LASTINCOLUMN = ""
            Else
                LASTINCOLUMN = .End(xlUp).Value
            End If
        End With
    End With
End Function
```

This function is complicated, so here are a few points that may help you understand it:

- `Application.Volatile` causes the function to be executed whenever the sheet is calculated.
- `Rows.Count` returns the number of rows in the worksheet. We used the `Count` property rather than hard-coding the value because not all worksheets have the same number of rows.
- `rng.Column` returns the column number of the upper-left cell in the `rng` argument.
- Using `rng.Parent` causes the function to work properly even if the `rng` argument refers to a different sheet or workbook.
- The `End` method (with the `xlUp` argument) is equivalent to activating the last cell in a column, pressing End, and then pressing the up-arrow key.
- The `IsEmpty` function checks whether the cell is empty. If so, it returns an empty string. Without this statement, an empty cell would be returned as 0.

The `LASTINROW` function follows. This function is similar to the `LASTINCOLUMN` function.

```
Function LASTINROW(rng As Range)
'    Returns the contents of the last non-empty cell in a row
    Application.Volatile
    With rng.Parent
        With .Cells(rng.Row, .Columns.Count)
            If Not IsEmpty(.Value) Then
                LASTINROW = .Value
            ElseIf IsEmpty(.End(xlToLeft)) Then
                LASTINROW = ""
            Else
                LASTINROW = .End(xlToLeft).Value
            End If
        End With
    End With
End Function
```

Does a string match a pattern?

The `ISLIKE` function is simple but also useful. This function returns TRUE if a text string matches a specified pattern.

```
Function ISLIKE(text As String, pattern As String) As Boolean
'    Returns true if the first argument is like the second
     ISLIKE = text Like pattern
End Function
```

The function is remarkably simple. It is essentially a wrapper that lets you take advantage of VBA's powerful Like operator in your formulas.

This ISLIKE function takes two arguments:

> text: A text string or a reference to a cell that contains a text string

> pattern: A string that contains wildcard characters according to the following list:

Character(s) in Pattern	Matches in Text
?	Any single character
*	Zero or more characters
#	Any single digit (0–9)
[charlist]	Any single character in charlist
[!charlist]	Any single character not in charlist

The following formula returns TRUE because * matches any number of characters. The formula returns TRUE if the first argument is any text that begins with *g*.

```
=ISLIKE("guitar","g*")
```

The following formula returns TRUE because ? matches any single character. If the first argument were "Unit12", the function would return FALSE.

```
=ISLIKE("Unit1","Unit?")
```

The next formula returns TRUE because the first argument is a single character in the second argument:

```
=ISLIKE("a","[aeiou]")
```

The following formula returns TRUE if cell A1 contains *a, e, i, o, u, A, E, I, O,* or *U*. Using the UPPER function for the arguments makes the formula not case-sensitive.

```
=ISLIKE(UPPER(A1), UPPER("[aeiou]"))
```

The following formula returns TRUE if cell A1 contains a value that begins with 1 and has exactly three digits (that is, any integer between 100 and 199):

```
=ISLIKE(A1,"1##")
```

Extracting the nth element from a string

EXTRACTELEMENT is a custom worksheet function (which you can also call from a VBA procedure) that extracts an element from a text string. For example, if a cell contains the following text, you can use the EXTRACTELEMENT function to extract any of the substrings between the hyphens.

```
123-456-787-0133-8844
```

The following formula, for example, returns 0133, which is the fourth element in the string. The string uses a hyphen (-) as the separator.

```
=EXTRACTELEMENT("123-456-787-0133-8844",4,"-")
```

The EXTRACTELEMENT function uses three arguments.

Txt: The text string from which you're extracting. It can be a literal string or a cell reference.

n: An integer that represents the element to extract.

Separator: A single character used as the separator.

> **NOTE**
>
> If you specify a space as the Separator argument, multiple spaces are treated as a single space, which is almost always what you want. If n exceeds the number of elements in the string, the function returns an empty string.

The VBA code for the EXTRACTELEMENT function follows:

```
Function EXTRACTELEMENT(Txt, n, Separator) As String
'     Returns the nth element of a text string, where the
'     elements are separated by a specified separator character
    Dim AllElements As Variant
    AllElements = Split(Txt, Separator)
    EXTRACTELEMENT = AllElements(n - 1)
End Function
```

This function uses the VBA Split function, which returns a variant array that contains each element of the text string. This array begins with 0 (not 1), so using n - 1 references the desired element.

Spelling out a number

The SPELLDOLLARS function returns a number spelled out in text, as on a check. For example, the following formula returns the string *One hundred twenty-three and 45/100 dollars*:

```
=SPELLDOLLARS(123.45)
```

Figure 7.20 shows some additional examples of the SPELLDOLLARS function. Column C contains formulas that use the function. For example, the formula in C1 is

```
=SPELLDOLLARS(A1)
```

Note that negative numbers are spelled out and enclosed in parentheses.

> **ON THE WEB**
>
> The SPELLDOLLARS function is too lengthy to list here, but you can view the complete listing in spelldollars function.xlsm on the book's website.

FIGURE 7.20

Examples of the SPELLDOLLARS function

	A	B	C
1	32		Thirty-Two and 00/100 Dollars
2	37.56		Thirty-Seven and 56/100 Dollars
3	-32		(Thirty-Two and 00/100 Dollars)
4	-26.44		(Twenty-Six and 44/100 Dollars)
5	-4		(Four and 00/100 Dollars)
6	1.87341		One and 87/100 Dollars
7	1.56		One and 56/100 Dollars
8	1		One and 00/100 Dollars
9	6.56		Six and 56/100 Dollars
10	12.12		Twelve and 12/100 Dollars
11	1000000		One Million and 00/100 Dollars
12	10000000000		Ten Billion and 00/100 Dollars
13	1111111111		One Billion One Hundred Eleven Million One Hundred Eleven Thousand One Hundred Eleven and 00/100 Dollars

A multifunctional function

The next example describes a technique that may be helpful in some situations: making a single worksheet function act like multiple functions. The following VBA listing is for a custom function called STATFUNCTION, which takes two arguments: the range (rng) and the operation (op). Depending on the value of op, the function returns a value computed using any of the following worksheet functions: AVERAGE, COUNT, MAX, MEDIAN, MIN, MODE, STDEV, SUM, or VAR.

For example, you can use this function in your worksheet as follows:

```
=STATFUNCTION(B1:B24,A24)
```

The result of the formula depends on the contents of cell A24, which should be a string such as Average, Count, or Max. You can adapt this technique for other types of functions.

```
Function STATFUNCTION (rng, op)
    Select Case UCase(op)
        Case "SUM"
            STATFUNCTION = WorksheetFunction.Sum(rng)
        Case "AVERAGE"
            STATFUNCTION = WorksheetFunction.Average(rng)
        Case "MEDIAN"
            STATFUNCTION = WorksheetFunction.Median(rng)
        Case "MODE"
            STATFUNCTION = WorksheetFunction.Mode(rng)
        Case "COUNT"
            STATFUNCTION = WorksheetFunction.Count(rng)
```

```
        Case "MAX"
            STATFUNCTION = WorksheetFunction.Max(rng)
        Case "MIN"
            STATFUNCTION = WorksheetFunction.Min(rng)
        Case "VAR"
            STATFUNCTION = WorksheetFunction.Var(rng)
        Case "STDEV"
            STATFUNCTION = WorksheetFunction.StDev(rng)
        Case Else
            STATFUNCTION = CVErr(xlErrNA)
    End Select
End Function
```

The SHEETOFFSET function

You probably know that Excel's support for 3D workbooks is limited. For example, if you need to refer to a different worksheet in a workbook, you must include the worksheet's name in your formula. Adding the worksheet name isn't a big problem . . . until you attempt to copy the formula across other worksheets. The copied formulas continue to refer to the original worksheet name, and the sheet references aren't adjusted as they would be in a true 3D workbook.

The example discussed in this section is the VBA SHEETOFFSET function, which enables you to address worksheets in a relative manner. For example, you can refer to cell A1 on the previous worksheet by using this formula:

```
=SHEETOFFSET(-1,A1)
```

The first argument represents the relative sheet, and it can be positive, negative, or zero. The second argument must be a reference to a single cell. You can copy this formula to other sheets, and the relative referencing will be in effect in all the copied formulas.

The VBA code for the SHEETOFFSET function follows:

```
Function SHEETOFFSET (Offset As Long, Optional Cell As Variant)
'   Returns cell contents at Ref, in sheet offset
    Dim WksIndex As Long, WksNum As Long
    Dim wks As Worksheet
    Application.Volatile
    If IsMissing(Cell) Then Set Cell = Application.Caller
    WksNum = 1
    For Each wks In Application.Caller.Parent.Parent.Worksheets
        If Application.Caller.Parent.Name = wks.Name Then
            SHEETOFFSET = Worksheets(WksNum + Offset).Range(Cell(1)
.Address)
            Exit Function
        Else
            WksNum = WksNum + 1
        End If
    Next wks
End Function
```

Returning the maximum value across all worksheets

If you need to determine the maximum value in cell B1 across a number of worksheets, you would use a formula such as this:

```
=MAX(Sheet1:Sheet4!B1)
```

This formula returns the maximum value in cell B1 for Sheet1, Sheet4, and all of the sheets in between. But what if you add a new sheet (Sheet5) after Sheet4? Your formula won't adjust automatically, so you need to edit the formula to include the new sheet reference.

```
=MAX(Sheet1:Sheet5!B1)
```

The MaxAllSheets function accepts a single-cell argument and returns the maximum value in that cell across all worksheets in the workbook. The formula that follows, for example, returns the maximum value in cell B1 for all sheets in the workbook:

```
=MAXALLSHEETS(B1)
```

If you add a new sheet, you don't need to edit the formula.

```
Function MAXALLSHEETS (cell)
    Dim MaxVal As Double
    Dim Addr As String
    Dim Wksht As Object
    Application.Volatile
    Addr = cell.Range("A1").Address
    MaxVal = -9.9E+307
    For Each Wksht In cell.Parent.Parent.Worksheets
        If Wksht.Name = cell.Parent.Name And _
          Addr = Application.Caller.Address Then
        ' avoid circular reference
        Else
            If IsNumeric(Wksht.Range(Addr)) Then
                If Wksht.Range(Addr) > MaxVal Then _
                   MaxVal = Wksht.Range(Addr).Value
            End If
        End If
    Next Wksht
    If MaxVal = -9.9E+307 Then MaxVal = 0
    MAXALLSHEETS = MaxVal
End Function
```

The For Each statement uses the following expression to access the workbook:

```
cell.Parent.Parent.Worksheets
```

The parent of the cell is a worksheet, and the parent of the worksheet is the workbook. Therefore, the For Each-Next loop cycles among all worksheets in the workbook. The first If statement inside the loop performs a check to see whether the cell being checked is the cell that contains the function. If so, that cell is ignored to avoid a circular reference error.

NOTE
You can easily modify this function to perform other cross-worksheet calculations, such as minimum, average, and sum.

Returning an array of nonduplicated random integers

The function in this section, RANDOMINTEGERS, returns an array of nonduplicated integers. The function is intended to be used in a multicell array formula.

```
{=RANDOMINTEGERS()}
```

Select a range and then enter the formula by pressing Ctrl+Shift+Enter. The formula returns an array of nonduplicated integers, arranged randomly. For example, if you enter the formula into a 50-cell range, the formulas will return nonduplicated integers from 1 to 50.

The code for RANDOMINTEGERS follows:

```
Function RANDOMINTEGERS()
    Dim FuncRange As Range
    Dim V() As Variant, ValArray() As Variant
    Dim CellCount As Double
    Dim i As Integer, j As Integer
    Dim r As Integer, c As Integer
    Dim Temp1 As Variant, Temp2 As Variant
    Dim RCount As Integer, CCount As Integer

'   Create Range object
    Set FuncRange = Application.Caller

'   Return an error if FuncRange is too large
    CellCount = FuncRange.Count
    If CellCount > 1000 Then
        RANDOMINTEGERS = CVErr(xlErrNA)
        Exit Function
    End If

'   Assign variables
    RCount = FuncRange.Rows.Count
    CCount = FuncRange.Columns.Count
    ReDim V(1 To RCount, 1 To CCount)
    ReDim ValArray(1 To 2, 1 To CellCount)

'   Fill array with random numbers
'   and consecutive integers
    For i = 1 To CellCount
        ValArray(1, i) = Rnd
        ValArray(2, i) = i
    Next i
```

```
'    Sort ValArray by the random number dimension
     For i = 1 To CellCount
         For j = i + 1 To CellCount
             If ValArray(1, i) > ValArray(1, j) Then
                 Temp1 = ValArray(1, j)
                 Temp2 = ValArray(2, j)
                 ValArray(1, j) = ValArray(1, i)
                 ValArray(2, j) = ValArray(2, i)
                 ValArray(1, i) = Temp1
                 ValArray(2, i) = Temp2
             End If
         Next j
     Next i

'    Put the randomized values into the V array
     i = 0
     For r = 1 To RCount
         For c = 1 To CCount
             i = i + 1
             V(r, c) = ValArray(2, i)
         Next c
     Next r
     RANDOMINTEGERS = V
End Function
```

Randomizing a range

The RANGERANDOMIZE function, which follows, accepts a range argument and returns an array that consists of the input range—in random order:

```
Function RANGERANDOMIZE(rng)
    Dim V() As Variant, ValArray() As Variant
    Dim CellCount As Double
    Dim i As Integer, j As Integer
    Dim r As Integer, c As Integer
    Dim Temp1 As Variant, Temp2 As Variant
    Dim RCount As Integer, CCount As Integer

'   Return an error if rng is too large
    CellCount = rng.Count
    If CellCount > 1000 Then
        RANGERANDOMIZE = CVErr(xlErrNA)
        Exit Function
    End If

'   Assign variables
    RCount = rng.Rows.Count
    CCount = rng.Columns.Count
```

```
        ReDim V(1 To RCount, 1 To CCount)
        ReDim ValArray(1 To 2, 1 To CellCount)

'       Fill ValArray with random numbers
'       and values from rng
        For i = 1 To CellCount
            ValArray(1, i) = Rnd
            ValArray(2, i) = rng(i)
        Next i

'       Sort ValArray by the random number dimension
        For i = 1 To CellCount
            For j = i + 1 To CellCount
                If ValArray(1, i) > ValArray(1, j) Then
                    Temp1 = ValArray(1, j)
                    Temp2 = ValArray(2, j)
                    ValArray(1, j) = ValArray(1, i)
                    ValArray(2, j) = ValArray(2, i)
                    ValArray(1, i) = Temp1
                    ValArray(2, i) = Temp2
                End If
            Next j
        Next i

'       Put the randomized values into the V array
        i = 0
        For r = 1 To RCount
            For c = 1 To CCount
                i = i + 1
                V(r, c) = ValArray(2, i)
            Next c
        Next r
        RANGERANDOMIZE = V
    End Function
```

The code is similar to that for the RANDOMINTEGERS function. Remember to enter this function as an array formula (by pressing Ctrl+Shift+Enter).

```
{=RANGERANDOMIZE(A2:A11)}
```

This formula returns the contents of A2:A11, but in a random order.

Sorting a range

The SORTED function accepts a single-column range argument and returns the range, sorted:

```
Function SORTED(Rng)
    Dim SortedData() As Variant
    Dim Cell As Range
```

```
        Dim Temp As Variant, i As Long, j As Long
        Dim NonEmpty As Long

    '   Transfer data to SortedData
        For Each Cell In Rng
            If Not IsEmpty(Cell) Then
                NonEmpty = NonEmpty + 1
                ReDim Preserve SortedData(1 To NonEmpty)
                SortedData(NonEmpty) = Cell.Value
            End If
        Next Cell

    '   Sort the array
        For i = 1 To NonEmpty
            For j = i + 1 To NonEmpty
                If SortedData(i) > SortedData(j) Then
                    Temp = SortedData(j)
                    SortedData(j) = SortedData(i)
                    SortedData(i) = Temp
                End If
            Next j
        Next i

    '   Transpose the array and return it
        SORTED = Application.Transpose(SortedData)
    End Function
```

Enter the SORTED function as an array formula (by pressing Ctrl+Shift+Enter). The SORTED function returns the contents of a range, sorted.

The SORTED function starts by creating an array named SortedData. This array contains all nonblank values in the argument range. Next, the array is sorted using a bubble sort algorithm. Because the array is a horizontal array, it must be transposed before it is returned by the function.

The SORTED function works with a range of any size, as long as it's in a single column or row. If the unsorted data is in a row, your formula needs to use Excel's TRANSPOSE function to display the sorted data horizontally. Here's an example:

```
=TRANSPOSE(SORTED(A16:L16))
```

Windows API Calls

VBA has the capability to use functions that are stored in *Dynamic Link Libraries* (DLLs). DLLs expose functions and procedures used by the Windows operating system so that other programs can reach out and call these functions and procedures programmatically. This is referred to as making an application programming interface call. The examples in this section illustrate the use of some common Windows API calls to DLLs.

Understanding API declarations

When making Windows API calls, you'll need to use an API declaration. An API declaration essentially tells Excel which Windows function or procedure you want to leverage, where it can be found, the parameters it takes, and what it returns.

For instance, the following API declaration calls the ability to play a sound file:

```
Public Declare Function PlayWavSound Lib "winmm.dll" _
    Alias "sndPlaySoundA" (ByVal LpszSoundName As String, _
    ByVal uFlags As Long) As Long
```

This tells Excel that the following:

- The function is public (it can be used from any module).
- The function is going to be referred to in the code as PlayWavSound.
- The function is found in the winmm.dll file.
- It goes by the name of sndPlaySoundA in the DLL. (This is case sensitive.)
- It takes two parameters: a String that specifies the name of the sound file and a Long number value that specifies any special method for playing the sound.

API declarations can be used just like any standard VBA function or procedure. The following example demonstrates how you would use the PlayWavSound API in a macro:

```
Public Declare PtrSafe Function PlayWavSound Lib "winmm.dll" _
    Alias "sndPlaySoundA"(ByVal LpszSoundName As String, _
    ByVal uFlags As Long) As LongPtr
Sub PlayChimes ()
    PlayWavSound "C:\Windows\Media\Chimes.wav", 0
End Sub
```

32-bit vs. 64-bit declarations

With the introduction of 64-bit versions of Microsoft Office, many of the Windows API declarations had to be adjusted to account for the 64-bit platform. This means that a user with a 64-bit version of Excel installed will not be able to run code with older API declarations.

To avoid compatibility issues, you can use an extended declaration technique that ensures your API calls will work on both 32-bit and 64-bit Excel. Take a moment to review this example, which conditionally calls the ShellExecute API:

```
#If VBA7 Then
Private Declare PtrSafe Function ShellExecute Lib "shell32.dll" Alias _
    "ShellExecuteA" (ByVal hwnd As LongPtr, ByVal lpOperation As String, _
    ByVal lpFile As String, ByVal lpParameters As String, ByVal lpDirectory _
    As String, ByVal nShowCmd As Long) As LongPtr
#Else
```

7

```
Private Declare Function ShellExecute Lib "shell32.dll" Alias "Shell-
ExecuteA" _
    (ByVal hwnd As Long, ByVal lpOperation As String, ByVal lpFile As _
    String, ByVal lpParameters As String, ByVal lpDirectory As String, _
    ByVal nShowCmd As Long) As Long
#End If
```

The pound sign (#) is used to mark conditional compilation. In this case, the first declaration will compile if the code is running on a 64-bit version of Excel. If the code is running on a 32-bit version of Excel, the second declaration will compile.

Determining file associations

In Windows, many file types are associated with a particular application. This association makes it possible to double-click the file to load it into its associated application.

The following function, named GetExecutable, uses a Windows API call to get the full path to the application associated with a particular file. For example, your system has many files with a .txt extension—one named Readme.txt is probably in your Windows directory right now. You can use the GetExecutable function to determine the full path of the application that opens when the file is double-clicked.

> **NOTE**
>
> Windows API declarations must appear at the top of your VBA module.

```
Private Declare PtrSafe Function FindExecutableA Lib "shell32.dll" _
    (ByVal lpFile As String, ByVal lpDirectory As String, _
    ByVal lpResult As String) As Long
Function GetExecutable(strFile As String) As String
    Dim strPath As String
    Dim intLen As Integer
    strPath = Space(255)
    intLen = FindExecutableA(strFile, "\", strPath)
    GetExecutable = Trim(strPath)
End Function
```

Figure 7.21 shows the result of calling the GetExecutable function, with an argument of the filename for an MP3 audio file. The function returns the full path of the application associated with the file.

> **ON THE WEB**
>
> This example is available on this book's website in the file association.xlsm file.

FIGURE 7.21

Determining the path and name of the application associated with a particular file

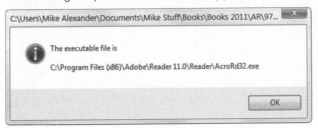

Determining default printer information

The example in this section uses a Windows API function to return information about the active printer. The information is contained in a single text string. The example parses the string and displays the information in a more readable format.

```vba
Private Declare PtrSafe Function GetProfileStringA Lib "kernel32" _
    (ByVal lpAppName As String, ByVal lpKeyName As String, _
    ByVal lpDefault As String, ByVal lpReturnedString As _
    String, ByVal nSize As Long) As Long

Sub DefaultPrinterInfo()
    Dim strLPT As String * 255
    Dim Result As String
    Dim ResultLength As Integer
    Dim Comma1 As Integer
    Dim Comma2 As Integer
    Dim Printer As String
    Dim Driver As String
    Dim Port As String
    Dim Msg As String
    Call GetProfileStringA _
      ("Windows", "Device", "", strLPT, 254)

    Result = Application.Trim(strLPT)
    ResultLength = Len(Result)

    Comma1 = InStr(1, Result, ",", 1)
    Comma2 = InStr(Comma1 + 1, Result, ",", 1)

'   Gets printer's name
    Printer = Left(Result, Comma1 - 1)

'   Gets driver
    Driver = Mid(Result, Comma1 + 1, Comma2 - Comma1 - 1)
```

7

```
'   Gets last part of device line
    Port = Right(Result, ResultLength - Comma2)

'   Build message
    Msg = "Printer:" & Chr(9) & Printer & Chr(13)
    Msg = Msg & "Driver:" & Chr(9) & Driver & Chr(13)
    Msg = Msg & "Port:" & Chr(9) & Port

'   Display message
    MsgBox Msg, vbInformation, "Default Printer Information"
End Sub
```

NOTE

The `ActivePrinter` property of the `Application` object returns the name of the active printer (and lets you change it), but there's no direct way to determine what printer driver or port is being used. That's why this function may be useful.

ON THE WEB

This example is available on this book's website in the `printer info.xlsm` file.

Determining video display information

The example in this section uses Windows API calls to determine a system's current video mode for the primary display monitor. If your application needs to display a certain amount of information on one screen, knowing the display size helps you scale the text accordingly. In addition, the code determines the number of monitors. If more than one monitor is installed, the procedure reports the virtual screen size.

```
Declare PtrSafe Function GetSystemMetrics Lib "user32" _
    (ByVal nIndex As Long) As Long

Public Const SM_CMONITORS = 80
Public Const SM_CXSCREEN = 0
Public Const SM_CYSCREEN = 1
Public Const SM_CXVIRTUALSCREEN = 78
Public Const SM_CYVIRTUALSCREEN = 79

Sub DisplayVideoInfo()
    Dim numMonitors As Long
    Dim vidWidth As Long, vidHeight As Long
    Dim virtWidth As Long, virtHeight As Long
    Dim Msg As String

    numMonitors = GetSystemMetrics(SM_CMONITORS)
    vidWidth = GetSystemMetrics(SM_CXSCREEN)
    vidHeight = GetSystemMetrics(SM_CYSCREEN)
```

```
        virtWidth = GetSystemMetrics(SM_CXVIRTUALSCREEN)
        virtHeight = GetSystemMetrics(SM_CYVIRTUALSCREEN)

        If numMonitors > 1 Then
            Msg = numMonitors & " display monitors" & vbCrLf
            Msg = Msg & "Virtual screen: " & virtWidth & " X "
            Msg = Msg & virtHeight & vbCrLf & vbCrLf
            Msg = Msg & "The video mode on the primary display is: "
            Msg = Msg & vidWidth & " X " & vidHeight
        Else
            Msg = Msg & "The video display mode: "
            Msg = Msg & vidWidth & " X " & vidHeight
        End If
        MsgBox Msg
    End Sub
```

ON THE WEB

This example is available on the book's website in the `video mode.xlsm` file.

Reading from and writing to the Registry

Most Windows applications use the Windows Registry database to store settings. Your VBA procedures can read values from the Registry and write new values to the Registry. Doing so requires the following Windows API declarations:

```
    Private Declare PtrSafe Function RegOpenKeyA Lib "ADVAPI32.DLL" _
        (ByVal hKey As Long, ByVal sSubKey As String, _
        ByRef hkeyResult As Long) As Long

    Private Declare PtrSafe Function RegCloseKey Lib "ADVAPI32.DLL" _
        (ByVal hKey As Long) As Long

    Private Declare PtrSafe Function RegSetValueExA Lib "ADVAPI32.DLL" _
        (ByVal hKey As Long, ByVal sValueName As String, _
        ByVal dwReserved As Long, ByVal dwType As Long, _
        ByVal sValue As String, ByVal dwSize As Long) As Long

    Private Declare PtrSafe Function RegCreateKeyA Lib "ADVAPI32.DLL" _
        (ByVal hKey As Long, ByVal sSubKey As String, _
        ByRef hkeyResult As Long) As Long

    Private Declare PtrSafe Function RegQueryValueExA Lib "ADVAPI32.DLL" _
        (ByVal hKey As Long, ByVal sValueName As String, _
        ByVal dwReserved As Long, ByRef lValueType As Long, _
        ByVal sValue As String, ByRef lResultLen As Long) As Long
```

7

ON THE WEB

On this book's website, in a file named `windows registry.xlsm`, you will find two wrapper functions that greatly simplify the task of working with the Registry: `GetRegistry` and `WriteRegistry`. You will also find examples on how to put these wrapper functions to use.

Reading from the Registry

The `GetRegistry` function returns a setting from the specified location in the Registry. It takes three arguments.

> `RootKey`: A string that represents the branch of the Registry to address. This string can be one of the following:
>
> `HKEY_CLASSES_ROOT`
>
> `HKEY_CURRENT_USER`
>
> `HKEY_LOCAL_MACHINE`
>
> `HKEY_USERS`
>
> `HKEY_CURRENT_CONFIG`
>
> `Path`: The full path of the Registry category being addressed.
>
> `RegEntry`: The name of the setting to retrieve.

Here's an example. If you'd like to find which graphic file, if any, is being used for the desktop wallpaper, you can call `GetRegistry` as follows. (Note that the arguments aren't case-sensitive.)

```
RootKey = "hkey_current_user"
    Path = "Control Panel\Desktop"
    RegEntry = "Wallpaper"
    MsgBox GetRegistry(RootKey, Path, RegEntry), _
        vbInformation, Path & "\RegEntry"
```

The message box will display the path and filename of the graphic file (or an empty string if wallpaper isn't used).

Writing to the Registry

The `WriteRegistry` function writes a value to the Registry at a specified location. If the operation is successful, the function returns `True`; otherwise, it returns `False`. `WriteRegistry` takes the following arguments (all of which are strings):

> `RootKey`: A string that represents the branch of the Registry to address. This string may be one of the following:
>
> `HKEY_CLASSES_ROOT`
>
> `HKEY_CURRENT_USER`
>
> `HKEY_LOCAL_MACHINE`

```
HKEY _ USERS

HKEY _ CURRENT _ CONFIG
```

Path: The full path in the Registry. If the path doesn't exist, it is created.

RegEntry: The name of the Registry category to which the value will be written. If it doesn't exist, it is added.

RegVal: The value that you're writing.

Here's an example that writes to the Registry a value representing the time and date Excel was started. The information is written in the area that stores Excel's settings.

```
Sub Workbook_Open()
    RootKey = "hkey_current_user"
    Path = "software\microsoft\office\15.0\excel\LastStarted"
    RegEntry = "DateTime"
    RegVal = Now()
    If WriteRegistry(RootKey, Path, RegEntry, RegVal) Then
        msg = RegVal & " has been stored in the registry."
    Else
        msg = "An error occurred"
    End If
    MsgBox msg
End Sub
```

If you store this routine in the ThisWorkbook module in your Personal Macro Workbook, the setting is automatically updated whenever you start Excel.

An easier way to access the Registry

If you want to use the Windows Registry to store and retrieve settings for your Excel applications, you don't have to bother with the Windows API calls. Rather, you can use the VBA GetSetting and SaveSetting functions. Using these functions is *much* easier than using the API calls.

These two functions are described in the Help system, so we won't cover the details here. However, it's important to understand that these functions work only with the following key name:

HKEY_CURRENT_USER\Software\VB and VBA Program Settings

In other words, you can't use these functions to access *any* key in the Registry. Rather, these functions are most useful for storing information about your Excel application that you need to maintain between sessions.

Part II

Advanced VBA Techniques

Working with Pivot Tables

IN THIS CHAPTER

Creating pivot tables with VBA

Looking at examples of VBA procedures that create pivot tables

Using VBA to create a worksheet table from a summary table

An Introductory Pivot Table Example

Excel's pivot table feature is, arguably, the most innovative and powerful feature in Excel. Pivot tables first appeared in Excel 5, and the feature has been improved in every subsequent version. This chapter is not an introduction to pivot tables. We assume that you're familiar with this feature and its terminology and that you know how to create and modify pivot tables manually.

As you probably know, creating a pivot table from a database or list enables you to summarize data in ways that otherwise would not be possible—and is amazingly fast and requires no formulas. You also can write VBA code to generate and modify pivot tables.

This section gets the ball rolling with a simple example of using VBA to create a pivot table.

Figure 8.1 shows a simple worksheet range that contains four fields: SalesRep, Region, Month, and Sales. Each record describes the sales for a particular sales representative in a particular month.

> **ON THE WEB**
>
> This workbook, named `simple pivot table.xlsm`, is available on the book's website.

FIGURE 8.1

This table is a good candidate for a pivot table.

	A	B	C	D
1	SalesRep	Region	Month	Sales
2	Amy	North	Jan	33,488
3	Amy	North	Feb	47,008
4	Amy	North	Mar	32,128
5	Bob	North	Jan	34,736
6	Bob	North	Feb	92,872
7	Bob	North	Mar	76,128
8	Chuck	South	Jan	41,536
9	Chuck	South	Feb	23,192
10	Chuck	South	Mar	21,736
11	Doug	South	Jan	44,834
12	Doug	South	Feb	32,002
13	Doug	South	Mar	23,932

Creating a pivot table

Figure 8.2 shows a pivot table created from the data, along with the PivotTable Fields task pane. This pivot table summarizes the sales performance by sales representative and month. This pivot table is set up with the following fields:

Region: A report filter field in the pivot table

SalesRep: A row field in the pivot table

Month: A column field in the pivot table

Sales: A values field in the pivot table that uses the SUM function

If you were to record a macro while building the pivot table in Figure 8.2, the macro recorder would generate code similar to the following:

```
Sub CreatePivotTable()
    Sheets.Add
    ActiveWorkbook.PivotCaches.Create _
        (SourceType:=xlDatabase, _
        SourceData:="Sheet1!R1C1:R13C4", _
        Version:=6).CreatePivotTable _
        TableDestination:="Sheet2!R3C1", _
        TableName:="PivotTable1", _
        DefaultVersion:=6
    Sheets("Sheet2").Select
    Cells(3, 1).Select
    With ActiveSheet.PivotTables("PivotTable1").PivotFields("Region")
        .Orientation = xlPageField
        .Position = 1
    End With
```

FIGURE 8.2

A pivot table created from the data in Figure 8.1

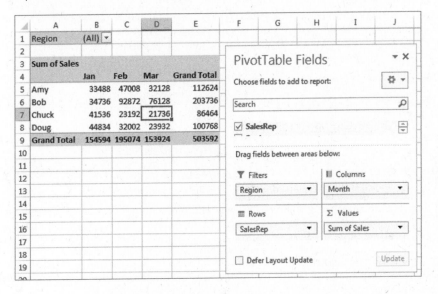

```
    With ActiveSheet.PivotTables("PivotTable1").PivotFields("SalesRep")
        .Orientation = xlRowField
        .Position = 1
    End With
    With ActiveSheet.PivotTables("PivotTable1").PivotFields("Month")
        .Orientation = xlColumnField
        .Position = 1
    End With
    ActiveSheet.PivotTables("PivotTable1").AddDataField _
        ActiveSheet.PivotTables("PivotTable1").PivotFields("Sales"), _
        "Sum of Sales", xlSum
End Sub
```

If you execute this macro, it will almost certainly end with an error. Examine the code, and you'll see that the macro recorder hard-coded the worksheet name (Sheet2) for the pivot table. If that sheet already exists (or if the new sheet that's added has a different name), the macro ends with an error. But a more serious problem is that the macro recorder also hard-coded the pivot table name. The new pivot table's name won't be PivotTable1 if the workbook has other pivot tables.

But even though the recorded macro doesn't work, it's not completely useless. The code provides lots of insight for writing code to generate pivot tables.

Data appropriate for a pivot table

A pivot table requires that your data be in the form of a rectangular database. You can store the database either in a worksheet range (which can be a table or just a normal range) or in an external database file. Although Excel can generate a pivot table from any database, not all databases benefit from this treatment.

In general, fields in a database table consist of two types.

Data Contains a value or data to be summarized. For the sales example, the Sales field is a data field.

Category Describes the data. For the sales data, the SalesRep, Region, and Month fields are category fields because they describe the data in the Sales field.

A database table that's appropriate for a pivot table is said to be *normalized*. In other words, each record (or row) contains information that describes the data.

A single database table can have any number of data fields and category fields. When you create a pivot table, you usually want to summarize one or more of the data fields. Conversely, the values in the category fields appear in the pivot table as rows, columns, or filters.

If you're not clear on the concept, check out the `normalized data.xlsx` workbook on this book's website. This workbook contains an example of a range of data before and after being normalized to make it suitable for a pivot table.

Examining the recorded code for the pivot table

VBA code that works with pivot tables can be confusing. To make any sense of the recorded macro, you need to know about a few relevant objects, all of which are explained in the Help system.

`PivotCaches`: A collection of `PivotCache` objects in a `Workbook` object (the data used by a pivot table is stored in a pivot cache)

`PivotTables`: A collection of `PivotTable` objects in a `Worksheet` object

`PivotFields`: A collection of fields in a `PivotTable` object

`PivotItems`: A collection of individual data items within a field category

`CreatePivotTable`: A method that creates a pivot table by using the data in a pivot cache

Cleaning up the recorded pivot table code

As with most recorded macros, the preceding example isn't as efficient as it could be. And, as noted, it's likely to generate an error. You can simplify the code to make it more understandable and also to prevent the error. The hand-crafted code that follows generates the same pivot table as the procedure previously listed:

```
Sub CreatePivotTable()
    Dim PTCache As PivotCache
    Dim PT As PivotTable
```

```
    '   Create the cache
        Set PTCache = ActiveWorkbook.PivotCaches.Create( _
            SourceType:=xlDatabase, _
            SourceData:=Range("A1").CurrentRegion)

    '   Add a new sheet for the pivot table
        Worksheets.Add

    '   Create the pivot table
        Set PT = ActiveSheet.PivotTables.Add( _
            PivotCache:=PTCache, _
            TableDestination:=Range("A3"))

    '   Specify the fields
        With PT
            .PivotFields("Region").Orientation = xlPageField
            .PivotFields("Month").Orientation = xlColumnField
            .PivotFields("SalesRep").Orientation = xlRowField
            .PivotFields("Sales").Orientation = xlDataField

            'no field captions
            .DisplayFieldCaptions = False
        End With
    End Sub
```

The CreatePivotTable procedure is simplified (and might be easier to understand) because it declares two object variables: PTCache and PT. A new PivotCache object is created by using the Create method. A worksheet is added, and it becomes the active sheet (the destination for the pivot table). Then a new PivotTable object is created by using the Add method of the PivotTables collection. The last section of the code adds the four fields to the pivot table and specifies their location within it by assigning a value to the Orientation property.

The original macro hard-coded both the data range used to create the PivotCache object ('Sheet1!R1C1:R13C4') and the pivot table location (Sheet2). In the CreatePivot-Table procedure, the pivot table is based on the current region surrounding cell A1. This ensures that the macro will continue to work properly if more data is added.

Adding the worksheet before the pivot table is created eliminates the need to hard-code the sheet reference. Yet another difference is that the handwritten macro doesn't specify a pivot table name. Because the PT object variable is created, your code doesn't ever have to refer to the pivot table by name.

> **NOTE**
> The code could be made more general through the use of indices rather than literal strings for the PivotFields collections. This way, if the user changes the column headings, the code will still work. For example, more general code would use PivotFields(1) rather than PivotFields('Region').

8

As always, the best way to master this topic is to record your actions in a macro to find out its relevant objects, methods, and properties. Then study the Help topics to understand how everything fits together. In almost every case, you'll need to modify the recorded macros. Or, after you understand how to work with pivot tables, you can write code from scratch and avoid the macro recorder.

Pivot table compatibility

If you plan to share a workbook that contains a pivot table with users of previous versions of Excel, you need to pay careful attention to compatibility. If you look at the recorded macro in the "Creating a pivot table" section, you see the following statement:

```
DefaultVersion:=6
```

If your workbook is in compatibility mode, the recorded statement is as follows:

```
DefaultVersion:=xlPivotTableVersion10
```

You'll also find that the recorded code is completely different because Microsoft has made significant changes in pivot tables beginning with Excel 2007.

Assume that you create a pivot table in Excel 2019 and give the workbook to a co-worker who has Excel 2003. The co-worker will see the pivot table, but it will not be refreshable. In other words, it's just a dead table of numbers.

To create a backward-compatible pivot table in Excel 2019, you must save your file in XLS format and then reopen it. After doing so, pivot tables that you create will work with versions prior to Excel 2007. But, of course, you won't be able to take advantage of all of the new pivot table features introduced in later versions of Excel.

Fortunately, Excel's Compatibility Checker will alert you regarding this type of compatibility issue (see the accompanying figure). However, it won't check your pivot table-related macros for compatibility. The macros in this chapter do *not* generate backward-compatible pivot tables.

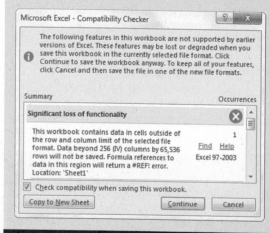

Creating a More Complex Pivot Table

In this section, we present VBA code to create a relatively complex pivot table.

Figure 8.3 shows part of a large worksheet table. This table has 15,840 rows and consists of hierarchical budget data for a corporation. The corporation has 5 divisions, and each division contains 11 departments. Each department has 4 budget categories, and each budget category contains several budget items. Budgeted and actual amounts are included for each of the 12 months. The goal is to summarize this information with a pivot table.

FIGURE 8.3

The data in this workbook will be summarized in a pivot table.

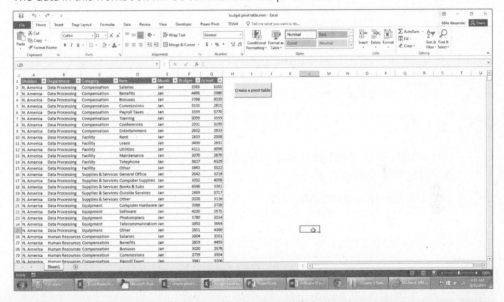

ON THE WEB

This workbook is available on the book's website in a file named `budget pivot table.xlsm`.

Figure 8.4 shows a pivot table created from the data. Note that the pivot table contains a calculated field named `Variance`. This field is the difference between the `Budget` amount and the `Actual` amount.

NOTE

Another option is to insert a new column in the table and create a formula to calculate the difference between the budget and actual amounts. If the data is from an external source (rather than in a worksheet), that option may not be possible.

FIGURE 8.4

A pivot table created from the budget data

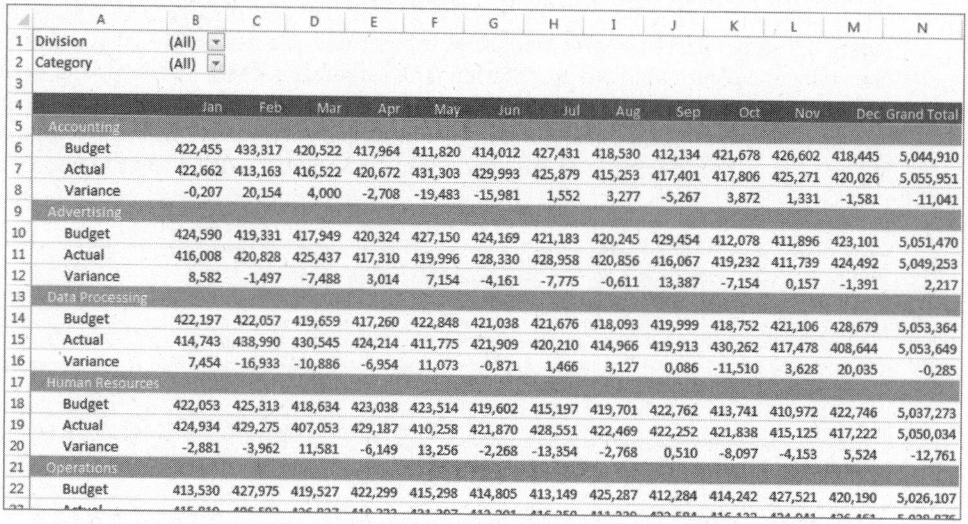

	A	B	C	D	E	F	G	H	I	J	K	L	M	N
1	Division	(All)												
2	Category	(All)												
3														
4		Jan	Feb	Mar	Apr	May	Jun	Jul	Aug	Sep	Oct	Nov	Dec	Grand Total
5	Accounting													
6	Budget	422,455	433,317	420,522	417,964	411,820	414,012	427,431	418,530	412,134	421,678	426,602	418,445	5,044,910
7	Actual	422,662	413,163	416,522	420,672	431,303	429,993	425,879	415,253	417,401	417,806	425,271	420,026	5,055,951
8	Variance	-0,207	20,154	4,000	-2,708	-19,483	-15,981	1,552	3,277	-5,267	3,872	1,331	-1,581	-11,041
9	Advertising													
10	Budget	424,590	419,331	417,949	420,324	427,150	424,169	421,183	420,245	429,454	412,078	411,896	423,101	5,051,470
11	Actual	416,008	420,828	425,437	417,310	419,996	428,330	428,958	420,856	416,067	419,232	411,739	424,492	5,049,253
12	Variance	8,582	-1,497	-7,488	3,014	7,154	-4,161	-7,775	-0,611	13,387	-7,154	0,157	-1,391	2,217
13	Data Processing													
14	Budget	422,197	422,057	419,659	417,260	422,848	421,038	421,676	418,093	419,999	418,752	421,106	428,679	5,053,364
15	Actual	414,743	438,990	430,545	424,214	411,775	421,909	420,210	414,966	419,913	430,262	417,478	408,644	5,053,649
16	Variance	7,454	-16,933	-10,886	-6,954	11,073	-0,871	1,466	3,127	0,086	-11,510	3,628	20,035	-0,285
17	Human Resources													
18	Budget	422,053	425,313	418,634	423,038	423,514	419,602	415,197	419,701	422,762	413,741	410,972	422,746	5,037,273
19	Actual	424,934	429,275	407,053	429,187	410,258	421,870	428,551	422,469	422,252	421,838	415,125	417,222	5,050,034
20	Variance	-2,881	-3,962	11,581	-6,149	13,256	-2,268	-13,354	-2,768	0,510	-8,097	-4,153	5,524	-12,761
21	Operations													
22	Budget	413,530	427,975	419,527	422,299	415,298	414,805	413,149	425,287	412,284	414,242	427,521	420,190	5,026,107

The code that created the pivot table

Here's the VBA code that created the pivot table:

```
Sub CreatePivotTable()
    Dim PTcache As PivotCache
    Dim PT As PivotTable

    Application.ScreenUpdating = False
'   Delete PivotSheet if it exists
    On Error Resume Next
    Application.DisplayAlerts = False
    Sheets("PivotSheet").Delete
    On Error GoTo 0

'   Create a Pivot Cache
    Set PTcache = ActiveWorkbook.PivotCaches.Create( _
        SourceType:=xlDatabase, _
        SourceData:=Range("A1").CurrentRegion.Address)

'   Add new worksheet
    Worksheets.Add
    ActiveSheet.Name = "PivotSheet"
    ActiveWindow.DisplayGridlines = False
```

```
'    Create the Pivot Table from the Cache
     Set PT = ActiveSheet.PivotTables.Add( _
       PivotCache:=PTcache, _
       TableDestination:=Range("A1"), _
       TableName:="BudgetPivot")

     With PT
'        Add fields
         .PivotFields("Category").Orientation = xlPageField
         .PivotFields("Division").Orientation = xlPageField
         .PivotFields("Department").Orientation = xlRowField
         .PivotFields("Month").Orientation = xlColumnField
         .PivotFields("Budget").Orientation = xlDataField
         .PivotFields("Actual").Orientation = xlDataField
         .DataPivotField.Orientation = xlRowField

'        Add a calculated field to compute variance
         .CalculatedFields.Add "Variance", "=Budget-Actual"
         .PivotFields("Variance").Orientation = xlDataField

'        Specify a number format
         .DataBodyRange.NumberFormat = "0,000"

'        Apply a style
         .TableStyle2 = "PivotStyleMedium2"

'        Hide Field Headers
         .DisplayFieldCaptions = False

'        Change the captions
         .PivotFields("Sum of Budget").Caption = " Budget"
         .PivotFields("Sum of Actual").Caption = " Actual"
         .PivotFields("Sum of Variance").Caption = " Variance"
     End With
End Sub
```

How the more complex pivot table works

The CreatePivotTable procedure starts by deleting the PivotSheet worksheet if it already exists. It then creates a PivotCache object, inserts a new worksheet named PivotSheet, and creates the pivot table from the PivotCache. The code then adds the following fields to the pivot table:

Category: A report filter (page) field

Division: A report filter (page) field

Department: A row field

Month: A column field

Budget: A data field

Actual: A data field

Note that the `Orientation` property of the `DataPivotField` is set to `xlRowField` in the following statement:

```
.DataPivotField.Orientation = xlRowField
```

This statement determines the overall orientation of the pivot table, and it represents the Sum Values field in the Pivot Table Fields task pane (see Figure 8.5). Try moving that field to the Columns section to see how it affects the pivot table layout.

FIGURE 8.5

The Pivot Table Fields task pane

Next, the procedure uses the `Add` method of the `CalculatedFields` collection to create the calculated field `Variance`, which subtracts the `Actual` amount from the `Budget` amount. This calculated field is assigned as a data field.

> **NOTE**
>
> To add a calculated field to a pivot table manually, use the PivotTable ⇨ Options ⇨ Calculations ⇨ Fields, Items, & Sets ⇨ Calculated Field command, which displays the Insert Calculated Field dialog box.

Finally, the code makes a few cosmetic adjustments.

- It applies a number format to the `DataBodyRange` (which represents the entire pivot table data).
- It applies a style.
- It hides the captions (equivalent to the PivotTable Tools ⇨ Analyze ⇨ Show ⇨ Field Headers command).
- It changes the captions displayed in the pivot table. For example, `Sum of Budget` is replaced by `Budget`. Note that the `Budget` string is preceded by a space. Excel doesn't allow you to change a caption that corresponds to a field name, so adding a space gets around this restriction.

> **NOTE**
>
> Remember to take full advantage of the macro recorder to learn about the various properties. Performing actions while recording a macro is an excellent way to expose the correct coding syntax that you need. The macro recorder, combined with the information in the Help system (and a fair amount of trial and error), will give you all of the information you need to create your own custom code.

Creating Multiple Pivot Tables

The final example creates a series of pivot tables that summarize data collected in a customer survey. That survey data consists of 150 rows. Each row contains the respondent's sex plus a numerical rating using a 1–5 scale for each of the 14 survey items.

> **ON THE WEB**
>
> This workbook, named `survey data pivot tables.xlsm`, is available on the book's website.

Figure 8.6 shows a few of the 28 pivot tables produced by the macro. Each survey item is summarized in two pivot tables (one showing percentages, and one showing the actual frequencies).

The VBA code that created the pivot tables follows:

```
Sub MakePivotTables()
'   This procedure creates 28 pivot tables
    Dim PTCache As PivotCache
    Dim PT As PivotTable
    Dim SummarySheet As Worksheet
    Dim ItemName As String
    Dim Row As Long, Col As Long, i As Long

    Application.ScreenUpdating = False
```

FIGURE 8.6

Several pivot tables created by a VBA procedure

	A	B	C	D	E	F	G	H	I
3		Female	Male	Grand Total			Female	Male	Grand Total
4	Strongly Disagree	28	40	68		Strongly Disagree	39.4%	50.6%	45.3%
5	Disagree	20	16	36		Disagree	28.2%	20.3%	24.0%
6	Undecided	15	9	24		Undecided	21.1%	11.4%	16.0%
7	Agree	6	14	20		Agree	8.5%	17.7%	13.3%
8	Strongly Agree	2		2		Strongly Agree	2.8%	0.0%	1.3%
9	Grand Total	71	79	150					
10									
11	Store hours are convenient					Store hours are convenient			
12	Count of Store hours are convenient					Count of Store hours are convenient			
13		Female	Male	Grand Total			Female	Male	Grand Total
14	Strongly Disagree	11	13	24		Strongly Disagree	15.5%	16.5%	16.0%
15	Disagree	7	11	18		Disagree	9.9%	13.9%	12.0%
16	Undecided	30	26	56		Undecided	42.3%	32.9%	37.3%
17	Agree	20	22	42		Agree	28.2%	27.8%	28.0%
18	Strongly Agree	3	7	10		Strongly Agree	4.2%	8.9%	6.7%
19	Grand Total	71	79	150					
20									
21	Stores are well-maintained					Stores are well-maintained			
22	Count of Stores are well-maintained					Count of Stores are well-maintained			
23		Female	Male	Grand Total			Female	Male	Grand Total
24	Strongly Disagree	7	14	21		Strongly Disagree	9.9%	17.7%	14.0%
25	Disagree	7	4	11		Disagree	9.9%	5.1%	7.3%
26	Undecided	16	14	30		Undecided	22.5%	17.7%	20.0%
27	Agree	29	29	58		Agree	40.8%	36.7%	38.7%
28	Strongly Agree	12	18	30		Strongly Agree	16.9%	22.8%	20.0%
29	Grand Total	71	79	150					

```
'   Delete Summary sheet if it exists
    On Error Resume Next
    Application.DisplayAlerts = False
    Sheets("Summary").Delete
    On Error GoTo 0

'   Add Summary sheet
    Set SummarySheet = Worksheets.Add
    ActiveSheet.Name = "Summary"

'   Create Pivot Cache
    Set PTCache = ActiveWorkbook.PivotCaches.Create( _
      SourceType:=xlDatabase, _
      SourceData:=Sheets("SurveyData").Range("A1"). _
      CurrentRegion)

    Row = 1
    For i = 1 To 14
      For Col = 1 To 6 Step 5 '2 columns
        ItemName = Sheets("SurveyData").Cells(1, i + 2)
        With Cells(Row, Col)
            .Value = ItemName
            .Font.Size = 16
        End With
```

```
'       Create pivot table
        Set PT = ActiveSheet.PivotTables.Add( _
          PivotCache:=PTCache, _
          TableDestination:=SummarySheet.Cells(Row + 1, Col))

'       Add the fields
        If Col = 1 Then 'Frequency tables
            With PT.PivotFields(ItemName)
              .Orientation = xlDataField
              .Name = "Frequency"
              .Function = xlCount
            End With
        Else ' Percent tables
            With PT.PivotFields(ItemName)
                .Orientation = xlDataField
                .Name = "Percent"
                .Function = xlCount
                .Calculation = xlPercentOfColumn
                .NumberFormat = "0.0%"
            End With
        End If

        PT.PivotFields(ItemName).Orientation = xlRowField
        PT.PivotFields("Sex").Orientation = xlColumnField
        PT.TableStyle2 = "PivotStyleMedium2"
        PT.DisplayFieldCaptions = False
        If Col = 6 Then
'           add data bars to the last column
            PT.ColumnGrand = False
            PT.DataBodyRange.Columns(3).FormatConditions. _
              AddDatabar
        With pt.DataBodyRange.Columns(3).FormatConditions(1)
          .BarFillType = xlDataBarFillSolid
          .MinPoint.Modify newtype:=xlConditionValueNumber,
newvalue:=0
          .MaxPoint.Modify newtype:=xlConditionValueNumber,
newvalue:=1
        End With
        End If
    Next Col
        Row = Row + 10
  Next i

'  Replace numbers with descriptive text
    With Range("A:A,F:F")
        .Replace "1", "Strongly Disagree"
        .Replace "2", "Disagree"
```

```
            .Replace "3", "Undecided"
            .Replace "4", "Agree"
            .Replace "5", "Strongly Agree"
        End With
    End Sub
```

Note that all of these pivot tables were created from a single `PivotCache` object.

The pivot tables are created in a nested loop. The `Col` loop counter goes from 1 to 6 by using the `Step` parameter. The instructions vary a bit for the second column of pivot tables. Specifically, the pivot tables in the second column do the following:

- Display the count as a percent of the column
- Do not show grand totals for the rows
- Are assigned a number format
- Display conditional formatting data bars

The `Row` variable keeps track of the starting row of each pivot table. The final step is to replace the numeric categories in columns A and F with text. For example, 1 is replaced with *Strongly Disagree*.

Creating a Reverse Pivot Table

A pivot table is a summary of data in a table. But what if you have a summary table and you'd like to create a normalized table from the summary? Figure 8.7 shows an example. Range B2:F14 contains a summary table—similar to a simple pivot table. Columns I:K contain a 48-row table created from the summary table. In the table, each row contains one data point, and the first two columns describe that data point. In other words, the transformed data is normalized. (See the sidebar "Data appropriate for a pivot table," earlier in this chapter.)

FIGURE 8.7

The summary table on the left will be converted to the table on the right.

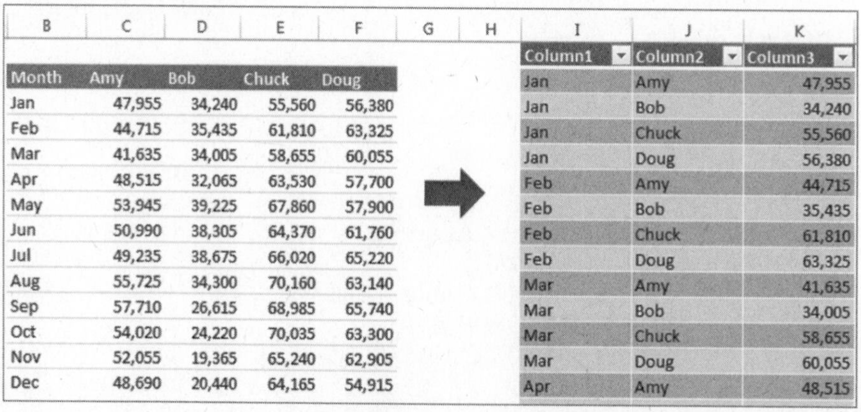

Month	Amy	Bob	Chuck	Doug
Jan	47,955	34,240	55,560	56,380
Feb	44,715	35,435	61,810	63,325
Mar	41,635	34,005	58,655	60,055
Apr	48,515	32,065	63,530	57,700
May	53,945	39,225	67,860	57,900
Jun	50,990	38,305	64,370	61,760
Jul	49,235	38,675	66,020	65,220
Aug	55,725	34,300	70,160	63,140
Sep	57,710	26,615	68,985	65,740
Oct	54,020	24,220	70,035	63,300
Nov	52,055	19,365	65,240	62,905
Dec	48,690	20,440	64,165	54,915

Column1	Column2	Column3
Jan	Amy	47,955
Jan	Bob	34,240
Jan	Chuck	55,560
Jan	Doug	56,380
Feb	Amy	44,715
Feb	Bob	35,435
Feb	Chuck	61,810
Feb	Doug	63,325
Mar	Amy	41,635
Mar	Bob	34,005
Mar	Chuck	58,655
Mar	Doug	60,055
Apr	Amy	48,515

Excel doesn't provide a way to transform a summary table into a normalized table, so it's a good job for a VBA macro. For example, the UserForm shown in Figure 8.8 gets the input and output ranges, and it also has an option to convert the output range to a table.

FIGURE 8.8

This dialog box asks the user for the ranges.

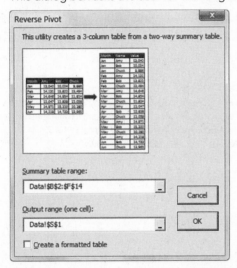

ON THE WEB

This workbook, named `reverse pivot table.xlsm`, is available on the book's website.

When the user clicks the OK button in the UserForm, VBA code validates the ranges and then calls the ReversePivot procedure with this statement:

```
Call ReversePivot(SummaryTable, OutputRange, cbCreateTable)
```

The statement passes three arguments.

SummaryTable: A Range object that represents the summary table

OutputRange: A Range object that represents the upper-left cell of the output range

cbCreateTable: The Checkbox object on the UserForm

This procedure will work for any size summary table. The number of data rows in the output table will be equal to (r-1) * (c-1), where r and c represent the number of rows and columns in SummaryTable.

The code for the ReversePivot procedure follows:

```
Sub ReversePivot(SummaryTable As Range, _
   OutputRange As Range, CreateTable As Boolean)
      Dim r As Long, c As Long
      Dim OutRow As Long, OutCol As Long

'     Convert the range
      OutRow = 2
      Application.ScreenUpdating = False
      OutputRange.Range("A1:C3") = Array("Column1", "Column2", _
"Column3")
      For r = 2 To SummaryTable.Rows.Count
         For c = 2 To SummaryTable.Columns.Count
            OutputRange.Cells(OutRow, 1) = SummaryTable.Cells(r, 1)
            OutputRange.Cells(OutRow, 2) = SummaryTable.Cells(1, c)
            OutputRange.Cells(OutRow, 3) = SummaryTable.Cells(r, c)
            OutputRange.Cells(OutRow, 3).NumberFormat = _
               SummaryTable.Cells(r, c).NumberFormat
            OutRow = OutRow + 1
         Next c
      Next r

'     Make it a table?
      On Error Resume Next
      If CreateTable Then _
        ActiveSheet.ListObjects.Add xlSrcRange, _
           OutputRange.CurrentRegion, , xlYes
      On Error Goto 0
End Sub
```

The procedure is fairly simple. The code loops through the rows and columns in the input range and then writes the data to the output range. The output range will always have three columns. The OutRow variable keeps track of the current row in the output range. Finally, if the user checked the check box, the output range is converted to a table by using the Add method of the ListObjects collection.

Working with Charts

Getting the Inside Scoop on Charts

Excel's charting feature lets you create a wide variety of charts using data that's stored in a worksheet. You have a great deal of control over nearly every aspect of each chart.

An Excel chart is simply packed with objects, each of which has its own properties and methods. Because of this, manipulating charts with Visual Basic for Applications (VBA) can be a bit of a challenge. In this chapter, we discuss the key concepts that you need to understand to write VBA code that generates or manipulates charts. The secret, as you'll see, is a good understanding of the object hierarchy for charts.

Chart locations

In Excel, a chart can be located in either of two places in a workbook.

- **As an embedded object on a worksheet:** A worksheet can contain any number of embedded charts.
- **In a separate chart sheet:** A chart sheet normally holds a single chart.

Most users create charts manually by using the commands in the Insert ➪ Charts group. But you can also create charts by using VBA. And, of course, you can use VBA to modify existing charts.

> **TIP**
>
> The fastest way to create a chart manually is to select your data and then press Alt+F1. Excel creates an embedded chart and uses the default chart type. To create a new default chart on a chart sheet, select the data and press F11.

A key concept when working with charts is the *active chart*, that is, the chart that's currently selected. When the user clicks an embedded chart or activates a chart sheet, a `Chart` object is activated. In VBA, the `ActiveChart` property returns the activated `Chart` object (if any). You can write code to work with this `Chart` object, much like you can write code to work with the `Workbook` object returned by the `ActiveWorkbook` property.

Here's an example: if a chart is activated, the following statement will display the `Name` property for the `Chart` object:

```
MsgBox ActiveChart.Name
```

If a chart isn't activated, the preceding statement generates an error.

> **NOTE**
>
> As you will see later in this chapter, you don't need to activate a chart to manipulate it with VBA.

The macro recorder and charts

As you have read in other chapters, you know that we often recommend using the macro recorder to learn about objects, properties, and methods. As always, recorded macros are best viewed as a learning tool. The recorded code will almost always steer you to the relevant objects, properties, and methods.

Compatibility note

The VBA code in this chapter uses the chart-related properties and methods that were introduced in Excel 2013. For example, Excel 2013 introduced the `AddChart2` method. The `AddChart` method still works, but we focus on the most recent changes, which are often much easier to use. As a result, some of the code presented here won't work with versions prior to Excel 2013.

The Chart object model

When you first start exploring the object model for a `Chart` object, you'll probably be confused—which isn't surprising because the object model *is* confusing. It's also deep.

For example, assume you want to change the title displayed in an embedded chart. The top-level object, of course, is the `Application` object (Excel). The `Application` object contains a `Workbook` object, and the `Workbook` object contains a `Worksheet` object. The

Worksheet object contains a ChartObject object, which contains a Chart object. The Chart object has a ChartTitle object, and the ChartTitle object has a Text property that stores the text displayed as the chart's title.

Here's another way to look at this hierarchy for an embedded chart:

```
Application
     Workbook
          Worksheet
               ChartObject
                    Chart
                         ChartTitle
```

Your VBA code must, of course, follow this object model precisely. For example, to set a chart's title to YTD Sales, you can write a VBA instruction like this:

```
Worksheets(1).ChartObjects(1).Chart.ChartTitle.Text = "YTD Sales"
```

This statement assumes the active workbook is the Workbook object. The statement works with the first object in the ChartObjects collection on the first worksheet. The Chart property returns the actual Chart object, and the ChartTitle property returns the ChartTitle object. Finally, you get to the Text property.

Note that the preceding statement will fail if the chart doesn't have a title. To add a default title (which displays the text Chart Title) to the chart, use this statement:

```
Worksheets("Sheet1").ChartObjects(1).Chart.HasTitle = True
```

For a chart sheet, the object hierarchy is a bit different because it doesn't involve the Worksheet object or the ChartObject object. For example, here's the hierarchy for the ChartTitle object for a chart in a chart sheet:

```
Application
     Workbook
          Chart
               ChartTitle
```

You can use this VBA statement to set the chart title in a chart sheet to YTD Sales:

```
Sheets("Chart1").ChartTitle.Text = "YTD Sales"
```

A chart sheet is essentially a Chart object, and it has no containing ChartObject object. Put another way, the parent object for an embedded chart is a ChartObject object, and the parent object for a chart on a separate chart sheet is a Workbook object.

Both of the following statements will display a message box that displays the word Chart:

```
MsgBox TypeName(Sheets("Sheet1").ChartObjects(1).Chart)
Msgbox TypeName(Sheets("Chart1"))
```

NOTE

When you create a new embedded chart, you're adding to the ChartObjects collection and the Shapes collection contained in a particular worksheet. (There is no Charts collection for a worksheet.) When you create a new chart sheet, you're adding to the Charts collection and the Sheets collection for a particular workbook.

Creating an Embedded Chart

A `ChartObject` is a special type of `Shape` object. Therefore, it's a member of the `Shapes` collection. To create a new chart, use the `AddChart2` method of the `Shapes` collection. The following statement creates an empty embedded chart with all default settings:

```
ActiveSheet.Shapes.AddChart2
```

The `AddChart2` method can use seven arguments (all are optional):

Style   A numeric code that specifies the style (or overall look) of the chart.

xlChartType   The type of chart. If omitted, the default chart type is used. Constants for all of the chart types are provided (for example, `xlArea` and `xlColumn-Clustered`).

Left   The left position of the chart, in points. If omitted, Excel centers the chart horizontally.

Top   The top position of the chart, in points. If omitted, Excel centers the chart vertically.

Width   The width of the chart, in points. If omitted, Excel uses 354.

Height   The height of the chart, in points. If omitted, Excel uses 210.

NewLayout   A numeric code that specifies the layout of the chart.

Here's a statement that creates a clustered column chart, using Style 201 and Layout 5, positioned 50 pixels from the left, 60 pixels from the top, 300 pixels wide, and 200 pixels high:

```
ActiveSheet.Shapes.AddChart2 201, xlColumnClustered, 50, 60,
300, 200, 5
```

In many cases, you may find it efficient to create an object variable when the chart is created. The following procedure creates a line chart that you can reference in code by using the `MyChart` object variable. Note that the `AddChart2` method specifies only the first two arguments. The other five arguments use default values.

```
Sub CreateChart()
    Dim MyChart As Chart
    Set MyChart = ActiveSheet.Shapes.AddChart2(212, xlLineMarkers)
.Chart
End Sub
```

A chart without data isn't useful. You can specify data for a chart in two ways.

- Select cells before your code creates the chart
- Use the `SetSourceData` method of the Chart object after the chart is created

Here's a simple procedure that selects a range of data and then creates a chart:

```
Sub CreateChart2()
    Range("A1:B6").Select
```

```
        ActiveSheet.Shapes.AddChart2 201, xlColumnClustered
    End Sub
```

The procedure that follows demonstrates the SetSourceData method. This procedure uses two object variables: DataRange (for the Range object that holds the data) and MyChart (for the Chart object). The MyChart object variable is set at the same time the chart is created.

```
Sub CreateChart3()
    Dim MyChart As Chart
    Dim DataRange As Range
    Set DataRange = ActiveSheet.Range("A1:B6")
    Set MyChart = ActiveSheet.Shapes.AddChart2.Chart
    MyChart.SetSourceData Source:=DataRange
End Sub
```

Note that the AddChart2 method has no arguments, so a default chart is created.

Creating a Chart on a Chart Sheet

The preceding section describes the basic procedures for creating an embedded chart. To create a chart directly on a chart sheet, use the Add2 method of the Charts collection. The Add2 method of the Charts collection uses several optional arguments, but these arguments specify the position of the chart sheet—not chart-related information.

The example that follows creates a chart on a chart sheet and specifies the data range and chart type:

```
Sub CreateChartSheet()
    Dim MyChart As Chart
    Dim DataRange As Range
    Set DataRange = ActiveSheet.Range("A1:C7")
    Set MyChart = Charts.Add2
    MyChart.SetSourceData Source:=DataRange
    ActiveChart.ChartType = xlColumnClustered
End Sub
```

Modifying Charts

Enhancements introduced with Excel 2013 make it easier than ever for end users to create and modify charts. For example, when a chart is activated, Excel displays three icons on the right side of the chart: Chart Elements (used to add or remove elements from the chart), Style & Color (used to select a chart style or change the color palette), and Chart Filters (used to hide series or data points).

Your VBA code can perform all the actions available from the new chart controls. For example, if you turn on the macro recorder while you add or remove elements from a chart, you'll see that the relevant method is SetElement (a method of the Chart object). This method takes one argument, and predefined constants are available. For example, to add primary horizontal gridlines to the active chart, use this statement:

```
ActiveChart.SetElement msoElementPrimaryValueGridLinesMajor
```

To remove the primary horizontal gridlines from the active chart, use this statement:

```
ActiveChart.SetElement msoElementPrimaryValueGridLinesNone
```

All of the constants are listed in the Help system, or you can use the macro recorder to discover them.

Use the ChartStyle property to change the chart to a predefined style. The styles are numbers, and no descriptive constants are available. For example, this statement changes the style of the active chart to Style 215:

```
ActiveChart.ChartStyle = 215
```

Valid values for the ChartStyle property are 1–48 and 201–248. The latter group consists of styles introduced in Excel 2013. Also, keep in mind that the actual appearance of the styles isn't consistent across Excel versions. For example, applying style 48 looks different in Excel 2010.

To change the color scheme used by a chart, set its ChartColor property to a value between 1 and 26. Here's an example:

```
ActiveChart.ChartColor = 12
```

When you combine the 96 ChartStyle values with the 26 ChartColor options, you have 2,496 combinations—enough to satisfy just about anyone. And if those prebuilt choices aren't enough, you have control over every element in a chart. For example, the following code changes the fill color for one point in a chart series:

```
With ActiveChart.FullSeriesCollection(1).Points(2).Format.Fill
    .Visible = msoTrue
    .ForeColor.ObjectThemeColor = msoThemeColorAccent2
    .ForeColor.TintAndShade = 0.4
    .ForeColor.Brightness = -0.25
    .Solid
End With
```

Again, recording your actions while you make changes to a chart will give you the object model information you need to write your code.

Using VBA to Activate a Chart

When a user clicks any area of an embedded chart, the chart is activated. Your VBA code can activate an embedded chart with the Activate method. Here's a VBA statement that's the equivalent of clicking an embedded chart to activate it:

```
ActiveSheet.ChartObjects("Chart 1").Activate
```

If the chart is on a chart sheet, use a statement like this:

```
Sheets("Chart1").Activate
```

Alternatively, you can activate a chart by selecting its containing shape:

```
ActiveSheet.Shapes("Chart 1").Select
```

When a chart is activated, you can refer to it your code by using the ActiveChart property (which returns a Chart object). For example, the following instruction displays the name of the active chart. If no active chart exists, the statement generates an error.

```
MsgBox ActiveChart.Name
```

To modify a chart with VBA, it's not necessary to activate it. The two procedures that follow have the same effect. That is, they change the embedded chart named Chart 1 to an area chart. The first procedure activates the chart before performing the manipulations; the second one doesn't.

```
Sub ModifyChart1()
    ActiveSheet.ChartObjects("Chart 1").Activate
    ActiveChart.ChartType = xlArea
End Sub

Sub ModifyChart2()
    ActiveSheet.ChartObjects("Chart 1").Chart.ChartType = xlArea
End Sub
```

Moving a Chart

A chart embedded on a worksheet can be converted to a chart sheet. To do so manually, just activate the embedded chart and choose Chart Tools ➪ Design ➪ Location ➪ Move Chart. In the Move Chart dialog box, select the New Sheet option and specify a name.

You can also convert an embedded chart to a chart sheet by using VBA. Here's an example that converts the first ChartObject on a worksheet named Sheet1 to a chart sheet named MyChart:

```
Sub MoveChart1()
    Sheets("Sheet1").ChartObjects(1).Chart. _
      Location xlLocationAsNewSheet, "MyChart"
End Sub
```

Unfortunately, you can't undo this action once the macro is triggered. However, you can use the following code to do the opposite of the preceding procedure, which converts the chart on a chart sheet named MyChart to an embedded chart on the worksheet named Sheet1.

```
Sub MoveChart2()
    Charts("MyChart").Location xlLocationAsObject, "Sheet1"
End Sub
```

9

> **NOTE**
> Using the `Location` method also activates the relocated chart.

Understanding Chart Names

Every `ChartObject` object has a name, and every `Chart` object contained in a `ChartObject` has a name. That statement seems straightforward, but chart names can be confusing. Create a new chart on `Sheet1` and activate it. Then activate the VBA Immediate window and type a few commands, shown here:

```
? ActiveSheet.Shapes(1).Name
Chart 1
? ActiveSheet.ChartObjects(1).Name
Chart 1
? ActiveChart.Name
Sheet1 Chart 1
? ActiveSheet.ChartObjects(1).Chart.Name
Sheet1 Chart 1
```

If you change the name of the worksheet, the name of the chart also changes to include the new sheet name. You can also use the Name box (to the left of the Formula bar) to change a `Chart` object's name and also change the name using VBA.

```
ActiveSheet.ChartObjects(1).Name = "New Name"
```

However, you can't change the name of a `Chart` object contained in a `ChartObject`. This statement generates an inexplicable "out of memory" error:

```
ActiveSheet.ChartObjects(1).Chart.Name = "New Name"
```

Oddly, Excel allows you to use the name of an existing `ChartObject`. In other words, you could have a dozen embedded charts on a worksheet, and every one of them can be named `Chart 1`. If you make a copy of an embedded chart, the new chart has the same name as the source chart.

Bottom line? Be aware of this quirk. If you find that your VBA charting macro isn't working, make sure you don't have two, identically named charts.

Using VBA to Deactivate a Chart

You can use the `Activate` method to activate a chart, but how do you deactivate (that is, deselect) a chart?

The only way to deactivate a chart using VBA is to select something other than the chart. For an embedded chart, you can use the `RangeSelection` property of the `ActiveWindow` object to deactivate the chart and select the range that was selected before the chart was activated.

```
ActiveWindow.RangeSelection.Select
```

To deactivate a chart on a chart sheet, just write code that activates a different sheet.

Determining Whether a Chart Is Activated

A common type of macro performs some manipulations on the active chart (the chart selected by a user). For example, a macro might change the chart's type, apply a style, add data labels, or export the chart to a graphics file.

The question is, how can your VBA code determine whether the user has actually selected a chart? By selecting a chart, we mean either activating a chart sheet or activating an embedded chart by clicking it. Your first inclination might be to check the TypeName property of the Selection, as in this expression:

```
TypeName(Selection) = "Chart"
```

In fact, this expression never evaluates to True. When a chart is activated, the actual selection will be an object within the Chart object. For example, the selection might be a Series object, a ChartTitle object, a Legend object, or a PlotArea object.

The solution is to determine whether ActiveChart is Nothing. If so, a chart isn't active. The following code checks to ensure that a chart is active. If not, the user sees a message and the procedure ends:

```
If ActiveChart Is Nothing Then
    MsgBox "Select a chart."
    Exit Sub
Else
    'other code goes here
End If
```

You may find it convenient to use a VBA function procedure to determine whether a chart is activated. The ChartIsSelected function, which follows, returns True if a chart sheet is active or if an embedded chart is activated, but it returns False if a chart isn't activated.

```
Private Function ChartIsActivated() As Boolean
    ChartIsActivated = Not ActiveChart Is Nothing
End Function
```

Deleting from the ChartObjects or Charts Collection

To delete a chart on a worksheet, you must know the name or index of the ChartObject or the Shape object. This statement deletes the ChartObject named Chart 1 on the active worksheet:

```
ActiveSheet.ChartObjects("Chart 1").Delete
```

Keep in mind that multiple ChartObjects can have the same name. If that's the case, you can delete a chart by using its index number.

```
ActiveSheet.ChartObjects(1).Delete
```

9

To delete all `ChartObject` objects on a worksheet, use the `Delete` method of the `ChartObjects` collection.

```
ActiveSheet.ChartObjects.Delete
```

You can also delete embedded charts by accessing the `Shapes` collection. The following statement deletes the shape named `Chart 1` on the active worksheet:

```
ActiveSheet.Shapes("Chart 1").Delete
```

This code deletes all embedded charts (and all other shapes) on the active sheet:

```
Dim shp as Shape
For Each shp In ActiveSheet.Shapes
    shp.Delete
Next shp
```

To delete a single chart sheet, you must know the chart sheet's name or index. The following statement deletes the chart sheet named `Chart1`:

```
Charts("Chart1").Delete
```

To delete all chart sheets in the active workbook, use the following statement:

```
ActiveWorkbook.Charts.Delete
```

Deleting sheets causes Excel to display a warning that data could be lost. The user must confirm the deletion before the macro can continue. You probably won't want to inundate the user with this warning prompt. To eliminate the prompt, use the `DisplayAlerts` property to temporarily turn alerts off before deleting.

```
Application.DisplayAlerts = False
ActiveWorkbook.Charts.Delete
Application.DisplayAlerts = True
```

Looping Through All Charts

In some cases, you may need to perform an operation on all charts. The following example applies changes to every embedded chart on the active worksheet. The procedure uses a loop to cycle through each object in the `ChartObjects` collection and then accesses the `Chart` object in each and changes several properties.

```
Sub FormatAllCharts()
    Dim ChtObj As ChartObject
    For Each ChtObj In ActiveSheet.ChartObjects
        With ChtObj.Chart
          .ChartType = xlLineMarkers
          .ApplyLayout 3
          .ChartStyle = 12
          .ClearToMatchStyle
          .SetElement msoElementChartTitleAboveChart
          .SetElement msoElementLegendNone
```

```
            .SetElement msoElementPrimaryValueAxisTitleNone
            .SetElement msoElementPrimaryCategoryAxisTitleNone
            .Axes(xlValue).MinimumScale = 0
            .Axes(xlValue).MaximumScale = 1000
            With .Axes(xlValue).MajorGridlines.Format.Line
                .ForeColor.ObjectThemeColor = msoThemeColorBackground1
                .ForeColor.TintAndShade = 0
                .ForeColor.Brightness = -0.25
                .DashStyle = msoLineSysDash
                .Transparency = 0
            End With
        End With
    Next ChtObj
End Sub
```

ON THE WEB

This example is available on the book's website in the `format all charts.xlsm` file.

Figure 9.1 shows four charts that use a variety of different formatting; Figure 9.2 shows the same charts after running the `FormatAllCharts` macro.

FIGURE 9.1

These charts use different formatting.

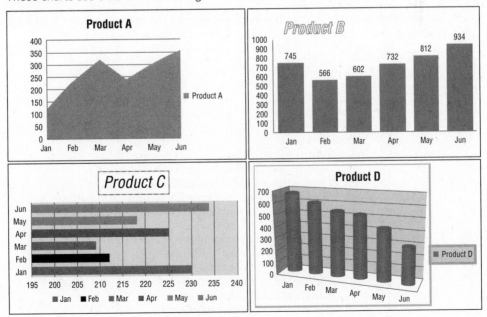

FIGURE 9.2

A simple macro applied consistent formatting to the four charts.

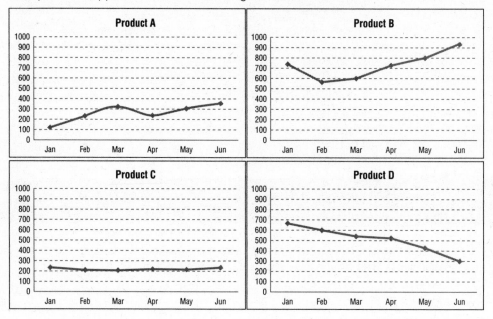

The following macro performs the same operation as the preceding `FormatAllCharts` procedure, but it works on all of the chart sheets in the active workbook:

```
Sub FormatAllCharts2()
    Dim cht as Chart
    For Each cht In ActiveWorkbook.Charts
        With cht
            .ChartType = xlLineMarkers
            .ApplyLayout 3
            .ChartStyle = 12
            .ClearToMatchStyle
            .SetElement msoElementChartTitleAboveChart
            .SetElement msoElementLegendNone
            .SetElement msoElementPrimaryValueAxisTitleNone
            .SetElement msoElementPrimaryCategoryAxisTitleNone
            .Axes(xlValue).MinimumScale = 0
            .Axes(xlValue).MaximumScale = 1000
            With .Axes(xlValue).MajorGridlines.Format.Line
                .ForeColor.ObjectThemeColor = msoThemeColorBackground1
                .ForeColor.TintAndShade = 0
                .ForeColor.Brightness = -0.25
                .DashStyle = msoLineSysDash
                .Transparency = 0
```

```
        End With
      End With
    Next cht
End Sub
```

Sizing and Aligning ChartObjects

A `ChartObject` object has standard positional (`Top` and `Left`) and sizing (`Width` and `Height`) properties that you can access with your VBA code. The Excel Ribbon has controls (in the Chart Tools ⇨ Format ⇨ Size group) to set the `Height` and `Width`, but not the `Top` and `Left`.

The following example resizes all `ChartObject` objects on a sheet so that they match the dimensions of the active chart. It also arranges the `ChartObject` objects into a user-specified number of columns.

```
Sub SizeAndAlignCharts()
    Dim W As Long, H As Long
    Dim TopPosition As Long, LeftPosition As Long
    Dim ChtObj As ChartObject
    Dim i As Long, NumCols As Long

    If ActiveChart Is Nothing Then
        MsgBox "Select a chart to be used as the base for the sizing"
        Exit Sub
    End If

    'Get columns
    On Error Resume Next
    NumCols = InputBox("How many columns of charts?")
    If Err.Number <> 0 Then Exit Sub
    If NumCols < 1 Then Exit Sub
    On Error GoTo 0

    'Get size of active chart
    W = ActiveChart.Parent.Width
    H = ActiveChart.Parent.Height

    'Change starting positions, if necessary
    TopPosition = 100
    LeftPosition = 20
    For i = 1 To ActiveSheet.ChartObjects.Count
        With ActiveSheet.ChartObjects(i)
            .Width = W
            .Height = H
            .Left = LeftPosition + ((i - 1) Mod NumCols) * W
            .Top = TopPosition + Int((i - 1) / NumCols) * H
```

```
        End With
    Next i
End Sub
```

If no chart is active, the user is prompted to activate a chart that will be used as the basis for sizing the other charts. We use an `InputBox` function to get the number of columns. The values for the `Left` and `Top` properties are calculated within the loop.

ON THE WEB

This workbook, named `size and align charts.xlsm`, is available on the book's website.

Creating Lots of Charts

The example in this section demonstrates how to automate the task of creating multiple charts. Figure 9.3 shows part of the data to be charted. The worksheet contains data for 50 people, and the goal is to create 50 charts, consistently formatted and nicely aligned.

FIGURE 9.3

Each row of data will be used to create a chart.

	A	B	C	D	E	F
1	Name	Day 1	Day 2	Day 3	Day 4	Day 5
2	Daisy Allen	37	56	70	72	88
3	Joe Perry	48	56	61	58	52
4	Joe Long	44	62	71	69	68
5	Stephen Mitchell	49	51	55	74	92
6	Thelma Carter	32	25	15	31	50
7	Susie Fitzgerald	47	67	85	92	99
8	Gerard Johnson	40	56	75	86	79
9	Mary Young	33	34	33	50	41
10	Robert Mcdonald	39	57	72	89	96
11	Robert Hall	39	54	49	45	41
12	Jennifer Head	58	50	43	45	56
13	Todd Fowler	32	42	40	42	55
14	Margaret Adams	56	71	75	72	71
15	William Smith	42	40	36	37	51
16	Douglas Taylor	45	46	46	56	67
17	Evelyn Reyes	39	36	41	34	49
18	Peter Gonzales	54	49	47	64	66
19	Victor Klein	36	42	33	50	43
20	Christopher Anderson	32	28	34	38	37
21	Raul Jones	31	25	30	22	33
22	Bernard Jones	45	48	52	66	67
23	Norma Young	53	67	57	50	64
24	Francis Valencia	49	68	65	68	64
25	Shannon Taylor	57	59	67	79	79

Sheet1 | Sheet2 | +

We start out by creating the CreateChart procedure, which accepts the following arguments:

rng: The range to be used for the chart

l: The left position for the chart

t: The top position for the chart

w: The width of the chart

h: The height of the chart

The CreateChart procedure uses these arguments to create a line chart with axis scale values ranging from 0 to 100.

```
Sub CreateChart(rng, l, t, w, h)
    With Worksheets("Sheet2").Shapes. _
        AddChart2(332, xlLineMarkers, l, t, w, h).Chart
            .SetSourceData Source:=rng
            .Axes(xlValue).MinimumScale = 0
            .Axes(xlValue).MaximumScale = 100
    End With
End Sub
```

Next, we can apply the procedure Make50Charts, which uses a For-Next loop to call CreateChart 50 times. Note that the chart data consists of the first row (the headers), plus data in a row from 2 through 50. We used the Union method to join these two ranges into one Range object, which is passed to the CreateChart procedure. The other tricky part is to determine the top and left position for each chart. This code does just that:

```
Sub Make50Charts()
    Dim ChartData As Range
    Dim i As Long
    Dim leftPos As Long, topPos As Long
'   Delete existing charts if they exist
    With Worksheets("Sheet2").ChartObjects
        If .Count > 0 Then .Delete
    End With

'   Initialize positions
    leftPos = 0
    topPos = 0

'   Loop through the data
    For i = 2 To 51
'       Determine the data range
        With Worksheets("Sheet1")
            Set ChartData = Union(.Range("A1:F1"), _
```

9

```
                .Range(.Cells(i, 1), .Cells(i, 6)))
            End With

'           Create a chart
            Call CreateChart(ChartData, leftPos, topPos, 180, 120)

'           Adjust positions
            If (i - 1) Mod 5 = 0 Then
                leftPos = 0
                topPos = topPos + 120
            Else
                leftPos = leftPos + 180
            End If
        Next i
    End Sub
```

Figure 9.4 shows some of the 50 charts.

FIGURE 9.4

A sampling of the 50 charts created by the macro

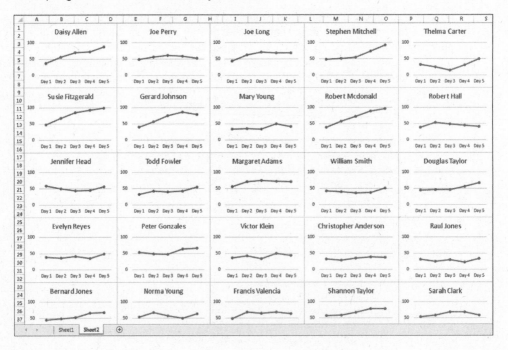

Exporting a Chart

In some cases, you may need an Excel chart in the form of a graphics file. For example, you may want to post the chart on a website. One option is to use a screen capture program and copy the pixels directly from the screen. Another choice is to write a simple VBA macro.

The procedure that follows uses the `Export` method of the `Chart` object to save the active chart as a GIF file:

```
Sub SaveChartAsGIF()
    Dim Fname as String
    If ActiveChart Is Nothing Then Exit Sub
    Fname = ThisWorkbook.Path & "\" & ActiveChart.Name & ".gif"
    ActiveChart.Export FileName:=Fname, FilterName:="GIF"
End Sub
```

Other choices for the `FilterName` argument are `"JPEG"` and `"PNG"`. Usually, GIF and PNG files look better. The Help system lists a third argument for the `Export` method: `Interactive`. If this argument is `True`, you're supposed to see a dialog box in which you can specify export options. However, this argument has no effect.

Keep in mind that the `Export` method will fail if the user doesn't have the specified graphics export filter installed. These filters are installed in the Office setup program.

Exporting all graphics

One way to export all graphic images from a workbook is to save the file in HTML format. Doing so creates a directory that contains GIF and PNG images of the charts, shapes, clip art, and even copied range images (created with Home ⇨ Clipboard ⇨ Paste ⇨ Picture (U)).

Here's a VBA procedure that automates the process. It works with the active workbook.

```
Sub SaveAllGraphics()
    Dim FileName As String
    Dim TempName As String
    Dim DirName As String
    Dim gFile As String

    FileName = ActiveWorkbook.FullName
    TempName = ActiveWorkbook.Path & "\" & _
        ActiveWorkbook.Name & "graphics.htm"
    DirName = Left(TempName, Len(TempName) - 4) & "_files"

'   Save active workbookbook as HTML, then reopen original
    ActiveWorkbook.Save
    ActiveWorkbook.SaveAs FileName:=TempName, FileFormat:=xlHtml
```

9

```
        Application.DisplayAlerts = False
        ActiveWorkbook.Close
        Workbooks.Open FileName

'       Delete the HTML file
        Kill TempName

'       Delete all but *.PNG files in the HTML folder
        gFile = Dir(DirName & "\*.*")
        Do While gFile <> ""
            If Right(gFile, 3) <> "png" Then Kill DirName & "\" & gFile
            gFile = Dir
        Loop

'       Show the exported graphics
        Shell "explorer.exe " & DirName, vbNormalFocus
    End Sub
```

The procedure starts by saving the active workbook. Then it saves the workbook as an HTML file, closes the file, and reopens the original workbook. Next, it deletes the HTML file because we're just interested in the folder that it creates (because that folder contains the images). The code then loops through the folder and deletes everything except the PNG files. Finally, it uses the Shell function to display the folder.

 See Chapter 11, "Working with External Data and Files," for more information about the file manipulation commands.

ON THE WEB

This example is available on the book's website in the `export all graphics.xlsm` file.

Changing the Data Used in a Chart

The examples presented so far in this chapter have used the SourceData property to specify the complete data range for a chart. In many cases, you'll want to adjust the data used by a particular chart series. To do so, access the Values property of the Series object. The Series object also has an XValues property that stores the category axis values.

NOTE

The Values property corresponds to the third argument of the SERIES formula, and the XValues property corresponds to the second argument of the SERIES formula. See the sidebar "Understanding a chart's SERIES formula."

Understanding a chart's SERIES formula

The data used in each series in a chart is determined by its SERIES formula. When you select a data series in a chart, the SERIES formula appears in the formula bar. This is not a real formula. In other words, you can't use it in a cell, and you can't use worksheet functions within the SERIES formula. You can, however, edit the arguments in the SERIES formula.

A SERIES formula has the following syntax:

```
=SERIES(series_name, category_labels, values, order, sizes)
```

The arguments that you can use in the SERIES formula are

- **series _ name:** Optional. A reference to the cell that contains the series name used in the legend. If the chart has only one series, the name argument is used as the title. This argument can also consist of text in quotation marks. If omitted, Excel creates a default series name (for example, Series 1).

- **category _ labels:** Optional. A reference to the range that contains the labels for the category axis. If omitted, Excel uses consecutive integers beginning with 1. For XY charts, this argument specifies the X values. A noncontiguous range reference is also valid. The ranges' addresses are separated by a comma and enclosed in parentheses. The argument could also consist of an array of comma-separated values (or text in quotation marks) enclosed in curly brackets.

- **values:** Required. A reference to the range that contains the values for the series. For XY charts, this argument specifies the Y values. A noncontiguous range reference is also valid. The ranges' addresses are separated by a comma and enclosed in parentheses. The argument could also consist of an array of comma-separated values enclosed in curly brackets.

- **order:** Required. An integer that specifies the plotting order of the series. This argument is relevant only if the chart has more than one series. For example, in a stacked column chart, this parameter determines the stacking order. Using a reference to a cell is not allowed.

- **sizes:** Only for bubble charts. A reference to the range that contains the values for the size of the bubbles in a bubble chart. A noncontiguous range reference is also valid. The ranges' addresses are separated by a comma and enclosed in parentheses. The argument could also consist of an array of values enclosed in curly brackets.

Range references in a SERIES formula are always absolute, and they always include the sheet name. For example:

```
=SERIES(Sheet1!$B$1,,Sheet1!$B$2:$B$7,1)
```

A range reference can consist of a noncontiguous range. If so, each range is separated by a comma, and the argument is enclosed in parentheses. In the following SERIES formula, the values range consists of B2:B3 and B5:B7:

```
=SERIES(,,(Sheet1!$B$2:$B$3,Sheet1!$B$5:$B$7),1)
```

You can substitute range names for the range references. If you do so (and the name is a workbook-level name), Excel changes the reference in the SERIES formula to include the workbook. Here's an example:

```
=SERIES(Sheet1!$B$1,,budget.xlsx!CurrentData,1)
```

Changing chart data based on the active cell

Figure 9.5 shows a chart that's based on the data in the row of the active cell. When the user moves the cell pointer, the chart is updated automatically.

FIGURE 9.5

This chart always displays the data from the row of the active cell.

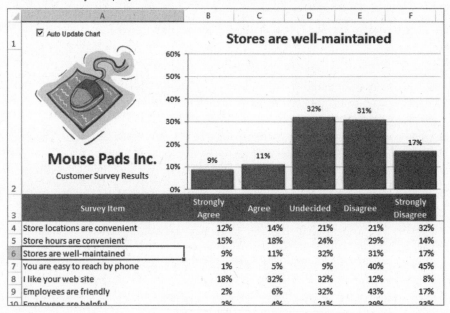

Survey Item	Strongly Agree	Agree	Undecided	Disagree	Strongly Disagree
Store locations are convenient	12%	14%	21%	21%	32%
Store hours are convenient	15%	18%	24%	29%	14%
Stores are well-maintained	9%	11%	32%	31%	17%
You are easy to reach by phone	1%	5%	9%	40%	45%
I like your web site	18%	32%	32%	12%	8%
Employees are friendly	2%	6%	32%	43%	17%
Employees are helpful	3%	4%	21%	39%	33%

This example uses an event handler for the Sheet1 object. The SelectionChange event occurs whenever the user changes the selection by moving the cell pointer. The event-handler procedure for this event (which is located in the code module for the Sheet1 object) is as follows:

```
Private Sub Worksheet_SelectionChange(ByVal Target As Excel.Range)
    If CheckBox1 Then Call UpdateChart
End Sub
```

In other words, every time the user moves the cell cursor, the Worksheet _ Selection-Change procedure is executed. If the Auto Update Chart check box (an ActiveX control on the sheet) is checked, this procedure calls the UpdateChart procedure, which follows:

```
Sub UpdateChart()
    Dim ChtObj As ChartObject
    Dim UserRow As Long
    Set ChtObj = ActiveSheet.ChartObjects(1)
```

```
        UserRow = ActiveCell.Row
        If UserRow < 4 Or IsEmpty(Cells(UserRow, 1)) Then
            ChtObj.Visible = False
        Else
            ChtObj.Chart.SeriesCollection(1).Values = _
                Range(Cells(UserRow, 2), Cells(UserRow, 6))
            ChtObj.Chart.ChartTitle.Text = Cells(UserRow, 1).Text
            ChtObj.Visible = True
        End If
    End Sub
```

The `UserRow` variable contains the row number of the active cell. The `If` statement checks that the active cell is in a row that contains data. (The data starts in row 4.) If the cell cursor is in a row that doesn't have data, the `ChartObject` object is hidden, and the underlying text is visible ("Cannot display chart"). Otherwise, the code sets the `Values` property for the `Series` object to the range in columns 2–6 of the active row. It also sets the `ChartTitle` object to correspond to the text in column A.

ON THE WEB

This example, named `chart active cell.xlsm`, is available on the book's website.

Using VBA to determine the ranges used in a chart

The previous example demonstrated how to use the `Values` property of a `Series` object to specify the data used by a chart series. This section discusses using VBA macros to identify the ranges used by a series in a chart. For example, you might want to increase the size of each series by adding a new cell to the range.

The following are the three properties that are relevant to this task:

- `Formula` property: Returns or sets the SERIES formula for the series. When you select a series in a chart, its SERIES formula is displayed in the formula bar. The `Formula` property returns this formula as a string.
- `Values` property: Returns or sets a collection of all the values in the series. This property can be specified as a range on a worksheet or as an array of constant values, but not as a combination of both.
- `XValues` property: Returns or sets an array of X values for a chart series. The `XValues` property can be set to a range on a worksheet or to an array of values, but it can't be a combination of both. The `XValues` property can also be empty.

If you create a VBA macro that needs to determine the data range used by a particular chart series, you might think that the `Values` property of the `Series` object is just the ticket. Similarly, the `XValues` property seems to be the way to get the range that contains the X values (or category labels). In theory, that way of thinking certainly *seems* correct. But in practice, it doesn't work.

When you set the `Values` property for a `Series` object, you can specify a `Range` object or an array. But when you read this property, an array is always returned. Unfortunately, the object model provides no way to get a `Range` object used by a `Series` object.

One possible solution is to write code to parse the SERIES formula and extract the range addresses. This task sounds simple, but it's actually difficult because a SERIES formula can be complex. The following are a few examples of valid SERIES formulas:

```
=SERIES(Sheet1!$B$1,Sheet1!$A$2:$A$4,Sheet1!$B$2:$B$4,1)
=SERIES(,,Sheet1!$B$2:$B$4,1)
=SERIES(,Sheet1!$A$2:$A$4,Sheet1!$B$2:$B$4,1)
=SERIES("Sales Summary",,Sheet1!$B$2:$B$4,1)
=SERIES(,{"Jan","Feb","Mar"},Sheet1!$B$2:$B$4,1)
=SERIES(,(Sheet1!$A$2,Sheet1!$A$4),(Sheet1!$B$2,Sheet1!$B$4),1)
=SERIES(Sheet1!$B$1,Sheet1!$A$2:$A$4,Sheet1!$B$2:$B$4,1,Sheet1!$C$2:$C$4)
```

As you can see, a SERIES formula can have missing arguments, use arrays, and even use noncontiguous range addresses. And, to confuse the issue even more, a bubble chart has an additional argument (for example, the last SERIES formula in the preceding list). Attempting to parse the arguments is certainly not a trivial programming task.

The solution is to use four custom VBA functions, each of which accepts one argument (a reference to a `Series` object) and returns a two-element array. These functions are the following:

- SERIESNAME_FROM_SERIES: The first array element contains a string that describes the data type of the first SERIES argument (`Range`, `Empty`, or `String`). The second array element contains a range address, an empty string, or a string.

- XVALUES_FROM_SERIES: The first array element contains a string that describes the data type of the second SERIES argument (`Range`, `Array`, `Empty`, or `String`). The second array element contains a range address, an array, an empty string, or a string.

- VALUES_FROM_SERIES: The first array element contains a string that describes the data type of the third SERIES argument (`Range` or `Array`). The second array element contains a range address or an array.

- BUBBLESIZE_FROM_SERIES: The first array element contains a string that describes the data type of the fifth SERIES argument (`Range`, `Array`, or `Empty`). The second array element contains a range address, an array, or an empty string. This function is relevant only for bubble charts.

Note you can get the fourth SERIES argument (plot order) directly by using the `Plot-Order` property of the `Series` object.

ON THE WEB

The VBA code for these functions is too lengthy to be listed here, but the code is available on the book's website in a file named `get series ranges.xlsm`. These functions are documented in such a way that they can be easily adapted to other situations.

The following example demonstrates the VALUES _ FROM _ SERIES function. It displays the address of the values range for the first series in the active chart.

```
Sub ShowValueRange()
    Dim Ser As Series
    Dim x As Variant
    Set Ser = ActiveChart.SeriesCollection(1)
    x = VALUES_FROM_SERIES(Ser)
    If x(1) = "Range" Then
        MsgBox Range(x(2)).Address
    End If
End Sub
```

The variable x is defined as a variant and will hold the two-element array that's returned by the VALUES _ FROM _ SERIES function. The first element of the x array contains a string that describes the data type. If the string is Range, the message box displays the address of the range contained in the second element of the x array.

The ContractAllSeries procedure follows. This procedure loops through the SeriesCollection collection and uses the XVALUE _ FROM _ SERIES and VALUES _ FROM _ SERIES functions to retrieve the current ranges. It then uses the Resize method to decrease the size of the ranges.

```
Sub ContractAllSeries()
    Dim s As Series
    Dim Result As Variant
    Dim DRange As Range
    For Each s In ActiveSheet.ChartObjects(1).Chart.SeriesCollection
        Result = XVALUES_FROM_SERIES(s)
        If Result(1) = "Range" Then
            Set DRange = Range(Result(2))
            If DRange.Rows.Count > 1 Then
                Set DRange = DRange.Resize(DRange.Rows.Count - 1)
                s.XValues = DRange
            End If
        End If
        Result = VALUES_FROM_SERIES(s)
        If Result(1) = "Range" Then
            Set DRange = Range(Result(2))
            If DRange.Rows.Count > 1 Then
                Set DRange = DRange.Resize(DRange.Rows.Count - 1)
                s.Values = DRange
            End If
        End If
    Next s
End Sub
```

The ExpandAllSeries procedure is similar. When executed, it expands each range by one cell.

Using VBA to Display Custom Data Labels on a Chart

Here's how to specify a range of data labels for a chart series:

1. Create your chart and select the data series that will contain labels from a range.

2. Click the Chart Elements icon to the right of the chart and choose Data Labels.

3. Click the arrow to right of the Data Labels item and choose More Options.

   The Label Options section of the Format Data Labels task pane is displayed.

4. Select Value From Cells.

   Excel prompts you for the range that contains the labels.

Figure 9.6 shows an example. We specify range C2:C7 as the data labels for the series. In the past, specifying a range as data labels had to be done manually or with a VBA macro.

FIGURE 9.6

Data labels from an arbitrary range show the percent change for each week.

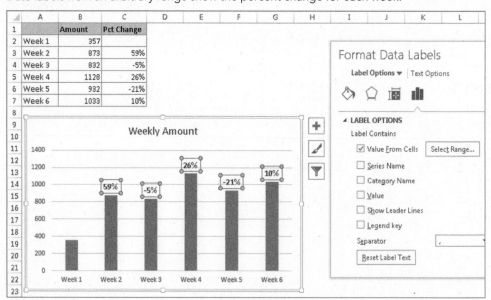

This feature is great but is not completely backward compatible. Figure 9.7 shows how the chart looks when opened in Excel 2010.

FIGURE 9.7

Data labels created from a range of data are not compatible with versions of Excel before 2013.

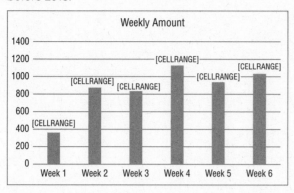

The remainder of this section describes how to use VBA to apply data labels using the values in a range. The data labels applied in this manner *are* compatible with previous versions of Excel.

Figure 9.8 shows an XY chart. It would be useful to display the associated name for each data point.

FIGURE 9.8

An XY chart that would benefit by having data labels

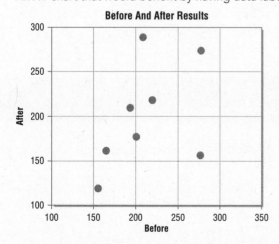

The `DataLabelsFromRange` procedure works with the first chart on the active sheet. It prompts the user for a range and then loops through the `Points` collection and changes the `Text` property to the values found in the range.

```vba
Sub DataLabelsFromRange()
    Dim DLRange As Range
    Dim Cht As Chart
    Dim i As Integer, Pts As Integer

'   Specify chart
    Set Cht = ActiveSheet.ChartObjects(1).Chart

'   Prompt for a range
    On Error Resume Next
    Set DLRange = Application.InputBox _
      (prompt:="Range for data labels?", Type:=8)
    If DLRange Is Nothing Then Exit Sub
    On Error GoTo 0

'   Add data labels
    Cht.SeriesCollection(1).ApplyDataLabels _
      Type:=xlDataLabelsShowValue, _
      AutoText:=True, _
      LegendKey:=False

'   Loop through the Points, and set the data labels
    Pts = Cht.SeriesCollection(1).Points.Count
    For i = 1 To Pts
        Cht.SeriesCollection(1). _
          Points(i).DataLabel.Text = DLRange(i)
    Next i
End Sub
```

ON THE WEB

This example, named `data labels.xlsm`, is available on the book's website.

Figure 9.9 shows the chart after running the `DataLabelsFromRange` procedure and specifying A2:A9 as the data range.

A data label in a chart can also consist of a link to a cell. To modify the `DataLabelsFromRange` procedure so that it creates cell links, just change the statement in the For-Next loop to the following:

```vba
Cht.SeriesCollection(1).Points(i).DataLabel.Text = _
        "=" & "'" & DLRange.Parent.Name & "'!" & _
        DLRange(i).Address(ReferenceStyle:=xlR1C1)
```

FIGURE 9.9

This XY chart has data labels, thanks to a VBA procedure.

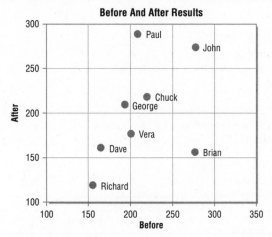

Displaying a Chart in a UserForm

In Chapter 15, "Advanced UserForm Techniques," we describe a way to display a chart in a UserForm. The technique saves the chart as a GIF file and then loads the GIF file into an Image control on the UserForm.

The example in this section uses that same technique but adds a new twist: the chart is created on the fly, and it uses the data in the row of the active cell.

The UserForm for this example is simple. It contains an Image control and a Command-Button (Close). The worksheet that contains the data has a button that executes the following procedure:

```
Sub ShowChart()
    Dim UserRow As Long
    UserRow = ActiveCell.Row
    If UserRow < 2 Or IsEmpty(Cells(UserRow, 1)) Then
        MsgBox "Move the cell pointer to a row that contains data."
        Exit Sub
    End If
    CreateChart (UserRow)
    UserForm1.Show
End Sub
```

Because the chart is based on the data in the row of the active cell, the procedure warns the user if the cell pointer is in an invalid row. If the active cell is appropriate, ShowChart calls the CreateChart procedure to create the chart and then displays the UserForm.

The CreateChart procedure accepts one argument, which represents the row of the active cell. This procedure originated from a macro recording and was cleaned up to make it more general.

```vba
Sub CreateChart(r)
    Dim TempChart As Chart
    Dim CatTitles As Range
    Dim SrcRange As Range, SourceData As Range
    Dim FName As String

    Set CatTitles = ActiveSheet.Range("A2:F2")
    Set SrcRange = ActiveSheet.Range(Cells(r, 1), Cells(r, 6))
    Set SourceData = Union(CatTitles, SrcRange)

'   Add a chart
    Application.ScreenUpdating = False
    Set TempChart = ActiveSheet.Shapes.AddChart2.Chart
        TempChart.SetSourceData Source:=SourceData

'   Fix it up
    With TempChart
        .ChartType = xlColumnClustered
        .SetSourceData Source:=SourceData, PlotBy:=xlRows
        .ChartStyle = 25
        .HasLegend = False
        .PlotArea.Interior.ColorIndex = xlNone
        .Axes(xlValue).MajorGridlines.Delete
        .ApplyDataLabels Type:=xlDataLabelsShowValue, LegendKey:=False
        .Axes(xlValue).MaximumScale = 0.6
        .ChartArea.Format.Line.Visible = False
    End With

'   Adjust the ChartObject's size
    With ActiveSheet.ChartObjects(1)
        .Width = 300
        .Height = 200
        .Activate
    End With

'   Save chart as GIF

    FName = Application.DefaultFilePath & Application.PathSeparator & _
"temp.gif"

    TempChart.Export Filename:=FName, filterName:="GIF"
    ActiveSheet.ChartObjects(1).Delete
    Application.ScreenUpdating = True
End Sub
```

When the `CreateChart` procedure ends, the worksheet contains a `ChartObject` with a chart of the data in the row of the active cell. However, the `ChartObject` isn't visible because `ScreenUpdating` is turned off. The chart is exported and deleted, and `Screen-Updating` is turned back on.

The final instruction of the `ShowChart` procedure loads the UserForm. The following is the `UserForm _ Initialize` procedure, which simply loads the GIF file into the `Image` control:

```
Private Sub UserForm_Initialize()
    Dim FName As String
    FName = Application.DefaultFilePath & _
        Application.PathSeparator & "temp.gif"
    UserForm1.Image1.Picture = LoadPicture(FName)
End Sub
```

Figure 9.10 illustrates the resulting UserForm when the macro is run.

FIGURE 9.10

A chart within a UserForm

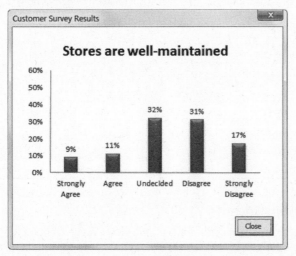

Understanding Chart Events

Excel supports several events associated with charts. For example, when a chart is activated, it generates an `Activate` event. The `Calculate` event occurs after the chart receives new or changed data. You can, of course, write VBA code that gets executed when a particular event occurs.

 Refer to Chapter 6, "Understanding Excel's Events," for additional information about events.

Table 9.1 lists all the chart events.

TABLE 9.1   Events Recognized by the Chart Object

Event	Action That Triggers the Event
`Activate`	A chart sheet or embedded chart is activated.
`Before-DoubleClick`	An embedded chart is double-clicked. This event occurs before the default double-click action.
`BeforeRightClick`	An embedded chart is right-clicked. The event occurs before the default right-click action.
`Calculate`	New or changed data is plotted on a chart.
`Deactivate`	A chart is deactivated.
`MouseDown`	A mouse button is pressed while the pointer is over a chart.
`MouseMove`	The position of the mouse pointer changes over a chart.
`MouseUp`	A mouse button is released while the pointer is over a chart.
`Resize`	A chart is resized.
`Select`	A chart element is selected.
`SeriesChange`	The value of a chart data point is changed.

An example of using Chart events

To program an event handler for an event taking place on a chart sheet, your VBA code must reside in the code module for the `Chart` object. To activate this code module, double-click the Chart item in the Project window. Then, in the code module, select Chart from the Object drop-down list on the left and select the event from the Procedure drop-down list on the right (see Figure 9.11).

> **NOTE**
>
> Because an embedded chart doesn't have its own code module, the procedure that we describe in this section works only for chart sheets. You can also handle events for embedded charts, but you must do some initial setup work that involves creating a class module. This procedure is described later in "Enabling events for an embedded chart."

FIGURE 9.11

Selecting an event in the code module for a Chart object

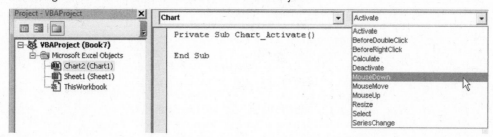

The example that follows simply displays a message when the user activates a chart sheet, deactivates a chart sheet, or selects any element on the chart. This is made possible with three event-handler procedures named as follows:

- Chart _ Activate: Executed when the chart sheet is activated
- Chart _ Deactivate: Executed when the chart sheet is deactivated
- Chart _ Select: Executed when an element on the chart sheet is selected

ON THE WEB

This workbook, named events - chart sheet.xlsm, is available on the book's website.

The Chart _ Activate procedure follows:

```
Private Sub Chart_Activate()
    Dim msg As String
    msg = "Hello " & Application.UserName & vbCrLf & vbCrLf
    msg = msg & "You are now viewing the six-month sales "
    msg = msg & "summary for Products 1-3." & vbCrLf & vbCrLf
    msg = msg & _
      "Click an item in the chart to find out what it is."
    MsgBox msg, vbInformation, ActiveWorkbook.Name
End Sub
```

This procedure displays a message whenever the chart is activated.

The Chart _ Deactivate procedure that follows also displays a message, but only when the chart sheet is deactivated:

```
Private Sub Chart_Deactivate()
    Dim msg As String
    msg = "Thanks for viewing the chart."
    MsgBox msg, , ActiveWorkbook.Name
End Sub
```

9

The `Chart _ Select` procedure that follows is executed whenever an item on the chart is selected:

```
Private Sub Chart_Select(ByVal ElementID As Long, _
   ByVal Arg1 As Long, ByVal Arg2 As Long)
   Dim Id As String
   Select Case ElementID
        Case xlAxis: Id = "Axis"
        Case xlAxisTitle: Id = "AxisTitle"
        Case xlChartArea: Id = "ChartArea"
        Case xlChartTitle: Id = "ChartTitle"
        Case xlCorners: Id = "Corners"
        Case xlDataLabel: Id = "DataLabel"
        Case xlDataTable: Id = "DataTable"
        Case xlDownBars: Id = "DownBars"
        Case xlDropLines: Id = "DropLines"
        Case xlErrorBars: Id = "ErrorBars"
        Case xlFloor: Id = "Floor"
        Case xlHiLoLines: Id = "HiLoLines"
        Case xlLegend: Id = "Legend"
        Case xlLegendEntry: Id = "LegendEntry"
        Case xlLegendKey: Id = "LegendKey"
        Case xlMajorGridlines: Id = "MajorGridlines"
        Case xlMinorGridlines: Id = "MinorGridlines"
        Case xlNothing: Id = "Nothing"
        Case xlPlotArea: Id = "PlotArea"
        Case xlRadarAxisLabels: Id = "RadarAxisLabels"
        Case xlSeries: Id = "Series"
        Case xlSeriesLines: Id = "SeriesLines"
        Case xlShape: Id = "Shape"
        Case xlTrendline: Id = "Trendline"
        Case xlUpBars: Id = "UpBars"
        Case xlWalls: Id = "Walls"
        Case xlXErrorBars: Id = "XErrorBars"
        Case xlYErrorBars: Id = "YErrorBars"
        Case Else:: Id = "Some unknown thing"
   End Select

   MsgBox "Selection type:" & Id & vbCrLf & Arg1 & vbCrLf & Arg2
End Sub
```

This procedure displays a message box that contains a description of the selected item, plus the values for `Arg1` and `Arg2`. When the `Select` event occurs, the `ElementID` argument contains an integer that corresponds to what was selected. The `Arg1` and `Arg2` arguments provide additional information about the selected item (see the Help system for details). The `Select Case` structure converts the built-in constants to descriptive strings.

Enabling events for an embedded chart

As we note in the preceding section, `Chart` events are automatically enabled for chart sheets but not for charts embedded in a worksheet. To use events with an embedded chart, you need to perform the following steps.

Create a class module

In the Visual Basic Editor (VBE) window, select your project in the Project window and choose Insert ⇨ Class Module. This step adds a new (empty) class module to your project. Then use the Properties window to give the class module a more descriptive name (such as `clsChart`). Renaming the class module isn't necessary but is a good practice.

Declare a public Chart object

The next step is to declare a `Public` variable that will represent the chart. The variable should be of type `Chart` and must be declared in the class module by using the `With-Events` keyword. If you omit the `WithEvents` keyword, the object will not respond to events. The following is an example of such a declaration:

```
Public WithEvents clsChart As Chart
```

Connect the declared object with your chart

Before your event-handler procedures will run, you must connect the declared object in the class module with your embedded chart. You do this by declaring an object of type `clsChart` (or whatever your class module is named). This should be a module-level object variable, declared in a regular VBA module (not in the class module). Here's an example:

```
Dim MyChart As New clsChart
```

Then you must write code to associate the `clsChart` object with a particular chart. The following statement accomplishes this task:

```
Set MyChart.clsChart = ActiveSheet.ChartObjects(1).Chart
```

After this statement is executed, the `clsChart` object in the class module points to the first embedded chart on the active sheet. Consequently, the event-handler procedures in the class module will execute when the events occur.

Write event-handler procedures for the chart class

In this section, we describe how to write event-handler procedures in the class module. Recall that the class module must contain a declaration such as the following:

```
Public WithEvents clsChart As Chart
```

After this new object has been declared with the WithEvents keyword, it appears in the Object drop-down list box in the class module. When you select the new object in the Object box, the valid events for that object are listed in the Procedure drop-down box on the right.

The following example is a simple event-handler procedure that is executed when the embedded chart is activated. This procedure simply pops up a message box that displays the name of the Chart object's parent (which is a ChartObject object).

```
Private Sub clsChart_Activate()
    MsgBox clsChart.Parent.Name & " was activated!"
End Sub
```

ON THE WEB

The book's website contains a workbook that demonstrates the concepts that we describe in this section. The file is `events - embedded chart.xlsm`.

Example: Using Chart events with an embedded chart

The example in this section provides a practical demonstration of the information presented in the previous section. The example shown in Figure 9.12 consists of an embedded chart that functions as a clickable image map. When chart events are enabled, clicking one of the chart columns activates a worksheet that shows detailed data for the region.

FIGURE 9.12

This chart serves as a clickable image map.

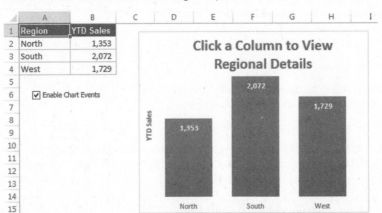

The workbook is set up with four worksheets. The sheet named Main contains the embedded chart. The other sheets are named North, South, and West. Formulas in B2:B4 sum the data in the respective sheets, and this summary data is plotted in the chart.

Clicking a column in the chart triggers an event, and the event-handler procedure activates the appropriate sheet so that the user can view the details for the desired region.

The workbook contains both a class module named EmbChartClass and a normal VBA module named Module1. For demonstration purposes, the Main worksheet also contains a check box control (from the Forms group). Clicking the check box executes the Check-Box1 _ Click procedure, which turns event monitoring on and off:

In addition, each of the other worksheets contains a button that executes the ReturnTo-Main macro that reactivates the Main sheet.

The complete listing of Module1 follows:

```
Dim SummaryChart As New EmbChartClass

Sub CheckBox1_Click()
    If Worksheets("Main").CheckBoxes("Check Box 1") = xlOn Then
        'Enable chart events
        Range("A1").Select
        Set SummaryChart.myChartClass = _
            Worksheets(1).ChartObjects(1).Chart
    Else
        'Disable chart events
        Set SummaryChart.myChartClass = Nothing
        Range("A1").Select
    End If
End Sub

Sub ReturnToMain()
'    Called by worksheet button
    Sheets("Main").Activate
    ActiveWindow.RangeSelection.Select
End Sub
```

The first instruction declares a new object variable SummaryChart to be of type Emb-ChartClass. As you will recall, this is the name of the class module. When the user clicks the Enable Chart Events button, the embedded chart is assigned to the SummaryChart object, which, in effect, enables the events for the chart. The contents of the class module for EmbChartClass follow:

```
Public WithEvents myChartClass As Chart

Private Sub myChartClass_MouseDown(ByVal Button As Long, _
    ByVal Shift As Long, ByVal X As Long, ByVal Y As Long)

    Dim IDnum As Long
    Dim a As Long, b As Long

'    The next statement returns values for
'    IDnum, a, and b
```

```
        myChartClass.GetChartElement X, Y, IDnum, a, b

'   Was a series clicked?
    If IDnum = xlSeries Then
        Select Case b
            Case 1
                Sheets("North").Activate
            Case 2
                Sheets("South").Activate
            Case 3
                Sheets("West").Activate
        End Select
    End If
    Range("A1").Select
End Sub
```

Clicking the chart generates a MouseDown event, which executes the myChartClass _
MouseDown procedure. This procedure uses the GetChartElement method to determine
what element of the chart was clicked. The GetChartElement method returns information about the chart element at specified X and Y coordinates (information that is available
through the arguments for the myChartClass _ MouseDown procedure).

On the Web

This workbook, named chart image map.xlsm, is available on the book's website.

Discovering VBA Charting Tricks

This section contains a few charting tricks that might be useful in your applications.
Others are simply for fun, or at the very least studying them could give you some new
insights into the object model for charts.

Printing embedded charts on a full page

When an embedded chart is selected, you can print the chart by choosing File ⇨ Print. The
embedded chart will be printed on a full page by itself (just as if it were on a chart sheet),
yet it will remain an embedded chart.

The following macro prints all embedded charts on the active sheet, and each chart is
printed on a full page:

```
Sub PrintEmbeddedCharts()
    Dim ChtObj As ChartObject
    For Each ChtObj In ActiveSheet.ChartObjects
        ChtObj.Chart.PrintOut
    Next ChtObj
End Sub
```

Creating unlinked charts

Normally, an Excel chart uses data stored in a range. Change the data in the range, and the chart is updated automatically. In some cases, you might want to unlink the chart from its data ranges and produce a *dead chart* (a chart that never changes). For example, if you plot data generated by various what-if scenarios, you might want to save a chart that represents some baseline so that you can compare it with other scenarios.

The three ways to create such a chart are as follows:

- **Copy the chart as a picture.** Activate the chart, and choose Home ⇨ Clipboard ⇨ Copy ⇨ Copy As Picture. Accept the defaults in the Copy Picture dialog box. Then click a cell and choose Home ⇨ Clipboard ⇨ Paste. The result will be a picture of the copied chart.
- **Convert the range references to arrays.** Click a chart series and then click the formula bar. Press F9 to convert the ranges to an array, and press Enter. Repeat these steps for each series in the chart.
- **Use VBA to assign an array rather than a range to the** XValues **or** Values **properties of the** Series **object.** This technique is described next.

The following procedure creates a chart by using arrays. The data isn't stored in the worksheet. As you can see, the SERIES formula contains arrays and not range references.

```
Sub CreateUnlinkedChart()
    Dim MyChart As Chart
    Set MyChart = ActiveSheet.Shapes.AddChart2.Chart
    With MyChart
        .SeriesCollection.NewSeries
        .SeriesCollection(1).Name = "Sales"
        .SeriesCollection(1).XValues = Array("Jan", "Feb", "Mar")
        .SeriesCollection(1).Values = Array(125, 165, 189)
        .ChartType = xlColumnClustered
        .SetElement msoElementLegendNone
    End With
End Sub
```

Because Excel imposes a limit to the length of a chart's SERIES formula, this technique works for only relatively small data sets.

The following procedure creates a picture of the active chart. (The original chart isn't deleted.) It works only with embedded charts.

```
Sub ConvertChartToPicture()
    Dim Cht As Chart
    If ActiveChart Is Nothing Then Exit Sub
    If TypeName(ActiveSheet) = "Chart" Then Exit Sub
    Set Cht = ActiveChart
    Cht.CopyPicture Appearance:=xlPrinter, _
        Size:=xlScreen, Format:=xlPicture
    ActiveWindow.RangeSelection.Select
```

9

```
        ActiveSheet.Paste
End Sub
```

When a chart is converted to a picture, you can create some interesting displays by choosing Picture Tools ⇨ Format ⇨ Picture Styles. See Figure 9.13 for an example.

FIGURE 9.13

After converting a chart to a picture, you can manipulate it by using a variety of formatting options.

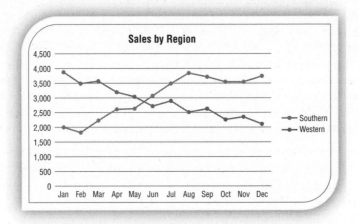

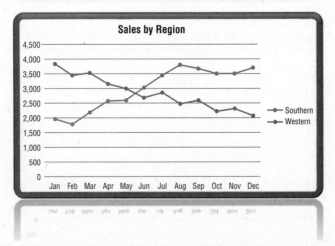

ON THE WEB

The two examples in this section are available on the book's website in the `unlinked chart.xlsm` file.

Displaying text with the MouseOver event

A common charting question deals with modifying chart tips. A *chart tip* is the small message that appears next to the mouse pointer when you move the mouse over an activated chart. The chart tip displays the chart element name and (for series) the value of the data point. The Chart object model does not expose these chart tips, so there is no way to modify them.

This section describes an alternative to chart tips. Figure 9.14 shows a column chart that uses the MouseOver event. When the mouse pointer is positioned over a column, the text box (a Shape object) in the upper-left corner displays information about the data point. The information is stored in a range and can consist of anything you like.

FIGURE 9.14

A text box displays information about the data point under the mouse pointer.

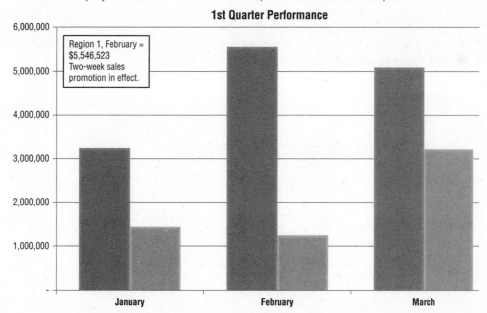

9

The event procedure that follows is located in the code module for the Chart sheet that contains the chart:

```
Private Sub Chart_MouseMove(ByVal Button As Long, ByVal Shift
As Long, _
   ByVal X As Long, ByVal Y As Long)
     Dim ElementId As Long
     Dim arg1 As Long, arg2 As Long
     On Error Resume Next
     ActiveChart.GetChartElement X, Y, ElementId, arg1, arg2
     If ElementId = xlSeries Then
         ActiveChart.Shapes(1).Visible = msoCTrue
         ActiveChart.Shapes(1).TextFrame.Characters.Text = _
           Sheets("Sheet1").Range("Comments").Offset(arg2, arg1)
     Else
         ActiveChart.Shapes(1).Visible = msoFalse
     End If
End Sub
```

This procedure monitors all mouse movements on the Chart sheet. The mouse coordinates are contained in the X and Y variables, which are passed to the procedure. The Button and Shift arguments aren't used in this procedure.

As in the previous example, the key component in this procedure is the GetChartElement method. If ElementId is xlSeries, the mouse pointer is over a series. The TextBox control is made visible and displays the text in a particular cell. This text contains descriptive information about the data point (see Figure 9.15). If the mouse pointer isn't over a series, the text box is hidden.

FIGURE 9.15

Range B7:C9 contains data point information that's displayed in the text box on the chart.

	A	B	C
1	Month	Region 1	Region 2
2	January	3,245,151	1,434,343
3	February	5,546,523	1,238,709
4	March	5,083,204	3,224,855
5			
6	Comments		
7		Region 1, January = $3,245,151	Region 2, January = $1,434,343
8		Region 1, February = $5,546,523 Two-week sales promotion in effect.	Region 2, February = $1,238,709
9		Region 1, March = $5,083,204	Region 2, March = $3,224,855 L.A. merger took place in week three.

The example workbook also contains a `Chart _ Activate` event procedure that turns off the normal ChartTip display, as well as a `Chart _ Deactivate` procedure that turns the settings back on. The `Chart _ Activate` procedure is as follows:

```
Private Sub Chart_Activate()
    Application.ShowChartTipNames = False
    Application.ShowChartTipValues = False
End Sub
```

Scrolling a chart

Figure 9.16 illustrates the example chart found in the `scrolling chart.xlsm` sample workbook. This chart displays only a portion of the source data, but it can be scrolled to show additional values.

FIGURE 9.16

An example of a scrollable chart

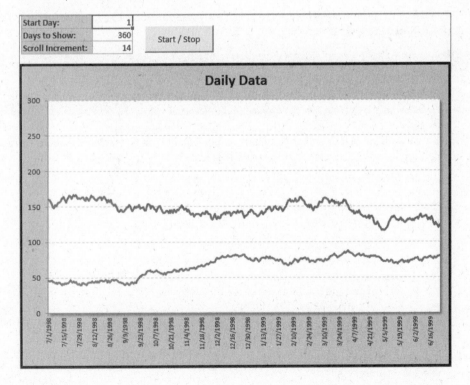

The workbook contains six names.

StartDay: A name for cell F1

NumDays: A name for cell F2

Increment: A name for cell F3 (used for automatic scrolling)

Date: A named formula:

```
=OFFSET(Sheet1!$A$1,StartDay,0,NumDays,1)
```

ProdA: A named formula:

```
=OFFSET(Sheet1!$B$1,StartDay,0,NumDays,1)
```

ProdB: A named formula:

```
=OFFSET(Sheet1!$C$1,StartDay,0,NumDays,1)
```

Each SERIES formula in the chart uses names for the category values and the data. The SERIES formula for the Product A series is as follows (note the workbook name and sheet name have been eliminated for clarity):

```
=SERIES($B$1,Date,ProdA,1)
```

The SERIES formula for the Product B series is as follows:

```
=SERIES($C$1,Date,ProdB,2)
```

Using these names enables the user to specify a value for StartDay and NumDays. The chart will display a subset of the data.

ON THE WEB

The book's website contains a workbook that includes this animated chart. The filename is `scrolling chart .xlsm`.

A relatively simple macro makes the chart scroll. The button in the worksheet executes the following macro that scrolls (or stops scrolling) the chart:

```
Public AnimationInProgress As Boolean

Sub AnimateChart()
    Dim StartVal As Long, r As Long
    If AnimationInProgress Then
        AnimationInProgress = False
        End
    End If
    AnimationInProgress = True
    StartVal = Range("StartDay")
    For r = StartVal To 5219 - Range("NumDays") Step Range("Increment")
        Range("StartDay") = r
        DoEvents
    Next r
```

```
        AnimationInProgress = False
    End Sub
```

The `AnimateChart` procedure uses a public variable (`AnimationInProgress`) to keep track of the animation status. The animation results from a loop that changes the value in the `StartDay` cell. Because the two chart series use this value, the chart is continually updated with a new starting value. The Scroll Increment setting determines how quickly the chart scrolls.

To stop the animation, we use an `End` statement rather than an `Exit Sub` statement. The `Exit Sub` statement doesn't work reliably in this scenario and may even crash Excel.

Working with Sparkline Charts

We conclude this chapter with a brief discussion of Sparkline charts, a feature introduced in Excel 2010. A *Sparkline* is a small chart displayed in a cell. A Sparkline lets the viewer quickly spot time-based trends or variations in data. Because they're so compact, Sparklines are often used in a group.

Figure 9.17 shows examples of the three types of Sparklines supported by Excel.

FIGURE 9.17

Sparkline examples

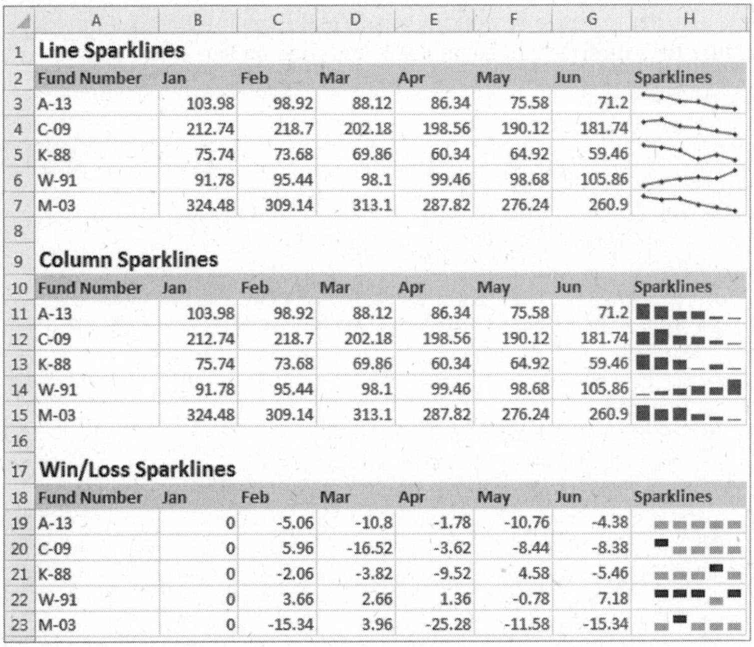

	A	B	C	D	E	F	G	H
1	**Line Sparklines**							
2	**Fund Number**	Jan	Feb	Mar	Apr	May	Jun	Sparklines
3	A-13	103.98	98.92	88.12	86.34	75.58	71.2	
4	C-09	212.74	218.7	202.18	198.56	190.12	181.74	
5	K-88	75.74	73.68	69.86	60.34	64.92	59.46	
6	W-91	91.78	95.44	98.1	99.46	98.68	105.86	
7	M-03	324.48	309.14	313.1	287.82	276.24	260.9	
8								
9	**Column Sparklines**							
10	**Fund Number**	Jan	Feb	Mar	Apr	May	Jun	Sparklines
11	A-13	103.98	98.92	88.12	86.34	75.58	71.2	
12	C-09	212.74	218.7	202.18	198.56	190.12	181.74	
13	K-88	75.74	73.68	69.86	60.34	64.92	59.46	
14	W-91	91.78	95.44	98.1	99.46	98.68	105.86	
15	M-03	324.48	309.14	313.1	287.82	276.24	260.9	
16								
17	**Win/Loss Sparklines**							
18	**Fund Number**	Jan	Feb	Mar	Apr	May	Jun	Sparklines
19	A-13	0	-5.06	-10.8	-1.78	-10.76	-4.38	
20	C-09	0	5.96	-16.52	-3.62	-8.44	-8.38	
21	K-88	0	-2.06	-3.82	-9.52	4.58	-5.46	
22	W-91	0	3.66	2.66	1.36	-0.78	7.18	
23	M-03	0	-15.34	3.96	-25.28	-11.58	-15.34	

9

As with most features, Microsoft added Sparklines to Excel's object model, which means you can work with Sparklines using VBA. At the top of the object hierarchy is the `Sparkline-Groups` collection, which is a collection of all `SparklineGroup` objects. A `Sparkline-Group` object contains `Sparkline` objects. Contrary to what you might expect, the parent of the `SparklineGroups` collection is a `Range` object, not a `Worksheet` object. Therefore, the following statement generates an error:

```
MsgBox ActiveSheet.SparklineGroups.Count
```

Rather, you need to use the `Cells` property (which returns a range object).

```
MsgBox Cells.SparklineGroups.Count
```

The following example lists the address of each Sparkline group on the active worksheet:

```
Sub ListSparklineGroups()
    Dim sg As SparklineGroup
    Dim i As Long
    For i = 1 To Cells.SparklineGroups.Count
        Set sg = Cells.SparklineGroups(i)
        MsgBox sg.Location.Address
    Next i
End Sub
```

Unfortunately, you can't use the `For Each` construct to loop through the objects in the `SparklineGroups` collection. You need to refer to the objects by their index number.

The following is another example of working with Sparklines in VBA. The `Sparkline-Report` procedure lists information about each Sparkline on the active sheet.

```
Sub SparklineReport()
    Dim sg As SparklineGroup
    Dim sl As Sparkline
    Dim SGType As String
    Dim SLSheet As Worksheet
    Dim i As Long, j As Long, r As Long

    If Cells.SparklineGroups.Count = 0 Then
        MsgBox "No sparklines were found on the active sheet."
        Exit Sub
    End If

    Set SLSheet = ActiveSheet
'   Insert new worksheet for the report
    Worksheets.Add
```

```
'    Headings
     With Range("A1")
         .Value = "Sparkline Report: " & SLSheet.Name & " in " _
             & SLSheet.Parent.Name
         .Font.Bold = True
         .Font.Size = 16
     End With
     With Range("A3:F3")
         .Value = Array("Group #", "Sparkline Grp Range", _
             "# in Group", "Type", "Sparkline #", "Source Range")
         .Font.Bold = True
     End With
     r = 4

     'Loop through each sparkline group
     For i = 1 To SLSheet.Cells.SparklineGroups.Count
         Set sg = SLSheet.Cells.SparklineGroups(i)
         Select Case sg.Type
             Case 1: SGType = "Line"
             Case 2: SGType = "Column"
             Case 3: SGType = "Win/Loss"
         End Select
         ' Loop through each sparkline in the group
         For j = 1 To sg.Count
             Set sl = sg.Item(j)
             Cells(r, 1) = i 'Group #
             Cells(r, 2) = sg.Location.Address
             Cells(r, 3) = sg.Count
             Cells(r, 4) = SGType
             Cells(r, 5) = j 'Sparkline # within Group
             Cells(r, 6) = sl.SourceData
             r = r + 1
         Next j
         r = r + 1
     Next i
 End Sub
```

Figure 9.18 shows a sample report generated from this procedure.

ON THE WEB

This workbook, named `sparkline report.xlsm`, is available on the book's website.

The result of running the `SparklineReport` procedure

	A	B	C	D	E	F	G
1	Sparkline Report: Sheet1 in sparkline report.xlsm						
2							
3	Group #	Sparkline	# in Group	Type	Sparkline	Source Range	
4	1	$N$22:N	10	Line	1	B22:M22	
5	1	$N$22:N	10	Line	2	B23:M23	
6	1	$N$22:N	10	Line	3	B24:M24	
7	1	$N$22:N	10	Line	4	B25:M25	
8	1	$N$22:N	10	Line	5	B26:M26	
9	1	$N$22:N	10	Line	6	B27:M27	
10	1	$N$22:N	10	Line	7	B28:M28	
11	1	$N$22:N	10	Line	8	B29:M29	
12	1	$N$22:N	10	Line	9	B30:M30	
13	1	$N$22:N	10	Line	10	B31:M31	
14							
15	2	$N$9:N	10	Column	1	B9:M9	
16	2	$N$9:N	10	Column	2	B10:M10	
17	2	$N$9:N	10	Column	3	B11:M11	
18	2	$N$9:N	10	Column	4	B12:M12	
19	2	$N$9:N	10	Column	5	B13:M13	
20	2	$N$9:N	10	Column	6	B14:M14	
21	2	$N$9:N	10	Column	7	B15:M15	
22	2	$N$9:N	10	Column	8	B16:M16	
23	2	$N$9:N	10	Column	9	B17:M17	
24	2	$N$9:N	10	Column	10	B18:M18	

Interacting with Other Applications

Understanding Microsoft Office Automation

Throughout this book, you've discovered how to leverage VBA to automate tasks, processes, and program flow. In this chapter, automation will take on a different meaning. *Automation* here will define the means of manipulating or controlling one application with another.

Why would you even want to control one application with another? Data-oriented processes quite often involve a succession of applications. It's not uncommon to see data being analyzed and aggregated in Excel, used in a PowerPoint presentation, and then e-mailed via Outlook.

The reality is that each Microsoft Office application has strengths that you routinely leverage through manual processes. With VBA, you can go further and automate the interactions between Excel and other Office applications.

Understanding the concept of binding

Each program in the Microsoft Office suite comes with its own Object Library. As you know, the *Object Library* is a kind of encyclopedia of all the objects, methods, and properties available in each Office application. Excel has its own object library, just as all the other Office applications have their own object library.

In order for Excel to be able to speak to another Office program, you have to bind it to that program. *Binding* is the process of exposing the Object Library for a server application to a client application. There are two types of binding: early binding and late binding.

Early binding

With *early binding*, you explicitly point a client application to the server application's Object Library to expose the server application's object model during design time or while programming. Then you use the exposed objects in your code to call a new instance of the server application as such:

```
Dim XL As Excel.Application
    Set XL = New Excel.Application
```

Early binding has several advantages.

- Because the objects are exposed at design time, the client application can compile your code before execution. This allows your code to run considerably faster than with late binding.
- Since the object library is exposed during design time, you have full access to the server application's object model in the Object Browser.
- You have the benefit of using IntelliSense. *IntelliSense* is the functionality you experience when you type a keyword and a dot (.) or an equal sign (=) and you see a pop-up list of the methods and properties available to you.
- You automatically have access to the server application's built-in constants.

To use early binding, you will need to create a reference to the appropriate object library by choosing the Tools ⇨ References command in the Visual Basic Editor (VBE). In the References dialog box (shown in Figure 10.1), find the Office application that you want to automate and then place a check next to it. The version of the available library on your system will be equal to your version of Office. So, for instance, if you are working with Office 2019, you will have the PowerPoint 17.0 library. If you have Office 2013, you will have the PowerPoint 15.0 library.

Late binding

Late binding is different in that you don't point a client application to a specific Object Library. Instead, you purposely keep things ambiguous, only using the CreateObject function to bind to the needed library at run-time or during program execution.

```
Dim XL As Object
    Set XL = CreateObject("Excel.Application")
```

FIGURE 10.1

Add a reference to the object library for the application that you are automating.

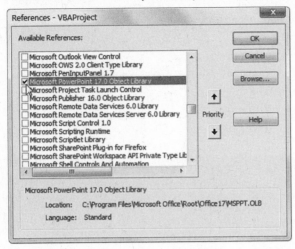

Late binding has one primary advantage. Late binding allows your automation procedures to be version-independent. That is to say, your automation procedure will not fail because of compatibility issues between multiple versions of a component.

For example, suppose you decide to use early binding and set a reference to the Excel Object Library on your system. The version of the available library on your system will be equal to your version of Excel. The problem is that if your users have a lower version of Excel on their machine, your automation procedure will fail. You do not have this problem with late binding.

GetObject vs. CreateObject

The VBA GetObject and CreateObject functions both return a reference to an object but work in different ways.

The CreateObject function creates an interface to a new instance of an application. Use this function when the application isn't running. If an instance of the application is already running, a new instance is started. For example, the following statement starts Excel, and the object returned in XLApp is a reference to the Excel.Application object that it created:

```
Set XLApp = CreateObject("Excel.Application")
```

The GetObject function is used either with an application that's already running or to start an application with a file already loaded. The following statement, for example, starts Excel with the file Myfile.xls already loaded. The object returned in XLBook is a reference to the Workbook object (the Myfile.xlsx file).

```
Set XLBook = GetObject("C:\Myfile.xlsx")
```

10

A simple automation example

The following example demonstrates how to create a Word object by using late binding. This procedure creates an instance of Word, displays the current version number, closes the Word application, and then destroys the object (thus freeing the memory that it used).

```
Sub GetWordVersion()
    Dim WordApp As Object
    Set WordApp = CreateObject("Word.Application")
    MsgBox WordApp.Version
    WordApp.Quit
    Set WordApp = Nothing
End Sub
```

> **NOTE**
>
> The Word object that's created in this procedure is invisible. If you'd like to see the object's window while it's being manipulated, set its Visible property to True, as follows:
>
> ```
> WordApp.Visible = True
> ```

This example can be adjusted to use early binding. Before doing so, we will need to activate the References dialog box in VBE (Tools ⇨ References) and set a reference to the Word object library. Once we set the appropriate reference, we can use the following code:

```
Sub GetWordVersion()
    Dim WordApp As New Word.Application
    MsgBox WordApp.Version
    WordApp.Quit
    Set WordApp = Nothing
End Sub
```

Automating Access from Excel

It typically doesn't occur to most Excel users to automate Access using Excel. Indeed, it's difficult for most of us to think of situations where this would even be necessary. Although there are admittedly few mind-blowing reasons to automate Access from Excel, you may find some of the automation tricks found in this section strangely appealing. Who knows? You may even implement a few of them.

Running an Access query from Excel

Here's a nifty macro for those of you who often copy and paste the results of your Microsoft Access queries into Excel. In this macro, you use a Data Access Object (DAO) to open and run an Access query in the background and output the results into Excel.

In this macro, you are pointing Excel to an Access database and pulling data from an existing Access query. You then store that query in a `Recordset` object, which you can use to populate your Excel spreadsheet.

ON THE WEB

This workbook, named `Running an Access Query from Excel.xlsm`, is available on the book's website.

NOTE

Since you are automating Access, you will need to set a reference to the Microsoft Access Object Library. To do so, open the VBE in Excel and select Tools ⇨ References. The Reference dialog box will activate. Scroll down until you find the entry Microsoft Access XX Object Library, where the *XX* is your version of Access. Place a check in the check box next to the entry.

```
Sub RunAccessQuery()

'Declare your variables
    Dim MyDatabase As DAO.Database
    Dim MyQueryDef As DAO.QueryDef
    Dim MyRecordset As DAO.Recordset
    Dim i As Integer
'Identify the database and query
    Set MyDatabase = DBEngine.OpenDatabase _
       ("C:\Temp\YourAccessDatabase.accdb")

    Set MyQueryDef = MyDatabase.QueryDefs("Your Query Name")

'Open the query
    Set MyRecordset = MyQueryDef.OpenRecordset


'Clear previous contents
     Sheets("Sheet1").Select
     ActiveSheet.Range("A6:K10000").ClearContents

'Copy the recordset to Excel
     ActiveSheet.Range("A7").CopyFromRecordset MyRecordset

'Add column heading names to the spreadsheet
    For i = 1 To MyRecordset.Fields.Count
        ActiveSheet.Cells(6, i).Value = MyRecordset.Fields(i - 1).Name
    Next i

End Sub
```

10

Running an Access macro from Excel

You can run Access macros from Excel using automation to fire the macro without opening Access. Not only is this technique useful for running those epic macros that involve a multistep series of 20 queries, but it can also come in handy for everyday tasks such as outputting Access data to an Excel file.

The following macro is a simple way to trigger an Access macro programmatically.

NOTE

You will need to set a reference to the Microsoft Access Object Library. To do so, open the VBE in Excel and select Tools ⁙ References. The Reference dialog box will activate. Scroll down until you find the entry Microsoft Access XX Object Library, where the *XX* is your version of Access. Place a check in the check box next to the entry.

```
Sub RunAccessMacro()

'Declare your variables
    Dim AC As Access.Application

'Start Access and open the target database
    Set AC = New Access.Application
            AC.OpenCurrentDatabase _
            ("C:\Temp\YourAccessDatabase.accdb")

'Run the Target Macro
    With AC
        .DoCmd.RunMacro "MyMacro"
        .Quit
    End With

End Sub
```

Automating Word from Excel

It's not unusual to see a Word document that contains a table that originated in Excel. In most cases, that table was simply copied and pasted directly into Word. While copying and pasting data from Excel into Word is indeed a valid form of integration, there are countless ways to integrate Excel and Word that go beyond copying and pasting data. This section offers a few examples that demonstrate techniques that you can leverage to integrate Excel and Word.

Sending Excel data to a Word document

If you find that you are constantly copying and pasting Excel data into Microsoft Word, you can use a macro to automate this task.

Before walking through the macro, it's important to go over a few set up steps:

1. To set up for a process like this, you must have a template Word document already created. In that document, create a bookmark tagging the location where you want your Excel data to be copied.

2. To create a bookmark in a Word document, place your cursor where you want the bookmark, select the Insert tab, and select Bookmark (found under the Links group). This will activate the Bookmark dialog box where you assign a name for your bookmark. Once the name has been assigned, click the Add button.

> **ON THE WEB**
>
> This workbook, named `Sending Excel Data to a Word Document.xlsm`, is available on the book's website. You will also find a document called `PasteTable.docx`. This document is a simple template that contains one bookmark called `DataTableHere`. In this example code, you copy a range to that `PasteTable.docx` template, using the `DataTableHere` bookmark to specify where to paste the copied range.

> **NOTE**
>
> You will need to set a reference to the Microsoft Word Object Library. To do so, open the Visual Basic Editor in Excel and select Tools ⇨ References. The Reference dialog box will activate. Scroll down until you find the entry Microsoft Word XX Object Library, where the *XX* is your version of Word. Place a check in the check box next to the entry.

```
Sub SendDataToWord()

'Declare your variables
    Dim MyRange As Excel.Range
    Dim wd As Word.Application
    Dim wdDoc As Word.Document
    Dim wdRange As Word.Range

'Copy the defined range
    Sheets("Revenue Table").Range("B4:F10").Copy

'Open the target Word document
    Set wd = New Word.Application
    Set wdDoc = wd.Documents.Open _
      (ThisWorkbook.Path & "\" & "PasteTable.docx")
    wd.Visible = True

'Set focus on the target bookmark
    Set wdRange = wdDoc.Bookmarks("DataTableHere").Range
```

10

```
'Delete the old table and paste new
    On Error Resume Next
    wdRange.Tables(1).Delete
    wdRange.Paste 'paste in the table
    On Error Goto 0

'Adjust column widths
    wdRange.Tables(1).Columns.SetWidth _
    (MyRange.Width / MyRange.Columns.Count), wdAdjustSameWidth

'Reinsert the bookmark
    wdDoc.Bookmarks.Add "DataTableHere", wdRange

'Memory cleanup
    Set wd = Nothing
    Set wdDoc = Nothing
    Set wdRange = Nothing

End Sub
```

Simulating Mail Merge with a Word document

One of the most requested forms of integration with Word is the mail merge. In most cases, *mail merge* refers to the process of creating one letter or document for each customer in a list of customers. For example, suppose you had a list of customers and you wanted to compose a letter to each customer. With mail merge, you can write the body of the letter one time and then run the Mail Merge feature in Word to create a letter for each customer automatically, affixing the appropriate, address, name, and other information to each letter.

If you are an automation buff, you can use a macro to simulate the Word Mail Merge function from Excel. The idea is relatively simple. You start with a template that contains bookmarks identifying where each element of contact information will go. With the template set to go, the idea is simply to loop through each contact in your contact list, assigning the component pieces of their contact information to the respective bookmarks.

ON THE WEB

This workbook, named `Simulating Mail Merge with a Word Document.xlsm`, is available on the book's website. You will also find a document called `MailMerge.docx`. This document has all the bookmarks needed to run the sample code shown here.

NOTE

You will need to set a reference to the Microsoft Word Object Library. To do so, open the Visual Basic Editor in Excel and select Tools ⇨ References. The Reference dialog box will activate. Scroll down until you find the entry Microsoft Word XX Object Library, where the *XX* is your version of Word. Place a check in the check box next to the entry.

```vb
Sub WordMailMerge()

'Declare your variables
    Dim wd As Word.Application
    Dim wdDoc As Word.Document
    Dim MyRange As Excel.Range
    Dim MyCell As Excel.Range
    Dim txtAddress As String
    Dim txtCity As String
    Dim txtState As String
    Dim txtPostalCode As String
    Dim txtFname As String
    Dim txtFullname As String


'Start Word and add a new document
    Set wd = New Word.Application
    Set wdDoc = wd.Documents.Add
    wd.Visible = True


'Set the range of your contact list
    Set MyRange = Sheets("Contact List").Range("A5:A24")


'Start the loop through each cell
    For Each MyCell In MyRange.Cells


'Assign values to each component of the letter
    txtAddress = MyCell.Value
    txtCity = MyCell.Offset(, 1).Value
    txtState = MyCell.Offset(, 2).Value
    txtPostalCode = MyCell.Offset(, 3).Value
    txtFname = MyCell.Offset(, 5).Value
    txtFullname = MyCell.Offset(, 6).Value

'Insert the structure of template document
    wd.Selection.InsertFile _
    ThisWorkbook.Path & "\" & "MailMerge.docx"


'Fill each relevant bookmark with respective value
    wd.Selection.Goto What:=wdGoToBookmark, Name:="Customer"
    wd.Selection.TypeText Text:=txtFullname

    wd.Selection.Goto What:=wdGoToBookmark, Name:="Address"
    wd.Selection.TypeText Text:=txtAddress
```

10

```
        wd.Selection.Goto What:=wdGoToBookmark, Name:="City"
        wd.Selection.TypeText Text:=txtCity

        wd.Selection.Goto What:=wdGoToBookmark, Name:="State"
        wd.Selection.TypeText Text:=txtState

        wd.Selection.Goto What:=wdGoToBookmark, Name:="Zip"
        wd.Selection.TypeText Text:=txtPostalCode

        wd.Selection.Goto What:=wdGoToBookmark, Name:="FirstName"
        wd.Selection.TypeText Text:=txtFname


    'Clear any remaining bookmarks
        On Error Resume Next
        wdDoc.Bookmarks("Address").Delete
        wdDoc.Bookmarks("Customer").Delete
        wdDoc.Bookmarks("City").Delete
        wdDoc.Bookmarks("State").Delete
        wdDoc.Bookmarks("FirstName").Delete
        wdDoc.Bookmarks("Zip").Delete
        On Error Goto 0

    'Go to the end, insert new page, and start with the next cell
        wd.Selection.EndKey Unit:=wdStory
        wd.Selection.InsertBreak Type:=wdPageBreak
        Next MyCell


    'Set cursor to beginning and clean up memory
        wd.Selection.HomeKey Unit:=wdStory
        wd.Activate
        Set wd = Nothing
        Set wdDoc = Nothing

    End Sub
```

Automating PowerPoint from Excel

It has been estimated that up to 50 percent of PowerPoint presentations contain data that has been copied straight out of Excel. This is not difficult to believe. It's often much easier to analyze and create charts and data views in Excel than in PowerPoint. Once those charts and data views have been created, why wouldn't you simply copy them into PowerPoint? The time and effort saved by copying directly from Excel is too good to pass up.

This section offers up a few techniques that can help you automate the process of getting your Excel data into PowerPoint.

Sending Excel data to a PowerPoint presentation

To help get a few fundamentals down, let's start simple and automate the creation of a PowerPoint presentation containing one slide with a title. In this example, you are copying a range from an Excel file and pasting that range into a slide in a newly created PowerPoint presentation.

ON THE WEB

This workbook, named `Sending Excel Data to a PowerPoint Presentation.xlsm`, is available on the book's website.

NOTE

You will need to set a reference to the Microsoft PowerPoint Object Library. Again, you can set the reference by opening the Visual Basic Editor in Excel and selecting Tools ⇨ References. Scroll down until you find the entry Microsoft PowerPoint XX Object Library, where the *XX* is your version of PowerPoint. Place a check in the check box next to the entry.

```
Sub CopyRangeToPresentation()

'Declare your variables
    Dim PP As PowerPoint.Application
    Dim PPPres As PowerPoint.Presentation
    Dim PPSlide As PowerPoint.Slide
    Dim SlideTitle As String

'Open PowerPoint and create new presentation
    Set PP = New PowerPoint.Application
    Set PPPres = PP.Presentations.Add
    PP.Visible = True
'Add new slide as slide 1 and set focus to it
    Set PPSlide = PPPres.Slides.Add(1, ppLayoutTitleOnly)
    PPSlide.Select

'Copy the range as a picture
    Sheets("Slide Data").Range("A2:J28").CopyPicture _
        Appearance:=xlScreen, Format:=xlPicture

'Paste the picture and adjust its position
    PPSlide.Shapes.Paste.Select
    PP.ActiveWindow.Selection.ShapeRange.Align msoAlignCenters, True
    PP.ActiveWindow.Selection.ShapeRange.Align msoAlignMiddles, True

'Add the title to the slide
    SlideTitle = "My First PowerPoint Slide"
    PPSlide.Shapes.Title.TextFrame.TextRange.Text = SlideTitle
```

10

```
'Memory Cleanup
    PP.Activate
    Set PPSlide = Nothing
    Set PPPres = Nothing
    Set PP = Nothing

End Sub
```

Sending all Excel charts to a PowerPoint presentation

It's not uncommon to see multiple charts on one worksheet. Many people have the need to copy charts to PowerPoint presentations. The macro here assists in that task, effectively automating the process of copying each one of these charts into its own slide.

In this macro, we loop through the `Activesheet.ChartObjects` collection to copy each chart as a picture into its own slide in a newly created PowerPoint presentation.

ON THE WEB

This workbook, named `Sending All Excel Charts to a PowerPoint Presentation.xlsm`, is available on the book's website.

NOTE

You will need to set a reference to the Microsoft PowerPoint Object Library. Again, you can set the reference by opening the Visual Basic Editor in Excel and selecting Tools ⇨ References. Scroll down until you find the entry Microsoft PowerPoint XX Object Library, where the XX is your version of PowerPoint. Place a check in the check box next to the entry.

```
Sub CopyAllChartsToPresentation()

'Declare your variables
    Dim PP As PowerPoint.Application
    Dim PPPres As PowerPoint.Presentation
    Dim PPSlide As PowerPoint.Slide
    Dim ppSlideCount As Long
    Dim i As Long

'Check for charts; exit if no charts exist
    Sheets("Slide Data").Select
    If ActiveSheet.ChartObjects.Count < 1 Then
        MsgBox "No charts exist in the active sheet"
        Exit Sub
    End If

'Open PowerPoint and create new presentation
    Set PP = New PowerPoint.Application
```

```
    Set PPPres = PP.Presentations.Add
    PP.Visible = True

'Start the loop based on chart count
    For i = 1 To ActiveSheet.ChartObjects.Count

        'Copy the chart as a picture
        ActiveSheet.ChartObjects(i).Chart.CopyPicture _
        Size:=xlScreen, Format:=xlPicture
        Application.Wait (Now + TimeValue("0:00:1"))

        'Count slides and add new slide as next available slide number
        ppSlideCount = PPPres.Slides.Count
        Set PPSlide = PPPres.Slides.Add(ppSlideCount + 1, ppLayoutBlank)
        PPSlide.Select

        'Paste the picture and adjust its position; Go to next chart
        PPSlide.Shapes.Paste.Select
        PP.ActiveWindow.Selection.ShapeRange.Align msoAlignCenters, True
        PP.ActiveWindow.Selection.ShapeRange.Align msoAlignMiddles, True
    Next i

'Memory Cleanup
    Set PPSlide = Nothing
    Set PPPres = Nothing
    Set PP = Nothing

End Sub
```

Convert a workbook into a PowerPoint Presentation

This last macro takes the concept of using Excel data in PowerPoint to the extreme. Open the sample workbook called `Convert a Workbook into a PowerPoint Presentation.xlsm`. In this workbook, you will notice that each worksheet contains its own data about a region. It's almost as if each worksheet is its own separate slide, providing information on a particular region.

The idea here is that you can build a workbook in such a way that it mimics a PowerPoint presentation; the workbook is the presentation itself, and each worksheet becomes a slide in the presentation. Once you do that, you can easily convert that workbook into an actual PowerPoint presentation using a bit of automation.

With this technique, you can build entire presentations in Excel where you have better analytical and automation tools. Then you can simply convert the Excel version of your presentation to a PowerPoint presentation.

10

NOTE

You will need to set a reference to the Microsoft PowerPoint Object Library. Again, you can set the reference by opening the Visual Basic Editor in Excel and selecting Tools ➪ References. Scroll down until you find the entry Microsoft PowerPoint XX Object Library, where the *XX* is your version of PowerPoint. Place a check in the check box next to the entry.

```vba
Sub SendWorkbookToPowerPoint()

'Declare your variables
    Dim pp As PowerPoint.Application
    Dim PPPres As PowerPoint.Presentation
    Dim PPSlide As PowerPoint.Slide
    Dim xlwksht As Excel.Worksheet
    Dim MyRange As String
    Dim MyTitle As String

'Open PowerPoint, add a new presentation and make visible
    Set pp = New PowerPoint.Application
    Set PPPres = pp.Presentations.Add
    pp.Visible = True

'Set the ranges for your data and title
    MyRange = "A1:I27"

'Start the loop through each worksheet
    For Each xlwksht In ActiveWorkbook.Worksheets
    xlwksht.Select
    Application.Wait (Now + TimeValue("0:00:1"))
    MyTitle = xlwksht.Range("C19").Value

'Copy the range as picture
    xlwksht.Range(MyRange).CopyPicture _
    Appearance:=xlScreen, Format:=xlPicture

'Count slides and add new slide as next available slide number
    SlideCount = PPPres.Slides.Count
    Set PPSlide = PPPres.Slides.Add(SlideCount + 1, ppLayoutTitleOnly)
    PPSlide.Select

'Paste the picture and adjust its position
    PPSlide.Shapes.Paste.Select
```

```
    pp.ActiveWindow.Selection.ShapeRange.Align msoAlignCenters, True
    pp.ActiveWindow.Selection.ShapeRange.Top = 100

'Add the title to the slide then move to next worksheet
    PPSlide.Shapes.Title.TextFrame.TextRange.Text = MyTitle
    Next xlwksht

'Memory Cleanup
    pp.Activate
    Set PPSlide = Nothing
    Set PPPres = Nothing
    Set pp = Nothing

End Sub
```

Automating Outlook from Excel

In this section, you'll discover a few examples of how you can integrate Excel and Outlook in a more automated fashion.

Mailing the active workbook as an attachment

The most fundamental Outlook task that we can perform through automation is sending an e-mail. In the example code shown here, the active workbook is sent to two e-mail recipients as an attachment.

> **ON THE WEB**
>
> This workbook, named `Mailing the Active Workbook as Attachment.xlsm`, is available on the book's website.

> **NOTE**
>
> You will need to set a reference to the Microsoft Outlook Object Library. You can set the reference by opening the Visual Basic Editor in Excel and selecting Tools ⇨ References. Scroll down until you find the entry Microsoft Outlook XX Object Library, where the *XX* is your version of Outlook. Place a check in the check box next to the entry.

```
    Sub EmailWorkbook()

'Declare your variables
    Dim OLApp As Outlook.Application
    Dim OLMail As Object

'Open Outlook start a new mail item
    Set OLApp = New Outlook.Application
```

10

```
    Set OLMail = OLApp.CreateItem(0)
    OLApp.Session.Logon

'Build your mail item and send
    With OLMail
        .To = "admin@datapigtechnologies.com; mike@datapigtechnologies
.com"
        .CC = ""
        .BCC = ""
        .Subject = "This is the Subject line"
        .Body = "Sample File Attached"
        .Attachments.Add ActiveWorkbook.FullName
        .Display  'Change to .Send to send without reviewing
    End With

'Memory cleanup
    Set OLMail = Nothing
    Set OLApp = Nothing

End Sub
```

Mailing a specific range as an attachment

You can imagine that you may not always want to send your entire workbook through e-mail. This macro demonstrates how you would send a specific range of data rather than the entire workbook.

ON THE WEB

This workbook, named `Mailing a Specific Range as Attachment.xlsm`, is available on the book's website.

NOTE

You will need to set a reference to the Microsoft Outlook Object Library. You can set the reference by opening the Visual Basic Editor in Excel and selecting Tools ➪ References. Scroll down until you find the entry Microsoft Outlook XX Object Library, where the *XX* is your version of Outlook. Place a check in the check box next to the entry.

```
Sub EmailRange()

'Declare your variables
    Dim OLApp As Outlook.Application
    Dim OLMail As Object

'Copy range, paste to new workbook, and save it
    Sheets("Revenue Table").Range("A1:E7").Copy
    Workbooks.Add
```

```
        Range("A1").PasteSpecial xlPasteValues
        Range("A1").PasteSpecial xlPasteFormats
        ActiveWorkbook.SaveAs ThisWorkbook.Path & "\TempRangeForEmail.xlsx"

    'Open Outlook start a new mail item
        Set OLApp = New Outlook.Application
        Set OLMail = OLApp.CreateItem(0)
        OLApp.Session.Logon

    'Build your mail item and send
        With OLMail
            .To = "admin@datapigtechnologies.com; mike@datapigtechnologies
    .com"
            .CC = ""
            .BCC = ""
            .Subject = "This is the Subject line"
            .Body = "Sample File Attached"
            .Attachments.Add (ThisWorkbook.Path & "\TempRangeForEmail.xlsx")
            .Display 'Change to .Send to send without reviewing
        End With

    'Delete the temporary Excel file
        ActiveWorkbook.Close SaveChanges:=True
        Kill ThisWorkbook.Path & "\TempRangeForEmail.xlsx"

    'Memory cleanup
        Set OLMail = Nothing
        Set OLApp = Nothing

    End Sub
```

Mailing a Single Sheet as an Attachment

This example demonstrates how you would send a specific worksheet of data rather than the entire workbook.

ON THE WEB

This workbook, named `Mailing a Single Sheet as an Attachment.xlsm`, is available on the book's website.

NOTE

You will need to set a reference to the Microsoft Outlook Object Library. You can set the reference by opening the Visual Basic Editor in Excel and selecting Tools ⇨ References. Scroll down until you find the entry Microsoft Outlook XX Object Library, where the *XX* is your version of Outlook. Place a check in the check box next to the entry.

10

```
Sub EmailWorkSheet()

'Declare your variables
    Dim OLApp As Outlook.Application
    Dim OLMail As Object

'Copy Worksheet, paste to new workbook, and save it
    Sheets("Revenue Table").Copy
    ActiveWorkbook.SaveAs ThisWorkbook.Path & "\TempRangeForEmail.xlsx"

'Open Outlook start a new mail item
    Set OLApp = New Outlook.Application
    Set OLMail = OLApp.CreateItem(0)
    OLApp.Session.Logon

'Build your mail item and send
    With OLMail
    .To = "admin@datapigtechnologies.com; mike@datapigtechnologies.com"
    .CC = ""
    .BCC = ""
    .Subject = "This is the Subject line"
    .Body = "Sample File Attached"
    .Attachments.Add (ThisWorkbook.Path & "\TempRangeForEmail.xlsx")
    .Display 'Change to .Send to send without reviewing
    End With

'Delete the temporary Excel file
    ActiveWorkbook.Close SaveChanges:=True
    Kill ThisWorkbook.Path & "\TempRangeForEmail.xlsx"

'Memory cleanup
    Set OLMail = Nothing
    Set OLApp = Nothing

End Sub
```

Mailing All E-mail Addresses in Your Contact List

Ever need to send out a mass mailing such as a newsletter or a memo? Instead of manually entering each of your contacts' e-mail addresses, you can run the following procedure. In this procedure, you send out one e-mail, automatically adding all the e-mail addresses in your contact list to the e-mail.

ON THE WEB

This workbook, named Mailing All Email Addresses in Your Contact List, is available on the book's website.

```
Sub EmailContactList()

'Declare your variables
    Dim OLApp As Outlook.Application
    Dim OLMail As Object
    Dim MyCell As Range
    Dim MyContacts As Range

'Define the range to loop through
    Set MyContacts = Sheets("Contact List").Range("H2:H21")

'Open Outlook
    Set OLApp = New Outlook.Application
    Set OLMail = OLApp.CreateItem(0)
    OLApp.Session.Logon

'Add each address in the contact list
    With OLMail
            For Each MyCell In MyContacts
                .BCC = .BCC & MyCell.Value & ";"
            Next MyCell

        .Subject = "Sample File Attached"
        .Body = "Sample file is attached"
        .Attachments.Add ActiveWorkbook.FullName
        .Display 'Change to .Send to send without reviewing

    End With

'Memory cleanup
    Set OLMail = Nothing
    Set OLApp = Nothing

End Sub
```

Starting Other Applications from Excel

You may find it necessary to launch other applications from Excel. For example, you might want to call up a Windows dialog box, open Internet Explorer, or execute a DOS batch file from Excel. Or, as an application developer, you may want to make it easy for a user to access the Windows Control Panel to adjust system settings.

10

In this section, you'll learn the fundamental functions needed to launch all kinds of programs from Excel.

Using the VBA Shell function

The VBA `Shell` function makes launching other programs relatively easy. The following is an example of VBA code that launches the Windows Calculator:

```
Sub StartCalc()
    Dim Program As String
    Dim TaskID As Double
    On Error Resume Next
    Program = "calc.exe"
    TaskID = Shell(Program, 1)
    If Err <> 0 Then
        MsgBox "Cannot start " & Program, vbCritical, "Error"
    End If
End Sub
```

The `Shell` function returns a task identification number for the application specified in the first argument. You can use this number later to activate the task. The second argument for the `Shell` function determines how the application is displayed. (1 is the code for a normal-size window that has the focus.) Refer to the Help system for other values for this argument.

If the `Shell` function isn't successful, it generates an error. Therefore, this procedure uses an `On Error` statement to display a message if the executable file can't be found or if some other error occurs.

It's important to understand that your VBA code doesn't pause while the application that was started with the `Shell` function is running. In other words, the `Shell` function runs the application *asynchronously*. If the procedure has more instructions after the `Shell` function is executed, these instructions are executed concurrently with the newly-loaded program. If any instruction requires user intervention (for example, displaying a message box), Excel's title bar flashes while the other application is active.

In some cases, you may want to launch an application with the `Shell` function, but you need your VBA code to pause until the application is closed. For example, the launched application might generate a file that is used later in your code. Although you can't pause the execution of your code, you *can* create a loop that does nothing except monitor the application's status. The example that follows displays a message box when the application launched by the `Shell` function has ended:

```
Declare PtrSafe Function OpenProcess Lib "kernel32" _
    (ByVal dwDesiredAccess As Long, _
    ByVal bInheritHandle As Long, _
    ByVal dwProcessId As Long) As Long
```

```
Declare PtrSafe Function GetExitCodeProcess Lib "kernel32" _
    (ByVal hProcess As Long, _
    lpExitCode As Long) As Long

Sub StartCalc2()
    Dim TaskID As Long
    Dim hProc As Long
    Dim lExitCode As Long
    Dim ACCESS_TYPE As Integer, STILL_ACTIVE As Integer
    Dim Program As String

    ACCESS_TYPE = &H400
    STILL_ACTIVE = &H103

    Program = "Calc.exe"
    On Error Resume Next

'   Shell the task
    TaskID = Shell(Program, 1)

'   Get the process handle
    hProc = OpenProcess(ACCESS_TYPE, False, TaskID)

    If Err <> 0 Then
        MsgBox "Cannot start " & Program, vbCritical, "Error"
        Exit Sub
    End If

    Do  'Loop continuously
'       Check on the process
        GetExitCodeProcess hProc, lExitCode
'       Allow event processing
        DoEvents
    Loop While lExitCode = STILL_ACTIVE

'   Task is finished, so show message
    MsgBox Program & " was closed"
End Sub
```

While the launched program is running, this procedure continually calls the GetExit-CodeProcess function from a Do Loop structure, testing for its returned value (lExit-Code). When the program is finished, lExitCode returns a different value, the loop ends, and the VBA code resumes executing.

ON THE WEB

Both of the previous examples are available on the book's website. The filename is start calculator.xlsm.

10

> **TIP**
>
> Another way to launch an app is to create a hyperlink in a cell (VBA not required). For example, this formula creates a hyperlink in a cell that, when clicked, runs the Windows Calculator program:
>
> ```
> =HYPERLINK("C:\Windows\System32\calc.exe","Windows Calculator")
> ```
>
> You need to make sure that the link points to the correct location. And you'll probably get at least one security warning when you click the link. This technique also works for files, and it loads the file into the default application for the file type. For example, clicking the hyperlink created by the following formula loads the file into the default app for text files:
>
> ```
> =HYPERLINK("C:\files\data.txt","Open the data file")
> ```

Displaying a folder window

The Shell function is also handy if you need to display a particular directory using File Explorer. For example, the statement that follows displays the folder of the active workbook (but only if the workbook has been saved):

```
If ActiveWorkbook.Path <> "" Then _
  Shell "explorer.exe " & ActiveWorkbook.Path, vbNormalFocus
```

Using the Windows ShellExecute API function

`ShellExecute` is a Windows application programming interface (API) function that is useful for starting other applications. Importantly, this function can start an application only if an associated filename is known (assuming that the file type is registered with Windows). For example, you can use `ShellExecute` to display a web document by starting the default web browser. Or, you can use an e-mail address to start the default e-mail client.

The API declaration follows (this code works only with Excel 2010 or later):

```
Private Declare PtrSafe Function ShellExecute Lib "shell32.dll" _
    Alias "ShellExecuteA" (ByVal hWnd As Long, _
    ByVal lpOperation As String, ByVal lpFile As String, _
    ByVal lpParameters As String, ByVal lpDirectory As String, _
    ByVal nShowCmd As Long) As Long
```

The following procedure demonstrates how to call the `ShellExecute` function. In this example, it opens a graphics file by using the graphics program that's set up to handle JPG files. If the result returned by the function is less than 32, an error occurred.

```
Sub ShowGraphic()
    Dim FileName As String
    Dim Result As Long
    FileName = ThisWorkbook.Path & "\flower.jpg"
```

```
        Result = ShellExecute(0&, vbNullString, FileName, _
            vbNullString, vbNullString, vbNormalFocus)
        If Result < 32 Then MsgBox "Error"
    End Sub
```

The next procedure opens a text file, using the default text file program:

```
Sub OpenTextFile()
    Dim FileName As String
    Dim Result As Long
    FileName = ThisWorkbook.Path & "\textfile.txt"
    Result = ShellExecute(0&, vbNullString, FileName, _
        vbNullString, vbNullString, vbNormalFocus)
    If Result < 32 Then MsgBox "Error"
End Sub
```

The following example is similar, but it opens a web URL by using the default browser:

```
Sub OpenURL()
    Dim URL As String
    Dim Result As Long
    URL = "http://spreadsheetpage.com"
    Result = ShellExecute(0&, vbNullString, URL, _
        vbNullString, vbNullString, vbNormalFocus)
    If Result < 32 Then MsgBox "Error"
End Sub
```

You can also use this technique with an e-mail address. The following example opens the default e-mail client (if one exists) and then addresses an e-mail to the recipient:

```
Sub StartEmail()
    Dim Addr As String
    Dim Result As Long
    Addr = "mailto:nobody@example.com"
    Result = ShellExecute(0&, vbNullString, Addr, _
        vbNullString, vbNullString, vbNormalFocus)
    If Result < 32 Then MsgBox "Error"
End Sub
```

> **ON THE WEB**
>
> These examples are available on the book's website in a file named `shellexecute examples.xlsm` in a folder called `shellexecute`. This file uses API declarations that are compatible with all versions of Excel.

Using AppActivate

You may find that if an application is already running, using the `Shell` function may start another instance of it. In most cases, however, you want to *activate* the instance that's running, not start another instance of it.

10

The following `StartCalculator` procedure uses the `AppActivate` statement to activate an application (in this case, the Windows Calculator) if it's already running. The argument for `AppActivate` is the caption of the application's title bar. If the `AppActivate` statement generates an error, Calculator is not running, and the routine starts the application.

```
Sub ActivateCalc()
    Dim AppFile As String
    Dim CalcTaskID As Double

    AppFile = "Calc.exe"
    On Error Resume Next
    AppActivate "Calculator"
    If Err <> 0 Then
        Err = 0
        CalcTaskID = Shell(AppFile, 1)
        If Err <> 0 Then MsgBox "Can't start Calculator"
    End If
End Sub
```

ON THE WEB

This example is available on the book's website. The filename is `start calculator.xlsm`.

Running Control Panel Dialog Boxes

Windows provides quite a few system dialog boxes and wizards, most of which are accessible from the Windows Control Panel. You might need to display one or more of these from your Excel application. For example, you might want to display the Windows Date and Time dialog box.

The key to running other system dialog boxes is to execute the `rundll32.exe` application by using the VBA `Shell` function.

The following procedure displays the Date and Time dialog box:

```
Sub ShowDateTimeDlg()
    Dim Arg As String
    Dim TaskID As Double
    Arg = "rundll32.exe shell32.dll,Control_RunDLL timedate.cpl"
    On Error Resume Next
    TaskID = Shell(Arg)
    If Err <> 0 Then
        MsgBox ("Cannot start the application.")
    End If
End Sub
```

The following is the general format for the `rundll32.exe` application:

```
rundll32.exe shell32.dll,Control_RunDLL filename.cpl, n,t
```

where:

- `filename.cpl`: The name of one of the Control Panel *.CPL files
- `n`: The zero-based number of the applet in the *.CPL file
- `t`: The number of the tab (for multitabbed applets)

ON THE WEB

A workbook that displays 12 additional Control Panel applets is available on this book's website. The filename is `control panel dialogs.xlsm`.

Working with External Data and Files

IN THIS CHAPTER

Working with external data connections

Using ActiveX Data Objects to get external data

Performing common file operations

Working with text files

Working with External Data Connections

External data is exactly what it sounds like: data that isn't located in the Excel workbook in which you're operating. Some examples of external data sources are text files, Access tables, SQL Server tables, and even other Excel workbooks.

There are numerous ways to get data into Excel. In fact, between the functionality found in the UI and the VBA/code techniques, there are too many techniques to focus on in one chapter. Instead, then, in this chapter we'll focus on a handful of techniques that can be implemented in most situations and that don't come with a lot of pitfalls and gotchas.

The first of those techniques is to use Excel's Power Query feature.

Power Query Basics

Power Query offers an intuitive mechanism to extract data from a wide variety of sources, perform complex transformations on that data, and then load the data into a workbook.

To start this basic review of Power Query, let's walk through a simple example. Imagine that you need to import Microsoft Corporation stock prices into Excel using Yahoo Finance. For this scenario, you need to perform a web query to pull the data needed from Yahoo Finance.

To start your query, follow these steps:

1. In a new Excel workbook, select the Get Data command in the Get & Transform Data group on the Data tab and then select From Other Sources ⇨ From Web (see Figure 11.1).

FIGURE 11.1

Starting a Power Query web query

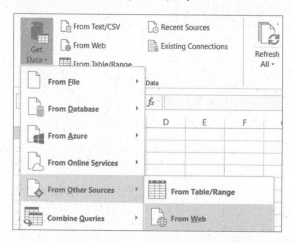

2. In the dialog box that appears, as shown in Figure 11.2, enter the URL for the data that you need; in this case, enter `http://finance.yahoo.com/q/hp?s=MSFT`.

FIGURE 11.2

Enter the target URL containing the data you need.

From Web

◉ Basic ○ Advanced

URL

`http://finance.yahoo.com/q/hp?s=MSFT`

| OK | Cancel |

3. After a bit of gyrating, the Navigator pane shown in Figure 11.3 appears. Here you select the data source you want to be extracted. You can click each table to see a preview of the data. In this case, the table labeled Table 2 holds the historical stock data you need, so click Table 2 and then click the Edit button.

FIGURE 11.3

Select the correct data source and then click the Edit button.

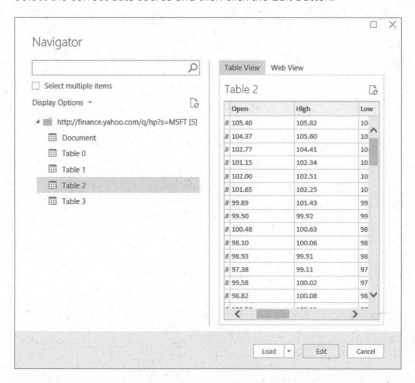

When you click the Edit button, a Power Query Editor window opens, which contains its own Ribbon and a preview pane that shows a preview of the data (see Figure 11.4). Here you can apply certain actions to shape, clean, and transform the data before importing.

FIGURE 11.4

The Power Query Editor window allows you to shape, clean, and transform data.

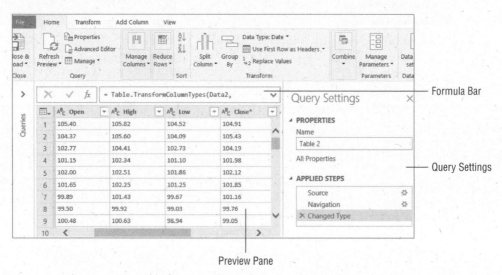

Preview Pane

The idea is to work with each column shown in the Power Query Editor, applying the necessary actions that will give you the data and structure that you need. You'll dive deeper into column actions later in this chapter. For now, you need to continue toward the goal of getting the last 30 days of stock prices for Microsoft Corporation.

4. Remove all the columns that you do not need by right-clicking each one and clicking Remove. (Besides the Date field, the only other columns that you need are the High, Low, and Close fields.) Alternatively, you can hold down the Ctrl key on your keyboard, select the columns that you want to keep, right-click any of the selected columns, and then choose Remove Other Columns (see Figure 11.5).

5. Make sure that the High, Low, and Close fields are formatted as proper numbers. To do this, hold down the Ctrl key on your keyboard, select the three columns, right-click one of the column headings, and then select Change Type ➪ Decimal Number. After you do this, you may notice that some of the rows show the word *Error*. These are rows that contained text values that could not be converted.

6. Remove the Error rows by selecting Remove Errors from the Column Actions list (next to the High field), as shown in Figure 11.6.

FIGURE 11.5

Select the columns that you want to keep and then select Remove Other Columns to get rid of the other columns.

FIGURE 11.6

You can click the Column Actions icon to select actions (such as Remove Errors) that you want applied to the entire data table.

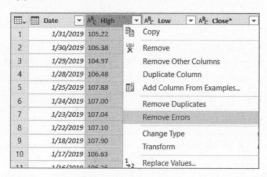

7. Once all the errors are removed, add a Week Of field that displays the week to which each date in the table belongs. To do this, right-click the Date field and select the Duplicate Column option. A new column (named Date – Copy) is added to the preview.

8. Right-click the newly added column, select the Rename option, and then rename the column **Week Of**.

9. Right-click the Week Of column that you just created, and select Transform ➪ Week ➪ Start of Week, as shown in Figure 11.7. Excel transforms the dates to display the start of the week for a given date.

10. When you've finished configuring your Power Query feed, save and output the results. To do this, click the Close & Load drop-down found on the Home tab of the Power Query Ribbon to reveal two options: Close & Load and Close & Load To.

FIGURE 11.7

The Power Query Editor can be used to apply transformation actions such as displaying the start of the week for a given date.

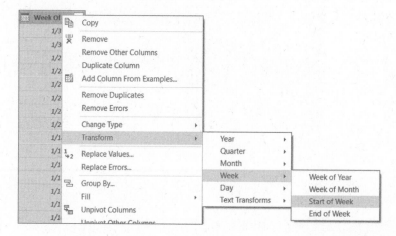

The Close & Load option saves your query and outputs the results to a new worksheet in your workbook as an Excel table. The Close & Load To option activates the Import Data dialog box, as shown in Figure 11.8, where you can choose to output the results to a specific worksheet or to the internal Data Model.

FIGURE 11.8

The Import Data dialog box gives you more control over how the results of queries are used.

The Import Data dialog box also enables you to save the query as a query connection only, which means you will be able to use the query in various in-memory processes without actually needing to output the results anywhere.

11. Select the New Worksheet option button to output your results as a table on a new worksheet in the active workbook.

At this point, you will have a table similar to the one shown in Figure 11.9, which can be used to produce the PivotTable you need.

FIGURE 11.9

Your final query pulled from the Internet: transformed, put into an Excel table, and ready to use in a PivotTable

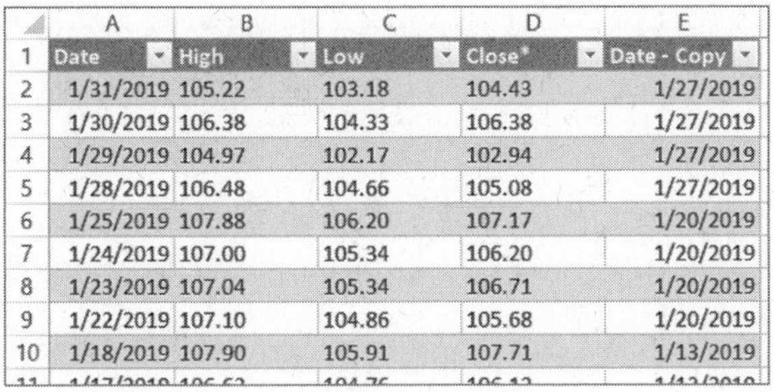

	A	B	C	D	E
1	Date	High	Low	Close*	Date - Copy
2	1/31/2019	105.22	103.18	104.43	1/27/2019
3	1/30/2019	106.38	104.33	106.38	1/27/2019
4	1/29/2019	104.97	102.17	102.94	1/27/2019
5	1/28/2019	106.48	104.66	105.08	1/27/2019
6	1/25/2019	107.88	106.20	107.17	1/20/2019
7	1/24/2019	107.00	105.34	106.20	1/20/2019
8	1/23/2019	107.04	105.34	106.71	1/20/2019
9	1/22/2019	107.10	104.86	105.68	1/20/2019
10	1/18/2019	107.90	105.91	107.71	1/13/2019
11	1/17/2019	106.63	104.76	106.12	1/13/2019

Take a moment to appreciate what Power Query allowed you to do just now. With a few clicks, you searched the Internet, found some base data, shaped the data to keep only the columns that you needed, and even manipulated that data to add an extra Week Of dimension to the base data. This is what Power Query is about: enabling you easily to extract, filter, and reshape data without the need for any programmatic coding skills.

The best part is that Power Query has the ability to connect to a wide array of data sources. Whether you need to pull data from an external website, a text file, a database system, Facebook, or a web service, Power Query can accommodate most, if not all, of your source data needs. You can see all of the available connection types by clicking the Get Data drop-down menu on the Data tab.

Power Query offers the ability to pull from a wide array of data sources.

From File   Pulls data from a specified Excel files, text files, CSV files, XML files, or folders

From Database   Pulls data from a database such as Microsoft Access, SQL Server, or SQL Server Analysis Services

From Azure   Pulls data from Microsoft's Azure Cloud services

From Online Services   Pulls data from cloud-based application services such as Facebook, Salesforce, and Microsoft Dynamics online

From Other Sources   Pulls data from a wide array of Internet, cloud, and other ODBC data sources

Understanding query steps

Power Query uses its own formula language, known as the *M* language, to codify your queries. As with macro recording, each action you take when working with Power Query results in code being written into a query step. Query steps are embedded M code, which allows your actions to be repeated each time you refresh your Power Query data.

You can see the query steps for your queries by activating the Query Settings pane in the Power Query Editor window (see Figure 11.10). Simply click the Query Settings command on the View tab of the Ribbon.

FIGURE 11.10

Query steps can be viewed and managed in the Applied Steps section of the Query Settings pane.

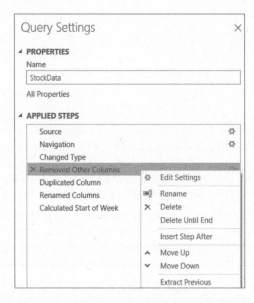

Note the Name box illustrated in Figure 11.10, where you can give your query a friendly name. In this example, we called our query StockData.

You can also check View ⇨ Layout ⇨ Formula Bar to enhance your analysis of each step with a formula bar that displays the syntax for a selected step.

Each query step represents an action that you took to get to a data table. You can click any step to see the underlying M code in the Power Query formula bar. For example, clicking the step called Removed Errors reveals the code for that step in the formula bar.

> **NOTE**
> When you click on a query step, the data shown in the preview pane is a preview of what the data looked like up to and including the step you clicked. For example, in Figure 11.10, clicking the step before the Removed Other Columns step lets you see what the data looked like before you removed the nonessential columns.

Refreshing Power Query data

It's important to note that Power Query data is not in any way connected to the source data used to extract it. A Power Query data table is merely a snapshot. In other words, as the source data changes, Power Query will not automatically keep up with the changes; you need to refresh your data manually.

If you chose to load your Power Query results to an Excel table in the existing workbook, you can manually refresh by right-clicking the table and selecting the Refresh option.

If you chose to load your Power Query data to the internal Data Model, you need to click Data ⇨ Queries & Connections ⇨ Queries & Connections and then right-click the target query in the task pane and select the Refresh option.

To get a bit more automated with the refreshing of your queries, you can configure your data sources to refresh your Power Query data automatically. To do so, follow these steps:

1. Go to the Data tab in the Excel Ribbon and select the Queries & Connections command. The Queries & Connections task pane appears.

2. Right-click the Power Query data connection that you want to refresh and then select the Properties option.

3. With the Properties dialog box open, select the Usage tab.

4. Set the options to refresh the chosen data connection.

Refresh Every X Minutes   Placing a check next to this option tells Excel to refresh the chosen data automatically every specified number of minutes. Excel will refresh all tables associated with that connection.

Refresh Data When Opening the File   Placing a check next to this option tells Excel to refresh the chosen data connection automatically upon opening the workbook. Excel will refresh all tables associated with that connection as soon as the workbook is opened.

These refresh options are useful when you want to ensure that your customers are working with the latest data. Of course, setting these options does not preclude the ability to refresh the data manually.

Managing existing queries

As you add various queries to a workbook, you will need a way to manage them. Excel accommodates this need by offering the Queries & Connections pane, which enables you to edit, duplicate, refresh, and generally manage all of the existing queries in the workbook. Activate the Queries & Connections pane by selecting the Queries & Connections command on the Data tab of the Excel ribbon.

You need to find the query with which you want to work and then right-click it to take any one of these actions:

Edit: Open the Query Editor, where you can modify the query steps.

Delete: Delete the selected query.

Refresh: Refresh the data in the selected query.

Load To: Activate the Import Data dialog box, where you can redefine where the selected query's results are used.

Duplicate: Create a copy of the query.

Reference: Create a new query that references the output of the original query.

Merge: Merge the selected query with another query in the workbook by matching specified columns.

Append: Append the results of another query in the workbook to the selected query.

Export Connection File: Create an .odc file to move or share the selected query.

Move to Group: Move the selected query into a logical group you create for better organization.

Move Up: Move the selected query up in the Queries & Connections pane.

Move Down: Move the selected query down in the Queries & Connections pane.

Show the Peek: Show a preview of the query results for the selected query.

Properties: Rename the query and add a friendly description.

The Queries & Connections pane is especially useful when your workbook contains several queries. Think of it as a kind of table of contents that allows you to easily find and interact with the queries in your workbook.

Using VBA to create dynamic connections

When building a custom query in Power Query, you are essentially doing nothing more than recording the syntax needed to return some desired result. Any syntax Power Query wrote for your query can be copied from the Advanced Editor and then used in VBA.

You can get to the Advanced Editor while in the Query Editor window (click the View tab of the ribbon and select Advanced Editor).

If you've followed along the with the first exercise, the Advanced Editor should look similar to Figure 11.11.

The takeaway here is that you don't have to be an expert on Power Query's M language to create and build external data queries dynamically with VBA.

For example, in Figure 11.12, you can select a stock symbol to change the Power Query Syntax in cell C6. Clicking the Refresh button will rebuild the Power Query connection with the new syntax.

FIGURE 11.11

FIGURE 11.11

The Advanced Editor window

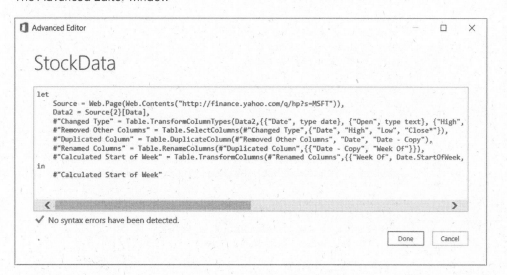

FIGURE 11.12

Designate a cell that will trap the criteria selection.

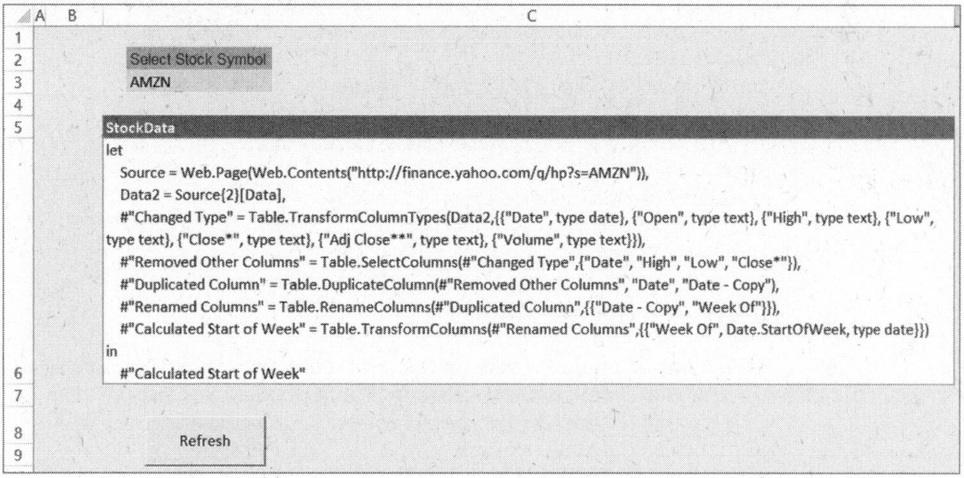

The following macro uses the `Workbook.Query` and `Workbook.Connection` objects to rebuild the query based on new syntax given:

```
Sub RefreshPowerQuery()
    Dim Qry As WorkbookQuery
    Dim QryName As String
    Dim QrySyntax As String
    Dim QryDesc As String
    Dim OutputSheet As Worksheet
    Dim ws As Worksheet

'Set variables
    QryName = ThisWorkbook.Sheets("Query Changer").Range("C5").Value
    QrySyntax = ThisWorkbook.Sheets("Query Changer").Range("C6").Value
    QryDesc = ThisWorkbook.Sheets("Query Changer").Range("C5").Value


'Delete Existing Query
    For Each Qry In ThisWorkbook.Queries
        If Qry.Name = QryName Then
            Set Qry = ThisWorkbook.Queries(QryName)
            Qry.Delete
        End If
    Next Qry

'Add New Query
    Set Qry = ThisWorkbook.Queries.Add(QryName, QrySyntax, QryDesc)

'Remove Old Sheet
    Application.DisplayAlerts = False
    For Each ws In ThisWorkbook.Worksheets
        If ws.Name = QryName Then ws.Delete
    Next ws
    Application.DisplayAlerts = True

'Add to New Sheet
    Set OutputSheet = Sheets.Add(After:=ActiveSheet)
    OutputSheet.Name = QryName

    With OutputSheet.ListObjects.Add(SourceType:=0, Source:= _
        "OLEDB;Provider=Microsoft.Mashup.OleDb.1;Data " & _
        "Source=$Workbook$;Location=" & Qry.Name _
        , Destination:=Range("$A$1")).QueryTable
        .CommandType = xlCmdDefault
        .CommandText = Array("SELECT * FROM [" & Qry.Name & "]")
        .RefreshOnFileOpen = False
        .BackgroundQuery = True
    End With
End Sub
```

If all went smoothly, you will have a nifty mechanism that allows for dynamic edits to the Power Query syntax for more flexible reporting.

Iterating through all connections in a workbook

You can also use the `Workbook.Connections` collection to iterate through all of the connection objects in a workbook and examine or modify their properties. For instance, the following macro populates a worksheet with a list of all connection objects in the current workbook, along with their associated connection strings and command texts:

```
Sub ListConnections()

    Dim i As Long
    Dim Cn As WorkbookConnection

    Worksheets.Add
    With ActiveSheet.Range("A1:C1")
        .Value = Array("Cn Name", "Connection String", "Command Text")
        .EntireColumn.AutoFit
    End With

    For Each Cn In ThisWorkbook.Connections
        i = i + 1

        Select Case Cn.Type
            Case Is = xlConnectionTypeODBC
                With ActiveSheet
                    .Range("A1").Offset(i, 0).Value = Cn.Name
                    .Range("A1").Offset(i, 1).Value = _
                      Cn.ODBCConnection.Connection
                    .Range("A1").Offset(i, 2).Value = _
                      Cn.ODBCConnection.CommandText
                End With

            Case Is = xlConnectionTypeOLEDB
                With ActiveSheet
                    .Range("A1").Offset(i, 0).Value = Cn.Name
                    .Range("A1").Offset(i, 1).Value = _
                      Cn.OLEDBConnection.Connection
```

```
                    .Range("A1").Offset(i, 2).Value = _
                        Cn.OLEDBConnection.CommandText
            End With
        End Select
    Next Cn
End Sub
```

Using ADO and VBA to Pull External Data

Another technique for working with external data is to use VBA with ActiveX Data Objects (ADO). Using the combination of ADO with VBA will allow you to work with external data sets in memory. This comes in handy when you need to perform complex, multilayered procedures and checks on external data sets but you don't want to create workbook connections or return those external data sets to the workbook.

When trying to grasp the basics of ADO, it helps to think of ADO as a tool that will help you accomplish two tasks: connect to a data source and specify the data set with which to work. In the following section, you will explore the fundamental syntax that you will need to know to do just that.

The connection string

The first thing you must do is to connect to a data source. To do this, you must give VBA few pieces of information. This information is passed to VBA in the form of a connection string. Here is an example connection string that points to an Access database:

```
"Provider=Microsoft.ACE.OLEDB.12.0;" & _
"Data Source= C:\MyDatabase.accdb;" & _
"User ID=Administrator;" & _
"Password=AdminPassword"
```

Don't be intimidated by all of the syntax here. A connection string is fundamentally nothing more than a text string that holds a series of variables (also called *arguments*), which VBA uses to identify and open a connection to a data source. Although connection strings can get pretty fancy, with a myriad of arguments and options, there are a handful of arguments that are commonly used when connecting to either Access or Excel.

For novices of ADO, it helps to focus on these commonly used arguments when working with connection strings: Provider, Data Source, Extended Properties, User ID, and Password.

Provider   The Provider argument tells VBA what type of data source with which you are working. When using Access or Excel as the data source, the Provider syntax will read as follows:

```
Provider=Microsoft.ACE.OLEDB.12.0
```

Data Source   The Data Source argument tells VBA where to find the database or workbook that contains the data needed. With the Data Source argument, you will pass the full path of the database or workbook. Here's an example:

```
Data Source=C:\Mydirectory\MyDatabaseName.accdb
```

Extended Properties   The Extended Properties argument is typically used when connecting to an Excel workbook. This argument tells VBA that the data source is something other than a database. When working with an Excel workbook, this argument reads as follows:

```
Extended Properties=Excel 12.0
```

User ID   The User ID argument is optional and used only if a user ID is required to connect to the data source.

```
User Id=MyUserId
```

Password   The Password argument is optional and used only if a password is required to connect to the data source.

```
Password=MyPassword
```

Take a moment now to examine a few examples of how these arguments are used in different connection strings.

Here's how to connect to an Access database:

```
"Provider=Microsoft.ACE.OLEDB.12.0;" & _
"Data Source= C:\MyDatabase.accdb"
```

Here's how to connect to an Access database with Password and User ID:

```
"Provider=Microsoft.ACE.OLEDB.12.0;" & _
"Data Source= C:\MyDatabase.accdb;" & _
"User ID=Administrator;" & _
"Password=AdminPassword"
```

Here's how to connect to an Excel workbook:

```
"Provider=Microsoft.ACE.OLEDB.12.0;" & _
"Data Source=C:\MyExcelWorkbook.xlsx;" & _
"Extended Properties=Excel 12.0"
```

Declaring a Recordset

In addition to building a connection to your data source, you will need to define the data set with which you need to work. In ADO, this data set is referred to as the *recordset*. A `Recordset` object is essentially a container for the records and fields returned from the data source. The most common way to define a `Recordset` object is to open an existing table or query using the following arguments:

```
Recordset.Open Source, ConnectString, CursorType, LockType
```

The `Source` argument specifies the data that is to be extracted. This is typically a table, a query, or a SQL statement that retrieves records. The `ConnectString` argument specifies the connection string used to connect to your chosen data source. The `CursorType` argument defines how a `Recordset` object allows you to move through the data to be extracted. The `CursorType` argument that are commonly used are as follows:

adOpenForwardOnly   This is the default setting; if you don't specify a `CursorType`, the `Recordset` object will automatically be `adOpenForwardOnly`. This `Cursor-Type` argument is the most efficient type because it allows you to move through the `Recordset` object in only one way: from beginning to end. This is ideal for reporting processes where data only needs to be retrieved and not traversed. Keep in mind that you cannot make changes to data when using this `CursorType`.

adOpenDynamic   This `CursorType` is typically used in processes where there is a need for looping, moving up and down through the data set, or the ability to see any edits made to the data set dynamically. This `CursorType` is typically memory- and resource-intensive, and it should be used only when needed.

adOpenStatic   This `CursorType` is ideal for the quick return of results, as it essentially returns a snapshot of your data. However, this is different from the `adOpen-ForwardOnly` `CursorType`, as it allows you to navigate the returned records. In addition, when using this `CursorType`, the data returned can be made updateable by setting its `LockType` to something other than `adLockReadOnly`.

The `LockType` argument lets you specify whether the data returned by the `Recordset` object can be changed. This argument is typically set to `adLockReadOnly` (the default setting) to indicate that there is no need to edit the data returned. Alternatively, you can set this argument to `adLockOptimistic`, which allows for the free editing of the data returned.

Referencing the ADO object library

With these basic ADO fundamentals under your belt, you're ready to create your own ADO procedure. However, before you do anything with ADO, you first need to set a reference to the ADO object library. Just as each Microsoft Office application has its own set of objects, properties, and methods, so does ADO. Since Excel does not inherently know the ADO object model, you will need to point Excel to the ADO reference library.

Start by opening a new Excel workbook and opening the Visual Basic Editor.

Once you are in the Visual Basic Editor, go up to the application menu and select Tools ⇨ References. This will open the References dialog box illustrated here in Figure 11.13. Scroll down until you locate the latest version of the Microsoft ActiveX Data Objects Library. Place a check mark beside this entry and click OK.

FIGURE 11.13

Select the latest version of the Microsoft ActiveX Data Objects Library.

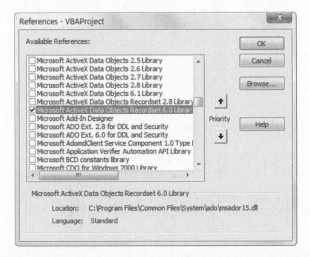

> **NOTE**
> It is normal to have several versions of the same library displayed in the References dialog box. It's generally best to select the latest version available. Note that versions after 2.8 are called the Microsoft ActiveX Data Objects Recordset Library.

After you click the OK button, you can open the References dialog box again to ensure that your reference is set. You will know that your selection took effect when the Microsoft ActiveX Data Objects Library is displayed at the top of the Reference dialog box with a check next to it.

Putting it all together in code

Now that you understand a few of the basics of ADO, take a look at how they come together in VBA. The following example code uses ADO to connect to an Access database and retrieve the Products table:

```
Sub GetAccessData()
    Dim MyConnect As String
    Dim MyRecordset As ADODB.Recordset

    MyConnect = "Provider=Microsoft.ACE.OLEDB.12.0;" & _
                "Data Source= C:\MyDir\MyDatabaseName.accdb"

    Set MyRecordset = New ADODB.Recordset

    MyRecordset.Open "Products", _
    MyConnect, adOpenStatic, adLockReadOnly

    Sheets("MySheetName").Range("A2").CopyFromRecordset _
    MyRecordset

    With ActiveSheet.Range("A1:C1")
        .Value = Array("Product", "Description", "Segment")
        .EntireColumn.AutoFit
    End With

End Sub
```

Now take a moment to understand what this macro is doing.

You first declare two variables: a string variable to hold the connection string and a Recordset object to hold the results of the data pull. In this example, the variable called MyConnect will hold the connection string identifying the data source. Meanwhile, the variable called MyRecordset will hold the data that is returned by the procedure.

Next, you define the connection string for the ADO procedure. In this scenario, you are connecting to the MyDatabaseName.accdb file found in the C:\MyDir\ directory. Once you have defined the data source, you can open the recordset and use MyConnect to return static read-only data.

Now you can use Excel's CopyFromRecordset method to get the data out of the recordset and into the spreadsheet. This method requires two pieces of information: the location of the data output and the Recordset object that holds the data. In this example, you are copying the data in the MyRecordset object onto the sheet called MySheetName (starting at cell A2).

Interestingly enough, the CopyFromRecordset method does not return column headers or field names. This forces one final action where you add column headers by simply defining them in an array and writing them to the active sheet.

With ADO and VBA, you can build all the necessary components one time in a nicely packaged macro and then simply forget about it. As long as the defined variables in your code (in other words, the data source path, the Recordset, the output path) do not change, then your ADO-based procedures will require virtually zero maintenance.

Using ADO with the active workbook

There are countless ways that you can use the fundamentals you have learned in this chapter. Of course, it would be impossible to go through every possibility here. However, there are some common scenarios where VBA can greatly enhance integration between Excel and Access.

Querying data from an Excel workbook

You can use an Excel workbook as a data source for your ADO procedures. To do so, you simply build a SQL statement that references the data within the Excel workbook. The idea is to pinpoint the data set in Excel to query by passing either a sheet name, a range of cells, or a named range to the SQL statement.

To query all the data on a specific worksheet, you pass the name of that worksheet followed by the dollar sign ($) as the table name in your SQL statement. Be sure to encapsulate the worksheet name with square brackets. Here's an example:

```
SELECT * FROM [MySheet$]
```

If the worksheet name contains spaces or characters that are not alphanumeric, you need to wrap the worksheet name in single quotes. Here's an example:

```
Select * from ['January;  Forecast vs. Budget$']
```

To query a range of cells within a given worksheet, you first identify the sheet as described above and then add the target range. Here's an example:

```
SELECT * FROM [MySheet$A1:G17]
```

To query a named range, simply use the name of the range as the table name in your SQL statement. Here's an example:

```
SELECT * FROM MyNamedRange
```

In the following example, the entire used range in the SampleData worksheet is queried to return only those records that belong to the North Region.

```
Sub GetData_From_Excel_Sheet()

    Dim MyConnect As String
    Dim MyRecordset As ADODB.Recordset
    Dim MySQL As String
```

```
MyConnect = "Provider=Microsoft.ACE.OLEDB.12.0;" & _
            "Data Source=" & ThisWorkbook.FullName & ";" & _
            "Extended Properties=Excel 12.0"

MySQL = " SELECT * FROM [SampleData$]" & _
        " WHERE Region ='NORTH'"

Set MyRecordset = New ADODB.Recordset
MyRecordset.Open MySQL, MyConnect, adOpenStatic, adLockReadOnly

  ThisWorkbook.Sheets.Add
  ActiveSheet.Range("A2").CopyFromRecordset MyRecordset

With ActiveSheet.Range("A1:F1")
    .Value = Array("Region", "Market", "Branch_Number", _
    "Invoice_Number", "Sales_Amount", "Contracted Hours")
    .EntireColumn.AutoFit
End With

End Sub
```

ON THE WEB

A working example of this code is available on the book's website in the workbook called `QueryDataFrom-Excel.xlsm`.

Appending records to an existing Excel table

There are often times when you don't necessarily want to overwrite the data in your Excel worksheet when you bring in fresh data. Instead, you may want to simply add or append data to the existing table. In a typical scenario, you hard-code the location or range where you want a given recordset to be copied. In these situations, this location must dynamically change to reflect the first empty cell in your worksheet. The following example code demonstrates this technique:

```
Sub Append_Results()

    Dim MyConnect As String
    Dim MyRecordset As ADODB.Recordset
    Dim MyRange As String

    MyConnect = "Provider=Microsoft.ACE.OLEDB.12.0;" & _
        "Data Source= C:\MyDir\MyDatabase.accdb"

    Set MyRecordset = New ADODB.Recordset
```

```
        MyRecordset.Open "Products", MyConnect, adOpenStatic

        Sheets("AppendData").Select
        MyRange = "A" & _
        ActiveSheet.Cells.SpecialCells(xlCellTypeLastCell).Row + 1

        ActiveSheet.Range(MyRange).CopyFromRecordset MyRecordset
    End Sub
```

Because you want to append data to an existing table, you need to determine dynamically the first available empty cell that can be used as the output location for the data pull. The first step in accomplishing this goal is to find the first empty row. This is relatively easy to do thanks to Excel's SpecialCells method.

Using the SpecialCells method, you can find the last used cell in the worksheet and then extract the row number of that cell. This gives you the last used row. To get the row number of the first empty row, you simply add 1; the next row down from the last used row will inherently be empty.

The idea is to concatenate the SpecialCells routine with a column letter (in this case A) to create a string that represents a range. For example, if the first empty row turns out to be 10, then the following code returns A10:

```
    "A" & ActiveSheet.Cells.SpecialCells(xlCellTypeLastCell).Row + 1
```

Trapping this answer in the MyRange string variable allows you to pass the answer to the CopyFromRecordset.

Working with Text Files

VBA contains a number of statements that allow low-level manipulation of files. These input/output (I/O) statements give you much more control over files than Excel's normal text file import and export options.

You can access a file in any of three ways.

Sequential access   By far the most common method. This type allows reading and writing individual characters or entire lines of data.

Random access   Used only if you're programming a database application, which is not often done using VBA.

Binary access   Used to read or write to any byte position in a file, such as when storing or displaying a bitmap image. This access method is rarely used in VBA.

Because random and binary access files are rarely used with VBA, this chapter focuses on sequential access files. In sequential access, your code starts reading from the beginning of the file and reads each line sequentially. For output, your code writes data to the end of the file.

> **NOTE**
>
> The method of reading and writing text files discussed in this book is the traditional data-channel approach. Another option is to use the object approach. The `FileSystemObject` object contains a `TextStream` object that can be used to read and write text files. The `FileSystemObject` object is part of Windows Scripting Host, which is disabled on some systems because of the malware potential associated with it.

Opening a text file

The VBA `Open` statement (not to be confused with the `Open` method of the `Workbooks` object) opens a file for reading or writing. Before you can read from or write to a file, you must open it.

The `Open` statement is versatile and has a complex syntax.

```
Open pathname For mode [Access access] [lock]  _
    As [#]filenumber [Len=reclength]
```

`pathname`: Required. The `pathname` part of the `Open` statement is straightforward. It simply contains the name and path (optional) of the file to be opened.

`mode`: Required. The file mode must be one of the following:

    `Append`: A sequential access mode that either allows the file to be read or allows data to be appended to the end of the file.

    `Input`: A sequential access mode that allows the file to be read but not written to.

    `Output`: A sequential access mode that allows the file to be read or written to. In this mode, a new file is always created. (An existing file with the same name is deleted.)

    `Binary`: A random access mode that allows data to be read or written to on a byte-by-byte basis.

    `Random`: A random access mode that allows data to be read or written in units determined by the `reclength` argument of the `Open` statement.

`access`: Optional. The `access` argument determines what can be done with the file. It can be `Read`, `Write`, or `Read Write`.

`lock`: Optional. The `lock` argument is useful for multiuser situations. The options are `Shared`, `Lock Read`, `Lock Write`, and `Lock Read Write`.

`filenumber`: Required. A file number ranging from 1 to 511. You can use the `FreeFile` function to get the next available file number. (Read about `FreeFile` in the upcoming section "Getting a file number.")

`reclength`: Optional. The record length (for random access files) or the buffer size (for sequential access files).

Reading a text file

The basic procedure for reading a text file with VBA consists of the following steps:

1. Open the file by using the `Open` statement.
2. Optional. Specify the position in the file by using the `Seek` function.
3. Read data from the file by using the `Input`, `Input #`, or `Line Input #` statement.
4. Close the file by using the `Close` statement.

Writing a text file

The basic procedure for writing a text file is as follows:

1. Open or create the file by using the `Open` statement.
2. Optional. Specify the position in the file by using the `Seek` function.
3. Write data to the file by using the `Write #` or `Print #` statement.
4. Close the file by using the `Close` statement.

Getting a file number

Most VBA programmers simply designate a file number in their `Open` statement. Here's an example:

```
Open "myfile.txt" For Input As #1
```

Then you can refer to the file in subsequent statements as #1.

If a second file is opened while the first is still open, you'd designate the second file as #2.

```
Open "another.txt" For Input As #2
```

Another approach is to use the VBA `FreeFile` function to get a file handle. Then you can refer to the file by using a variable. Here's an example:

```
FileHandle = FreeFile
Open "myfile.txt" For Input As FileHandle
```

Determining or setting the file position

For sequential file access, you rarely need to know the current location in the file. If for some reason you need to know this information, you can use the `Seek` function.

Excel's text file import and export features

Excel can directly read and write three types of text files.

Comma-separated value (CSV) files Columns of data are separated by a comma, and each row of data ends in a carriage return character. For some non-English versions of Excel, a semicolon rather than a comma is used.

PRN Columns of data are aligned by character position, and each row of data ends in a carriage return. These files are also known as *fixed-width files*.

TXT (tab-delimited) files Columns of data are separated by tab characters, and each row of data ends in a carriage return.

When you attempt to open a text file with the File ➪ Open command, the Text Import Wizard might appear to help you delineate the columns. If the text file is tab-delimited or comma-delimited, Excel usually opens the file without displaying the Text Import Wizard. If the data isn't interpreted correctly, close the file and try renaming it to use a .txt extension.

The Text to Columns Wizard (accessed by choosing Data ➪ Data Tools ➪ Text to Columns) is identical to the Text Import Wizard, but it works with data stored in a single worksheet column.

Statements for reading and writing

VBA provides several statements to read and write data to a file.

Three statements are used for reading data from a sequential access file.

Input: Reads a specified number of characters from a file

Input #: Reads data as a series of variables, with variables separated by a comma

Line Input #: Reads a complete line of data (delineated by a carriage return character, a linefeed character, or both)

Two statements are used for writing data to a sequential access file.

Write #: Writes a series of values, with each value separated by a comma and enclosed in quotes. If you end the statement with a semicolon, a carriage return/linefeed sequence is not inserted after each value. Data written with Write # is usually read from a file with an Input # statement.

Print #: Writes a series of values, with each value separated by a tab character. If you end the statement with a semicolon, a carriage return/linefeed sequence isn't inserted after each value. Data written with Print # is usually read from a file with a Line Input # or an Input statement.

Text File Manipulation Examples

This section contains a number of examples that demonstrate various techniques that manipulate text files.

Importing data in a text file

The code in the following example reads a text file and then places each line of data in a single cell (beginning with the active cell):

```
Sub ImportData()
    Open "c:\data\textfile.txt" For Input As #1
    r = 0
    Do Until EOF(1)
        Line Input #1, data
        ActiveCell.Offset(r, 0) = data
        r = r + 1
    Loop
    Close #1
End Sub
```

In most cases, this procedure won't be very useful because each line of data is simply dumped into a single cell. It is easier just to open the text file directly by using File ⇨ Open.

Exporting a range to a text file

The example in this section writes the data in a selected worksheet range to a CSV text file. Although Excel can export data to a CSV file, it exports the entire worksheet. This macro works with a specified range of cells.

```
Sub ExportRange()
    Dim Filename As String
    Dim NumRows As Long, NumCols As Integer
    Dim r As Long, c As Integer
    Dim Data
    Dim ExpRng As Range

    Set ExpRng = Selection
    NumCols = ExpRng.Columns.Count
    NumRows = ExpRng.Rows.Count
    Filename = Application.DefaultFilePath & "\textfile.csv"
    Open Filename For Output As #1
        For r = 1 To NumRows
```

```
            For c = 1 To NumCols
                Data = ExpRng.Cells(r, c).Value
                If IsNumeric(Data) Then Data = Val(Data)
                If IsEmpty(ExpRng.Cells(r, c)) Then Data = ""
                If c <> NumCols Then
                    Write #1, Data;
                Else
                    Write #1, Data
                End If
            Next c
        Next r
    Close #1
    MsgBox ExpRng.Count & " cells were exported to " _
      & Filename, vbInformation
End Sub
```

Note that the procedure uses two `Write` # statements. The first statement ends with a semicolon, so a return/linefeed sequence isn't written. For the last cell in a row, however, the second `Write` # statement doesn't use a semicolon, which causes the next output to appear on a new line.

You used a variable named `Data` to store the contents of each cell. If the cell is numeric, the variable is converted to a value. This step ensures that numeric data won't be stored with quotation marks. If a cell is empty, its `Value` property returns 0. Therefore, the code also checks for a blank cell (by using the `IsEmpty` function) and substitutes an empty string instead of a 0.

On the Web

These exporting and importing examples are available on the book's website in the `export and import csv .xlsm` file.

Importing a text file to a range

The example in this section reads the CSV file created in the preceding example and then stores the values beginning at the active cell in the active worksheet. The code reads each character and essentially parses the line of data, ignoring quote characters and looking for commas to delineate the columns.

```
Sub ImportRange()
    Dim ImpRng As Range
    Dim Filename As String
    Dim r As Long, c As Integer
    Dim txt As String, Char As String * 1
    Dim Data
    Dim i As Integer
```

```
Set ImpRng = ActiveCell
On Error Resume Next
Filename = Application.DefaultFilePath & "\textfile.csv"
Open Filename For Input As #1
If Err <> 0 Then
    MsgBox "Not found: " & Filename, vbCritical, "ERROR"
    Exit Sub
End If
r = 0
c = 0
txt = ""
Application.ScreenUpdating = False
Do Until EOF(1)
    Line Input #1, Data
    For i = 1 To Len(Data)
        Char = Mid(Data, i, 1)
        If Char = "," Then 'comma
            ActiveCell.Offset(r, c) = txt
            c = c + 1
            txt = ""
        ElseIf i = Len(Data) Then 'end of line
            If Char <> Chr(34) Then txt = txt & Char
            ActiveCell.Offset(r, c) = txt
            txt = ""
        ElseIf Char <> Chr(34) Then
            txt = txt & Char
        End If
    Next i
    c = 0
    r = r + 1
Loop
Close #1
Application.ScreenUpdating = True
End Sub
```

> **NOTE**
>
> The preceding procedure works with most data, but it has a flaw: it doesn't handle data that contains a comma or a quote character. But commas resulting from formatting are handled correctly (they're ignored). In addition, an imported date will be surrounded by number signs, for example, #2019-05-12#.

Logging Excel usage

The example in this section writes data to a text file every time Excel is opened and closed. For this example to work reliably, the procedure must be located in a workbook that's opened every time you start Excel. Storing the macro in your Personal Macro Workbook is an excellent choice.

The following procedure, stored in the code module for the `ThisWorkbook` object, is executed when the file is opened:

```
Private Sub Workbook_Open()
    Open Application.DefaultFilePath & "\excelusage.txt" For
Append As #1
    Print #1, "Started " & Now
    Close #1
End Sub
```

The procedure appends a new line to a file named `excelusage.txt`. The new line contains the current date and time and might look something like this:

```
Started 11/16/2013 9:27:43 PM
```

The following procedure is executed before the workbook is closed. It appends a new line that contains the word *Stopped* along with the current date and time.

```
Private Sub Workbook_BeforeClose(Cancel As Boolean)
    Open Application.DefaultFilePath & "\excelusage.txt" _
      For Append As #1
    Print #1, "Stopped " & Now
    Close #1
End Sub
```

ON THE WEB

A workbook that contains these procedures is available on the book's website in the `excel usage log.xlsm` file.

Refer to Chapter 6, "Understanding Excel's Events," for more information about event-handler procedures, such as `Workbook _ Open` and `Workbook _ BeforeClose`.

Filtering a text file

The example in this section demonstrates how to work with two text files at once. The `FilterFile` procedure that follows reads a text file (`infile.txt`) and copies only the rows that contain a specific text string (`"January"`) to a second text file (`output.txt`):

```
Sub FilterFile()

    Dim TextToFind As String
    Dim Filtered As Long
    Dim data As String

    Open ThisWorkbook.Path & "\infile.txt" For Input As #1
    Open Application.DefaultFilePath & "\output.txt" For Output As #2
    If Err <> 0 Then
```

```
        MsgBox "Error reading or writing a file."
        Exit Sub
    End If
    TextToFind = "January"
    Filtered = 0
    Do While Not EOF(1)
        Line Input #1, data
        If InStr(1, data, TextToFind) Then
            Filtered = Filtered + 1
            Print #2, data
        End If
    Loop
    Close 'Close all files
    MsgBox Filtered & " lines were written to:" & vbNewLine & _
        Application.DefaultFilePath & "\output.txt"

End Sub
```

ON THE WEB

This example, named `filter text file.xlsm`, is available on the book's website.

Performing Common File Operations

Many applications that you develop for Excel require working with external files. For example, you might need to get a listing of files in a directory, delete files, or rename files. Excel can import and export several types of text files. In many cases, however, Excel's built-in text file handling isn't sufficient. For example, you might want to paste a list of filenames into a range or export a range of cells to a simple Hypertext Markup Language (HTML) file.

In this chapter, you explore how to use Visual Basic for Applications (VBA) to perform common (and not so common) file operations and work directly with text files.

Excel provides two ways to perform common file operations.

- **Use traditional VBA statements and functions:** This method works for all versions of Excel.
- **Use the** `FileSystemObject` **object, which uses the Microsoft Scripting Library:** This method works for Excel 2000 and later.

CAUTION

Some earlier versions of Excel also supported the use of the `FileSearch` object. That feature was removed, beginning with Excel 2007. If you execute an old macro that uses the `FileSearch` object, the macro will fail.

In the sections that follow, you explore these two methods and some examples.

Using VBA file-related statements

The VBA statements that you can use to work with files are summarized in Table 11.1. Most of these statements are straightforward, and all are described in the Help system.

TABLE 11.1   VBA File-Related Statements

Command	What It Does
ChDir	Changes the current directory
ChDrive	Changes the current drive
Dir	Returns a filename or directory that matches a specified pattern or file attribute
FileCopy	Copies a file
FileDateTime	Returns the date and time when a file was last modified
FileLen	Returns the size of a file in bytes
GetAttr	Returns a value that represents an attribute of a file
Kill	Deletes a file
MkDir	Creates a new directory
Name	Renames a file or directory
RmDir	Removes an empty directory
SetAttr	Changes an attribute for a file

The remainder of this section consists of examples that demonstrate some of the file manipulation commands.

A VBA function to determine whether a file exists

The following function returns True if a particular file exists and False if it doesn't exist. If the Dir function returns an empty string, the file couldn't be found, so the function returns False.

```
Function FileExists(fname) As Boolean
    FileExists = Dir(fname) <> ""
End Function
```

The argument for the FileExists function consists of a full path and filename. The function can be used in a worksheet or called from a VBA procedure. Here's an example:

```
MyFile = "c:\budgeting\budget notes.docx"
Msgbox FileExists(MyFile)
```

A VBA function to determine whether a path exists

The following function returns True if a specified path exists and False otherwise:

```
Function PathExists(pname) As Boolean
'    Returns TRUE if the path exists
```

```
    On Error Resume Next
    PathExists = (GetAttr(pname) And vbDirectory) = vbDirectory
End Function
```

The pname argument is a string that contains a directory (without a filename). The trailing backslash in the pathname is optional. Here's an example of calling the function:

```
MyFolder = "c:\users\john\desktop\downloads\"
MsgBox PathExists(MyFolder)
```

ON THE WEB

The FileExists and PathExists functions are available on the book's website in the file functions .xlsm file.

A VBA procedure to display a list of files in a directory

The following procedure displays (in the active worksheet) a list of files in a particular directory, along with the file size and date:

```
Sub ListFiles()
    Dim Directory As String
    Dim r As Long
    Dim f As String
    Dim FileSize As Double
    Directory = "f:\excelfiles\budgeting\"
    r = 1
'    Insert headers
    Cells(r, 1) = "FileName"
    Cells(r, 2) = "Size"
    Cells(r, 3) = "Date/Time"
    Range("A1:C1").Font.Bold = True
'    Get first file
    f = Dir(Directory, vbReadOnly + vbHidden + vbSystem)
    Do While f <> ""
        r = r + 1
        Cells(r, 1) = f
        'Adjust for filesize > 2 gigabytes
        FileSize = FileLen(Directory & f)
        If FileSize < 0 Then FileSize = FileSize + 4294967296#
        Cells(r, 2) = FileSize

        Cells(r, 3) = FileDateTime(Directory & f)
'    Get next file
        f = Dir()
    Loop
End Sub
```

Note that the procedure uses the `Dir` function twice. The first time (used with an argument), it retrieves the first matching filename found. Subsequent calls (without an argument) retrieve additional matching filenames. When no more files are found, the `Dir` function returns an empty string.

The `Dir` function also accepts wildcard file specifications in its first argument. To get a list of Excel files, for example, you could use a statement such as this:

```
f = Dir(Directory & "*.xl??", vbReadOnly + vbHidden + vbSystem)
```

This statement retrieves the name of the first `*.xl??` file in the specified directory. The wildcard specification returns a four-character extension that begins with XL. For example, the extension could be `.xlsx`, `.xltx`, or `.xlam`. The second argument for the `Dir` function lets you specify the attributes of the files (in terms of built-in constants). In this example, the `Dir` function retrieves filenames that have no attributes, read-only files, hidden files, and system files.

To also retrieve Excel files in earlier formats (for example, `.xls` and `.xla` files), use the following wildcard specification:

```
*.xl*
```

Table 11.2 lists the built-in constants for the `Dir` function.

TABLE 11.2   File Attribute Constants for the Dir Function

Constant	Value	Description
vbNormal	0	Files with no attributes. This is the default setting and is always in effect.
vbReadOnly	1	Read-only files.
vbHidden	2	Hidden files.
vbSystem	4	System files.

Constant	Value	Description
vbVolume	8	Volume label. If any other attribute is specified, this attribute is ignored.
vbDirectory	16	Directories. This attribute doesn't work. Calling the Dir function with the vbDirectory attribute doesn't continually return subdirectories.

CAUTION

If you use the Dir function to loop through files and call another procedure to process the files, make sure that the other procedure doesn't use the Dir function. Only one "set" of Dir calls can be active at any time.

A recursive VBA procedure to display a list of files in nested directories

The example in this section creates a list of files in a specified directory, including its subdirectories. This procedure is unusual because it calls itself—a method known as *recursion*.

```
Public Sub RecursiveDir(ByVal CurrDir As String)

    Dim Dirs() As String
    Dim NumDirs As Long
    Dim FileName As String
    Dim PathAndName As String
    Dim i As Long
    Dim Filesize As Double

'   Make sure path ends in backslash
    If Right(CurrDir, 1) <> "\" Then CurrDir = CurrDir & "\"

'   Put column headings on active sheet
    Cells(1, 1) = "Path"
    Cells(1, 2) = "Filename"
    Cells(1, 3) = "Size"
    Cells(1, 4) = "Date/Time"
    Range("A1:D1").Font.Bold = True

'   Get files
    On Error Resume Next
    FileName = Dir(CurrDir & "*.*", vbDirectory)
    Do While Len(FileName) <> 0
      If Left(FileName, 1) <> "." Then 'Current dir
        PathAndName = CurrDir & FileName
        If (GetAttr(PathAndName) And vbDirectory) = vbDirectory Then
          'store found directories
            ReDim Preserve Dirs(0 To NumDirs) As String
            Dirs(NumDirs) = PathAndName
```

```
        NumDirs = NumDirs + 1
    Else
      'Write the path and file to the sheet
      Cells(WorksheetFunction.CountA(Range("A:A")) + 1, 1) = CurrDir
      Cells(WorksheetFunction.CountA(Range("B:B")) + 1, 2) = FileName
      'adjust for filesize > 2 gigabytes
      Filesize = FileLen(PathAndName)
      If Filesize < 0 Then Filesize = Filesize + 4294967296#
      Cells(WorksheetFunction.CountA(Range("C:C")) + 1, 3) = Filesize
      Cells(WorksheetFunction.CountA(Range("D:D")) + 1, 4) = _
          FileDateTime(PathAndName)
    End If
  End If
    FileName = Dir()
  Loop
  ' Process the found directories, recursively
  For i = 0 To NumDirs - 1
      RecursiveDir Dirs(i)
  Next i
End Sub
```

The procedure takes one argument, CurrDir, which is the directory being examined. Information for each file is displayed in the active worksheet. As the procedure loops through the files, it stores the subdirectory names in an array named Dirs. When no more files are found, the procedure calls itself using an entry in the Dirs array for its argument. When all directories in the Dirs array have been processed, the procedure ends.

Because the RecursiveDir procedure uses an argument, it must be executed from another procedure by using a statement like this:

```
Call RecursiveDir("c:\directory\")
```

ON THE WEB

The book's website contains a version of this procedure that allows you to select a directory from a dialog box. The filename is recursive file list.xlsm.

Using the FileSystemObject object

The FileSystemObject object is a member of Windows Scripting Host and provides access to a computer's file system. This object is often used in script-oriented web pages (for example, VBScript and JavaScript) and can be used with Excel 2000 and later versions.

> **CAUTION**
> Windows Scripting Host can potentially be used to spread computer viruses and other malware, so it may be disabled on some systems. In addition, some antivirus software products have been known to interfere with Windows Scripting Host. Therefore, use caution if you're designing an application that will be used on many different systems.

The name `FileSystemObject` is a bit misleading because it includes a number of objects, each designed for a specific purpose.

Drive: A drive or a collection of drives

File: A file or a collection of files

Folder: A folder or a collection of folders

TextStream: A stream of text that is read from, written to, or appended to a text file

The first step in using the `FileSystemObject` object is to create an instance of the object. You can perform this task in two ways: early binding or late binding.

The late binding method uses two statements like this:

```
Dim FileSys As Object
    Set FileSys = CreateObject("Scripting.FileSystemObject")
```

Note that the `FileSys` object variable is declared as a generic `Object` rather than as an actual object type. The object type is resolved at run-time.

The early binding method of creating the object requires that you set up a reference to Windows Script Host Object Model. You do this by using Tools ➪ References in VBE. After you've established the reference, create the object by using statements like these:

```
Dim FileSys As FileSystemObject
Set FileSys = CreateObject("Scripting.FileSystemObject")
```

Using the early binding method enables you to take advantage of the VBE Auto List Members feature to help you identify properties and methods as you type. In addition, you can use Object Browser (by pressing F2) to learn more about the object model.

The examples that follow demonstrate various tasks using the `FileSystemObject` object.

Using FileSystemObject to determine whether a file exists

The `Function` procedure that follows accepts one argument (the path and filename) and returns `True` if the file exists:

```
Function FileExists3(fname) As Boolean
    Dim FileSys As Object 'FileSystemObject
    Set FileSys = CreateObject("Scripting.FileSystemObject")
    FileExists3 = FileSys.FileExists(fname)
End Function
```

The function creates a new `FileSystemObject` object named `FileSys` and then accesses the `FileExists` property for that object.

Using FileSystemObject to determine whether a path exists

The `Function` procedure that follows accepts one argument (the path) and returns `True` if the path exists:

```
Function PathExists2(path) As Boolean
    Dim FileSys As Object 'FileSystemObject
    Set FileSys = CreateObject("Scripting.FileSystemObject")
    PathExists2 = FileSys.FolderExists(path)
End Function
```

Using FileSystemObject to list information about all available disk drives

The example in this section uses `FileSystemObject` to retrieve and display information about all disk drives. The procedure loops through the `Drives` collection and writes various property values to a worksheet.

```
Sub ShowDriveInfo()
    Dim FileSys As FileSystemObject
    Dim Drv As Drive
    Dim Row As Long
    Set FileSys = CreateObject("Scripting.FileSystemObject")
    Cells.ClearContents
    Row = 1
'   Column headers
    Range("A1:F1") = Array("Drive", "Ready", "Type", "Vol. Name", _
        "Size", "Available")
    On Error Resume Next
'   Loop through the drives
    For Each Drv In FileSys.Drives
        Row = Row + 1
        Cells(Row, 1) = Drv.DriveLetter
        Cells(Row, 2) = Drv.IsReady
        Select Case Drv.DriveType
            Case 0: Cells(Row, 3) = "Unknown"
            Case 1: Cells(Row, 3) = "Removable"
            Case 2: Cells(Row, 3) = "Fixed"
            Case 3: Cells(Row, 3) = "Network"
            Case 4: Cells(Row, 3) = "CD-ROM"
            Case 5: Cells(Row, 3) = "RAM Disk"
        End Select
```

```
            Cells(Row, 4) = Drv.VolumeName
            Cells(Row, 5) = Drv.TotalSize
            Cells(Row, 6) = Drv.AvailableSpace
        Next Drv
        'Make a table
        ActiveSheet.ListObjects.Add xlSrcRange, _
          Range("A1").CurrentRegion, , xlYes
    End Sub
```

 Chapter 7, "VBA Programming Examples and Techniques," describes another method of getting drive information by using Windows API functions.

Zipping and Unzipping Files

Perhaps the most commonly used type of file compression is the zip format. Even Excel 2007 (and later) files are stored in the zip format (although they don't use the `.zip` extension). A zip file can contain any number of files and even complete directory structures. The content of the files determines the degree of compression. For example, JPG image files and MP3 audio files are already compressed, so zipping these file types has little effect on the file size. Text files, on the other hand, usually shrink quite a bit when compressed.

> **ON THE WEB**
> The examples in this section are available on the book's website in files named `zip files.xlsm` and `unzip a file.xlsm`.

Zipping files

The example in this section demonstrates how to create a zip file from a group of user-selected files. The `ZipFiles` procedure displays a dialog box so that the user can select the files. It then creates a zip file named `compressed.zip` in Excel's default directory.

```
    Sub ZipFiles()
        Dim ShellApp As Object
        Dim FileNameZip As Variant
        Dim FileNames As Variant
        Dim i As Long, FileCount As Long

    '   Get the file names
        FileNames = Application.GetOpenFilename _
            (FileFilter:="All Files (*.*),*.*", _
             FilterIndex:=1, _
             Title:="Select the files to ZIP", _
             MultiSelect:=True)
```

```vba
'   Exit if dialog box canceled
    If Not IsArray(FileNames) Then Exit Sub

    FileCount = UBound(FileNames)
    FileNameZip = Application.DefaultFilePath & "\compressed.zip"

    'Create empty Zip File with zip header
    Open FileNameZip For Output As #1
    Print #1, Chr$(80) & Chr$(75) & Chr$(5) & Chr$(6) & String(18, 0)
    Close #1

    Set ShellApp = CreateObject("Shell.Application")
    'Copy the files to the compressed folder

    For i = LBound(FileNames) To UBound(FileNames)
        DoEvents
        ShellApp.Namespace(FileNameZip).CopyHere FileNames(i)

        'Keep script waiting until Compressing is done
        On Error Resume Next
        Do Until ShellApp.Namespace(FileNameZip).items.Count = i
          DoEvents
          Application.Wait (Now + TimeValue("0:00:01"))
        Loop
        Application.StatusBar = "File " & i & " of " & UBound(FileNames)
    Next i

    If MsgBox(FileCount & " files were zipped to:" & _
        vbNewLine & FileNameZip & vbNewLine & vbNewLine & _
        "View the zip file?", vbQuestion + vbYesNo) = vbYes Then _
        Shell "Explorer.exe /e," & FileNameZip, vbNormalFocus
End Sub
```

The ZipFiles procedure creates a file named compressed.zip and writes a string of characters, which identify it as a zip file. Next, a Shell.Application object is created, and the code uses its CopyHere method to copy the files to the zip archive. The next section of the code is a Do Until loop, which checks the number of files in the zip archive every second. This step is necessary because copying the files could take some time, and if the procedure ends before the files are copied, the zip file will be incomplete (and probably corrupt).

When the number of files in the zip archive matches the number that should be there, the loop ends, and users are presented with a message box asking if they want to see the files. Clicking the Yes button opens a Windows Explorer window that shows the zipped files.

> **CAUTION**
>
> The ZipFiles procedure presented here was kept simple to make it easy to understand. The code does no error checking and is not flexible. For example, there is no option to choose the zip filename or location, and the current compressed.zip file is always overwritten without warning. It's certainly no replacement for the zipping tools built into Windows, but it's an interesting demonstration of what you can do with VBA.

Unzipping a file

The example in this section performs the opposite function of the preceding example. It asks the user for a ZIP filename and then unzips the files and puts them in a directory named Unzipped, located in Excel's default file directory.

```vba
Sub UnzipAFile()
    Dim ShellApp As Object
    Dim TargetFile
    Dim ZipFolder

    '   Target file & temp dir
    TargetFile = Application.GetOpenFilename _
        (FileFilter:="Zip Files (*.zip), *.zip")
    If TargetFile = False Then Exit Sub

    ZipFolder = Application.DefaultFilePath & "\Unzipped\"

    '   Create a temp folder
    On Error Resume Next
    RmDir ZipFolder
    MkDir ZipFolder
    On Error GoTo 0

    '   Copy the zipped files to the newly created folder
    Set ShellApp = CreateObject("Shell.Application")
    ShellApp.Namespace(ZipFolder).CopyHere _
        ShellApp.Namespace(TargetFile).items

    If MsgBox("The file was unzipped to:" & _
        vbNewLine & ZipFolder & vbNewLine & vbNewLine & _
        "View the folder?", vbQuestion + vbYesNo) = vbYes Then _
        Shell "Explorer.exe /e," & ZipFolder, vbNormalFocus
End Sub
```

The UnzipAFile procedure uses the GetOpenFilename method to get the zip file. It then creates the new folder and uses the Shell.Application object to copy the contents of the zip file to the new folder. Finally, the user can choose to display the new directory.

Part III

Working with UserForms

IN THIS PART

Leveraging Custom Dialog Boxes

IN THIS CHAPTER

Using an input box to get user input

Using a message box to display messages or to get a simple response

Selecting a file from a dialog box

Selecting a directory

Displaying Excel's built-in dialog boxes

Alternatives to UserForms

Dialog boxes are a key user interface element in many Windows programs. Virtually every Windows program uses them, and most users have a good understanding of how they work. UserForms are one way for Excel developers to create custom dialog boxes. However, VBA provides alternative methods to display built-in dialog boxes with minimal programming required.

Before we get into creating UserForms (beginning with Chapter 13, "Introducing UserForms"), you might find it helpful to understand some of Excel's built-in tools that display dialog boxes. The sections that follow describe various dialog boxes that you can display using VBA without creating a UserForm.

Using an Input Box

An *input box* is a simple dialog box that allows the user to make a single entry. For example, you can use an input box to let the user enter text or a number or even select a range. You can generate an input box in two ways: by using the VBA InputBox function and by using the InputBox method of the Application object. We explain each method in the sections that follow.

Using the VBA InputBox function

The syntax for VBA's InputBox function is as follows:

```
InputBox(prompt[,title][,default][,xpos][,ypos][,helpfile, context])
```

- `Prompt`: Required. The text displayed in the input box.
- `Title`: Optional. The caption displayed in the title bar of the input box. If you omit it, "Microsoft Excel" is displayed.
- `Default`: Optional. The default value to be displayed in the input box.
- `XPos, YPos`: Optional. The screen coordinates of the upper-left corner of the input box.
- `HelpFile, Context`: Optional. The help file and help topic.

The `InputBox` function prompts the user for a single piece of information. The function always returns a String, so your code may need to convert the results to a value, if that's what your procedure expects.

The prompt tells the user what to enter in the entry field. It can be up to 1,024 characters long, but generally a shorter prompt is more user-friendly. In addition to the prompt, you can provide a title for the dialog box. The title should tell the user the purpose of the dialog box, and the prompt should tell the user how to use the dialog box. If you provide a default value, the dialog box will display with that value, and that can help speed data entry. You can specify the dialog box's display position on the screen and a custom help topic, although these are lesser-used parameters. If you include the help parameters, the input box displays a Help button.

The following example, which generates the dialog box shown in Figure 12.1, uses the VBA `InputBox` function to ask the user for his or her full name. The code then extracts the first name and displays a greeting in a message box.

```
[c12Sub GetName()
    Dim UserName As String
    Dim FirstSpace As Long
    Do Until Len(UserName) > 0
        UserName = InputBox("Enter your full name: ", _
            "Identify Yourself")
    Loop
    FirstSpace = InStr(UserName, Space(1))
    If FirstSpace > 0 Then
        UserName = Left$(UserName, FirstSpace - 1)
    End If
    MsgBox "Hello " & UserName
End Sub
```

FIGURE 12.1

The VBA InputBox function at work

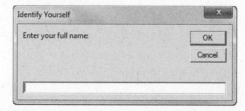

Note that this InputBox function is written in a Do Until loop to ensure that something is entered when the input box appears. If the user clicks Cancel or doesn't enter any text, UserName contains an empty string, and the input box reappears. The procedure then attempts to extract the first name by searching for the first space character (by using the InStr function) and then using the Left function to extract all characters before the first space. If a space character isn't found, the entire name is used as entered.

The following code shows the same procedure with two changes. First, the UserName property of the Application object is supplied as the default value to the dialog box. If the name with which the user has signed into Office is correct, they only have to click OK and don't have to enter anything. If not, they can change the default property to whatever they want. Next, the Split function is used to split the text into an array wherever there is a space. Then the first array element (the (0) in the code) is returned. If the user enters Joe Smith, Joe is the first element of the array, and Smith is the second.

```
Sub GetNameSplit()
   Dim UserName As String
   Do Until Len(UserName) > 0
      UserName = InputBox("Enter your full name: ", _
         "Identify Yourself", Application.UserName)
   Loop
   MsgBox "Hello " & Split(UserName, Space(1))(0)
End Sub
```

If the user enters a name with no space, the array created by Split will have only one element. The code will still work because it uses the first element. If you wanted to use a different element, you would have to make sure that it existed first. Using Split isn't necessarily a better way than InStr to split up a name, just a different one.

The following is another example of the VBA InputBox function, with the result shown in Figure 12.2. The user is asked to fill in the missing word. This example also illustrates the use of named arguments. The prompt text is retrieved from a worksheet cell and is assigned to a variable (Prompt).

```
[c12Sub GetWord()
    Dim TheWord As String
    Dim Prompt As String
    Dim Title As String
    Prompt = Range("A1").Value
    Title = "What's the missing word?"
    TheWord = InputBox(Prompt:=Prompt, Title:=Title)
    If UCase(TheWord) = "BATTLEFIELD" Then
        MsgBox "Correct."
    Else
        MsgBox "That is incorrect."
    End If
End Sub
```

FIGURE 12.2

Using the VBA InputBox function with a long prompt

As we mentioned, the `InputBox` function always returns a string. If the string returned by the `InputBox` function looks like a number, you can convert it to a value by using the VBA `Val` function or just perform a mathematical operation on the string.

The following code uses the `InputBox` function to prompt for a numeric value. It uses the built-in `IsNumeric` function to determine whether the string can be interpreted as a number. If so, it displays the user's input multiplied by 12.

```
Sub GetValue()
    Dim Monthly As String
    Monthly = InputBox("Enter your monthly salary:")
    If Len(Monthly) > 0 And IsNumeric(Monthly) Then
        MsgBox "Annualized: " & Monthly * 12
    Else
        MsgBox "Invalid input"
    End If
End Sub
```

ON THE WEB

The four examples in this section are available on the book's website in the `InputBox Function.xlsm` file.

Using the Application.InputBox method

Using Excel's `InputBox` method rather than the VBA `InputBox` function offers three advantages.

- You can specify the data type returned. (It doesn't have to be a String.)

- The user can specify a worksheet range by dragging in the worksheet.
- Input validation is performed automatically.

The syntax for the `InputBox` method is as follows:

```
InputBox(Prompt [,Title] [,Default] [,Left] [,Top] [,HelpFile,
HelpContextID] [,Type])
```

- `Prompt`: Required. The text displayed in the input box.
- `Title`: Optional. The caption in the title bar of the input box. If you omit it, "Microsoft Excel" is displayed.
- `Default`: Optional. The value that is prefilled in the input box.
- `Left, Top`: Optional. The screen coordinates of the upper-left corner of the window.
- `HelpFile, HelpContextID`: Optional. The help file and help topic.
- `Type`: Optional. A code for the data type returned, as listed in Table 12.1.

> **NOTE**
>
> The `Left`, `Top`, `HelpFile`, and `HelpContextID` arguments are no longer supported. You can specify these arguments, but they have no effect.

TABLE 12.1   Codes to Determine the Data Type Returned by Excel's InputBox Method

Code	Meaning
0	A formula
1	A number
2	A string (text)
4	A logical value (`True` or `False`)
8	A cell reference, as a range object
16	An error value, such as #N/A
64	An array of values

The `InputBox` method is versatile. To allow more than one data type to be returned, use the sum of the pertinent codes. For example, to display an input box that can accept text or numbers, set `type` equal to 3 (that is, 1 + 2, or *number* plus *text*). If you use 8 for the `type` argument, the user can enter a cell or range address (or a named cell or range) manually or point to a range in the worksheet.

The `EraseRange` procedure, which follows, uses the `InputBox` method to allow the user to select a range to erase (see Figure 12.3). The user can either type the range address manually or use the mouse to select the range in the sheet.

FIGURE 12.3

Using the InputBox method to specify a range

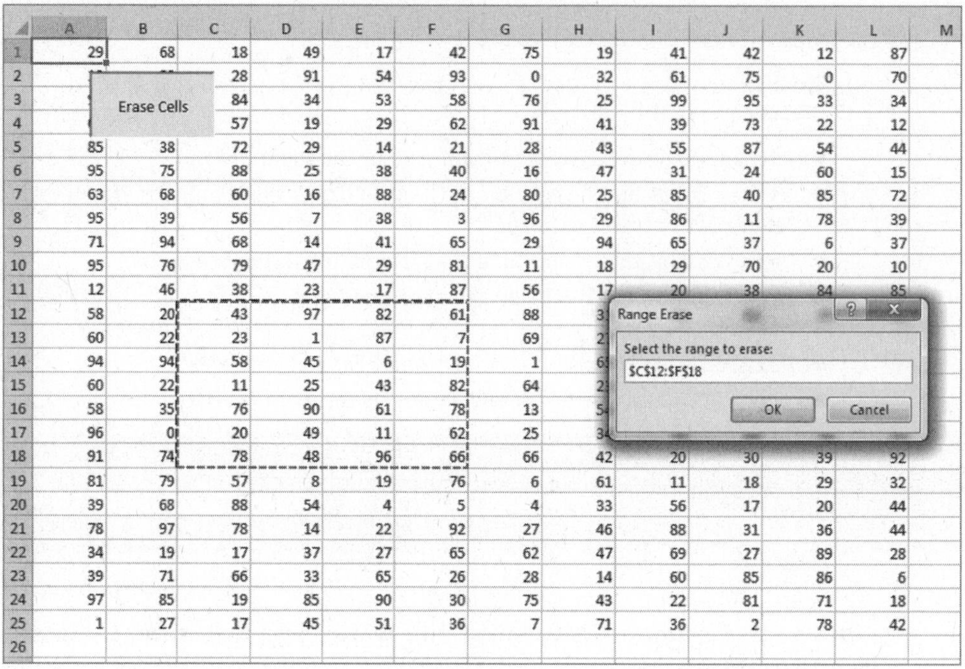

	A	B	C	D	E	F	G	H	I	J	K	L	M
1	29	68	18	49	17	42	75	19	41	42	12	87	
2			28	91	54	93	0	32	61	75	0	70	
3		Erase Cells	84	34	53	58	76	25	99	95	33	34	
4			57	19	29	62	91	41	39	73	22	12	
5	85	38	72	29	14	21	28	43	55	87	54	44	
6	95	75	88	25	38	40	16	47	31	24	60	15	
7	63	68	60	16	88	24	80	25	85	40	85	72	
8	95	39	56	7	38	3	96	29	86	11	78	39	
9	71	94	68	14	41	65	29	94	65	37	6	37	
10	95	76	79	47	29	81	11	18	29	70	20	10	
11	12	46	38	23	17	87	56	17	20	38	84	85	
12	58	20	43	97	82	61	88	3					
13	60	22	23	1	87	7	69	2					
14	94	94	58	45	6	19	1	6					
15	60	22	11	25	43	82	64	2					
16	58	35	76	90	61	78	13	5					
17	96	0	20	49	11	62	25	3					
18	91	74	78	48	96	66	66	42	20	30	39	92	
19	81	79	57	8	19	76	6	61	11	18	29	32	
20	39	68	88	54	4	5	4	33	56	17	20	44	
21	78	97	78	14	22	92	27	46	88	31	36	44	
22	34	19	17	37	27	65	62	47	69	27	89	28	
23	39	71	66	33	65	26	28	14	60	85	86	6	
24	97	85	19	85	90	30	75	43	22	81	71	18	
25	1	27	17	45	51	36	7	71	36	2	78	42	
26													

Range Erase dialog box:
Select the range to erase:
$C$12:$F$18
OK   Cancel

The InputBox method with a Type argument of 8 returns a Range object (note the Set keyword). This range is then erased (by using the ClearContents method). The default value displayed in the input box is the current selection's address. If the user clicks Cancel instead of selecting a range, the InputBox method returns the Boolean value False. A Boolean value can't be assigned to a range, so On Error Resume Next is used to ignore the error. Finally, the contents are cleared, and the range is selected only if a range was entered; that is, the UserRange variable isn't Nothing.

```
Sub EraseRange()
    Dim UserRange As Range
    On Error Resume Next
        Set UserRange = Application.InputBox _
            (Prompt:="Select the range to erase:", _
            Title:="Range Erase", _
            Default:=Selection.Address, _
            Type:=8)
    On Error GoTo 0
    If Not UserRange Is Nothing Then
        UserRange.ClearContents
        UserRange.Select
    End If
End Sub
```

Yet another advantage of using the InputBox method is that Excel performs input valida-tion automatically. If you enter something other than a range address in the GetRange example, Excel displays a message and lets the user try again (see Figure 12.4).

FIGURE 12.4

Excel's InputBox method performs validation automatically

The following code is similar to the GetValue procedure in the preceding section, but this procedure uses the Inputbox method rather than the InputBox function. Although the type argument is set to 1 (a numeric value), the Monthly variable is declared as a variant. That way, the Monthly variable can hold False without causing an error if the user clicks Cancel. If the user makes a non-numeric entry, Excel displays a message and lets the user try again (see Figure 12.5).

```
Sub GetValue2()
    Dim Monthly As Variant
    Monthly = Application.InputBox _
        (Prompt:="Enter your monthly salary:", _
         Type:=1)
    If Monthly <> False Then
        MsgBox "Annualized: " & Monthly * 12
    End If
End Sub
```

FIGURE 12.5

Another example of validating an entry in Excel's InputBox

425

NOTE

Note in Figure 12.5 that the user prefixed the number with USD for U.S. dollars. Excel doesn't recognize that as a number and correctly reported that it's not valid. However, because USD1024 is a valid range reference, that range is selected. Excel attempts to process the entry before it validates it against the `Type` argument.

ON THE WEB

The two examples in this section are available on the book's website in a file named `Inputbox Method.xlsm`.

Using the VBA MsgBox Function

VBA's `MsgBox` function is an easy way to display a message to the user or to get a simple response (such as OK or Cancel). We use the `MsgBox` function in many of the examples in this book as a way to display a variable's value.

Keep in mind that `MsgBox` is a function, and your code stops running until the message box is dismissed by the user.

TIP

When a message box is displayed, you can press Ctrl+C to copy the contents of the message box to the Windows Clipboard.

The syntax for `MsgBox` is as follows:

```
MsgBox(prompt [,buttons] [,title] [,helpfile, context])
```

- `Prompt`: Required. The text displayed in the message box.
- `Buttons`: Optional. A numeric expression that determines which buttons and icon are displayed in the message box (see Table 12.2).
- `Title`: Optional. The caption in the message box window. If you omit it, "Microsoft Excel" is displayed.
- `HelpFile, Context`: Optional. The help file and help topic.

You can easily customize your message boxes because of the flexibility of the `buttons` argument. (Table 12.2 lists some of the constants that you can use for this argument.) You can specify which buttons to display, whether an icon appears, and which button is the default.

TABLE 12.2   **Constants Used for Buttons in the MsgBox Function**

Constant	Value	Description
vbOKOnly	0	Display only an OK button.
vbOKCancel	1	Display OK and Cancel buttons.
vbAbortRetryIgnore	2	Display Abort, Retry, and Ignore buttons.
vbYesNoCancel	3	Display Yes, No, and Cancel buttons.
vbYesNo	4	Display Yes and No buttons.
vbRetryCancel	5	Display Retry and Cancel buttons.
vbCritical	16	Display Critical Message icon.
vbQuestion	32	Display Warning Query icon.
vbExclamation	48	Display Warning Message icon.
vbInformation	64	Display Information Message icon.
vbDefaultButton1	0	First button is default.
vbDefaultButton2	256	Second button is default.
vbDefaultButton3	512	Third button is default.
vbDefaultButton4	768	Fourth button is default.
vbSystemModal	4096	All applications are suspended until the user responds to the message box (might not work under all conditions).
vbMsgBoxHelpButton	16384	Display a Help button. To display help when this button is clicked, use the helpfile and context arguments.

You can use the MsgBox function by itself (simply to display a message) or assign its result to a variable. The MsgBox function returns a value representing the button clicked by the user. The following example displays a message and an OK button, but it doesn't return a result:

```
Sub MsgBoxDemo()
    MsgBox "Macro finished with no errors."
End Sub
```

Note that the single argument is not enclosed in parentheses because the MsgBox result is not assigned to a variable.

To get a response from a message box, you can assign the results of the MsgBox function to a variable. In this situation, the arguments must be in parentheses. The following code uses some built-in constants (described in Table 12.3) to make it easier to work with the values returned by MsgBox:

```
Sub GetAnswer()
    Dim Ans As Long
```

```
    Ans = MsgBox("Continue?", vbYesNo)
    Select Case Ans
        Case vbYes
'           ...[code if Ans is Yes]...
        Case vbNo
'           ...[code if Ans is No]...
    End Select
End Sub
```

TABLE 12.3   Constants Used for MsgBox Return Value

Constant	Value	Button Clicked
vbOK	1	OK
vbCancel	2	Cancel
vbAbort	3	Abort
vbRetry	4	Retry
vbIgnore	5	Ignore
vbYes	6	Yes
vbNo	7	No

The variable returned by the MsgBox function is a Long data type. Actually, you don't even need to use a variable to use the result of a message box. The following procedure is another way of coding the GetAnswer procedure:

```
Sub GetAnswer2()
    If MsgBox("Continue?", vbYesNo) = vbYes Then
'       ...[code if Ans is Yes]...
    Else
'       ...[code if Ans is No]...
    End If
End Sub
```

The following function example uses a combination of constants to display a message box with a Yes button, a No button, and a question mark icon; the second button is designated as the default button (see Figure 12.6). For simplicity, I assigned these constants to the Config variable.

```
Private Function ContinueProcedure() As Boolean
    Dim Config As Long
    Dim Ans As Long
    Config = vbYesNo + vbQuestion + vbDefaultButton2
    Ans = MsgBox("An error occurred. Continue?", Config)
    ContinueProcedure = Ans = vbYes
End Function
```

FIGURE 12.6

The button argument of the MsgBox function determines which buttons appear.

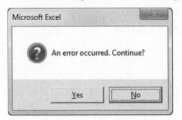

You can call the `ContinueProcedure` function from another procedure. For example, the following statement calls the `ContinueProcedure` function (which displays the message box). If the function returns `False` (that is, the user selects No), the procedure ends. Otherwise, the next statement is executed.

```
If Not ContinueProcedure() Then Exit Sub
```

The width of the message box depends on your video resolution. Figure 12.7 shows a message box displaying lengthy text with no forced line breaks.

FIGURE 12.7

Displaying lengthy text in a message box

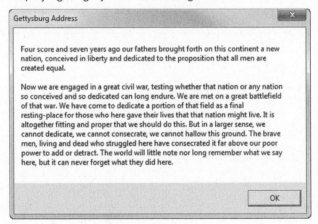

If you'd like to force a line break in the message, use the `vbNewLine` constant in the text. The following example displays the message in three lines:

```
Sub MultiLine()
    Dim Msg As String
    Msg = "This is the first line." & vbNewLine & vbNewLine
    Msg = Msg & "This is the second line." & vbNewLine
```

```
        Msg = Msg & "And this is the last line."
        MsgBox Msg
    End Sub
```

You can also insert a tab character by using the vbTab constant. The following procedure uses a message box to display the values in a 12 × 3 range of cells in A1:C12 (see Figure 12.8). It separates the columns by using a vbTab constant and inserts a new line by using the vbNewLine constant. The MsgBox function accepts a maximum string length of 1,023 characters, which will limit the number of cells that you can display. Also, note that the tab stops are fixed, so if a cell contains more than 11 characters, the columns won't be aligned.

```
Sub ShowRange()
    Dim Msg As String
    Dim r As Long, c As Long
    Msg = ""
    For r = 1 To 12
        For c = 1 To 3
            Msg = Msg & Cells(r, c).Text
            If c <> 3 Then Msg = Msg & vbTab
        Next c
        Msg = Msg & vbNewLine
    Next r
    MsgBox Msg
End Sub
```

FIGURE 12.8

This message box displays text with tabs and line breaks.

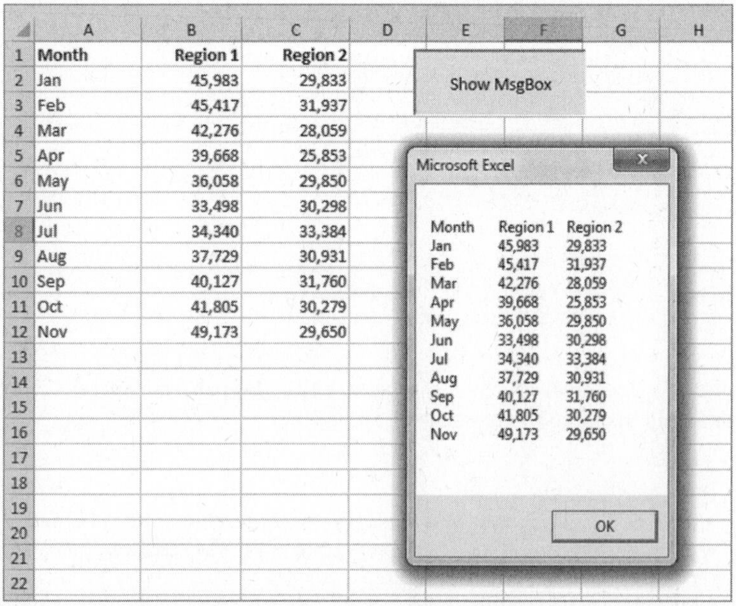

ON THE WEB

Examples from this section are available on the book's website in a file named `MsgBox Function.xlsm`.

 Chapter 14, "Looking at UserForm Examples," includes a `UserForm` example that emulates the `MsgBox` function.

Using the Excel GetOpenFilename Method

If your application needs to ask the user for a filename, you can use the `InputBox` function. But this approach is tedious and error-prone because the user must type (or paste) the filename (with no browsing capability). A better approach is to use the `Application`
`.GetOpenFilename` method, which ensures that your application gets a valid filename (as well as its complete path).

This method displays the normal Open dialog box, but it does *not* actually open the selected file. Rather, the method returns a string that contains the filename and path selected by the user. Then you can write code to do whatever you want with the filename.

The syntax for the `GetOpenFilename` method is as follows:

```
Application.GetOpenFilename(FileFilter, FilterIndex, Title,
ButtonText, MultiSelect)
```

- `FileFilter`: Optional. A string that limits what types of files are shown in the Open dialog.
- `FilterIndex`: Optional. The index number of the default file-filtering criteria.
- `Title`: Optional. The title of the dialog box. If omitted, the title is `Open`.
- `ButtonText`: For Macintosh only.
- `MultiSelect`: Optional. If `True`, you can select multiple files. The default value is `False`.

The `FileFilter` argument determines what file types appear in the dialog box's Files of Type drop-down list. The argument consists of pairs of file filter strings followed by the wildcard file filter specification, with each part and each pair separated by commas. If omitted, this argument defaults to the following:

```
"All Files (*.*),*.*"
```

Note that the first part of this string (`All Files (*.*)`) is the text displayed in the Files of Type drop-down list. The second part (`*.*`) determines which files are displayed.

The following instruction assigns a string to a variable named `Filt`. You can then use this string as a `FileFilter` argument for the `GetOpenFilename` method. In this case, the dialog box will allow the user to select from four file types (plus an All Files option). Note

12

that we used the VBA line continuation sequence to set up the `Filt` variable; doing so makes it much easier to work with this rather complicated argument.

```
Filt = "Text Files (*.txt),*.txt," & _
       "Lotus Files (*.prn),*.prn," & _
       "Comma Separated Files (*.csv),*.csv," & _
       "ASCII Files (*.asc),*.asc," & _
       "All Files (*.*),*.*"
```

The `FilterIndex` argument specifies which `FileFilter` is the default, and the `Title` argument is text that is displayed in the title bar. If the `MultiSelect` argument is `True`, the user can select multiple files, all of which are returned in an array.

The following example prompts the user for a filename. It defines five file filters.

```
Sub GetImportFileName()
    Dim Filt As String
    Dim FilterIndex As Long
    Dim Title As String
    Dim FileName As Variant

'   Set up list of file filters
    Filt = "Text Files (*.txt),*.txt," & _
           "Lotus Files (*.prn),*.prn," & _
           "Comma Separated Files (*.csv),*.csv," & _
           "ASCII Files (*.asc),*.asc," & _
           "All Files (*.*),*.*"

'   Display *.* by default
    FilterIndex = 5

'   Set the dialog box caption
    Title = "Select a File to Import"

'   Get the file name
    FileName = Application.GetOpenFilename _
        (FileFilter:=Filt, _
         FilterIndex:=FilterIndex, _
         Title:=Title)

'   Exit if dialog box canceled
    If FileName <> False Then
'       Display full path and name of the file
        MsgBox "You selected " & FileName
    Else
        MsgBox "No file was selected."
    End If
End Sub
```

Figure 12.9 shows the dialog box that appears when this procedure is executed and the user selects the Text Files filter.

FIGURE 12.9

The GetOpenFilename method displays a dialog box used to specify a file.

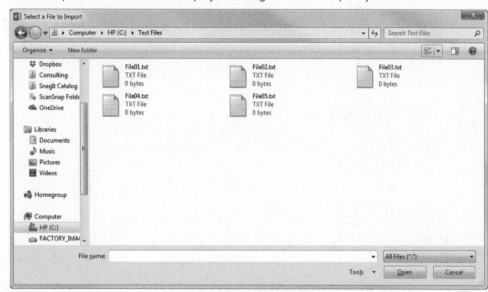

The following example is similar to the preceding one. The difference is that the user can press Ctrl or Shift and select multiple files when the dialog box is displayed. The code checks for the Cancel button click by determining whether `FileName` is an array. If the user doesn't click Cancel, the result is an array that consists of at least one element. In this example, a list of the selected files is displayed in a message box.

```
Sub GetImportFileName2()
    Dim Filt As String
    Dim FilterIndex As Long
    Dim FileName As Variant
    Dim Title As String
    Dim Msg As String
'   Set up list of file filters
    Filt = "Text Files (*.txt),*.txt," & _
           "Lotus Files (*.prn),*.prn," & _
           "Comma Separated Files (*.csv),*.csv," & _
           "ASCII Files (*.asc),*.asc," & _
           "All Files (*.*),*.*"
```

```
'    Display *.* by default
     FilterIndex = 5

'    Set the dialog box caption
     Title = "Select a File to Import"

'    Get the file name
     FileName = Application.GetOpenFilename _
         (FileFilter:=Filt, _
          FilterIndex:=FilterIndex, _
          Title:=Title, _
          MultiSelect:=True)

     If IsArray(FileName) Then
'        Display full path and name of the files
         Msg = Join(FileName, vbNewLine)
         MsgBox "You selected:" & vbNewLine & Msg
     Else
'        Exit if dialog box canceled
         MsgBox "No file was selected."
     End If
End Sub
```

When `MultiSelect` is `True`, the `FileName` variable will be an array, even if only one file was selected.

ON THE WEB

The two examples in this section are available on the book's website in the `Prompt for File.xlsm` file.

Using the Excel GetSaveAsFilename Method

The `GetSaveAsFilename` method displays a Save As dialog box and lets the user select (or specify) a location and filename as if the user were saving a file. Like the `GetOpenFilename` method, the `GetSaveAsFilename` method returns a filename and path but doesn't take any action.

The syntax for this method is as follows:

```
Application.GetSaveAsFilename(InitialFilename, FileFilter,
  FilterIndex, Title, ButtonText)
```

The arguments are as follows:

- `InitialFilename`: Optional. A string that is prefilled in the File name box.
- `FileFilter`: Optional. A string that determines what shows in the Save as type dropdown.

- `FilterIndex`: Optional. The index number of the default file-filtering criteria.
- `Title`: Optional. The title of the dialog box.
- `ButtonText`: For Macintosh only.

Prompting for a Folder

If you need to get a filename, the simplest solution is to use the `GetOpenFileName` method, as we described earlier. But if you need to get a folder name only (no file), you can use Excel's `FileDialog` object.

The following procedure displays a dialog box that allows the user to select a folder. The selected folder name (or `Canceled`) is then displayed by using the `MsgBox` function.

```
Sub GetAFolder ()
    With Application.FileDialog(msoFileDialogFolderPicker)
        .InitialFileName = Application.DefaultFilePath & "\"
        .Title = "Select a location for the backup"
        .Show
        If .SelectedItems.Count = 0 Then
            MsgBox "Canceled"
        Else
            MsgBox .SelectedItems(1)
        End If
    End With
End Sub
```

The `FileDialog` object lets you specify the starting folder by providing a value for the `InitialFileName` property. In this example, the code uses Excel's default file path as the starting folder.

Displaying Excel's Built-in Dialog Boxes

Code that you write in VBA can execute many Excel Ribbon commands. And, if the command normally leads to a dialog box, your code can "make choices" in the dialog box (although the dialog box itself isn't displayed). For example, the following VBA statement is equivalent to choosing the Home ⇨ Editing ⇨ Find & Select ⇨ Go To command, specifying the range A1:C3, and clicking OK:

```
Application.Goto Reference:=Range("A1:C3")
```

But when you execute this statement, the Go To dialog box never appears (which is almost always what you want).

In some cases, however, you may want to display one of Excel's built-in dialog boxes so that the user can make the choices. You can do so by writing code that executes a Ribbon command.

12

> **NOTE**
>
> Using the `Dialogs` collection of the `Application` object is another way to display an Excel dialog box. However, Microsoft has not kept this feature up-to-date, so we don't even discuss it. The method we describe in this section is a much better solution.

In early versions of Excel, programmers created custom menus and toolbars by using the `CommandBar` object. In Excel 2007 and newer versions, the `CommandBar` object is still available, but it doesn't work like it has in the past.

The `CommandBar` object has also been enhanced, beginning with Excel 2007. You can use the `CommandBar` object to execute Ribbon commands using VBA. Many of the Ribbon commands display a dialog box. For example, the following statement displays the Unhide dialog box (see Figure 12.10):

```
Application.CommandBars.ExecuteMso "SheetUnhide"
```

FIGURE 12.10

This dialog box was displayed with a VBA statement.

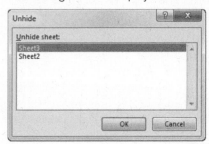

Keep in mind that your code cannot get any information about the user's action. For example, when this statement is executed, there is no way to know which sheet was selected or whether the user clicked the Cancel button. And, of course, code that executes a Ribbon command is not compatible with versions prior to Excel 2007.

The `ExecuteMso` method accepts one argument: an `idMso` parameter, which represents a Ribbon control. Unfortunately, these parameters aren't listed in the Help system.

If you try to display a built-in dialog box in an incorrect context, Excel displays an error message. For example, here's a statement that displays the Format Number dialog box:

```
Application.CommandBars.ExecuteMso "NumberFormatsDialog"
```

If you execute this statement when it's not appropriate (for example, when a shape is selected), Excel displays an error message because that dialog box is appropriate only for worksheet cells.

Excel has thousands of commands. How can you find the name of the one you need? One way is to use the Customize Ribbon tab of the Excel Options dialog box (right-click any Ribbon control and choose Customize the Ribbon from the shortcut menu). Virtually every command available in Excel is listed in the left panel. Find the command you need, hover your mouse cursor over it, and you'll see its command name in parentheses in the tooltip. Figure 12.11 shows how to find the idMso command in order to display the Define Name dialog box.

FIGURE 12.11

Using the Customize Ribbon panel to identify a command name

Here's the command to display the Define Name dialog box:

```
Application.CommandBars.ExecuteMso "NameDefine"
```

Executing An Old Menu Item Directly

You can display a built-in dialog box by using the `ExecuteMso` method. Another way to display a built-in dialog box requires knowledge of the pre–Excel 2007 toolbars, which are officially known as `CommandBar` objects. Although Excel no longer uses `CommandBar` objects, they're still supported for compatibility.

The following statement, for example, is equivalent to selecting the Format ➪ Sheet ➪ Unhide command in the Excel 2003 menu:

```
Application.CommandBars("Worksheet Menu Bar"). _
  Controls("Format").Controls("Sheet"). _
  Controls("Unhide...").Execute
```

When executed, this statement displays the Unhide dialog box. Note that the menu item captions must match exactly (including the three dots following `Unhide`).

Here's another example. This statement displays the Format Cells dialog box:

```
Application.CommandBars("Worksheet Menu Bar"). _
    Controls("Format").Controls("Cells...").Execute
```

It's probably not a good idea to rely on `CommandBar` objects because they may be removed from a future version of Excel.

Displaying a Data Form

Many people use Excel to manage lists in which the information is arranged in tabular form. Excel offers a simple way to work with this type of data through the use of a built-in data entry form that Excel can create automatically. This data form works with either a normal range of data or a range that has been designated as a table (by choosing the Insert ➪ Tables ➪ Table command). Figure 12.12 shows an example of a data form in use.

Making the data form accessible

For some reason, the command to access the data form isn't on the Excel Ribbon. To access the data form from Excel's user interface, you must add it to your Quick Access toolbar or to the Ribbon. The following are instructions to add this command to the Quick Access toolbar.

FIGURE 12.12

Some users prefer to use Excel's built-in data form for data-entry tasks.

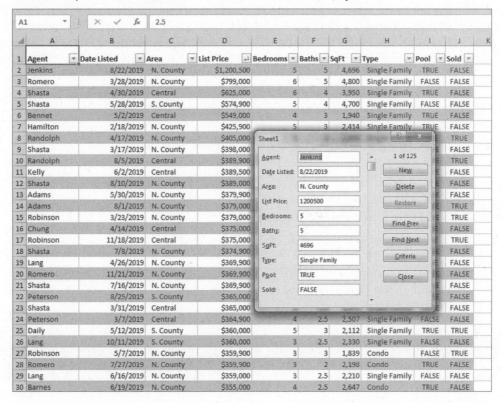

Adding the Form Command to the Quick Access Toolbar

1. Right-click the Quick Access toolbar, and choose Customize Quick Access Toolbar.
   The Customize the Quick Access Toolbar panel of the Excel Options dialog box appears.
2. In the Choose Commands From drop-down list, select Commands Not in the Ribbon.
3. In the list box on the left, select Form.
4. Click the Add button to add the selected command to your Quick Access toolbar.
5. Click OK to close the Excel Options dialog box.

After performing these steps, a new icon will appear on your Quick Access toolbar.

To use a data form, you must arrange your data so that Excel can recognize it as a table. Start by entering headings for the columns in the first row of your data entry range. Select any cell in the table, and click the Form button on your Quick Access toolbar. Excel then displays a dialog box customized to your data. You can use the Tab key to move between text boxes and supply information. If a cell contains a formula, the formula result appears as text (not as an edit box). In other words, you can't modify formulas from the data entry form.

When you complete the data form, click the New button. Excel enters the data into a row in the worksheet and clears the dialog box for the next row of data.

Displaying a data form by using VBA

Use the ShowDataForm method to display Excel's data form. The only requirement is that the data table must begin in cell A1. Alternatively, the data range can have a range name of Database.

The following code displays the data form:

```
Sub DisplayDataForm()
    ActiveSheet.ShowDataForm
End Sub
```

This macro will work even if the Form command has not been added to the Ribbon or the Quick Access toolbar.

ON THE WEB

A workbook with this example is available on the book's website in the Data Form Example.xlsm file.

Introducing UserForms

How Excel Handles Custom Dialog Boxes

Excel makes creating custom dialog boxes for your applications relatively easy. In fact, you can duplicate the look and feel of many of Excel's dialog boxes. You use a UserForm to create a custom dialog box, and you access UserForms in the Visual Basic Editor (VBE).

This is the typical sequence you'll follow when you create a UserForm:

1. Insert a new UserForm into your workbook's VBA project.

2. Add controls to the UserForm.

3. Adjust some of the properties of the controls that you added.

4. Write event-handler procedures for some of the controls.

   An event-handler procedure is a one tied to a particular event, such as a button click. When the user clicks the button, the procedure runs. You create these procedures in the UserForm's code module.

5. Write a procedure that will display the UserForm.

   This procedure will be located in a standard VBA module (not in the code module for the UserForm).

6. Add a way to make it easy for the user to execute the procedure that you created in step 5.

   You can add a button to a worksheet, create a shortcut menu command, and so on.

Inserting a New UserForm

To insert a new UserForm, activate the VBE (press Alt+F11), select your workbook's project from the Project Explorer, and then choose Insert ⟹ UserForm. The VBE gives each new UserForm a default name, such as UserForm1, UserForm2, and so on.

FIGURE 13.1

The Properties window for an empty UserForm

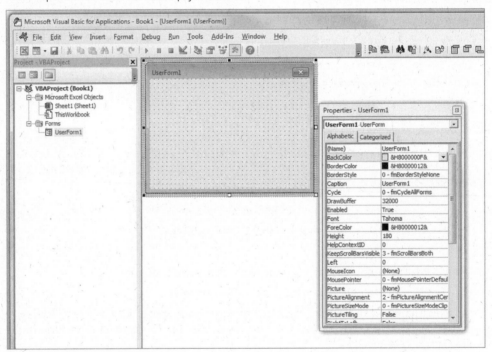

A workbook can have any number of UserForms, and each UserForm holds a single custom dialog box.

Adding Controls to a UserForm

To add controls to a UserForm, use the Toolbox, as shown in Figure 13.2. (VBE doesn't have menu commands that add controls.) If the Toolbox isn't displayed, choose View ➪ Toolbox. The Toolbox is a floating window, so you can move it to a convenient location.

FIGURE 13.2

Use the Toolbox to add controls to a UserForm.

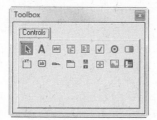

Click the Toolbox button that corresponds to the control that you want to add and then click inside the dialog box to create the control (using its default size). Or, you can click the control and then drag in the dialog box to specify the dimensions for the control.

When you add a new control, it's assigned a name that combines the control type with the numeric sequence for that type of control. For example, if you add a CommandButton control to an empty UserForm, it's named CommandButton1. If you then add a second CommandButton control, it's named CommandButton2.

> **TIP**
>
> Renaming all the controls that you'll be manipulating with your VBA code is a good idea. Doing so lets you refer to meaningful names (such as lbxProducts) rather than generic names (such as ListBox1). To change the name of a control, use the Properties window in VBE. Just select the object and change the (Name) property.

Toolbox Controls

In the sections that follow, we briefly describe the controls available to you in the Toolbox.

> **ON THE WEB**
>
> Figure 13.3 shows a UserForm that contains one of each control. This workbook, named All Userform Controls.xlsm, is available on the book's website.

13

FIGURE 13.3

This UserForm displays all of the controls.

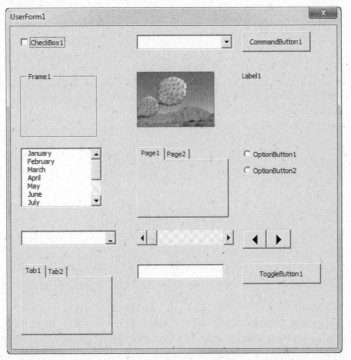

> **TIP**
>
> Your UserForms can also use other ActiveX controls that aren't included with Excel. See "Customizing the Toolbox" later in this chapter.

CheckBox

A `CheckBox` control is useful for getting a binary choice: yes or no, true or false, on or off, and so on. When a check box is checked, it has a value of `True`; when it's not checked, the check box value is `False`.

`CheckBox` controls have a `TripleState` property that when set to `True` causes the check box to have one of three values: `True`, `False`, or `Null`. This is useful when you don't want to influence a user's choice by having the check box initially set to either `True` or `False`.

ComboBox

A `ComboBox` control presents a list of items in a drop-down box and displays only one item at a time. Unlike a `ListBox` control, you can set up a combo box to allow the user to enter a value that doesn't appear in the list of items.

CommandButton

Every dialog box that you create will probably have at least one `CommandButton` control. Usually, your UserForms will have one button labeled OK and another labeled Cancel.

Frame

A `Frame` control is used to enclose other controls. You enclose controls either for aesthetic purposes or to group a set of controls logically. A `Frame` control is particularly useful when the dialog box contains more than one set of `OptionButton` controls.

Image

You can use an `Image` control to display a graphic image, which can come from a file or can be pasted from the Clipboard. You may want to use an `Image` control to display your company's logo in a dialog box. The graphics image is stored in the workbook. That way, if you distribute your workbook to someone else, you don't have to include a copy of the graphics file.

> **CAUTION**
>
> Some graphics files are very large, and using such images can make your workbook increase dramatically in size. For best results, use graphics sparingly or use small graphics files.

Label

A `Label` control simply displays text in your dialog box.

ListBox

The `ListBox` control presents a list of items, and the user can select an item (or multiple items). `ListBox` controls are very flexible. For example, you can specify a worksheet range that holds the list box items, and this range can consist of multiple columns. Or, you can fill the list box with items by using VBA.

MultiPage

A `MultiPage` control lets you create tabbed dialog boxes. Excel's built-in Format Cells dialog box uses a `MultiPage` control. By default, a `MultiPage` control has two pages, but you can add any number of additional pages.

13

OptionButton

OptionButton controls are useful when the user needs to select one item from a small number of choices. Option buttons are always used in groups of at least two. When one option button is selected, the other option buttons in its group are deselected.

If your UserForm contains more than one set of option buttons, the option buttons in each set must share a unique GroupName property value. Otherwise, all option buttons become part of the same set. Alternatively, you can enclose the option buttons in a Frame control, which automatically groups the option buttons contained in the frame.

RefEdit

The RefEdit control is used when you need to let the user select a range in a worksheet. This control accepts a typed range address or a range address generated by pointing to the range in a worksheet.

ScrollBar

The ScrollBar control is similar to a SpinButton control. The difference is that the user can drag the scroll bar button to change the control's value in larger increments. The ScrollBar control is most useful for selecting a value that extends across a wide range of possible values.

SpinButton

The SpinButton control lets the user select a value by clicking either of two arrows: one to increase the value and the other to decrease the value. A spin button is often used with a text box or label, which displays the current value of the spin button. A spin button can be oriented horizontally or vertically.

TabStrip

A TabStrip control is similar to a MultiPage control, but it's not as easy to use. A TabStrip control, unlike a MultiPage control, doesn't serve as a container for other objects. Generally, if the layout of your form is the same for each page and only the data changes, a tab strip is appropriate. If your layout changes for each page, use a multi page.

TextBox

A TextBox control lets the user type text or a value.

ToggleButton

A ToggleButton control has two states: on and off. Clicking the button toggles between these two states, and the button changes its appearance. Its value is either True (pressed) or `False` (not pressed). Like check boxes, toggle buttons have a `TripleState` property that allows a `Null` value.

Using controls on a worksheet

You can embed many of the UserForm controls directly into a worksheet. You can access these controls by using Excel's Developer ⇨ Controls ⇨ Insert command. Adding such controls to a worksheet requires much less effort than creating a UserForm. In addition, you may not have to create any macros because you can link a control to a worksheet cell. For example, if you insert a `CheckBox` control on a worksheet, you can link it to a particular cell by setting its `LinkedCell` property. When the check box is checked, the linked cell displays `TRUE`. When the check box is unchecked, the linked cell displays `FALSE`.

The accompanying figure shows a worksheet that contains some ActiveX controls. This workbook, named `ActiveX Worksheet Controls.xlsx`, is available on this book's website. The workbook uses linked cells and contains no macros.

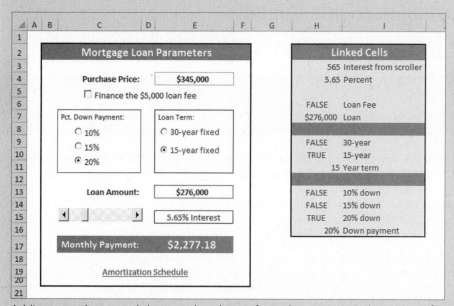

Adding controls to a worksheet can be a bit confusing because controls can come from two sources.

Form controls These controls are insertable objects.

ActiveX controls These controls are a subset of those that are available for use on UserForms.

You can use the controls from either of these sources, but it's important that you understand the distinctions between them. The Form controls work much differently than the ActiveX controls.

Continues

continued

When you add an ActiveX control to a worksheet, Excel goes into *design mode*. In this mode, you can adjust the properties of any controls on your worksheet, add or edit event-handler procedures for the control, or change its size or position. To display the Properties window for an ActiveX control, use the Developer ➪ Controls ➪ Properties command.

You can attach any macro to a Form control button. If you use an ActiveX `CommandButton`, clicking it will execute its event-handler procedure (for example, `CommandButton1_Click`) in the code module for the sheet it's on—you can't attach just any macro to it.

When Excel is in design mode, you can't try the controls. To test the controls, you must exit design mode by clicking the Developer ➪ Controls ➪ Design mode button (which is a toggle).

Adjusting UserForm Controls

After you place a control in a UserForm, you can move and resize the control by using standard mouse techniques.

TIP

You can select multiple controls by holding down the Ctrl key while selecting individual controls, Shift-clicking to select all controls between the first control and last control, or by clicking and dragging to lasso a group of controls.

A UserForm can contain vertical and horizontal gridlines (displayed as dots) that help you align the controls that you add. When you add or move a control, it *snaps* to the grid to help you line up the controls. If you don't like to see these gridlines, you can turn them off by choosing Tools ➪ Options in VBE. In the Options dialog box, select the General tab and set your desired options in the Form Grid Settings section. These gridlines are for design only and do not appear when the dialog box is displayed to the user.

The Format menu in the VBE window provides several commands to help you precisely align and space the controls in a dialog box. The Align and Make Same Size menus also appear on the context menu when you right-click a control. Before you use these commands, select the controls with which you want to work. These commands work just as you'd expect, so we don't explain them here. Figure 13.4 shows a dialog box with several `OptionButton` controls about to be aligned. Figure 13.5 shows the controls after they are aligned and assigned equal vertical spacing.

FIGURE 13.4

Use the Format ⇨ Align command to change the alignment of controls.

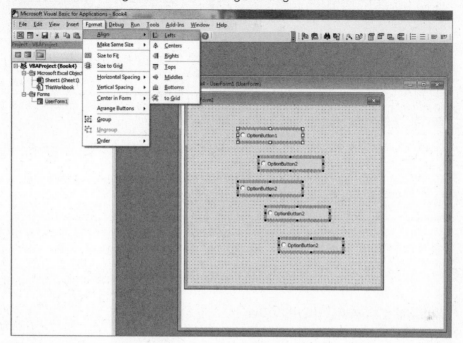

FIGURE 13.5

The OptionButton controls, aligned and evenly spaced

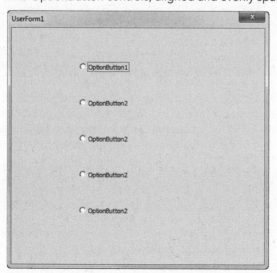

Adjusting a Control's Properties

Every control has a number of properties that determine how the control looks and behaves. You can change a control's properties as follows:

- At design time, when you're developing the UserForm. You use the Properties window to make design time changes.
- During run-time, when the UserForm is being displayed for the user. You use VBA instructions to change a control's properties at run-time.

Whether you set a property at design time or run-time is highly dependent on what your application is trying to do. Generally, though, set properties at design time when you can and at run-time when you have to. While having values set at design time is faster, most speed gains won't be noticeable. The best reason to set properties at design time is because the less code you have, the fewer bugs you can have.

Using the Properties window

In the VBE, the Properties window adjusts to display the properties of the selected item (which can be a control or the UserForm itself). In addition, you can select a control from the drop-down list at the top of the Properties window. Figure 13.6 shows the Properties window for an OptionButton control.

To change a property, just click it and enter the desired value. For some properties a downward-pointing arrow appears when that property is selected, allowing you to select a value from a list. For example, the TextAlign property can have any of the following values: 1 - fmTextAlignLeft, 2 - fmTextAlignCenter, or 3 - fmTextAlignRight.

A few properties (for example, Font and Picture) display a small button with an ellipsis when selected. Click the button to display a dialog box associated with the property.

FIGURE 13.6

The Properties window for an OptionButton control

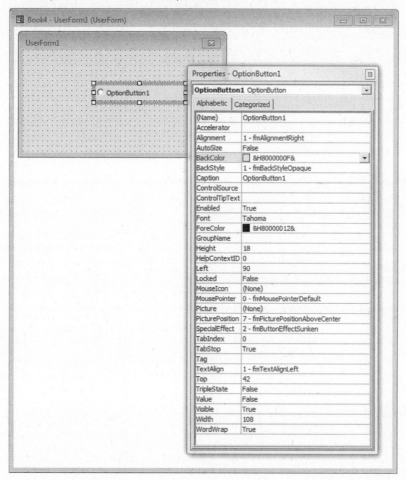

The Image control's Picture property is worth mentioning because you can either select a graphic file that contains the image or paste an image from the Clipboard. When pasting an image, first copy it to the Clipboard and then select the Picture property for the Image control and press Ctrl+V to paste the Clipboard contents.

NOTE

If you select two or more controls at once, the Properties window displays only the properties that are common to the selected controls.

> **TIP**
> The UserForm itself has many properties that you can adjust. Some of these properties are then used as defaults for controls that you add to the UserForm. For example, if you change the UserForm `Font` property, all controls you subsequently add to the UserForm will use that font. Note, however, that controls already on the UserForm aren't affected.

Common properties

Although each control has its own unique set of properties, many controls have some common properties. For example, every control has a `(Name)` property and properties that determine its size and position (`Height`, `Width`, `Left`, and `Right`).

> You will see the `Me` keyword used in code samples in this chapter and others. In a class module, such as a UserForm, the `Me` keyword is a shortcut reference to the instance of the class. That is, `Me` refers to the UserForm that contains it.
>
> Instead of typing `Userform1.CheckBox1.Value`, you can type **`Me.CheckBox1.Value`**. Of course, you don't have to specify the UserForm at all inside of its own code module, so you could also simply type **`CheckBox1.Value`**. The main advantage of using `Me` is that it brings up IntelliSense, allowing you easier access to all of the form's properties and controls.

If you're going to manipulate a control by using VBA, you'll want to provide a meaningful name for the control. For example, the first `OptionButton` control that you add to a UserForm has a default name of `OptionButton1`. You refer to this object in your code with a statement such as the following:

```
Me.OptionButton1.Value = True
```

But if you give the `OptionButton` control a more meaningful name (such as `optLandscape`), you can use a statement such as this one:

```
Me.optLandscape.Value = True
```

> **TIP**
> Many people find it helpful to use a name that also identifies the type of object. The preceding example uses `opt` as the prefix to identify the control as an `OptionButton` control. See the "Using a Naming Convention" sidebar later in this chapter for more information.

You can adjust the properties of several controls at once. For example, you might have several `OptionButton` controls that you want left-aligned. You can simply select all of them and then change the `Left` property in the Properties box. All of the selected controls will then take on that new `Left` property value.

The best way to learn about the various properties for a control is to use the Help system. Simply click a property in the Properties window and press F1.

Using a naming convention

Many developers use a naming convention when assigning names to controls on a UserForm. It's not necessary, but it makes referring to the controls easier when you write code and identifying controls easier when you set the tab order (explained later in the chapter). If you share a code base or if someone else is tasked with maintaining your code, a naming convention can help the other person navigate your code more easily.

The most common naming conventions use a prefix that indicates the control's type followed by a descriptive name. There are no standard prefixes, so pick what works for you and use it consistently. The following example naming convention uses a three-letter prefix and a descriptive name:

Control	Prefix	Example
CheckBox	chk	chkActive
ComboBox	cbx	cbxLocations
CommandButton	cmd	cmdCancel
Frame	frm	frmType
Image	img	imgLogo
Label	lbl	lblLocations
ListBox	lbx	lbxMonths
MultiPage	mpg	mpgPages
OptionButton	opt	optOrientation
RefEdit	ref	refRange
ScrollBar	scr	scrLevel
SpinButton	spb	spbAmount
TabStrip	tab	tabTabs
TextBox	tbx	tbxName
ToggleButton	tgb	tgbActive

One advantage to using a naming convention is to get a list of controls with the Auto List Members feature. You can use the Me keyword in a UserForm's code module to refer to the UserForm. When you type **Me** followed by a dot, the VBE lists all the properties of the UserForm and all of its controls. You can begin typing a control's name to limit the list based on what you type.

The following figure shows the Auto List Members window when you type **me.tbx**. You can see in the figure that five text boxes are listed next to each other (because they have the same prefix) and their descriptive names makes it easy for you to know which control to select.

Continues

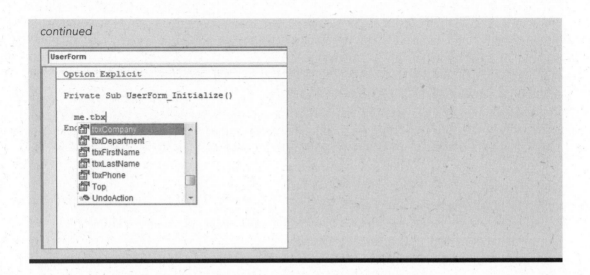

Accommodating keyboard users

Many users prefer to navigate through a dialog box by using the keyboard: the Tab and Shift+Tab keystrokes cycle through the controls, and pressing a *hot key* (an underlined letter) operates the control. To make sure that your dialog box works properly for keyboard users, you must consider two issues: tab order and accelerator keys.

Changing the tab order of controls

The *tab order* determines the sequence in which the controls are activated when the user presses Tab or Shift+Tab. It also determines which control has the initial *focus*. If a user is entering text in a TextBox control, for example, the TextBox has the focus. If the user clicks an OptionButton control, the OptionButton has the focus. The control that's first in the tab order has the focus when a dialog box is first displayed.

To set the tab order of your controls, choose View ➪ Tab Order or right-click the UserForm and choose Tab Order from the shortcut menu. In either case, Excel displays the Tab Order dialog box, which lists all of the controls in the same order in which controls pass the focus between each other in the UserForm. To move a control, select it and click the Move Up or Move Down button. You can choose more than one control (by Shift- or Ctrl-clicking) and move them all at once.

Alternatively, you can set an individual control's position in the tab order by using the Properties window. The first control in the tab order has a TabIndex property of 0. Changing the TabIndex property for a control may also affect the TabIndex property of other controls. These adjustments are made automatically to ensure that no control has a

TabIndex value greater than the number of controls. If you want to remove a control from the tab order, set its TabStop property to False.

> **NOTE**
>
> Some controls, such as Frame and MultiPage, act as containers for other controls. The controls inside a container have their own tab order. To set the tab order for a group of OptionButton controls inside a Frame control, select the Frame control before you choose the View ↕ Tab Order command. Figure 13.7 shows the Tab Order dialog box when a Frame is selected.

FIGURE 13.7

Use the Tab Order dialog box to specify the tab order of the controls in a Frame control.

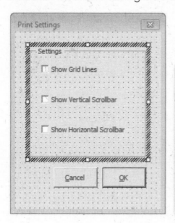
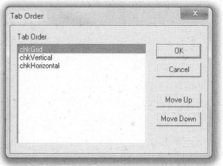

Setting hot keys

You can assign an accelerator key, or hot key, to most dialog box controls. An accelerator key allows the user to access the control by pressing Alt and the hot key. Use the Accelerator property in the Properties window for this purpose.

> **TIP**
>
> Some controls, such as a TextBox, don't have an Accelerator property because they don't display a caption. You still can allow direct keyboard access to these controls by using a Label control. Assign an accelerator key to the label, and put it before the text box in the tab order.

Testing a UserForm

You'll usually want to test your UserForm while you're developing it. You can test a UserForm in three ways, without actually calling it from a VBA procedure.

- Choose the Run ➪ Run Sub/UserForm command.
- Press F5.
- Click the Run Sub/UserForm button on the Standard toolbar.

These three techniques all trigger the UserForm's Initialize event. When a dialog box is displayed in this test mode, you can try the tab order and the accelerator keys.

Displaying a UserForm

To display a UserForm from VBA, you create a procedure that uses the Userform.Show method. If your UserForm is named UContacts, the following procedure displays the dialog box on that form:

```
Sub AddEditContacts()
    UContacts.Show
End Sub
```

This procedure must be in a standard VBA module and not in the code module for the UserForm.

When the UserForm is displayed, it remains visible on-screen until it's dismissed. Usually, you'll add a CommandButton control to the UserForm that executes a procedure that dismisses the UserForm. The procedure can either unload the UserForm (with the Unload command) or hide the UserForm (with the UserForm.Hide method). This concept will become clearer as you work through various examples in this and subsequent chapters. The following examples demonstrate two ways to dismiss a UserForm:

```
Private Sub cmdOK_Click()
    Unload Me
    'The form is removed from memory
End Sub

Private Sub cmdOK_Click()
    Me.Hide
    'The calling procedure can still access the form's properties
End Sub
```

Adjusting the display position

The StartUpPosition property of the UserForm object determines where on the screen the dialog box will be displayed. You can specify this property in the Properties box or at run-time. The default value is 1 – CenterOwner, which displays the dialog box in the center of the Excel window.

If you use a dual-monitor system, however, you'll find that sometimes the StartUpPosition property seems to be ignored. Specifically, if the Excel window is on the secondary monitor, the UserForm may appear on the left edge of the primary window.

The following code ensures that the UserForm is always displayed in the center of the Excel window:

```
With UserForm1
  .StartUpPosition = 0
  .Left = Application.Left + (0.5 * Application.Width) - (0.5 *
.Width)
  .Top = Application.Top + (0.5 * Application.Height) - (0.5 *
.Height)
  .Show
End With
```

Displaying a modeless UserForm

By default, UserForms are displayed modally. This means the UserForm must be dismissed before the user can do anything in the worksheet. You can also display a modeless UserForm. When a modeless UserForm is displayed, the user can continue working in Excel, and the UserForm remains visible. To display a modeless UserForm, use the following syntax:

```
UserForm1.Show vbModeless
```

There are several examples in the following chapters demonstrating modal and modeless UserForms.

> **NOTE**
>
> The single-document interface introduced in Excel 2013 affects modeless UserForms. In versions prior to 2013, a modeless UserForm is visible regardless of which workbook window is active. In Excel 2013 and later, a modeless UserForm is associated with the workbook window that's active when the UserForm appears. If you switch to a different workbook window, the UserForm may not be visible. Chapter 15, "Implementing Advanced UserForm Techniques," has an example that demonstrates how to make a modeless UserForm visible in all workbook windows.

Displaying a UserForm based on a variable

In some cases, you may have several UserForms, and your code makes a decision regarding which of them to display. If the name of the UserForm is stored as a string variable, you can use the Add method to add the UserForm to the UserForms collection and then use the Show method of the UserForms collection. Here's an example that assigns the name of a UserForm to the MyForm variable and then displays the UserForm:

```
MyForm = "UserForm1"
UserForms.Add(MyForm).Show
```

13

Loading a UserForm

VBA also has a `Load` statement. Loading a UserForm loads it into memory and triggers the UserForm's `Initialize` event. However, the dialog box is not visible until you use the `Show` method. To load a UserForm, use a statement like this:

```
Load UserForm1
```

If you have a complex UserForm that takes a bit of time to initialize, you might want to load it into memory before it's needed so that it will appear more quickly when you use the `Show` method. In the majority of situations, however, you don't need to use the `Load` statement. Like the `Show` method, the `Load` statement should be used in a standard module, not in the code module of the UserForm you're trying to load.

About event-handler procedures

After the UserForm is displayed, the user interacts with it—selecting an item from a list box, clicking a command button, and so on. In official terminology, the user *triggers an event*. For example, clicking a command button triggers the `Click` event for the `CommandButton` control. You need to write procedures that execute when these events occur. These procedures are sometimes known as *event-handler procedures*.

> **NOTE**
>
> Event-handler procedures must be located in the code module for the UserForm. However, your event-handler procedure can call another procedure that's located in a standard VBA module.

Your VBA code can change the properties of the controls while the UserForm is displayed (that is, at run-time). For example, you could assign to a `ListBox` control a procedure that changes the text in a label when an item is selected. This type of manipulation is the key to making dialog boxes interactive and will become clearer later in this chapter.

Closing a UserForm

To close a UserForm, use the `Unload` command, as shown in this example:

```
Unload UserForm1
```

Or, if the code is located in the code module for the UserForm, you can use the following:

```
Unload Me
```

In this case, the keyword `Me` refers to the UserForm. Using `Me` rather than the UserForm's name eliminates the need to modify your code if you change the name of the UserForm.

Normally, your VBA code should include the `Unload` command after the UserForm has performed its actions. For example, your UserForm may have a `CommandButton` control that functions as an OK button. Clicking this button executes a procedure, and one of the statements in the procedure will unload the UserForm. The UserForm remains visible on the screen until the procedure that contains the Unload statement finishes.

When a UserForm is unloaded, its controls are reset to their original values. In other words, your code won't be able to access the user's choices after the UserForm is unloaded. If the user's choice must be used later (after the UserForm is unloaded), you need to store the value in a Public variable, declared in a standard VBA module. Or, you could store the value in a worksheet cell or even in the Windows registry.

> **NOTE**
>
> A UserForm is automatically unloaded when the user clicks the Close button (the X in the UserForm title bar). This action also triggers a UserForm QueryClose event, followed by a UserForm Terminate event.

UserForms also have a Hide method. When you invoke this method, the UserForm disappears, but it remains loaded in memory so that your code can still access the various properties of the controls. Here's an example of a statement that hides a UserForm:

```
UserForm1.Hide
```

Or, if the code is in the code module for the UserForm, you can use the following:

```
Me.Hide
```

If you'd like your UserForm to disappear immediately while its macro is executing, use the Hide method at the top of the procedure. For example, in the following procedure, the UserForm disappears immediately when CommandButton1 is clicked. The last statement in the procedure unloads the UserForm.

```
Private Sub CommandButton1_Click()
  Me.Hide
  Application.ScreenUpdating = True
  For r = 1 To 10000
    ActiveSheet.Cells(r, 1) = r
  Next r
  Unload Me
End Sub
```

In this example, ScreenUpdating is set to True to force Excel to hide the UserForm completely. Without that statement, the UserForm may actually remain visible.

In Chapter 15, we describe how to display a progress indicator, which takes advantage of the fact that a UserForm remains visible while the macro executes.

13

Creating a UserForm: An Example

If you've never created a UserForm, you might want to walk through the example in this section. The example includes step-by-step instructions for creating a simple dialog box and the VBA procedures necessary for it to function.

This example uses a UserForm to obtain two pieces of information: a person's name and gender. The dialog box uses a text box to get the name and three option buttons to get the gender (Male, Female, or Unknown). The information collected in the dialog box is then sent to the next blank row in a worksheet.

Creating the UserForm

Figure 13.8 shows the completed UserForm for this example.

FIGURE 13.8

This dialog box asks the user to enter a name and a gender.

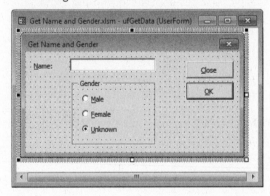

For best results, start with a new workbook with only one worksheet in it. Then follow these steps:

1. Press Alt+F11 to activate VBE.
2. In the Project Explorer, select the workbook's project and choose Insert ➪ UserForm to add an empty UserForm.

   The UserForm's (Name) and Caption properties will have their default value: UserForm1.
3. Use the Properties window to change the UserForm's (Name) property to ufGetData and its Caption property to Get Name and Gender.

   (If the Properties window isn't visible, press F4.)
4. Add a Label control, and adjust the properties as follows:

Property	Value
Name	lblName
Accelerator	N
Caption	Name:
TabIndex	0

5. Add a TextBox control, and adjust the properties as follows:

Property	Value
Name	tbxName
TabIndex	1

6. Add a Frame control, and adjust the properties as follows:

Property	Value
Name	frmGender
Caption	Gender
TabIndex	2

7. Add an OptionButton control inside the frame, and adjust the properties as follows:

Property	Value
Accelerator	M
Caption	Male
Name	optMale
TabIndex	0

8. Add another OptionButton control inside the frame, and adjust the properties as follows:

Property	Value
Accelerator	F
Caption	Female
Name	optFemale
TabIndex	1

13

9. Add yet another `OptionButton` control inside the frame, and adjust the properties as follows:

Property	Value
Accelerator	U
Caption	Unknown
Name	optUnknown
TabIndex	2
Value	True

10. Add a `CommandButton` control outside the frame, and adjust the properties as follows:

Property	Value
Accelerator	O
Caption	OK
Default	True
Name	cmdOK
TabIndex	3

11. Add another `CommandButton` control, and adjust the properties as follows:

Property	Value
Accelerator	C
Caption	Close
Cancel	True
Name	cmdClose
TabIndex	4

> **TIP**
>
> When you're creating several controls that are similar, you may find it easier to copy an existing control rather than create a new one. To copy a control, press Ctrl while you drag the control to make a new copy of it. Then adjust the properties for the copied control.

Writing code to display the dialog box

Next, you add an ActiveX CommandButton control to the worksheet. This button will execute a procedure that displays the UserForm. Here's how to do this:

1. Activate Excel.

    (Alt+F11 is the shortcut key combination.)

2. Choose Developer ➪ Controls ➪ Insert, and click CommandButton from the ActiveX Controls section (the bottom group of controls).

3. Drag in the worksheet to create the button.

    If you like, you can change the caption for the worksheet button. To do so, right-click the button and choose CommandButton Object ➪ Edit from the shortcut menu. You can then edit the text that appears on the button. To change other properties of the object, right-click and choose Properties. Then make the changes in the Properties box.

4. Double-click the CommandButton control.

    This step activates VBE. More specifically, the code module for the worksheet will be displayed, with an empty event-handler procedure for the Click event of the worksheet's CommandButton control.

5. Enter a single statement in the CommandButton1_Click procedure (see Figure 13.9).

This short procedure uses the Show method of ufGetData to display the UserForm.

FIGURE 13.9

The CommandButton1_Click procedure is executed when the button on the worksheet is clicked.

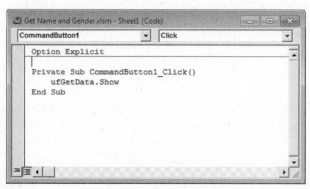

Testing the dialog box

The next step is to reactivate Excel and try the procedure that displays the dialog box.

> **NOTE**
>
> When you click the command button on the worksheet, you'll find that nothing happens. Instead, the button is selected. That's because Excel is still in design mode—which happens automatically when you insert an ActiveX control. To exit design mode, click the Design Mode button in the Developer ⮂ Controls group. To make any changes to your `CommandButton` control, you'll need to put Excel back into design mode.

When you exit design mode, clicking the button will display the UserForm (see Figure 13.10).

FIGURE 13.10

The CommandButton's Click event procedure displays the UserForm.

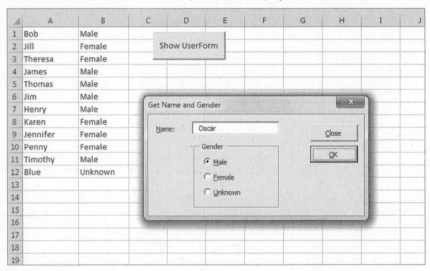

When the dialog box is displayed, enter some text in the text box and click OK. Nothing happens, which is understandable because you haven't yet created an event-handler procedure for the OK button.

> **NOTE**
>
> Click the X (Close) button in the UserForm title bar to dismiss the dialog box.

Adding event-handler procedures

In this section, we explain how to write the procedures that will handle the events that occur while the UserForm is displayed. To continue the example, do the following:

1. Press Alt+F11 to activate VBE.

2. Make sure that the UserForm is displayed, and double-click the `CommandButton` control captioned Close.

   This step activates the code window for the UserForm and inserts an empty procedure named `cmdClose_Click`. Note that this procedure consists of the object's name, an underscore character, and the event that it handles.

3. Modify the procedure as follows. (This is the event handler for the `Click` event of the `cmdClose CommandButton` control.)

```
Private Sub cmdClose_Click()
  Unload Me
End Sub
```

   This procedure, which is executed when the user clicks the Close button, simply unloads the UserForm.

4. Press Shift+F7 to redisplay UserForm1 (or click the View Object icon at the top of the Project Explorer window).

5. Double-click the OK button, and enter the following procedure. (This is the event handler for the `cmdOK` button's `Click` event.)

```
Private Sub cmdOK_Click()
    Dim lNextRow As Long
    Dim wf As WorksheetFunction

    Set wf = Application.WorksheetFunction

'   Make sure a name is entered
    If Len(Me.tbxName.Text) = 0 Then
        MsgBox "You must enter a name."
        Me.tbxName.SetFocus
    Else
'   Determine the next empty row
        lNextRow = wf.CountA(Sheet1.Range("A:A")) + 1
'   Transfer the name
        Sheet1.Cells(lNextRow, 1) = Me.tbxName.Text

'   Transfer the gender
        With Sheet1.Cells(lNextRow, 2)
            If Me.optMale.Value Then .Value = "Male"
            If Me.optFemale.Value Then .Value = "Female"
            If Me.optUnknown.Value Then .Value = "Unknown"
        End With
```

```
'    Clear the controls for the next entry
     Me.tbxName.Text = vbNullString
     Me.optUnknown.Value = True
     Me.tbxName.SetFocus
  End If
End Sub
```

6. Activate Excel and click the button again to display the UserForm and then run the procedure again.

    You'll find that the UserForm controls now function correctly. You can use them to add new names to the two-column list in the worksheet.

Here's how the `cmdOK_Click` procedure works: First, the procedure makes sure that something was entered in the text box. If nothing is entered (the length of the text is 0), it displays a message and sets the focus back to the text box. If something was entered, it uses the Excel COUNTA function to determine the next blank cell in column A. Next, it transfers the text from the text box to column A. It then uses a series of `If` statements to determine which option button was selected and writes the appropriate text (Male, Female, or Unknown) to column B. Finally, the dialog box is reset to make it ready for the next entry. Note that clicking OK doesn't close the dialog box. To end data entry (and unload the UserForm), click the Close button.

The finished dialog box

After you've entered the two event-handler procedures, you'll find that the dialog box works flawlessly. (Don't forget to test the hot keys.) In real life, you'd probably need to collect more information than just the name and gender. The same basic principles apply; you would just need to deal with more UserForm controls.

ON THE WEB

A workbook with this example is available on this book's website in the `Get Name and Gender.xlsm` file.

Each `UserForm` control (as well as the UserForm itself) is designed to respond to certain types of events, and a user or Excel can trigger these events. For example, clicking a button generates a `Click` event for the control. You can write code that is executed when a particular event occurs.

Some actions generate multiple events. For example, clicking the up arrow of a `SpinButton` control generates a `SpinUp` event and also a `Change` event. When a UserForm is displayed by using the `Show` method, Excel generates an `Initialize` event and an `Activate` event for the UserForm. (Actually, the `Initialize` event occurs when the UserForm is loaded into memory and before it's actually displayed.)

 Excel also supports events associated with a `Sheet` object, `Chart` objects, and the `ThisWorkbook` object. We discuss these types of events in Chapter 6, "Understanding Excel's Events."

Learning about events

To find out which events are supported by a particular control, do the following:

1. Add a control to a UserForm.

2. Double-click the control to activate the code module for the UserForm.

   VBE inserts an empty event-handler procedure for the default event for the control.

3. Click the drop-down list in the upper-right corner of the module window.

   You see a complete list of events for the control. Figure 13.11 shows the list of events for a CheckBox control.

FIGURE 13.11

The event list for a CheckBox control

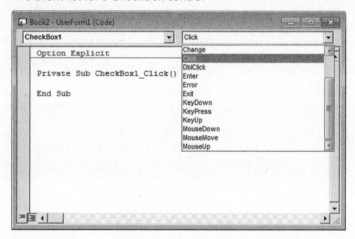

4. Select an event from the list.

   VBE creates an empty event-handler procedure for you.

To find out specific details about an event, consult the Help system. The Help system also lists the events available for each control.

> **CAUTION**
>
> Event-handler procedures incorporate the name of the object in the procedure's name. If you change the name of a control, you'll also need to make the appropriate changes to the control's event-handler procedure(s), because the name changes aren't performed automatically. To make things easy on yourself, it's a good idea to provide names for your controls before you begin creating event-handler procedures.

A UserForm has quite a few events. Here are the events associated with showing and unloading a UserForm:

`Initialize`   Occurs when a UserForm is loaded but before it's shown. It doesn't occur if the UserForm was previously hidden.

`Activate`   Occurs when a UserForm is shown.

`Deactivate`   Occurs when a UserForm is deactivated but doesn't occur if the form is hidden.

`QueryClose`   Occurs before a UserForm is unloaded.

`Terminate`   Occurs after the UserForm is unloaded.

> **NOTE**
>
> Sometimes, it's important that you choose the appropriate event for your event-handler procedure and that you understand the order in which the events occur. Using the `Show` method invokes the `Initialize` and `Activate` events (in that order). Using the `Load` command invokes only the `Initialize` event. Using the `Unload` command triggers the `QueryClose` and `Terminate` events (in that order), but using the `Hide` method doesn't trigger either event.

> **ON THE WEB**
>
> The book's website contains the `Userform Events.xlsm` workbook, which monitors all of these events and displays a message box when an event occurs. If you're confused about UserForm events, studying the code in this workbook should clear things up.

SpinButton events

To help clarify the concept of events, this section takes a close look at the events associated with a `SpinButton` control. Some of these events are associated with other controls, and some are unique to the `SpinButton` control.

> **ON THE WEB**
>
> The book's website contains a workbook that demonstrates the sequence of events that occur for a `SpinButton` control and the UserForm that contains it. The workbook, named `Spinbutton Events.xlsm`, contains a series of event-handler routines—one for each `SpinButton` and `UserForm` event. Each routine simply displays a message box that tells you which event just fired.

Table 13.1 lists all the events for the `SpinButton` control.

TABLE 13.1 **SpinButton Events**

Event	Description
AfterUpdate	Occurs after the control is changed through the user interface
BeforeDragOver	Occurs when a drag-and-drop operation is in progress
BeforeDropOrPaste	Occurs when the user is about to drop or paste data onto the control
BeforeUpdate	Occurs before the control is changed
Change	Occurs when the Value property changes
Enter	Occurs before the control receives the focus from a control on the same UserForm
Error	Occurs when the control detects an error and can't return the error information to a calling program
Exit	Occurs immediately before a control loses the focus to another control on the same form
KeyDown	Occurs when the user presses a key and the object has the focus
KeyPress	Occurs when the user presses any key that produces a typeable character
KeyUp	Occurs when the user releases a key and the object has the focus
SpinDown	Occurs when the user clicks the lower (or left) SpinButton arrow
SpinUp	Occurs when the user clicks the upper (or right) SpinButton arrow

A user can operate a spin button by clicking it with the mouse or (if the control has the focus) by using the arrow keys.

Mouse-initiated events

When the user clicks the upper spin button arrow, the following events occur in this order:

1. Enter (triggered only if the spin button did not already have the focus)
2. Change
3. SpinUp

Keyboard-initiated events

The user can also press Tab to set the focus to the spin button and then use the arrow keys to increment or decrement the control. If so, the following events occur (in this order):

1. Enter (occurs when the spin button gets the focus)
2. KeyUp (from releasing the Tab key)

13

3. `KeyDown`

4. `Change`

5. `SpinUp` (or `SpinDown`)

6. `KeyUp`

What about code-initiated events?

The `SpinButton` control can also be changed by VBA code, which also triggers the appropriate event(s). For example, the following statement sets the `spbDemo.Value` property to `0` and also triggers the `Change` event for the `SpinButton` control, but only if its value was not already 0:

```
Me.spbDemo.Value = 0
```

You might think that you could disable events by setting the `EnableEvents` property of the `Application` object to `False`. Unfortunately, this property applies only to events that involve true Excel objects: `Workbooks`, `Worksheets`, and `Charts`.

Pairing a SpinButton with a TextBox

A `SpinButton` control has a `Value` property, but this control doesn't have a caption in which to display its value. In many cases, however, you'll want the user to see the spin button value. And sometimes you'll want the user to be able to change the spin button value directly instead of clicking the spin button repeatedly.

The solution is to pair a spin button with a text box, which enables the user to specify a value either by typing it in the text box directly or by clicking the spin button to increment or decrement the value in the text box.

Figure 13.12 shows a simple example. The `SpinButton` control's `Min` property is `-10`, and its `Max` property is `10`. Clicking the spin button's arrows will change its value to an integer between −10 and 10.

FIGURE 13.12

This SpinButton is paired with a TextBox.

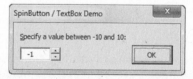

The code required to link a spin button with a text box is relatively simple. It's basically a matter of writing event-handler procedures to ensure that the SpinButton control's Value property is always in sync with the TextBox control's Text property. In the following code, the controls have their default names (SpinButton1 and TextBox1).

The following procedure is executed whenever the SpinButton control's Change event is triggered. That is, the procedure is executed when the user clicks the spin button or changes its value by pressing an arrow key.

```
Private Sub SpinButton1_Change()
    Me.TextBox1.Text = Me.SpinButton1.Value
End Sub
```

The procedure assigns the SpinButton control's Value to the Text property of the TextBox control. If the user enters a value directly in the text box, its Change event is triggered and the following procedure is executed:

```
Private Sub TextBox1_Change()
    Dim NewVal As Long

    If IsNumeric(Me.TextBox1.Text) Then
        NewVal = Val(Me.TextBox1.Text)
        If NewVal >= Me.SpinButton1.Min And _
            NewVal <= Me.SpinButton1.Max Then _
            Me.SpinButton1.Value = NewVal
    End If
End Sub
```

This procedure starts by determining whether the entry in the text box is a number. If so, the procedure continues and the text is assigned to the NewVal variable. The next statement determines whether the value is within the proper range for the spin button. If so, the SpinButton control's Value property is set to the value entered in the text box. If the entry is not numeric or is out of range, nothing happens.

The example is set up so that clicking the OK button (which is named OKButton) transfers the spin button value to the active cell. The event handler for this CommandButton control's Click event is as follows:

```
Private Sub OKButton_Click()
'   Enter the value into the active cell
    If CStr(Me.SpinButton1.Value) = Me.TextBox1.Text Then
        ActiveCell = Me.SpinButton1.Value
        Unload Me
    Else
        MsgBox "Invalid entry.", vbCritical
        Me.TextBox1.SetFocus
        Me.TextBox1.SelStart = 0
        Me.TextBox1.SelLength = Len(Me.TextBox1.Text)
    End If
End Sub
```

13

This procedure does one final check: it makes sure that the text entered in the text box matches the spin button's value. This check is necessary in the case of an invalid entry. For example, if the user enters **3r** in the text box, the spin button's value would not be changed and the result placed in the active cell would not be what the user intended. Note that the SpinButton's Value property is converted to a string by using the CStr function. This conversion ensures that the comparison won't generate an error if a value is compared with text. If the spin button's value doesn't match the text box's contents, a message box is displayed. Notice that the focus is set to the TextBox object, and the contents are selected (by using the SelStart and SelLength properties). This setup makes it easy for the user to correct the entry.

About the Tag property

Every UserForm and control has a Tag property. This property doesn't represent anything specific and, by default, is empty. You can use the Tag property to store information for your own use.

For example, you may have a series of TextBox controls in a UserForm. The user may be required to enter text in some but not all of them. You can use the Tag property to identify (for your own use) which fields are required. In this case, you can set the Tag property to a string such as Required. Then when you write code to validate the user's entries, you can refer to the Tag property.

The following example is a function that examines all TextBox controls on UserForm1 and returns the number of required TextBox controls that are empty: if the function returns a number greater than 0, it means that all required fields were not completed.

```
Function EmptyCount() As Long
  Dim ctl As Control

  EmptyCount= 0
  For Each ctl In UserForm1.Controls
    If TypeName(ctl) = "TextBox" Then
      If ctl.Tag = "Required" Then
        If Len(ctl.Text) = 0 Then
          EmptyCount = EmptyCount + 1
        End If
      End If
    End If
  Next ctl
End Function
```

As you work with UserForms, you'll probably think of other uses for the Tag property.

Referencing UserForm Controls

When working with controls on a UserForm, the event-handler VBA code is usually contained in the code window for the UserForm. In such a case, you do not need to qualify references to the controls because the controls are assumed to belong to the UserForm.

You can also refer to UserForm controls from a general VBA module. To do so, you need to qualify the reference to the control by specifying the UserForm name. For example, consider the following procedure, which is located in a standard module. It simply displays the UserForm named `UserForm1`.

```
Sub GetData()
  UserForm1.Show
End Sub
```

Assume that `UserForm1` contains a text box (named `TextBox1`), and you want to provide a default value for the text box. You could modify the procedure as follows:

```
Sub GetData()
  UserForm1.TextBox1.Value = "John Doe"
  UserForm1.Show
End Sub
```

Another way to set the default value is to take advantage of the UserForm's `Initialize` event. You can write code in the `UserForm_Initialize` procedure, which is located in the code module for the UserForm. Here's an example:

```
Private Sub UserForm_Initialize()
  Me.TextBox1.Value = "John Doe"
End Sub
```

Note that when the control is referenced in the code module for the UserForm, you can use the `Me` keyword instead of the UserForm name. In fact, when you're in the UserForm's code module, you aren't required to use the `Me` keyword. If you omit it, VBA assumes that you're referencing the control on the form you're in. However, qualifying references to controls does have an advantage: it allows you to take advantage of the Auto List Members feature, which lets you choose the control names from a drop-down list.

13

TIP

Rather than use the actual name of the UserForm, it's preferable to use `Me`. Then, if you change the name of the UserForm, you won't need to replace the references in your code.

Understanding the controls collection

The controls on a UserForm make up a collection. For example, the following statement displays the number of controls on UserForm1:

```
MsgBox UserForm1.Controls.Count
```

VBA does *not* maintain a collection of each control type. For example, there is no collection of CommandButton controls. However, you can determine the type of control by using the TypeName function. The following procedure uses a For Each structure to loop through the Controls collection and then displays the number of CommandButton controls on UserForm1:

```
Sub CountButtons()
  Dim cbCount As Long
  Dim ctl as Control

  cbCount = 0
  For Each ctl In UserForm1.Controls
    If TypeName(ctl) = "CommandButton" Then cbCount = cbCount + 1
  Next ctl
  MsgBox cbCount
End Sub
```

Customizing the Toolbox

When a UserForm is active in VBE, the Toolbox displays the controls that you can add to the UserForm. If the Toolbox isn't visible, choose View ➪ Toolbox to display it. This section describes ways to customize the Toolbox.

Adding new pages to the Toolbox

The Toolbox initially contains a single tab named Controls. Right-click this tab and choose New Page to add a new tab to the Toolbox. You can also change the text displayed on the tab by choosing Rename from the shortcut menu.

Customizing or combining controls

A handy feature lets you customize a control and then save it for future use. You can, for example, create a command button that's set up to serve as an OK button. Set the following properties to customize the CommandButton control: Width, Height, Caption, Default, and Name. Then drag the customized button to the Toolbox to create a new control. Right-click the new control to rename it or change its icon.

You can also create a new Toolbox entry that consists of multiple controls. For example, you can create two command buttons that represent a UserForm's OK and Cancel buttons. Customize them as you like and then select them both and drag them to the Toolbox. Then, you can use this new Toolbox control to add two customized buttons in one fell swoop.

This type of customization also works with controls that act as containers. For example, create a `Frame` control and add four customized option buttons, neatly spaced and aligned. Then drag the frame to the Toolbox to create a customized `Frame` control.

To help identify customized controls, right-click the control and choose Customize *xxx* from the shortcut menu (where *xxx* is the control's name). You see a new dialog box that lets you change the tooltip text, edit the icon, or load a new icon image from a file.

> **TIP**
>
> You may want to place your customized controls on a separate page in the Toolbox. Then you can export the entire page so that you can share it with other Excel users. To export a Toolbox page, right-click the tab and choose Export Page.

Figure 13.13 shows a new page with eight customized controls:

- A frame with four option buttons
- A text box and spinner
- Six check boxes
- A "critical" red X icon
- An exclamation point icon
- A question mark icon
- An Information icon
- Two command buttons

The four icons are the same images displayed by the `MsgBox` function.

> **ON THE WEB**
>
> You can find these customized controls on the book's website in the `newcontrols.pag` file. To import the PAG file as a new page in your Toolbox, right-click a tab, choose Import Page, and then locate and choose the file.

Adding other ActiveX controls

UserForms can use other ActiveX controls developed by Microsoft or other vendors. To add an additional ActiveX control to the Toolbox, right-click the Toolbox and choose Additional Controls. You see the dialog box shown in Figure 13.14.

FIGURE 13.13

The Toolbox, with a new page of controls

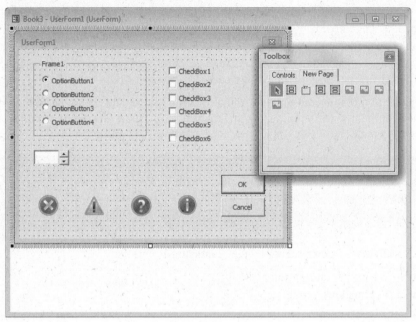

FIGURE 13.14

The Additional Controls dialog box lets you add other ActiveX controls.

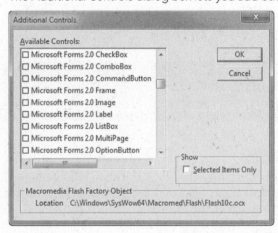

The Additional Controls dialog box lists all ActiveX controls installed on your system. Select the control(s) that you want to add and then click OK to add an icon for each selected control.

> **CAUTION**
>
> Most ActiveX controls installed on your system will probably not work in Excel UserForms. Also, some controls require a license to use them in an application. If you (or the users of your application) aren't licensed to use a particular control, an error will occur.

Creating UserForm Templates

You may find that when you design a new UserForm, you tend to add the same controls each time. For example, every UserForm might have two command buttons that serve as OK and Cancel buttons. In the preceding section, we describe how to create a new control that combines these two (customized) buttons into a single control. Another option is to create your UserForm template and then export it so that you can import it into other projects. An advantage is that the event-handler code for the controls is stored with the template.

Start by creating a UserForm that contains all of the controls and customizations that you'd need to reuse in other projects. Then make sure that the UserForm is selected and choose File ⇨ Export File (or press Ctrl+E). You'll be prompted for a filename.

Then, when you start your next project, choose File ⇨ Import File to load the saved UserForm.

Emulating Excel's dialog boxes

The look and feel of Windows dialog boxes differs from program to program. When developing applications for Excel, it's best to try to mimic Excel's dialog box style whenever possible.

A good way to learn how to create effective dialog boxes is to try to copy one of Excel's dialog boxes down to the smallest detail. For example, make sure that you get all the hot keys defined and be sure that the tab order is the same. To re-create one of Excel's dialog boxes, you need to test it under various circumstances and see how it behaves. Analyzing Excel's dialog boxes will definitely improve your own dialog boxes.

On the other hand, you'll find that it's impossible to duplicate some of Excel's dialog boxes. For example, it's not possible to duplicate the Convert Text to Columns Wizard dialog box, which is displayed when you choose Data ⇨ Data Tools ⇨ Text to Columns. This dialog box uses controls that are not available to VBA users.

A UserForm Checklist

Before you unleash a UserForm on end users, be sure that everything is working correctly. The following checklist should help you identify potential problems:

- Are similar controls the same size?
- Are the controls evenly spaced?
- Is the dialog box overwhelming? If so, you may want to group the controls by using a MultiPage control.
- Can every control be accessed with a hot key?
- Are any hot keys duplicated?
- Is the tab order set correctly?
- Will your VBA code take appropriate action if the user presses Esc or clicks the Close button on the UserForm?
- Is any text misspelled?
- Does the dialog box have an appropriate caption?
- Will the dialog box display properly at all video resolutions?
- Are the controls grouped logically (by function)?
- Do ScrollBar and SpinButton controls allow only valid values?
- Does the UserForm use any controls that might not be installed on every system?
- Are ListBox controls set properly (single, multi, or extended)?

If you have a smaller group of users who can test your form before you send it to a wider group, this can be helpful in finding problems.

Looking at UserForm Examples

IN THIS CHAPTER

Using a UserForm for a simple menu

Selecting ranges from a UserForm

Using a UserForm as a splash screen

Changing the size of a UserForm while it's displayed

Zooming and scrolling a sheet from a UserForm

Understanding various techniques that involve a `ListBox` control

Using an external control

Using the `MultiPage` control

Animating a `Label` control

Creating a UserForm "Menu"

Sometimes, you might want to use a UserForm as a type of menu. In other words, the UserForm presents some options, and the user makes a choice. This section presents two ways to do this: by using command buttons and by using a list box.

 Chapter 15 contains additional examples of more advanced UserForm techniques.

Using CommandButtons in a UserForm

Figure 14.1 shows an example of a UserForm that uses command buttons as a simple menu.

FIGURE 14.1

This dialog box uses command buttons as a menu.

Setting up this sort of UserForm is easy, and the code behind the UserForm is straightforward. Each command button has its own procedure for its `Click` event. For example, the following procedure is executed when `CommandButton1` is clicked:

```
Private Sub CommandButton1_Click()
    Me.Hide
    Macro1
    Unload Me
End Sub
```

This procedure hides the UserForm, runs a procedure called `Macro1`, and then closes the UserForm. The other buttons have similar event-handler procedures.

Using a list box in a UserForm

Figure 14.2 shows another example that uses a list box as a menu.

FIGURE 14.2

This dialog box uses a list box as a menu.

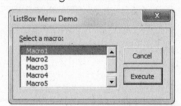

This style is easier to maintain because you can easily add new menu items without adjusting the size of the UserForm. Before the UserForm is displayed, its `Initialize` event-handler procedure is called. This procedure, which follows, uses the `AddItem` method to add six items to the list box:

```
Private Sub UserForm_Initialize()
    With Me.ListBox1
```

480

```
            .AddItem "Macro1"
            .AddItem "Macro2"
            .AddItem "Macro3"
            .AddItem "Macro4"
            .AddItem "Macro5"
            .AddItem "Macro6"
        End With
    End Sub
```

The Execute button also has a procedure to handle its Click event, shown here:

```
    Private Sub ExecuteButton_Click()
        Select Case Me.ListBox1.ListIndex
            Case -1
                MsgBox "Select a macro from the list."
                Exit Sub
            Case 0: Macro1
            Case 1: Macro2
            Case 2: Macro3
            Case 3: Macro4
            Case 4: Macro5
            Case 5: Macro6
        End Select
        Unload Me
    End Sub
```

This procedure accesses the ListIndex property of the ListBox control to determine which item is selected. The procedure uses a Select Case structure to execute the appropriate macro. If ListIndex is -1, nothing is selected in the list box, and the user sees a message.

In addition, this UserForm has a procedure to handle the double-click event for the list box. Double-clicking an item in the list box executes the corresponding macro.

ON THE WEB
The two examples in this section are available on the book's website in the Userform Menus.xlsm file.

14

 Chapter 15 shows a similar example in which you can use a UserForm to simulate a toolbar.

Selecting Ranges from a UserForm

Many of Excel's built-in dialog boxes allow the user to specify a range. For example, the Goal Seek dialog box (displayed by choosing Data ⇨ Forecast ⇨ What-If Analysis ⇨ Goal Seek) asks the user to select two single-cell ranges. The user can either type the range addresses (or names) directly or use the mouse to point and click in a sheet to make a range selection.

Your UserForms can also provide this type of functionality, thanks to the RefEdit control. The RefEdit control doesn't look exactly like the range selection control used in Excel's built-in dialog boxes, but it works in a similar manner. If the user clicks the small button on the right side of the control, the dialog box disappears temporarily and a small range selector is displayed—which is exactly what happens with Excel's built-in dialog boxes.

> **NOTE**
>
> Unfortunately, the RefEdit control has a few quirks that still haven't been fixed. You'll find that this control doesn't allow the user to use shortcut range-selection keys (for example, pressing End, followed by Shift and the down arrow, will not select cells to the end of the column). In addition, the control is mouse-centric. After clicking the small button on the right side of the control (to hide the dialog box temporarily), you're limited to mouse selections only. You can't use the keyboard to make a selection.

Figure 14.3 shows a UserForm that contains a RefEdit control. This dialog box enables the user to perform a simple mathematical operation on all nonformula (and nonempty) cells in the selected range. The operation that's performed corresponds to the selected option button.

FIGURE 14.3

The RefEdit control allows the user to select a range.

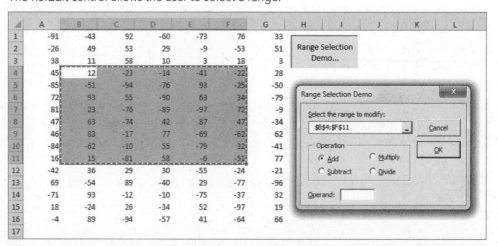

> **ON THE WEB**
>
> This example is available on the book's website in a file named Range Selection Demo.xlsm.

The following are a few things to keep in mind when using a `RefEdit` control:

- The `RefEdit` control returns a text string that represents a range address. You can convert this string to a `Range` object by using a statement such as the following:

```
Set UserRange = Range(Me.RefEdit1.Text)
```

- Initializing the `RefEdit` control to display the current range selection is good practice. You can do so in the `UserForm_Initialize` procedure by using a statement such as the following:

```
Me.RefEdit1.Text = ActiveWindow.RangeSelection.Address
```

- For best results, avoid using a `RefEdit` control inside a `Frame` or `MultiPage` control. Doing so may cause Excel to crash.

- Don't assume that `RefEdit` will always return a valid range address. Pointing to a range isn't the only way to get text into this control. The user can type any text and can also edit or delete the displayed text. Therefore, you need to make sure that the range is valid. The following code is an example of a way to check for a valid range. If an invalid range is detected, the user is given a message, and the focus is set to the `RefEdit` control so that the user can try again.

```
On Error Resume Next
Set UserRange = Range(Me.refRange.Text)
If Err.Number <> 0 Then
    MsgBox "Invalid range selected"
    Me.refRange.SetFocus
    Exit Sub
End If
On Error GoTo 0
```

- The user can also click the worksheet tabs while selecting a range with the `RefEdit` control. Therefore, you can't assume that the selection is on the active sheet. However, if a different sheet is selected, the range address is preceded by a sheet name. Here's an example:

```
Sheet2!$A$1:$C$4
```

- If you need to get a single cell selection from the user, you can isolate the upper-left cell of a selected range by using a statement such as the following:

```
Set OneCell = Range(Me.RefEdit1.Text).Cells(1)
```

 As we discuss in Chapter 12, you can also use Excel's `InputBox` method to allow the user to select a range.

Creating a Splash Screen

Some developers like to display introductory information when their application is opened. This display is commonly known as a *splash screen*.

You can create a splash screen for your Excel application with a UserForm. This example is essentially a UserForm that is displayed automatically when the workbook is opened and then dismisses itself after five seconds.

ON THE WEB

This book's website contains a workbook that demonstrates this procedure in a file named `Splash Screen .xlsm`.

Follow these instructions to create a splash screen for your project:

1. Create your workbook.
2. Activate the Visual Basic Editor (VBE) and insert a new UserForm into the project.

   The code in this example assumes that this form is named `frmSplash`.
3. Place any controls that you like on `frmSplash`.

   For example, you may want to insert an `Image` control that has your company's logo. Figure 14.4 shows an example.

FIGURE 14.4

This splash screen is displayed briefly when the workbook is opened.

4. Insert the following procedure into the code module for the `ThisWorkbook` object:

```
Private Sub Workbook_Open()
    frmSplash.Show
End Sub
```

5. Insert the following procedure into the code module for `frmSplash`.

   For a delay other than five seconds, change the argument for the `TimeSerial` function.

```
Private Sub UserForm_Activate()
    Application.OnTime Now + _
        TimeSerial(0,0,5), "KillTheForm"
End Sub
```

6. Insert the following procedure into a general VBA module:

```
Private Sub KillTheForm()
    Unload frmSplash
End Sub
```

   When the workbook is opened, the `Workbook_Open` procedure is executed. The procedure in step 4 displays the UserForm. At that time, the UserForm's `Activate` event occurs, which triggers the `UserForm_Activate` procedure (see step 5). This procedure uses the `Application.OnTime` method to execute a procedure named `KillTheForm` at a particular time. In this case, the time is five seconds after the activation event. The `KillTheForm` procedure simply unloads the UserForm.

7. As an option, you can add a small command button named `cmdCancel`, set its `Cancel` property to `True`, and insert the following event-handler procedure in the UserForm's code module:

```
Private Sub cmdCancel_Click()
    Unload Me
End Sub
```

   Doing so lets the user cancel the splash screen before the time has expired by pressing Esc. In the example, a small button is placed behind another object so that it's not visible.

CAUTION

Keep in mind that the splash screen isn't displayed until the workbook is entirely loaded. In other words, if you'd like to display the splash screen to give the user something to look at while a large workbook is loading, this technique won't fill the bill.

14

If your application needs to run some VBA procedures at startup, you can display the UserForm *modeless* so that the code will continue running while the UserForm is displayed. To do so, change the `Workbook_Open` procedure as follows:

```
Private Sub Workbook_Open()
    frmSplash.Show vbModeless
    ' other code goes here
End Sub
```

Disabling a UserForm's Close Button

When a UserForm is displayed, clicking the Close button (the X in the upper-right corner) will unload the form. You might have a situation in which you don't want the Close button to unload the form. For example, you might require that the UserForm be closed only by clicking a particular command button.

Although you can't actually disable the Close button, you can prevent the UserForm from closing if the user clicks it. You can do so by monitoring the UserForm's `QueryClose` event.

The following procedure, which is located in the code module for the UserForm, is executed before the form is closed (that is, when the `QueryClose` event occurs):

```
Private Sub UserForm_QueryClose _
  (Cancel As Integer, CloseMode As Integer)
    If CloseMode = vbFormControlMenu Then
        MsgBox "Click the OK button to close the form."
        Cancel = True
    End If
End Sub
```

The `UserForm_QueryClose` procedure uses two arguments. The `CloseMode` argument contains a value that indicates the cause of the `QueryClose` event. If `CloseMode` is equal to `vbFormControlMenu` (a built-in constant), the user clicked the Close button. If a message is displayed, the `Cancel` argument is set to `True`, and the form isn't actually closed.

Preventing Breaking Out of the Macro

Keep in mind that a user can press Ctrl+Break to break out of the macro. In this example, pressing Ctrl+Break while the UserForm is displayed dismisses the UserForm. To prevent this occurrence, execute the following statement prior to displaying the UserForm:

```
Application.EnableCancelKey = xlDisabled
```

Make sure that your application is debugged before you add this statement. Otherwise, you'll find that it's impossible to break out of an accidental endless loop.

Changing a UserForm's Size

Many applications use dialog boxes that change their own size. For example, Excel's Find and Replace dialog box (displayed when you choose Home ➪ Editing ➪ Find & Select ➪ Replace) adjusts its height when the user clicks the Options button.

The example in this section demonstrates how to get a UserForm to change its size dynamically. Changing a dialog box's size is done by altering the `Width` or `Height` property of the UserForm object. This example displays a list of worksheets in the active workbook and lets the user select which sheets to print.

 Refer to Chapter 15 for an example that allows the user to change the UserForm's size by dragging the lower-right corner.

Figure 14.5 shows the two states of the dialog box: as it is first displayed and after the user clicks the Options button. Note that the button's caption changes, depending on the size of the UserForm.

FIGURE 14.5

A dialog box before and after displaying options

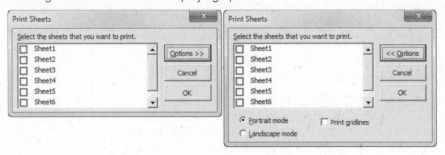

While you're creating the UserForm, set it to its largest size to enable you to work with the controls. Then use the UserForm_Initialize procedure to set the UserForm to its default (smaller) size.

The code uses two constants, defined at the top of the module:

```
Const SmallSize As Long = 124
Const LargeSize As Long = 164
```

The following is the event handler that's executed when the CommandButton named cmdOptions is clicked:

```
Private Sub cmdOptions_Click()
    Const OptionsHidden As String = "Options >>"
    Const OptionsShown As String = "<< Options"

    If Me.cmdOptions.Caption = OptionsHidden Then
        Me.Height = LargeSize
        Me.cmdOptions.Caption = OptionsShown
    Else
        Me.Height = SmallSize
        Me.cmdOptions.Caption = OptionsHidden
    End If
End Sub
```

This procedure examines the Caption property of the command button and sets the UserForm's Height property accordingly.

NOTE

When controls aren't displayed because they're outside the visible portion of the UserForm, the accelerator keys for such controls continue to function. In this example, the user can press the Alt+L hot key (to select landscape mode) even if that option isn't visible. To block access to nondisplayed controls, you can write code to disable the controls when they aren't displayed.

ON THE WEB

The example in this section is available on the book's website in the file named Change Userform Size .xlsm.

Zooming and Scrolling a Sheet from a UserForm

The example in this section demonstrates how to use ScrollBar controls to allow sheet scrolling and zooming while a dialog box is displayed. Figure 14.6 shows how the example dialog box is set up. When the UserForm is displayed, the user can adjust the worksheet's zoom factor (from 10% to 400%) by using the scroll bar at the top. The two scroll bars in the bottom section of the dialog box allow the user to scroll the worksheet horizontally and vertically.

FIGURE 14.6

Here, scroll bars allow zooming and scrolling of the worksheet.

ON THE WEB

This example, named `Zoom and Scroll Sheet.xlsm`, is available on the book's website.

The code for this example is remarkably simple. The controls are initialized in the `UserForm_Initialize` procedure, which follows:

```
Private Sub UserForm_Initialize()
    Me.lblZoom.Caption = ActiveWindow.Zoom & "%"
'   Zoom
    With Me.scbZoom
        .Min = 10
        .Max = 400
        .SmallChange = 1
        .LargeChange = 10
        .Value = ActiveWindow.Zoom
    End With

'   Horizontally scrolling
    With Me.scbColumns
        .Min = 1
        .Max = ActiveSheet.UsedRange.Columns.Count
        .Value = ActiveWindow.ScrollColumn
        .LargeChange = 25
        .SmallChange = 1
    End With

'   Vertically scrolling
    With Me.scbRows
        .Min = 1
```

```
            .Max = ActiveSheet.UsedRange.Rows.Count
            .Value = ActiveWindow.ScrollRow
            .LargeChange = 25
            .SmallChange = 1
        End With
    End Sub
```

This procedure sets various properties of the `ScrollBar` controls by using values based on the active window.

When the `scbZoom` control is used, the `scbZoom_Change` procedure (which follows) is executed. This procedure sets the `ScrollBar` control's `Value` property to the `ActiveWindow`'s `Zoom` property value. It also changes a label to display the current zoom factor.

```
    Private Sub scbZoom_Change()
        With ActiveWindow
            .Zoom = Me.scbZoom.Value
            Me.lblZoom = .Zoom & "%"
            .ScrollColumn = Me.scbColumns.Value
            .ScrollRow = Me.scbRows.Value
        End With
    End Sub
```

Worksheet scrolling is accomplished by the two procedures that follow. These procedures set the `ScrollRow` or `ScrollColumn` property of the `ActiveWindow` object equal to the appropriate `ScrollBar` control value.

```
    Private Sub scbColumns_Change()
        ActiveWindow.ScrollColumn = Me.scbColumns.Value
    End Sub

    Private Sub scbRows_Change()
        ActiveWindow.ScrollRow = Me.scbRows.Value
    End Sub
```

> **TIP**
>
> If you use the `Scroll` event rather than the `Change` event in the preceding procedures, the event will be triggered when the scroll bars are dragged—resulting in smooth zooming and scrolling. To use the `Scroll` event, just make the procedure names `scbColumns_Scroll` and `scbRows_Scroll()`, respectively.

Exploring ListBox Techniques

The `ListBox` control is versatile, but it can be tricky to work with. This section contains a number of examples that demonstrate common techniques that involve the `ListBox` control.

The following are a few points to keep in mind when working with `ListBox` controls. Examples in the sections that follow demonstrate many of these points:

- You can retrieve the items in a list box from a range of cells (specified by the `RowSource` property), or you can add them by using VBA code (using the `AddItem` or `List` methods).
- You can set up a list box to allow a single selection or multiple selections. You use the `MultiSelect` property to specify whether the user can select more than one item.
- If a list box isn't set up for a multiple selection, you can link the value of the list box to a worksheet cell by using the `ControlSource` property.
- You can display a list box with no items selected (the `ListIndex` property will be -1). However, after an item is selected, the user can't deselect all items. The exception is if the `MultiSelect` property is `True`.
- A list box can contain multiple columns (controlled by the `ColumnCount` property) and even a descriptive header (controlled by the `ColumnHeads` property).
- The vertical height of a list box displayed in a UserForm window at design time isn't always the same as the vertical height when the UserForm is displayed.
- You can display the items in a list box either as check boxes (if multiple selections are allowed) or as option buttons (if a single selection is allowed). The display type is controlled by the `ListStyle` property.

For complete details on the properties and methods for a `ListBox` control, consult the Help system.

Adding items to a ListBox control

Before displaying a UserForm that uses a `ListBox` control, you need to fill the list box with items. You can fill a listbox at design time using items stored in a worksheet range or at run-time using VBA.

The two examples in this section presume the following:

- You have a UserForm named `UserForm1`.
- This UserForm contains a `ListBox` control named `ListBox1`.
- The workbook contains a sheet named `Sheet1`, and range A1:A12 contains the items to be displayed in the list box.

Adding items to a list box at design time

To add items to a list box at design time, the list box items must be stored in a worksheet range. Use the `RowSource` property to specify the range that contains the list box items.

Figure 14.7 shows the Properties window for a `ListBox` control. The `RowSource` property is set to `Sheet1!A1:A12`. When the UserForm is displayed, the list box will contain the 12 items in this range. The items appear in the list box at design time as soon as you specify the range for the `RowSource` property.

FIGURE 14.7

Setting the RowSource property at design time

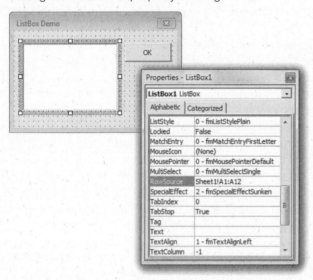

Ensuring the Proper Range Is Used

In most cases, you'll want to include the worksheet name when you specify the `RowSource` property; otherwise, the list box will use the specified range on the active worksheet. In some cases, you may need to qualify the range fully by including the workbook name. Here's an example:

`[budget.xlsx]Sheet1!A1:A12`

A better practice is to define a workbook-level name for the range and use that name in your code. This habit will ensure that the proper range is used even if rows above the range are added or deleted.

Adding items to a list box at run-time

To add list box items at run-time, you have three choices.

- Set the `RowSource` property to a range address by using code.
- Write code that uses the `AddItem` method to add the list box items.
- Assign an array to the `List` property of the `ListBox` control.

As you might expect, you can set the RowSource property through code rather than with the Properties window. For example, the following procedure sets the RowSource property for a list box before displaying the UserForm. In this case, the items consist of the cell entries in a range named Categories in the Budget worksheet.

```
UserForm1.ListBox1.RowSource = "Budget!Categories"
    UserForm1.Show
```

If the list box items aren't contained in a worksheet range, you can write VBA code to fill the list box before the dialog box appears. The following procedure fills the list box with the names of the months by using the AddItem method:

```
Sub ShowUserForm2()
'   Fill the list box
    With UserForm1.ListBox1
        .RowSource=""
        .AddItem "January"
        .AddItem "February"
        .AddItem "March"
        .AddItem "April"
        .AddItem "May"
        .AddItem "June"
        .AddItem "July"
        .AddItem "August"
        .AddItem "September"
        .AddItem "October"
        .AddItem "November"
        .AddItem "December"
    End With
    UserForm1.Show
End Sub
```

CAUTION

In the preceding code, note that the RowSource property is set to an empty string. This setting avoids a potential error that occurs if the Properties window has a nonempty RowSource setting. If you try to add items to a list box that has a non-null RowSource setting, you'll get a "Permission denied" error.

You can also retrieve items from a range and use the AddItem method to add them to the list box. Here's an example that fills a list box with the contents of A1:A12 on Sheet1:

```
For Row = 1 To 12
  UserForm1.ListBox1.AddItem Sheets("Sheet1").Cells(Row, 1)
Next Row
```

Using the List property is even simpler. The statement that follows has the same effect as the preceding For Next loop:

```
UserForm1.ListBox1.List = _
    Application.Transpose(Sheets("Sheet1").Range("A1:A12"))
```

This example uses the `Transpose` function because the `List` property expects a horizontal array, and the range is in a column rather than a row.

You can use the `List` property also if your data is stored in a one-dimensional array. For example, assume that you have an array named `MyList` that contains 50 elements. The following statement will create a 50-item list in `ListBox1`:

```
UserForm1.ListBox1.List = MyList
```

VBA has an `Array` function and a `Split` function, both of which return a one-dimensional array. You can assign the results of one of those functions to the List property, as in these examples:

```
UserForm1.ListBox1.List = Array("January", "February", _
    "March", "April", "May", "June", "July", "August", _
    "September", "October", "November", "December")
UserForm1.ListBox1.List = Split("Mon Tue Wed Thu Fri Sat Sun")
```

ON THE WEB

The examples in this section are available on the book's website in the file named `Listbox Fill.xlsm`.

Adding only unique items to a list box

In some cases, you may need to fill a list box with *unique* (nonduplicated) items from a list. For example, assume that you have a worksheet that contains customer data. One of the columns might contain the state (see Figure 14.8). You'd like to fill a list box with the state names of your customers, but you don't want to include duplicate state names.

One fast and efficient technique involves using a `Collection` object. After creating a new `Collection` object, you can add items to the object with the following syntax:

```
object.Add item, key, before, after
```

The `key` argument, if used, must be a unique text string that you can later use to access that member of the collection. The important word here is *unique*. If you attempt to add a nonunique key to a collection, an error occurs, and the item isn't added. You can take advantage of this situation and use it to create a collection that consists only of unique items.

The following procedure starts by declaring a `Collection` object named `NoDupes`. It assumes that a range named `States` contains a list of items, some of which may be duplicated.

FIGURE 14.8

A `Collection` object is used to fill a list box with the unique items from column B.

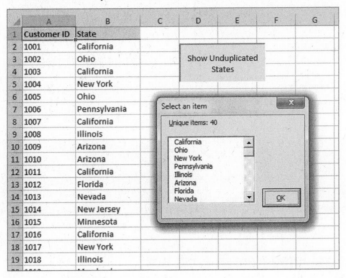

The code loops through the cells in the range and attempts to add the cell's value to the `NoDupes` collection. It also uses the cell's value (converted to a string) for the key argument. Using the `On Error Resume Next` statement causes VBA to ignore the error that occurs if the key isn't unique. When an error occurs, the item isn't added to the collection, which is just what you want. The procedure then transfers the items in the `NoDupes` collection to the list box. The UserForm also contains a label that displays the number of unique items.

```
Sub RemoveDuplicates1()
    Dim AllCells As Range, Cell As Range
    Dim NoDupes As Collection
    Dim Item As Variant

    Set NoDupes = New Collection

    On Error Resume Next
    For Each Cell In Range("State").Cells
        NoDupes.Add Cell.Value, CStr(Cell.Value)
    Next Cell
    On Error GoTo 0
```

```
'       Add the non-duplicated items to a ListBox
        For Each Item In NoDupes
            UserForm1.ListBox1.AddItem Item
        Next Item

'       Display the count
        UserForm1.Label1.Caption = "Unique items: " & NoDupes.Count

'       Show the UserForm
        UserForm1.Show
    End Sub
```

ON THE WEB

This example, named `Listbox Unique Items1.xlsm`, is available on the book's website. A workbook named `Listbox Unique Items2.xlsm` has a slightly more sophisticated version of this technique and displays the items sorted.

Determining the selected item in a list box

The examples in the preceding sections merely display a UserForm with a list box filled with various items. These procedures omit a key point: how to determine which item or items were selected by the user.

NOTE

The example in this section assumes a single-selection `ListBox` object—one whose `MultiSelect` property is set to 0.

To determine which item was selected, access the `ListBox` control's `Value` property. The statement that follows, for example, displays the text of the selected item in `ListBox1`.

```
MsgBox Me.ListBox1.Value
```

If no item is selected, this statement will generate an error.

If you need to know the position of the selected item in the list (rather than the content of that item), you can access the `ListBox` control's `ListIndex` property. The following example uses a message box to display the item number of the selected list box item:

```
MsgBox "You selected item #" & Me.ListBox1.ListIndex
```

If no item is selected, the `ListIndex` property will return -1.

NOTE

The numbering of items in a list box begins with 0, not 1. Therefore, the `ListIndex` of the first item is 0, and the `ListIndex` of the last item is equivalent to the value of the `ListCount` property minus 1.

Determining multiple selections in a list box

A `ListBox` control's `MultiSelect` property can be any of three values:

- 0 **(fmMultiSelectSingle):** Only one item can be selected. This setting is the default.
- 1 **(fmMultiSelectMulti):** One or more items can be selected. Press the spacebar or click an item to select or deselect it.
- 2 **(fmMultiSelectExtended):** Press Ctrl and click to select multiple items. Shift-clicking extends the selection from the previously selected item to the current item. You can also use Shift and one of the arrow keys to extend the selected items.

If the list box allows multiple selections (that is, if its `MultiSelect` property is either 1 or 2), trying to access the `ListIndex` or `Value` property will result in an error. Instead, you need to use the `Selected` property, which returns an array whose first item has an index of 0. For example, the following statement displays `True` if the first item in the list box list is selected:

```
MsgBox ListBox1.Selected(0)
```

ON THE WEB

This book's website contains a workbook that demonstrates how to identify the selected item(s) in a list box. It works for single-selection and multiple-selection list boxes. The file is named `Listbox Selected Items.xlsm`.

The following code, from the example workbook on the website, loops through each item in the list box. If the item was selected, the item's text is appended to a variable called `Msg`. Finally, the names of all selected items are displayed in a message box.

```
Private Sub cmdOK_Click()
    Dim Msg As String
    Dim i As Long

    If Me.ListBox1.ListIndex = -1 Then
        Msg = "Nothing"
    Else
        For i = 0 To Me.ListBox1.ListCount - 1
            If ListBox1.Selected(i) Then _
                Msg = Msg & Me.ListBox1.List(i) & vbNewLine
        Next i
    End If
    MsgBox "You selected: " & vbNewLine & Msg
    Unload Me
End Sub
```

Figure 14.9 shows the result when multiple list box items are selected.

FIGURE 14.9

This message box displays a list of items selected in a list box.

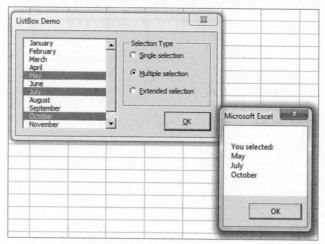

Multiple lists in a single list box

This example demonstrates how to create a list box in which the contents change depending on the user's selection from a group of OptionButtons.

The list box gets its items from a worksheet range. The procedures that handle the `Click` event for the `OptionButton` controls simply set the `ListBox` control's `RowSource` property to a different range. One of these procedures follows:

```
Private Sub optMonths_Click()
    Me.ListBox1.RowSource = "Sheet1!Months"
End Sub
```

Figure 14.10 shows the UserForm.

Clicking the option button named `optMonths` changes the `RowSource` property of the `ListBox` control to use a range named `Months` on `Sheet1`.

ON THE WEB

This example, named `Listbox Multiple Lists.xlsm`, is available on the book's website.

List box item transfer

Some applications require a user to select several items from a list. It's often useful to create a new list of the selected items and display the new list in another list box. For an example of this situation, check out the Quick Access Toolbar tab of the Excel Options dialog box.

Figure 14.11 shows a dialog box with two list boxes. The Add button adds the item selected in the left list box to the right list box. The Remove button removes the selected item from the list on the right. A check box determines the behavior when a duplicate item is added to the list. Namely, if the Allow Duplicates checkbox isn't marked, the item is removed from the From list so that it can't be added again.

FIGURE 14.10

The contents of this list box depend on the option button selected.

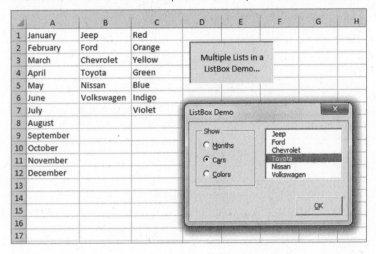

FIGURE 14.11

Building a list from another list

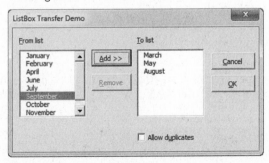

The code for this example is simple. Here's the procedure that is executed when the user clicks the Add button:

```
Private Sub cmdAdd_Click()
    'Add the value
```

499

```
        Me.lbxTo.AddItem Me.lbxFrom.Value
        If Not Me.chkDuplicates.Value Then
            'If duplicates aren't allowed, remove the value
            Me.lbxFrom.RemoveItem Me.lbxFrom.ListIndex
        End If
        EnableButtons
    End Sub
```

The code for the Remove button is similar.

```
    Private Sub cmdRemove_Click()
        If Not Me.chkDuplicates.Value Then
            Me.lbxFrom.AddItem Me.lbxTo.Value
        End If
        Me.lbxTo.RemoveItem Me.lbxTo.ListIndex
        EnableButtons
    End Sub
```

Note that neither routine checks to make sure that an item is actually selected. Instead, each button's Enabled property is set to False at design time. Another procedure, EnableButtons, is called to enable the buttons only when it's appropriate.

In addition to calling EnableButtons from cmdAdd_Click and cmdRemove_Click, both ListBox's Change events also call it. The ListBox control's Change event procedures and the EnableButtons procedure are shown here:

```
    Private Sub lbxFrom_Change()
        EnableButtons
    End Sub

    Private Sub lbxTo_Change()
        EnableButtons
    End Sub

    Private Sub EnableButtons()
        Me.cmdAdd.Enabled = Me.lbxFrom.ListIndex > -1
        Me.cmdRemove.Enabled = Me.lbxTo.ListIndex > -1
    End Sub
```

The ListIndex property is compared to -1, which returns True or False. That value is assigned to the Enabled property to allow the user to click a button only when an item is selected.

ON THE WEB

This example, named `Listbox Item Transfer.xlsm`, is available on the book's website.

Moving items in a list box

Often, the order of items in a list is important. The example in this section demonstrates how to allow the user to move items up or down in a list box. The VBE uses this type of technique to let you control the tab order of the items in a UserForm. (Right-click a UserForm, and choose Tab Order from the shortcut menu.)

Figure 14.12 shows a dialog box that contains a list box and two CommandButtons. Clicking the Move Up button moves the selected item up in the ListBox; clicking the Move Down button moves the selected item down.

FIGURE 14.12

The buttons allow the user to move items up or down in the ListBox.

The event-handler procedures for the two CommandButtons follow:

```
Private Sub cmdUp_Click()
    Dim lSelected As Long
    Dim sSelected As String

    '   Store the currently selected item
        lSelected = Me.lbxItems.ListIndex
        sSelected = Me.lbxItems.Value

    '   Remove the selected item
        Me.lbxItems.RemoveItem lSelected
    '   Add back the item one above
        Me.lbxItems.AddItem sSelected, lSelected - 1
    '   Reselect the moved item
        Me.lbxItems.ListIndex = lSelected - 1
    End Sub

Private Sub cmdDown_Click()
    Dim lSelected As Long
    Dim sSelected As String
```

14

```
'   Store the currently selected item
    lSelected = Me.lbxItems.ListIndex
    sSelected = Me.lbxItems.Value

'   Remove the selected item
    Me.lbxItems.RemoveItem lSelected
'   Add back the item one below
    Me.lbxItems.AddItem sSelected, lSelected + 1
'   Reselect the moved item
    Me.lbxItems.ListIndex = lSelected + 1
End Sub
```

The up and down buttons are disabled by default (their `Enabled` properties are set to `False` at design time). The `Click` event of the `ListBox` control is used to enable the buttons only when it's appropriate for them to be clicked. The `cmdDown` button is enabled only when something is selected (the `ListIndex` property is 0 or greater) and the item selected is not the last item. The `cmdUp` control is similarly enabled, except that it tests that the item selected isn't the first item. The event procedure follows:

```
Private Sub lbxItems_Click()
    Me.cmdDown.Enabled = Me.lbxItems.ListIndex > -1 _
        And Me.lbxItems.ListIndex < Me.lbxItems.ListCount - 1
    Me.cmdUp.Enabled = Me.lbxItems.ListIndex > -1 _
        And Me.lbxItems.ListIndex > 0
End Sub
```

Rapid clicking of the Move Up or the Move Down button doesn't reliably register as multiple clicks because VBA recognizes it as a double-click instead of two single clicks. To accommodate this, two more procedures that respond to the `DblClick` event for each button were added. These procedures simply call the appropriate `Click` event procedure listed previously.

Working with multicolumn ListBox controls

The list box examples so far have had only a single column for their items. You can, however, create a list box that displays multiple columns and (optionally) column headers. Figure 14.13 shows an example of a multicolumn list box that gets its data from a worksheet range.

ON THE WEB

This example, named `Listbox Multicolumn1.xlsm`, is available on the book's website.

FIGURE 14.13

This ListBox displays a three-column list with column headers.

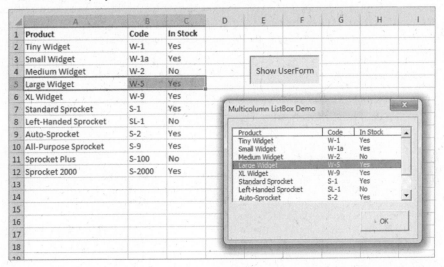

To set up a multicolumn list box that uses data stored in a worksheet range, follow these steps:

1. Make sure that the `ListBox` control's `ColumnCount` property is set to the correct number of columns.

2. Specify the correct multicolumn range in the Excel worksheet as the `ListBox` control's `RowSource` property.

3. If you want to display column headers, set the `ColumnHeads` property to `True`.

   Do not include the column headings on the worksheet in the range setting for the `RowSource` property. VBA will instead automatically use the row directly above the first row of the `RowSource` range.

4. Adjust the column widths by assigning a series of values, specified in *points* (1/72 of 1 inch) and separated by semicolons, to the `ColumnWidths` property. This will almost always require some trial and error.

   For example, for a three-column list box, the `ColumnWidths` property might be set to the following text string:

   ```
   110 pt;40 pt;30 pt
   ```

5. Specify the appropriate column as the `BoundColumn` property.

   The bound column specifies which column is referenced when an instruction polls the `ListBox` control's `Value` property.

To fill a list box with multicolumn data without using a range, you first create a two-dimensional array and then assign the array to the ListBox control's List property. The following statements demonstrate this using a 12-row-by-2-column array named Data. The two-column list box shows the month names in column 1 and the number of the days in the month in column 2 (see Figure 14.14). Note that the procedure sets the ColumnCount property to 2.

```
Private Sub UserForm_Initialize()
    Dim i As Long
    Dim Data(1 To 12, 1 To 2) As String
    Dim ThisYear As Long
    ThisYear = Year(Now)
'   Fill the list box
    For i = 1 To 12
        Data(i, 1) = Format(DateSerial(ThisYear, i, 1), "mmmm")
        Data(i, 2) = Day(DateSerial(ThisYear, i + 1, 0))
    Next i
    Me.ListBox1.ColumnCount = 2
    Me.ListBox1.List = Data
End Sub
```

FIGURE 14.14

A two-column ListBox filled with data stored in an array

NOTE

There is no way to specify column headers for the ColumnHeads property when the list source is a VBA array.

Using a list box to select worksheet rows

The example in this section displays a list box that consists of the entire used range of the active worksheet (see Figure 14.15). The user can select multiple items in the list box. Clicking the All button selects all items, and clicking the None button deselects all items. Clicking OK selects those corresponding rows in the worksheet. You might find that selecting multiple noncontiguous rows is easier when using this method rather than by pressing Ctrl while you click the row borders.

FIGURE 14.15

This list box makes selecting rows in a worksheet easy.

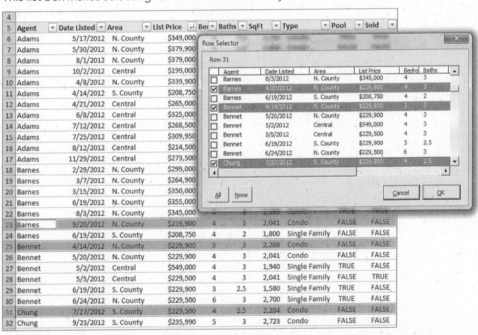

Selecting multiple items is possible because the `ListBox` control's `MultiSelect` property is set to `1 - fmMultiSelectMulti`. The checkboxes on each item are displayed because the `ListBox` control's `ListStyle` property is set to `1 - fmListStyleOption`.

The UserForm's `Initialize` procedure follows. This procedure creates a `Range` object named `rng` that consists of the active sheet's used range. Additional code sets the `ListBox` control's `ColumnCount` and `RowSource` properties and adjusts the `ColumnWidths` property so that the list box columns are proportional to the column widths in the worksheet.

```
Private Sub UserForm_Initialize()
    Dim ColCnt As Long
    Dim rng As Range
    Dim ColWidths As String
    Dim i As Long

    ColCnt = ActiveSheet.UsedRange.Columns.Count
    Set rng = ActiveSheet.UsedRange
    With Me.lbxRange
        .ColumnCount = ColCnt
        .RowSource = _
            rng.Offset(1).Resize(rng.Rows.Count - 1).Address
        For i = 1 To .ColumnCount
            ColWidths = ColWidths & rng.Columns(i).Width & ";"
        Next i
        .ColumnWidths = ColWidths
        .ListIndex = 0
    End With
End Sub
```

The All and None buttons (named `cmdAll` and `cmdNone`, respectively) have simple event-handler procedures.

```
Private Sub cmdAll_Click()
    Dim i As Long
    For i = 0 To Me.lbxRange.ListCount - 1
        Me.lbxRange.Selected(i) = True
    Next i
End Sub

Private Sub cmdNone_Click()
    Dim i As Long
    For i = 0 To Me.lbxRange.ListCount - 1
        Me.lbxRange.Selected(i) = False
    Next i
End Sub
```

The `cmdOK_Click` procedure follows. This procedure creates a `Range` object named `RowRange` that consists of the rows that correspond to the selected items in the list box. To determine whether a row was selected, the code examines the `Selected` property of the `ListBox` control. Note that it uses the `Union` function to add ranges to the `RowRange` object.

```
Private Sub cmdOK_Click()
    Dim RowRange As Range
    Dim i As Long
```

```
      For i = 0 To Me.lbxRange.ListCount - 1
          If Me.lbxRange.Selected(i) Then
              If RowRange Is Nothing Then
                  Set RowRange = ActiveSheet.UsedRange.Rows(i + 2)
              Else
                  Set RowRange = Union(RowRange, _
                      ActiveSheet.UsedRange.Rows(i + 2))
              End If
          End If
      Next i
      If Not RowRange Is Nothing Then RowRange.Select
      Unload Me
  End Sub
```

Using a list box to activate a sheet

The example in this section is just as useful as it is instructive. This example uses a multicolumn list box to display a list of sheets in the active workbook. The columns represent the following:

- The sheet's name
- The type of sheet (worksheet, chart sheet, or Excel 5/95 dialog sheet)
- The number of nonempty cells in the sheet
- Whether the sheet is visible

Figure 14.16 shows an example of the dialog box.

The code in the `UserForm_Initialize` procedure (which follows) creates a two-dimensional array and collects the information by looping through the sheets in the active workbook. It then transfers this array to the list box.

```
  Public OriginalSheet As Object

  Private Sub UserForm_Initialize()
      Dim SheetData() As String, Sht As Object
      Dim ShtCnt As Long, ShtNum As Long, ListPos As Long

      Set OriginalSheet = ActiveSheet
      ShtCnt = ActiveWorkbook.Sheets.Count
      ReDim SheetData(1 To ShtCnt, 1 To 4)
      ShtNum = 1
      For Each Sht In ActiveWorkbook.Sheets
          If Sht.Name = ActiveSheet.Name Then _
            ListPos = ShtNum - 1
          SheetData(ShtNum, 1) = Sht.Name
          Select Case TypeName(Sht)
              Case "Worksheet"
                  SheetData(ShtNum, 2) = "Sheet"
                  SheetData(ShtNum, 3) = _
                      Application.CountA(Sht.Cells)
```

14

```
            Case "Chart"
                    SheetData(ShtNum, 2) = "Chart"
                    SheetData(ShtNum, 3) = "N/A"
            Case "DialogSheet"
                    SheetData(ShtNum, 2) = "Dialog"
                    SheetData(ShtNum, 3) = "N/A"
        End Select
        If Sht.Visible Then
            SheetData(ShtNum, 4) = "True"
        Else
            SheetData(ShtNum, 4) = "False"
        End If
        ShtNum = ShtNum + 1
    Next Sht
    With Me.lbxSheets
        .ColumnWidths = "100 pt;30 pt;40 pt;50 pt"
        .List = SheetData
        .ListIndex = ListPos
    End With
End Sub
```

FIGURE 14.16

This dialog box lets the user activate a sheet.

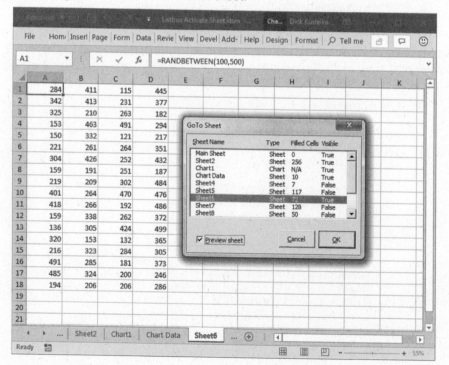

The `lbxSheets_Click` procedure follows:

```
Private Sub lbxSheets_Click()
    If Me.chkPreview.Value Then _
        Sheets(Me.lbxSheets.Value).Activate
End Sub
```

The value of the `CheckBox` control (named `chkPreview`) determines whether the selected sheet is previewed when the user clicks an item in the list box.

Clicking the OK button (named `cmdOK`) executes the `cmdOK_Click` procedure, which follows:

```
Private Sub cmdOK_Click()
    Dim UserSheet As Object
    Set UserSheet = Sheets(Me.lbxSheets.Value)
    If UserSheet.Visible Then
        UserSheet.Activate
    Else
        If MsgBox("Unhide sheet?", _
          vbQuestion + vbYesNoCancel) = vbYes Then
            UserSheet.Visible = True
            UserSheet.Activate
        Else
            OriginalSheet.Activate
        End If
    End If
    Unload Me
End Sub
```

The `cmdOK_Click` procedure creates an object variable that represents the selected sheet. If the sheet is visible, it's activated. If it's not visible, the user is presented with a message box asking whether it should be unhidden. If the user responds in the affirmative, the sheet is unhidden and activated. Otherwise, the original sheet (stored in a public object variable named `OriginalSheet`) is activated.

Double-clicking an item in the ListBox has the same result as clicking the OK button. The `lbxSheets_DblClick` procedure, which follows, simply calls the `cmdOK_Click` procedure:

```
Private Sub lbxSheets_DblClick(ByVal Cancel As MSForms.ReturnBoolean)
    cmdOK_Click
End Sub
```

ON THE WEB

This example is available on the book's website in the file named `Listbox Activate Sheet.xlsm`.

14

Using a text box to filter a list box

If your list box has a large number of items, you can provide a way to filter the list box so that you don't have to scroll through so many entries. Figure 14.17 shows a list box whose entries have been filtered by a text box.

FIGURE 14.17

Use a text box to filter a list box.

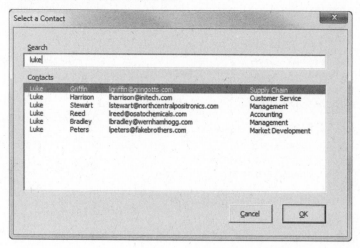

The UserForm uses a procedure named `FillContacts`, shown next, to add items to the list box. `FillContacts` accepts an optional argument that's used to filter the contacts. If you don't supply the `sFilter` argument, all 1,000 contacts are shown; otherwise, only those contacts that match the filter are shown.

```
Private Sub FillContacts(Optional sFilter As String = "*")
    Dim i As Long, j As Long

    'Clear any existing entries in the ListBox
    Me.lbxContacts.Clear
    'Loop through all the rows and columns of the contact list
    For i = LBound(maContacts, 1) To UBound(maContacts, 1)
        For j = 1 To 4
            'Compare the contact to the filter
            If UCase(maContacts(i, j)) Like _
                UCase("*" & sFilter & "*") Then

                'Add it to the ListBox
                With Me.lbxContacts
                    .AddItem maContacts(i, 1)
                    .List(.ListCount - 1, 1) = maContacts(i, 2)
```

```
                    .List(.ListCount - 1, 2) = maContacts(i, 3)
                    .List(.ListCount - 1, 3) = maContacts(i, 4)
            End With
            'If any column matched, skip the rest of the columns
            'and move to the next contact
            Exit For
        End If
    Next j
Next i
'Select the first contact
If Me.lbxContacts.ListCount > 0 Then Me.lbxContacts.ListIndex = 0
End Sub
```

First, FillContacts clears any existing entries out of the list box. Next, the procedure loops through all of the rows and the four columns of an array and compares each value to sFilter. The procedure uses the Like operator and surrounds sFilter with asterisks so that you can type any part of the value and still get a match. To make the filter case-insensitive, it converts both values to uppercase using the UCase function. If any of the values (first name, last name, email, or department) matches the filter, that contact is added to the list box.

The maContacts array that FillContacts uses is created in the UserForm_ Initialize event. The event's code fills the array using a table on Sheet1 called tblContacts. Then it calls FillContacts with no filter argument so that all contacts are shown initially. The code for the Initialize event follows:

```
Private maContacts As Variant

Private Sub UserForm_Initialize()
    maContacts = Sheet1.ListObjects("tblContacts").DataBodyRange
.Value
    FillContacts
End Sub
```

Finally, the Change event for the text box also calls FillContacts. But instead of omitting the filter, this event supplies whatever text is currently in the text box. The Change event is one simple line of code.

```
Private Sub tbxSearch_Change()
    FillContacts Me.tbxSearch.Text
End Sub
```

This is a good example of using something other than an event procedure in the UserForm code module to do the work. Instead of duplicating code in the UserForm_Initialize event and the tbxSearch_Change event, the two events simply call FillContacts.

ON THE WEB

This example is available on the book's website in the file named Listbox Filter.xlsm.

Using the MultiPage Control in a UserForm

The MultiPage control is useful for UserForms that must display many controls because it enables you to group choices and place each group on a separate tab.

Figure 14.18 shows an example of a UserForm that contains a MultiPage control. In this case, the control has three pages, each with its own tab.

FIGURE 14.18

MultiPage groups your controls on pages, making them accessible from a tab.

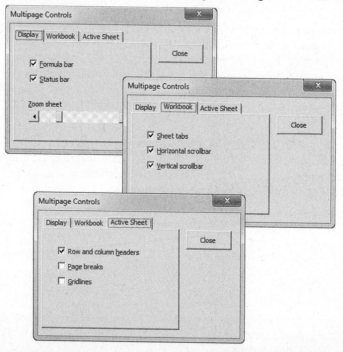

NOTE

The Toolbox also contains a control named TabStrip, which resembles a MultiPage control. However, unlike the MultiPage control, the TabStrip control isn't a container for other objects. If the layout of your controls doesn't change when the user clicks a tab (but the values do), use a TabStrip. If the layout changes, use a MultiPage.

Using a `MultiPage` control can be tricky. The following are some things to keep in mind when using this control:

- The tab (or page) that's displayed up front is determined by the control's `Value` property. A value of 0 displays the first tab, a value of 1 displays the second tab, and so on.
- By default, a `MultiPage` control has two pages. To add a new page in the VBE, right-click a tab and choose New Page from the shortcut menu.
- When you're working with a `MultiPage` control, just click a tab to set the properties for that particular page. The Properties window will display the properties that you can adjust.
- You may find it difficult to select the actual `MultiPage` control because clicking the control selects a page within the control. To select the control itself, click its border. Or, you can use the Tab key to cycle among all the controls. Yet another option is to choose the `MultiPage` control from the drop-down list in the Properties window.
- If your `MultiPage` control has lots of tabs, you can set its `MultiRow` property to `True` to display the tabs in more than one row.
- If you prefer, you can display buttons instead of tabs. Just change the `Style` property to 1. If the `Style` property value is 2, the `MultiPage` control won't display tabs or buttons and you'll have to write code that provides a means for switching tabs.
- The `TabOrientation` property determines the location of the tabs on the `MultiPage` control.

Using an External Control

The example in this section uses the Windows Media Player ActiveX control. Although this control isn't an Excel control (it's installed with Windows), it works fine in a UserForm.

> **CAUTION**
>
> ActiveX controls contain code. If that code is malicious, it could damage your computer. For that reason, Excel warns you when add an external ActiveX control to your UserForm. If you don't trust the control's author, don't add the control.

To make this control available, add a UserForm to a workbook and follow these steps:

1. Activate the VBE.
2. Right-click the Toolbox and choose Additional Controls.

   Choose View ⇨ Toolbox if the Toolbox isn't visible.

3. In the Additional Controls dialog box, scroll down and place a check mark next to Windows Media Player.

4. Click OK.

Your Toolbox will display a new control.

Figure 14.19 shows the Windows Media Player control in a UserForm, along with the Property window. The URL property represents the media item being played (music or video). If the item is on your hard drive, the URL property will contain the full path along with the filename.

FIGURE 14.19

The Windows Media Player control in a UserForm

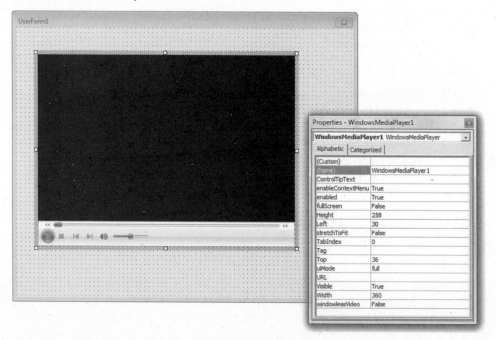

Figure 14.20 shows this control being used. The video is showing a visualization that changes in time to the audio. A list box is filled with MP3 audio filenames. Clicking the Play button plays the selected file. Clicking the Close button stops the sound and closes the UserForm. This UserForm is displayed modeless, so the user can continue working when the dialog box is displayed.

ON THE WEB

This example is available on the book's website in the `Mediaplayer.xlsm` file, which is in a separate directory that includes public domain MP3 sound files.

FIGURE 14.20

The Windows Media Player control

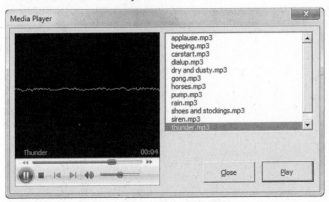

This example was easy to create. The UserForm_Initialize procedure adds the MP3 filenames to the ListBox. To keep things simple, it reads the files that are in the same directory as the workbook. A more versatile approach is to let the user select a directory.

```
Private Sub UserForm_Initialize()
    Dim FileName As String
'   Fill listbox with MP3 files
    FileName = Dir(ThisWorkbook.Path & "\*.mp3", vbNormal)
    Do While Len(FileName) > 0
        Me.lbxMedia.AddItem FileName
        FileName = Dir()
    Loop
    Me.lbxMedia.ListIndex = 0
End Sub
```

The cmdPlay_Click event-handler code consists of a single statement, which assigns the selected filename to the URL property of the WindowsMediaPlayer1 object.

```
Private Sub cmdPlay_Click()
'   URL property loads track, and starts player
    WindowsMediaPlayer1.URL = _
        ThisWorkbook.Path & "\" & _
        Me.lbxMedia.List(Me.lbxMedia.ListIndex)
End Sub
```

You can probably think of lots of enhancements for this simple application. Also note that this control responds to many events.

14

Animating a Label

The final example in this chapter demonstrates how to animate a Label control. The UserForm shown in Figure 14.21 is an interactive random number generator.

FIGURE 14.21

Generating a random number

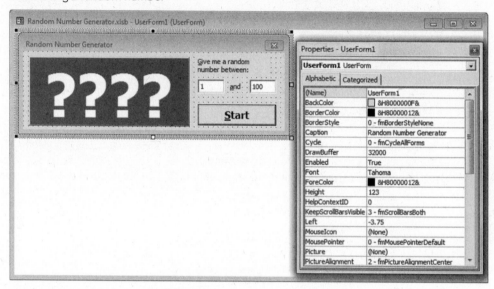

Two text boxes hold the lower and upper values for the random number. A label initially displays four question marks, but the text is animated to show random numbers when the user clicks the Start button. The Start button changes to a Stop button, and clicking it again stops the animation and displays the random number. Figure 14.22 shows the dialog box displaying a random number between -1,000 and 1000.

FIGURE 14.22

A random number has been chosen.

The code that's attached to the button is as follows:

```
Private Stopped As Boolean

Private Sub cmdStartStop_Click()
    Dim Low As Double, Hi As Double
    Dim wf As WorksheetFunction

    Set wf = Application.WorksheetFunction

    If Me.cmdStartStop.Caption = "Start" Then
'       validate low and hi values
        If Not IsNumeric(Me.tbxStart.Text) Then
            MsgBox "Non-numeric starting value.", vbInformation
            With Me.tbxStart
                .SelStart = 0
                .SelLength = Len(.Text)
                .SetFocus
            End With
            Exit Sub
        End If

        If Not IsNumeric(Me.tbxEnd.Text) Then
            MsgBox "Non-numeric ending value.", vbInformation
            With Me.tbxEnd
                .SelStart = 0
                .SelLength = Len(.Text)
                .SetFocus
            End With
            Exit Sub
        End If

'       Make sure they aren't in the wrong order
        Low = wf.Min(Val(Me.tbxStart.Text), Val(Me.tbxEnd.Text))
        Hi = wf.Max(Val(Me.tbxStart.Text), Val(Me.tbxEnd.Text))

'       Adjust font size, if necessary
        Select Case _
            wf.Max(Len(Me.tbxStart.Text), Len(Me.tbxEnd.Text))

            Case Is < 5: Me.lblRandom.Font.Size = 72
            Case 5: Me.lblRandom.Font.Size = 60
            Case 6: Me.lblRandom.Font.Size = 48
            Case Else: Me.lblRandom.Font.Size = 36
        End Select

        Me.cmdStartStop.Caption = "Stop"
        Stopped = False
        Randomize
```

14

```
            Do Until Stopped
                Me.lblRandom.Caption = _
                    Int((Hi - Low + 1) * Rnd + Low)
                DoEvents ' Causes the animation
            Loop
        Else
            Stopped = True
            Me.cmdStartStop.Caption = "Start"
        End If
    End Sub
```

Because the button serves two purposes (starting and stopping), the procedure uses a module-level variable, Stopped, to keep track of the state. The first part of the procedure consists of two If-Then structures to validate the contents of the text box. Two more statements ensure that the low value is in fact less than the high value. The next section adjusts the label's font size, based on the maximum value. The Do Until loop is responsible for generating and displaying the random numbers.

Note the DoEvents statement. This statement causes Excel to "yield" to the operating system. Without the statement, the label wouldn't display each random number as it's generated. In other words, the DoEvents statement makes the animation possible.

The UserForm also contains a command button that serves as a Cancel button. This control is positioned off the UserForm so that it's not visible. This CommandButton control has its Cancel property set to True, so pressing Esc is equivalent to clicking the button. Its click event-handler procedure simply sets the Stopped variable to True and unloads the UserForm.

```
    Private Sub cmdCancel_Click()
        Stopped = True
        Unload Me
    End Sub
```

ON THE WEB

This example, named Random Number Generator.xlsm, is available on the book's website.

Implementing Advanced UserForm Techniques

IN THIS CHAPTER

Using modeless UserForms

Displaying a progress indicator

Creating a wizard—an interactive series of dialog boxes

Creating a function that emulates VBA's MsgBox function

Allowing users to move UserForm controls

Displaying a UserForm with no title bar

Simulating a toolbar with a UserForm

Emulating a task pane with a UserForm

Allowing users to resize a UserForm

Handling multiple controls with a single event handler

Using a dialog box to select a color

Displaying a chart in a UserForm

Creating puzzles and games with UserForms

A Modeless Dialog Box

Most dialog boxes that you encounter are *modal* dialog boxes, which you must dismiss from the screen before the user can do anything with the underlying application. Some dialog boxes, however, are *modeless*, which means that the user can continue to work in the application while the dialog box is displayed.

To display a modeless UserForm, use a statement such as the following:

```
UserForm1.Show vbModeless
```

The keyword vbModeless is a built-in constant that has a value of 0. Therefore, the following statement works identically:

```
UserForm1.Show 0
```

Figure 15.1 shows a modeless dialog box that displays information about the active cell. When the dialog box is displayed, the user is free to move the cell cursor, activate other sheets, and perform other Excel actions. The information displayed in the dialog box changes when the active cell changes.

FIGURE 15.1

This modeless dialog box remains visible while the user continues working.

▲	A	B	C	D	E	F	G	H	I	J	K
1	10/7/2018										
2											
3	Product	Sales	Units	Per Unit	Pct of Total						
4	Widgets	$1,322.50	20	$66.13	89.7%			InfoBox			
5	Shapholytes	$902.44	6	$150.41	204.1%						
6	Hinkers	$322.40	8	$40.30	54.7%						
7	Ralimongers	$32.00	1	$32.00	43.4%						
8	Total:	$2,579.34	35	$73.70							
9											
10											
11											
12											
13											
14											
15											
16											
17											
18											

Cell: D7

Formula:	=B7/C7
Number Format:	$#,##0.00_);($#,##0.00)
Locked:	True

Close

The key to making this UserForm work is determining when to update the information in the dialog box. To do so, the code in the example monitors two workbook events: Sheet-SelectionChange and SheetActivate. These event-handler procedures are located in the code module for the ThisWorkbook object.

 Refer to Chapter 6, "Understanding Excel's Events," for additional information about events.

The event-handler procedures are simple.

```
Private Sub Workbook_SheetSelectionChange _
  (ByVal Sh As Object, ByVal Target As Range)
    UpdateBox
End Sub
```

```
Private Sub Workbook_SheetActivate(ByVal Sh As Object)
    UpdateBox
End Sub
```

The two previous procedures call the UpdateBox procedure, which follows:

```
Sub UpdateBox()
    With UserForm1
'       Make sure a worksheet is active
        If TypeName(ActiveSheet) <> "Worksheet" Then
            .lblFormula.Caption = "N/A"
            .lblNumFormat.Caption = "N/A"
            .lblLocked.Caption = "N/A"
        Else
            .Caption = "Cell: " & _
                ActiveCell.Address(False, False)
'           Formula
            If ActiveCell.HasFormula Then
                .lblFormula.Caption = ActiveCell.Formula
            Else
                .lblFormula.Caption = "(none)"
            End If
'           Number format
            .lblNumFormat.Caption = ActiveCell.NumberFormat
'           Locked
            .lblLocked.Caption = ActiveCell.Locked
        End If
    End With
End Sub
```

The UpdateBox procedure changes the UserForm's caption to show the active cell's address; then it updates the three Label controls (lblFormula, lblNumFormat, and lblLocked).

The following are a few points to help you understand how this example works:

- The UserForm is displayed modeless so that you can still access the worksheet while it's displayed.
- Code at the top of the procedure checks to make sure that the active sheet is a worksheet. If the sheet isn't a worksheet, the Label controls are assigned the text N/A.
- The workbook monitors the active cell by using the SheetSelectionChange event (which is located in the ThisWorkbook code module).
- The information is displayed in Label controls on the UserForm.

Figure 15.2 shows a more sophisticated version of this example. This version displays quite a bit of additional information about the selected cell. The code is too lengthy to display here, but you can view the well-commented code in the example workbook.

15

521

FIGURE 15.2

This modeless UserForm displays various pieces of information about the active cell.

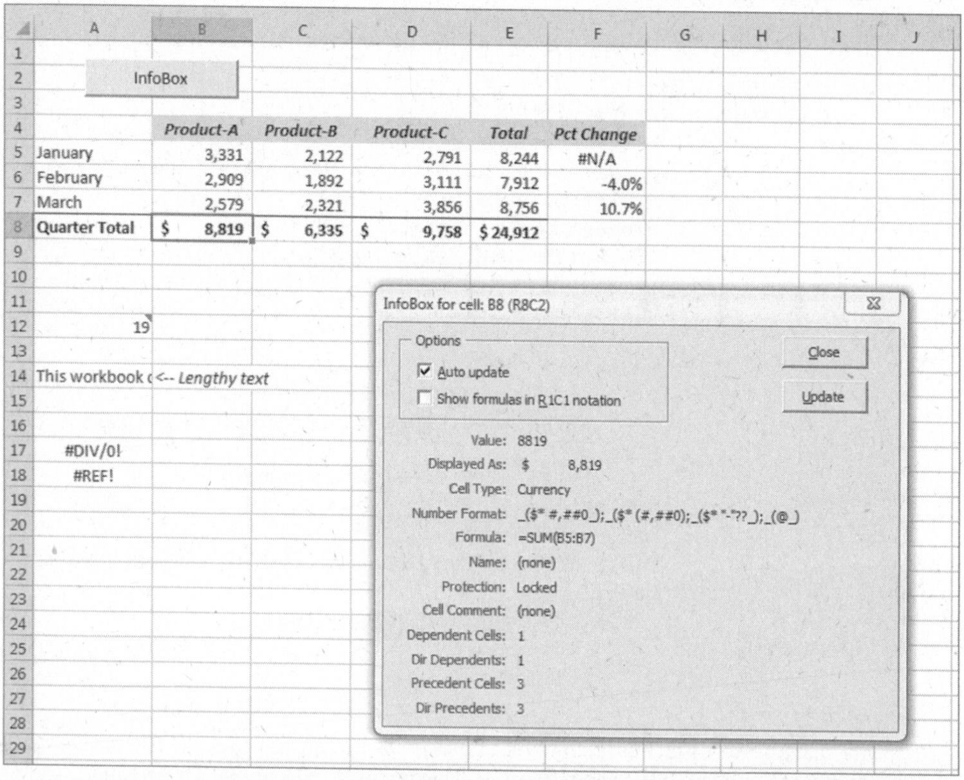

> **ON THE WEB**
>
> This example, named `Modeless Userform2.xlsm`, is available on the book's website.

The following are some key points about this more sophisticated version:

- The UserForm has a check box (Auto Update). When this check box is selected, the UserForm is updated automatically. When Auto Update isn't turned on, the user can use the Update button to refresh the information.
- The workbook uses a class module to monitor two events for all open workbooks: the `SheetSelectionChange` event and the `SheetActivate` event. As a result, the code to display the information about the current cell is executed automatically whenever these events occur in any workbook (assuming that the Auto Update option is in effect). Some actions (such as changing a cell's number format) do not trigger either of these events. Therefore, the UserForm also contains an Update button.

Refer to Chapter 20, "Leveraging Class Modules," for more information about class modules.

- The counts displayed for the cell precedents and dependents fields include cells in the active sheet only because of a limitation of the Precedents and Dependents properties.
- Because the length of the information will vary, VBA code is used to size and vertically space the labels—and also to change the height of the UserForm if necessary.

Modeless UserForms in Excel 2019

The single-document interface, which was introduced in Excel 2013, adds a new wrinkle to modeless UserForms. When a modeless UserForm is displayed, it's associated with the active workbook window. So, if you switch to a different workbook window, the modeless dialog box may not be visible. Even if it *is* visible, it will not work as you intended if a different workbook is active.

If you would like a modeless UserForm to be available in all workbook windows, you need to do some extra work. A workbook (Modeless SDI.xlsm) on the book's website demonstrates this technique.

The example uses a Windows API function to get the Windows handle of the modeless UserForm. The workbook uses a class module to monitor all Window Activate events. When a window is activated, another Windows API function sets the UserForm's parent to the new workbook window. As a result, the UserForm always appears on top of the active window.

Windows API functions vary depending on whether you use 32-bit or 64-bit Excel. See Chapter 21, "Understanding Compatibility Issues," for more information.

Displaying a Progress Indicator

One of the most common requests among Excel developers is to create a progress indicator. A typical *progress indicator* is a graphical thermometer-type display that shows how much of a task is remaining, such as a lengthy macro.

In this section, we describe how to create three types of progress indicators:

- A progress bar on a UserForm that's called by a separate macro (a stand-alone progress indicator)
- A progress bar that's integrated into the same UserForm that initiates the macro
- A progress bar on a UserForm that shows tasks being completed, rather than a graphical bar

Using a progress indicator requires that your code gauge how far along your macro is in completing its given task. How you do this will vary depending on the macro. For example, if your macro writes data to cells and you know the number of cells that will be written to, it's a simple matter to write code that calculates the percent completed. Even if you can't accurately gauge the progress of a macro, it's a good idea to give the user some indication that the macro is still running and Excel hasn't crashed.

15

> **CAUTION**
>
> A progress indicator will slow down your macro a bit because of the extra overhead of having to update it. If speed is absolutely critical, you might prefer not to use one.

Displaying progress in the status bar

A simple way to display the progress of a macro is to use Excel's status bar. The advantage is that a status bar is easy to program. However, the disadvantage is that most users aren't accustomed to watching the status bar and may not see the indicator.

To write text to the status bar, use a statement such as the following:

```
Application.StatusBar = "Please wait..."
```

You can, of course, update the status bar while your macro progresses. For example, if you have a variable named Pct that represents the percent completed, you can write code that periodically executes a statement such as this:

```
Application.StatusBar = "Processing... " & Pct & "% Completed"
```

You can also display information about where the code is. If you're working with a number of cells, you can display each cell's address in the status bar. Or, if you're opening some files, you can display the file name. It doesn't necessarily tell the user how far along the code is, but it does tell them that it's still running.

You can simulate a graphical progress indicator in the status bar by repeating a character as your code progresses. The VBA function Chr$(149) produces a solid dot character, and the String() function will repeat any character a specified number of times. The following statement shows up to 50 dots:

```
Application.StatusBar = String(Int(Pct * 50), Chr$(149))
```

When your macro finishes, you must reset the status bar to its normal state with the following statement:

```
Application.StatusBar = False
```

If you don't reset the status bar, the final message will continue to be displayed.

Creating a stand-alone progress indicator

This section describes how to set up a stand-alone progress indicator—that is, one that isn't initiated by displaying a UserForm—to show the progress of a macro. The macro in the following example clears the worksheet and writes 20,000 random numbers to a range of cells:

```
Sub GenerateRandomNumbers()
'   Inserts random numbers on the active worksheet
    Const RowMax As Long = 500
    Const ColMax As Long = 40
    Dim r As Long, c As Long
    If TypeName(ActiveSheet) <> "Worksheet" Then Exit Sub
    Cells.Clear
```

```
        For r = 1 To RowMax
            For c = 1 To ColMax
                Cells(r, c) = Int(Rnd * 1000)
            Next c
        Next r
    End Sub
```

After you make a few modifications to this macro (described in the next section), the User-Form, shown in Figure 15.3, displays the progress.

FIGURE 15.3

A UserForm displays the progress of a macro.

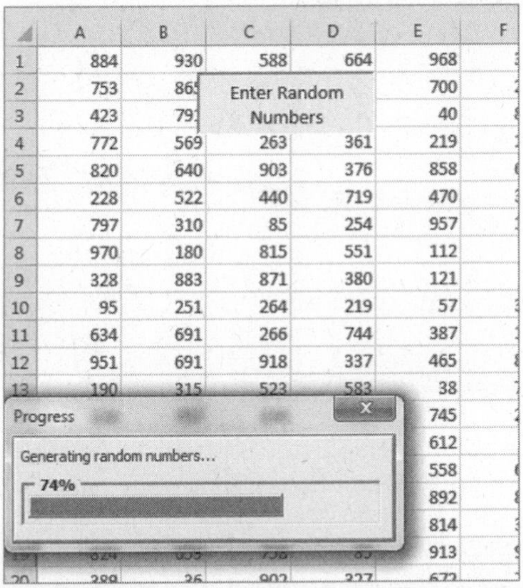

ON THE WEB

This example, named `Progress Indicator1.xlsm`, is available on the book's website.

Building the stand-alone progress indicator UserForm

Follow these steps to create the UserForm that will be used to display the progress of your task:

1. Insert a new UserForm, change its `Name` property to `UProgress`, and change its `Caption` property to `Progress`.

2. Add a `Frame` control, and name it `frmProgress`.

3. Add a `Label` control inside the frame, name it `lblProgress`, remove the label's caption, and make its background color (`BackColor` property) something that will stand out.

The label's size doesn't matter for now.

4. (Optional) Add another label above the frame to describe what's going on.

5. Adjust the UserForm and controls so that they look something like Figure 15.4.

FIGURE 15.4

This UserForm will serve as a progress indicator.

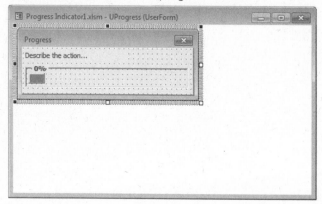

You can, of course, apply any other type of formatting to the controls. For example, the `SpecialEffect` property for the `Frame` control was changed to make it appear sunken.

Creating the code that increments the progress bar

When the form is first called, its `Initialize` event is triggered. The following event procedure sets the color of the progress bar to red and sets its initial width to `0`:

```
Private Sub UserForm_Initialize()
    With Me
        .lblProgress.BackColor = vbRed
        .lblProgress.Width = 0
    End With
End Sub
```

The form's `SetDescription` method is used to add some text above the progress bar to let the user know what's going on. If you chose not to include this label on your form, you don't need to include this procedure.

```
Public Sub SetDescription(Description As String)
    Me.lblDescription.Caption = Description
End Sub
```

The form's `UpdateProgress` method sets the frame's caption and increases the width of the progress label. As the calling procedure progresses, higher percentages are passed into `UpdateProgress`, and the label widens. Note that the `UpdateProgress` method uses the `Repaint` method of the `UserForm` object. Without this statement, the changes to the label would not be updated.

```
Public Sub UpdateProgress(PctDone As Double)
    With Me
        .frmProgress.Caption = Format(PctDone, "0%")
        .lblProgress.Width = PctDone * (.frmProgress.Width - 10)
        .Repaint
    End With
End Sub
```

TIP

An additional accoutrement is to make the progress bar color match the workbook's current theme. To do so, just add this statement to the `ShowUserForm` procedure:

```
.lblProgress.BackColor = ActiveWorkbook.Theme. _
    ThemeColorScheme.Colors(msoThemeAccent1)
```

Calling the stand-alone progress indicator from your code

The modified version of the `GenerateRandomNumbers` procedure (which was presented earlier) follows. Note that additional code shows the form and updates its controls to indicate progress.

```
Sub GenerateRandomNumbers()
'   Inserts random numbers on the active worksheet
    Dim Counter As Long
    Dim r As Long, c As Long
    Dim PctDone As Double
    Const RowMax As Long = 500
    Const ColMax As Long = 40

    If TypeName(ActiveSheet) <> "Worksheet" Then Exit Sub
    ActiveSheet.Cells.Clear
    UProgress.SetDescription "Generating random numbers..."
    UProgress.Show vbModeless
    Counter = 1
    For r = 1 To RowMax
        For c = 1 To ColMax
            ActiveSheet.Cells(r, c) = Int(Rnd * 1000)
            Counter = Counter + 1
        Next c
        PctDone = Counter / (RowMax * ColMax)
        UProgress.UpdateProgress PctDone
```

```
        Next r
        Unload UProgress
    End Sub
```

The `GenerateRandomNumbers` procedure calls the form's `SetDescription` property and shows the form modeless so that the remaining code continues to run. The procedure then executes two loops to write random values to cells, keeping count as it goes. In the outer loop, the procedure calls the form's `UpdateProgress` method, which takes one argument (the `PctDone` variable, which represents the progress of the macro). `PctDone` will contain a value between `0` and `1`. At the end of the procedure, the form is unloaded.

Benefits of a stand-alone progress indicator

You now have a `UserForm` that you can call from any procedure where you want to show progress. Simply show the form modeless, and call the `UpdateProgress` method in the appropriate place in your code. There's nothing in this `UserForm` that ties it to a particular calling procedure. The only requirement is that you send it increasing percentages, and the form takes care of the rest.

In the calling procedure, you need to figure out how to determine the percentage completed and assign it to the `PctDone` variable. In this example, you know how many cells you are going to fill and you only need to keep a count of how many have already been filled to calculate the progress. This calculation will be different for other calling procedures. If your code runs in a loop (as in this example), determining the percentage completed is easy. If your code is not in a loop, you might need to estimate the progress completed at various points in your code.

Showing a progress indicator that's integrated into a UserForm

In the preceding example, you called a progress indicator UserForm that was completely separate from your calling procedure. You may prefer to include the progress indicator directly on the UserForm that's running the code. In this section, we'll show you a couple of options for including a professional-looking progress indicator right on your form.

On the Web

This book's website demonstrates this technique in the `Progress Indicator2.xlsm` file.

As in the previous example, this one enters random numbers into a worksheet. The difference here is that the application contains a UserForm that allows the user to specify the number of rows and columns for the random numbers (see Figure 15.5).

Modifying your UserForm for a progress indicator with a MultiPage control

The first technique will display a progress indicator on another page of a `MultiPage` control. This step assumes you have a UserForm all set up. You'll add a `MultiPage` control. The first page of the `MultiPage` control will contain all of your original UserForm controls. The second page will contain the controls that display the progress indicator. When the macro begins executing, VBA code will change the `Value` property of the `MultiPage` control, effectively to hide the original controls and display the progress indicator.

FIGURE 15.5

The user specifies the number of rows and columns for the random numbers.

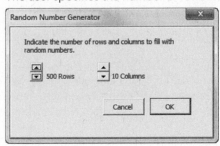

The first step is to add a MultiPage control to your UserForm. Next, move all the existing controls on the UserForm to Page1 of the MultiPage control.

Then activate Page2 of the MultiPage control, and set it up as shown in Figure 15.6. This is essentially the same combination of controls used in the example in the previous section.

FIGURE 15.6

Page2 of the MultiPage control will display the progress indicator.

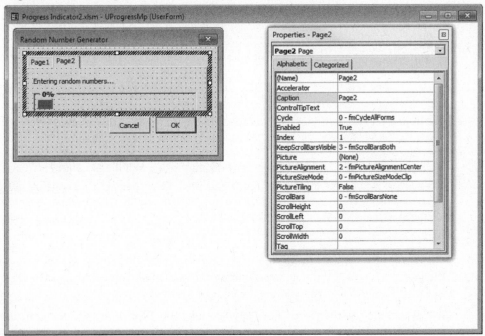

15

Follow these steps to set up the MultiPage control:

1. Add a Frame control, and name it frmProgress.

2. Add a Label control inside the frame, name it lblProgress, remove the label's caption, and make its background color red.

3. (Optional) Add another label to describe what's going on.

4. Next, activate the MultiPage control itself (not a page on the control) and set its Style property to 2 – fmTabStyleNone. (This will hide the tabs.) You'll probably need to adjust the size of the MultiPage control to account for the fact that the tabs aren't displayed.

TIP

The easiest way to select the MultiPage control when the tabs are hidden is to use the drop-down list in the Properties window. To select a particular page, specify a Value for the MultiPage control: 0 for Page1, 1 for Page2, and so on.

Inserting the UpdateProgress procedure for a progress indicator with a MultiPage control

Insert the following procedure in the code module for the UserForm:

```
Sub UpdateProgress(Pct)
    With Me
        .frmProgress.Caption = Format(Pct, "0%")
        .frmProgress.Width = Pct * (.frmProgress.Width - 10)
        .Repaint
    End With
End Sub
```

The UpdateProgress procedure is called from the macro that's executed when the user clicks the OK button and performs the updating of the progress indicator.

Modifying your procedure for a progress indicator with a MultiPage control

You need to modify the procedure that is executed when the user clicks the OK button—the Click event-handler procedure for the button named cmdOK_Click. First, insert the following statement at the top of your procedure:

```
Me.mpProgress.Value = 1
```

This statement activates Page2 of the MultiPage control (the page that displays the progress indicator). If you named your MultiPage control something other than mpProgress, you'll need to adjust the code to use your name.

In the next step, you're pretty much on your own. You need to write code to calculate the percent completed and assign this value to a variable named PctDone. Most likely, this calculation will be performed inside a loop. Then insert the following statement, which will update the progress indicator:

```
UpdateProgress PctDone
```

How a progress indicator with a MultiPage control works

Using a MultiPage control as a progress indicator is straightforward, and, as you've seen, it involves only one UserForm. The code switches pages of the MultiPage control and converts your normal dialog box into a progress indicator. Because the MultiPage tabs are hidden, it doesn't even resemble a MultiPage control.

Showing a progress indicator without using a MultiPage control

The second technique is simpler because it doesn't use a MultiPage control. Rather, the progress indicator is stored at the bottom of the UserForm, but the UserForm's height is reduced so that the progress indicator controls aren't visible. When it's time to display the progress indicator, the UserForm's height is increased, which makes the progress indicator visible.

Figure 15.7 shows the UserForm in the VBE.

FIGURE 15.7

The progress indicator will be hidden by reducing the height of the UserForm.

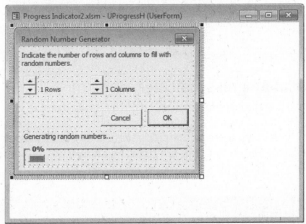

The Height property of the UserForm is 177. However, before the UserForm is displayed, the VBA code changes the Height property to 130 (which means that the progress indicator controls aren't visible to the user). When the user clicks OK, the VBA code changes the Height property to 177 with the following statement:

```
Me.Height = 177
```

Figure 15.8 shows the UserForm with the progress indicator section unhidden.

15

FIGURE 15.8

The progress indicator in action

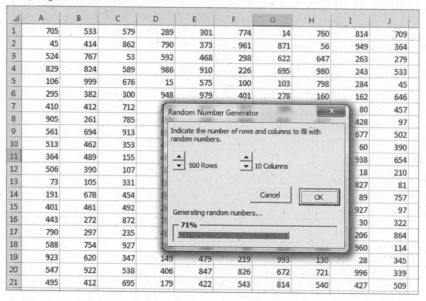

Creating a nongraphical progress indicator

The preceding examples showed graphical progress indicators by increasing the width of a label. If you have a smaller number of steps, you may prefer to show a description of the steps as they're completed. The following procedure processes a small number of text files in a folder. Instead of showing a progress bar, you can list the names of the files as they are processed.

```
Sub ProcessFiles()

    Dim sFile As String, lFile As Long
    Const sPATH As String = "C:\Test Files\"

    sFile = Dir(sPATH & "*.txt")
    Do While Len(sFile) > 0
        ImportFile sFile
        sFile = Dir
    Loop

End Sub
```

The procedure finds all of the text files in a directory and calls another procedure that imports them. What happens to the file isn't important, merely that there are a finite number of steps to be completed.

Creating the UserForm to display the steps

Figure 15.9 shows the simple UserForm in the VBE. It has only two controls: a label to describe what's happening and a list box to list the steps.

FIGURE 15.9

The steps are listed in a ListBox control.

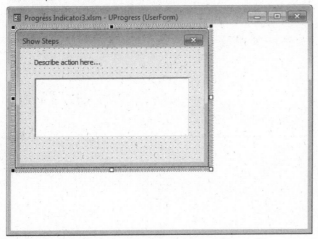

The code behind the UserForm is equally simple. You change the descriptive label by calling the SetDescription procedure. As the calling procedure progresses, you call the AddStep procedure to add an item to the ListBox. The TopIndex property of the List-Box object keeps the most recent steps visible if the ListBox isn't tall enough.

```
Public Sub AddStep(sStep As String)
    With Me.lbxSteps
        .AddItem sStep
        .TopIndex = Application.Max(.ListCount, .ListCount - 6)
    End With
    Me.Repaint
End Sub
```

Modifying the calling procedure to use the progress indicator

The ProcessFiles procedure shown next has been modified to use the progress indicator as it processes files. First, the UserForm's Caption property is set to indicate what process is occurring. Next, the SetDescription method is called so that the user knows what's appearing in the ListBox control. The Show method includes the vbModeless parameter that allows the calling procedure to continue executing. Inside the loop, the `AddStep` method adds filenames to indicate progress. Figure 15.10 shows the UserForm in action.

```
Sub ProcessFiles()
    Dim sFile As String, lFile As Long
    Const sPATH As String = "C:\Text Files\"

    sFile = Dir(sPATH & "*.txt")
    UProgress.Caption = "Processing File Progress"
    UProgress.SetDescription "Completed files..."
    UProgress.Show vbModeless

    Do While Len(sFile) > 0
        ImportFile sFile
        UProgress.AddStep sPATH & sFile
        sFile = Dir
    Loop
    Unload UProgress
End Sub
```

FIGURE 15.10

Files are added to the list to show progress.

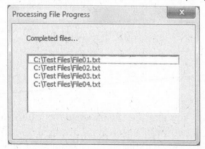

This progress indicator is similar to the stand-alone progress indicator shown in a previous section. It doesn't care about what are the steps to your procedure. You can process files, fill ranges on a worksheet, or perform any number of steps. By changing the `Caption` property and calling the `SetDescription` method, you can customize this progress indicator for whatever process you're completing.

Creating Wizards

Many applications incorporate wizards to guide users through an operation. Excel's Text Import Wizard is a good example. A *wizard* is essentially a series of dialog boxes that solicit information from the user. Sometimes, the user's choices in earlier dialog boxes influence the contents of later dialog boxes. In most wizards, the user is free to go forward or backward through the dialog box sequence or to click the Finish button to accept all defaults.

You can create wizards by using VBA and a series of UserForms. However, it's more efficient to create a wizard using a single UserForm and a `MultiPage` control with the tabs hidden.

Figure 15.11 shows an example of a simple four-step wizard, which consists of a single User-Form that contains a `MultiPage` control. Each step of the wizard displays a different page in the `MultiPage` control.

FIGURE 15.11

This four-step wizard uses a MultiPage control.

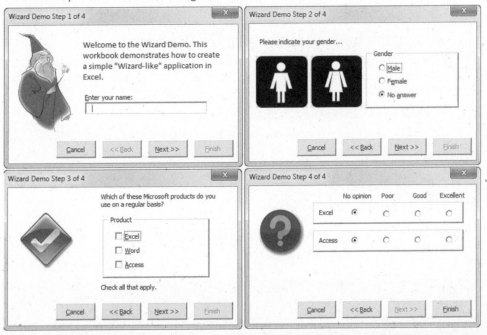

ON THE WEB

The wizard example in this section is available on the book's website in a file named `Wizard Demo.xlsm`.

The sections that follow describe how we created the sample wizard.

Setting up the MultiPage control for the wizard

Start with a new UserForm and add a `MultiPage` control. By default, this control contains two pages. Right-click the MultiPage tab and insert enough new pages to handle your wizard (one page for each wizard step). This example is a four-step wizard, so the

15

MultiPage control has four pages. The captions of the MultiPage tabs are irrelevant because they won't be seen. The MultiPage control's Style property will eventually be set to 2 - fmTabStyleNone.

> **TIP**
>
> While working on the UserForm, you'll want to keep the MultiPage tabs visible to make it easier to access various pages.

Next, add the desired controls to each page of the MultiPage control. These controls will, of course, vary depending on your application. You may need to resize the MultiPage control while you work to have room for the controls.

Adding the buttons to the wizard's UserForm

Now add the buttons that control the progress of the wizard. These buttons are placed outside the MultiPage control because they're used while any of the pages are displayed. Most wizards have four buttons.

Cancel Cancels the wizard and performs no action.

Back Returns to the previous step. During step 1 of the wizard, this button should be disabled.

Next Advances to the next step. During the last wizard step, this button should be disabled.

Finish Finishes the wizard.

In the example, these command buttons are named cmdCancel, cmdBack, cmdNext, and cmdFinish.

> **NOTE**
>
> In some cases, the user is allowed to click the Finish button at any time and accept the defaults for items that were skipped. In other cases, the wizard requires a user response for some items, so the Finish button is disabled until all required input is made. This example requires an entry in the text box in step 1.

Programming the wizard's buttons

Each of the four wizard buttons requires a procedure to handle its Click event. The event handler for the cmdCancel control follows:

```
Private Sub cmdCancel_Click()
    Dim Msg As String
    Dim Ans As Long
    Msg = "Cancel the wizard?"
```

```
      Ans = MsgBox(Msg, vbQuestion + vbYesNo, APPNAME)
      If Ans = vbYes Then Unload Me
   End Sub
```

This procedure uses a MsgBox function (see Figure 15.12) to verify that the user really wants to exit. If the user clicks the Yes button, the UserForm is unloaded with no action taken. This type of verification, of course, is optional.

FIGURE 15.12

Clicking the Cancel button displays a confirmation message box.

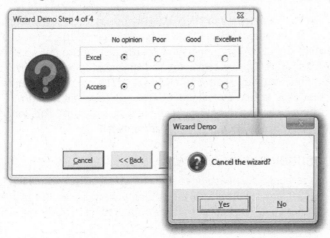

The event-handler procedures for the Back and Next buttons follow:

```
Private Sub cmdBack_Click()
    Me.mpgWizard.Value = Me.mpgWizard.Value - 1
    UpdateControls
End Sub

Private Sub cmdNext_Click()
    Me.mpgWizard.Value = Me.mpgWizard.Value + 1
    UpdateControls
End Sub
```

These two procedures are simple. They change the Value property of the MultiPage control and then call another procedure named UpdateControls (which follows).

The UpdateControls procedure is responsible for enabling and disabling the cmdBack and cmdNext controls.

```
Sub UpdateControls()
'    Enable back if not on page 1
    Me.cmdBack.Enabled = Me.mpgWizard.Value > 0
```

15

```
'     Enable next if not on the last page
      Me.cmdNext.Enabled = Me.mpgWizard.Value < Me.mpgWizard.Pages.Count - 1

'     Update the caption
      Me.Caption = APPNAME & " Step " _
        & Me.mpgWizard.Value + 1 & " of " _
        & Me.mpgWizard.Pages.Count

'     the Name field is required
      Me.cmdFinish.Enabled = Len(Me.tbxName.Text) > 0
End Sub
```

The procedure checks the `Value` property of the `MultiPage` control to see what page is showing. If the first page is showing, the `Enabled` property of `cmdBack` is set to `False`. If the last page is showing, the `Enabled` property of `cmdNext` is set to `False`. Next, the procedure changes the UserForm's caption to display the current step and the total number of steps. `APPNAME` is a public constant, defined in `Module1`. The procedure then examines the name field on the first page (a text box named `tbxName`). This field is required, so if it's empty, the user can't click the Finish button. If the text box is empty (the length of its contents is zero), `cmdFinish` is disabled; otherwise, it's enabled.

Programming dependencies in a wizard

In some wizards, a user's response on a particular step can affect what's displayed in a subsequent step. In this example, the user indicates which products they use in step 3 and then rate those products in step 4. The option buttons for a product's rating are visible only if the user has indicated a particular product.

Programmatically, you accomplish this task by monitoring the `MultiPage` control's `Change` event. Whenever the value of the `MultiPage` control is changed (by clicking the Back button or the Next button), the `mpgWizard_Change` procedure is executed. If the `MultiPage` control is on the last tab (step 4), the procedure examines the values of the `CheckBox` controls in step 3 and makes the appropriate adjustments in step 4.

In this example, the code uses two arrays of controls—one for the product `CheckBox` controls (step 3) and one for the `Frame` controls (step 4). The code uses a `For-Next` loop to hide the frames for the products that aren't used and then adjusts their vertical positioning. If none of the check boxes in step 3 are checked, everything in step 4 is hidden except a label that displays `Click Finish to exit` (if a name is entered in step 1) or `A name is required in Step 1` (if a name isn't entered in step 1). The `mpgWizard_Change` procedure follows:

```
Private Sub mpgWizard_Change()
    Dim TopPos As Long
    Dim FSpace As Long
    Dim AtLeastOne As Boolean
    Dim i As Long
```

```vba
    '    Set up the Ratings page?
    If Me.mpgWizard.Value = 3 Then
        '    Create an array of CheckBox controls
        Dim ProdCB(1 To 3) As MSForms.CheckBox
        Set ProdCB(1) = Me.chkExcel
        Set ProdCB(2) = Me.chkWord
        Set ProdCB(3) = Me.chkAccess

        '    Create an array of Frame controls
        Dim ProdFrame(1 To 3) As MSForms.Frame
        Set ProdFrame(1) = Me.frmExcel
        Set ProdFrame(2) = Me.frmWord
        Set ProdFrame(3) = Me.frmAccess

        TopPos = 22
        FSpace = 8
        AtLeastOne = False

        '    Loop through all products
        For i = 1 To 3
            If ProdCB(i).Value Then
                ProdFrame(i).Visible = True
                ProdFrame(i).Top = TopPos
                TopPos = TopPos + ProdFrame(i).Height + FSpace
                AtLeastOne = True
            Else
                ProdFrame(i).Visible = False
            End If
        Next i

        '    Uses no products?
        If AtLeastOne Then
            Me.lblHeadings.Visible = True
            Me.imgRating.Visible = True
            Me.lblFinishMsg.Visible = False
        Else
            Me.lblHeadings.Visible = False
            Me.imgRating.Visible = False
            Me.lblFinishMsg.Visible = True
            If Len(Me.tbxName.Text) = 0 Then
                Me.lblFinishMsg.Caption = _
                    "A name is required in Step 1."
            Else
                Me.lblFinishMsg.Caption = _
                    "Click Finish to exit."
            End If
        End If
    End If
End Sub
```

15

Performing the task with the wizard

When the user clicks the Finish button, the wizard performs its task: transferring the information from the UserForm to the next empty row in the worksheet. This procedure, named cmdFinish_Click, is straightforward. It starts by determining the next empty worksheet row and assigns this value to a variable (r). The remainder of the procedure simply translates the values of the controls and enters data into the worksheet.

```
Private Sub cmdFinish_Click()
    Dim r As Long

    r = Application.WorksheetFunction. _
      CountA(Range("A:A")) + 1

'    Insert the name
    Cells(r, 1) = Me.tbxName.Text

'    Insert the gender
    Select Case True
        Case Me.optMale.Value: Cells(r, 2) = "Male"
        Case Me.optFemale: Cells(r, 2) = "Female"
        Case Me.optNoAnswer: Cells(r, 2) = "Unknown"
    End Select

'    Insert usage
    Cells(r, 3) = Me.chkExcel.Value
    Cells(r, 4) = Me.chkWord.Value
    Cells(r, 5) = Me.chkAccess.Value

'    Insert ratings
    If Me.optExcelNo.Value Then Cells(r, 6) = ""
    If Me.optExcelPoor.Value Then Cells(r, 6) = 0
    If Me.optExcelGood.Value Then Cells(r, 6) = 1
    If Me.optExcelExc.Value Then Cells(r, 6) = 2
    If Me.optWordNo.Value Then Cells(r, 7) = ""
    If Me.optWordPoor.Value Then Cells(r, 7) = 0
    If Me.optWordGood.Value Then Cells(r, 7) = 1
    If Me.optWordExc.Value Then Cells(r, 7) = 2
    If Me.optAccessNo.Value Then Cells(r, 8) = ""
    If Me.optAccessPoor.Value Then Cells(r, 8) = 0
    If Me.optAccessGood.Value Then Cells(r, 8) = 1
    If Me.optAccessExc.Value Then Cells(r, 8) = 2

    Unload Me
End Sub
```

After you test your wizard and everything is working properly, you can set the MultiPage control's Style property to 2 - fmTabStyleNone to hide the tabs.

Emulating the MsgBox Function

The VBA MsgBox function (discussed in Chapter 12, "Leveraging Custom Dialog Boxes") is a bit unusual because, unlike most functions, it displays a dialog box. But, similar to other functions, it also returns a value: an integer that represents which button the user clicked.

This section describes a custom function that emulates the VBA MsgBox function. On first thought, creating such a function might seem easy. Think again! The MsgBox function is extraordinarily versatile because of the arguments that it accepts. Consequently, creating a function to emulate MsgBox is no small feat.

NOTE

The point of this exercise is not to create an alternative messaging function. Rather, it's to demonstrate how to develop a complex function that also incorporates a UserForm. However, some people might like the idea of being able to customize their messages. If so, you'll find that this function is easy to customize. For example, you can change the font, colors, button text, and so on.

The pseudo-MsgBox function is named MyMsgBox. The emulation is close but not perfect. The MyMsgBox function has the following limitations:

- It does not support the Helpfile argument (which adds a Help button that, when clicked, opens a help file).
- It does not support the Context argument (which specifies the context ID for the help file).
- It does not support the *system modal* option, which puts everything in Windows on hold until you respond to the dialog box.
- It does not play a sound when it is called.

The syntax for MyMsgBox is as follows:

```
MyMsgBox(prompt[, buttons] [, title])
```

This syntax is the same as the MsgBox syntax except that it doesn't use the last two optional arguments (Helpfile and Context). MyMsgBox also uses the same predefined constants as MsgBox: vbOKOnly, vbQuestion, vbDefaultButton1, and so on.

NOTE

If you're not familiar with the VBA MsgBox function, consult the Help system to become acquainted with its arguments.

MsgBox emulation: MyMsgBox code

The MyMsgBox function uses a UserForm named UMsgBox. The function itself, which follows, sets up the UserForm according to the arguments passed to the function. It calls several other procedures to make many of the settings.

```
Function MyMsgBox(ByVal Prompt As String, _
    Optional ByVal Buttons As Long, _
    Optional ByVal Title As String) As Long
'    Emulates VBA's MsgBox function
'    Does not support the HelpFile or Context arguments
    With UMsgBox
'       Do the Caption
        If Len(Title) > 0 Then .Caption = Title _
            Else .Caption = Application.Name
        SetImage Buttons
        SetPrompt Prompt
        SetButtons Buttons
        .Height = .cmdLeft.Top + 64
        SetDefaultButton Buttons
        .Show
    End With
    MyMsgBox = UMsgBox.UserClick
End Function
```

On the Web

The complete code for the MyMsgBox function is too lengthy to list here, but it's available in a workbook named Msgbox Emulation.xlsm, available on the book's website. The workbook is set up so that you can easily try various options.

Figure 15.13 shows MyMsgBox in use. It looks similar to the VBA message box, but we used a different font for the message text and also used some different icons.

FIGURE 15.13

The result of the MsgBox emulation function

If you use a multiple monitor system, the position of the displayed UserForm may not be centered in Excel's window. To solve that problem, use the following code to display UMsgBox:

```
With UMsgBox
    .StartUpPosition = 0
    .Left = Application.Left + (0.5 * Application.Width) -
(0.5 * .Width)
    .Top = Application.Top + (0.5 * Application.Height) - (0.5
* .Height)
    .Show
End With
```

Here's the code to execute the function:

```
Prompt = "You have chosen to save this workbook" & vbCrLf
Prompt = Prompt & "on a drive that is not available to"  & vbCrLf
Prompt = Prompt & "all employees." & vbCrLf & vbCrLf
Prompt = Prompt & "OK to continue?"
Buttons = vbQuestion + vbYesNo
Title = "Network Location Notice"
Ans = MyMsgBox(Prompt, Buttons, Title)
```

How the MyMsgBox function works

The MyMsgBox function examines the arguments and does the following:

- Determines which, if any, image to display (and hides the others)
- Determines which button(s) to display (and hides the others)
- Determines which button is the default button
- Centers the buttons in the dialog box
- Determines the captions for the command buttons
- Determines the position of the text within the dialog box
- Determines the width and height of the dialog box (by using an API function call to get the video resolution)
- Displays the UserForm

Interpreting the second argument (buttons) is challenging. This argument can consist of a number of constants added together. For example, the second argument can be something like this:

```
VbYesNoCancel + VbQuestion + VbDefaultButton3
```

This argument creates a three-button MsgBox (with Yes, No, and Cancel buttons), displays the question mark icon, and makes the third button the default button. The actual argument is 547 (3 + 32 + 512).

To determine what to display on the UserForm, the function uses a technique called Bitwise And. Each of the three arguments can be one of a series of numbers, and those numbers don't overlap with the other arguments. The six types of buttons that you can display are numbered 0 to 5. If you add up all of the numbers 0 to 5, you get 15. The lowest value of the possible icon values is 16, which is one more than all of the buttons put together.

15

One of the procedures called by `MyMsgBox` is named `SetDefaultButtons` and is shown next. It uses `Bitwise And` by comparing the `Buttons` argument to a constant, such as `vbDefaultButton3`. If the result of the `Bitwise And` is equal to `vbDefaultButton3`, then you can be sure that `vbDefaultButton3` was one of the choices that made up the `Buttons` argument, regardless of any other choices included in that argument.

```
Private Sub SetDefaultButton(Buttons As Long)
    With UMsgBox
        Select Case True
            Case (Buttons And vbDefaultButton4) = vbDefaultButton4
                .cmdLeft.Default = True
                .cmdLeft.TabIndex = 0
            Case (Buttons And vbDefaultButton3) = vbDefaultButton3
                .cmdRight.Default = True
                .cmdRight.TabIndex = 0
            Case (Buttons And vbDefaultButton2) = vbDefaultButton2
                .cmdMiddle.Default = True
                .cmdMiddle.TabIndex = 0
            Case Else
                .cmdLeft.Default = True
                .cmdLeft.TabIndex = 0
        End Select
    End With
End Sub
```

The UserForm (shown in Figure 15.14) contains four `Label` controls. Each of these `Label` controls has an image, which was pasted into the `Picture` property. The UserForm also has three `CommandButton` controls and a `TextBox` control.

FIGURE 15.14

The UserForm for the MyMsgBox function

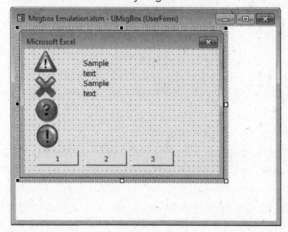

Three additional event-handler procedures are included (one for each CommandButton). These routines determine which button was clicked and return a value for the function by setting a value for the UserClick variable.

Using the MyMsgBox function

To use this function in your own project, export the MyMsgBoxMod module and the UMsgBox UserForm. Then import these two files into your project. You can then use the MyMsgBox function in your code just as you'd use the MsgBox function.

A UserForm with Movable Controls

The UserForm shown in Figure 15.15 contains three Image controls. The user can use the mouse to drag these images around in the dialog box. The example in this section will help you understand mouse-related events.

FIGURE 15.15

You can drag and rearrange the three Image controls by using the mouse.

15

Each `Image` control has two associated event procedures: `MouseDown` and `MouseMove`. The event procedures for the `Image1` control are shown here. (The others are identical except for the control names.)

```
Private Sub Image1_MouseDown(ByVal Button As Integer, _
    ByVal Shift As Integer, ByVal X As Single, ByVal Y As Single)
'   Starting position when button is pressed
    OldX = X
    OldY = Y
    Image1.ZOrder 0
End Sub

Private Sub Image1_MouseMove(ByVal Button As Integer, _
    ByVal Shift As Integer, ByVal X As Single, ByVal Y As Single)
'   Move the image
    If Button = 1 Then
        Image1.Left = Image1.Left + (X - OldX)
        Image1.Top = Image1.Top + (Y - OldY)
    End If
End Sub
```

When the mouse button is pressed, the `MouseDown` event occurs, and the X and Y positions of the mouse pointer are stored. Two public variables are used to keep track of the original position of the controls: `OldX` and `OldY`. This procedure also sets the `ZOrder` property to zero, which puts the image on top of the others.

When the mouse is being moved, the `MouseMove` event occurs repeatedly. The event procedure checks the mouse button. If the `Button` argument is 1, it means that the left mouse button is depressed. If so, then the `Image` control is shifted relative to its old position.

Also note that the mouse pointer changes when it's over an image. That's because the `MousePointer` property is set to 15 - `fmMousePointerSizeAll`, a mouse pointer style that's commonly used to indicate that an item can be dragged.

A UserForm with No Title Bar

Excel provides no direct way to display a UserForm without its title bar. But this feat is possible with the help of a few API functions. Figure 15.16 shows a UserForm with no title bar.

FIGURE 15.16

This UserForm lacks a title bar.

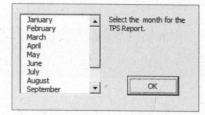

Figure 15.17 shows another example of a UserForm without a title bar. This dialog box contains an `Image` control and a `CommandButton` control.

FIGURE 15.17

Another UserForm without a title bar

Displaying a UserForm without a title bar requires four windows API functions: `GetWindowLong`, `SetWindowLong`, `DrawMenuBar`, and `FindWindowA` (see the example file for the function declarations). The `UserForm_Initialize` procedure calls these functions:

```
Private Sub UserForm_Initialize()
    Dim lngWindow As Long, lFrmHdl As Long
    lFrmHdl = FindWindowA(vbNullString, Me.Caption)
    lngWindow = GetWindowLong(lFrmHdl, GWL_STYLE)
    lngWindow = lngWindow And (Not WS_CAPTION)
    Call SetWindowLong(lFrmHdl, GWL_STYLE, lngWindow)
    Call DrawMenuBar(lFrmHdl)
End Sub
```

One problem is that the user has no way to reposition a dialog box without a title bar. The solution is to use the `MouseDown` and `MouseMove` events, as described in the preceding section.

15

NOTE

Because the `FindWindowA` function uses the UserForm's caption, this technique won't work if the `Caption` property is set to an empty string.

Simulating a Toolbar with a UserForm

This section describes how to create an alternative to the Ribbon: a modeless UserForm that simulates a floating toolbar. Figure 15.18 shows a UserForm that you can use to allow your users to interact with your application. It uses Windows API calls to make the title bar a bit shorter than normal, and it also displays the UserForm with square (rather than rounded) corners. The Close button is also smaller.

FIGURE 15.18

A UserForm set up to function as a toolbar

G	H	I	J	K	L	M	N
123	237	53	79	320	21	338	296
134	339	313	291	188	275	273	256
276	237	262	227	216	293	278	126
186	232	65	247	64	92	36	145
90	8	256	209	220	347	119	173
239	317	294	334	59	341	54	11
56	51	312	106	263	37	209	35
201	83	348	101	92	208	236	342
310	344					20	193
342	149					329	103
267	27					173	78
315	182					257	58
323	52	294	28				212
342	150	120	167	184	23	263	237
115	251	246	209	333	266	98	156
99	195	100	86	270	92	193	14
249	153	181	226	123	241	268	311
301	214	346	315	114	62	29	193
265	295	45	241	172	263	272	219
165	132	238	246	19	287	210	283
219	263	118	266	299	330	157	84
94	180	7	119	195	13	52	191

UserForm Posing As A Toolbar

Click here to exceute Macro 5

ON THE WEB

This example, named `Simulated Toolbar.xlm`, is available on the book's website.

The UserForm contains eight `Image` controls, and each executes a macro. Figure 15.19 shows the UserForm in the VBE. Note the following:

- The controls aren't aligned.
- The images displayed are not necessarily the final images.

- The UserForm isn't the final size.
- The title bar is the standard size.

FIGURE 15.19

The UserForm that simulates a toolbar

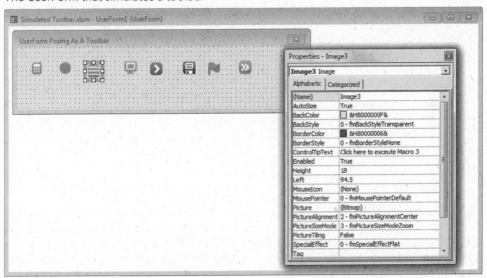

The VBA code takes care of the cosmetic details, including borrowing images from Excel's Ribbon. For example, this statement assigns an image to the Image1 control:

```
Image1.Picture = Application.CommandBars. _
    GetImageMso("ReviewAcceptChange", 32, 32)
```

See Chapter 17, "Working with the Ribbon," for more information about accessing images from the Ribbon.

The code also aligns the controls and adjusts the size of the UserForm to eliminate wasted space. In addition, the code uses Windows API functions to make the UserForm's title bar smaller—just like a real toolbar. To make the UserForm look even more like a toolbar, the ControlTipText property of each Image control has been set so that a toolbar-like tooltip displays when the mouse cursor is hovered over the control.

If you open the example file, you'll also notice that the images increase in size slightly when the mouse cursor is hovered over them. That's because each Image control has an

15

associated `MouseMove` event handler that changes the size. Here's the `MouseMove` event handler procedure for `Image1` (the others are identical):

```
Private Sub Image1_MouseMove(ByVal Button As Integer, _
    ByVal Shift As Integer, ByVal X As Single, ByVal Y As Single)
    Call NormalSize
    Image1.Width = 26
    Image1.Height = 26
End Sub
```

This procedure calls the `NormalSize` procedure, which returns each image to its normal size:

```
Private Sub NormalSize()
'    Make all controls normal size
    Dim ctl As Control
    For Each ctl In Controls
        ctl.Width = 24
        ctl.Height = 24
    Next ctl
End Sub
```

The net effect is that the user gets some visual feedback when the mouse cursor moves over a control—just like a real toolbar. The toolbar simulation only goes so far, however. You can't resize the UserForm (for example, to make the images display vertically rather than horizontally). And, of course, you can't dock the pseudo-toolbar to one of the Excel window borders.

Emulating a Task Pane with a UserForm

The UserForm in Figure 15.20 is an attempt to emulate the look of a built-in task pane. The example is the same as the modeless UserForm example at the beginning of the chapter (refer to Figure 15.2). You can move the UserForm by dragging its title (the same way you move a task pane). The UserForm also has an X (Close) button in the upper-right corner. And, like a task pane, it displays a vertical scrollbar only when needed.

The task pane shown in the figure has a white background. The color of the task pane background varies, depending on the Office theme (specified in the General tab of the Excel Options dialog box). The background of the control is transparent, and the following code sets the background color:

```
Me.BackColor = RGB(255, 255, 255)
Frame1.BackColor = RGB(255, 255, 255)
Frame2.BackColor = RGB(255, 255, 255)
```

Frame controls cannot have a transparent background, so the background color of the two `Frame` controls had to be set separately.

FIGURE 15.20

A UserForm designed to look like a task pane

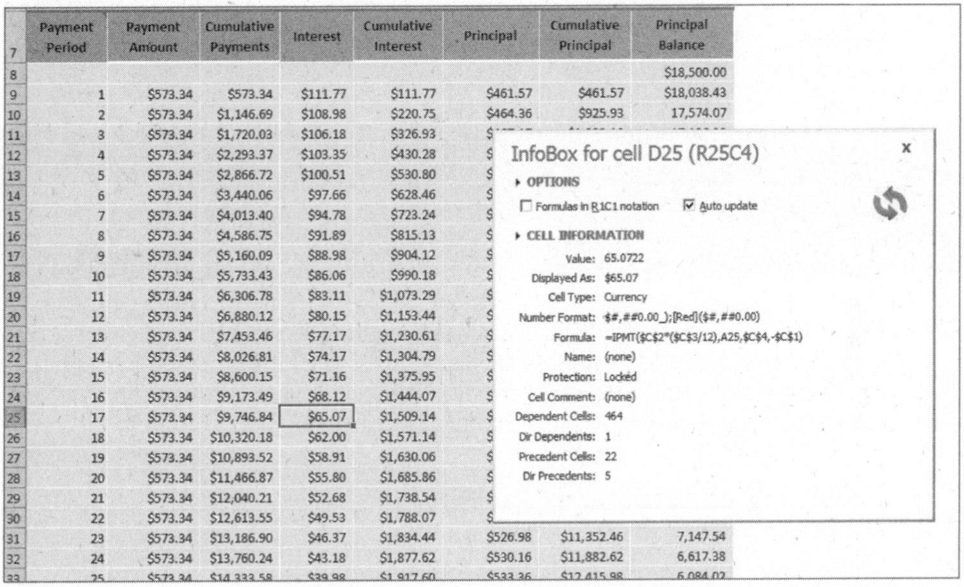

To create a UserForm that has a background color that matches the Light Gray theme, use this expression:

```
RGB(240, 240, 240)
```

To emulate the Dark Gray theme, use this expression:

```
RGB(222, 222, 222)
```

The UserForm has the basic look of a task pane, but it falls short in terms of behavior. For example, the sections cannot be collapsed, and it's not possible to dock the UserForm to the side of the screen. Also, it's not resizable by the user—but it could be (see the next section).

ON THE WEB

This example, named `Emulate Task Pane.xlsm`, is available on the book's website.

A Resizable UserForm

Excel uses several resizable dialog boxes. For example, you can resize the Name Manager dialog box by clicking and dragging the bottom-right corner.

15

If you'd like to create a resizable UserForm, you'll eventually discover that there's no direct way to do it. One solution is to resort to Windows API calls. That method works, but it's complicated to set up and doesn't generate any events, so your code can't respond when the UserForm is resized. In this section, we present a much simpler technique for creating a user-resizable UserForm.

Figure 15.21 shows the UserForm that's described in this section. It contains a `ListBox` control that displays data from a worksheet. The scrollbars on the list box indicate that the list box contains information that doesn't fit. In addition, a (perhaps) familiar sizing control appears in the bottom-right corner of the dialog box.

FIGURE 15.21

This UserForm is resizable.

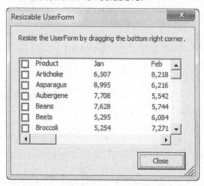

Figure 15.22 shows the same UserForm after the user resized it. The size of the list box is also increased, and the Close button remains in the same relative position. You can stretch this UserForm to the limits of your monitor.

The sizing control at the bottom-right corner is actually a `Label` control that displays a single character: the letter *o* (character 111) from the Marlett font, character set 2. This control (named `objResizer`) is added to the UserForm in the `UserForm_Initialize` procedure at run-time.

FIGURE 15.22

The UserForm after it was increased

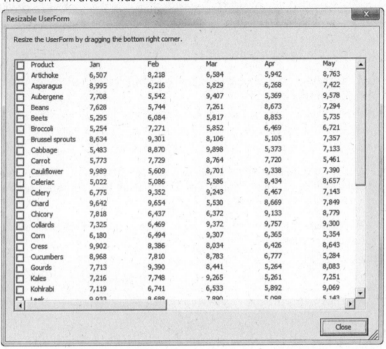

```
Private Sub UserForm_Initialize()
'     Add a resizing control to bottom right corner of UserForm
      Set objResizer = Me.Controls.Add("Forms.label.1", MResizer, True)
      With objResizer
          .Caption = Chr(111)
          .Font.Name = "Marlett"
          .Font.Charset = 2
          .Font.Size = 14
          .BackStyle = fmBackStyleTransparent
          .AutoSize = True
          .ForeColor = RGB(100, 100, 100)
          .MousePointer = fmMousePointerSizeNWSE
          .ZOrder
          .Top = Me.InsideHeight - .Height
          .Left = Me.InsideWidth - .Width
      End With
End Sub
```

15

> **NOTE**
>
> Although the `Label` control is added at run-time, the event-handler code for the object is contained in the module. Including code for an object that doesn't exist is not a problem.

This technique relies on these facts:

- The user can move a control on a UserForm (see "A UserForm with Movable Controls," earlier in this chapter).
- Events exist that can identify mouse movements and pointer coordinates. Specifically, these events are `MouseDown` and `MouseMove`.
- VBA code can change the size of a UserForm at run-time, but a user cannot.

Do a bit of creative thinking about these facts, and you see that it's possible to translate the user's movement of a `Label` control into information that you can use to resize a UserForm.

When the user clicks the `objResizer` `Label` object, the `objResizer_MouseDown` event-handler procedure is executed.

```
Private Sub objResizer_MouseDown(ByVal Button As Integer, _
    ByVal Shift As Integer, ByVal X As Single, ByVal Y As Single)
    If Button = 1 Then
        LeftResizePos = X
        TopResizePos = Y
    End If
End Sub
```

This procedure executes only if the left mouse button is pressed (that is, the `Button` argument is 1) and the cursor is on the `objResizer` label. The X and Y mouse coordinates at the time of the button click are stored in module-level variables: `LeftResizePos` and `TopResizePos`.

Subsequent mouse movements fire the `MouseMove` event, and the `objResizer_MouseMove` event handler kicks into action. Here's an initial take on this procedure:

```
Private Sub objResizer_MouseMove(ByVal Button As Integer, _
    ByVal Shift As Integer, ByVal X As Single, ByVal Y As Single)
    If Button = 1 Then
        With objResizer
            .Move .Left + X - LeftResizePos, .Top + Y - TopResizePos
            Me.Width = Me.Width + X - LeftResizePos
            Me.Height = Me.Height + Y - TopResizePos
            .Left = Me.InsideWidth - .Width
            .Top = Me.InsideHeight - .Height
        End With
    End If
End Sub
```

If you study the code, you'll see that the UserForm's Width and Height properties are adjusted based on the movement of the objResizer Label control. Figure 15.23 shows how the UserForm looks after the user moves the Label control down and to the right.

FIGURE 15.23

The VBA code converts Label control movements into new Width and Height properties for the UserForm.

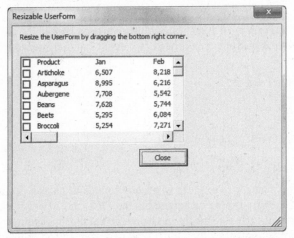

The problem, of course, is that the other controls in the UserForm don't respond to the UserForm's new size. The list box should be expanded, and the command button should be relocated so that it remains in the lower-right corner.

More VBA code is needed to adjust the controls in the UserForm when the UserForm size is changed. The location for this new code is in the objResizer_MouseMove event-handler procedure. The statements that follow do the job:

```
'   Adjust the ListBox
    On Error Resume Next
    With ListBox1
        .Width = Me.Width - 37
        .Height = Me.Height - 100
    End With
    On Error GoTo 0

'   Adjust the Close Button
    With CloseButton
        .Left = Me.Width - 85
        .Top = Me.Height - 54
    End With
```

These two controls are adjusted relative to the UserForm's size (the Me keyword is used to refer to the UserForm). After adding this new code, the dialog box works like a charm. The user can make the dialog box as large as needed, and the controls correspondingly adjust.

It should be clear that the most challenging part of creating a resizable dialog box is figuring out how to adjust the controls. When you have more than two or three controls, the code can get complicated.

Handling Multiple UserForm Controls with One Event Handler

Every command button on a UserForm must have its own procedure to handle its events. For example, if you have two command buttons, you'll need two event-handler procedures for the controls' Click events.

```
Private Sub CommandButton1_Click()
' Code goes here
End Sub

Private Sub CommandButton2_Click()
' Code goes here
End Sub
```

In other words, you can't assign a macro to execute when *any* command button is clicked. Each Click event handler is hardwired to its command button. You can, however, have each event handler call another all-inclusive macro in the event-handler procedures, but you'll need to pass an argument to indicate which button was clicked. In the following examples, clicking either CommandButton1 or CommandButton2 executes the Button-Click procedure, and the single argument tells the ButtonClick procedure which button was clicked.

```
Private Sub CommandButton1_Click()
    Call ButtonClick(1)
End Sub

Private Sub CommandButton2_Click()
    Call ButtonClick(2)
End Sub
```

If your UserForm has many command buttons, setting up all of these event handlers can get tedious. You might prefer to have a single procedure that can determine which button was clicked and take the appropriate action.

This section describes a way around this limitation by using a class module to define a new class.

ON THE WEB

This example, named Multiple Buttons.xlsm, is available on the book's website.

The following steps describe how to re-create the example UserForm shown in Figure 15.24:

1. Create your UserForm as usual and add several command buttons. (The example contains 16 CommandButton controls.) This example assumes that the form is named UserForm1.

FIGURE 15.24

Multiple command buttons with a single event-handler procedure

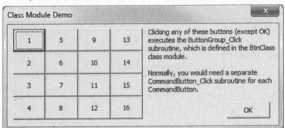

2. Insert a class module into your project (choose Insert ⇨ Class Module), give it the name BtnClass, and enter the following code:

```
Public WithEvents ButtonGroup As MsForms.CommandButton

Private Sub ButtonGroup_Click()
    Dim Msg As String
    Msg = "You clicked " & ButtonGroup.Name & vbCrLf & vbCrLf
    Msg = Msg & "Caption: " & ButtonGroup.Caption & vbCrLf
    Msg = Msg & "Left Position: " & ButtonGroup.Left & vbCrLf
    Msg = Msg & "Top Position: " & ButtonGroup.Top & vbCrLf
    MsgBox Msg, vbInformation, ButtonGroup.Name
End Sub
```

You will need to customize the ButtonGroup_Click procedure.

> **TIP**
>
> You can adapt this technique to work with other types of controls. You need to change the type name in the Public WithEvents declaration. For example, if you have option buttons instead of command buttons, use a declaration statement like this:
>
> ```
> Public WithEvents ButtonGroup As MsForms.OptionButton
> ```

3. Insert a standard VBA module, and enter the following code:

```
Sub ShowDialog()
    UserForm1.Show
End Sub
```

15

This routine simply displays the UserForm.

4. In the code module for the UserForm, enter the UserForm_Initialize code that follows:

```
Dim Buttons() As New BtnClass

Private Sub UserForm_Initialize()
    Dim ButtonCount As Long
    Dim ctl As Control

'   Create the Button objects
    ButtonCount = 0
    For Each ctl In Me.Controls
        If TypeName(ctl) = "CommandButton" Then
            'Skip the OK Button
            If ctl.Name <> "cmdOK" Then
                ButtonCount = ButtonCount + 1
                ReDim Preserve Buttons(1 To ButtonCount)
                Set Buttons(ButtonCount).ButtonGroup = ctl
            End If
        End If
    Next ctl
End Sub
```

This procedure is triggered by the UserForm's Initialize event. Note that the code excludes the button named cmdOK from the button group. Therefore, clicking the OK button doesn't execute the ButtonGroup_Click procedure.

After performing these steps, you can execute the ShowDialog procedure to display the UserForm. Clicking any CommandButton (except the OK button) executes the Button-Group_Click procedure. Figure 15.25 shows an example of the message displayed when a button is clicked.

FIGURE 15.25

The ButtonGroup_Click procedure describes the button that was clicked.

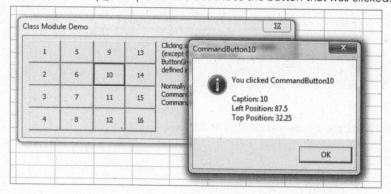

Selecting a Color in a UserForm

The example in this section is a function that displays a dialog box (similar in concept to the MyMsgBox function, presented earlier). The function, named GetAColor, returns a color value.

```
Function GetAColor() As Variant
    UGetAColor.Show
    GetAColor = UGetAColor.ColorValue
    Unload UGetAColor
End Function
```

You can use the GetAColor function with a statement like the following:

```
UserColor = GetAColor()
```

Executing this statement displays the UserForm. The user selects a color and clicks OK. The function then assigns the user's selected color value to the UserColor variable.

The UserForm, shown in Figure 15.26, contains three ScrollBar controls—one for each of the color components (red, green, and blue). The value range for each scroll bar is from 0 to 255. The module contains procedures for the ScrollBar Change events. For example, here's the procedure that's executed when the first scroll bar is changed:

```
Private Sub scbRed_Change()
    Me.lblRed.BackColor = RGB(Me.scbRed.Value, 0, 0)
    UpdateColor
End Sub
```

The UpdateColor procedure adjusts the color sample displayed, and it also updates the RGB values.

FIGURE 15.26

This dialog box lets the user select a color by specifying the red, green, and blue components.

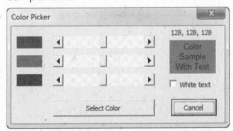

The `GetAColor` UserForm has another twist: it remembers the last color that was selected. When the function ends, the three scroll bar values are stored in the Windows Registry, using this code (`APPNAME` is a string defined in `Module1`):

```
SaveSetting APPNAME, "Colors", "RedValue", Me.scbRed.Value
SaveSetting APPNAME, "Colors", "BlueValue", Me.scbBlue.Value
SaveSetting APPNAME, "Colors", "GreenValue", Me.scbGreen.Value
```

`SaveSetting` will create the folders and keys in the registry if they don't already exist. The `UserForm_Initialize` procedure retrieves these values and assigns them to the scroll bars:

```
Me.scbRed.Value = GetSetting(APPNAME, "Colors", "RedValue", 128)
Me.scbGreen.Value = GetSetting(APPNAME, "Colors", "GreenValue", 128)
Me.scbBlue.Value = GetSetting(APPNAME, "Colors", "BlueValue", 128)
```

The last argument for the `GetSetting` function is the default value, which is used if the Registry key is not found. In this case, each color defaults to 128, which produces middle gray.

The `SaveSetting` and `GetSetting` functions always use this Registry key:

```
HKEY_CURRENT_USER\Software\VB and VBA Program Settings\
```

Figure 15.27 shows the Registry data, displayed with the Windows `Regedit.exe` program.

FIGURE 15.27

The user's scroll bar values are stored in the Windows Registry and retrieved the next time the `GetAColor` function is used.

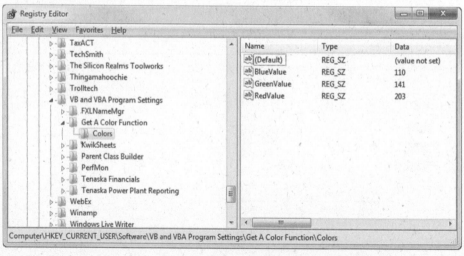

Displaying a Chart in a UserForm

Excel provides no direct way to display a chart in a UserForm. You can, of course, copy the chart and paste it to the `Picture` property of an `Image` control, but this creates a static image of the chart, so it won't display any changes that are made to the chart.

This section describes a technique to display a chart in a UserForm. Figure 15.28 shows a UserForm with a chart displayed in an `Image` object. The chart resides on a worksheet, and the UserForm always displays the current chart. This technique works by copying the chart to a temporary graphics file and then uses the `LoadPicture` function to specify that file for the Image control's `Picture` property.

FIGURE 15.28

A UserForm can display "live" charts.

To display a chart in a UserForm, follow these general steps:

1. Create your chart or charts as usual.
2. Insert a UserForm and then add an `Image` control.
3. Write VBA code to save the chart as a GIF file and then set the `Image` control's `Picture` property to the GIF file. You need to use VBA's `LoadPicture` function to do this task.
4. Add other bells and whistles as desired. For example, the UserForm in the demo file contains controls that let you change the chart type. Alternatively, you could write code to display multiple charts.

15

Saving a chart as a GIF file

The following code demonstrates how to create a GIF file (named `temp.gif`) from a chart (in this case, the first chart object on the sheet named `Data`):

```
Set CurrentChart = Sheets("Data").ChartObjects(1).Chart
Fname = ThisWorkbook.Path & "\temp.gif"
CurrentChart.Export FileName:=Fname, FilterName:="GIF"
```

Changing the Image control's Picture property

If the `Image` control on the UserForm is named `Image1`, the following statement loads the image (represented by the Fname variable) into the `Image` control:

```
Me.Image1.Picture = LoadPicture(Fname)
```

> **NOTE**
>
> This technique works fine, but you may notice a slight delay when the chart is saved and then retrieved. On a fast system, however, this delay is hardly noticeable.

Making a UserForm Semitransparent

Normally, a UserForm is opaque—it completely hides whatever is underneath it. However, you can make a UserForm semitransparent, such that the user can see the worksheet under the UserForm.

Creating a semitransparent UserForm requires a number of Windows API functions. You can set the transparency level using values that range from 0 (UserForm is invisible) to 255 (UserForm is completely opaque, as usual). Values in between 0 and 255 specify a level of semitransparency.

Figure 15.29 shows an example of a UserForm with a transparency level of about 128.

> **ON THE WEB**
>
> This workbook is available on the book's website. The filename is `Semitransparent Userform.xlsm`.

What good is a semitransparent UserForm? You've probably seen websites that use the light-box effect. The web page is dimmed (as if the lights are lowered), and an image or a pop-up is displayed. This effect serves to focus the user's attention on a specific item on the screen.

FIGURE 15.29

A semitransparent UserForm

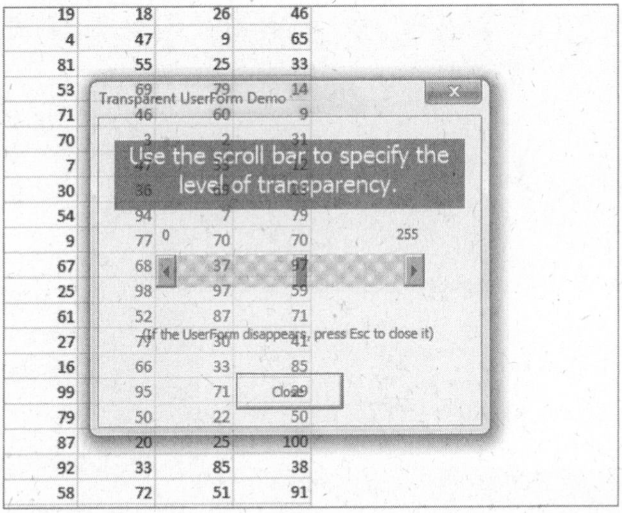

Figure 15.30 shows an Excel workbook that uses the light-box effect. Excel's window is dimmed, but the message box is displayed normally. How does it work? It starts with a UserForm with a black background. Then there is code to resize and position the UserForm so that it covers the entire Excel window. Here's the code to accomplish the cover-up:

```
With Me
    .Height = Application.Height
    .Width = Application.Width
    .Left = Application.Left
    .Top = Application.Top
End With
```

Then, the semitransparent UserForm is made transparent, which gives Excel's window a dimmed appearance. The message box (or another UserForm) is displayed on top of the semitransparent UserForm.

ON THE WEB

This workbook is available on the book's website in the `Excel Light-box.xlsm` file.

A Puzzle on a UserForm

The example in this section is a familiar sliding puzzle, displayed on a UserForm (see Figure 15.31). This puzzle was invented by Noyes Chapman in the late 1800s. In addition to providing a few minutes of amusement, you may find the coding instructive.

15

FIGURE 15.30

Creating a light-box effect in Excel

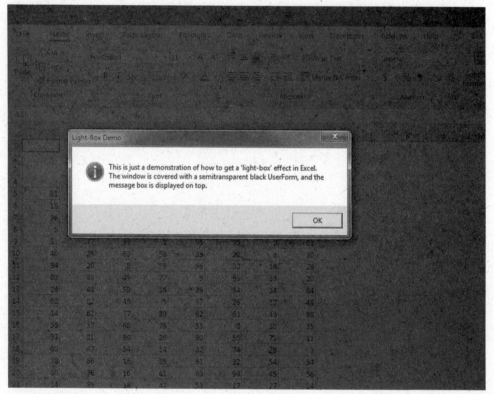

FIGURE 15.31

A sliding tile puzzle in a UserForm

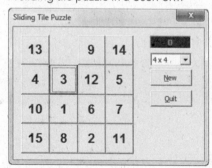

The goal is to arrange the shuffled tiles (`CommandButton` controls) in numerical order. Click a button next to the empty space, and the button moves to the empty space. The `ComboBox` control lets the user choose from three configurations: 3 × 3, 4 × 4, and 5 × 5. The New button shuffles the tiles, and a `Label` control keeps track of the number of moves.

This application uses a class module to handle all button events (see "Handling Multiple UserForm Controls with One Event Handler," earlier in this chapter).

The VBA code is lengthy, so it's not listed here. Here are a few points to keep in mind when examining the code:

- The `CommandButton` controls are added to the UserForm via code. The number and size of the buttons are determined by the combo box value.
- The tiles are shuffled by simulating a few thousand random clicks on the buttons. Another option is simply to assign random numbers, but that could result in some unsolvable games.
- The blank space in the tile grid is actually a `CommandButton` control with its `Visible` property set to `False`.
- The class module contains one event procedure (`MouseUp`), which is executed whenever the user clicks a tile.
- When the user clicks a command button tile, its `Caption` is swapped with the hidden button. The code doesn't actually move any buttons.

ON THE WEB

This workbook, named `Sliding Tile Puzzle.xlsm`, is available on the book's website.

Video Poker on a UserForm

Finally, here is proof that Excel doesn't have to be boring. Figure 15.32 shows a UserForm set up as a casino-style video poker game.

FIGURE 15.32

A feature-packed video poker game

The game features the following:

- A choice between two games: Joker's Wild and Jacks or Better
- A chart that shows your winning (or losing) history
- The capability to change the payoffs
- Help (displayed on a worksheet)
- An emergency button that quickly hides the UserForm

All that's missing is the casino noise.

ON THE WEB

This workbook, named `Video Poker.xlsm`, is available on the book's website.

As you might expect, the code is much too lengthy to list here, but if you examine the workbook, you'll find lots of useful UserForm tips—including a class module example.

Part IV

Developing Excel Applications

IN THIS PART

Creating and Using Add-Ins

What Is an Add-In?

One of Excel's most useful features for developers is the capability to create add-ins. Creating add-ins adds a professional touch to your work, and add-ins offer several key advantages over standard workbook files.

Generally speaking, a *spreadsheet add-in* is something added to a spreadsheet application to give it additional functionality. Excel ships with several add-ins. Examples include the *Analysis ToolPak* (which adds statistical and analysis capabilities) and *Solver* (which performs advanced optimization calculations).

Some add-ins also provide new worksheet functions that you can use in formulas. With a well-designed add-in, the new features blend in well with the original interface, so they appear to be part of Excel.

Comparing an add-in with a standard workbook

Any knowledgeable Excel user can create an add-in from an Excel workbook file; no additional software or programming tools are required. You can convert any workbook file to an add-in, but not every workbook is appropriate for an add-in. An Excel add-in is basically a normal XLSM workbook with the following differences:

- The IsAddin property of the ThisWorkbook object is True. By default, this property is False.
- The workbook window is hidden in such a way that it can't be unhidden by choosing the View ➪ Window ➪ Unhide command. This means you can't display worksheets or chart sheets contained in an add-in unless you write code to copy the sheet to a standard workbook.
- An add-in isn't a member of the Workbooks collection. Rather, it's a member of the AddIns collection. However, you *can* access an add-in through the Workbooks collection (see "XLAM file VBA collection membership," later in this chapter).
- You install and uninstall add-ins by using the Add-ins dialog box. When an add-in is installed, it remains installed across Excel sessions.
- The Macro dialog box (invoked by choosing Developer ➪ Code ➪ Macros or View ➪ Macros ➪ Macros) doesn't display the names of the macros contained in an add-in.
- When you write formulas, you can use a custom worksheet function stored in an add-in without having to precede the function's name with the source add-in's filename.

NOTE

In the past, Excel allowed you to use any extension for an add-in. Beginning with Excel 2007, you can still use any extension for an add-in, but if the extension is not XLA or XLAM, you will see the warning shown in Figure 16.1. This prompt occurs even if the add-in is an installed add-in that opens automatically when Excel starts, and even if the file is in a trusted location.

FIGURE 16.1

Excel warns you if an add-in uses a nonstandard file extension.

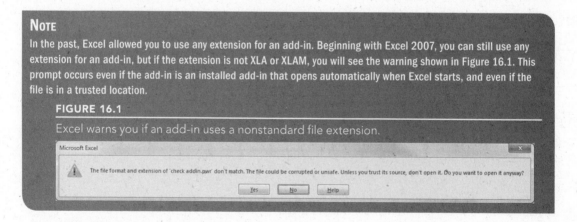

Why create add-ins?

You might decide to convert your Excel application into an add-in for any of the following reasons:

To restrict access to your code and worksheets When you distribute an application as an add-in and you protect its VBA project with a password, users can't view or modify the sheets or the VBA code in the workbook. Therefore, if you use proprietary techniques in your application, you can prevent anyone from copying the code—or at least make it more difficult to do so.

To separate your VBA code from your data If you send a macro-enabled workbook to a user that contains both code and data, it's difficult to update the code. The user may have added data or changed existing data. If you send another workbook with updated code, the data changes will be lost.

To make deploying your application easier You can put an add-in on a network share and have users load it from there. If changes are required, you can replace the add-in on the network share, and when the users restart Excel, the new add-in will load.

To avoid confusion If a user loads your application as an add-in, the file isn't visible, and it is, therefore, less likely to confuse novice users or get in the way. Unlike a hidden workbook, an add-in can't be unhidden.

To simplify access to worksheet functions Custom worksheet functions stored in an add-in do not need to include the add-in's filename. For example, if you store a custom function named MOVAVG in a workbook named Newfuncs.xlsm, you must use syntax like the following to use this function in a formula that's in a different workbook:

```
=Newfuncs.xlsm!MOVAVG(A1:A50)
```

But if this function is stored in an add-in file that's open, you can use much simpler syntax because you don't need to include the file reference.

```
=MOVAVG(A1:A50)
```

To provide easier access for users After you identify the location of your add-in, it appears in the Add-ins dialog box with a friendly name and a description of what it does.

To gain better control over loading Add-ins can be opened automatically when Excel starts, regardless of the directory in which they are stored.

To avoid displaying prompts when unloading When an add-in is closed, the user is never prompted to save changes.

NOTE

The capability to use add-ins is determined by the user's security settings in the Add-ins tab of the Trust Center dialog box (see Figure 16.2). To display this dialog box, choose Developer ➪ Code ➪ Macro Security. Or, if the Developer tab isn't displayed, choose File ➪ Options ➪ Trust Center and then click the Trust Center Settings button.

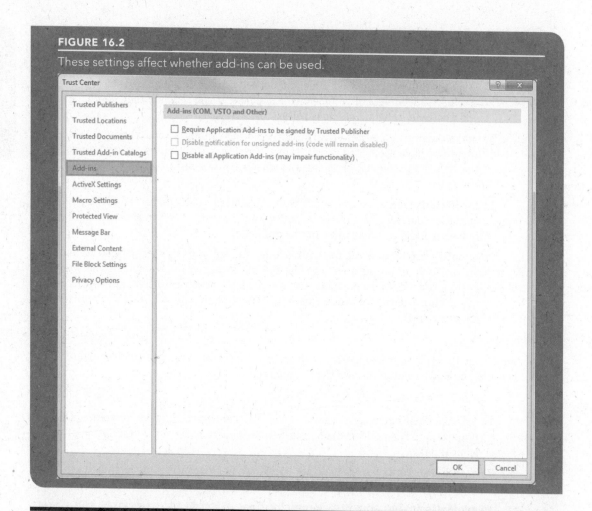

FIGURE 16.2

These settings affect whether add-ins can be used.

About COM add-ins

Excel also supports Component Object Model (COM) add-ins. These files have a .dll or .exe file extension. A COM add-in can be written so that it works with all Office applications that support add-ins. An additional advantage is that the code is compiled, so the original source isn't viewable. Unlike XLAM add-ins, a COM add-in can't contain Excel sheets or charts. COM add-ins are developed in Visual Basic .NET. Discussion of creating COM add-in procedures is well beyond the scope of this book.

Understanding Excel's Add-in Manager

The most efficient way to load and unload add-ins is with Excel's Add-ins dialog box, which you access by using any of the following methods:

- Choose File ⇨ Options ⇨ Add-ins. Then, in the Excel Options dialog box, choose Excel Add-ins from the Manage drop-down box and click Go.

- Choose Developer ➪ Add-Ins ➪ Excel Add-ins. Note that, by default, the Developer tab is not visible. At least one file must be open for this Ribbon button to be enabled.
- Press Alt+TI, a shortcut key sequence used in earlier versions of Excel that still works. At least one file must be open for this shortcut to work.

Figure 16.3 shows the Add-ins dialog box. The list contains the names of all add-ins that Excel knows about, and check marks identify installed add-ins. You can open (install) and close (uninstall) add-ins from this dialog box by selecting or deselecting the check boxes. When you uninstall an add-in, it is not removed from your system. It remains in the list in case you want to install it later. Use the Browse button to locate additional add-ins and add them to the list.

FIGURE 16.3

The Add-ins dialog box

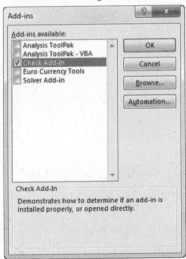

> **CAUTION**
>
> You can open most add-in files also by choosing the File ➪ Open command. Because an add-in is never the active workbook, however, you can't close an add-in by choosing File ➪ Close. You can remove the add-in only by exiting and restarting Excel or by executing VBA code to close the add-in. Here's an example:
>
> ```
> Workbooks("myaddin.xlam").Close
> ```
>
> Opening an add-in with the File ➪ Open command opens the file but does not officially install the add-in.

When you open an add-in, you might notice something different about Excel. In almost every case, the user interface changes in some way: Excel displays either a new command on the Ribbon or new menu items on a shortcut menu. For example, when the Analysis

ToolPak add-in is installed, it gives you a new command: Data ⇨ Analysis ⇨ Data Analysis. When you install Excel's Euro Currency Tools add-in, you get a new group in the Formulas tab: Solutions.

If the add-in contains only custom worksheet functions, the new functions appear in the Insert Function dialog box.

> **NOTE**
>
> If you open an add-in created in a version before Excel 2007, any user interface modifications made by the add-in won't appear as they were intended to appear. Rather, you must access the user interface items (menus and tool-bars) by choosing Add-Ins ⇨ Menu Commands or Add-Ins ⇨ Custom Toolbars.

Creating an Add-In

You can convert any workbook to an add-in, but not all workbooks are appropriate candidates for add-ins. First, an add-in must contain macros. (Otherwise, it's useless.)

Generally, a workbook that benefits most from being converted to an add-in is one that contains general-purpose macro procedures. A workbook that consists only of worksheets would be inaccessible as an add-in because worksheets within add-ins are hidden from the user. You can, however, write code that copies all or part of a sheet from your add-in to a visible workbook.

Creating an add-in from a workbook is simple. The following steps describe the procedure for creating an add-in from a normal workbook file:

1. Develop your application, and make sure that everything works properly.

2. Include a way to execute the macro or macros in the add-in.

 See Chapter 17, "Working with the Ribbon," and Chapter 18, "Working with Shortcut Menus," for more information about modifying Excel's user interface.

3. Activate the Visual Basic Editor (VBE), and select the workbook in the Project window.

4. Choose Tools ⇨ *xxx* Properties (where *xxx* represents the name of the project), click the Protection tab, and select the Lock Project for Viewing check box. Then enter a password (twice), and click OK.

   This step is necessary only if you want to prevent others from viewing or modifying your macros or UserForms.

5. Reactivate Excel, and choose File ⇨ Info to display the properties of the workbook.

6. Enter a brief descriptive title in the Title field and a longer description in the Comments field.

This step isn't required, but it makes the add-in easier to use by displaying descriptive text in the Add-ins dialog box.

7. Choose File ⇨ Save As ⇨ Browse to display the Save As dialog box.

8. In the Save As dialog box, select Excel Add-In (*.xlam) from the Save as Type drop-down list.

   Excel proposes the standard add-ins directory, but you can save the add-in to any location.

9. Click Save.

   A copy of the workbook is saved (with an .xlam extension), and the original workbook remains open.

10. Close the original workbook and then install the add-in version.

11. Test the add-in to make sure that it works correctly.

If your add-in doesn't work, make changes to your code—and don't forget to save your changes. Because an add-in doesn't appear in an Excel window, you must save it from the VBE.

CAUTION

A workbook being converted to an add-in must have at least one worksheet, and a worksheet must be the active sheet when you create the add-in. If a chart sheet is active, the option to save the workbook as an add-in does not appear in the Save As dialog box.

A few words about passwords

Microsoft has never promoted Excel as a product that creates applications in which the source code is secure. The password feature provided in Excel is sufficient to prevent casual users from accessing parts of your application that you'd like to keep hidden. However, if you must be absolutely sure that no one ever sees your code or formulas, Excel isn't your best choice as a development platform.

An Add-In Example

In this section, we discuss the steps involved in creating a useful add-in. The example uses a utility that exports charts to separate graphic files. The utility adds a new group (Export Charts) to the Home tab (and can be accessed also by pressing Ctrl+Shift+E). Figure 16.4 shows the main dialog box for this utility. This is a fairly complicated utility, and you might want to take some time to see how it works.

FIGURE 16.4

The Export Charts workbook will make a useful add-in.

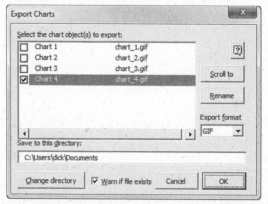

In this example, you'll be working with an application that has already been developed and debugged. The workbook consists of the following items:

A worksheet named Sheet1 This sheet is not used, but it must be present because every add-in must have at least one worksheet.

A UserForm named UExport This dialog box serves as the primary user interface. The code module for this UserForm contains several event-handler procedures.

A UserForm named URename This dialog box is displayed when the user clicks the Rename button to change the filename of a chart to be exported.

A UserForm named USplash This dialog box is displayed when the workbook is opened. It briefly describes how to access the Export Charts utility, and it also contains a Don't Show This Message Again check box.

A VBA module named Module1 This module contains several procedures, including the main procedure (named StartExportCharts), which displays the UExport dialog box.

ThisWorkbook code module This module contains a Workbook_Open procedure that reads the saved settings and displays a start-up message.

XML code to customize the Ribbon This customization was done outside Excel. See Chapter 17 for more information about customizing the Ribbon by using RibbonX.

Adding descriptive information for the example add-in

To enter a title and description for your add-in, choose File ⇨ Info. Enter a title, such as **Export Charts**, for the add-in in the Title field. This text will appear in the list in the Add-ins dialog box. In the Comments field, enter a description of the add-in. If you don't see the Comments field, click the Show All Properties link. This information will appear at the bottom of the Add-ins dialog box when the add-in is selected.

Adding a title and description for the add-in is optional, but it is highly recommended.

Creating an add-in

To create an add-in, do the following:

1. Activate the VBE, and select the future add-in workbook in the Project window.
2. Choose Debug ⇨ Compile.

   This step forces a compilation of the VBA code, and it also identifies any syntax errors so that you can correct them. When you save a workbook as an add-in, Excel creates the add-in even if it contains syntax errors.

3. Choose Tools ⇨ *xxx* Properties (where *xxx* represents the name of the project) to display the Project Properties dialog box, click the General tab, and enter a new name for the project.

   By default, all VB projects are named *VBProject*. In this example, the project name is changed to *ExpCharts*. This step is optional but recommended.

4. Save the workbook one last time using its *.XLSM name.

   Strictly speaking, this step isn't necessary, but it gives you an XLSM backup (with no password) of your XLAM add-in file.

5. With the Project Properties dialog box still displayed, click the Protection tab, select the Lock Project for Viewing check box, and enter a password (twice). Click OK.

   The code will remain viewable, and the password protection will take effect the next time the file is opened. If you don't need to protect the project, you can skip this step.

6. In Excel, choose File ⇨ Save As ⇨ Browse.

   Excel displays its Save As dialog box.

7. In the Save as Type drop-down list, select Excel Add-In (*.xlam).
8. Click Save.

   A new add-in file is created, and the original XLSM version remains open.

When you create an add-in, Excel proposes the standard add-ins directory, but add-ins can be located in any directory.

About Excel's Add-in Manager

You install and uninstall add-ins by using Excel's Add-ins dialog box. This dialog box lists the names of all available add-ins. Those with check marks are installed.

In VBA terms, the Add-ins dialog box lists the `Title` property of each `AddIn` object in the `AddIns` collection. Each add-in that appears with a check mark has its `Installed` property set to `True`.

You can install an add-in by selecting its check box, and you can uninstall an installed add-in by removing the check mark. To add an add-in to the list, use the Browse button to locate its file. By default, the Add-ins dialog box lists files of the following types:

XLAM: An Excel 2007 or newer add-in created from an XLSM file

XLA: A pre–Excel 2007 add-in created from an XLS file

XLL: A stand-alone compiled DLL file

If you click the Automation button, you can browse for COM add-ins. Note that the Automation Servers dialog box will probably list many files, including COM add-ins that don't work with Excel.

You can include an add-in file in the `AddIns` collection with the `Add` method of the VBA `AddIns` collection, but you can't remove one by using VBA. You can also open an add-in from within VBA code by setting the `AddIn` object's `Installed` property to `True`. Setting it to `False` closes the add-in.

The Add-in Manager stores the installed status of the add-ins in the Windows Registry when you exit Excel. Therefore, all add-ins that are installed when you close Excel are automatically opened the next time you start Excel.

Installing an add-in

To avoid confusion, close the XLSM workbook before installing the add-in created from that workbook.

To install an add-in, do the following:

1. Choose File ⇨ Options, and click the Add-Ins tab.

2. Choose Excel Add-Ins from the Manage drop-down list and then click Go (or press Alt+TI).

   Excel displays the Add-ins dialog box.

3. Click the Browse button, and locate and double-click the add-in that you just created.

   After you find your new add-in, the Add-ins dialog box displays the add-in in its list. As shown in Figure 16.5, the Add-ins dialog box also displays the descriptive information that you provided in the Document Properties panel.

4. Click OK to close the dialog box and open the add-in.

FIGURE 16.5

The Add-ins dialog box with the new add-in selected

When the Export Charts add-in is installed, a new tab named Power Chart is created with two controls. One control displays the Export Charts dialog box; the other displays the help file.

You can use the add-in also by pressing its shortcut key combination: Ctrl+Shift+E.

Testing the add-in

After installing the add-in, it's a good idea to perform some additional testing. For this example, open a new workbook and create some charts to try the various features in the Export Charts utility. Do everything you can think of to try to make the add-in fail. Better yet, seek the assistance of someone unfamiliar with the application to give it a crash test.

If you discover any errors, you can correct the code in the add-in (the original file is not required). After making changes, save the file by choosing File ⇨ Save in the VBE.

Distributing an add-in

You can distribute this add-in to other Excel users simply by giving them a copy of the XLAM file (they don't need the XLSM version) along with instructions on how to install it. If you locked the file with a password, your macro code cannot be viewed or modified by others unless they know the password.

Modifying an add-in

If you need to modify an add-in, first open it and then unlock the VB project if you applied a password. To unlock it, activate VBE and then double-click its project's name in the Project window. You'll be prompted for the password. Make your changes and then save the file from VBE (choose File ⇨ Save).

If you create an add-in that stores its information in a worksheet, you must set its `IsAddIn` property to `False` before you can view that workbook in Excel. You do this in the Properties window shown in Figure 16.6 when the `ThisWorkbook` object is selected. After you make your changes, set the `IsAddIn` property back to `True` before you save the file. If you leave the `IsAddIn` property set to `False`, Excel won't let you save the file with the XLAM extension.

FIGURE 16.6

Making an add-in not an add-in

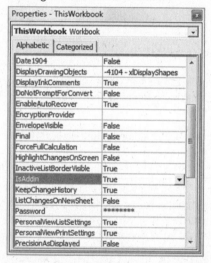

Creating an add-in: a checklist

Before you release your add-in to the world, take a few minutes to run through this checklist:

- Did you test your add-in with all supported platforms and Excel versions?
- Did you give your VB project a new name? By default, every project is named *VBProject*. It's a good idea to give your project a more meaningful name.
- Does your add-in make any assumptions about the user's directory structure or directory names?

- When you use the Add-ins dialog box to load your add-in, is its name and description correct and appropriate?
- If your add-in uses VBA functions that aren't designed to be used in a worksheet, have you declared the functions as Private? If not, these functions will appear in the Insert Function dialog box.
- Did you remember to remove all Debug.Print statements from your code?
- Did you force a recompile of your add-in to ensure that it contains no syntax errors?
- Did you account for any international issues?
- Is your add-in file optimized for speed? See "Optimizing the Performance of Add-Ins" later in this chapter.

Comparing XLAM and XLSM Files

This section begins by comparing an XLAM add-in file with its XLSM source file. Later in this chapter, we discuss methods that you can use to optimize the performance of your add-in.

For starters, an add-in based on an XLSM source file is the same size as the original. The VBA code in XLAM files isn't optimized, so faster performance isn't among the benefits of using an add-in.

XLAM file VBA collection membership

An add-in is a member of the AddIns collection, but it isn't an official member of the Workbooks collection. However, you *can* refer to an add-in by using the Workbooks method of the Application object and supplying the add-in's filename as its index. The following instruction creates an object variable that represents an add-in named myaddin.xlam:

```
Dim TestAddin As Workbook
Set TestAddin = Workbooks("myaddin.xlam")
```

Add-ins cannot be referenced by an index number in the Workbooks collection. If you use the following code to loop through the Workbooks collection, the myaddin.xlam workbook isn't displayed:

```
Dim w as Workbook

For Each w in Application.Workbooks
  MsgBox w.Name
Next w
```

The following `For-Next` loop, on the other hand, displays `myaddin.xlam`—assuming that Excel "knows" about it—in the Add-ins dialog box:

```
Dim a as Addin

For Each a in Application.AddIns
    MsgBox a.Name
Next a
```

Visibility of XLSM and XLAM files

Ordinary workbooks are displayed in one or more windows. For example, the following statement displays the number of windows for the active workbook:

```
MsgBox ActiveWorkbook.Windows.Count
```

You can manipulate the visibility of each window for a workbook by choosing the View ➪ Window ➪ Hide command (in Excel) or by changing the `Visible` property using VBA. The following code hides all windows for the active workbook:

```
Dim Win As Window

For Each Win In ActiveWorkbook.Windows
    Win.Visible = False
Next Win
```

Add-in files are never visible, and they don't have windows, even though they have unseen worksheets. Consequently, add-ins don't appear in the windows list when you choose the View ➪ Window ➪ Switch Windows command. If `myaddin.xlam` is open, the following statement returns 0:

```
MsgBox Workbooks("myaddin.xlam").Windows.Count
```

Worksheets and chart sheets in XLSM and XLAM files

Add-in files, like normal workbook files, can have any number of worksheets or chart sheets. But to convert an XLSM file to an add-in, the file must have at least one worksheet. In many cases, this worksheet will be empty.

When an add-in is open, your VBA code can access its sheets as if they were in an ordinary workbook. Because add-in files aren't part of the `Workbooks` collection, however, you must always reference an add-in by its name and not by an index number. The following example displays the value in cell A1 of the first worksheet in `myaddin.xla`, which is assumed to be open:

```
MsgBox Workbooks("myaddin.xlam").Worksheets(1).Range("A1").Value
```

If your add-in contains a worksheet that you'd like the user to see, you can either copy the sheet to an open workbook or create a new workbook from the sheet.

The following code, for example, copies the first worksheet from an add-in and places it in the active workbook (as the last sheet):

```
Sub CopySheetFromAddin()
    Dim AddinSheet As Worksheet
    Dim NumSheets As Long
    Set AddinSheet = Workbooks("myaddin.xlam").Sheets(1)
    NumSheets = ActiveWorkbook.Sheets.Count
    AddinSheet.Copy After:=ActiveWorkbook.Sheets(NumSheets)
End Sub
```

Note that this procedure works even if the VBA project for the add-in is protected with a password.

Creating a new workbook from a sheet within an add-in is even simpler.

```
Sub CreateNewWorkbook()
    Workbooks("myaddin.xlam").Sheets(1).Copy
End Sub
```

> **NOTE**
>
> The previous examples assume that the code is in a file other than the add-in file. VBA code within an add-in should always use `ThisWorkbook` to qualify references to sheets or ranges within the add-in. For example, the following statement is assumed to be in a VBA module in an add-in file. This statement displays the value in cell A1 on Sheet 1.
>
> ```
> MsgBox ThisWorkbook.Sheets("Sheet1").Range("A1").Value
> ```

Accessing VBA procedures in an add-in

Accessing the VBA procedures in an add-in is a bit different from accessing procedures in a normal XLSM workbook. First, when you choose the View ⇨ Macros ⇨ Macros command, the Macro dialog box doesn't display the names of macros that are in open add-ins. It's almost as if Excel were trying to prevent you from accessing them.

> **TIP**
>
> If you know the name of the procedure in the add-in, you can enter it directly in the Macro dialog box and click Run to execute it. The `Sub` procedure must be in a standard VBA module and not in a code module for an object.

Because procedures contained in an add-in aren't listed in the Macro dialog box, you must provide other means to access them. Your choices include direct methods (such as shortcut keys and Ribbon commands) as well as indirect methods (such as event handlers). One such candidate, for example, may be the `OnTime` method, which executes a procedure at a specific time of day.

You can use the `Run` method of the `Application` object to execute a procedure in an add-in. Here's an example:

```
Application.Run "myaddin.xlam!DisplayNames"
```

Another option is to use the Tools ⇨ References command in VBE to enable a reference to the add-in. Then you can refer directly to one of its procedures in your VBA code without the filename qualifier. In fact, you don't need to use the `Run` method; you can call the procedure directly as long as it's not declared as `Private`. The following procedure executes a procedure named `DisplayNames` in an add-in that has been added as a reference:

```
Sub RunTheAddingCode()
    DisplayNames
End Sub
```

> **NOTE**
>
> Even when a reference to the add-in has been established, its macro names don't appear in the Macro dialog box.

Function procedures defined in an add-in work just like those defined in an XLSM workbook. They're easy to access because Excel displays their names in the Insert Function dialog box under the User Defined category (by default). The only exception is if the `Function` procedure was declared with the `Private` keyword; then the function doesn't appear there. That's why it's a good idea to declare custom functions as `Private` if they will be used only by other VBA procedures and aren't designed to be used in worksheet formulas.

You can use worksheet functions contained in add-ins without the workbook name qualifier. For example, if you have a custom function named MOVAVG stored in the file new-funcs.xlsm, you'd use the following instruction to address the function from a worksheet in a different workbook:

```
=newfuncs.xlsm!MOVAVG(A1:A50)
```

But if this function is stored in an add-in file that's open, you can omit the file reference and write the following instead:

```
=MOVAVG(A1:A50)
```

Keep in mind that a workbook that uses a function defined in an add-in will have a link to that add-in. Therefore, the add-in must be available whenever that workbook is used.

Sleuthing a protected add-in

The Macro dialog box doesn't display the names of procedures contained in add-ins. But what if you'd like to run such a procedure? You can't run a procedure if you don't know its name, but you can find its name by using the Object Browser.

To illustrate, install the Euro Currency Tools add-in. This add-in is distributed with Excel, and it is password-protected so you can't view the code. When installed, the add-in creates a new group, called Solutions, on the Formulas tab of the Ribbon. When you click the Euro Conversion button, the Euro Conversion dialog box is displayed. This dialog box lets you convert a range that contains currencies.

To determine the name of the procedure that displays this dialog box, follow these steps:

1. Activate VBE and then select the EUROTOOL.XLAM project in the Project window.

2. Press F2 to activate Object Browser.

3. In the Libraries drop-down list, select EuroTool, which displays all of the classes in the EUROTOOL.XLAM add-in, as depicted here.

Continues

(continued)

4. Select various items in the Classes list to see what class they are and the members that they contain.

You see that this add-in has quite a few worksheets. Excel allows you to copy sheets from protected add-ins, so if you'd like to take a look at one of the worksheets, use the Immediate window and copy the worksheet to a new workbook using a statement like this:

```
Workbooks("eurotool.xlam").Sheets(1).Copy
```

Or, to examine all of the worksheets, execute this statement, which converts the add-in to a standard workbook:

```
Workbooks("eurotool.xlam").IsAddin = False
```

The following figure shows a portion of the workbook. This sheet (and the others) contains information used to localize the add-in for different languages.

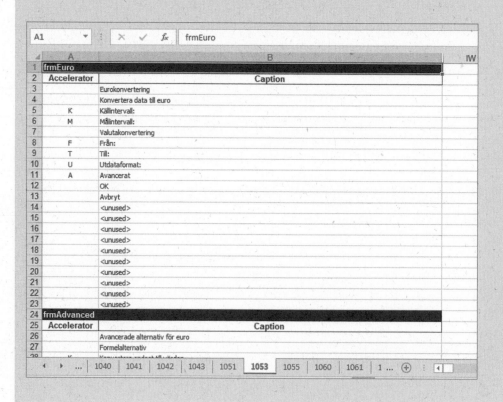

That's interesting, but it doesn't help identify the procedure name we're seeking.

This add-in has a lot of procedures, but none of the ones in the standard modules displays the dialog box. There is a member listed in the `ThisWorkbook` code module called `EuroConversionWizard`. You can't execute that directly because it's an object's code module. You can, however, use the `Run` method to execute it, as shown in the following statement:

```
Application.Run "eurotool.xlam!ThisWorkbook.EuroConversionWizard"
```

Executing this statement displays the Euro Conversion dialog box, just as if you'd clicked the button on the Ribbon.

Armed with this information, you can write VBA code to display the Euro Conversion dialog box—assuming, of course, that you can think of a reason to do so.

Manipulating Add-Ins with VBA

In this section, we present information that can help you write VBA procedures that manipulate add-ins.

The `AddIns` collection consists of all of the add-ins that Excel knows about. These add-ins can be either installed or not. The Add-ins dialog box lists all members of the `AddIns` collection. Those entries accompanied by a check mark are installed.

> **NOTE**
>
> Beginning with Excel 2010, an additional collection is available: `AddIns2`. This collection is the same as the `Add-Ins` collection, but it also includes add-ins that were opened using the File ⇨ Open command. In the past, accessing these add-ins required an XLM macro.

Adding an item to the AddIns collection

The add-in files that make up the `AddIns` collection can be stored anywhere. Excel maintains a partial list of these files and their locations in the Windows Registry. For Excel 2019, this list is stored here:

```
HKEY_CURRENT_USER\Software\Microsoft\Office\16.0\Excel\Add-in Manager
```

You can use the Windows Registry Editor (`regedit.exe`) to view this Registry key. Note that the standard add-ins shipped with Excel do not appear in this Registry key. In addition, add-in files stored in the following directory also appear in the list but aren't listed in the Registry:

```
C:\Program Files\Microsoft Office\root\Office16\Library
```

Note that the path on your system may be different depending on the version of Windows you are using. You can add a new `AddIn` object to the `AddIns` collection either manually or programmatically. To add a new add-in to the collection manually, display the Add-ins dialog box, click the Browse button, and locate the add-in.

To add a new member to the `AddIns` collection with VBA, use the collection's `Add` method. Here's an example:

```
Application.AddIns.Add "c:\files\newaddin.xlam"
```

After the preceding instruction is executed, the `AddIns` collection has a new member, and the Add-ins dialog box shows a new item in its list. If the add-in already exists in the collection, nothing happens, and an error isn't generated.

If the add-in is on removable media (for example, a CD-ROM), you can also copy the file to Excel's library directory with the `Add` method. The following example copies `myaddin` `.xlam` from drive E and adds it to the `AddIns` collection. The second argument (set to `True`, in this case) specifies whether the add-in should be copied. If the add-in resides on a hard drive, the second argument can be ignored.

```
Application.AddIns.Add "e:\myaddin.xla", True
```

NOTE

Adding a new file to the `AddIns` collection does not install it. To install the add-in, set its `Installed` property to `True`.

CAUTION

The Windows Registry doesn't get updated until Excel closes normally. Therefore, if Excel ends abnormally (that is, if it crashes), the add-in's name won't get added to the Registry, and the add-in won't be part of the `AddIns` collection when Excel restarts.

Removing an item from the AddIns collection

Oddly, there is no direct way to remove an add-in from the `AddIns` collection. The `AddIns` collection doesn't have a `Delete` or `Remove` method. One way to remove an add-in from the Add-ins dialog box is to edit the Windows Registry database (using `regedit.exe`).

After you do this, the add-in won't appear in the Add-ins dialog box the next time you start Excel. Note that this method isn't guaranteed to work with all add-in files.

Another way to remove an add-in from the `AddIns` collection is to delete, move, or rename its XLAM (or XLA) file. You'll get a warning like the one shown in Figure 16.7 the next time you try to install or uninstall the add-in, along with an opportunity to remove it from the `AddIns` collection.

FIGURE 16.7

One way to remove a member of the AddIns collection

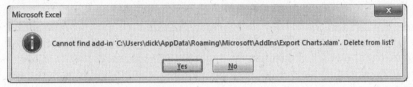

AddIn object properties

An `AddIn` object is a single member of the `AddIns` collection. For example, to display the filename of the first member of the `AddIns` collection, use the following:

```
Msgbox AddIns(1).Name
```

An `AddIn` object has 15 properties, which you can read about in the Help system. Of these properties, 5 are hidden. Some of the terminology is a bit confusing, so we discuss a few of the more important properties in the sections that follow.

The Name property of an AddIn object

The `Name` property holds the filename of the add-in. `Name` is a read-only property, so you can't change the name of the file by changing the `Name` property.

The Path property of an AddIn object

The `Path` property holds the drive and path where the add-in file is stored. It doesn't include a final backslash or the filename.

The FullName property of an AddIn object

The `FullName` property holds the add-in's drive, path, and filename. This property is redundant because this information is also available from the `Name` and `Path` properties. The following instructions produce the same message:

```
MsgBox AddIns(1).Path & "\" & AddIns(1).Name
MsgBox AddIns(1).FullName
```

The Title property of an AddIn object

The `Title` property is a hidden property that holds a descriptive name for the add-in. The `Title` property is what appears in the Add-ins dialog box. This property is set when Excel reads the file's Title property from Windows and can't be changed in code. You can add or change the `Title` property of an add-in by first setting the `IsAddin` property to `False` (so the add-in will appear as a normal workbook in Excel) and then choosing File ➪ Info and changing Title in the Backstage area. Don't forget to set the `IsAddin` property back to `True` and save the add-in from the VBE. Because Excel reads file properties only when an add-in is installed, it won't know about this change until you uninstall and reinstall the add-in (or restart Excel).

Of course, you can also change any file property (including Title) through Windows Explorer. Right-click the add-in file in Windows Explorer and choose Properties from the shortcut menu. Then click the Details tab and make the change. If the file is open in Excel, changes you make in Windows Explorer won't be saved, so uninstall it or close Excel before using this method.

Typically, a member of a collection is addressed by way of its `Name` property setting. The `AddIns` collection is different; it uses the `Title` property instead. The following example displays the filename for the Analysis ToolPak add-in (that is, `analys32.xll`), whose `Title` property is `Analysis ToolPak`.

```
Sub ShowName()
    MsgBox AddIns("Analysis Toolpak").Name
End Sub
```

You can also reference a particular add-in with its index number if you happen to know it. In the vast majority of cases, however, you will want to refer to an add-in by using its `Title` property.

The Comments property of an AddIn object

The `Comments` property stores text that is displayed in the Add-ins dialog box when a particular add-in is selected. Like `Title`, `Comments` is read from the file property of the same name and can't be changed in code. To change it, use either of the methods described in the preceding section. Comments can be as long as 255 characters, but the Add-ins dialog box can display only about 100 characters.

The Installed property of an AddIn object

The `Installed` property is `True` if the add-in is currently installed, that is, if it has a check mark in the Add-ins dialog box. Setting the `Installed` property to `True` opens the add-in. Setting it to `False` unloads it. Here's an example of how to install (that is, open) the Analysis ToolPak add-in with VBA:

```
Sub InstallATP()
    AddIns("Analysis ToolPak").Installed = True
End Sub
```

After this procedure is executed, the Add-ins dialog box displays a check mark next to Analysis ToolPak. If the add-in is already installed, setting its Installed property to True has no effect. To remove this add-in (uninstall it), simply set the Installed property to False.

CAUTION

If an add-in was opened with the File ➪ Open command, it isn't considered to be installed. Consequently, its Installed property is False. An add-in is installed only if it appears in the Add-ins dialog box, with a check mark next to its name.

The ListAllAddIns procedure that follows creates a table that lists all members of the AddIns collection and displays the following properties: Name, Title, Installed, Comments, and Path.

```
Sub ListAllAddins()
    Dim ai As AddIn
    Dim Row As Long
    Dim Table1 As ListObject
    Dim sh As Worksheet

    Set sh = ActiveSheet
    sh.Cells.Clear
    sh.Range("A1:E1") = Array("Name", "Title", "Installed", _
      "Comments", "Path")
    Row = 2
    On Error Resume Next
      For Each ai In Application.AddIns
        sh.Cells(Row, 1) = ai.Name
        sh.Cells(Row, 2) = ai.Title
        sh.Cells(Row, 3) = ai.Installed
        sh.Cells(Row, 4) = ai.Comments
        sh.Cells(Row, 5) = ai.Path
        Row = Row + 1
      Next ai
    On Error GoTo 0
    sh.Range("A1").Select
    sh.ListObjects.Add
    sh.ListObjects(1).TableStyle = _
      "TableStyleMedium2"
    sh.ListObjects(1).Range.EntireColumn.AutoFit
End Sub
```

Figure 16.8 shows the result of executing this procedure. If you modify the code to use the AddIns2 collection, the table will also include add-ins that were opened using the File ➪ Open command (if any). The AddIns2 collection is available only in Excel 2010 and newer.

FIGURE 16.8

A table that lists information about all members of the `AddIns` collection

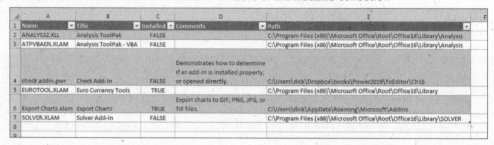

Name	Title	Installed	Comments	Path
ANALYS32.XLL	Analysis ToolPak	FALSE		C:\Program Files (x86)\Microsoft Office\Root\Office16\Library\Analysis
ATPVBAEN.XLAM	Analysis ToolPak - VBA	FALSE		C:\Program Files (x86)\Microsoft Office\Root\Office16\Library\Analysis
check addin.pwr	Check Add-In	FALSE	Demonstrates how to determine if an add-in is installed properly, or opened directly.	C:\Users\dick\Dropbox\books\Power2019\ToEditor\Ch16
EUROTOOL.XLAM	Euro Currency Tools	TRUE		C:\Program Files (x86)\Microsoft Office\Root\Office16\Library
Export Charts.xlam	Export Charts	TRUE	Export charts to GIF, PNG, JPG, or TIF files.	C:\Users\dick\AppData\Roaming\Microsoft\AddIns
SOLVER.XLAM	Solver Add-in	FALSE		C:\Program Files (x86)\Microsoft Office\Root\Office16\Library\SOLVER

ON THE WEB

This procedure is available on the book's website in the `List Add-in Information.xlsm` file.

NOTE

You can determine whether a particular workbook is an add-in by accessing its `IsAddIn` property. This property isn't read-only, so you can also convert a workbook to an add-in by setting the `IsAddIn` property to `True`. Conversely, you can convert an add-in to a workbook by setting the `IsAddIn` property to `False`. After doing so, the add-in's worksheets will be visible in Excel—even if the add-in's VBA project is protected. By using this technique, you can see that most of the dialog boxes in `SOLVER.XLAM` are old Excel 5/95 dialog sheets, not UserForms. Also, `SOLVER.XLAM` contains more than 15,000 defined names.

Accessing an add-in as a workbook

You can open an XLAM add-in file by using the Add-ins dialog box or by choosing the File ⇨ Open command. The former method is preferred because when you open an add-in with the File ⇨ Open command, its `Installed` property is *not* set to `True`. Therefore, you can't close the file by using the Add-ins dialog box. In fact, the only way to close such an add-in is with a VBA statement such as the following:

```
Workbooks("myaddin.xlam").Close
```

CAUTION

Using the `Close` method on an installed add-in removes the add-in from memory, but it does *not* set its `Installed` property to `False`. Therefore, the Add-ins dialog box still lists the add-in as installed, which can be confusing. The proper way to remove an installed add-in is to set its `Installed` property to `False`.

As you may have surmised, Excel's add-in capability is quirky. This component (except for the addition of the `AddIns2` collection) hasn't been improved in many years. Therefore, as a developer, you need to pay particular attention to issues involving installing and uninstalling add-ins.

AddIn object events

An `AddIn` object has two events: `AddInInstall` (occurs when the add-in is installed) and `AddInUninstall` (occurs when it is uninstalled). You can write event-handler procedures for these events in the `ThisWorkbook` code module for the add-in.

The following example is displayed as a message when the add-in is installed:

```
Private Sub Workbook_AddInInstall()
    MsgBox ThisWorkbook.Name & " add-in has been installed."
End Sub
```

> **CAUTION**
>
> Don't confuse the `AddInInstall` event with the `Open` event. The `AddInInstall` event occurs only when the add-in is first installed—not every time it is opened. If you need to execute code every time the add-in is opened, use a `Workbook _ Open` procedure.

 For additional information about events, see Chapter 6, "Understanding Excel's Events."

Optimizing the Performance of Add-Ins

If you ask a dozen Excel programmers to automate a particular task, chances are that you'll get a dozen different approaches. Most likely, not all of these approaches will perform equally well.

You can use the following tips to ensure that your code runs as quickly as possible. These tips apply to all VBA code, not just the code in add-ins.

- **Set the `Application.ScreenUpdating` property to** `False` when writing data to a worksheet or performing any other actions that cause changes to the display.
- **Declare the data type for all variables used and avoid variants whenever possible.** Use an `Option Explicit` statement at the top of each module to force yourself to declare all variables.
- **Create object variables to avoid lengthy object references.** For example, if you're working with a `Series` object for a chart, create an object variable by using code like this:

```
Dim S1 As Series
Set S1 = ActiveWorkbook.Sheets(1).ChartObjects(1)._
    Chart.SeriesCollection(1)
```

- **Whenever possible, declare object variables as a specific object type**—not `As Object`.
- **Use the `With-End With` construct,** when appropriate, to set multiple properties or call multiple methods for a single object.
- **Remove all extraneous code.** This tip is especially important if you've used the macro recorder to create procedures.
- **Manipulate data with VBA arrays rather than worksheet ranges,** if possible. Reading and writing to a worksheet usually takes much longer than manipulating data in memory. However, for best results, test both options.
- **Consider setting the calculation mode to Manual** if your code writes lots of data to worksheets. Doing so may increase the speed significantly. Here is code that changes the calculation mode to manual and back to its original setting after the code is run:

```
lCalcMode = Application.Calculation
Application.Calculation = xlCalculationManual
'Your code goes here
Application.Calculation = lCalcMode
```

- **Avoid linking UserForm controls to worksheet cells.** Doing so may trigger a recalculation whenever the user changes the UserForm control.
- **Compile your code before creating the add-in.** Doing so may increase the file size slightly, but it eliminates the need for Excel to compile the code before executing the procedures.

Special Problems with Add-Ins

Add-ins are great, but you should realize by now that there's no free lunch. Add-ins present their share of problems—or should we say *challenges?* In this section, we discuss some issues you need to know about if you'll be developing add-ins for widespread user distribution.

Ensuring that an add-in is installed

In some cases, you may need to ensure that your add-in is installed properly—that is, opened using the Add-ins dialog box and not the File ⇨ Open command. This section describes a technique that determines how an add-in was opened and gives the user an opportunity to install the add-in if it is not properly installed.

If the add-in isn't properly installed, the code displays a message (see Figure 16.9). Clicking Yes installs the add-in. Clicking No leaves the file open but doesn't install it. Clicking Cancel closes the file.

FIGURE 16.9

When attempting to open the add-in incorrectly, the user sees this message.

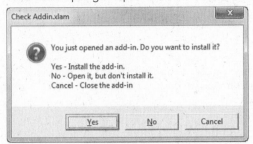

The code that follows is the code module for the add-in's `ThisWorkbook` object. This technique relies on the fact that the `AddInInstall` event occurs before the `Open` event for the workbook.

```
Dim InstalledProperly As Boolean

Private Sub Workbook_AddinInstall()
    InstalledProperly = True
End Sub

Private Sub Workbook_Open()
    Dim ai As AddIn, newAi As AddIn
    Dim msg As String
    Dim ans As Long

    'Was just installed using the Add-ins dialog box?
    If InstalledProperly Then Exit Sub

    'Is it in the AddIns collection?
    For Each ai In AddIns
      If ai.Name = ThisWorkbook.Name Then
        If ai.Installed Then
          MsgBox "This add-in is properly installed.", _
            vbInformation, ThisWorkbook.Name
          Exit Sub
        End If
      End If
    Next ai

    'It's not in AddIns collection, prompt user.
    msg = "You just opened an add-in. Do you want to install it?"
    msg = msg & vbNewLine
```

```
msg = msg & vbNewLine & "Yes - Install the add-in. "
msg = msg & vbNewLine & "No - Open it, but don't install it."
msg = msg & vbNewLine & "Cancel - Close the add-in"
ans = MsgBox(msg, vbQuestion + vbYesNoCancel, ThisWorkbook.Name)

Select Case ans
  Case vbYes
    ' Add it to the AddIns collection and install it.
    Set newAi = Application.AddIns.Add(ThisWorkbook.FullName)
    newAi.Installed = True
  Case vbNo
    'no action, leave it open
  Case vbCancel
    ThisWorkbook.Close
End Select
End Sub
```

The procedure covers the following possibilities:

- The add-in was opened automatically because it was installed in a previous session (it was listed in the Add-ins dialog and displayed a check mark). The user doesn't see a message.

- The user uses the Add-ins dialog box to install the add-in. The user doesn't see a message.

- The add-in was opened manually (by using File ⇨ Open) and is not a member of the AddIns collection. The user sees the message and must take one of the three actions.

- The add-in was opened manually, is a member of the AddIns collection, but it is not installed (not displayed with a check mark). The user sees the message and must take one of the three actions.

By the way, you can also use this code as a way to simplify the installation of an add-in that you give to someone. Just tell them to double-click the add-in's filename (which opens it in Excel) and respond Yes to the prompt. Better yet, modify the code so that the add-in is installed without a prompt.

ON THE WEB

This add-in, named Check Addin.xlam, is available on the book's website. Try opening it using both methods (with the Add-ins dialog box and by choosing File ⇨ Open).

Referencing other files from an add-in

If your add-in uses other files, you need to be especially careful when distributing the application. You can't assume anything about the storage structure of the system on which users will run the application. The easiest approach is to insist that all files for the application be copied to a single directory. Then you can use the Path property of your application's workbook to build path references to all other files.

For example, if your application uses a custom help file, be sure that the help file is copied to the same directory as the application itself. Then you can use a procedure like the following to make sure that the help file can be located:

```
Sub GetHelp()
    Application.Help ThisWorkbook.Path & "\userhelp.chm"
End Sub
```

If your application uses application programming interface (API) calls to standard Windows DLLs, you can assume that these can be found by Windows. But if you use custom DLLs, the best practice is to make sure that they're installed in the Windows\System directory (which might or might not be named Windows\System). You'll need to use the GetSystemDirectory Windows API function to determine the exact path of the System directory.

Working with the Ribbon

IN THIS CHAPTER

Looking at the Excel Ribbon UI from a user's perspective

Using VBA to work with the Ribbon

Customizing the Ribbon with RibbonX code

Looking at examples of workbooks that modify the Ribbon

Using boilerplate code for creating an old-style toolbar

Ribbon Basics

Beginning with Microsoft Office 2007, the primary user interface was changed from menus and toolbars to the *Ribbon*. While there are similarities between toolbars and the Ribbon, the Ribbon is radically different, particularly when it comes to VBA.

The Ribbon consists of a hierarchy of tabs, groups, and controls. The tabs appear across the top. Each tab consists of one or more groups, and each group consists of one or more controls.

Tabs These are the top objects in the Ribbon hierarchy. You use tabs to separate the most fundamental operations into logical groups. The default Ribbon contains the Home, Insert, Page Layout, Formulas, Data, Review, View, and Help tabs. You can add controls to existing tabs or create new tabs. For example, you might make a new tab with your company's name that contains controls for code that's specific to your company's operations.

Groups These are the second highest objects in the Ribbon hierarchy. Groups contain any of the number of different types of controls, and they are used to separate operations logically that are supported by a Ribbon tab. The default Formulas tab contains the Function Library, Defined Names, Formula Auditing, and Calculation groups. You don't have to include only related controls in a group, but it helps the user navigate the Ribbon more easily if you do.

Controls This level of the Ribbon hierarchy is where the action is. You interact with Excel or your custom VBA code through controls. The Ribbon supports a variety of controls, many of which are discussed in this chapter.

The Ribbon supports many types of controls. While we don't discuss every type of control in this chapter, we do discuss the ones that you are likely to use. If you're used to the older menus and toolbars, you'll appreciate the flexibility that the Ribbon controls offer. Figure 17.1 shows the default Page Layout tab with a good selection of control types.

FIGURE 17.1

The Page Layout tab contains many different control types.

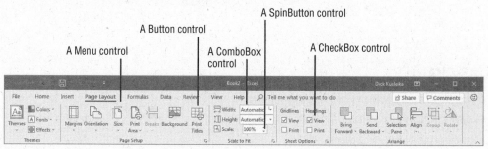

Here is a brief description of some of the controls:

Button   The Button control is the most basic Ribbon control, and it will be most familiar to you if you used the older toolbar user interface. You click a button and it performs an action. The Cut button on the Home tab performs the built-in cut action. Your custom buttons can be used to execute a macro that you've written.

SplitButton   The SplitButton control is similar to the Button control, but with an added feature. It is split, either horizontally or vertically, into a button part and a list part. You can click the button part to perform an action, just like the Button control. The list part, represented by an arrow, shows a list of similar buttons. The Paste SplitButton on the Home tab is a good example. The button part performs the normal paste operation. If you click the arrow to show the list, you can choose a different paste operation such as Paste Values or Paste Formatting.

CheckBox   The CheckBox control is similar to a check box on a UserForm. It appears as an empty box when unchecked and contains a check mark when checked. The View Gridlines controls in the Page Layout ⇨ Sheet Options group is a good example of a checkbox.

ComboBox   The ComboBox control is another familiar control if you've used User-Forms. Like the UserForm control with the same name, you can type text into the text box part of a ComboBox (called an EditBox in the Ribbon) or select an item from a list. The NumberFormat control in the Home ⇨ Number group is a good example of a ComboBox control. For example, you can type **Currency** directly in the text box portion or click the drop-down arrow and select a number format from the list.

Menu The Menu control displays a list of other controls. You can include a Button, SplitButton, CheckBox, or even another Menu control in the list. It differs from a SplitButton because when you click it, it always displays the list. That is, it does not have the option of having a default control. The Conditional Formatting control on the Home tab is an example of a Menu control.

There are several other controls offered by the Ribbon, including the ToggleButton, Gallery, EditBox, dynamicMenu, and Label controls. Some of these controls are used in this chapter. To learn more about these and the other controls, visit Microsoft's website at https://msdn.microsoft.com/en-us/library/bb386089.aspx.

Customizing the Ribbon

Excel provides a couple of ways to add your macros to the Ribbon. These methods don't give you the flexibility that creating a custom Ribbon does, but what they lack in customization, they make up for in simplicity.

Adding a button to the Ribbon

The simplest way to use the Ribbon to execute your code is to add your macro to a custom group using Excel's Customize Ribbon interface. In a new workbook, insert a module and add the following simple procedure:

```
Public Sub HelloWorld()
   MsgBox "Hello World!"
End Sub
```

ON THE WEB

This workbook, named Custom Ribbon and QAT.xlsm, is available on the book's website.

Return to Excel, right-click anywhere on the Ribbon, and choose Customize the Ribbon to display the Customize Ribbon tab in the Excel Options dialog box. The Customize Ribbon tab primarily consists of two lists. The list on the left contains all of the possible commands, and the list on the right shows what the Ribbon currently looks like.

At the top of these lists are drop-down boxes that allow you to filter them, making the command you're looking for easier to find. From the drop-down above the commands list, choose Macros, as shown in Figure 17.2. Now the left list shows all of the macros that are available to add to the Ribbon, including the HelloWorld procedure that you just created.

You can't add your macro to just anywhere on the Ribbon. Excel prevents you from changing its built-in groups. To add your macro, you must create a custom group.

FIGURE 17.2

The Customize Ribbon tab allows you to add macros to the Ribbon.

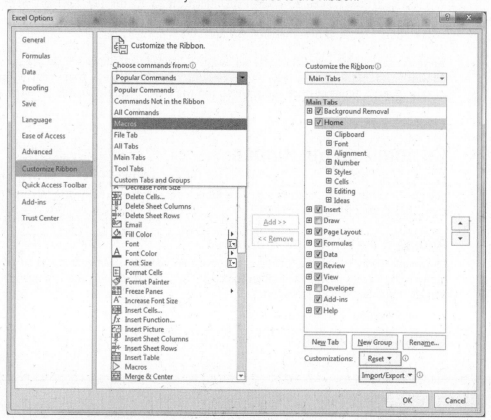

Adding your macro to a custom group on the Ribbon

Follow these steps to add the `HelloWorld` procedure to a custom group on the Home tab:

1. Select the Home tab in the right list of the Customize Ribbon tab. If you don't see the Home tab, select Main Tabs from the drop-down above this list.

2. Click the New Group button below the list to add a custom group to the Home tab.

3. The new group is named New Group (Custom) by default. Click the Rename button to change the group's name to **MyGroup**.

4. With the custom group selected, choose the HelloWorld entry in the left list and click the Add>> button. Your HelloWorld macro now appears below the custom group.

5. Select the HelloWorld entry in the right list and click the Rename button. In the Rename dialog box, you can change the label of the control and change the icon from the default macro icon. Figure 17.3 shows the Rename dialog box where the blue information icon is selected and the Display Name value is changed to include a space between *Hello* and *World*.

6. Click OK to close the Excel Options dialog box.

FIGURE 17.3

The Rename dialog lets you choose an icon for your Ribbon button.

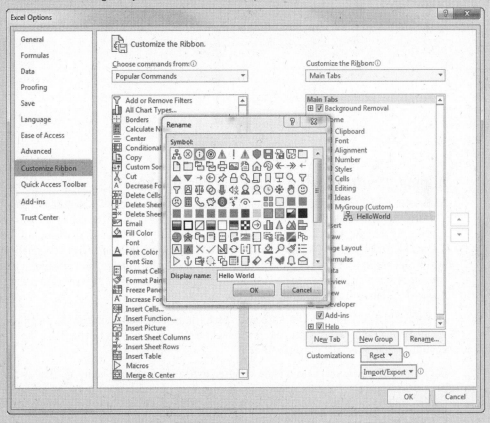

The Home tab now contains a custom group called MyGroup, and that group contains one control labeled Hello World. Figure 17.4 shows the new control and the message box that's displayed when it's clicked.

FIGURE 17.4

The custom Ribbon button executes the HelloWorld macro.

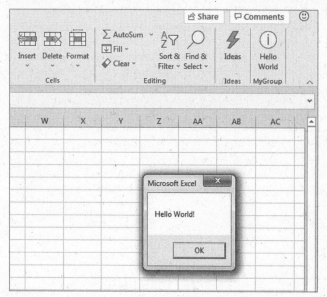

Adding a button to the Quick Access toolbar

Another method for accessing your macros is to add them to the *Quick Access toolbar* (QAT). The QAT is a list of buttons that's always visible regardless of which tab is showing on the Ribbon. By default, the QAT appears above the tabs on the Ribbon, but it can also be shown below the Ribbon. If you prefer to show the QAT below the Ribbon, click the small down arrow on the right of the QAT and choose Show Below the Ribbon from the menu. Or, you can, right-click anywhere on the QAT or the Ribbon and choose Show Quick Access Toolbar below the Ribbon from the shortcut menu.

By default, the QAT shows the AutoSave, Save, Undo, and Redo commands. In this example, we'll add the HelloWorld procedure from the preceding section to the QAT. The steps are similar to adding a button to the Ribbon.

Click the QAT down arrow, and choose More Commands from the menu to display the Quick Access Toolbar tab of the Excel Options dialog. Note how similar this tab is to the Customize Ribbon tab from the preceding section. It has a list of commands on the left and the current state of the QAT on the right.

Next, select Macros from the drop-down box above the left list. The HelloWorld procedure now appears in the list. Select HelloWorld from the left list, and click the Add>> button to add it to the QAT (see Figure 17.5). Unlike customizing the Ribbon, there is no Rename button. To customize a QAT button, click the Modify button to choose an icon and change

FIGURE 17.5

You can add a macro to the Quick Access toolbar.

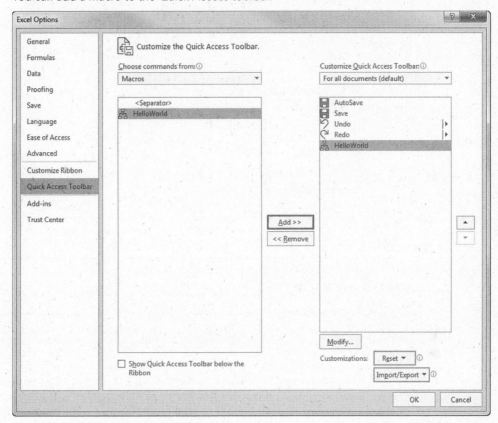

the name. The QAT doesn't actually display names. Changing Display Name in the Modify Button dialog changes what's shown in the tooltip when you hover over the button.

When you return to Excel's main window, the QAT will include a new button that executes your HelloWorld procedure. Figure 17.6 shows the QAT and the results of clicking the new button.

Understanding the limitations of Ribbon customization

Now that you have a custom button on both the Ribbon and the QAT, you can easily execute the HelloWorld procedure. When you save and close the workbook that contains HelloWorld, the buttons on the Ribbon and QAT may still be there under certain circumstances. If you click either of those buttons when the workbook is closed, Excel will attempt to open the workbook. If Excel can't find it because you moved or renamed the workbook, you get a message that Excel can't find your macro (see Figure 17.7).

FIGURE 17.6

The new QAT button executes your macro.

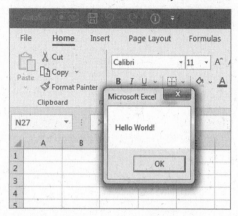

FIGURE 17.7

Excel can't find the macro associated with the Ribbon button.

One way to prevent this message is include your macro in an add-in that's always loaded. See Chapter 16, "Creating and Using Add-Ins," for how to create an add-in. If you want the buttons to appear only when the workbook is opened or you want to use Ribbon controls other than the `Button` control, you have to create a custom Ribbon in your workbook.

Unlike the Ribbon, the QAT has a method for showing a control only when a particular workbook is open. There is a drop-down on the right side of the Customize the Quick Access Toolbar dialog. If you choose the default "For all documents," the control will stay on the QAT regardless of what workbooks are open or active. The other option in the drop-down is For ActiveWorkbook.xlsm, where `ActiveWorkbook.xlsm` is the name of the active workbook. If you choose this option, the control will show on the QAT only when that particular workbook is active.

Creating a Custom Ribbon

You can't modify the Ribbon solely using VBA. Rather, you must write RibbonX code and insert the code into the workbook file—outside of Excel. You can, however, create VBA macros that are executed when a custom Ribbon control is activated.

RibbonX code is Extensible Markup Language (XML) that describes the controls, including where on the Ribbon they're displayed, what they look like, and what happens when they're activated. This book covers only a small portion of RibbonX—the topic is complex enough to be the subject of an entire book.

Adding a button to an existing tab

This section contains a step-by-step walk-through that will create two controls in a custom group on the Data tab of the Ribbon. You'll use the Custom UI Editor for Microsoft Office, an application created by Microsoft, to insert the XML for the new Ribbon into a workbook.

ON THE WEB

You can download a free copy of the Custom UI Editor for Microsoft Office from here:

`http://openxmldeveloper.org/blog/b/openxmldeveloper/archive/2006/05/26/customuieditor`
`.aspx`

The Custom UI Editor requires .NET version 3.0, which is not available via the normal Microsoft channels. If you don't have version 3.0 installed on your computer, you can still download it from Microsoft's website at the following location:

`https://www.microsoft.com/en-us/download/details.aspx?id=3005`

See your errors

Before you do any work with Ribbon customization, you should enable the display of RibbonX errors. Access the Excel Options dialog box (File ⇨ Options) and click the Advanced tab. Scroll down to the General section, and select Show Add-in User Interface Errors.

When this setting is enabled, RibbonX errors (if any) are displayed when the workbook opens, which is helpful for debugging.

Using RibbonX code to modify the Ribbon

Follow these steps to create a workbook that contains RibbonX code that modifies the Ribbon:

1. Create a new Excel workbook, and insert a standard module.
2. Save the workbook as macro-enabled, and name it `Ribbon Modification.xlsm`.
3. Close the workbook.
4. Launch the Custom UI Editor for Microsoft Office.
5. Open `Ribbon Modification.xlsm` by clicking the Open button on the Custom UI Editor toolbar and navigating to the file.

Continues

(continued)

6. From the Insert menu, choose Office 2010 Custom UI Part. This will add a `customUI14.xml` entry under your workbook in the tree view on the left.

7. In the main window, type the code shown in Figure 17.8. XML is case-sensitive, so be sure to type it exactly as displayed.

FIGURE 17.8

XML to create two buttons in a custom group

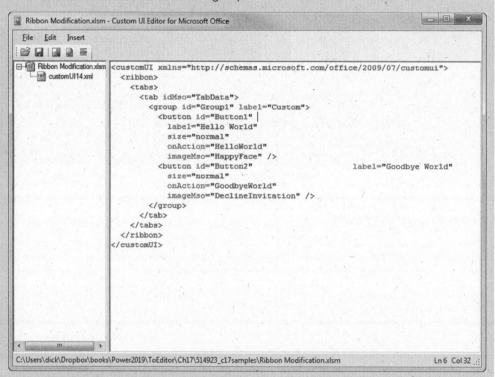

8. Click the Validate button on the toolbar to make sure that the XML is valid. The editor will display a `Custom UI is well formed` message if there are no errors.

9. Click the Generate Callbacks button on the toolbar. Figure 17.9 shows the procedures that you'll need for the buttons to work. Copy these procedures to the Clipboard so that you can paste them into the workbook later.

FIGURE 17.9

The editor generates VBA code to use in your workbook.

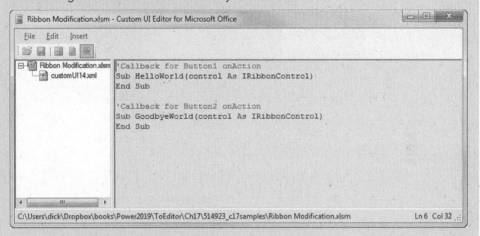

10. Double-click the `customUI.xml` entry in the tree view to return to the XML window.

11. Choose File ⇨ Save and then choose File ⇨ Close.

12. Activate Excel and open the workbook.

13. Press Alt+F11 to open the VBE, and paste the callback procedures that you copied in step 9 into the module you created in step 1.

14. Add a MsgBox line to each procedure, as shown in Figure 17.10.

FIGURE 17.10

Modify the callback procedures in the VBE.

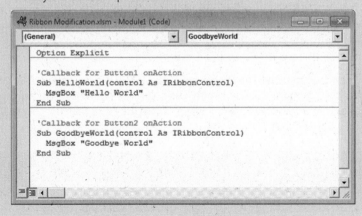

15. Return to Excel, activate the Data tab, and click your new buttons to test that they work (see Figure 17.11).

FIGURE 17.11

Two new buttons added to the Data tab

It's important to understand that the Ribbon modification is document-specific. In other words, the new Ribbon group is displayed only when the workbook that contains the RibbonX code is the active workbook. This is a major departure from how UI modifications worked in versions before Excel 2007.

TIP

To display Ribbon customizations when any workbook is active, convert the workbook to an add-in file or add the RibbonX code to your Personal Macro Workbook.

The RibbonX code

The RibbonX code used in this example is XML. Excel can read this XML and convert it into UI elements, such as tabs, groups, and buttons. XML consists of data between opening and closing tags (or, in some cases, within self-closing tags). The first line defines the schema in a customUI tag—this tells Excel how to read the XML. The last line is the closing tag for the customUI tag.

```
<customUI xmlns="http://schemas.microsoft.com/office/2009/07/
customui">

</customUI>
```

Everything between these two tags is interpreted as RibbonX code by Excel. The next line, the `ribbon` tag, defines that you want to work with the Ribbon. Its closing tag is the second-to-last line. The XML is hierarchical, just like the Ribbon. You can see in Figure 17.8 that the button tags are contained in the group tag, the group tag is contained in a tab tag, the tab tag is contained in the tabs tag, and the tabs tag is contained in the ribbon tag.

Tags also contain attributes. The tab tag contains an `idMso` attribute that tells Excel which tab to use.

```
<tab idMso="TabData">
```

Each built-in tab and group has a unique `idMso`. In this example, `TabData` tells Excel that you want to work in the built-in Data tab.

On the Web

You can get a complete list of `idMso` values for built-in Ribbon elements on Microsoft's website at www.microsoft.com/en-us/download/confirmation.aspx?id=727.

Custom elements, like the group and button tags, use the `id` attribute rather than `idMso`. You can use any value for the `id` attribute, such as `Group1` and `Button1` in this example, as long as it's unique. The following lists the attributes used in the example and a brief description of what they do:

> `idMso`: The unique identifier of a built-in UI element.
>
> `id`: A unique identifier, created by you, for custom elements.
>
> `label`: The text that accompanies the control in the Ribbon.
>
> `size`: Button controls can be large, normal, or small.
>
> `onAction`: The name of the VBA procedure to run when the button is clicked.
>
> `imageMso`: The identifier of a built-in image. You can use built-in images on your custom buttons. See the "Using imageMso images" sidebar for more information.

A complete list of attributes for all the UI elements would be too long to show here. You can find many examples of RibbonX on the Web and change them to suit your needs.

> **NOTE**
>
> RibbonX code is case-sensitive. For example, if you use IMAGEMSO instead of `imageMso`, your RibbonX code won't work properly.

Callback procedures

VBA responds to user actions using events (see Chapter 6, "Understanding Excel's Events"). The Ribbon uses a different technique: *callback procedures*. The buttons in this example are tied to the VBA code via the OnAction attribute. Most controls have an OnAction attribute, and the action is different for different controls. A button's action is a click, but a check box's action is a check or uncheck.

Most attributes have a corresponding callback attribute, generally with a get prefix. For example, the label attribute sets the text that displays for the control. There is also a getLabel attribute. You set the getLabel attribute to the name of a VBA procedure that determines what text is displayed. We'll discuss dynamic controls later in this chapter, but for now understand that callback procedures are not limited to OnAction.

Both VBA procedures in this example contain an argument named control, which is an IRibbonControl object. This object has three properties, which you can access in your VBA code.

- Context: A handle to the active window containing the Ribbon that triggered the callback. For example, use the following expression to get the name of the workbook that contains the RibbonX code:

  control.Context.Caption
- Id: Contains the name of the control, specified as its Id parameter.
- Tag: Contains any arbitrary text associated with the control.

The VBA callback procedures can be as simple or as complex as necessary.

The CUSTOM UI part

In step 6 of the "Using RibbonX code to modify the Ribbon" instructions, you inserted a customUI part for Office 2010. This choice makes the workbook incompatible with Excel 2007 and earlier. The other option on the Insert menu is Office 2007 Custom UI Part. Put the RibbonX code in an Office 2007 Custom UI part if you know that you need to support Excel 2007.

Microsoft makes new Custom UI Parts available when it changes the Ribbon in a way that requires one. Don't look for a 2019 Custom UI Part. This version of Office continues to use the Office 2010 Custom UI Part.

Using imageMso images

Microsoft Office provides more than 1,000 named images that are associated with various commands. You can specify any of these images for your custom Ribbon controls—if you know the image's name.

The accompanying figure shows a workbook that contains the names of all of the imageMso images for various versions of Office. Scroll through the image names, and you'll see 50 images at a time (in small or large size), beginning with the image name in the active cell. This workbook, named Mso Image Browser.xlsm, is available on the book's website.

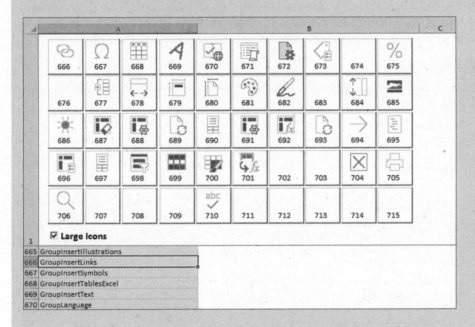

You can also use these images in an Image control placed on a UserForm. The following statement assigns the imageMso image named ReviewAcceptChanges to the Picture property of a UserForm Image control named Image1. The size of the image is specified as 32×32 pixels.

```
Image1.Picture = Application.CommandBars. _
  GetImageMso("ReviewAcceptChange", 32, 32)
```

Adding a check box to an existing tab

This section contains another example of using RibbonX to modify the UI. This workbook creates a new group on the Page Layout tab and adds a check box that toggles the display of page breaks.

> **NOTE**
>
> Although Excel has more than 1,700 commands, it doesn't have a command that toggles the page break display. After printing or previewing a worksheet, the only way to hide the page break display is to use the Excel Options dialog box. Therefore, the example in this section has some practical value.

This example is a bit tricky because it requires that the new Ribbon control be in sync with the active sheet. For example, if you activate a worksheet that doesn't display page breaks, the check box should be in its deselected state. If you activate a worksheet that displays page breaks, the check box should be selected. Furthermore, page breaks aren't relevant for a chart sheet, so the control should be disabled if you activate a chart sheet.

The RibbonX code

The RibbonX code that adds a new group (with a `CheckBox` control) to the Page Layout tab follows:

```
<customUI
    xmlns="http://schemas.microsoft.com/office/2006/01/customui"
    onLoad="Initialize">
  <ribbon>
    <tabs>
      <tab idMso="TabPageLayoutExcel">
        <group id="Group1" label="Custom">
          <checkBox id="Checkbox1"
            label="Page Breaks"
            onAction="TogglePageBreakDisplay"
            getPressed="GetPressed"
            getEnabled="GetEnabled"/>
        </group>
      </tab>
    </tabs>
  </ribbon>
</customUI>
```

This RibbonX code references four VBA callback procedures (each of which is described later).

- `Initialize`: Executed when the workbook is opened
- `TogglePageBreakDisplay`: Executed when the user clicks the check box
- `GetPressed`: Executed when the control is invalidated (the user activates a different sheet)
- `GetEnabled`: Executed when the control is invalidated (the user activates a different sheet)

Figure 17.12 shows the new control, placed in a group named Custom.

FIGURE 17.12

This check box control is always in sync with the page break display of the active sheet.

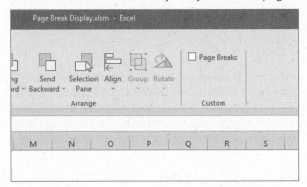

The VBA code

The `CustomUI` tag includes an `onLoad` parameter, which specifies the `Initialize` VBA callback procedure, as follows (this code is in a standard VBA module):

```
Public MyRibbon As IRibbonUI

Sub Initialize(Ribbon As IRibbonUI)
    'Executed when the workbook loads
    Set MyRibbon = Ribbon
End Sub
```

The `Initialize` procedure creates an `IRibbonUI` object named `MyRibbon`. Note that `MyRibbon` is a `Public` variable, so it's accessible from other procedures in the module.

The `ThisWorkbook` module contains a simple event procedure that is executed whenever a worksheet is activated. It calls the `CheckPageBreakDisplay` procedure.

```
Private Sub Workbook_SheetActivate(ByVal Sh As Object)
    CheckPageBreakDisplay
End Sub
```

The `CheckPageBreakDisplay` procedure *invalidates* the check box. In other words, it destroys any data associated with that control.

```
Sub CheckPageBreakDisplay()
    'Executed when a sheet is activated
    MyRibbon.InvalidateControl ("Checkbox1")
End Sub
```

When a control is invalidated, the `GetPressed` and `GetEnabled` procedures are called.

```
Sub GetPressed(control As IRibbonControl, ByRef returnedVal)
    'Executed when the control is invalidated
    On Error Resume Next
```

```
    returnedVal = ActiveSheet.DisplayPageBreaks
End Sub

Sub GetEnabled(control As IRibbonControl, ByRef returnedVal)
    'Executed when the control is invalidated
    returnedVal = TypeName(ActiveSheet) = "Worksheet"
End Sub
```

Note that the returnedVal argument is passed ByRef. This means that your code is able to change the value—and that's exactly what happens. In the GetPressed procedure, the returnedVal variable is set to the status of the DisplayPageBreaks property of the active sheet. The result is that the control's Pressed parameter is True if page breaks are displayed (and the control is selected). Otherwise, the control isn't selected.

In the GetEnabled procedure, the returnedVal variable is set to True if the active sheet is a worksheet (as opposed to a chart sheet). Therefore, the control is enabled only when the active sheet is a worksheet.

The only other VBA procedure is the onAction procedure, TogglePageBreakDisplay, which is executed when the user selects or deselects the check box.

```
Sub TogglePageBreakDisplay(control As IRibbonControl, pressed
As Boolean)
    'Executed when check box is clicked
    On Error Resume Next
    ActiveSheet.DisplayPageBreaks = pressed
End Sub
```

The pressed argument is True if the user selects the check box and False if the user deselects the check box. The code sets the DisplayPageBreaks property accordingly.

Ribbon controls demo

Figure 17.13 shows a custom Ribbon tab (My Stuff) with five groups of controls. In this section, we briefly describe the RibbonX code and the VBA callback procedures.

FIGURE 17.13

A new Ribbon tab with five groups of controls

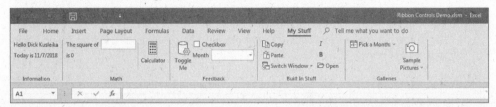

Creating a new tab

The following RibbonX code creates the new tab:

```
<ribbon>
  <tabs>
    <tab id="CustomTab" label="My Stuff">
    </tab>
  </tabs>
</ribbon>
```

TIP

If you'd like to create a minimal UI, the `ribbon` tag has a `startFromScratch` attribute. If set to `True`, all of the built-in tabs are hidden.

```
<ribbon startFromScratch="true" >
```

Creating a Ribbon group

The code in the `Ribbon Controls Demo.xlsm` example creates five groups on the My Stuff tab. Here's the code that creates the five groups:

```
<group  id="grpInfo" label="Information">
</group>

<group  id="grpMath" label="Math">
</group>

<group  id="grpFeedback" label="Feedback">
</group>

<group  id="grpBuiltIn" label="Built In Stuff">
</group>

<group  id="grpGalleries" label="Galleries">
</group>
```

These pairs of `<group>` and `</group>` tags are located between the `<tab>` and `</tab>` tags that create the new tab.

Creating controls

The following is the RibbonX code that creates the controls in the first group (Information). Figure 17.14 shows these controls on the Ribbon.

FIGURE 17.14

A Ribbon group with two labels.

```
<group id="grpInfo" label="Information">
  <labelControl id="lblUser" getLabel="getlblUser"/>
  <labelControl id="lblDate" getLabel="getlblDate"/>
</group>
```

Two `label` controls each have an associated VBA callback procedure (named `getlblUser` and `getlblDate`). These procedures are as follows:

```
Sub getlblUser(control As IRibbonControl, ByRef returnedVal)
  returnedVal = "Hello " & Application.UserName
End Sub

Sub getlblDate(control As IRibbonControl, ByRef returnedVal)
  returnedVal = "Today is " & Date
End Sub
```

When the RibbonX code is loaded, these two procedures are executed, and the captions of the `label` controls are dynamically updated with the user's name and the date.

Figure 17.15 shows the controls in the second group, labeled Math.

FIGURE 17.15

An editBox control in a custom Ribbon group

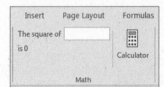

The RibbonX for the Math group follows:

```
<group id="grpMath" label="Math">
  <editBox id="ebxSquare"
    showLabel="true"
    label="The square of"
    onChange="ebxSquare_Change"/>

  <labelControl id="lblSquare"
    getLabel="getlblSquare"/>
  <separator id="sepMath"/>
  <button id="btnCalc"
    label="Calculator"
    size="large"
    onAction="ShowCalculator"
    imageMso="Calculator"/>
</group>
```

The editBox control has an onChange callback procedure named ebxSquare _ Change, which updates a label to display the square of the number entered. The ebxSquare _ Change procedure is as follows:

```
Private sq As Double

Sub ebxSquare_Change(control As IRibbonControl, text As String)
  sq = Val(text) ^ 2
  MyRibbon.Invalidate
End Sub
```

The label control showing the result is updated when MyRibbon is invalidated. Invalidating the Ribbon causes all of the controls to reinitialize. This procedure sets the sq variable to the square of the number entered, which is used by the label in the next procedure.

The label control has a getLabel callback procedure named getlblSquare. When the Ribbon is invalidated, this procedure is run. For an example of how to invalidate the Ribbon, see the "Adding a check box to an existing tab" section earlier in this chapter.

```
Sub getlblSquare(control As IRibbonControl, ByRef returnedVal)
  returnedVal = "is " & sq
End Sub
```

The separator control, sepMath, adds a vertical line to separate the squaring controls from the last control. The last control in this group is a simple button. Its onAction parameter executes a VBA procedure named ShowCalculator, which uses the VBA Shell function to display the Windows calculator.

```
Sub ShowCalculator(control As IRibbonControl)
  On Error Resume Next
  Shell "calc.exe", vbNormalFocus
  If Err.Number <> 0 Then MsgBox "Can't start calc.exe"
End Sub
```

17

Figure 17.16 shows the controls in the third group, labeled Feedback.

FIGURE 17.16

Three controls in a custom Ribbon group.

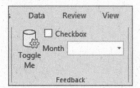

The RibbonX code for the third group is as follows:

```
<group  id="grpFeedback" label="Feedback">
  <toggleButton id="ToggleButton1"
    size="large"
    imageMso="FileManageMenu"
    label="Toggle Me"
    onAction="ToggleButton1_Click"/>

  <checkBox id="Checkbox1"
    label="Checkbox"
    onAction="Checkbox1_Change"/>

  <comboBox id="Combo1"
    label="Month"
    onChange="Combo1_Change">
    <item id="Month1" label="January"/>
    <item id="Month2" label="February"/>
    <item id="Month3" label="March"/>
    <item id="Month4" label="April"/>
    <item id="Month5" label="May"/>
    <item id="Month6" label="June"/>
    <item id="Month7" label="July"/>
    <item id="Month8" label="August"/>
    <item id="Month9" label="September"/>
    <item id="Month10" label="October"/>
    <item id="Month11" label="November"/>
    <item id="Month12" label="December"/>
  </comboBox>
</group>
```

The group contains a toggleButton, a checkBox, and a comboBox control. These controls are straightforward. Each has an associated callback procedure that simply displays the status of the control.

```
Sub ToggleButton1_Click(control As IRibbonControl, pressed
As Boolean)
  MsgBox "Toggle value: " & pressed
End Sub
```

```
Sub Checkbox1_Change(control As IRibbonControl, pressed As Boolean)
    MsgBox "Checkbox value: " & pressed
End Sub

Sub Combo1_Change(control As IRibbonControl, text As String)
    MsgBox text
End Sub
```

ON THE WEB

The `comboBox` control also accepts user-entered text. If you want to limit the choices to those that you provide, use a `dropDown` control.

The controls in the fourth group consist of built-in controls, as shown in Figure 17.17. To include a built-in control in a custom group, you just need to know its name (the `idMso` parameter).

FIGURE 17.17

This group contains built-in controls.

The RibbonX code is as follows:

```
<group id="grpBuiltIn" label="Built In Stuff">
    <control idMso="Copy" label="Copy"/>
    <control idMso="Paste" label="Paste" enabled="true"/>
    <control idMso="WindowSwitchWindowsMenuExcel"
        label="Switch Window"/>
    <control idMso="Italic"/>
    <control idMso="Bold"/>
    <control idMso="FileOpen"/>
</group>
```

These controls don't have callback procedures because they perform the standard action.

Figure 17.18 shows the final group of controls, which consists of two galleries.

FIGURE 17.18

This Ribbon group contains two galleries.

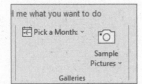

The RibbonX code for these two gallery controls is as follows:

```
<group id="grpGalleries" label="Galleries">
  <gallery id="galAppointments"
    imageMso="ViewAppointmentInCalendar"
    label="Pick a Month:"
    columns="2" rows="6"
    onAction="MonthSelected">
    <item id="January" label="January"
      imageMso="QuerySelectQueryType"/>
    <item id="February" label="February"
      imageMso="QuerySelectQueryType"/>
    <item id="March" label="March"
      imageMso="QuerySelectQueryType"/>
    <item id="April" label="April"
      imageMso="QuerySelectQueryType"/>
    <item id="May" label="May"
      imageMso="QuerySelectQueryType"/>
    <item id="June" label="June"
      imageMso="QuerySelectQueryType"/>
    <item id="July" label="July"
      imageMso="QuerySelectQueryType"/>
    <item id="August" label="August"
      imageMso="QuerySelectQueryType"/>
    <item id="September" label="September"
      imageMso="QuerySelectQueryType"/>
    <item id="October" label="October"
      imageMso="QuerySelectQueryType"/>
    <item id="November" label="November"
      imageMso="QuerySelectQueryType"/>
    <item id="December" label="December"
      imageMso="QuerySelectQueryType"/>
    <button id="Today"
      label="Today..."
      imageMso="ViewAppointmentInCalendar"
      onAction="ShowToday"/>
  </gallery>
  <gallery id="galPictures"
    label="Sample Pictures"
    columns="4"
    itemWidth="100" itemHeight="125"
    imageMso="Camera"
    onAction="galPictures_Click"
    getItemCount="galPictures_ItemCount"
    getItemImage="galPictures_ItemImage"
    size="large"/>
</group>
```

Figure 17.19 shows the first gallery, a list of month names in two columns.

FIGURE 17.19

A gallery that displays month names, plus a button

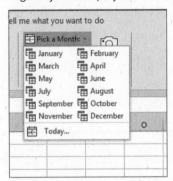

The `onAction` parameter executes the `MonthSelected` callback procedure, which displays the selected month (which is stored as the `id` parameter).

```
Sub MonthSelected(control As IRibbonControl, _
    id As String, index As Integer)

    MsgBox "You selected " & id
End Sub
```

The Pick a Month gallery also contains a button control with its own callback procedure (labeled Today) at the bottom.

```
Sub ShowToday(control As IRibbonControl)
    MsgBox "Today is " & Date
End Sub
```

The second gallery, shown in Figure 17.20, displays eight images, saved as JPG files.

These images are stored in a folder named `demopics` in the same folder as the workbook. The gallery uses the `getItemImage` callback procedure to fill the images. When the Ribbon is first loaded, the `onLoad` callback procedure, shown next, creates an array of image files in the directory, counts them, and stores the information in module-level variables, `aFiles()` and `ImgCnt`, so that the other callback procedures can read them.

```
Private ImgCnt As Long
Private aFiles() As String
Private sPath As String

Sub ribbonLoaded(ribbon As IRibbonUI)
    Set MyRibbon = ribbon
```

```
Dim sFile As String
sPath = ThisWorkbook.Path & "\demopics\"
sFile = Dir(sPath & "*.jpg")

Do While Len(sFile) > 0
  ImgCnt = ImgCnt + 1
  ReDim Preserve aFiles(1 To ImgCnt)
  aFiles(ImgCnt) = sFile
  sFile = Dir
Loop
End Sub
```

FIGURE 17.20

A gallery of images

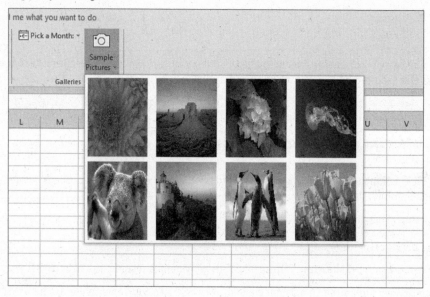

When the gallery is clicked, the getItemCount callback procedure, named galPictures_ItemCount, reads the ImgCnt variable, and galPictures_ItemImage is called that many times. Each time it's called, the index argument is increased by one. VBA's LoadPicture function is used to insert the images into the gallery.

```
Sub galPictures_ItemCount(control As IRibbonControl, _
  ByRef returnedVal)

  returnedVal = ImgCnt
End Sub
```

```
Sub galPictures_ItemImage(control As IRibbonControl, _
  index As Integer, ByRef returnedVal)

  Set returnedVal = LoadPicture(sPath & aFiles(index + 1))
End Sub
```

Note that dynamic controls, such as galleries, start their index at zero.

A dynamicMenu control example

One of the most interesting Ribbon controls is the dynamicMenu control. This control lets your VBA code feed XML data into the control, which provides the basis for menus that change based on context.

Setting up a dynamicMenu control isn't a simple task, but this control probably offers the most flexibility in terms of using VBA to modify the Ribbon dynamically.

This section describes a simple dynamicMenu control demo that displays a different menu for each of the three worksheets in a workbook. Figure 17.21 shows the menu that appears when Sheet1 is active. When a sheet is activated, a VBA procedure sends XML code specific to the sheet. For this demo, the XML code is stored directly in the worksheets to make it easier to read. Alternatively, the XML markup can be stored as a string variable in your code.

FIGURE 17.21

The dynamicMenu control lets you create a menu that varies depending on the context.

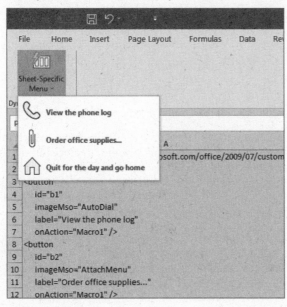

The RibbonX code that creates the new tab, the new group, and the `dynamicMenu` control follows:

```
<customUI xmlns="http://schemas.microsoft.com/
office/2009/07/customui"
    onLoad="ribbonLoaded">
  <ribbon>
  <tabs>
    <tab id="CustomTab" label="Dynamic">
        <group id="group1" label="Dynamic Menu Demo">
          <dynamicMenu id="DynamicMenu"
                getContent="dynamicMenuContent"
                imageMso="RegionLayoutMenu"
                size = "large"
                label="Sheet-Specific Menu"/>
        </group>
    </tab>
    </tabs>
    </ribbon>
</customUI>
```

This example needs a way to invalidate the Ribbon whenever the user activates a new sheet. You can use the same method used for the page break display example earlier in this chapter (see "Adding a check box to an existing tab"). Specifically, you declare a `Public` variable, `MyRibbon`, of type `IRibbonUI`. Use the `Workbook_SheetActivate` event procedure to call the `UpdateDynamicRibbon` procedure whenever a new sheet is activated.

```
Sub UpdateDynamicRibbon()
    'Invalidate the Ribbon to force a call to dynamicMenuContent
    On Error Resume Next
    MyRibbon.Invalidate
    If Err.Number <> 0 Then
      MsgBox "Lost the Ribbon object. Save and reload."
    End If
End Sub
```

The `UpdateDynamicRibbon` procedure invalidates the `MyRibbon` object, which forces a call to the VBA callback procedure named `dynamicMenuContent` (a procedure referenced by the `getContent` parameter in the RibbonX code). Note the error-handling code. Some edits to your VBA code destroy the `MyRibbon` object, which is created when the workbook is opened. Attempting to invalidate an object that doesn't exist causes an error, and the message box informs the user that the workbook must be saved and reopened.

The `dynamicMenuContent` procedure follows. This procedure loops through the cells in column A of the active sheet, reads the XML code, and stores it in a variable named `XMLcode`. When all of the XML has been appended, it's passed to the `returnedVal` argument. The net effect is that the `dynamicMenu` control has new code, so it displays a different set of menu options.

```
Sub dynamicMenuContent(control As IRibbonControl, _
  ByRef returnedVal)

  Dim r As Long
  Dim XMLcode As String
  'Read the XML markup from the active sheet
  For r = 1 To Application.CountA(Range("A:A"))
    XMLcode = XMLcode & ActiveSheet.Cells(r, 1).Value & " "
  Next r
  returnedVal = XMLcode
End Sub
```

ON THE WEB

The workbook that contains this example is available on the book's website in the `Dynamic Menu.xlsm` file.

17

More on Ribbon customization

This section concludes with some additional points to keep in mind as you explore the wonderful world of Excel Ribbon customization.

- When you're working with the Ribbon, make sure you turn on the display of error messages. Refer to the "See your errors" sidebar, earlier in this chapter.

- Remember that RibbonX code is case-sensitive.

- All of the named control IDs are in English, and they're the same across all language versions of Excel. Therefore, Ribbon modifications work regardless of what language version of Excel is used.

- Ribbon modifications appear only when the workbook that contains the RibbonX code is active. To make Ribbon modifications appear for all workbooks, the RibbonX code must be in an add-in.

- The built-in controls scale themselves when the Excel window is resized. Custom controls do not scale in Excel 2007, but they do in Excel 2010 and later.

- You cannot add or remove controls from a built-in Ribbon group.

- You can, however, hide tabs. The RibbonX code that follows hides three tabs.

```
<customUI xmlns="http://schemas.microsoft.com/office/2009/07/customui">
<ribbon>
  <tabs>
    <tab idMso="TabPageLayoutExcel" visible="false"/>
    <tab idMso="TabData" visible="false"/>
    <tab idMso="TabReview" visible="false"/>
  </tabs>
</ribbon>
</customUI>
```

- You can also hide groups within a tab. Here's the RibbonX code that hides four groups on the Insert tab:

```
<customUI xmlns="http://schemas.microsoft.com/office/2009/07/customui">
<ribbon>
  <tabs>
    <tab idMso="TabInsert">
      <group idMso="GroupInsertTablesExcel" visible="false"/>
      <group idMso="GroupInsertIllustrations" visible="false"/>
      <group idMso="GroupInsertLinks" visible="false"/>
      <group idMso="GroupInsertText" visible="false"/>
    </tab>
  </tabs>
</ribbon>
</customUI>
```

■ You can assign your own macro to a built-in control. This is known as *repurposing the control*. The RibbonX code that follows intercepts three built-in commands:

```
<customUI xmlns="http://schemas.microsoft.com/office/2009/07/customui">
<commands>
  <command idMso="FileSave" onAction="mySave"/>
  <command idMso="FilePrint" onAction="myPrint"/>
  <command idMso="FilePrintQuick" onAction="myPrint"/>
</commands>
</customUI>
```

■ You can also write RibbonX code to disable one or more built-in controls. The code that follows disables the Insert ClipArt command:

```
<customUI xmlns="http://schemas.microsoft.com/office/2009/07/customui">
<commands>
  <command idMso="ClipArtInsert" enabled="false"/>
</commands>
</customUI>
```

■ If you have two or more workbooks (or add-ins) that add controls to the same custom Ribbon group, you must make sure they both use the same namespace. Do this in the <CustomUI> tag at the top of the RibbonX code.

Using VBA with the Ribbon

As you've seen in this chapter, the typical workflow when working with the Ribbon is to create the RibbonX code and use callback procedures to respond to user actions. There are other ways to interact with the Ribbon with VBA, but they are limited.

The following is a list of what you can do with the Ribbon using VBA:

■ Determine whether a particular control is enabled

■ Determine whether a particular control is visible

■ Determine whether a particular control is pressed (for toggle buttons and check boxes)

■ Get a control's label, screen tip, or supertip (a more detailed description of the control)

■ Display the image associated with a control

■ Execute the command associated with a particular control

Accessing a Ribbon control

All told, Excel has more than 1,700 Ribbon controls. Every Ribbon control has a name, and you use that name when you work with the control using VBA.

For example, the statement that follows displays a message box that shows the Enabled status of the `ViewCustomViews` control. (This control is located in the View ⇨ Workbook Views group.)

```
MsgBox Application.CommandBars.GetEnabledMso("ViewCustomViews")
```

Normally, this control is enabled. But if the workbook contains a table (created by choosing Insert ⇨ Tables ⇨ Table), the `ViewCustomViews` control is disabled. In other words, a workbook can use either the Custom Views feature or the Tables feature but not both.

Determining the name of a particular control is a manual task. First, display the Customize Ribbon tab of the Excel Options dialog box. Locate the control in the list box on the left and then hover the mouse pointer over the item. The control's name appears in a pop-up screen tip, in parentheses (see Figure 17.22).

FIGURE 17.22

Using the Customize Ribbon tab of the Excel Options dialog box to determine the name of a control

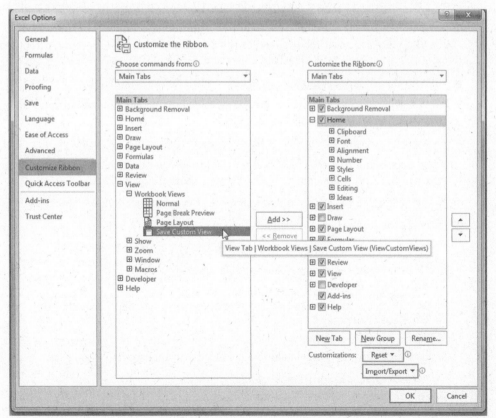

Unfortunately, it's not possible to write VBA code to loop through all of the controls on the Ribbon and display a list of their names.

Working with the Ribbon

The preceding section provided an example of using the GetEnabledMso method of the CommandBars object. The following is a list of all methods relevant to working with the Ribbon via the CommandBars object. All of these methods take one argument: idMso, which is a String data type and represents the name of the command. You must know the name—using index numbers is not possible.

- ExecuteMso: Executes a control
- GetEnabledMso: Returns True if the specified control is enabled
- GetImageMso: Returns the image for a control
- GetLabelMso: Returns the label for a control
- GetPressedMso: Returns True if the specified control is pressed (applies to check box and toggle button controls)
- GetScreentipMso: Returns the screen tip for a control (the text that appears in the control)
- GetSupertipMso: Returns the supertip for a control (the description of the control that appears when you hover the mouse pointer over the control)

The VBA statement that follows toggles the Selection task pane (a feature introduced in Excel 2007 that facilitates selecting objects on a worksheet):

```
Application.CommandBars.ExecuteMso "SelectionPane"
```

The following statement displays the Paste Special dialog box (and will display an error message if the Windows Clipboard is empty):

```
Application.CommandBars.ExecuteMso "PasteSpecialDialog"
```

Here's a command that tells you whether the formula bar is visible (it corresponds to the state of the Formula Bar control in the View ⇨ Show group):

```
MsgBox Application.CommandBars.GetPressedMso "ViewFormulaBar"
```

To toggle the formula bar, use this statement:

```
Application.CommandBars.ExecuteMso "ViewFormulaBar"
```

To make sure that the formula bar is visible, use this code:

```
With Application.CommandBars
  If Not .GetPressedMso("ViewFormulaBar") Then .ExecuteMso
"ViewFormulaBar"
End With
```

To make sure that the formula bar is not visible, use this code:

```
With Application.CommandBars
  If .GetPressedMso("ViewFormulaBar") Then .ExecuteMso
"ViewFormulaBar"
End With
```

Or don't bother with the Ribbon and set the `DisplayFormulaBar` property of the `Application` object either to `True` or `False`. This statement displays the formula bar (or has no effect if the formula bar is already visible):

```
Application.DisplayFormulaBar = True
```

The statement that follows displays `True` if the Merge & Center control is enabled. (This control is disabled if the sheet is protected or if the active cell is in a table.)

```
MsgBox Application.CommandBars.GetEnabledMso("MergeCenter")
```

The following VBA code adds an ActiveX Image control to the active worksheet and uses the `GetImageMso` method to display the binoculars icon from the Find & Select control in the Home ⇨ Editing group:

```
Sub ImageOnSheet()
  Dim MyImage As OLEObject

  Set MyImage = ActiveSheet.OLEObjects.Add _
    (ClassType:="Forms.Image.1", _
    Left:=50, _
    Top:=50)
  With MyImage.Object
    .AutoSize = True
    .BorderStyle = 0
    .Picture = Application.CommandBars. _
      GetImageMso("FindDialog", 32, 32)
  End With
End Sub
```

To display the Ribbon icon in an `Image` control (named `Image1`) on a UserForm, use this procedure:

```
Private Sub UserForm_Initialize()
  With Image1
    .Picture = Application.CommandBars.GetImageMso _
      ("FindDialog", 32, 32)
    .AutoSize = True
  End With
End Sub
```

Activating a tab

Microsoft provides no direct way to activate a Ribbon tab from VBA. But if you really need to do so, using `SendKeys` is your only option. The `SendKeys` method simulates keystrokes. The keystrokes required to activate the Home tab are Alt+H. These keystrokes display the keytips in the Ribbon. To hide the keytips, press F6. Using this information, the following statement sends the keystrokes required to activate the Home tab:

```
Application.SendKeys "%h{F6}"
```

To avoid the display of keytips, turn off screen updating:

```
Application.ScreenUpdating = False
```

```
Application.SendKeys "%h{F6}"
Application.ScreenUpdateing=True
```

> **CAUTION**
>
> As always, use `SendKeys` as a last resort and understand that `SendKeys` may not be perfectly reliable. For example, if you execute the previous example while a UserForm is displayed, the keystrokes will be sent to the User-Form, not to the Ribbon.

Creating an Old-Style Toolbar

Excel 2019 will still display menus and toolbars written using pre-2007 methods. We strongly recommend that you use the Ribbon in your projects for many reasons, not the least of which is the richer controls that the Ribbon offers. But if you have to maintain existing code that uses the old-style toolbars, you will have to know how they work.

In this section, we provide boilerplate code that you can adapt as needed. We don't offer much in the way of explanation. For more information about `CommandBar` objects, search the Web or consult the Excel 2003 edition of this book. `CommandBar` objects can be much more powerful than the example presented here.

Limitations of old-style toolbars

If you decide to create a toolbar, be aware of the following limitations:

- The toolbar can't be free-floating.
- The toolbar will always appear in the Add-Ins ⇨ Custom Toolbars group (along with any other toolbars).
- Excel ignores some `CommandBar` properties and methods.

Code to create a toolbar

> **NOTE**
>
> In versions prior to Excel 2013, custom toolbars are visible regardless of which workbook is active. Since Excel 2013, however, a custom toolbar is visible only in the workbook in which it was created—and also in new workbooks created while the original workbook is active.

The code in this section assumes you have a workbook with two macros (named `Macro1` and `Macro2`). It also assumes that you want the toolbar to be created when the workbook is opened and deleted when the workbook is closed.

In the `ThisWorkbook` code module, enter the following procedures. The first one calls the procedure that creates the toolbar when the workbook is opened. The second calls the procedure to delete the toolbar when the workbook is closed.

```
Private Sub Workbook_Open()
  CreateToolbar
End Sub

Private Sub Workbook_BeforeClose(Cancel As Boolean)
  DeleteToolbar
End Sub
```

 In Chapter 6, we describe a potentially serious problem with the Workbook _ BeforeClose event. Excel's Do you want to save ... prompt is displayed *after* the Workbook _ BeforeClose event handler runs. So if the user clicks Cancel, the workbook remains open but the custom menu items have already been deleted. In Chapter 6, we also present a way to get around this problem.

The CreateToolbar procedure follows:

```
Const TOOLBARNAME As String = "MyToolbar"

Sub CreateToolbar()
  Dim TBar As CommandBar
  Dim Btn As CommandBarButton

' Delete existing toolbar (if it exists)
  On Error Resume Next
    CommandBars(TOOLBARNAME).Delete
  On Error GoTo 0

' Create toolbar
  Set TBar = CommandBars.Add
  With TBar
    .Name = TOOLBARNAME
    .Visible = True
  End With

' Add a button
  Set Btn = TBar.Controls.Add(Type:=msoControlButton)
  With Btn
    .FaceId = 300
    .OnAction = "Macro1"
    .Caption = "Macro1 Tooltip goes here"
  End With

' Add another button
  Set Btn = TBar.Controls.Add(Type:=msoControlButton)
  With Btn
    .FaceId = 25
    .OnAction = "Macro2"
    .Caption = "Macro2 Tooltip goes here"
  End With
End Sub
```

Figure 17.23 shows the two-button toolbar.

FIGURE 17.23

An old-style toolbar, located in the Custom Toolbars group of the Add-Ins tab

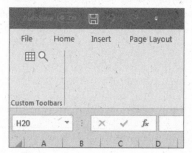

The module-level constant, TOOLBARNAME, stores the toolbar's name. This name is used also in the DeleteToolbar procedure, so using a constant ensures that both procedures work with the same name.

The procedure starts by deleting the existing toolbar that has the same name (if such a toolbar exists). Including this statement is useful during development and also eliminates the error you get if you attempt to create a toolbar using a duplicate name.

The toolbar is created by using the Add method of the CommandBars object. The two buttons are added by using the Add method of the Controls object. Each button has three properties.

- FaceID: A number that determines the image displayed on the button. Chapter 18, "Working with Shortcut Menus," contains more information about FaceID images.
- OnAction: The macro executed when the button is clicked.
- Caption: The screen tip that appears when you hover the mouse pointer over the button.

Tip

Rather than set the FaceID property, you can set the Picture property using any of the imageMso images. For example, the following statement displays a green check mark:

```
.Picture = Application.CommandBars.GetImageMso _
    ("AcceptInvitation", 16, 16)
```

For more information about imageMso images, see the sidebar "Using imageMso images."

When the workbook is closed, the `Workbook_BeforeClose` event procedure fires, which calls `DeleteToolbar`.

```
Sub DeleteToolbar()
   On Error Resume Next
      CommandBars(TOOLBARNAME).Delete
   On Error GoTo 0
End Sub
```

Note that the toolbar is *not* deleted from workbook windows that were opened after the toolbar was created.

Working with Shortcut Menus

CommandBar Overview

A `CommandBar` object is used for three Excel user interface elements.

- Custom toolbars
- Custom menus
- Customs shortcut (right-click) menus

When you write VBA code to customize a menu or a toolbar, Excel intercepts that code and ignores many of your commands. Menu and toolbar customizations performed with the `CommandBar` object appear in the Add-Ins ⇨ Menu Commands group or the Add-Ins ⇨ Custom Toolbars group. So, for all practical purposes, the `CommandBar` object in Excel is now limited to shortcut menu operations.

In this section, we provide some background information about `CommandBar` objects.

CommandBar types

Excel supports three types of `CommandBar` objects, differentiated by their `Type` property. The `Type` property can be any of these three values:

- `msoBarTypeNormal`: A toolbar (`Type` = 0)
- `msoBarTypeMenuBar`: A menu bar (`Type` = 1)
- `msoBarTypePopUp`: A shortcut menu (`Type` = 2)

Even though toolbars and menu bars aren't used in Excel 2007 and later, these UI elements are still included in the object model for compatibility with older applications. However, attempting to display a CommandBar object of type 0 or 1 has no effect in Excel versions after Excel 2003. In Excel 2003, for example, the following statement displays the Standard toolbar:

```
CommandBars("Standard").Visible = True
```

In later versions of Excel, that statement is ignored.

This chapter focuses exclusively on type 2 CommandBar objects (shortcut menus).

Listing shortcut menus

The ShowShortcutMenuNames procedure that follows, which loops through all CommandBar objects, lists the 67 shortcut menus that exist in Excel 2019. To limit the list only to shortcut menus, the code checks the Type property to see whether its value is msoBarTypePopUp (a built-in constant that has a value of 2).

```
Sub ShowShortcutMenuNames()
   Dim Row As Long
   Dim cbar As CommandBar

   Row = 1
   For Each cbar In CommandBars
     If cbar.Type = msoBarTypePopup Then
        Cells(Row, 1) = cbar.Index
        Cells(Row, 2) = cbar.Name
        Cells(Row, 3) = cbar.Controls.Count
        Row = Row + 1
     End If
   Next cbar
End Sub
```

Figure 18.1 shows part of the output from this procedure. The shortcut menu index values range from 22 to 156. Also, note that not all of the names are unique. For example, CommandBar objects 36 and 39 both have a Name value of Cell because right-clicking a cell gives a different shortcut menu when the worksheet is in page break preview mode.

FIGURE 18.1

A simple macro generates a list of all shortcut menus.

	A	B	C	D
1	22	PivotChart Menu	6	
2	35	Workbook tabs	16	
3	36	Cell	34	
4	37	Column	15	
5	38	Row	15	
6	39	Cell	27	
7	40	Column	21	
8	41	Row	21	
9	42	Ply	11	
10	43	XLM Cell	20	
11	44	Document	9	
12	45	Desktop	5	
13	46	Nondefault Drag and Drop	11	
14	47	AutoFill	12	
15	48	Button	12	
16	49	Dialog	4	
17	50	Series	5	
18	51	Plot Area	8	
19	52	Floor and Walls	3	
20	53	Trendline	2	

Referring to CommandBars

You can reference a particular CommandBar object by its Index or Name property. For example, the expressions that follow both refer to the shortcut menu that is displayed when you right-click a column letter in Excel 2019:

```
Application.CommandBars(37)
Application.CommandBars("Column")
```

The CommandBars collection is a member of the Application object. When you reference this collection in a regular VBA module or in a module for a sheet, you can omit the reference to the Application object. For example, the following statement (contained in a standard VBA module) displays the name of the object in the CommandBars collection that has an index of 42:

```
MsgBox CommandBars(42).Name
```

When you reference the CommandBars collection from a code module for a This-Workbook object, you must precede it with a reference to the Application object, like this:

```
MsgBox Application.CommandBars(42).Name
```

> **CAUTION**
>
> Unfortunately, the index numbers for CommandBar objects have not always remained constant across the different Excel versions. Therefore, using names rather than index numbers is more reliable. Names are also more readable and lead to more maintainable code.

Referring to Controls in a CommandBar

A `CommandBar` object contains `Control` objects, which are buttons or menus. You can refer to a control by its `Index` property or by its `Caption` property. Here's a simple procedure that displays the caption of the first menu item on the Cell shortcut menu:

```
Sub ShowCaption()
    MsgBox CommandBars("Cell").Controls(1).Caption
End Sub
```

The following procedure displays the `Caption` property for each control in the shortcut menu that appears when you right-click a sheet tab (that shortcut menu is named `Ply`):

```
Sub ShowCaptions()
    Dim txt As String
    Dim ctl As CommandBarControl

    For Each ctl In CommandBars("Ply").Controls
        txt = txt & ctl.Caption & vbNewLine
    Next ctl
    MsgBox txt
End Sub
```

When you execute this procedure, you see the message box shown in Figure 18.2. The ampersand is used to indicate the underlined letter in the text—the keystroke that will execute the menu item.

FIGURE 18.2

Displaying the `Caption` property for controls

In some cases, Control objects on a shortcut menu contain other Control objects. For example, the Filter control on the Cell right-click menu contains other controls. The Filter control is a submenu, and the additional items are submenu items.

The statement that follows displays the first submenu item in the Filter submenu:

```
MsgBox CommandBars("Cell").Controls("Filter").Controls(1).Caption
```

Finding a control

If you're writing code that will be used by a different language version of Excel, avoid using the Caption property to access a particular shortcut menu item. The Caption property is language-specific, so your code will fail if the user has a different language version of Excel.

Instead, use the FindControl method with the ID of the control (which is language-independent). For example, assume that you want to disable the Cut menu on the shortcut menu that appears when you right-click a column letter. If your workbook will be used only by people who have the English version of Excel, this statement will do the job:

```
CommandBars("Column").Controls("Cut").Enabled = False
```

To ensure that the command will work with non-English versions, you need to know the ID of the control. The following statement will tell you that the ID is 21:

```
MsgBox CommandBars("Column").Controls("Cut").ID
```

Then, to disable that control, use this statement:

```
CommandBars("Column").FindControl(ID:=21).Enabled = False
```

The CommandBar names are not regionalized, so a reference to CommandBars("Column") will always work. If two or more command bars have the same name, the first one is used.

Properties of CommandBar Controls

CommandBar controls have a number of properties that determine how the controls look and work. This list contains some of the more useful properties for CommandBar controls:

- Caption: The text displayed for the control. If the control shows only an image, the Caption property appears when you move the mouse pointer over the control.
- ID: A unique numeric identifier for the control.
- FaceID: A number that represents a built-in graphic image displayed next to the control's text.
- Type: A value that determines whether a control is a button (msoControl-Button) or a submenu (msoControlPopup).
- Picture: A graphics image displayed next to the control's text. This property is useful if you want to display a graphic from the Ribbon.

18

- BeginGroup: True if a separator bar appears before the control.
- OnAction: The name of a VBA macro that executes when the user clicks the control.
- BuiltIn: True if the control is an Excel built-in control.
- Enabled: True if the control can be clicked.
- Visible: True if the control is visible. Many of the shortcut menus contain hidden controls.
- ToolTipText: Text that appears when the user moves the mouse pointer over the control. (This is not applicable for shortcut menus.)

Displaying All Shortcut Menu Items

The ShowShortcutMenuItems procedure that follows creates a table that lists all the first-level controls on every shortcut menu. For each control, the table includes the shortcut menu's Index and Name values, plus the ID, Caption, Type, Enabled, and Visible property values.

```
Sub ShowShortcutMenuItems()
    Dim Row As Long
    Dim Cbar As CommandBar
    Dim ctl As CommandBarControl

    Range("A1:G1") = Array("Index", "Name", "ID", "Caption", _
        "Type", "Enabled", "Visible")
    Row = 2
    Application.ScreenUpdating = False

    For Each Cbar In Application.CommandBars
        If Cbar.Type = 2 Then
            For Each ctl In Cbar.Controls
                Cells(Row, 1) = Cbar.Index
                Cells(Row, 2) = Cbar.Name
                Cells(Row, 3) = ctl.ID
                Cells(Row, 4) = ctl.Caption
                If ctl.Type = 1 Then
                    Cells(Row, 5) = "Button"
                Else
                    Cells(Row, 5) = "Submenu"
                End If
                Cells(Row, 6) = ctl.Enabled
                Cells(Row, 7) = ctl.Visible
                Row = Row + 1
```

```
      Next ctl
    End If
  Next Cbar

    ActiveSheet.ListObjects.Add(xlSrcRange, _
      Range("A1").CurrentRegion, , xlYes).Name = "Table1"
  End Sub
```

Figure 18.3 shows a portion of the output.

FIGURE 18.3

Listing the items in all shortcut menus

	A	B	C	D	E	F	G
1	Index	Name	ID	Caption	Type	Enabled	Visible
2	22	PivotChart Menu	460	Field Setti&ngs	Button	TRUE	TRUE
3	22	PivotChart Menu	1604	&Options...	Button	FALSE	TRUE
4	22	PivotChart Menu	459	&Refresh Data	Button	TRUE	TRUE
5	22	PivotChart Menu	3956	&Hide PivotChart Field Buttons	Button	FALSE	TRUE
6	22	PivotChart Menu	30254	For&mulas	Submenu	TRUE	TRUE
7	22	PivotChart Menu	5416	Remo&ve Field	Button	FALSE	TRUE
8	35	Workbook tabs	957	Sheet1	Button	TRUE	TRUE
9	35	Workbook tabs	957	&Sheet List	Button	TRUE	FALSE
10	35	Workbook tabs	957	&Sheet List	Button	TRUE	FALSE
11	35	Workbook tabs	957	&Sheet List	Button	TRUE	FALSE
12	35	Workbook tabs	957	&Sheet List	Button	TRUE	FALSE
13	35	Workbook tabs	957	&Sheet List	Button	TRUE	FALSE
14	35	Workbook tabs	957	&Sheet List	Button	TRUE	FALSE
15	35	Workbook tabs	957	&Sheet List	Button	TRUE	FALSE
16	35	Workbook tabs	957	&Sheet List	Button	TRUE	FALSE
17	35	Workbook tabs	957	&Sheet List	Button	TRUE	FALSE
18	35	Workbook tabs	957	&Sheet List	Button	TRUE	FALSE
19	35	Workbook tabs	957	&Sheet List	Button	TRUE	FALSE
20	35	Workbook tabs	957	&Sheet List	Button	TRUE	FALSE
21	35	Workbook tabs	957	&Sheet List	Button	TRUE	FALSE
22	35	Workbook tabs	957	&Sheet List	Button	TRUE	FALSE
23	35	Workbook tabs	957	&Sheet List	Button	TRUE	FALSE
24	36	Cell	21	Cu&t	Button	TRUE	TRUE
25	36	Cell	19	&Copy	Button	TRUE	TRUE
26	36	Cell	22	&Paste	Button	TRUE	TRUE
27	36	Cell	21437	Paste &Special...	Button	TRUE	TRUE
28	36	Cell	3624	&Paste Table	Button	TRUE	TRUE

ON THE WEB

This example, named `Show Shortcut Menu Items.xlsm`, is available on the book's website.

18

Using VBA to Customize Shortcut Menus

In this section, we present some practical examples of VBA code that manipulates Excel's shortcut menus. These examples, which can be modified to suit your needs, will give you an idea of the types of things you can do with shortcut menus.

Shortcut menu and the single-document interface

In Excel versions prior to 2013, if your code modified a shortcut menu, that modification was in effect for all workbooks. For example, if you added a new item to the Cell right-click menu, that new item would appear when you right-clicked a cell in *any* workbook. In other words, shortcut menu modifications were at the *application* level.

Beginning in Excel 2013, Excel uses a single-document interface, which affects shortcut menus. Changes that you make to shortcut menus affect only the active workbook window. When you execute the code that modifies the shortcut menu, the shortcut menu for windows other than the active window will not be changed. This behavior is a radical departure from how things worked in previous versions of Excel.

And another twist: if the user opens a workbook (or creates a new workbook) when the active window displays the modified shortcut menu, the new workbook will also display the modified shortcut menu. In other words, new windows display the same shortcut menus as the window that was active when the new window was opened. If you write code to delete the shortcut menus, they are deleted only in the original workbook.

Even if a shortcut menu modification is intended to be used only in a single workbook, there's still a potential problem: if the user opens a new workbook, that new workbook will display the customized shortcut menus. Therefore, you might need to modify your code so that the macros executed by the shortcut menus work only in the workbook for which they were designed.

If you want to use a custom shortcut menu as a way to execute a macro in an add-in, that menu item will be available only in workbooks that are opened *after* the add-in is opened.

Customizing shortcut menus with RibbonX code

You can also use RibbonX code to customize shortcut menus. When a workbook is opened that contains such code, the shortcut menu changes affect only that workbook. To make shortcut menu modifications in all workbooks, place the RibbonX code in an add-in.

Here's a simple example of RibbonX code that modifies the Cell right-click menu. As shown in the accompanying figure, the code adds a shortcut menu item after the Hyperlink menu item.

```
<customUI xmlns="http://schemas.microsoft.com/office/2009/07/
customui">
  <contextMenus>
    <contextMenu idMso="ContextMenuCell">
      <button id="FileName_MyMenuItem"
        label="Run My Macro..."
```

```
            insertAfterMso="HyperlinkInsert"
            onAction="MyMacro"
            imageMso="AdvancedFileProperties"/>
      </contextMenu>
    </contextMenus>
</customUI>
```

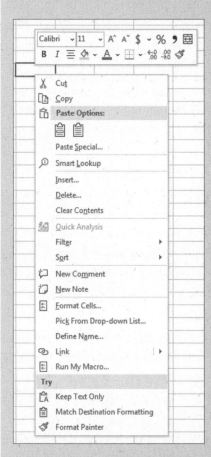

Using RibbonX to modify shortcut menus was introduced in Excel 2010, so this technique doesn't work with Excel 2007.

As we explain in Chapter 17, "Working with the Ribbon," you need to use a separate program to add RibbonX code.

Resetting a Shortcut Menu

The Reset method restores a shortcut menu to its original, default condition. The following procedure resets the Cell shortcut menu to its normal state:

```
Sub ResetCellMenu()
   CommandBars("Cell").Reset
End Sub
```

In the current version of Excel, the Reset method affects the Cell shortcut menu only in the active window.

As noted previously, Excel has two shortcut menus named Cell. The preceding code resets only the first one (index of 36). To reset the second Cell shortcut menu, you can use its index number (39) instead of its name. Remember, however, the index numbers aren't consistent across Excel versions. Here's a better procedure to reset both instances of the Cell shortcut menu in the active window:

```
Sub ResetCellMenu()
   Dim cbar As CommandBar

   For Each cbar In Application.CommandBars
      If cbar.Name = "Cell" Then cbar.Reset
   Next cbar
End Sub
```

The following procedure resets all built-in shortcut menus to their original states:

```
Sub ResetAllShortcutMenus()
   Dim cbar As CommandBar

   For Each cbar In Application.CommandBars
      If cbar.Type = msoBarTypePopup Then
         cbar.Reset
         cbar.Enabled = True
      End If
   Next cbar
End Sub
```

In Excel 2019, the ResetAllShortcutMenus procedure works only with the active window. To reset the shortcut menus in all open windows, the code gets a bit more complex.

```
Sub ResetAllShortcutMenus2()
   ' Works with all windows
   Dim cbar As CommandBar
   Dim activeWin As Window
   Dim win As Window

   ' Remember current active window
   Set activeWin = ActiveWindow
```

```
  ' Loop through each visible window
  Application.ScreenUpdating = False
  For Each win In Windows
    If win.Visible Then
      win.Activate
      For Each cbar In Application.CommandBars
        If cbar.Type = msoBarTypePopup Then
          cbar.Reset
          cbar.Enabled = True
        End If
      Next cbar
    End If
  Next win
  ' Activate original window
  activeWin.Activate
  Application.ScreenUpdating = True
End Sub
```

The code starts by keeping track of the active window and storing it as an object variable
(activeWin). The code then loops through all open windows and activates each one, but it
skips hidden windows because activating a hidden window makes it visible. For each active
window, it loops through each CommandBar object and resets those that are shortcut
menus. Finally, the code reactivates the original window.

ON THE WEB

Both versions of the ResetAllShortcutMenus procedure are available on the book's website in the Reset
All Shortcut Menus.xlsm file.

18

Disabling a shortcut menu

The Enabled property lets you disable an entire shortcut menu. For example, you can set
this property so that right-clicking a cell does not display the normal shortcut menu. The
following statement disables the Cell shortcut menu for the workbook in the active window:

```
Application.CommandBars("Cell").Enabled = False
```

To reenable the shortcut menu, set its Enabled property to True. Resetting a shortcut
menu does not enable it.

If you want to disable *all* shortcut menus in the active window, use the following
procedure:

```
Sub DisableAllShortcutMenus()
  Dim cb As CommandBar

  For Each cb In CommandBars
    If cb.Type = msoBarTypePopup Then _
      cb.Enabled = False
  Next cb
End Sub
```

Disabling shortcut menu items

You may want to disable one or more items on certain shortcut menus while your application is running. When an item is disabled, its text appears in light gray, and clicking it has no effect. The following procedure disables the Hide menu item from the Row and Column shortcut menus in the active window:

```
Sub DisableHideMenuItems()
    CommandBars("Column").Controls("Hide").Enabled = False
    CommandBars("Row").Controls("Hide").Enabled = False
End Sub
```

This procedure doesn't prevent a user from using other methods to hide rows or columns, such as the Format command in the Home ⇨ Cells group.

Adding a new item to the Cell shortcut menu

The AddToShortcut procedure that follows adds a new menu item to the Cell shortcut menu: Toggle Wrap Text. Recall that Excel has two Cell shortcut menus. This procedure modifies the normal right-click menu but not the right-click menu that appears in page break preview mode.

```
Sub AddToShortCut()
'   Adds a menu item to the Cell shortcut menu (active workbook)
    Dim Bar As CommandBar
    Dim NewControl As CommandBarButton

    DeleteFromShortcut
    Set Bar = CommandBars("Cell")
    Set NewControl = Bar.Controls.Add _
      (Type:=msoControlButton)

    With NewControl
      .Caption = "Toggle &Wrap Text"
      .OnAction = "ToggleWrapText"
      .Picture = Application.CommandBars.GetImageMso _
          ("WrapText", 16, 16)
      .Style = msoButtonIconAndCaption
    End With
End Sub
```

Figure 18.4 shows the new menu item displayed after right-clicking a cell.

The first command, after the declaration of a couple of variables, calls the DeleteFrom-Shortcut procedure (listed later in this section). This statement ensures that only one Toggle Wrap Text menu item appears on the shortcut Cell menu. Note that the underlined hot key for this menu item is W, not T, because T is already used by the Cut menu item.

FIGURE 18.4

The Cell shortcut menu with a custom menu item

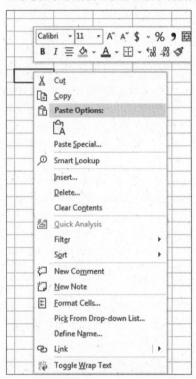

The `Picture` property is set by referencing the image used on the Ribbon for the Wrap Text command. Refer to Chapter 17 for more information about images used in Ribbon commands.

The macro executed when the menu item is selected is specified by the `OnAction` property. In this case, the macro is named `ToggleWrapText`.

```
Sub ToggleWrapText()
    On Error Resume Next
    CommandBars.ExecuteMso "WrapText"
    If Err.Number <> 0 Then MsgBox "Could not toggle Wrap Text"
End Sub
```

This procedure simply executes the `WrapText` Ribbon command. If an error occurs (for example, the worksheet is protected), the user gets a message.

The `DeleteFromShortcut` procedure removes the new menu item from the Cell shortcut menu.

```
Sub DeleteFromShortcut()
    On Error Resume Next
    CommandBars("Cell").Controls("Toggle &Wrap Text").Delete
End Sub
```

In most cases, you want to add and remove the shortcut menu additions automatically: add the shortcut menu item when the workbook is opened and delete the menu item when the workbook is closed. Just add these two event procedures to the `ThisWorkbook` code module:

```
Private Sub Workbook_Open()
    AddToShortCut
End Sub
```

```
Private Sub Workbook_BeforeClose(Cancel As Boolean)
    DeleteFromShortcut
End Sub
```

The `Workbook_Open` procedure is executed when the workbook is opened, and the `Work-book_BeforeClose` procedure is executed when you close the workbook but before the workbook is actually closed. It's just what the doctor ordered.

By the way, if shortcut menus are used only in Excel 2019, you don't need to remove them when the workbook closes because the shortcut menu modifications are applied only to the active workbook window.

ON THE WEB

The workbook described in this section is available on the book's website in the `Add to Cell Shortcut`
`.xlsm` file. The file also includes a version of the macro that adds the new shortcut menu item to all open windows.

Adding a submenu to a shortcut menu

The example in this section adds a submenu with three options to the Cell shortcut menu of the active window. Figure 18.5 shows the worksheet after right-clicking a cell. Each submenu item executes a macro that changes the case of text in the selected cells.

The code that creates the submenu and submenu items is as follows:

```
Sub AddSubmenu()
    Dim Bar As CommandBar
    Dim NewMenu As CommandBarControl
    Dim NewSubmenu As CommandBarButton

    DeleteSubmenu
    Set Bar = CommandBars("Cell")
```

FIGURE 18.5

This shortcut menu has a submenu with three submenu items.

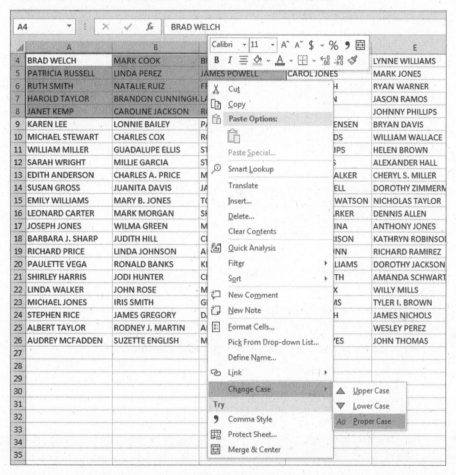

```
'   Add submenu
Set NewMenu = Bar.Controls.Add _
    (Type:=msoControlPopup, _
     temporary:=True)
NewMenu.Caption = "Ch&ange Case"
NewMenu.BeginGroup = True

'   Add first submenu item
Set NewSubmenu = NewMenu.Controls.Add _
    (Type:=msoControlButton)
With NewSubmenu
```

```
                    .FaceId = 38
                    .Caption = "&Upper Case"
                    .OnAction = "MakeUpperCase"
            End With

      '     Add second submenu item
            Set NewSubmenu = NewMenu.Controls.Add _
              (Type:=msoControlButton)
            With NewSubmenu
                    .FaceId = 40
                    .Caption = "&Lower Case"
                    .OnAction = "MakeLowerCase"
            End With

      '     Add third submenu item
            Set NewSubmenu = NewMenu.Controls.Add _
              (Type:=msoControlButton)
            With NewSubmenu
                    .FaceId = 476
                    .Caption = "&Proper Case"
                    .OnAction = "MakeProperCase"
            End With
      End Sub
```

The submenu is added first, and its Type property is msoControlPopup. Then the three submenu items are added, and each has a different OnAction property.

The code to delete the submenu is much simpler, as shown here:

```
      Sub DeleteSubmenu()
         On Error Resume Next
         CommandBars("Cell").Controls("Cha&nge Case").Delete
      End Sub
```

ON THE WEB

The workbook described in this section is available on the book's website in the `Shortcut with Submenu .xlsm` file.

Limiting a shortcut menu to a single workbook

As previously noted, in Excel 2019, shortcut menu modifications are applied only to the active workbook window (workbook A). For example, you might add a new item to the Cell right-click menu in workbook A. But if the user opens a new workbook when workbook A is active, the new workbook will also display the modified shortcut menu. If you want the shortcut menu to work only when workbook A is active, you can add some code to the macro that's executed by the shortcut menu.

Finding FaceID images

The icon that's displayed on a shortcut menu item is determined by one of two property settings.

- **Picture**: This option lets you use an `imageMso` from the Ribbon. For an example, see "Adding a new item to the Cell shortcut menu" earlier in this chapter.
- **FaceID**: This option is the easiest because the `FaceID` property is just a numeric value that represents one of hundreds of images.

But how do you find out which number corresponds to a particular `FaceID` image? Excel doesn't provide a way, so this book's website contains a workbook that lets you enter beginning and ending `FaceID` numbers. Click a button, and the images are displayed in the worksheet. Each image has a name that corresponds to its `FaceID` value. See the accompanying figure, which shows `FaceID` values from 1 to 500. The workbook is named `Show Faceids.xlsm`.

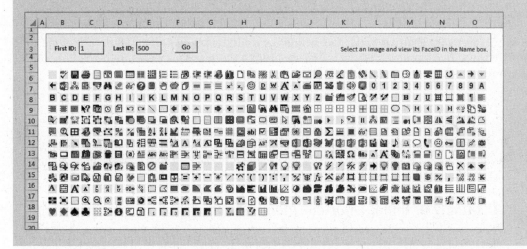

Assume that you wrote code that adds a shortcut menu that, when clicked, executes the `MyMacro` procedure. To limit this procedure to only the workbook in which it's defined, use code like this:

```
Sub MyMacro()
   If Not ActiveWorkbook Is ThisWorkbook Then
     MsgBox "This shortcut menu doesn't work here."
   Else
     ' [Macro code goes here]
   End If
End Sub
```

Shortcut Menus and Events

The examples in this section demonstrate various shortcut menu programming techniques used with events.

 We discuss event programming in Chapter 6, "Understanding Excel's Events."

Adding and deleting menus automatically

If you need to modify a shortcut menu when a workbook is opened, use the Workbook_ Open event. The following code, stored in the code module for the ThisWorkbook object, executes the ModifyShortcut procedure (not shown here):

```
Private Sub Workbook_Open()
    ModifyShortcut
End Sub
```

To return the shortcut to its state before the modification, use a procedure such as the following. This procedure, which is executed before the workbook closes, calls the Restore-Shortcut procedure (not shown here):

```
Private Sub Workbook_BeforeClose(Cancel As Boolean)
    RestoreShortcut
End Sub
```

If this code is used exclusively in Excel 2013 or later, it's not necessary to restore the shortcut menus when the workbook is closed because the modifications are applied only to the active workbook and disappear when the workbook is closed.

Disabling or hiding shortcut menu items

When a shortcut menu item is disabled, its text appears in a faint shade of gray, and clicking it has no effect. When a menu item is hidden, it doesn't appear on the shortcut menu. You can, of course, write VBA code to enable or disable shortcut menu items. Similarly, you can write code to hide shortcut menu items. The key is tapping into the correct event.

The following code, for example, disables the Change Case shortcut menu item (which was added to the Cells menu) when Sheet2 is activated. This procedure is located in the code module for Sheet2.

```
Private Sub Worksheet_Activate()
    CommandBars("Cell").Controls("Change Case").Enabled = False
End Sub
```

To enable the menu item when Sheet2 is deactivated, add the following procedure to its code module. The net effect is that the Change Case menu item is available at all times except when Sheet2 is active.

```
Private Sub Worksheet_Deactivate()
    CommandBars("Cell").Controls("Change Case").Enabled = True
End Sub
```

To hide the menu item rather than disable it, simply set the `Visible` property to `False` instead of the `Enabled` property.

Creating a context-sensitive shortcut menu

You can create a new shortcut menu and display it in response to a particular event. The code that follows creates a shortcut menu named MyShortcut and adds six menu items to it. Each menu item has its `OnAction` property set to execute a simple procedure that displays one of the tabs in the Format Cells dialog box (see Figure 18.6).

FIGURE 18.6

A new shortcut menu appears only when the user right-clicks a cell in the shaded area of the worksheet.

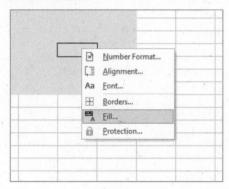

```
Sub CreateShortcut()
    Dim myBar As CommandBar
    Dim myItem As CommandBarControl

    DeleteShortcut
    Set myBar = CommandBars.Add _
        (Name:="MyShortcut", Position:=msoBarPopup, Temporary:=True)

    Set myItem = myBar.Controls.Add(Type:=msoControlButton)
    With myItem
        .Caption = "&Number Format..."
        .OnAction = "ShowFormatNumber"
        .FaceId = 1554
    End With
```

```
            Set myItem = myBar.Controls.Add(Type:=msoControlButton)
            With myItem
                .Caption = "&Alignment..."
                .OnAction = "ShowFormatAlignment"
                .FaceId = 194
            End With

            Set myItem = myBar.Controls.Add(Type:=msoControlButton)
            With myItem
                .Caption = "&Font..."
                .OnAction = "ShowFormatFont"
                .FaceId = 309
            End With

            Set myItem = myBar.Controls.Add(Type:=msoControlButton)
            With myItem
                .Caption = "&Borders..."
                .OnAction = "ShowFormatBorder"
                .FaceId = 149
                .BeginGroup = True
            End With

            Set myItem = myBar.Controls.Add(Type:=msoControlButton)
            With myItem
                .Caption = "&Fill..."
                .OnAction = "ShowFormatPatterns"
                .FaceId = 687
            End With

            Set myItem = myBar.Controls.Add(Type:=msoControlButton)
            With myItem
                .Caption = "&Protection..."
                .OnAction = "ShowFormatProtection"
                .FaceId = 225
            End With
        End Sub
```

After the shortcut menu is created, you can display it by using the ShowPopup method. The following procedure, located in the code module for a Worksheet object, is executed when the user right-clicks in a cell within the range named data:

```
Private Sub Worksheet_BeforeRightClick _
    (ByVal Target As Excel.Range, Cancel As Boolean)

    If Union(Target.Range("A1"), Range("data")).Address = _
        Range("data").Address Then
        CommandBars("MyShortcut").ShowPopup
        Cancel = True
    End If
End Sub
```

If the active cell is within a range named data when the user right-clicks, the `MyShort-cut` menu appears. Setting the `Cancel` argument to `True` ensures that the normal shortcut menu isn't displayed. Note that the mini toolbar isn't displayed.

You can also display this shortcut menu without even using the mouse. Create a simple procedure and assign a shortcut key by using the Options button in the Macro dialog box.

```
Sub ShowMyShortcutMenu()
  ' Ctrl+Shift+M shortcut key
  CommandBars("MyShortcut").ShowPopup
End Sub
```

ON THE WEB

The book's website contains an example (named `Context-sensitive Shortcut Menu.xlsm`) that creates a new shortcut menu and displays it in place of the normal Cell shortcut menu.

18

Providing Help for Your Applications

Help for Your Excel Applications

If you develop a nontrivial application in Excel, you may want to consider building in some sort of help for end users. Doing so makes the users feel more comfortable with the application and could eliminate some support e-mails from users with basic questions. Another advantage is that help is always available. That is, the instructions for using your application can't be misplaced or buried under a pile of books.

You can provide help for your Excel applications in a number of ways, ranging from simple to complex. The method you choose depends on your application's scope and complexity and how much effort you're willing to put into this phase of development. Some applications might require only a brief set of instructions on how to start them. Others may benefit from a full-blown searchable Help system. Most often, applications need something in between.

This chapter classifies user help into two categories.

Unofficial Help system   This method of displaying help uses standard Excel components (such as a UserForm). Or you can simply display the support information in a text file, Word document, or PDF file.

Official Help system   This Help system uses a compiled HTML file (with a .chm extension) produced by Microsoft's HTML Help Workshop.

Creating a compiled help file isn't a trivial task, but it is worth the effort if your application is complex or if it will be used by a large number of people.

About the examples in this chapter

Many of the examples in this chapter use a common workbook application to demonstrate various ways of providing help. The application uses data stored in a worksheet to generate and print form letters.

As you can see in the following figure, cells display the total number of records in the database (C2, calculated by a formula), the current record number (C3), the first record to print (C4), and the last record to print (C5). To display a particular record, the user enters a value in cell C3. To print a series of form letters, the user specifies the first and last record numbers in cells C4 and C5.

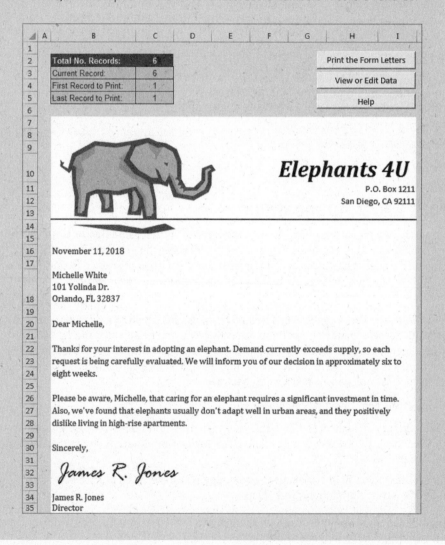

The application is simple, but it does consist of several discrete components. We use this example to demonstrate various ways of displaying context-sensitive help.

The form letter workbook consists of the following components:

- Form: A worksheet that contains the text of the form letter.
- Data: A worksheet that contains a seven-field table of customer information.
- HelpSheet: A worksheet that's present only in the examples that store help text on a worksheet.
- PrintMod: A VBA module that contains macros to print the form letters.
- HelpMod: A VBA module that contains macros that control the help display. The content of this module varies depending on the type of help being demonstrated.
- UHelp: Present only if the help technique involves a UserForm.

Help Systems That Use Excel Components

Perhaps the most straightforward method of providing help to your users is to use the features in Excel itself. The primary advantage of this method is that you don't need to learn how to create HTML help files, which can be a major undertaking and might take longer to develop than your application.

In this section, we provide an overview of some help techniques that use the following built-in Excel components:

Cell comments Using comments is about as simple as it gets.

A text box control A short macro is all it takes to toggle the display of a text box that shows help information.

A worksheet An easy way to add help is to insert a worksheet, enter your help information, and name its tab *Help*. When the user clicks the tab, the worksheet is activated.

A custom UserForm A number of techniques involve displaying help text in a UserForm.

Using cell comments for help

Perhaps the simplest way to provide user help is to use cell comments. This technique is most appropriate for describing the type of input that's expected in a cell. When the user

19

moves the mouse pointer over a cell that contains a comment, the comment appears in a small window, like a tooltip (see Figure 19.1). Another advantage is that this technique doesn't require macros.

FIGURE 19.1

Using cell comments to display help

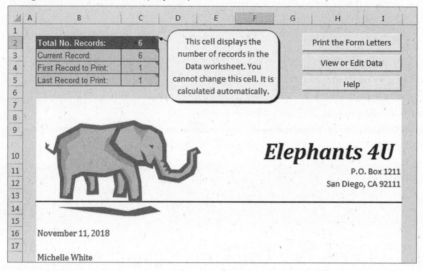

The automatic display of cell comments is an option. The following VBA instruction, which can be placed in a Workbook_Open procedure, ensures that cell comment indicators are displayed for cells that contain comments:

```
Application.DisplayCommentIndicator = xlCommentIndicatorOnly
```

ON THE WEB

A workbook that demonstrates the use of cell comments is available on the book's website in the `cell comments\formletter.xlsm` file.

TIP

Cell comments can also display images. Right-click the comment's border, and choose Format Comment from the shortcut menu. In the Format Comment dialog box, select the Colors and Lines tab. Click the Color drop-down list and select Fill Effects. In the Fill Effects dialog box, click the Picture tab and then click the Select Picture button to choose the image file.

As an alternative to cell comments, you can use Excel's Data ➪ Data Tools ➪ Data Validation command, which displays a dialog box that lets you specify validation criteria for a cell or range. You can just ignore the data validation aspect and use the Input Message tab of the Data Validation dialog box to specify a message that's displayed when the cell is activated. This text is limited to 255 characters.

Using a text box for help

Using a text box to display help information is also easy to implement. Simply create a text box by choosing Insert ⇨ Text ⇨ Text Box, enter the help text, and format it to your liking.

TIP

In lieu of a text box, you can use a different shape and add text to it. Choose Insert ⇨ Illustrations ⇨ Shapes and choose a shape. Then just starting typing the text.

Figure 19.2 shows an example of a shape set up to display help information. A shadow effect makes the object appear to float above the worksheet.

FIGURE 19.2

Using a shape object with text to display help for the user

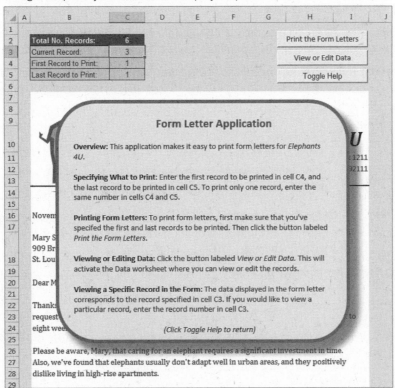

Most of the time, you won't want the text box to be visible. Therefore, you can add a button to your application to execute a macro that toggles the Visible property of the text box. An example of such a macro follows. In this case, the TextBox control is named HelpText.

```
Sub ToggleHelp()
  ActiveSheet.TextBoxes("HelpText").Visible = _
    Not ActiveSheet.TextBoxes("HelpText").Visible
End Sub
```

ON THE WEB

A workbook that demonstrates using a text box for help is available on the book's website in the `textbox\form-letter.xlsm` file.

Using a worksheet to display help text

Another easy way to add help to your application is to create a macro that activates a separate worksheet that holds the help information. Just attach the macro to a button control and—*voilà!*—quick-and-dirty help.

Figure 19.3 shows a sample help worksheet. We designed the range that contains the help text to simulate a page from a yellow notebook pad—a touch that you may or may not like.

To keep the user from scrolling around the HelpSheet worksheet, the macro sets the ScrollArea property of the worksheet. Because this property isn't stored with the workbook, it must be set when the worksheet is activated.

```
Sub ShowHelp()
  'Activate help sheet
  Worksheets("HelpSheet").Activate
  ActiveSheet.ScrollArea = "A1:C35"
  Range("A1").Select
End Sub
```

The worksheet is protected to prevent the user from changing the text and selecting cells, and the first row is frozen so that the Return to the Form button is always visible, regardless of how far down the sheet the user scrolls.

The main disadvantage of using this technique is that the help text isn't visible along with the main work area. One possible solution is to write a macro that opens a new window to display the sheet.

FIGURE 19.3

An easy method is to put user help in a separate worksheet.

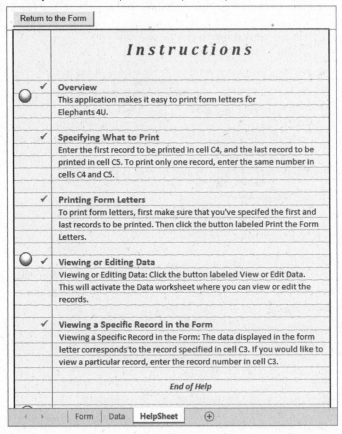

Displaying help in a UserForm

Another way to provide help to the user is to display the text in a UserForm. In this section, I describe several techniques that involve UserForms.

Using Label controls to display help text

Figure 19.4 shows a UserForm that contains two Label controls: one for the title and one for the help text. A SpinButton control enables the user to navigate among the topics. The text itself is stored in a worksheet, with topics in column A and text in column B. A macro transfers the text from the worksheet to the Label controls.

FIGURE 19.4

Clicking one of the arrows on the SpinButton changes the text displayed in the labels.

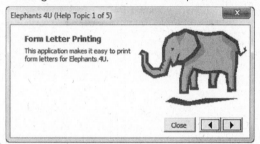

Clicking the SpinButton control executes the following procedure. This procedure sets the Caption property of the two Label controls to the text in the appropriate row of the worksheet (named HelpSheet).

```
Private Sub sbTopics_Change()
  Dim HelpTopic As Long

  HelpTopic = Me.sbTopics.Value
  Me.lblTitle.Caption = _
    Sheets("HelpSheet").Cells(HelpTopic, 1).Value

  Me.lblTopic.Caption = _
    Sheets("HelpSheet").Cells(HelpTopic, 2).Value

  Me.Caption = APPNAME & " (Help Topic " & HelpTopic & " of " _
    & Me.sbTopics.Max & ")"
End Sub
```

Here, APPNAME is a global constant that contains the application's name.

ON THE WEB

A workbook that demonstrates this technique is available on the book's website in the `userform1\formletter`
`.xlsm` file.

Using Control tips in a UserForm

Every UserForm control has a `ControlTipText` property, which can store brief descriptive text. When the user moves the mouse pointer over a control, the Control tip (if any) is displayed in a pop-up window. See the accompanying figure.

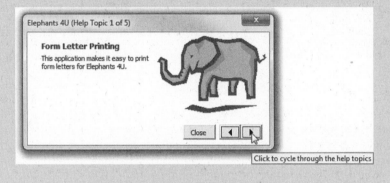

Using a scrolling label to display help text

The next technique displays help text in a single `Label` control. Because a `Label` control can't contain a vertical scroll bar, the label is placed inside a `Frame` control, which *can* contain a scroll bar. Figure 19.5 shows an example of a UserForm set up in this manner. The user can scroll through the text by using the frame's scroll bar.

FIGURE 19.5

Inserting a Label control inside a Frame control adds scrolling to the label.

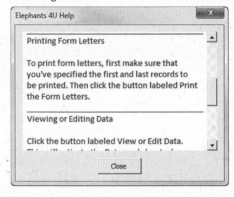

The text displayed in the label is read from a worksheet named `HelpSheet` when the User-Form is initialized. Here's the `UserForm_Initialize` procedure for this worksheet:

```
Private Sub UserForm_Initialize()
    Dim LastRow As Long
    Dim r As Long
    Dim txt As String

    Me.Caption = APPNAME & " Help"
    LastRow = Sheets("HelpSheet").Cells(Rows.Count, 1).End(xlUp).Row
    txt = ""

    For r = 1 To LastRow
        txt = txt & Sheets("HelpSheet").Cells(r, 1).Text & vbCrLf
    Next r

    With Me.lblMain
        .Top = 0
        .Caption = txt
        .Width = 260
        .AutoSize = True
    End With

    Me.frmMain.ScrollHeight = Me.lblMain.Height
    Me.frmMain.ScrollTop = 0
End Sub
```

Note that the code adjusts the frame's `ScrollHeight` property to ensure that the scrolling covers the complete height of the label. Again, `APPNAME` is a global constant that contains the application's name.

Because a label can't display formatted text, underscore characters are used in the `Help-Sheet` worksheet to delineate the help topic titles.

ON THE WEB

A workbook that demonstrates this technique is available on the book's website in a file named `userform2\ formletter.xlsm`.

Using a ComboBox control to select a help topic

The example in this section improves upon the preceding example. Figure 19.6 shows a UserForm that contains a `ComboBox` control and a `Label` control. The user can select a topic from the drop-down combo box or view the topics sequentially by clicking the Previous or Next button.

FIGURE 19.6

Using a drop-down list control to select a help topic

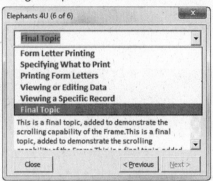

This example is a bit more complex than the example in the preceding section, but it's also much more flexible. It uses the label-within-a-scrolling-frame technique (described previously) to support help text of any length.

The help text is stored in a worksheet named HelpSheet in two columns (A and B). The first column contains the topic headings, and the second column contains the text. The combo box items are added in the UserForm_Initialize procedure. The CurrentTopic variable is a module-level variable that stores an integer that represents the help topic.

```
Private Sub UpdateForm()
    Me.cbxTopics.ListIndex = CurrentTopic - 1
    Me.Caption = APPNAME & _
      " (" & CurrentTopic & " of " & TopicCount & ")"

    With Me.lblMain
      .Caption = HelpSheet.Cells(CurrentTopic, 2).Value
      .AutoSize = False
      .Width = 212
      .AutoSize = True
    End With

    With Me.frmMain
      .ScrollHeight = Me.lblMain.Height + 5
      .ScrollTop = 1
    End With

    If CurrentTopic = 1 Then
      Me.cmdNext.SetFocus
    ElseIf CurrentTopic > TopicCount Then
```

```
        Me.cmdPrevious.SetFocus
    End If

    Me.cmdPrevious.Enabled = CurrentTopic > 1
    Me.cmdNext.Enabled = CurrentTopic < TopicCount
End Sub
```

ON THE WEB

A workbook that demonstrates this technique is available on the book's website in the `userform3\form-letter.xlsm` file.

Displaying Help in a Web Browser

This section describes two ways to display user help in a web browser.

Using HTML files

Yet another way to display help for an Excel application is to create one or more HTML files and provide a hyperlink that displays the file in the default web browser. The HTML files can be stored locally or on your corporate intranet. You can create the hyperlink to the help file in a cell (macros not required). Figure 19.7 shows an example of help in a browser.

FIGURE 19.7

Displaying help in a web browser

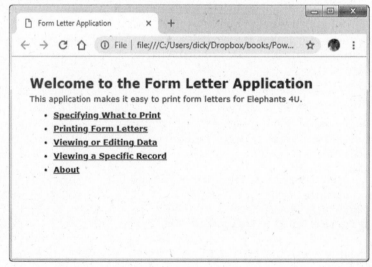

Easy-to-use HTML editors are readily available, and your HTML-based Help system can be as simple or as complex as necessary. A disadvantage is that you may need to distribute a large number of HTML files. One solution to this problem is to use an MHTML file, which we describe next.

Another advantage of this method is that you can change your help files without having to redeploy the entire application. For example, if you find an error in your help file, you can replace just the file with the correction in it.

ON THE WEB

A workbook that demonstrates this technique is available on the book's website in the `web browser\form-letter.xlsm` file.

Using an MHTML file

MHTML, which stands for MIME Hypertext Markup Language, is a web archive format. MHTML files can be displayed by Microsoft Internet Explorer (and a few other browsers).

The nice thing about using an MHTML file for an Excel Help system is that you can create these files in Excel. Just create your help text using any number of worksheets. Then choose File ⇨ Save As, click the Save As Type drop-down list, and select Single File Web Page (*.mht; *.mhtml). VBA macros aren't saved in this format.

In Excel, you can create a hyperlink to display the MHTML file.

Figure 19.8 shows an MHTML file displayed in Internet Explorer. Note that the bottom of the file contains tabs that link to the help topics. These tabs correspond to the worksheet tabs in the Excel workbook used to create the MHTML file.

ON THE WEB

A workbook that demonstrates this technique is available on the book's website in the `mhtml_file\form-letter.xlsm` file. Also included is the workbook used to create the MHTML file (`helpsource.xlsx`). Apparently, some versions of Internet Explorer won't display an MHTML file that's hyperlinked from a Microsoft Office file if the filename or path includes space characters. The example on the book's website uses a Windows API function (`ShellExecute`) to display the MHTML file if the hyperlink fails.

19

CAUTION

If you save a multisheet Excel workbook as an MHTML file, the file will contain JavaScript code, which may generate a security warning when the file is opened.

FIGURE 19.8

Displaying an MHTML file in a web browser

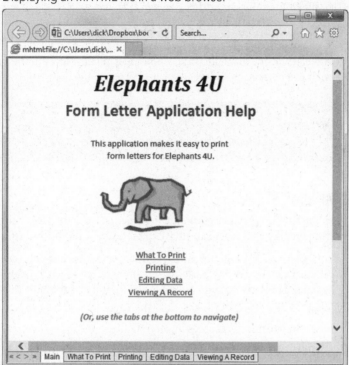

Using the HTML Help System

One of the most common Help systems used in Windows applications is compiled HTML Help, which creates CHM files. In this section, we briefly describe the HTML help-authoring system. Details on creating such Help systems are well beyond the scope of this book. However, you'll find lots of information and examples online.

> **NOTE**
>
> If you plan to develop a large-scale Help system, we strongly recommend that you purchase a help-authoring software product. Help-authoring software makes it much easier to develop help files because the software takes care of many of the tedious details for you. Many products are available, including freeware, shareware, and commercial offerings.

A compiled HTML Help system transforms a series of HTML files into a compact Help system. Additionally, you can create a combined table of contents and index as well as use keywords for advanced hyperlinking capability. HTML Help can also use additional tools, such as graphics files, ActiveX controls, scripting, and Dynamic HTML (DHTML). Figure 19.9 shows an example of a simple HTML Help system.

FIGURE 19.9

An example of HTML Help

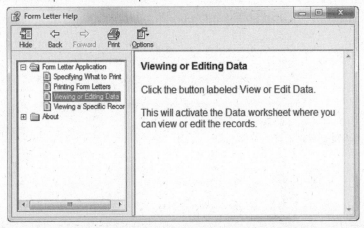

On the Web

A workbook that demonstrates this technique is available on the book's website in the `html help\formletter.xlsm` file.

HTML Help is displayed by HTML Help Viewer, which uses the layout engine of Internet Explorer. The information is displayed in a window, and the table of contents, index, and search tools are displayed in a separate pane. In addition, the help text can contain standard hyperlinks that display another topic or even a document on the Internet. It's also important that HTML Help can access files stored on a website so that you can direct users to more up-to-date information.

You need a special compiler (HTML Help Workshop) to create an HTML Help system. HTML Help Workshop, along with lots of additional information, is available free from Microsoft's website. Navigate to the following page for more information and downloads:

https://docs.microsoft.com/en-us/previous-versions/windows/desktop/htmlhelp/
microsoft-html-help-1-4-sdk

Figure 19.10 shows HTML Help Workshop with the project file that created the Help system shown in Figure 19.9.

19

FIGURE 19.10

Using HTML Help Workshop to create a help file

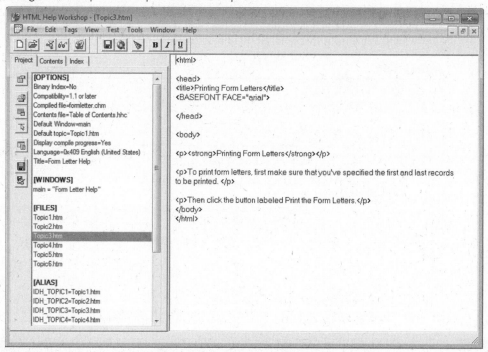

Using the Help method to display HTML Help

Use the `Help` method of the `Application` object to display a help file—either a WinHelp HLP file or an HTML Help CHM file. This method works even if the help file doesn't have context IDs defined.

The syntax for the `Help` method is as follows:

```
Application.Help(helpFile, helpContextID)
```

Both arguments are optional. If the name of the help file is omitted, Excel's help file is displayed. If the context ID argument is omitted, the specified help file is displayed with the default topic.

The following example displays the default topic of `myapp.chm`, which is assumed to be in the same directory as the workbook from which it's called. Note that the second argument is omitted.

```
Sub ShowHelpContents()
  Application.Help ThisWorkbook.Path & "\myapp.chm"
End Sub
```

The following instruction displays the help topic with a context ID of 1002 from an HTML help file named myapp.chm:

```
Application.Help ThisWorkbook.Path & "\myapp.chm", 1002
```

Associating a help file with your application

You can associate a particular HTML help file with your Excel application in one of two ways: by using the Project Properties dialog box or by writing VBA code.

In Visual Basic Editor (VBE), choose Tools ⇨ *xxx* Properties (where *xxx* corresponds to your project's name). In the Project Properties dialog box, click the General tab and specify a compiled HTML help file for the project. This file should have a .chm extension.

The statement that follows demonstrates how to associate a help file with your application by using a VBA statement. The following instruction sets up an association with myfuncs .chm, which is assumed to be in the same directory as the workbook:

```
ThisWorkbook.VBProject.HelpFile = ThisWorkbook.Path & "\myfuncs.chm"
```

> **NOTE**
>
> If this statement generates an error, you must enable programmatic access to VBA projects. In Excel, choose Developer ⇨ Code ⇨ Macro Security to display the Trust Center dialog box. Then select the option labeled Trust Access to the VBA Project Object Model.

When a help file is associated with your application, you can call up a particular help topic in the following situations:

- When the user presses F1 while a custom worksheet function is selected in the Insert Function dialog box.
- When the user presses F1 while a UserForm is displayed. The help topic associated with the control that has the focus is displayed.

Associating a help topic with a VBA function

If you create custom worksheet functions with VBA, you might want to associate a help file and context ID with each function. After these items are assigned to a function, the help topic can be displayed from the Insert Function dialog box by pressing F1.

19

Activity

To specify a context ID for a custom worksheet function, follow these steps:

1. Create the function as usual.

2. Make sure that your project has an associated help file (refer to the preceding section).

3. In VBE, press F2 to activate the Object Browser.

4. Select your project from the Project/Library drop-down list.

5. In the Classes window, select the module that contains your function.

6. In the Members Of window, select the function.

7. Right-click the function and then select Properties from the shortcut menu.

   The Member Options dialog box is displayed, as shown in Figure 19.11.

FIGURE 19.11

Specify a context ID for a custom function.

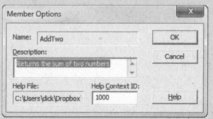

8. Enter the context ID of the help topic for the function.

You can also enter a description of the function.

> **NOTE**
>
> The Member Options dialog box doesn't let you specify the help file. It always uses the help file associated with the project.

You may prefer to write VBA code that sets up the context ID and help file for your custom functions. You can do this by using the MacroOptions method.

The following procedure uses the MacroOptions method to specify a description, help file, and context ID for two custom functions (AddTwo and Squared). You need to execute this macro only one time.

```
Sub SetOptions()
  ' Set options for the AddTwo function
  Application.MacroOptions Macro:="AddTwo", _
```

```
        Description:="Returns the sum of two numbers", _
        HelpFile:=ThisWorkbook.Path & "\myfuncs.chm", _
        HelpContextID:=1000, _
        ArgumentDescriptions:=Array("The first number to add", _
        "The second number to add")

    ' Set options for the Squared function
    Application.MacroOptions Macro:="Squared", _
        Description:="Returns the square of an argument", _
        HelpFile:=ThisWorkbook.Path & "\myfuncs.chm", _
        HelpContextID:=2000, _
        ArgumentDescriptions:=Array("The number to be squared")
End Sub
```

After executing these procedures, the user can get help directly from the Insert Function dialog box by clicking the Help on This Function hyperlink.

ON THE WEB

A workbook that demonstrates this technique is available on the book's website in the `function help\` `myfuncs.xlsm` file.

Leveraging Class Modules

What Is a Class Module?

For many VBA programmers, the concept of a class module is a mystery. This feature can be confusing, but the examples in this chapter will help to make it less mysterious.

A *class module* is a special type of VBA module that you can insert in a VBA project. Basically, a class module enables the programmer (you) to create a new object. As you should know by now, programming Excel really boils down to manipulating objects. A class module allows you to create new objects, along with corresponding properties, methods, and events.

At this point, you might be asking, "Do I really need to create new objects?" The answer is "No." You don't *need* to, but you might want to after you understand some of the benefits of doing so. In many cases, a class module simply serves as a substitute for functions or procedures, but it could be a more convenient and manageable alternative. In other cases, however, you'll find that a class module is the only way to accomplish a particular task.

The following are some typical uses for class modules:

To encapsulate code and improve readability By moving all of your code related to payroll, for example, into custom objects representing employees and paychecks, you can keep your code more organized.

To handle events of objects not exposed by Excel Examples of this include application events, chart events, or query table events. Chapter 15, "Implementing Advanced UserForm Techniques," shows an example of using application events.

To encapsulate a Windows application programming interface (API) function to make it easier to use in your code   For example, you can create a class that makes it easy to detect or set the state of the Num Lock or Caps Lock key. Or, you can create a class that simplifies access to the Windows Registry.

To enable multiple objects in a UserForm to execute a single procedure   Normally, each object has its own event handler. The example in Chapter 15 demonstrates how to use a class module so that multiple command buttons have a single Click event-handler procedure.

To create reusable components that can be imported into other projects   After you create a general-purpose class module, you can import it into other projects to reduce your development time.

Built-in class modules

If you've been following the examples in this book so far, then you've already used a class module. Excel automatically creates a class module for the Workbook object, each Worksheet object, and any UserForm objects. That's right: the ThisWorkbook module is just a class module. And when you insert a UserForm into your project, you're inserting a class module.

The difference between a UserForm's class module and a custom class module is that the UserForm has a user-interface component (the form and its controls) that a custom class module doesn't have. However, you can create properties and methods in a UserForm's class module to extend its functionality, because it's just a class module.

Custom class modules

The remainder of this chapter deals with creating custom class modules. Unlike built-in class modules, where Excel defines the object and its properties and methods, custom class modules allow you to define them. What custom objects you create depends on your application. If you're writing a contact manager application, you might have a Company class and a Contact class. For a sales commission calculator, you might have a Salesperson class and an Invoice class. One of the benefits of class modules is that you can design them to fit your specific needs perfectly.

Classes and objects

The terms *class* and *object* are used interchangeably by many VBA developers. They are very closely related, but there is a minor distinction. A class module defines an object, but it's not the actual object.

Think of a class module as a blueprint for a house. The blueprint describes all of the properties and dimensions of the house, but it's not a house. You can create a bunch of houses from one blueprint. Similarly, you can create a bunch of objects from one class.

Objects, properties, and methods

It's helpful to think of objects, properties, and methods in terms of grammar. The *objects* are the nouns. They are things. They may represent tangible things like an employee, a customer, or a dump truck. They may also represent intangible things like a transaction. When you're designing your application using a class module, start by identifying the objects that live in your domain.

Objects have *properties*. Properties are the adjectives in the grammar analogy. They describe the characteristics of an object. One characteristic of a house is how many cars fit in the garage. If you create a house class, you might also create a GarageCarCount property. Similarly, you might create an ExteriorColor property that holds the color of the paint used on the outside of the house. You don't have to create a property for every conceivable characteristic of an object. You only create properties for characteristics that are important to your application. As an example, Excel has a Font object that has a Size property. You can read this property to determine the font size, or you can set this property to change the font size.

Finally, *methods* are the verbs of the class grammar. Methods describe actions that the class module takes. In general, there are two types of methods: methods that change more than one property at a time and methods that interact with the outside world. Excel's Workbook object has a Name property. You can read the Name property, but you can't change it. To change the Name property, you have to use a method (like Save or SaveAs) because the outside world, namely, the operating system, cares about the actual name of the workbook.

Creating a NumLock Class

One of the benefits of class modules is to give complicated, hard-to-use code (like Windows APIs) a better interface. Detecting or changing the state of the Num Lock key requires a couple of Windows API functions and is fairly complicated. You can put the API functions into a class module and build your own properties and methods that are far easier to use than the API functions.

In this section, we provide step-by-step instructions for creating a useful, albeit simple, class module. This class module creates a NumLock class that has one property (Value) and one method (Toggle).

After the class is created, your VBA code can determine the current state of the Num Lock key by using an instruction such as the following, which displays the Value property:

```
MsgBox clsNumLock.Value
```

In addition, your code can toggle the Num Lock key by using the Toggle method:

```
clsNumLock.Toggle
```

20

The class is designed so that you can't simply set the Value property. The Value property isn't just a value that you're storing in a class, but the actual state of the keyboard. To change the Value property, you define a method that interacts with the keyboard via the Windows API, and that changes the property value. It's important to understand that a class module contains the code that *defines* the object, including its properties and methods. You can then create an instance of this object in other VBA code modules and manipulate its properties and methods.

To understand better the process of creating a class module, you might want to follow the instructions in the following sections. Start with an empty workbook.

Inserting a class module

Activate Visual Basic Editor (VBE), and choose Insert ⇨ Class Module. This step adds an empty class module named Class1. If the Properties window isn't displayed, press F4 to display it. Then change the name of the class module to CNumLock (see Figure 20.1).

FIGURE 20.1

An empty class module named CNumLock

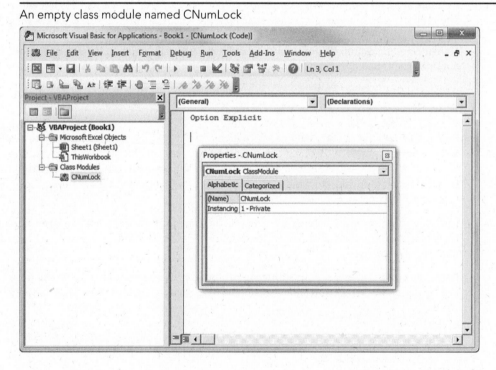

Adding VBA code to the class module

In the next step, you create the code for the Value property. To detect or change the state of the Num Lock key, the class module needs the Windows API declarations that detect and set the Num Lock key. That code follows.

```
Private Declare PtrSafe Sub keybd_event Lib "user32" _
    (ByVal bVk As Byte, _
    ByVal bScan As Byte, _
    ByVal dwFlags As Long, ByVal dwExtraInfo As Long)

Private Declare PtrSafe Function GetKeyboardState Lib "user32" _
    (pbKeyState As Byte) As Long
Private Declare PtrSafe Function SetKeyboardState Lib "user32" _
    (lppbKeyState As Byte) As Long

'Constant declarations
Const VK_NUMLOCK = &H90
```

Next, you need a procedure that retrieves the current state of the Num Lock key. This is called the *Value property* of the object in this example, but you can use any name for the property. To retrieve the state, insert the following Property Get procedure:

```
Public Property Get Value() As Boolean
    ' Get the current state
    Dim Keys(0 To 255) As Byte

    GetKeyboardState Keys(0)
    Value = CBool(Keys(VK_NUMLOCK))
End Property
```

 The details of Property procedures are described later in this chapter, in the "Programming properties of objects" section.

This procedure, which uses the GetKeyboardState Windows API function to determine the current state of the Num Lock key, is called whenever VBA code reads the Value property of the object. For example, after the object is created, a VBA statement such as this executes the Property Get procedure:

```
MsgBox clsNumLock.Value
```

If the Value property were read/write, you would need a Property Let procedure to go with your Property Get. Since we're setting the Value property via the Toggle method, there is no Property Let procedure.

20

Next, you need a procedure to toggle the `NumLock` state. This procedure is called the `Toggle` method.

```
Public Sub Toggle()
    ' Toggles the state
    ' Simulate Key Press
    keybd_event VK_NUMLOCK, &H45, KEYEVENTF_EXTENDEDKEY Or 0, 0

    ' Simulate Key Release
    keybd_event VK_NUMLOCK, &H45, KEYEVENTF_EXTENDEDKEY _
      Or KEYEVENTF_KEYUP, 0
End Sub
```

Note that `Toggle` is a standard `Sub` procedure (not a `Property Let` or `Pr[...]` procedure). A VBA statement such as the following one toggles the state of t[...] Lock object by executing the `Toggle` procedure:

```
clsNumLock.Toggle
```

Using the CNumLock class

Before you can use the `CNumLock` class, you must create an instance of the object. The following statement, which resides in a standard VBA module (not the class module), does just that:

```
Dim clsNumLock As CNumLock
```

Note that the object type is `CNumLock` (that is, the name of the class module). The object variable can have any name, but this example uses the convention of prefixing class modules with a capital `C` and prefixing the object variables that are derived from those class modules with `cls`. So, the `CNumLock` class is instantiated as the `clsNumLock` object variable.

The following procedure reads the `Value` property of the `clsNumLock` object, toggles the value, reads the value again, and displays a message to the user describing what just happened.

```
Public Sub NumLockTest()
    Dim clsNumLock As CNumLock
    Dim OldValue As Boolean

    Set clsNumLock = New CNumLock
    OldValue = clsNumLock.Value
    clsNumLock.Toggle
    DoEvents
    MsgBox "Num Lock was changed from " & _
      OldValue & " to " & clsNumLock.Value
End Sub
```

Figure 20.2 shows the result of running `NumLockTest`. Using the `NumLock` class is much simpler than dealing directly with the API functions. After you create a class module, you can reuse it in any other project simply by importing the class module.

FIGURE 20.2

A message box shows the change in status of the Num Lock key.

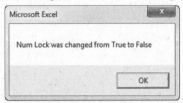

ON THE WEB

The completed class module for this example is available on the book's website. The workbook, named `Keyboard Class.xlsm`, also contains a class module to detect and set the state of the Caps Lock key and the Scroll Lock key.

Coding Properties, Methods, and Events

The example in the preceding section demonstrates how to create a new object class with a single read-only property named `Value` and a single method named `Toggle`. An object class can contain any number of properties, methods, and events.

The name that you use for the class module in which you define the object class is also the name of the object class. By default, class modules are named `Class1`, `Class2`, and so on. You'll want to provide a more meaningful name for your object class.

Programming properties of objects

Most objects have at least one property, and you can give them as many as you need. After a property is defined and the object is created, you can use it in your code using the standard dot syntax.

```
object.property
```

The VBE Auto List Members option works with objects defined in a class module, which makes it easier to select properties or methods when writing code.

Properties for the object that you define can be read-only, write-only, or read/write. You define a read-only property with a single procedure, using the Property Get keywords. Here's an example of a Property Get procedure:

```
Public Property Get FileNameOnly() As String
  Dim Sep As String, LastSep As Long

  Sep = Application.PathSeparator
  LastSep = InStrRev(FullName, Sep)
  FileNameOnly = Right(FullName, Len(FullName) - LastSep)
End Property
```

You may have noticed that a Property Get procedure works like a Function procedure. The code performs calculations and then returns a property value that corresponds to the procedure's name. In this example, the procedure's name is FileNameOnly. The property value returned is the filename part of a path string (contained in a Public variable named FullName). For example, if FullName is c:\data\myfile.txt, the procedure returns a property value of myfile.txt. The FileNameOnly procedure is called when VBA code references the object and property.

For read/write properties, you create two procedures: a Property Get procedure (which reads a property value) and a Property Let procedure (which writes a property value). The value being assigned to the property is treated as the final argument (or the only argument) of a Property Let procedure.

Two example procedures follow:

```
Dim XLFile As Boolean

Property Get SaveAsExcelFile() As Boolean
  SaveAsExcelFile = XLFile
End Property

Property Let SaveAsExcelFile(bVal As Boolean)
  XLFile = bVal
End Property
```

> **NOTE**
>
> Use Property Set in place of Property Let when the property is an object data type.

A Public variable in a class module can also be used as a property of the object. In the preceding example, the Property Get and Property Let procedures could be eliminated and replaced with this module-level declaration:

```
Public SaveAsExcelFile As Boolean
```

In the unlikely event that you need to create a write-only property, you create a single Property Let procedure with no corresponding Property Get procedure.

The previous examples use a Boolean module-level variable named XLFile. The Property Get procedure simply returns the value of this variable as the property value. If the object were named FileSys, for example, the following statement would display the current value of the SaveAsExcelFile property:

```
MsgBox FileSys.SaveAsExcelFile
```

The Property Let statement, on the other hand, accepts an argument and uses the argument to change the value of a property. For example, you could write a statement such as the following to set the SaveAsExcelFile property to True:

```
FileSys.SaveAsExcelFile = True
```

In this case, the value True is passed to the Property Let statement, thus changing the property's value.

You'll need to create a variable that represents the value for each property that you define within your class module.

> **NOTE**
>
> Normal procedure-naming rules apply to property procedures, and you'll find that VBA won't let you use some names if they are reserved words. If you get a syntax error when creating a property procedure, try changing the name of the procedure.

Programming methods for objects

A method for an object class is programmed by using a standard Sub or Function procedure placed in the class module. An object might or might not use methods. Your code executes a method by using standard notation.

```
object.method
```

Like any other VBA method, a method that you write for an object class will perform some type of action. The following procedure is an example of a method that saves a workbook in one of two file formats, depending on the value of the XLFile variable. As you can see, nothing about this procedure is special.

```
Sub SaveFile()
  If XLFile Then
    ActiveWorkbook.SaveAs FileName:=FName, _
      FileFormat:=xlWorkbookNormal
  Else
    ActiveWorkbook.SaveAs FileName:=FName, _
      FileFormat:=xlCSV
  End If
End Sub
```

20

Class module events

Every class module has two events: `Initialize` and `Terminate`. The `Initialize` event occurs when a new instance of the object is created; the `Terminate` event occurs when the object is destroyed. You might want to use the `Initialize` event to set default property values.

The frameworks for these event-handler procedures are as follows:

```
Private Sub Class_Initialize()
   ' Initialization code goes here
End Sub

Private Sub Class_Terminate()
   ' Termination code goes here
End Sub
```

An object is *destroyed* (and the memory it uses is freed) when the procedure or module in which it is declared finishes executing. You can destroy an object at any time by setting it to `Nothing`. The following statement, for example, destroys the object named `MyObject`:

```
Set MyObject = Nothing
```

Exposing a QueryTable Event

Excel automatically creates class modules for some objects, like `ThisWorkbook` and `Sheet1`. These class modules expose events like `Workbook_SheetActivate` and `Worksheet_SelectionChange`. Other objects in the Excel object model have events, but you have to create a custom class module to expose them. In this section, we'll show you how to expose the events of a `QueryTable` object.

Figure 20.3 shows a worksheet with a web query that starts in cell A5. The web query pulls financial information from a website. The only thing that's missing is the date when this web query was last updated so that you can know whether the prices are current.

In VBA, a web query is a `QueryTable` object. The `QueryTable` object has two events: `BeforeRefresh` and `AfterRefresh`. Those events are pretty well named, and you've probably already figured out when they fire.

To be able to use the `QueryTable` events, you need to do the following:

- Create a custom class module.
- Declare a `QueryTable` using the `WithEvents` keyword.
- Write the event procedure code.
- Create a `Public` variable to keep the object in scope.
- Create a procedure to instantiate the class.

FIGURE 20.3

A web query for financial information

	A	B	C	D	E	F	G	H	I
1									
2									
3									
4									
5	Currency	Last	Day High	Day Low	% Change	Bid	Ask		
6	EUR/USD	1.1191	1.1197	1.1181	0.02%	1.1191	1.1192		
7	GBP/USD	1.5145	1.5151	1.5138	0.01%	1.5145	1.515		
8	USD/JPY	120.45	120.49	120.39	-0.01%	120.45	120.47		
9	USD/CHF	0.9759	0.9766	0.9742	0.12%	0.9759	0.9769		
10	USD/CAD	1.3087	1.309	1.3076	0.03%	1.3087	1.3093		
11	AUD/USD	0.7077	0.7088	0.7075	-0.06%	0.7077	0.7085		
12									
13	DOW	16,776.43	304.06	1.85%					
14	S&P 500	1,987.05	35.69	1.83%					
15	NASDAQ	4,781.26	73.49	1.56%					
16	TR US Index	178.53	3.32	1.89%					
17									
18	EUR/USD	1.1191	0.02%						
19	GBP/USD	1.5145	0.01%						
20	USD/JPY	120.45	-0.01%						
21									
22									
23	Gold	1,135.60	1	0.09%					
24	Oil	46.32	0.06	0.13%					
25	Corn	393.75	4.5	1.16%					

Those are the basic steps for exposing events of any object that supports events. (Not all of them do.) When you use the `WithEvents` keyword, VBA will only let you declare objects that support events.

Activity

Follow these steps to add a message to a worksheet informing the user when a web query was last updated:

1. In the VBE, choose Insert ⇨ Class Module to insert a new class module.
2. Press F4 to go to the Properties window, and name the module CQueryEvents.
3. Type the following code in the class module:

```
Private WithEvents qt As QueryTable


Public Property Get QTable() As QueryTable
   Set QTable = qt

End Property
```

Continues

continued

```
Public Property Set QTable(rQTable As QueryTable)
  Set qt = rQTable
End Property
```

The first line declares a module-level variable that will store the web query. You can see that it was declared with the `WithEvents` keyword. Next, `Property Get` and `Property Set` procedures are written so that you can set the variable from outside of the class.

4. From the drop-downs at the top of the code pane (see Figure 20.4), select qt and After-Refresh. This will insert the `Sub` and `End Sub` statements for the event module. If the VBE inserts statements for the default event procedure, `BeforeRefresh` in this case, you can delete them.

FIGURE 20.4

The code pane lists available events.

5. Type the following code into the event procedure:

```
Private Sub qt_AfterRefresh(ByVal Success As Boolean)
  If Success Then

    Me.QTable.Parent.Range("A1").Value = _
      "Last updated: " & Format(Now, "mm-dd-yyyy hh:mm:ss")
  End If
End Sub
```

The event procedure has a built-in argument, Success, that is True if the query updated without errors. Now that the class is set up, you need to create an object based on it.

6. Insert a standard module (Insert ➪ Module). You can accept the default name of Module1 for this exercise or change it if you want.

7. Type the following code into the module:

```
Public clsQueryEvents As CQueryEvents


Sub Auto_Open()
  Set clsQueryEvents = New CQueryEvents
  Set clsQueryEvents.QTable = Sheet1.QueryTables(1)
End Sub
```

A globally scoped variable (declared with the Public keyword) will stay in scope for as long as the worksheet is open. This means that the class will continue to "listen" for events until you close the workbook. The Auto_Open procedure runs when the workbook is first opened. It creates the clsQueryEvents object and then sets the events variable to the web query on Sheet1.

8. Run Auto_Open from the Immediate Window or by pressing F5 in the VBE.

That's it. You now have code that will run after the web query on Sheet1 is refreshed. You can click Refresh All on the Data tab of the Ribbon to test the code. If you followed the steps, you should see something similar to Figure 20.5.

Continues

20

continued

FIGURE 20.5

After a web query is refreshed, the last update time is recorded.

	A	B	C	D	E	F	G
1	Last updated: 11-12-2018 19:00:54						
2							
3							
4							
5	Currency	Last	Day High	Day Low	% Change	Bid	Ask
6	EUR/USD	1.1222	1.1232	1.1217	0.04%	1.1222	1.1225
7	GBP/USD	1.285	1.2861	1.2842	0.02%	1.285	1.2855
8	USD/JPY	113.63	113.86	113.63	-0.18%	113.63	113.64
9	USD/CHF	1.0101	1.0111	1.0101	-0.06%	1.0101	1.0107
10	USD/CAD	1.3242	1.3248	1.3238	-0.02%	1.3242	1.3245
11	AUD/USD	0.7165	0.7178	0.7165	-0.10%	0.7165	0.7168
12							
13	DOW	25,387.18	-602.12	-2.32%			
14	S&P 500	2,726.22	-54.79	-1.97%			
15	NASDAQ	7,200.87	-206.03	-2.78%			
16	TR US Index	240.99	-4.83	-1.96%			

ON THE WEB

A workbook named `Query Table Events.xlsm` is available on this book's website. It contains the web query used in the example in this section. Another workbook, named `Query Table Events Complete.xlsm`, contains the web query and the completed code.

Creating a Class to Hold Classes

One of the benefits of using class modules is to organize your code according to the objects the code affects. You may, for instance, create a `CEmployee` class for your code that deals with employees. But you probably don't have just one employee. Often, you create many objects from one class, and a great way to keep track of them is within another class.

In this section, you'll learn how to create parent classes and child classes in a commission-calculating application. You'll create a `CSalesRep` child class and keep track of all instances of it in a `CSalesReps` class. (Naming the parent class as the plural of the child class is a common convention.) Similarly, you'll create a `CInvoices` parent class to hold `CInvoice` objects.

ON THE WEB

A workbook with all of the data and code for this section is available on this book's website. The workbook is named `Commission Calc.xlsm`.

Creating the CSalesRep and CSalesReps classes

Figure 20.6 shows two tables. The first table lists all the sales representatives and some commission information. The second table is a list of invoices. Start by creating a CSales-Rep class module and include the following code:

```
Private mSalesRepID As Long
Private mSalesRep As String
Private mCommissionRate As Double
Private mThreshold As Double

Public Property Let SalesRepID(ByVal lSalesRepID As Long)
  mSalesRepID = lSalesRepID
End Property

Public Property Get SalesRepID() As Long
   SalesRepID = mSalesRepID
End Property

Public Property Let SalesRep(ByVal sSalesRep As String)
  mSalesRep = sSalesRep
End Property

Public Property Get SalesRep() As String
   SalesRep = mSalesRep
End Property

Public Property Let CommissionRate( _
  ByVal dCommissionRate As Double)
  mCommissionRate = dCommissionRate
End Property

Public Property Get CommissionRate() As Double
   CommissionRate = mCommissionRate
End Property

Public Property Let Threshold(ByVal dThreshold As Double)
  mThreshold = dThreshold
End Property

Public Property Get Threshold() As Double
   Threshold = mThreshold
End Property
```

You'll notice that there is a private variable for every column in the sales rep table and a Property Get and Property Let statement for every variable. Next, add another class module named CSalesReps. This will be the parent class that holds all of the CSales-Rep objects.

FIGURE 20.6

Excel tables hold the information for the objects.

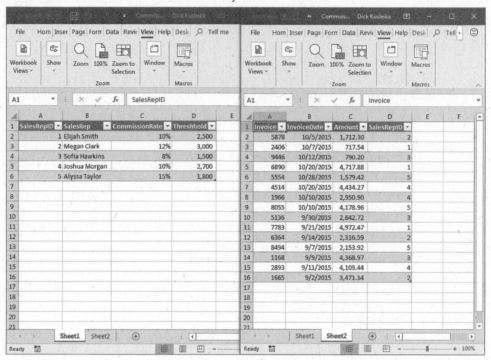

In the parent class, create a `Collection` variable that will hold all of the children.

```
Private mSalesReps As New Collection
```

Now you need to add a way to get the children into the collection. Create an `Add` method, an `Item` property, and a `Count` property in the `CSalesReps` class module using this following code:

```
Public Sub Add(clsSalesRep As CSalesRep)
  mSalesReps.Add clsSalesRep, CStr(clsSalesRep.SalesRepID)
End Sub

Public Property Get Count() As Long
  Count = mSalesReps.Count
End Property

Public Property Get Item(lId As Long) As CSalesRep
  Set Item = mSalesReps(lId)
End Property
```

You might notice that all you've done is mimic the Collection object's Add method and Item and Count properties. The Collection object's key argument must be a unique string, so you used the SalesRepID property and the CStr() function to ensure that the key is unique and a string.

That's all there is to creating a parent class. Simply add a Collection variable and mimic whichever of the Collection's properties and methods you need.

Creating the CInvoice and CInvoices classes

The following is the code for the CInvoice class:

```
Private mInvoice As String
Private mInvoiceDate As Date
Private mAmount As Double

Public Property Let Invoice(ByVal sInvoice As String)
    mInvoice = sInvoice
End Property

Public Property Get Invoice() As String
    Invoice = mInvoice
End Property

Public Property Let InvoiceDate(ByVal dtInvoiceDate As Date)
    mInvoiceDate = dtInvoiceDate
End Property

Public Property Get InvoiceDate() As Date
    InvoiceDate = mInvoiceDate
End Property

Public Property Let Amount(ByVal dAmount As Double)
    mAmount = dAmount
End Property

Public Property Get Amount() As Double
    Amount = mAmount
End Property
```

We won't go into as much detail on CInvoice because, like CSalesRep, it simply creates a property for every column in the table. But it doesn't create one for the SalesRepID column, and you'll see why later in this section. The following code is in the CInvoices class module:

```
Private mInvoices As New Collection

Public Sub Add(clsInvoice As CInvoice)
    mInvoices.Add clsInvoice, clsInvoice.Invoice
End Sub
```

20

```
Public Property Get Count() As Long
   Count = mInvoices.Count
End Property
```

Like `CSalesReps`, this class has a `Collection`, an `Add` method, and a `Count` property. It doesn't have an `Item` property because that's not currently needed. But you can add an `Item` property later if the application requires it. Now you have two parent classes and two child classes. The final step before you can start creating objects is to define the relationship between them. In `CSalesRep`, include the following code:

```
Private mInvoices As New CInvoices

Public Property Get Invoices() As CInvoices
   Set Invoices = mInvoices
End Property
```

Now the hierarchy is `CSalesReps` ⇨ `CSalesRep` ⇨ `CInvoices` ⇨ `CInvoice`.

Filling the parent classes with objects

With your classes defined, you can create new `CSalesRep` and `CInvoice` objects and add them to their respective parent classes. The following two procedures do just that.

```
Public Sub FillSalesReps(ByRef clsSalesReps As CSalesReps)
   Dim i As Long
   Dim clsSalesRep As CSalesRep
   Dim loReps As ListObject

   Set loReps = Sheet1.ListObjects(1)
   'loop through all the sales reps
   For i = 1 To loReps.ListRows.Count
     'create a new sales rep object
     Set clsSalesRep = New CSalesRep

     'Set the properties     With loReps.ListRows(i).Range
       clsSalesRep.SalesRepID = .Cells(1).Value
       clsSalesRep.SalesRep = .Cells(2).Value
       clsSalesRep.CommissionRate = .Cells(3).Value
       clsSalesRep.Threshold = .Cells(4).Value
     End With

     'Add the child to the parent class
     clsSalesReps.Add clsSalesRep
     'Fill invoices for this rep
     FillInvoices clsSalesRep
   Next i
End Sub
```

```
Public Sub FillInvoices(ByRef clsSalesRep As CSalesRep)
   Dim i As Long
   Dim clsInvoice As CInvoice
   Dim loInv As ListObject

   'create a variable for the table
   Set loInv = Sheet2.ListObjects(1)

   'loop through the invoices table
   For i = 1 To loInv.ListRows.Count
     With loInv.ListRows(i).Range
       'Only if it's for this rep, add it
       If .Cells(4).Value = clsSalesRep.SalesRepID Then
         Set clsInvoice = New CInvoice
         clsInvoice.Invoice = .Cells(1).Value
         clsInvoice.InvoiceDate = .Cells(2).Value
         clsInvoice.Amount = .Cells(3).Value
         clsSalesRep.Invoices.Add clsInvoice
       End If
     End With
   Next i
End Sub
```

The first procedure accepts a CSalesReps argument. This is the class at the top of the hierarchy. The procedure loops through all of the rows in the sales rep table, creates a new CSalesRep object, sets the properties of the new object, and adds it to the parent class.

Inside the loop, the FillSalesReps procedure calls FillInvoices and passes it a CSalesRep object. Only those invoices that relate to the CSaleRep object are created and added to it. There isn't just one CInvoices parent class like there's only one CSalesReps class. Instead, each CSalesRep has its own CInvoices instance that holds the invoices that relate to it. This relationship of using a parent class like CInvoices acting as a child to another class is a complicated but powerful coding technique.

Calculating the commissions

Insert a new standard module, and type the following code to calculate the commission and output the results:

```
Public Sub CalculateCommission()
   Dim clsSalesReps As CSalesReps
   Dim i As Long

   'Create a new parent object and fill it with child objects
   Set clsSalesReps = New CSalesReps
   FillSalesReps clsSalesReps

   'Loop through all the reps and print commissions
   For i = 1 To clsSalesReps.Count
     With clsSalesReps.Item(i)
```

20

```
        Debug.Print .SalesRep, _
          Format(.Commission, "$#,##0.00")
      End With
    Next i
  End Sub
```

You may have noticed that the previous procedure uses a `Commission` property that has not yet been created. In the `CSalesRep` class, insert the following code to create a `Commission` property:

```
Public Property Get Commission() As Double
  If Me.Invoices.Total < Me.Threshhold Then
    Commission = 0
  Else
    Commission = (Me.Invoices.Total - Me.Threshhold) _
      * Me.CommissionRate
  End If
End Property
```

If the total of all of the invoices is less than the threshold, this procedure sets the commission to zero. Otherwise, the total sales in excess of the threshold is multiplied by the commission rate. To get the total of the invoices, this property uses a `Total` property from `CInvoices`. Since you haven't created that property yet, insert the following code into `CInvoices` to do so:

```
Public Property Get Total() As Double
  Dim i As Long

  For i = 1 To mInvoices.Count
    Total = Total + mInvoices.Item(i).Amount
  Next i
End Property
```

Figure 20.7 shows the output in the Immediate Window from running `Calculate-Commissions`. You probably noticed that using the class module requires a little more setup than writing normal procedures. Besides, for an application as simple as this, it may not be worth the effort. As your applications get more complicated, however, you'll find that organizing your code in class modules will make it more readable, easier to maintain, and easier to modify should the need arise.

FIGURE 20.7

The commission calculation is output to the Immediate Window.

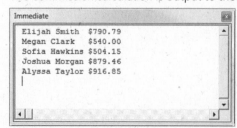

Understanding Compatibility Issues

What Is Compatibility?

Compatibility is an often-used term among computer people. In general, it refers to how well software performs under various conditions. These conditions might be defined in terms of hardware, software, or a combination of the two. For example, software written for Windows may not run directly on other operating systems, such as macOS or Linux.

In this chapter, we discuss a more specific compatibility issue involving how your Excel 2019 applications will work with earlier versions of Excel for Windows and Excel for Mac. The fact that two versions of Excel might use the same file format isn't always enough to ensure complete compatibility between the contents of their files. For example, Excel 97, Excel 2000, Excel 2002, Excel 2003, and Excel 2008 for Mac all use the same file format, but compatibility problems are rampant. Just because a particular version of Excel can open a worksheet file or an add-in doesn't guarantee that that version of Excel can carry out the VBA macro instructions contained within it. Another example: Excel 2019 and Excel 2007 both use the same file format. If your application uses features that were introduced in Excel 2010 or newer, you can't expect that Excel 2007 users will magically have access to these new features.

Excel is a moving target, and you can't guarantee complete compatibility. In most cases, you must do quite a bit of additional work to achieve compatibility.

Types of Compatibility Problems

You need to be aware of several categories of potential compatibility problems. These issues are listed here and discussed further in this chapter:

File format issues   You can save workbooks in several different Excel file formats. Earlier versions of Excel might not be able to open workbooks that were saved in a newer version's file format. For more information about sharing Excel 2007 through Excel 2019 files, see the sidebar "The Microsoft Office Compatibility Pack."

New feature issues   It should be obvious that you can't use a feature introduced in a particular version of Excel in previous versions of Excel.

Microsoft issues   Microsoft itself is responsible for some types of compatibility issues. For example, as we note in Chapter 18, "Working with Shortcut Menus," index numbers for shortcut menus haven't remained consistent across Excel versions.

Windows versus Mac issues   If your application must work on both platforms, plan to spend lots of time ironing out various compatibility problems. Also, note that VBA was removed in Excel 2008 for Mac but then came back in Excel 2011 for Mac.

Bit issues   Excel 2010 was the first version of Excel that's available in both 32-bit and 64-bit editions. If your VBA code uses API functions, you'll need to be aware of some potential problems if the code must run in both 32-bit and 64-bit Excel, as well as other versions of Excel.

International issues   If your application will be used by those who use a different language version of Excel, you must address a number of issues.

After reading this chapter, it should be clear that you can ensure compatibility in only one way: test your application on every target platform and with every target version of Excel.

Microsoft Office Compatibility Pack

If you plan to share your Excel 2019 application with others who use an Excel version older than Excel 2007, you have two choices.

- Always save your files in the older XLS file format.
- Make sure that the recipients of your files have installed Microsoft Office Compatibility Pack.

Microsoft Office Compatibility Pack is a free download available at www.microsoft.com. When it's installed, Office 2003 users can open, edit, and save documents, workbooks, and presentations in the new file formats for Word, Excel, and PowerPoint.

Keep in mind that this compatibility pack doesn't endow earlier versions of Excel with any of the new features in Excel 2007 and newer versions. It simply allows those users to open and save files in the new file format.

Avoid Using New Features

If your application must work with both Excel 2019 and earlier versions, you need to avoid any features that were added after the earliest Excel version that you will support. Another alternative is to incorporate the new features selectively. In other words, your code can determine which version of Excel is being used and then take advantage of the new features or not.

VBA programmers must be careful not to use any objects, properties, or methods that aren't available in earlier versions. In general, the safest approach is to develop your application for the lowest version number. For compatibility with Excel 2003 and newer, you should use Excel 2003 for development; then test thoroughly by using newer versions.

Determining Excel's version number

The Version property of the Application object returns the version of Excel. The returned value is a string, so you might need to convert it to a value. Use the VBA Val function to make the conversion. The following function, for example, returns True if the user is running Excel 2007 or newer:

```
Function XL12OrLater()
  XL12OrLater = Val(Application.Version) >= 12
End Function
```

Excel 2007 is version 12, Excel 2010 is version 14, Excel 2013 is version 15, and Excel 2016 is version 16. You might expect Excel 2019 to be version 17—and you wouldn't be alone. But Application.Version still returns 16 in Excel 2019. We presume that this is an error, but Microsoft has neither acknowledged this nor indicated that this will get fixed. Don't be surprised if it gets fixed in the future, but for now there's no easy way to distinguish Excel 2016 and Excel 2019.

A useful feature introduced in Excel 2007 is the Compatibility Checker, shown in Figure 21.1. Display this dialog box by choosing File ⇨ Info ⇨ Check for Issues ⇨ Check Compatibility. Compatibility Checker identifies any compatibility issues that might cause a problem if the file is opened using an earlier version of Excel.

FIGURE 21.1

Compatibility Checker

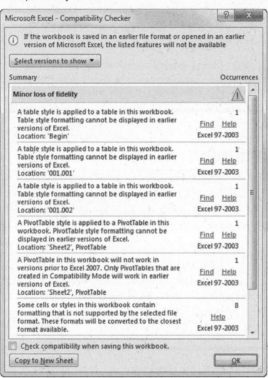

Unfortunately, the Compatibility Checker doesn't look at the VBA code, which is a prime candidate for compatibility problems. However, you can download Microsoft Office Code Compatibility Inspector (search for it at www.microsoft.com). This tool installs as an add-in and adds new commands to the Developer tab. It may help you locate potential compatibility problems in your VBA code. Inspector adds comments to your code to identify potential problems and also creates a report. The Microsoft Office Code Compatibility Inspector was written for Office 2010, and apparently it has not been updated since (but it still installs). Figure 21.2 shows a summary report.

FIGURE 21.2

A summary report from Microsoft Office Code Compatibility Inspector

But Will It Work on a Mac?

Excel for Mac represents a small proportion of the total Excel market, and many developers choose simply to ignore it. The good news is that the file format is compatible across both platforms. The bad news is that the features supported aren't identical, and VBA macro compatibility is far from perfect. And, as we noted, Excel 2008 for Mac had no support for VBA.

You can write VBA code to determine on which platform your application is running. The following function accesses the OperatingSystem property of the Application object and returns True if the operating system is any version of Windows (that is, if the returned string contains the text Win):

```
Function WindowsOS() As Boolean
    WindowsOS = Application.OperatingSystem Like "*Win*"
End Function
```

Subtle (and not so subtle) differences exist between the Windows versions and the Mac versions of Excel. Many of these differences are cosmetic (for example, different default fonts), but others are more serious. For example, Excel for Mac doesn't include ActiveX controls. Also, some Mac versions use the 1904 date system as the default, but Excel for Windows uses the 1900 date system by default, so workbooks that use dates could be off by four years.

Another limitation concerns Windows API functions: they won't work with Excel for Mac. If your application depends on such functions, you need to develop a workaround.

Here's an example of a potential compatibility problem: If your code deals with paths and filenames, you need to construct your path with the appropriate path separator (a colon for the Mac, a backslash for Windows). A better approach is to avoid hard-coding the path separator character and instead use VBA to determine it. The following statement assigns the path separator character to a variable named PathSep:

```
PathSep = Application.PathSeparator
```

After this statement is executed, your code can use the `PathSep` variable in place of a hard-coded colon or backslash.

Rather than try to make a single file compatible with both platforms, most developers choose to develop on one platform and then modify the application so that it works on the other platform. In some situations, you'll probably need to maintain two separate versions of your application.

You can make sure that your application is compatible with a particular Mac version of Excel in only one way: by testing it thoroughly on a Mac—and being prepared to develop some workarounds for procedures that don't work correctly.

On the Web

Ron de Bruin, a Microsoft Excel MVP in the Netherlands, created a web page with many examples relevant to VBA compatibility between Excel for Mac and Excel for Windows. The URL for the web page is `www.rondebruin.nl/mac.htm`.

Dealing with 64-Bit Excel

Starting with version 2010, you can install Excel as a 32-bit application or as a 64-bit application. The latter works only if you're running a 64-bit version of Windows. The 64-bit version can handle much larger workbooks because it takes advantage of the larger address space in 64-bit Windows.

Most users don't need the 64-bit version of Excel because they don't work with massive amounts of data in a workbook. Remember, the 64-bit version offers no performance boost. Some operations may actually be slower in the 64-bit version.

In general, workbooks and add-ins created using the 32-bit version will work fine in the 64-bit version. Note, however, that ActiveX controls will not work in the 64-bit version. Also, if the workbook contains VBA code that uses Windows API functions, the 32-bit API function declarations won't compile in the 64-bit version.

For example, the following declaration works with 32-bit Excel versions but causes a compile error with 64-bit Excel:

```
Declare Function GetWindowsDirectoryA Lib "kernel32" _
    (ByVal lpBuffer As String, ByVal nSize As Long) As Long
```

The following declaration works with Excel 2010 and newer (both 32-bit and 64-bit) but causes a compile error in previous versions of Excel:

```
Declare PtrSafe Function GetWindowsDirectoryA Lib "kernel32" _
    (ByVal lpBuffer As String, ByVal nSize As Long) As Long
```

To use this API function in both 32-bit and 64-bit Excel, you must declare two versions of the function by using two conditional compiler directives.

- VBA7 returns True if your code is using version 7 of VBA (which is included in Office 2010 and newer).
- Win64 returns True if the code is running in 64-bit Excel.

Here's an example of how to use these directives to declare an API function that's compatible with 32-bit and 64-bit Excel:

```
#If VBA7 And Win64 Then
    Declare PtrSafe Function GetWindowsDirectoryA Lib "kernel32" _
        (ByVal lpBuffer As String, ByVal nSize As Long) As Long
#Else
    Declare Function GetWindowsDirectoryA Lib "kernel32" _
        (ByVal lpBuffer As String, ByVal nSize As Long) As Long
#End If
```

The first Declare statement is used when VBA7 and Wind64 are both True, which is the case only for 64-bit Excel 2010 and newer. In all other versions, the second Declare statement is used.

Creating an International Application

The final compatibility concern deals with language issues and international settings. Excel is available in many different language versions. The following statement displays the country code for the version of Excel:

```
MsgBox Application.International(xlCountryCode)
```

The United States/English version of Excel has a country code of 1. Other country codes are listed in Table 21.1.

TABLE 21.1 Excel Country Codes

Country Code	Country/Region	Language
1	United States	English
7	Russia	Russian
30	Greece	Greek
31	The Netherlands	Dutch
33	France	French
34	Spain	Spanish
36	Hungary	Hungarian
39	Italy	Italian
42	Czech Republic	Czech
45	Denmark	Danish

Continues

TABLE 21.1 *(continued)*

Country Code	Country/Region	Language
46	Sweden	Swedish
47	Norway	Norwegian
48	Poland	Polish
49	Germany	German
55	Brazil	Portuguese
66	Thailand	Thai
81	Japan	Japanese
82	Korea	Korean
84	Vietnam	Vietnamese
86	People's Republic of China	Simplified Chinese
90	Turkey	Turkish
91	India	Indian
92	Pakistan	Urdu
351	Portugal	Portuguese
358	Finland	Finnish
886	Taiwan	Traditional Chinese
966	Saudi Arabia	Arabic
972	Israel	Hebrew
982	Iran	Farsi

Excel also supports language packs, so a single copy of Excel can display any number of different languages. The language comes into play in two areas: the user interface and the execution mode.

You can determine the current language used by the user interface by using a statement such as this:

```
Msgbox Application.LanguageSettings.LanguageID(msoLanguageIDUI)
```

The language ID for English U.S. is 1033.

If your application will be used by those who speak another language, you need to ensure that the proper language is used in your dialog boxes. Also, you need to identify the user's decimal and thousands separator characters. In the United States, these are almost always a period and a comma, respectively. However, users in other countries might have their systems set up to use other characters. Yet another issue is date and time formatting: the United States is one of the few countries that uses the month/day/year format.

If you're developing an application that will be used only by people within your company, you probably won't need to be concerned with international compatibility. But if your company has offices throughout the world or you plan to distribute your application outside your country, you need to address a number of issues to ensure that your application will work properly. We discuss these issues in the following sections.

Multilanguage Applications

An obvious consideration involves the language used in your application. For example, if you use one or more dialog boxes, you probably want the text to appear in the language of the user. Fortunately, changing the language isn't too difficult (assuming, of course, that you or someone you know can translate your text).

> **ON THE WEB**
>
> The book's website contains an example that demonstrates how to allow the user to choose from three languages in a dialog box: English, Spanish, or German. The example is in the `Multilingual Wizard.xlsm` file.

The first step of the multilingual wizard contains three option buttons that enable the user to select a language. The text for the three languages is stored in a worksheet.

The `UserForm _ Initialize` procedure contains code that attempts to guess the user's language by checking the `International` property:

```
Select Case Application.International(xlCountryCode)
   Case 34 'Spanish
     UserLanguage = 2
   Case 49 'German
     UserLanguage = 3
   Case Else 'default to English
     UserLanguage = 1 'default
End Select
```

Figure 21.3 shows the UserForm displaying text in all three languages.

FIGURE 21.3

The wizard demo in English, Spanish, and German

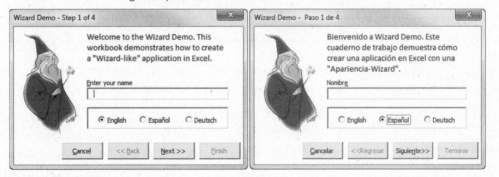

FIGURE 21.3 *(continued)*

VBA Language Considerations

In general, you need not be concerned with the language in which you write your VBA code. Excel uses two object libraries: the Excel object library and the VBA object library. When you install Excel, it registers the English language version of these object libraries as the default libraries (regardless of the language version of Excel).

Using Local Properties

If your code will display worksheet information, such as a formula or a range address, you probably want to use the local language. For example, the following statement displays the formula in cell A1:

```
MsgBox Range("A1").Formula
```

For international applications, a better approach is to use the FormulaLocal property rather than the Formula property:

```
MsgBox Range("A1").FormulaLocal
```

Several other properties also have local versions. These are shown in Table 21.2. (Refer to the Help system for specific details.)

TABLE 21.2 Properties That Have Local Versions

Property	Local Version	Return Contents
Address	AddressLocal	Address
Category	CategoryLocal	Function category (XLM macros only)
Formula	FormulaLocal	Formula
FormulaR1C1	FormulaR1C1Local	Formula, using R1C1 notation
Name	NameLocal	Name
NumberFormat	NumberFormatLocal	Number format
RefersTo	RefersToLocal	Reference
RefersToR1C1	RefersToR1C1Local	Reference, using R1C1 notation

Identifying System Settings

Generally, you can't assume that the end user's system is set up like the system on which you develop your application. For international applications, you need to be aware of the following settings:

Decimal separator   The character used to separate the decimal portion of a value

Thousands separator   The character used to delineate every three digits in a value

List separator   The character used to separate items in a list

You can determine the current separator settings by accessing the `International` property of the `Application` object. For example, the following statement displays the decimal separator, which won't always be a period:

```
MsgBox Application.International(xlDecimalSeparator)
```

The 45 international settings that you can access with the `International` property are listed in Table 21.3.

TABLE 21.3   Constants for the International Property

Constant	What It Returns
xlCountryCode	Country version of Microsoft Excel
xlCountrySetting	Current country setting in the Windows Control Panel
xlDecimalSeparator	Decimal separator
xlThousandsSeparator	Thousands separator
xlListSeparator	List separator
xlUpperCaseRowLetter	Uppercase row letter (for R1C1-style references)
xlUpperCaseColumnLetter	Uppercase column letter
xlLowerCaseRowLetter	Lowercase row letter
xlLowerCaseColumnLetter	Lowercase column letter
xlLeftBracket	Character used instead of the left bracket ([) in R1C1-style relative references
xlRightBracket	Character used instead of the right bracket (]) in R1C1-style references
xlLeftBrace	Character used instead of the left brace ({) in array literals
xlRightBrace	Character used instead of the right brace (}) in array literals
xlColumnSeparator	Character used to separate columns in array literals
xlRowSeparator	Character used to separate rows in array literals

Continues

TABLE 21.3 *(continued)*

Constant	What It Returns
xlAlternateArraySeparator	Alternate array item separator to be used if the current array separator is the same as the decimal separator
xlDateSeparator	Date separator (/)
xlTimeSeparator	Time separator (:)
xlYearCode	Year symbol in number formats (y)
xlMonthCode	Month symbol (m)
xlDayCode	Day symbol (d)
xlHourCode	Hour symbol (h)
xlMinuteCode	Minute symbol (m)
xlSecondCode	Second symbol (s)
xlCurrencyCode	Currency symbol
xlGeneralFormatName	Name of the General number format
xlCurrencyDigits	Number of decimal digits to be used in currency formats
xlCurrencyNegative	A value that represents the currency format for negative currency values
xlNoncurrencyDigits	Number of decimal digits to be used in noncurrency formats
xlMonthNameChars	Always returns three characters for backward-compatibility; abbreviated month names are read from Microsoft Windows and can be any length
xlWeekdayNameChars	Always returns three characters for backward-compatibility; abbreviated weekday names are read from Microsoft Windows and can be any length
xlDateOrder	An integer that represents the order of date elements
xl24HourClock	True if the system is using 24-hour time; False if the system is using 12-hour time
xlNonEnglishFunctions	True if the system isn't displaying functions in English
xlMetric	True if the system is using the metric system; False if the system is using the English measurement system
xlCurrencySpaceBefore	True if a space is added before the currency symbol
xlCurrencyBefore	True if the currency symbol precedes the currency values; False if it follows them
xlCurrencyMinusSign	True if the system is using a minus sign for negative numbers; False if the system is using parentheses
xlCurrencyTrailingZeros	True if trailing zeros are displayed for zero currency values
xlCurrencyLeadingZeros	True if leading zeros are displayed for zero currency values

Constant	What It Returns
xlMonthLeadingZero	True if a leading zero is displayed in months (when months are displayed as numbers)
xlDayLeadingZero	True if a leading zero is displayed in days
xl4DigitYears	True if the system is using four-digit years; False if the system is using two-digit years
xlMDY	True if the date order is month-day-year for dates displayed in the long form; False if the date order is day/month/year
xlTimeLeadingZero	True if a leading zero is displayed in times

Date and Time Settings

If your application writes formatted dates and will be used in other countries, you might want to make sure that the date is in a format familiar to the user. The best approach is to specify a date by using the VBA DateSerial function and let Excel take care of the formatting details. (It will use the user's short date format.)

The following procedure uses the DateSerial function to assign a date to the StartDate variable. This date is then written to cell A1 with the local short date format.

```
Sub WriteDate()
  Dim StartDate As Date
  StartDate = DateSerial(2016, 4, 15)
  Range("A1").Value = StartDate
End Sub
```

If you need to do any other formatting for the date, you can write code to do so after the date has been entered in the cell. Excel provides several named date and time formats, plus quite a few named number formats. The Help system describes all of these formats (search for *named date/time formats* or *named numeric formats*).

Part V

Appendix: VBA Statements and Functions Reference

VBA Statements and Functions Reference

T his appendix contains a complete listing of all Visual Basic for Applications (VBA) statements (Table A.1) and built-in functions (Table A.2). For details, consult Excel's online help.

VBA Statements

VBA statements are keywords defined in the Visual Basic for Applications specification that make up the VBA language. Statements are used to control program flow, manipulate data, handle errors, communicate with the file system, and act as labels. In contrast, functions primarily return a value or values.

TABLE A.1   Summary of VBA Statements

Statement	Action
AppActivate	Activates an application window
Beep	Sounds a tone through the computer's speaker
Call	Transfers control to another procedure
ChDir	Changes the current directory
ChDrive	Changes the current drive
Close	Closes a text file
Const	Declares a constant value
Date	Sets the current system date
Declare	Declares a reference to an external procedure in a Dynamic Link Library (DLL)
DefBool	Sets the default data type to Boolean for variables that begin with specified letters
DefByte	Sets the default data type to Byte for variables that begin with specified letters

Continues

TABLE A.1 *(continued)*

Statement	Action
DefCur	Sets the default data type to `Currency` for variables that begin with specified letters
DefDate	Sets the default data type to `Date` for variables that begin with specified letters
DefDec	Sets the default data type to `Decimal` for variables that begin with specified letters
DefDbl	Sets the default data type to `Double` for variables that begin with specified letters
DefInt	Sets the default data type to `Integer` for variables that begin with specified letters
DefLng	Sets the default data type to `Long` for variables that begin with specified letters
DefLngLng	Sets the default data type to `LongLong` for variables that begin with specified letters
DefLngPtr	Sets the default data type to `LongPtr` for variables that begin with specified letters
DefObj	Sets the default data type to `Object` for variables that begin with specified letters
DefSng	Sets the default data type to `Single` for variables that begin with specified letters
DefStr	Sets the default data type to `String` for variables that begin with specified letters
DefVar	Sets the default data type to `Variant` for variables that begin with specified letters
DeleteSetting	Deletes a section or key setting from an application's entry in the Windows Registry
Dim	Declares variables and (optionally) their data types
Do-Loop	Loops through a set of instructions
End	Used by itself, exits the program; also used to end a block of statements that begin with `If`, `With`, `Sub`, `Function`, `Property`, `Type`, or `Select`
Enum	Declares a type for enumeration
Erase	Reinitializes an array
Error	Simulates a specific error condition
Event	Declares a user-defined event
Exit Do	Exits a block of `Do-Loop` code
Exit For	Exits a block of `For-Next` code

Statement	Action
Exit Function	Exits a Function procedure
Exit Property	Exits a property procedure
Exit Sub	Exits a subroutine procedure
FileCopy	Copies a file
For Each-Next	Loops through a set of instructions for each member of a series
For-Next	Loops through a set of instructions a specific number of times
Function	Declares the name and arguments for a Function procedure
Get	Reads data from a text file
GoSub...Return	Branches to and returns from a procedure
GoTo	Branches to a specified statement within a procedure
If-Then-Else	Processes statements conditionally
Implements	Specifies an interface or class that will be implemented in a class module
Input #	Reads data from a sequential text file
Kill	Deletes a file from a disk
Let	Assigns the value of an expression to a variable or property
Line Input #	Reads a line of data from a sequential text file
Load	Loads an object but doesn't show it
Lock...Unlock	Controls access to a text file
LSet	Left-aligns a string within a string variable
Mid	Replaces characters in a string with other characters
MkDir	Creates a new directory
Name	Renames a file or directory
On Error	Gives specific instructions for what to do in the case of an error
On...GoSub	Branches, based on a condition
On...GoTo	Branches, based on a condition
Open	Opens a text file
Option Base	Sets the default lower limit for arrays
Option Compare	Declares the default comparison mode when comparing strings
Option Explicit	Forces declaration of all variables in a module
Option Private	Indicates that an entire module is Private
Print #	Writes data to a sequential file
Private	Declares a local variable
Property Get	Declares the name and arguments of a Property Get procedure

Continues

TABLE A.1 *(continued)*

Statement	Action
Property Let	Declares the name and arguments of a Property Let procedure
Property Set	Declares the name and arguments of a Property Set procedure
Public	Declares a public variable
Put	Writes a variable to a text file
RaiseEvent	Fires a user-defined event
Randomize	Initializes the random number generator
ReDim	Changes the dimensions of an array
Rem	Specifies a line of comments (same as an apostrophe ['])
Reset	Closes all open text files
Resume	Resumes execution when an error-handling routine finishes
RmDir	Removes an empty directory
RSet	Right-aligns a string within a string variable
SaveSetting	Saves or creates an application entry in the Windows Registry
Seek	Sets the position for the next access in a text file
Select Case	Processes statements conditionally
SendKeys	Sends keystrokes to the active window
Set	Assigns an object reference to a variable or property
SetAttr	Changes attribute information for a file
Static	Declares variables at the procedure level so that the variables retain their values as long as the code is running
Stop	Pauses the program
Sub	Declares the name and arguments of a Sub procedure
Time	Sets the system time
Type	Defines a custom data type
Unload	Removes an object from memory
While...Wend	Loops through a set of instructions as long as a certain condition remains true
Width #	Sets the output line width of a text file
With	Sets a series of properties for an object
Write #	Writes data to a sequential text file

Functions

Functions are code that is built in to the VBA standard library. A function may accept zero, one, or multiple arguments and returns a value (although the value maybe something complex, like an object).

You can use Excel's worksheet functions directly in your VBA code. Excel worksheet functions that don't have a VBA equivalent are methods of the WorksheetFunction object. For example, VBA doesn't have a function to convert radians to degrees, but Excel has a worksheet function for this procedure, so you can use a VBA instruction such as the following:

```
Deg = Application.WorksheetFunction.Degrees(3.14)
```

> **NOTE**
> Excel 2019 has no new VBA functions.

TABLE A.2 **Summary of VBA Functions**

Function	Action
Abs	Returns the absolute value of a number
Array	Returns a variant containing an array
Asc	Converts the first character of a string to its ASCII value
Atn	Returns the arctangent of a number
CallByName	Executes a method, or sets or returns a property of an object
CBool	Converts an expression to a Boolean data type
CByte	Converts an expression to a Byte data type
CCur	Converts an expression to a Currency data type
CDate	Converts an expression to a Date data type
CDbl	Converts an expression to a Double data type
CDec	Converts an expression to a Decimal data type
Choose	Selects and returns a value from a list of arguments
Chr	Converts a character code to a string
CInt	Converts an expression to an Integer data type
CLng	Converts an expression to a Long data type
CLngLng	Converts an expression to a LongLong data type
CLngPtr	Converts an expression to a LongPtr data type
Cos	Returns the cosine of a number

Continues

TABLE A.2 *(continued)*

Function	Action
CreateObject	Creates an Object Linking and Embedding (OLE) Automation object
CSng	Converts an expression to a `Single` data type
CStr	Converts an expression to a `String` data type
CurDir	Returns the current path
CVar	Converts an expression to a `variant` data type
CVDate	Converts an expression to a `Date` data type (for compatibility, not recommended)
CVErr	Returns a user-defined error value that corresponds to an error number
Date	Returns the current system date
DateAdd	Adds a time interval to a date
DateDiff	Returns the time interval between two dates
DatePart	Returns a specified part of a date
DateSerial	Converts a date to a serial number
DateValue	Converts a string to a date
Day	Returns the day of the month of a date
DDB	Returns the depreciation of an asset
Dir	Returns the name of a file or directory that matches a pattern
DoEvents	Yields execution so the operating system can process other events
Environ	Returns an operating environment string
EOF	Returns `True` if the end of a text file has been reached
Error	Returns the error message that corresponds to an error number
Exp	Returns the base of natural logarithms (*e*) raised to a power
FileAttr	Returns the file mode for a text file
FileDateTime	Returns the date and time when a file was last modified
FileLen	Returns the number of bytes in a file
Filter	Returns a subset of a string array, filtered
Fix	Returns the integer portion of a number
Format	Displays an expression in a particular format
FormatCurrency	Returns an expression formatted with the system currency symbol
FormatDateTime	Returns an expression formatted as a date or time
FormatNumber	Returns an expression formatted as a number
FormatPercent	Returns an expression formatted as a percentage
FreeFile	Returns the next available file number when working with text files

Function	Action
FV	Returns the future value of an annuity
GetAllSettings	Returns a list of settings and values from the Windows Registry
GetAttr	Returns a code representing a file attribute
GetObject	Retrieves an OLE Automation object from a file
GetSetting	Returns a specific setting from the application's entry in the Windows Registry
Hex	Converts from decimal to hexadecimal
Hour	Returns the hour of a time
IIf	Evaluates an expression and returns one of two parts
Input	Returns characters from a sequential text file
InputBox	Displays a box to prompt a user for input
InStr	Returns the position of a string within another string
InStrRev	Returns the position of a string within another string from the end of the string
Int	Returns the integer portion of a number
IPmt	Returns the interest payment for a given period of an annuity
IRR	Returns the internal rate of return for a series of cash flows
IsArray	Returns True if a variable is an array
IsDate	Returns True if a variable is a date
IsEmpty	Returns True if a variable has not been initialized
IsError	Returns True if an expression is an error value
IsMissing	Returns True if an optional argument was not passed to a procedure
IsNull	Returns True if an expression contains a Null value
IsNumeric	Returns True if an expression can be evaluated as a number
IsObject	Returns True if an expression references an OLE Automation object
Join	Combines strings contained in an array
LBound	Returns the smallest subscript for a dimension of an array
LCase	Returns a string converted to lowercase
Left	Returns a specified number of characters from the left of a string
Len	Returns the number of characters in a string
Loc	Returns the current read or write position of a text file
LOF	Returns the number of bytes in an open text file
Log	Returns the natural logarithm of a number
LTrim	Returns a copy of a string with no leading spaces
Mid	Returns a specified number of characters from a string

Continues

TABLE A.2 *(continued)*

Function	Action
Minute	Returns the minute of a time
MIRR	Returns the modified internal rate of return for a series of periodic cash flows
Month	Returns the month of a date as a number
MonthName	Returns the month of a date as a string
MsgBox	Displays a modal message box
Now	Returns the current system date and time
NPer	Returns the number of periods for an annuity
NPV	Returns the net present value of an investment
Oct	Converts from decimal to octal
Partition	Returns a string representing a range in which a value falls
Pmt	Returns a payment amount for an annuity
Ppmt	Returns the principal payment amount for an annuity
PV	Returns the present value of an annuity
QBColor	Returns a red/green/blue (RGB) color code
Rate	Returns the interest rate per period for an annuity
Replace	Returns a string in which a substring is replaced with another string
RGB	Returns a number representing an RGB color value
Right	Returns a specified number of characters from the right of a string
Rnd	Returns a random number between 0 and 1
Round	Returns a rounded number
RTrim	Returns a copy of a string with no trailing spaces
Second	Returns the seconds portion of a specified time
Seek	Returns the current position in a text file
Sgn	Returns an integer that indicates the sign of a number
Shell	Runs an executable program
Sin	Returns the sine of a number
SLN	Returns the straight-line depreciation for an asset for a period
Space	Returns a string with a specified number of spaces
Spc	Positions output when printing to a file
Split	Returns a one-dimensional array containing a number of substrings
Sqr	Returns the square root of a number
Str	Returns a string representation of a number
StrComp	Returns a value indicating the result of a string comparison

Function	Action
StrConv	Returns a converted string
String	Returns a repeating character or string
StrReverse	Returns a string, reversed
Switch	Evaluates a list of Boolean expressions and returns a value associated with the first True expression
SYD	Returns the sum-of-years' digits depreciation of an asset for a period
Tab	Positions output when printing to a file
Tan	Returns the tangent of a number
Time	Returns the current system time
Timer	Returns the number of seconds since midnight
TimeSerial	Returns the time for a specified hour, minute, and second
TimeValue	Converts a string to a time serial number
Trim	Returns a string without leading spaces and/or trailing spaces
TypeName	Returns a string that describes the data type of a variable
UBound	Returns the largest available subscript for a dimension of an array
UCase	Converts a string to uppercase
Val	Returns the number formed from any initial numeric characters of a string
VarType	Returns a value indicating the subtype of a variable
Weekday	Returns a number indicating a day of the week
WeekdayName	Returns a string indicating a day of the week
Year	Returns the year of a date

Index

Symbols and Numerics

= (equal sign), 76
64-bit Excel, 704–705
64-bit functions, 179

A

`AbortProc` variable, 186
absolute references, macros, 23–26
Access, 354–356
`Activate` event, 190, 191, 197
`Activate` method, 310–311
activating charts, 310–311
active cell, chart data, 324–325
active chart, 306, 313
active workbook, ADO in, 395–397
ActiveX controls, 8, 9
   versus form controls, 11
   Toolbox, 475–477
`AddIn` object, 589–593
`AddinInstall` event, 190
add-ins, 569
   accessing as workbook, 592–593
   Add-in Manager, 572–580
   COM, 572
   creating, 574–575, 577
   descriptive information, 577
   distributing, 579
   files, 6
   installation, 578–579
   modifying, 580
   password-protected, 14
   performance, 593–594
   procedures, 583–587
   reasons for, 570–572
   testing, 579
   troubleshooting, 594–597
   versus workbooks, 569–570
`AddIns` collection
   adding items, 587–588
   removing items, 588–589

Add-ins dialog box, 573–574
`AddinUninstall` event, 190
ADO (ActiveX Data Objects), external data and
   active workbook and, 395–397
   code, 394–395
   connection string, 390–392
   object library references, 392–394
   recordsets, 392
`AfterCalculate` event, 207
`AfterSave` event, 190
alignment
   `ChartObject` object, 317–318
   controls, 448–450
`ALLBOLD` function, 264–265
Analysis TookPak, 569
`And` operator, 77
`AnimateChart` procedure, 347
`AppActivate`, 373–374
application development, 4
   distribution, 16–17
   documentation, 16
   Help system, 16
   installed version of Excel, 17
   language, 17–18
   planning, 6–7
   system speed and, 18
   testing, 12
   updates, 17
   user interface, 7–11
   video mode and, 18
   visual appeal, 15
`Application` object, 43, 45–46
application-level events
   `AfterCalculate`, 207
   enabling, 206–208
   monitoring, 209–210
   `NewWorkbook`, 207
   `OnKey`, 212–215
   `OnTime`, 210–211
   `SheetActivate`, 207
   `SheetBeforeDoubleClick`, 207

ranges
  arrays
    one-dimensional, 241–242
    transferring to, 242–243
  cells
    counting selected, 228
    data types, 236–238
    prompting for values, 223–224
    selecting by value, 243–244
    values in, 225–226
  charts, determining, 325–327
  copying, 218–219
    noncontiguous, 244–246
    variably sized, 219–221
  data labels, 328–331
  InputBox method and, 424
  looping, 230–233
  monitoring for changes, 199–203
  moving, 219
  randomizing, 276–277
  in ranges, 236
  reading, 238–239
  referencing, 222
  resizing, 223
  rows, 233–236
  selecting, 221–222
    pausing macros, 226–228
    from Userforms, 481–483
  sorting, 277–278
  type, 228–230
  values, counting cells, 267–268
  writing, 238–239
  writing to, 239–241
read-only recommended workbooks, 14
Record Macro dialog box, 20, 110–111
  Description option, 21
  Macro Name option, 20
  Shortcut Key option, 21
  Store Macro In option, 21
recording macros, 20–27
Recordset object, 392
recursion, 409–410
ReDim statement, 79
RefEdit control, 446, 482–483
referenced workbooks, 114–115
references
  cell references *versus* arguments, 158
  properties, 53
References dialog box, 114, 354

relative references, macros, 26–27
Rem keyword, 64
REMOVEVOWELS function, 145, 147
reserved words, 65
Resize property, 223
reverse pivot tables, 302–304
ReversePivot procedure, 302–304
Ribbon
  buttons
    adding, 601–604, 607–610
    Quick Access toolbar, 604–605
  controls, 599
    access, 629–630
    Button, 600
    CheckBox, 600
    ComboBox, 600
    demo, 616–625
    dynamicMenu, 625–627
    Menu, 601
    SplitButton, 600
  customizing, 8
    creating custom, 606–628
    limitations, 605–606
  groups, 599
  imageMso images, 613
  procedures, 111
  RibbonX code, 607–611
    callback procedures, 612
    check boxes, 613–616
    Custom UI, 612
  tabs, 599
    activating, 631
RmDir statement, 406
rows
  deleting, empty, 233–234
  duplicating, 234–236
  hiding, 14
Run Sub/UserForm command, 109

S

SAYIT function, 265
scope
  procedures, 107–108
  variables, 70–72
ScrollBar control, 10–11, 446
scrolling, charts, 345–347
security, 7
  macros, 28